Exploring Early Childhood

Readings in Theory and Practice

Exploring Early Childhood

Readings in Theory and Practice

MARGOT KAPLAN-SANOFF

RENÉE YABLANS-MAGID

Beaver College

Macmillan Publishing Co., Inc.
New York

Collier Macmillan Publishers
London

Macmillan Publishing Co., Inc.
866 Third Avenue, New York, New York 10022

Collier Macmillan Canada, Ltd.

Library of Congress Cataloging in Publication Data

Kaplan-Sanoff, Margot.
  Exploring early childhood.

  Includes bibliographical references and index.
  1. Education, Preschool.   2. Child Development.
I. Magid, Renee, joint author.   II. Title.
LB1140.2.K366   372'.21   80-19636
ISBN 0-02-361940-6

Printing: 1 2 3 4 5 6 7 8   Year: 1 2 3 4 5 6 7 8

**To Robby and David
With Love and Thanks**

Preface

Because early childhood development is currently one of the most rapidly expanding fields in education and psychology, few textbooks have been able to keep up with the recent flow of new information and ideas. This book of readings, although by no means exhaustive, is meant to provide an organized approach to the study of early childhood. It explores not only the most recent theories in child development but also their practical application.

The book is divided into three sections—an introduction to early childhood, a review of the four major content areas in the field, and an introduction to the administration of early childhood centers. The introductory section provides several major readings on the theoretical approaches to early childhood development. It raises such issues as the role of intrinsic motivation in cognitive development and the connection between environmental variables and learning. The second section of the text explores the current theories of infant and early childhood development in the four major categories of growth—motor, social, language, and cognitive development. In addition to the theoretical aspects presented, each chapter also includes recent projects, teaching techniques, and programs based upon those theories. Part III discusses the important issues involved in administering early childhood centers. Preceding the chapters on administration is a brief, basic overview of the process of administration that acquaints the reader with the logical sequence of planning, operating, and evaluating a center.

In selecting the readings, careful consideration was given to choosing articles from a variety of disciplines. The articles represent ideas not only from the field of education but also from business administration, psychology, and pediatric medicine. Rather than choosing only those articles that are consistent with a single philosophical orientation, the editors tried to select readings from a wide array of theoretical perspectives. Attention was given to including contemporary readings as well as major seminal studies in theory and research. Indeed several of the articles are published for the first time in this book.

Exploring Early Childhood was not designed with any one type of course or student in mind. Rather it was the editors' intention to compile a book of readings that can be used at both the undergraduate and graduate levels either as the primary text or as a secondary text in conjunction with others. As a primary text, the book offers a logical and systematic approach to the field of early childhood development. Whereas most primary texts currently available tend to provide little more than a broad overview of the subject matter, this book introduces the student in an organized fashion to the sophisticated analysis of the major writers in early childhood. As a secondary source book, *Exploring Early Childhood* can be used to supplement the general discussion provided in a basic text by acquainting students with a variety of viewpoints compiled within a single text. When employed as a secondary source book, it is not necessary for students to read the material in any particular order. Furthermore, the book is meant to serve as a permanent reference for students as they pursue their professional careers. In this regard, the book can be used as general required reading within a student's total program of study.

In the hope that students will use this text as something more than mere required reading, the editors have employed a system of cross-referencing, indicating with an asterisk those references cited within a reading that also appear in the text. Thus a student can read independently other related articles cited in the assigned reading. In addition, the Appendix contains a list of the names and addresses of research centers and agencies that publish and report work in the field of early childhood development; students may write for information directly to a cited source. Finally, the editors acknowledge the use of the general term "he" throughout the book to provide continuity of writing style; however, in all cases the term "he" is meant to represent both male and female roles.

The editors would also like to take this opportunity to thank the many people who helped in the organization and publication of this book. Our greatest debt is to the authors whose articles are represented here. Because many of the articles originally appeared in *Young Children*, we wish to thank the National Association for the Education of Young Children (NAEYC) for their generous cooperation. And of course we must acknowledge the valuable role our students played in providing both the impetus and the encouragement to complete this project. Special thanks to Ellen Feldman, Donna Greenberg, Bobbi Cornman, JoAnn Finkle, Katie Sturgill, and H. Johnson for their assistance in typing, handling correspondence, and proofreading.

M. K. S.
R. Y. M.

Contents

PART II
CONTENT AREAS IN EARLY
CHILDHOOD

MOTOR DEVELOPMENT IN EARLY
CHILDHOOD 87

Contents

PART III
INTRODUCTION TO EARLY CHILDHOOD ADMINISTRATION

Contents

THE EVALUATION PROCESS 471

Introduction to Early Childhood Part I

HISTORICAL PERSPECTIVES
AND THEORETICAL APPROACHES
IN EARLY CHILDHOOD

Within the last decade, the field of early childhood has grown from one primarily concerned with preschool development to one that spans such diverse issues as infant stimulation, cognitive assessment, and enriched play environments. Similarly, research has expanded to include topics as disparate as neurological influence and interactional factors. Although it is impossible within the scope of any book to discuss all the varied perspectives and approaches that inform early childhood development, one can identify several distinct themes that serve to unify the viewpoints presented by the literature in the field.

The first theme stresses the interdependence between one area of development and all the other areas of growth. No longer can we speak of social skills as being separate from cognitive awareness, nor can we consider language development as isolated from the social and cognitive milieu from which it evolves. Motor, social, language, and cognitive development are all intimately related—each one affecting the others.

The second theme explores the origins of competence, delineating how children develop feelings of control and mastery over the people, events, and objects in their environment. Detailed studies of infant and child growth have provided insight into the processes by which a child manipulates the objects in his world and learns to communicate his understanding of how those objects work through language and symbolic expression. Also of great concern to researchers and educators are the methods by which adults can facilitate the development of competence through discovery, learning, spontaneous play, and supportive adult-child interactions.

The third theme relates directly to our assumptions about how children learn. Theoretical differences in teaching and research strategies stem from the debate over whether learning involves an essentially passive child who is taught through direct reinforcement or an intrinsically motivated learner who actively explores the environment. These two radically different strategies, often referred to as the process/product dichotomy, have radically different implications for curriculum development, staff training, and environmental design.

In order to understand the significance of these three themes, it is important at the outset to understand the major historical events and theoretical orientations that have influenced research and educational programs for young children. The readings in this first chapter are divided into two sections. The first section provides a historical overview of early childhood development. For example, Katz looks at both the past and present assumptions behind the education of young children, and she argues for the establishment of appropriate goals for early childhood.

However, when considering the issues related to a specific discipline, it is crucial to review not only past events but also future goals and perspectives; in the field of early childhood those perspectives include the politics and reality of child care. Gaffney's article summarizes the need for a nationwide early childhood program, whereas Divoky's advocates the examination of alternatives before delegating the sole responsibility for child care to either the public schools or the social service agencies.

A brief introduction to several theoretical approaches is offered in the second section of this chapter in the readings by Case, Elkind, Hunt, Bruner, and Bijou. Each of these articles presents a major theoretical argument. For example, Bruner's seminal work defines self-discovery learning and its importance for problem solving, recall, and motivation. In addition, these articles highlight the inescapable influence of Jean Piaget, B. F. Skinner, and Maria Montessori on theoretical discussions of early childhood development.

LILLIAN G. KATZ

1. Perspectives on Early Childhood Education

When you look back at the early days of Head Start and other early childhood program plans, the original ideas of the program designers seem both naive and oversimplified. The early designers based their plans on several premises. The first was that the preschool years are the most formative ones in children's development. Secondly, that those years should be full of stimulation or enrichment. Thirdly, that the children of families who are poor do not have enough stimulation or enrichment, and finally, that this supposed lack of stimulation causes children of the poor to be unresponsive to schooling. They hoped that a summer of enrichment would give children a headstart to later schooling.[1]

Now, seven years later, are these ideas still accepted? Judging from the current scene and recent experience, the most obvious error in the thinking of the original designers was that poor children are understimulated. This is very rarely the case. Poor children frequently have rich environments—rich in social, cultural, and linguistic experiences—as rich in meaning and complexity as the environments of children who are in a better-off socioeconomic position.[2]

Many children who are poor are overstimulated. They very commonly suffer from insufficient adult help in making sense out of their rich environments. It is in this sense that many poor children can be said to "starve in the midst of plenty" and appear to be understimulated.[3]

A second early idea that proved to be in error involves our stereotyping of a "poor" child. There is no "poor" child as such. There are just as many individual differences among children who are poor—of every ethnic group—as there are among middle-class white American children. The volumes of research which are processed through our Clearinghouse reveal in numerous tables and charts that individual differences are found in every

From Lillian G. Katz, "Perspectives on Early Childhood Education," *The Educational Forum*, Vol. 37 (May 1973), pp. 393-98. Reprinted by permission of Kappa Delta Pi, an Honor Society in Education, owners of the copyright.

[1]M.E. Akers, "Prologues: The Why of Early Childhood Education," in I. Gordon (ed.), *Early Childhood Education*, The Seventy-first Yearbook of the National Society for the Study of Education (Chicago: University of Chicago Press, 1972); and J. O. Miller, "Early Childhood Education Program and Research Support Literature: A State of the Art Review," in *National Program on Early Childhood Education* (St. Louis, Mo.: CEMREL, Inc., 1972).

[2]S. Baratz and J. C. Baratz, "Early Childhood Intervention: The Social Science Base of Institutional Racism," *Harvard Educational Review*, 40, 1:29-50 (February, 1970).

[3]A. P. Streissguth and H. L. Bee, "Mother-child Interactions and Cognitive Development in Children," in W. W. Hartup (ed.), *The Young Child: Reviews of Research*, Vol. 2 (Washington, D.C.: National Association for the Education of Young Children, 1972).

population on every human characteristic! Interestingly enough, we forgot that among both rich and poor there are many children who feel unloved. Similarly, we overlook the fact that among the poor, parents differ from each other just as wealthy parents do. Today we know that there are very few generalizations that can be made about people who are poor.[4]

One of the few generalizations we can make, based on our own experiences and across the world, is that wherever you are, if you are poor your chances of serious health problems increase.[5] Another which seems to hold for industrial nations is that the poorer you are the more powerless you feel.

There is one other very consistent finding, although there are strong arguments about this one. Children's language development, which is crucial to so many other aspects of development, seems to be slowed down with increasing poverty. There are many different ways to interpret this. Definitive answers to questions raised by this finding will be some time in coming.[6]

We also know now that one summer of enrichment, or even one year of enrichment, is not enough to help children. My own view is that we oversold early childhood education, and that in one year it cannot be expected to overcome all the ill-effects of poverty on children or change the society which needs changing. Another point I want to make about overselling early childhood education is that children need good education from the earliest years and throughout their years of growth—for 18 or 20 years. A community must care very deeply about the education of all of its children all through their development.

Now I would like to look at the research and development work of recent years in terms of a set of distinctions which I find useful.

In terms of the proliferation of curriculum models—at least 25 clearly identifiable ones—we see increasing polarization of curriculum goals. We seem to have foregone the intention to prepare the preschooler for schooling, and are now introducing such schooling earlier and earlier in the child's life. I find it helpful, in looking at curriculum goals, to make a distinction between academic and intellectual goals. Academic goals have to do with helping children to become pupils, helping them learn to conform to the daily routines of classroom life, and strengthening their motivation to achieve. These goals are important, but they are not the same as intellectual goals. Intellectual goals are those which help the child to become a learner (rather than pupil), an enquirer, an investigator and which help the child to learn to study. Intellectual goals have to do with strengthening motivation for learning rather than motivation for achieving.

We have customarily stated the goals of education in academic terms,

[4]M. Cole and J. S. Bruner, "Preliminaries to a Theory of Cultural Differences," in I. Gordon (ed.), *op. cit.*

[5]H. G. Birch and J. D. Gussow, *Disadvantaged Children: Health, Nutrition and School Failure* (New York: Harcourt, Brace and World and Grune & Stratton, 1970).

[6]S. M. Ervin-Tripp, "Children's Sociolinguistic Competence and Dialect Diversity," in I. Gordon (ed.), *op. cit.*

i.e., to help children to acquire skills, particularly the proverbial three R's. There is impressive evidence that we do know how to reach these goals with young children. The results achieved by the application of operant conditioning techniques and token economy systems indicate that we have at our disposal some very powerful techniques that "work." But it seems to me that the real problem in education is to help children—in fact, all people, young or old—acquire the skills, knowledge, *and* personal resources they need in such a way as to strengthen, safeguard, and enhance their sense of self-worth, dignity, and self-respect, and encourage curiosity, compassion, and tenderness. We must fashion an education that will achieve the mutually inclusive goals of acquiring skills, knowledge, and personal strengths and resources.

It may be that latent awareness of the importance of addressing academic and intellectual and personal goals together is one of the factors behind the current interest in Open Education. Here I would like to introduce another distinction, namely, the distinction between classes which are open and classes which are empty.

The goal of the open classroom approach is to help children make sense out of their own experiences, their own environments, and their own feelings. It is an approach which helps children to acquire the basic skills of learning as *tools* with which to examine, analyze, record, observe, measure, explore, describe, and organize their experiences. These seem to me to be developmentally appropriate intellectual goals for young children. It is an approach to education which is open to children's own interests, but not open in terms of the standards with which those interests are pursued. In the empty classroom everything is treated as equally worth doing, equally worth knowing, or equally worthless. It may be open to all interests, but no expectations or standards of work are expressed, no demands are made, and no conformity is required.

Good open education for young children can help children to make sense out of their experience. So many of the children we are trying to help live in complex, unpredictable—and rich—environments. It seems to me that if you cannot understand most of the events around you, you come to feel stupid. There are many children who wander through their universe feeling overwhelmed, feeling that they never can or will understand it. In the good open classroom teachers alert children to those events and phenomena in the children's own environments which are worth knowing about, which are important, and which, when understood, could help the child to organize his own experience.

Here I would like to introduce another distinction, namely, between being an authoritarian teacher and an authoritative teacher. An authoritarian teacher is one who makes demands on children, sets expectations for children, insists on conformity to arbitrary requirements without support, warmth, encouragement, or explanation. On the other hand, the authoritative teacher combines both warmth and strength, encouragement and exactingness, conformity and explanation. These qualities must all come together. In addition to combining these qualities the authoritative teacher treats children's opinions and feelings as valid. She is sensitive to their feelings and opinions, but she is not pushed around by them. Children need adults, and need to be loved by people they can perceive as strong. The love from a strong person who is himself or herself self-respecting is crucial for development. To withhold making demands and setting reasonable standards and expectations is to abdicate the authority ascribed to adults.[7]

Another distinction I would like to make is between teaching and performing. This is a difficult distinction to define. Perhaps the best way to approach it is to share my concern about teachers who do what they do in order to please a third person who is not even there. Often they say that what they're doing, let's say in kindergarten, is done because the first grade teacher who will receive her pupils, expects her to "cover" it. This is a type of "education for afterlife"—always rationalizing today's pedagogy in terms of the next life. Sometimes teachers tell me they do such and such because of the "parents." On further questioning it often turns out to be one vocal parent from among 30 contented or indifferent ones. Of course there is always the "administration" to blame. Far too often it is the janitor who causes teachers' behavior. Then again the testers or evaluators from downtown cause teacher behavior. The list of obtrusive others for whom teachers perform is a long one. How can we teach if we are constantly performing? Teaching requires a high degree of vigilance and awareness of the minds, feelings, and wishes of each individual child. On stage, one must be aware of the audience, and thereby one misses the complex cues embedded in the children's behavior.

This takes me to another distinction, namely, the distinction between children having fun and children getting satisfaction. To provide children with programs of activities that are fun is too cheap a goal. We must offer children the chance to gain the kind of satisfaction that comes from problem solving, from problem posing, from hard work, from effort, and from mastery, and we are unfair to children when we fail to encourage them to tackle the difficult and, occasionally, the tedious.

Here I would like to add a very similar distinction between excitement and learning. Most of us have a fairly even level of activity, although for each individual that typical level varies. If you picture this level as a sort of straight line, and then introduce into the environment of someone at his own typical level of activity an exciting experience, the level of activity goes up. However, it cannot be maintained. It has to come down. What concerns me is that when the activity level comes down, it does not come down to the earlier level. It goes below this level, and it is then that depression and mistrust set in and apathy is common. What you have to do in order to get moving again is to find an activity that is twice as exciting as the first one and you are thus constantly on a spiral of thrills.

One of the major concerns, it seems to me, is that the real work of this world is not exciting. We like to portray the lives of physicians and lawyers as constant series of peak experiences. But the real health of our communities is maintained by physicians who give you booster shots and who look at sore throats, perhaps 200 a week; looking at sore throats cannot be exciting. Furthermore, the physician who maintains the community's

[7]D. Baumrind, "Current Patterns of Parental Authority," *Developmental Psychology Monographs*, 4, 1:1-103 (1971).

health looks at each sore throat alertly so as to catch potentially significant indicators of serious complications.

It seems to me that instead of trying to get children excited we should foster their capacity to find the universe interesting. Strengthening children's capacities for sustained interest and effort would be more worthy of them. We have to remember that introducing things to children because they are exciting, that is, aiming for cheap goals, is a pervasive quality of our whole society. Notice how often people use the term "exciting" around you. People have learned to expect that. We seem to have taught the children who are now adolescents to expect to be excited, to be entertained and titillated. But one cannot learn much that way. Learning means getting involved and pursuing a line of reasoning or thought or inquiry. If we teach our children to expect thrills each day we seriously handicap them. In early childhood programs—and in other segments of our society—we have become accustomed to settling for cheap thrills and quick success, which may in fact be hollow success.

In the recent years of rapid expansion in early childhood education, we exaggerated its power to overcome longstanding social, psychological, and economic problems. We now need to take stock of what we have learned and settle down to the long labor ahead of us.

References

Akers, M. E. "Prologues: The Why of Early Childhood Education." In *Early Childhood Education*, The Seventy-first Yearbook for the Study of Education, edited by I. Gordon. Chicago: University of Chicago Press, 1972.

Baratz, S. and Baratz, J. C. "Early Childhood Intervention: The Social Science Base of Institutional Racism. *Harvard Educational Review 40* (1970): 29–50.

Baumrind, D. Current Patterns of Parental Authority. *Developmental Psychology Monograph 4* (1971): 1–103.

Birch, H. G., and Gussow, J. D. *Disadvantaged Children: Health, Nutrition and School Failure*. New York: Harcourt, Brace and Grune & Stratton, 1970.

Cole, M., and Bruner, J. S. "Preliminaries to a Theory of Cultural Differences." In *Early Childhood Education*, The Seventy-first Yearbook for the Study of Education, edited by I. Gordon. Chicago: University of Chicago Press, 1972.

Ervin-Tripp, S. M. Children's Sociolinguistic Competence and Dialect Diversity. In *Early Childhood Education*, The Seventy-first Yearbook for the Study of Education, edited by I. Gordon. Chicago: University of Chicago Press, 1972.

Miller, J. O. Early Childhood Education Program and Research Support Literature: A State of the Art Review." In *National Program on Early Childhood Education*. St. Louis: CEMREL, Inc., 1972.

Streissguth, A. P., and Bee, H. L. "Mother-Child Interactions and Cognitive Development in Children." In *The Young Child: Reviews of Research*, Vol. 2, edited by W. W. Hartup. Washington, D.C.: National Association for the Education of Young Children, 1972.

2. Early Childhood Education: Who's Doing What to Whom, and Why?

One of the biggest and potentially most misdirected discoveries made by public education recently is that children under five do not *have* to be *pre*schoolers. No more are under-fives *assumed* to be outside educational policy and resources; no more are they automatically granted the status of fledglings who belong to mother and the nest.

The discovery that every preschooler is a potential schooler seems to have been "made" during the last five years. President Nixon vetoed a $2.1 billion child-development bill in 1971 and the public was not outraged. Nixon claimed the bill would lead to the breakdown of the family and to "sovietization," and while the public may not have bought that argument, it did seem suspicious of organizing and institutionalizing preschoolers and of removing them from what many people saw to be a world of maternal protection and innocent domesticity.

And yet the same voices that once talked about the folly of public intervention in the lives of young children now are asking, sometimes eagerly: How can we get the job done?

This change in attitude and some of the reasons behind it involve a story that is complicated and not always encouraging. The change may have been initiated by research—beginning with Benjamin Bloom's work at the University of Chicago—which led many people to conclude that the first five years of life are the very time when much, if not most, of learning goes on. The change probably was aided by Head Start. This naive, if well-meant, national campaign to equalize educational opportunity by prepping impoverished three- and four-year-olds for school success found itself to be too little and too late, forcing social planners to think about intervening even earlier in the lives of kids and their families. And changes in society at large—the feminist movement, a rethinking of parental roles and family styles, the economy—helped make young children a social as well as educational issue.

As soon as one-, two-, three- and four-year-olds were considered as a group that could be reached, they were transmuted into a potential market. Publishers and other education-business folk went about building an industry of early childhood curricula and related "learning materials"; of screening and diagnostic schemes to uncover high risk indicators and developmental delays; of research projects to investigate the significance of every perinatal factor and piece of infant behavior; and of plans and programs to educate, train, support and mold toddlers and their parents.

Schools wanted a piece of the action, too.

THE SCHOOLS MAKE THEIR CLAIM

Albert Shanker and his American Federation of Teachers have launched a major campaign (Educare) to corner the under-fives market for public school teachers. With school enrollments declining, budgets strapped, and massive numbers of teachers unemployed, Shanker sees the early childhood field as a growth area for schools and their staffs. The AFT estimates that universally accessible early childhood education for the nation's 10.4 million three- to five-year-olds would put 150,000 to 200,000 teachers to work immediately, plus provide jobs for another 400,000 persons. At the national level, the AFT campaign is focusing on eventual passage of the still dormant Child and Family Services Act of 1975, a bill that would provide $1.8 billion over three years for a national network of comprehensive child care programs for poor and middle-class families. The AFT wants public schools, and not social and child-development agencies, to control these programs, and AFT intends to try to kill the legislation if public school sponsorship isn't part of the package.

At the national level, AFT already has lined up its support. Early in 1976, Shanker held a press conference in which seven other major educational organizations—including the National School Boards Association, the American Association of School Administrators, the American Association of Colleges of Teacher Education, the National Congress of Parents and Teachers, and even a somewhat reluctant National Education Association—fell in line with the AFT in committing themselves to public school sponsorship of early childhood services. "If this nation," the group declared, "is to develop a truly comprehensive system of early childhood development services, we think that the public school system should have a major responsibility for its delivery and for coordinating other essential health, diagnostic, parent education, and counseling services."

There is more than a little support for Shanker's position in influential federal circles. The most outspoken supporter of the schools' claim to the early childhood field has been Edwin W. Martin, director of the U.S. Office of Education's Bureau of Education for the Handicapped, which already funds preschool programs to the tune of $22 million, a third of that money under public school auspices.

"It's a logical extension," Martin maintains. "The public school system is the only broad-based, stable social service system you've got. Sure, you can run good programs under social service auspices, but it's a patchwork approach. And yes, the schools are weak in parental involvement, but there's no reason to believe they're absolutely unbending or unresponsive. If the schools are deputized for the job, they'll do it."

Day-care and child-development spokesmen, however, are highly skeptical about the ability of public schools to reach younger children. Theodore Taylor, executive director of the Day Care and Child Development Council of America, Inc., notes the special needs of preschool children: "These children are obviously largely not verbal. Understanding them and establishing two-way communication with them requires not only some study and experience, but also special insights and sensibilities. Indeed, a great number of those who are most effective . . . in the field more than make up for any lack in formal study by a combination of experience and sensitivity. Many good teachers have comparable sensitivities . . . but [these] are supported by or ancillary to verbal communication. I suggest that few good eighth grade teachers could readily convert to teaching three- and four-year-olds." The AFT argues back that in-service training programs, continuing education and retraining opportunities for teachers and paraprofessionals could make the conversion possible.

But Taylor also has a concern that can't be answered so easily: "The educational system is in chaos and cannot deal with its own problems. Why should we believe that [the system] can give the children in their early years any better service than [it has given] to elementary and secondary age children?"

Jule M. Sugarman, a veteran of the child care field and now chief administrative officer of the city of Atlanta, suggests somewhat more gently that each state and community should have the option to choose that administrative vehicle that is best able to do the job at the local level. Early childhood programs are essentially different from those now operated by the public schools, Sugarman notes, but schools might be selected for sponsorship *if* they can show that they have the willingness and flexibility to involve parents, concern themselves with developmental issues, hire people with differing backgrounds, conduct programs in different kinds of facilities, operate during hours that fit the needs of parents and children, and work with other agencies. Schools must prove their merit, though, and compete with other potential sponsors.

The president of the American Federation of State, County, and Municipal Employees, Jerry Wurf, makes a similar case: "It would be a mistake to fall into the trap of accepting the argument that because existing child care delivery systems and programs have inadequacies, other mechanisms and institutions, such as the schools, would do a better job. Any delivery system will have some problems. What is needed is one that has the best chance of establishing a system of accountability and flexibility. State and local government prime sponsorship would do that." Employees of these state and local governments, of course, are the members of Wurf's union.

In this early rush for early childhood education, is everyone simply pursuing vested interests? Shanker responds to this type of charge by saying, "Unions are at their finest when they find issues representing a good combination of self-interest and public interest."

WE KNOW LITTLE, AND PUT EVEN LESS TO WORK

What, then, is best for the public interest? What is best for the children? What works best for preschoolers from greatly differing backgrounds?

What do parents want for their children and for themselves? What do we really know about how toddlers learn? In the heat of battle for the control of early childhood education, these questions seem to melt away.

Because we recently have learned a good deal about the significance of the early years, there is a tendency to think we know a lot. But as Harvard psychologist Sheldon White, who did a major study of the nation's child care programs, said: "I'm not impressed at all. My God, we don't even understand what we mean when we say 'children's learning.' " Colleague Jerome Kagan concurs: "In the last decade we have learned more about the first five years of life than had been learned in 300 years before. Compared with a subject like physics, however, we are somewhere between the 15th and 16th centuries."

One thing the early childhood field has "learned" and made a wholesale purchase of is the developmental model of psychiatry and psychology, which has it that children move naturally from one phase of growth to another; that the Western norms of development are a universal model; that, as psychologist Arnold J. Sameroff of the University of Rochester describes it, "behaviors necessarily build on each other to produce a continuity of functioning from conception to adulthood."

The widespread assumption in the early childhood field is that future functioning can be rather nicely predicted by a study of behavior and influences at an earlier age, that early screening and testing can show us where a child is heading, that certain factors—whether they be traumas or benefits—affect all children in somewhat the same way. But the evidence is just beginning to come in that child development may be a much more complicated business than this model suggests, that the most sophisticated kinds of predictions of how children will function as adults can be wrong, that early conflicts and difficulties may be as good a preparation for later competence as a harmonious, supportive family life, and that the uniqueness of children often confounds the norms psychologists use to measure intelligence, abilities and social adjustment.

Sameroff's review of the literature and the most recent research on early childhood education now leads him to conclude that the "hypothesized 'continuity' in development from early trauma to later deviancy does not appear to hold." Nor do environmental factors—the personality of the parent, the parent's child-rearing beliefs and practices—alone tell much about the outcome of the child. Sameroff surmises: "Evidence for qualitative continuities and stabilities in development appear to be artifacts of an incomplete analysis of the child in [his] environment."

ECE MOVES INTO THE HOME

In spite of the fragility of what we think we know, in spite of the failures of most compensatory preschool programs to maintain their gains, in spite of contradictory research findings on whether group care is a positive, neutral or harmful arrangement for young children, new programs for preschoolers are beginning every day, with the public schools claiming a good number of them. Last year, then U.S. Commissioner of Education Terrel

H. Bell found $2.9 million in discretionary Title III funds to underwrite 52 pilot programs in which public elementary schools are used as a base for training parents of preschoolers to do the early education job at home. The Early Childhood Education Outreach programs, as they're called, typically offer a combination of home visits and classes for preschoolers and their parents. They're modest in cost because no custodial care is involved. And unlike most of the current federal efforts in early childhood education, Outreach is not aimed at some special target population, such as the handicapped or disadvantaged, but at all families with preschoolers within a community.

Bell's stated reason for starting the Outreach programs is basic: There are a lot of important things preschoolers can learn, and the schools, with their surplus of teachers, are able and willing to teach them.

At the Lenox School in southeast Washington, D.C., where dismal housing projects offer a view of the Capitol's dome, the Outreach project is housed in two rooms that look just like what they are—elementary classrooms with the desks removed. On a typical morning, six youngsters, ranging in age from two-and-a-half to four, attend a class taught by Eunice B. Cobb, a former remedial reading teacher. As the mothers sit quietly in the background, the youngsters pledge the flag, chant "How Are You Today?" and report on the weather. "Put on your listening ears!" Cobb orders, and then gets down to the matter at hand, a highly directed session of finding triangles and squares in clothing, then naming the colors of socks. With ruler in hand, Cobb keeps the tempo of the drill brisk, reprimands a child whose attention wanders briefly, has the youngsters stretch and bounce on cue, and physically pulls and yanks them about in the acting out of a nursery rhyme.

The mothers seem mutely accepting of the heavy-handed approach, and when it's their turn to run skill drill sessions with one or two children, they use an equally hard-sell and formal approach to get the youngsters to match numbers, colors and shapes and to color neatly the prescribed ditto sheets. The children are enormously cooperative and well-behaved during the hour of "learning," but when a freeplay break comes, they let off steam with car races, fantasy plays and wrestling. Neither the staff nor the mothers seem much interested in the free-play activity, except to keep it within bounds: "Let's not play so rough." At clean-up time, a youngster volunteers to put away a small plastic truck for a classmate, but this act of cooperation is aborted by Cobb, who reruns the scene so the truck user ends up putting away the toy. "We have to teach our children a certain amount of responsibility," she explains.

Nowhere is there any sense that two- and three-year-olds might have needs special to their age, that exploration and discovery and social transactions might be the most appropriate learning experiences for the youngsters. There are no wood blocks, easels, small animals in cages, open-ended play equipment, corners for playing house or any other indicators of a desire to capture the interests of kids. "The idea for the program came from the prekindergarten and kindergarten teachers," explains Jennie T. Gross, the program director and Lenox principal. "Some of our youngsters are very immature in kindergarten, and we need to pretrain them. We know we've got to get the children earlier and mold them a little differently."

"Maybe I'm a little regimented," Cobb explains, "but I've got to show them that everything in here is learning, even using a napkin and fork at lunchtime. When we made cookies, they saw the circles. In here, in this program, repetition is the thing—review, review, review."

For youngsters whose families don't bring them to the school-based program, there's a fledgling home visiting program in which Clara L. Herndon, an amiable former school secretary, visits two homes on a typical morning. On her first call one day last winter at a tiny, dark home thick with stale air, she is awaited by Kevin, an alert and polite child with a tight cough. He's in his underwear. "I bet you've got some homework for me," she greets him, noting that he is "well advanced, on lesson 14" in matching items. As Kevin's mother, dressed in a housecoat and slippers, disappears into the kitchen to make a late breakfast for herself, Kevin recites the pledge to the flag, sing-songs a patriotic ditty, gives Herndon a free-form drawing he's done instead of the dittoed picture he was supposed to crayon, matches scraps of paper meant to look like eggs and bacon and toast and butter, and chooses the Hamburgler doll from the pair of dolls Herndon has brought from the program's modest toy library. Herndon isn't clear on Kevin's age; she reports he's three but the boy's mother says he just turned five, the age he looks to be. It isn't clear why he isn't in kindergarten or prekindergarten at Lenox—something about a serious physical problem that wouldn't let Kevin tolerate normal school activity.

At the second home, where the furniture and carpets stuffed into the miniature living room are all sheathed in plastic, Charles and a cousin are being watched over by a busily cleaning grandmother. A bouncy, charming, curious boy, Charles doesn't yet know his colors and can count only to five. He does know about Hot Wheels and Ronald McDonald and Batman. He tries to talk about Hot Wheels and Evel Knievel, but neither his grandmother nor Herndon is familiar enough with these totems of TV-watching preschoolers to pick up on his enthusiasm. Herndon shows him what is supposed to be a paper leaf: "What's this?" "A monster," the boy responds quickly. "His imagination is terrific," Herndon smiles, getting him quickly back to the matching of leaves and squirrels and to coloring inside the lines.

SOPHISTICATED PROGRAMS IN AFFLUENT COMMUNITIES

Although the Lenox program is simple-minded and primitive in its approach to preparing youngsters for the rigors of school, its intention, at least, is not so different from the original goals of the most celebrated and sophisticated of the preschool projects now in operation: the Brookline Early Education Project in Massachusetts. BEEP was conceived back in 1969 when the Boston suburb's superintendent of schools Robert I. Sperber thought that getting the kids into school at four years of age might be the answer to what he considered the inordinate amounts of time and money that his affluent system was spending on remedial and compensatory programs for older students. Sperber went to Burton White, the psychologist who heads the Harvard Graduate School of Education's Preschool Project, for advice on such a program, and was told that reaching children at three or four years of age was too late for guaranteeing "successful educational careers."

What finally emerged in 1972 was an intricately designed demonstration and research project which is intervening in and monitoring the development of 285 youngsters from conception to school entrance at five. The stated goals of the program are to help parents "provide an optimum learning environment" during this period and to assess how each child progresses by running him through an enormously fulsome diagnostic program of medical, psychological and developmental tests, screens and interviews that make note of everything from the mother's "emotional responsiveness" to the normalcy of every possible neurological response to the child's "social orientation" at each stage.

With its sponsorship by the prestigious Brookline schools, its ties with the Harvard Graduate School of Education and Children's Hospital Medical Center in Boston, and its $2 million in support from the Carnegie Corporation of New York and the Robert Wood Johnson Foundation, BEEP was fated from the start to become a national model for school-sponsored early childhood programs. Any number of school districts are considering some version of the program, and districts in St. Louis and Madison, Wisconsin, have committed themselves to similar efforts. The problem is that, now in midstream, BEEP seems to be having serious questions about where the program is going.

BEEP's education component, founded on Burton White's model of child rearing, assumes a suburban mother eager to learn from the experts how to become the kind of classy, involved child rearer that would elevate her job to a kind of profession. Mothers of young children should not work out of the house full time, says White. "I am totally convinced . . . any other kind of job, be it formal or informal, working as an engineer somewhere, working as the president of a bank, working as a career professional in designing, or in the arts, cannot compete (in humanistic terms) with the job of helping a child make the most of his potential for a rich life. I do not think any job is more important . . . than [this] one."

White gets away with what he's saying by conceding that not every well-educated woman glows with the satisfaction of full-time mothering. For "a great number of our very best-put-together" women it means "a miserable average day," he admits, but the reason the job is "more stressful and far less rewarding than it could be" is not because it's inherently physically exhausting, emotionally trying or intellectually empty, but because these mothers aren't good enough at it. They "do not know how to do the job," White reveals, and their ignorance ranges from not knowing how to baby-proof a room to not knowing the stages of a toddler's development. His remedy for those ignorant and consequently unhappy mothers is information and more information, training before and on the job, and a full acceptance of their role as the "first educational delivery system" for their children. Because if the mother doesn't do her job, he warns, "there may be little the professional can do to save the child from mediocrity." The bottom line plays on pure guilt: If you're not good and happy at this mothering/teaching job, your child is fated to be an academic also-ran.

White has even been so bold as to pin down and promote the style of mothering that will produce an "A" child—one who will prove exceptionally competent in school—as opposed to a so-so "B" or an incompetent "C". Mothers produce "A's" by designing a physical environment that's safe enough so a child can explore freely while setting limits on dangerous or annoying behavior. More important, they act as "consultants" to their youngsters in brief but frequent episodes throughout the day, talking to them to provide, help or comfort, or to share a discovery. For White, the quality and purposefulness of the mother's days don't seem to matter. She is a kind of given who can be trained to perform key tasks, and if she does them well, she has done all that matters.

To test White's thesis, BEEP's original intention was to spare nothing in funds and expertise to inform, enlighten and train a group of volunteering mothers to see if they could be programmed to bring about in youngsters the "optimal physical and intellectual growth during the preschool years." BEEP mothers, it was planned, would have all the professional expertise available to tell them how to become "professional mothers" with the most "competent" children. Even visions of higher IQs danced in some heads.

Now, three years later, White no longer is affiliated with the project he spawned, and at the BEEP headquarters, located in an old Victorian mansion stocked with Creative Playthings and file drawers crammed with developmental assessments, staff members are quick to point out that this project doesn't necessarily endorse White's ideas.

What mothers want, more than information on infant stimulation or learning strategies, BEEP found, is lots of support in the isolation, stress and messiness of their daily lives with small children; instead of a blueprint for superior child rearing, mothers ask for individually tailored help for family and personal problems (BEEP made more social service referrals than medical referrals in its first three years); the mothers need a receptive ear from people who share their dilemmas and fears, not a patronizing voice from self-styled experts; and instead of guidelines that will make them more anxious about their competence, mothers need an atmosphere that will minimize the myths and presuppositions about mothering. White clearly doesn't like the emphasis on service: "BEEP was not conceived as a social work program," he argues.

If BEEP has modified its support style, it's had to change even more drastically its original belief that the use of "the best assessment techniques available" would uncover scores of medical and developmental problems which, the theory went, were the reasons kids ended up "learning disabled" or otherwise dysfunctional in school. BEEP seems in the process of discrediting all the retrospective studies that blame undetected neurological and physical problems for later classroom performance.

BEEP's diagnostic armada has turned up only four previously unknown "hard" neurologic findings and only one speech problem among its 285 subjects. In a control group of 155 30-month-old children, only two previously unknown neurologic findings were discovered. BEEP director

Donald Pierson now admits that the early emphasis on medical-based problems was unwarranted and inappropriate, conceding, "We're finding very few significant deficits that don't get picked up in the newborn nursery."

Then what is it about BEEP that does make sense? What models can it offer to other systems? Pierson says some mothers like occasional home visits while many others appreciate a drop-in center where they can talk to other mothers and share their experiences. No one would disagree that such voluntary services would be nice to have. But it's not clear why it's taking more than $2 million to learn this. It's not clear to BEEP or anyone else why such services should be sponsored by the school system, except as a public relations device to counter the distrust many parents feel as their children enter school.

Although most of the school systems inspired by BEEP and the early childhood push are waiting for federal or foundation funding, the Clayton (Missouri) school system began an infant program last year with $63,000 of its own money, even though the district has a $500,000 spending deficit. Superintendent Earl W. Hobbs first cited the usual educational rationale for early intervention, even in the upper-middle-class families typical of his suburban district: "There's a growing amount of research that suggests that kids, in terms of overall development, make it or don't depending upon what their parents do with them between the ages one and three. . . . One of our main purposes is to give parents all the help they need in properly coping with this crucial stage of life of their child."

And then he spoke openly of the motive of improving public relations for his enterprise: "Like a business, a school system that does not continually meet its consumer's needs slowly dies. We see this as a shot of adrenaline in our program at a time [when] we are tightening our belts and reassessing old programs."

Clearly, the positive community response suggests that Hobbs is onto something. Clayton residents with babies and toddlers have lined up to pay $50 for eight sessions of discussion and observation; the price is twice that for nonresidents. The well-educated Clayton mothers do not need basic information about developmental stages and child rearing; they've read all the books and picked up on the trends. What they seem to need, and what project coordinator Barbara Geno, a former kindergarten teacher, knows to give them, is reassurance that they're doing a good job, that they're not alone in their anxieties, that it's OK to relax a little. Geno doesn't know why the suburban mothers tend toward such anxiety, but as a working mother she can empathize with them. "Middle-class mothers are most susceptible to uncertainties," she said, "and we can loosen them up a bit. We may produce better cognitive skills through the program, but that's not really our goal. Our real results aren't testable. My point of view is that schools don't teach much, so they have to be fun and be a challenge, and a place that can be a support system for families, not one that's ac-cusatory of families." Apparently we have a school system offering a few social services in the hope of improving its image in the community, of getting people to think that school is a warm, helpful, "fun" place.

In the absence of massive federal or state funds for early childhood programs, projects similar in design to those in Clayton or the District of Columbia may be what school systems opt for: voluntary, short-range efforts, comparatively modest in cost because there's no attempt to provide child care. Such projects assume a full-time parent to do that job. Rather than pretending to deal with the needs of the six million preschool children with working parents, they build on the traditional mother-and-child-at-home model. They make mom an extension of the school, a kind of volunteer early childhood teacher. Few school boards are going to turn away from such a low-budget approach to readying kids for school while making parents allies of the system.

Much more politically controversial and financially demanding are school programs that go the step beyond to replace the parent as caretaker or teacher. Yet these are the very programs that count for working parents seeking day-care teachers and for paraprofessionals seeking jobs. (The difference between "day care" and "early childhood education" is a matter of emphasis, of political thrust, and of a style of operation. As Anna B. Mayer and Alfred J. Kahn note in *Day Care As a Social Instrument: A Policy Paper*, the caring and educating functions "are inextricably woven in the dynamism of child growth and development.")

A few systems, like the one in Mount Diablo, California, are making plans to provide low-cost custodial day care for parents without outside financial help or the hiring of high-cost teachers. But most districts will wait till the battle over the preschoolers gets fought out at the national level and outside funding is available.

SCHOOLS DO THEIR THING AT CHILD CARE CENTERS

While opinions about the ability of the schools to operate good early childhood programs are plentiful, concrete examples are rare. Perhaps the best precedent, one that does not bode well for the schools' future in child care, is that of California's Children Centers. For the past 30 years, California has operated a statewide system of high-quality day-care centers, mainly for the children of single and poor parents. Although officially under education department auspices, the centers traditionally have maintained a surprising amount of autonomy, functioning quite separately from the school systems of which they are a part. As W. Norton Grubb and Marvin Lazerson note in a history of the centers, most public school personnel disregard the centers, seeing them as "tolerable babysitters, at best," and often as antieducational institutions run by amateurs. Most often the centers seemed to flourish in the shadow of this indifference, attracting "large numbers of teachers who were dedicated to young children, who dislike[d] the regimentation of children in the elementary schools, and who reveled in the freedom they were allowed in the centers. . . . They could emphasize play and the child's social development, responsibility of health care and some liaison with parents as distinct alternatives to existing public school practices. . . . To center personnel, the centers were more responsive to children than the schools were."

With the coming of federal funds, the increased prestige of early childhood education, and the scramble for teaching jobs, all of this is now changing. The centers are becoming, in character and goals, part of the school systems to which they're connected: more bureaucratic, obsessive about credentials and professionalism, more concerned with teaching specific cognitive skills that make for school readiness. For Grubb and Lazerson, the evolution of the centers into "a mechanism for preparing children for elementary schools is disastrous. . . . Indeed, the most likely trend is that the methods and goals of the elementary school will be extended downward to child care: that order will replace the centers' enlivened chaos, that rote instruction will replace individual patterns of exploration, that conformity and neatness will replace spontaneity and creativity."

For Rae Breton, a 25-year veteran of the Children Centers and head teacher of a model center, the passing of the old days seems a tragedy. "We usually got the basement," she recalls, "but we could do damn well what we pleased in that basement. We could experiment and enjoy and discover. We made caves and were cavemen, painted the damn bricks and grew mushrooms, had a teahouse and made root beer that blew up, kept a goose and a lamb, did all the good things. We had people with a fine gift for children. Sure, lots of them didn't have degrees, but they had skills and fun in their souls. Our children have had a bad reputation in school, of course. They were too lively and clannish; they got into trouble." As for the present, she finds herself drowning in bureaucratic routines and paperwork, being sent teachers "who have lots of education but are unaware and are tight, tight, tight, like a new shoe, or even worse, who hate kids, really hate them."

Breton and many early childhood specialists see the goals and styles of good day-care and preschool programs as quite different, and often in conflict, with those of the public schools. If so, the kinds of teaching skills and quality programs that make an elementary school successful cannot simply be retooled to meet the needs of younger children. And for all the schools that are not doing as well by older children as might be expected, the taking on of a program with an entirely different orientation and demands would be pure hubris.

The wisest people in the early childhood field—from Jean Piaget to master teachers in nursery schools—tell us that pushing children into academic subjects too early is not only unproductive but dangerous. "If you force a child to learn specific content before he is ready," they warn, "he will develop a long-term attitude about school that may be negative." Benjamin Bloom notes that "learning to learn should not be confused with the early teaching of the child to read, to spell or even to do simple arithmetic. Learning to learn is far more basic. Simply put, it means developing the child's view of adults as sources of information and ideas, and, most importantly, motivating that child to find pleasure in the act of learning itself."

If what young children should be learning has nothing to do with basic skill drills, pencil-and-paper activities, or the other kinds of exercises that fill most primary grade schedules and that most schools think of as education, the schools better think long and hard before they take on these children in their most vulnerable and critical years of growth.

If, on the other hand, a school system is sophisticated enough to avoid "pretraining" for first grade and chooses by default the social service approach that Brookline and Clayton seem to be pursuing, their course may be even more treacherous. Whatever their strengths, even the best schools have no great expertise in family counseling, therapy or social work. Nor should they. To further blur the role of the school and confuse its function will not serve it well in the long run. There is no reason to expect school to serve the whole family well when it is not doing its job for that family's child.

And if the education profession and its ancillaries are allowed to treat the nation's youngest as simply another market—for balancing school budgets, solving unemployment problems, selling slick curriculum packages or filling union rosters—we may be enriching one generation while threatening the next.

MATTHEW W. GAFFNEY

3. Present Imperatives for Public Parenting

As the United States approaches the evening of the century, nothing seems more predictable in the field of education than the widespread adoption of prekindergarten schooling for all. The evidence is in: The early years of life are crucial to future learnings. The need is clear. If the nation is ever to reach the goal of equality of educational opportunity, the early inequalities of intellectual stimulation must be rectified. The knowledges and skills of how to conduct an effective program have been worked out and are in practice in many sections of the country. Those most concerned about the future well-being of the nation are in agreement. The time has come to act.

The steady decline in the birthrate so evident in the early seventies has set some serious priorities for the eighties. One of the most persuasive theories of economics is the doctrine of scarcity. When things become more scarce, they become more precious. The falling enrollment in elementary schools, spreading now to high schools and ultimately to colleges, generates problems far beyond those of the professional educators facing empty

With permission from Matthew W. Gaffney.

classrooms and closed school buildings. People are important. If there are fewer people, then each person is more valuable. Parental attention is increased. The economy faces the fact of fewer workers and consumers. The nation that has relied on the brains and muscle of its youth for survival must face a reordering of some of its priorities.

The time has come to sound a tocsin. Professional educators, teachers, administrators and boards of education must take the leadership in pointing out the problem and its solution on a national scale. We cannot afford to wait for a Pied Piper to teach us the lesson of Hamelin Town.

Ordinary people watchers have always known that the child is father to the man, that the early years are crucial in the development of certain skills, especially in the development of personality traits.

It was Benjamin S. Bloom's extensive research in the late 1950s, culminating in the landmark study *Stability and Change in Human Characteristics* in 1964, that firmly and scientifically established the importance of the early years. In what is now recognized as one of the outstanding contributions to the science of education is the proof of the tremendous importance of the first few years of life for all that follows. His findings also reveal that change in many characteristics becomes more and more difficult with increasing age, and only the most powerful environmental conditions are likely to produce significant changes at later stages of life.

Bloom writes:

growth and development are not in equal units per unit of time. . . . we note that for some characteristics there is as much quantitative growth in a single year at one period in an individual's development as there is in eight to ten years at other stages in his development. The importance of the influences which affect the growth of such characteristics is likely to be far greater in the periods of most rapid development than it is, at least quantitatively, in the periods of least rapid development.

He concludes from his studies that the early environment is of crucial importance for three reasons. The first is based on the very rapid growth of selected characteristics in the early years when variation in the environment is so important because it shapes these characteristics in their most rapid periods of formation. The second concerns the sequential nature of much of human development, the hierarchical building of one skill upon another. And the third reason stems from learning theory observed in practice: It is much easier to learn something new than it is to stamp out one set of learned behaviors and replace it with a new set.

A steady progression of studies continues to confirm what Dr. Bloom made so clear regarding the importance of the early years. Craig T. Ramey and Frances A. Campbell, in "Compensatory Education for Disadvantaged Children" in *School Review* (February 1979), reported extensively on a project that was designed to extend scientific and educational understanding of the factors affecting the growth and development of children in the country's lowest socioeconomic strata. Known as the Carolina Abecedarian Project, it was a longitudinal early continuing educational program beginning with children six, twelve, and eighteen months old. The results indicate that the children in the experimental group were six times less likely to have a significant developmental delay than were their matched counterparts not in the program. They summarize that supplemental education within the project appears to have improved vastly the odds for intellectual normality in the disadvantaged child.

The famous Head Start program of the 1960s has survived remarkably well in terms of the number of continuing programs, although the title has lost it original meaning and impact. Government-supported early childhood nursery schools for welfare families will no doubt be extended in the area of child care in those communities where it is not now provided.

The need exists for community programs beyond those provided for those on welfare. Peter Morrison, in "Beyond the Baby Boom" in *The Futurist* (April 1979), points out that in 1977, 46 percent of wives were in the labor force, compared with only 24 percent in 1950. This increase has been especially noteworthy among mothers, 49 percent of whom were in the labor force in 1976, compared with 30 percent in 1960. An issue of the *Christian Science Monitor* (February 26, 1979), reviewing this problem of the empty home, estimated that there are six million working women with youngsters under six. Yet nationally, it is reported, less than 10 percent of the working mothers with preschoolers use center-based care.

The need exists. That early intervention does have a positive effect is clear. Perhaps what will finally move our society is a growing realization that there is an almost incalculable value to the nation in securing the maximum development of our children. As Daniel Webster once said, "The intelligence of the people is the security of the nation."

The *National Assessment of Educational Progress Newsletter* of February 1979, examining current data predicting the status of United States scientists of the future, reports:

Even as readers acknowledge the scope and utility of this science report, many will be disturbed by the jarring reminder of what differences in socioeconomic status and sex mean to many young Americans in terms of science achievement. . . . Early intervention is essential. Unfortunately, it is the parents of the disadvantaged who are least likely to have either the training resources or time needed to create the kind of environment that the (NAEP) data seem to suggest is beneficial. . . . Just as the government now recognizes the need to provide nutritional assistance to poor Americans, so it must provide individual education assistance to disadvantaged families. . . . If our children are to be ready for the 21st century, we must begin to prepare them now.

The Newsletter might well have closed with the truism, "You are your brother's keeper, and if you don't, he will keep you in trouble." And that is even more true of "your brother's children."

One of the most chilling observations on the effect of the scarcity of youth was made by a high-ranking officer in the Department of Defense. He pointed out that if the United States is to maintain its armed forces at their current size, one out of every three eighteen-year-old males will have to be in the armed forces by 1985.

Quantity of youth we do not have, but quality improvement in those we do have is well within our grasp. At the national level, the efforts for early childhood education improvement have already begun. Eventually, the tragic shortage of youngsters who are reaching the maximum of their possible potential will move our state and local governmental leaders to action. Early childhood care and training is a national investment as well as a humanitarian effort.

We have a self-proven federal program. Begun in 1964 as part of the Economic Opportunity Act, project Head Start is still with us. Doris Wallace, writing in *Education Before Five* (1977), summarized the program:

Of one thing there is little doubt: that parents and communities thoroughly approve of Head Start. . . . Cutbacks have been resisted and there appears to be a universal wish to extend the program. . . . Further, the very existence of Head Start emphasizes recognition of the early years; and indeed Head Start has provided the impetus to programs for older children—that is Follow Through—as well as for younger children, for example, parent-child centers and, more recently, the Child and Family Resource program. . . . It can, on many grounds, then, be considered a national program that has worked.

The machinery is in place for a nationwide move to achieve pre-kindergarten experiences as well as kindergarten schooling for every child. The local board of education is a national pattern. Establishing local advisory councils to these boards is a growing trend. Local boards not only have the power to act, but also have a source of funding. The decline in enrollments has left many school districts with a surplus of classrooms and underused or surplus buildings. The former teacher shortage has now turned to a teacher surplus. Teacher-training institutions are emptying. The decade of the eighties will need only local leadership to bring about this necessary fundamental change in American education.

THEORETICAL APPROACHES IN EARLY CHILDHOOD

J. McV. HUNT

4. The Epigenesis of Intrinsic Motivation and Early Cognitive Learning

Even as late as 15 years ago, a symposium on the stimulation of early cognitive learning would have been almost impossible. It would have been taken by most people as a sign that both participants and members of the audience were too soft-headed to be considered seriously. Even as late as 15 years ago, there was simply no point in talking about such a matter, for no possibility of altering cognitive capacity, or intelligence, was conceived to exist. To be sure, there was, before World War II, some evidence that suggested, even strongly, that cognitive capacities might be modified by early experience; but such evidence as existed was "too loose" to convince anyone who embraced the assumptions that intelligence is fixed and that development is predetermined (see Hunt, 1961.)[1] These two assumptions—and I believed and taught them just as did most of us—were considered to be among the marks of a "sound" and "hard-headed" psychologist. Had we psychologists absorbed the implications of Johannsen's (1903)[2] distinction between the genotype and the phenotype and his notion that the phenotype is always a product of continuous, on-going, organism—environment interaction, we should never have held these two assumptions with such certainty; but of the two fathers of the science of genetics we know only Mendel. Since World War II, however, the various investigations of the effects of infantile experience has piled up sufficient evidence to nearly destroy the credibility of these two dominant assumptions of our post-Darwinian tradition.

The change in conceptions started with the work of Sigmund Freud, but it has recently taken some abrupt new turns. Freud's (1905)[3] theory of psychosexual development attributed great importance to the effects of early infantile experience and especially to the preverbal fates of instinctive modes of pleasure-getting. The earliest studies of the effects of infantile

From J. McV. Hunt, "The Epigenesis of Intrinsic Motivation and Early Cognitive Learning," in *Current Research in Motivation*, ed. Ralph N. Haber (New York: Holt, Rinehart & Winston, 1966), pp. 355–370. Reprinted by permission of J. McV. Hunt and Holt, Rinehart & Winston, Inc. This paper was originally prepared for the symposium on the Stimulation of Early Cognitive Learning, chaired by J. R. Braun and presented at the Annual Meeting of the American Psychological Association, Philadelphia, Pennsylvania, 30 August 1963. It was written with the support of Public Health Service Grant MH K6-18,567.

experience assumed these effects to be on the emotional rather than on the intellectual aspects of personality (Hunt, 1941).[4] Yet the studies of the effects of the richness of environmental variations encountered during infancy on adult maze-learning ability in rats (Hebb, 1947)[5] and in dogs (Thompson & Heron, 1954)[6] have proved to be most regularly reproducible. These studies stemmed from the neuropsychological theorizing of Donald Hebb (1949)[7] and his distinction between "early learning," in which "cell-assemblies" are developed, and "later learning," in which these assemblies are connected in various kinds of "phase sequences." The studies showed that those rats encountering the larger number of environmental variations during infancy received higher scores on the Hebb-Williams (1946)[8] maze-test of animal intelligence than did those encountering fewer variations (see Forgays & Forgays, 1952; Forgus, 1954; Hymovitch, 1952).[9]

In Hebb's (1947)[10] original study of this kind, the number of variations in environment ranged from the many supplied by pet-reared rats in a human home to the few supplied by cage-rearing in the laboratory. A similar approach was employed by Thompson & Heron (1954)[11], and dogs pet-reared from weaning until eight months of age proved to be markedly superior in performance on the Hebb-Williams test at 18 months of age (after ten months with their cage-reared litter-mates in a dog pasture) to those litter-mates individually cage-reared from weaning to eight months. In fact, the pet-reared dogs appeared to differ more from their cage-reared litter-mates than did the pet-reared rats from their litter-mates. From this I am inclined to infer that the degree of the adult effect of such infantile experience increases as one goes up the vertebrate scale. I tend to attribute this apparent increase in the effect of infantile experience to the increasing proportion of the brain that is without direct connections with receptor input and/or motor output (see Pribram, 1960).[12] I refer here, of course, to the notion of the A/S ratio first put forth by Hebb (1949).[13]

This notion, that the degree of effect of the richness of variations in environment encountered during infancy on adult cognitive capacities increases with the size of the A/S ratio, suggests that the results of these animal studies should probably generalize to the human species. Incontrovertible evidence concerning this suggestion is hard to come by. Nevertheless, a combination of observations strongly supports the suggestion that such early experience has marked effects on the rate of human development and perhaps also has effects on the level of adult intellectual ability.

First, the evidence concerning effects of early experience upon the rate of human intellectual development is fairly compelling. It has long been noted that children being reared in orphanages show retardation in both their functional development and their motivational apathy. These observations were long discounted because of the notion that only those genotypically inferior remain in orphanages, but the well-known studies of René Spitz (1945, 1946)[14] helped to rule out this attribution of the retardation to a selection of genotypes. Unfortunately, Spitz's observations could be discounted on other grounds (see Pinneau, 1955).[15] More recently, however, Wayne Dennis (1960),[16] whose prejudices would appear from his previous writings to favor the traditional assumptions of "fixed intelligence" and "predetermined development," has found two orphanages in Teheran where retardation is even more extreme than that reported by Spitz. Of those infants in their second year, 60 percent were still unable to sit up alone; of those in their fourth year, 85 percent were still unable to walk alone. Moreover, while children typically creep on all fours rather than scoot, as did the children in a third orphanage in Teheran (one for demonstration purposes), those in these two typically chose scooting. By way of explanation, Spitz emphasized the emotional factors associated with lack of mothering (a one-to-one interpersonal relationship) as the basis for the greater retardation observed at "foundling home" than at "nursery." Dennis, on the other hand, has attributed the extreme retardation in sitting and walking to lack of learning opportunities, or more specifically, to the "paucity of handling, including failure of attendants to place children in the sitting position and the prone position" (1960, p. 58).[17] These may well be important factors, but I suspect that yet another factor is of sufficient importance to deserve specific investigative attention—namely, a paucity of variation in auditory and visual inputs, or, perhaps I should say a paucity of meaningful variation in these inputs. On the visual side, these Teheran infants (i.e., those in the orphanages in which 90 percent of the children are recorded as having been under one month of age at the time of admission) had plenty of light, but they continually faced homogeneous off-whiteness interrupted only by passing attendants who seldom stopped to be perceived. On the auditory side, while the noise level of the surrounding city was high and cries of other children were numerous, seldom did clear variations in sound come with such redundancy as to become recognizable and very seldom did such sound variations herald any specific changes in visual input. Thus, opportunities for the development of specific variations in either type of input and opportunities for auditory-visual coordinations were lacking. Moreover, since no toys were provided, the children had little opportunity to develop intentional behavior calculated to make interesting spectacles last. Dennis has reported the most extreme case of mass retardation of which I know. Although signs of malnutrition were present, Dennis was inclined not to consider it a major factor because of the vigor he observed in such automatisms as head shaking and rocking back and forth, and because he could see no way in which malnutrition could call forth scooting rather than creeping. Moreover, the role of heredity was minimized by the facts that the children in the demonstration orphanage, where retardation was much less marked, came from the one admitting neonates, and that they were probably chosen from those most retarded at the time of transfer.

Second, the evidence concerning the permanence of such effects is highly suggestive if less compelling than that concerning rate of development. Whether or not such retardation as that observed in Teheran inevitably leaves a permanent deficit cannot be stated with certainty. You will recall that Dennis observed that once these children in the orphanage learned to walk, they appeared to walk and run as well as other children do. But do not most intellectual and social functions demand a much more broadly integrated and more finely differentiated set of autonomous central processes than do such motor functions as walking and running? Certainly this is suggested by the fact that the dogs pet-reared by Thompson and Heron (1954)[18] are much superior to those cage-reared in solving various problems in the Hebb-Williams mazes even after a period of ten months of running free in the dog pasture. Moreover, permanence of the effects of infantile experience is also strongly suggested by the results of Goldfarb's (see 1955)[19] studies, in which adolescents, orphanage-reared for approximately their first three years, showed lower IQs, less rich fantasies, less tendency to take and hold onto a task, and more social problems than did adolescents (matched with those orphanage-reared for educational and socioeducational status of their mothers) who were reared in foster homes for those first three years. And again, permanence of intellectual deficit is also suggested by the finding in Israel that children of Jewish immigrants from the Orient persist in their scholastic inferiority to children of Jewish immigrants from Western countries, and by the observations that children from the slums in America persist in scholastic inferiority to children from middle-class parents even though the slum children may be advanced at least in motor development at ages from one to two years. In spite of these strong suggestions, it would be exceedingly interesting to have direct evidence from test performances at adolescence of these orphanage-reared Iranians for comparison with the test performances of family-reared Iranians or of adolescents reared in the demonstration orphanage. It is also important to determine whether the intellectual deficit from defective early experience is irreversible, or persists because of the way in which human children are usually treated once they achieve certain ages. If the latter alternative is the case, it should be possible to devise corrective experiences to overcome the deficit. This would be restudying the issues that concerned Itard and Seguin. Getting the evidence necessary to decide such issues is exceedingly difficult.

EARLY COGNITIVE LEARNING AND THE DEVELOPMENT OF INTRINSIC MOTIVATION

Combining such bits of evidence as I have indicated with the geneticist's conception of genotype-environment interaction and with the biologist's notion of organism-environment interaction now makes it quite sensible to attempt to stimulate early cognitive learning. This evidence, however, hardly indicates how to go about it. Perhaps the most fruitful source of suggestions about how to proceed comes from an examination of the relationship between the development of intrinsic motivation and early cognitive learning.

Changes in Traditional Assumptions of Motivation

One of the leading traditional assumptions about motivation, namely, that painful stimulation during infancy leads inevitably (through something like Pavlovian conditioning) to increased proclivity to anxiousness and to reduced capacity for adaptation or learning, has been called into serious question by evidence from studies of the effects of painful infantile experience. Various investigators have found that rats submitted to painful electric shock, like those handled and petted, defecate and urinate less in an unfamiliar situation than do those left unmolested in the maternal nest (see Denenberg, 1959, 1962; Denenberg & Karas, 1960; Denenberg, Morton, Kline, & Grota, 1962; Levine, 1956, 1957, 1958, 1959).[20] If proneness to defecate or urinate in an unfamiliar situation is an index to anxiousness, these findings appear to deny the notion that anxiousness is an inevitable consequence of painful stimulation and to suggest that painful stimulation may be a special case of the principle that variation in inputs helps to immunize an animal to fear of the strange. Moreover, investigators have found that encounters with electric shock before weaning may increase the adult ability of rats to learn, at least when this ability is indexed by means of the number of trials required to establish an avoidance response to painful stimulation (see Brookshire, 1958; Brookshire, Littman, & Stewart, 1961; Denenberg, 1959; Denenberg & Bell, 1960; Denenberg & Karas, 1960; Levine, 1956, 1958; Levine, Chevalier, & Korchin, 1956).[21] Encounters with painful electric shock in infancy appear to share with petting and handling the same kind of effects upon avoidance conditioning just as they share similar effects upon later defecation and urination in an unfamiliar situation. At least, this appears to be true for rats, but it may not be true for mice (see Lindzey, Lykken, & Winston, 1960).[22]

Perhaps this surprising similarity in the effects of painful stimulation and in the effects of petting and handling is an artifact of comparing the effects of each of these kinds of encounters with the effect of leaving the infant rat unmolested in the maternal nest. In such comparisons, painful shock, petting, and handling all constitute variations in receptor inputs or in environmental encounters. It has been argued that these various kinds of input are equivalent in their effects on still unweaned rat pups and that it is only stimulation per se that counts in early infancy (Levine, 1959).[23] This, however, can hardly be so, for Salama & Hunt (1964)[24] have found that rats shocked daily during their second ten days of life show substantially less "fixation" effect of shock at the choice-point in a T-maze than do their litter-mates that were petted or handled. The petted and handled rats in this experiment showed "fixation" effects that did not differ significantly from those of litter-mates left unmolested in the maternal nest. The findings of this experiment show that some of the effects of shock in early infancy differ markedly from those of petting and handling, but the fact that shock in infancy reduces rather than increases the "fixation" effects of shock at the choice-point in the maze is again highly dissonant with the assumption that painful stimulation must inevitably increase proclivity to anxiousness. Long ago, the Spartans based their child-rearing on the principle that infants should be exposed to pain and cold to toughen them against future encounters with such exigencies. The evidence may indicate that they were not entirely wrong. On the other hand, the status of this issue is hardly such as to warrant any abrupt change in our tradition of protective tenderness toward our young.

Another change in our conception of motivation derives from recognition that there is a motivating system inherent in an organism's informational interaction with the environment. Although it is quite clear that painful stimulation, homeostatic needs, and sex all constitute genuine motivating systems, a very large share of an organism's interaction with the environment is informational in character. It occurs through the distance receptors, the eyes and the ears, and, to a much lesser degree, through touch. Elsewhere I have documented the basis for the notion that a motivating system inheres within this informational interaction (Hunt, 1963a).[25] For instance, the Russian investigators have found both an emotional aspect and an attentional aspect to even an infant mammal's response to change in visual or auditory input. This is what they call the "orienting response." The emotional aspect of this "orienting response" can be registered by such expressive indicators as vascular changes (plethysmograph), changes in blood pressure (sphygmomanometer), changes in heart rate (cardiotachometer), changes in palmar sweating (electrical conductance of the skin), changes in muscular tension (electromyograph), and changes in brain potentials (electroencephalogram). For these changes, see Razran (1961).[26] The attentional aspect can be seen in the cessation of ongoing activities and the efforts to turn to the source of input. The fact that this "orienting response" is present at birth, or as soon as the ears are cleared and the eyes are open, indicates that it is a fundamental, ready-made mechanism. The fact that this response has both emotional and attentional aspects indicates, at least to me, that it is motivational, and the fact that the "orienting response" occurs to changes of ongoing inputs through the eyes and ears indicates that its motivational power is intrinsic within the organism's informational interaction with the environment.

Stage One in the Epigenesis of Intrinsic Motivation: The "Orienting Response."

Indications of the motivational importance of this "orienting response" and of encounters with variations in inputs derive from the marked retardation observed in children whose auditory and visual inputs have been severely restricted. Here the extreme retardation observed by Dennis (1960)[27] in the Teheran orphanages has the dramatic import, if I am correct, that the major factor in its causation lies in homogeneity of reception input. Furthermore, in light of our traditional behavioristic belief that the observable motor response is all-important in development, it is worth noting that the marked retardation that I am attributing to homogeneity of input does not occur with inhibition of motor function during the first year. Again, this latter observation is by Dennis, or by Dennis & Dennis (1940). You will recall that the distribution of ages for the onset of walking in Hopi children cradled for their first year did not differ from the distribution of ages for onset of walking in Hopi children reared in an unrestrained fashion. While the motions of the legs and arms of the cradled infants were restrained during most of their waking hours, the fact that these cradled infants were often carried about, once they were 40 days old, means that they probably encountered an enriched variety of redundant changes in auditory and visual input. Such a comparison suggests that it may be changes in perceptual input rather than opportunity for motor response that is most important in the motivation of psychological development during the earliest months (see also Fiske & Maddi, 1961).[28]

First Suggestion for Stimulating Early Cognitive Learning

This brings me to my first concrete suggestion for stimulating cognitive development during the earliest months, and the process can begin at the child's birth. I suggest that the circumstances be so arranged that the infant will encounter a high variety of redundant changes of auditory, visual, and tactual inputs.

But this suggestion needs elaboration. While changes in ongoing stimulation are probably of basic motivational importance, it may not be mere change in itself that is sufficient to foster cognitive development; redundance of the input changes and of intermodal sequences of input changes are probably necessary. Piaget's (1936)[29] observations of his own infants suggest that, during approximately the first half-year, one of the major accomplishments of interaction with the environment consists in the coordination of what are at birth largely independent sensorimotor systems. According to Piaget, these systems include sucking, listening, looking, grasping, vocalizing, and wriggling. Without use, any one of these systems will wane. As is well known to any farm boy who has pail-fed a calf, the sucking wanes after ten days or two weeks of pail-feeding and the calf can be trusted completely among fresh cows with full udders. Moreover, the work of Alexander Wolf (1943)[30] and of Gauron & Becker (1959)[31] on the effects of depriving infant rats of audition and vision on the readiness of these systems to respond in adulthood, coupled with the work of Brattgård (1952)[32] and of Riesen (1947, 1958, 1961)[33] showing that the visual system fails to develop properly when rabbits and chimpanzees are reared in darkness, indicates that this principle holds for listening and looking as well as sucking. Parenthetically, I should add that the role of organism-environment interaction in early development appears also to be tied biochemically with later capacity to synthesize RNA, as the work of Brattgård (1952),[34] Hydén (1959),[35] and others (see Riesen, 1961)[36] appears to indicate. Perhaps the earliest of such interactions serve chiefly to sustain and to strengthen and develop the individual ready-made sensorimotor organizations or, as Piaget terms them, the "reflexive schemata." Very shortly, under typical circumstances, however, the sounds that evoke listening come to evoke looking, and the things seen come to evoke grasping and reaching, and the things grasped come to evoke sucking, etc. Such changes indicate progress in the coordination of the originally separate systems. During this phase, which is the second stage in Piaget's (1936)[37] system, the progressive organization of schemata consists chiefly in such coordination, and it appears to consist in sequential organization, of which Pavlov's *conditioning* and Guthrie's *contiguity learning* are special cases.

If one tries to imagine how one can introduce redundant changes in visual and auditory inputs in order to provide for the sequential coordination of listening with looking, of looking with reaching, etc., one finds it no easy matter without actually having on hand human beings whose approaches and withdrawals supply the auditory-input changes that are regularly followed by visual-input changes. I have found myself wondering if the emphasis on mothering may not have a somewhat justified explanation in that it is the human infant's informational interaction with this coming and going of the mother than provides the perceptual basis for this coordination of relatively independent schemata.

Stage Two in the Epigenesis of Intrinsic Motivation

But the nature of this intrinsic motivational process changes with experience. Any attempt to stimulate early cognitive learning must, I believe, take this change in form, or epigenesis, into account if it is to be at all successful. Moreover, if this epigenesis is taken into account, the circumstances encountered by the infant should not only motivate a rapid rate of cognitive development but should contribute substantially to the satisfaction the infant gets from life. As observers of infant development have long noted, the human infant appears to learn spontaneously, that is, in the absence of the traditional extrinsic motivators, and to get superb enjoyment from the process (see Baldwin, 1895; Bühler, 1918, 1928; Hendrick, 1943; Mittleman, 1954).[38] This is a new notion to most of us, but it is also old. For instance, it was implicit in the "self-activity" of Froebel (1887)[39] and in the "intrinsic interest" of Dewey (1900).[40] Moreover, Maria Montessori (1909),[41] to whose work I shall return shortly, built her system of education for young children on the notion that children have a spontaneous interest in learning.

In what appears to be the first major transition in the structure of intrinsic motivation, the infant, while continuing to respond to changes in ongoing stimulation, comes to react toward the cessation of inputs which have been encountered repeatedly in a fashion designed to continue them or to bring them back onto perceptual ken. Piaget (1936)[42] called this a "reversal transformation." He considered it to be the beginnings of intention. Each of you who has ever dandled an infant on your knee is familiar with at least one example: when you stop your motion, the infant starts a motion of his own that resembles yours, and when you start again, the infant stops. The prevalence of infants' actions that are instigated by an absence of repeatedly encountered changes in input suggests, at least to me, that the repeated encounters with a given pattern of change in receptor input lead to recognition that provides one basis, and I believe it an important one, for cathexis, emotional attachment, and positive reinforcement (see Hunt, 1963b).[43] My colleague Morton Weir prefers to refer to what attracts the infant as "predictability." Perhaps this is the better term. I have, however, preferred "recognition" because I suspect that what is happening is that the repeated encounters with a pattern of change in ongoing input serve to build into the storage of the posterior intrinsic system of the cerebrum a coded schema that can be matched to an input from the repeatedly encountered pattern of change. As the pattern is becoming recognizable, or when it is newly recognized, I suspect it provides a joyful basis of cathexis and positive reinforcement. I believe, at least tentatively, that it is this recognition that is one of the most consistent evokers of the infant's smile. Such an interpretation gains some support from the fact that maternal separation and encounters with unfamiliar persons bring little emotional disturbance, anxiety, or grief until the second half of the first year of life (Freud & Burlingham, 1944).[44] In fact, these observations of emotional disturbance are important indicators that the cathexis or maternal attachment has been formed. It is this emotional disturbance that supports the observation that an infant acts to retain or to obtain a pattern of familiar input that attests his cathexis of that pattern. Moreover, it should be noted that emotional distress accompanies maternal deprivation only after the age at which objects have begun to acquire permanence for the child. Presumably this permanence of objects is based on the development, in the course of repeated encounters with a pattern of change in input, of a set of semiautonomous central processes that can represent the pattern deriving from an encounter with an object.

Parenthetically, may I suggest also that the following-response within what is called "imprinting" may well be a special case of this more general principle that emotional attachment grows out of the recognition coming from repeatedly encountering an object, place, or person; the fact that the following-response occurs after a shorter period of perceptual contact with an object in a species such as the grey-leg goose, or in the sheep or deer, than is required in species such as the chimpanzee or man suggests that the number of encounters, or duration of perceptual contact, required may well be a matter of the portion of the brain without direct connections with receptors or motor units, or what Hebb (1949)[45] has termed the A/S ratio.

Out of such observations comes the empirical principle, which I have imbibed from Piaget (1936),[46] that "the more an infant has seen and heard, the more he wants to see and hear." The avidity of an infant's interest in the world may be seen to be in large part a function of the variety of situations he has encountered repeatedly. Moreover, it would appear to be precisely the absence of such avid interest that constitutes the regularly observed apathy of orphanage-reared children who have encountered only a very limited variety of situations. It may well be that this seeking of inputs that have been made familiar by repeated encounters is what motivates the behavior Dennis & Dennis (1941)[47] have termed "autogenous." Outstanding examples of such behavior are the hand-watching and the repetitive vocalizations called "babbling." It is, apparently, seeking to see the hands that motivates the motions to keep them within view, thereby providing the beginnings of eye-hand coordination. It is, apparently, seeking to hear voice sounds that motivates spontaneous vocalizing and keeps it going, thereby providing the infant with a beginning of ear-vocal coordination.

Second Suggestion for the Stimulation of Early Cognitive Learning

This brings me to my second suggestion for fostering early cognitive learning. It comes in connection with the development of intrinsically motivated intentions or plans, as the terms *intention* and *plan* are utilized by Miller, Galanter, & Pribram (1960).[48] In fact, it is in connection with this development of intrinsically motivated intentions or plans that one basis for this change in the conception of motivation may be seen. Psychologists and psychoanalysts have conceived of actions, habits, defenses, and even of every thought system, as an attempt to reduce or eliminate stimulation or excitation within the nervous system arising out of painful stimulation, homeostatic need, or sex. To anyone who has observed and pondered the struggle of a young infant to reach and grasp some object he sees, it is extremely difficult to find such an extrinsic motivational basis for his reaching and grasping. What is suggested by Piaget's observations is that in the course of repeated encounters with an object, there comes a point at which seeing that object becomes an occasion for grasping it. In this coordination between looking and grasping, it would appear that grasping the object becomes a goal even though it is quite unrelated to pain, to homeostatic need, or to sex. Once an infant has the grasping goal of an object he has seen repeatedly, his various other motor schemata of striking, pushing, and even locomotion become also means to achieve this goal. Anyone who ponders this phenomenon in the light of the traditional theory of extrinsic motives will ask, "but why grasp the object?" And, "why grasp one object rather than another?" My tentative answer to these questions is that the object has become attractive with the new-found recognition that comes with repeated visual or auditory encounters. While reading Piaget's (1936, 1937)[49] observations, one gets the impression that a smile very frequently precedes the effort to grasp, as if the infant were saying, "I know what you are, I'll take hold of you." Of course, nothing is so explicit; he has no language; he is merely manifesting a kind of primordial plan or intention. It is my hypothesis that this primordial intention is instigated by recognitive perception. If this hypothesis is true, then once an infant is ready to grasp things and to manipulate them, it is important that he have perceptual access to things he can grasp. It is important that there be a variety of such things that he has encountered earlier. The more varied the objects that are available, the more interest the infant will have in his world and the more sources of attractive novelty he will have later on.

As already indicted, it is probably also important that the infant have an opportunity to interact with human beings as well as with inanimate objects. Perhaps one of the chief functions of early interaction with human beings is to make the vocalized phones of the parental language and the gestures of communication familiar, for one of the most common forms of action designed to hold onto newly recognized inputs is imitation. (This conception of imitation differs radically from that given by Miller & Dollard (1941),[50] but it does not deny that their conception may be true under certain circumstances.) Such imitation is important for socialization and for intellectual development because the roots of human culture reside in the sounds of language and the various gestures of communication. An infant imitates first those phones and gestures that are highly familiar to him. In fact, one of the most feasible ways to start an interactive relationship with a young infant is to make one of the sounds that he is making regularly or to perform one of his characteristic gestures. The very fact that the sounds or gestures are the infant's helps to insure his recognition of them. Seeing them in another person commonly brings delighted interest and, not infrequently, imitative effort to recover them when the adult has stopped. The infant's jouncing in the dandling relationship is a special case of such imitative effort. Again we have a kind of encounter hard to arrange without involving human beings. This paucity of encounters that can be arranged without human beings supports the idea that the stories of feral men, including Romulus and Remus, are probably myths.

Stage Three in the Epigenesis of Intrinsic Motivation

The second major transformation in intrinsic motivation appears to occur when repeatedly encountered objects, places, and events become "old stuff." The infant then becomes interested in *novelty*. The breakdown of the meaning of a given input with repeated perceptual encounters and the monotony that comes with repeated participation in given events are phenomena that psychologists have long observed (see Titchener, 1926, p. 425).[51] Hebb (1949, p. 224),[52] moreover, has observed that a major source of pleasure resides in encountering something new within the framework of the familiar. The sequence—of "orienting response" to stimulus change, recognition with repeated encounters, and interest in the variations within the familiar—may well be one in the interaction of an organism with each completely new class of environmental phenomena. What look like stages in the development of the first year may possibly be derived from the fact that an infant tends to be repeatedly encountering a fairly extended variety of situations at a fairly consistent rate. In any event, in his observations of his own children, Piaget (1936)[53] noted that this interest in novelty appears toward the end of the first year.

There are those who dislike the very notion of such an epigenesis in the structure of motivation. There are those who seek single explanatory principles. Some have tried to explain this series of transformations in terms either of a process in which the new is continually becoming familiar or of a process whereby the earlier interest in the familiar exists because recognizability itself is novel at this phase. We may someday get a biochemical understanding of this phenomenon, but such attempts to find a unitary psychological principle of explanation are probably doomed to failure. Numerous studies indicate very clearly that organisms first respond to change in ongoing inputs. It is less certain that they next prefer the familiar, but the evidence is abundant that they later prefer objects and situations that are relatively less familiar than others available (see Dember, Earl, & Paradise, 1957; Hebb & Mahut, 1955; Montgomery, 1952, 1953a.)[54] There is one instance in which a study shows that the lowly rat will endure even the pain of electric shock to get from his familiar nest-cage to an unfamiliar situation where there are novel objects to manipulate (Nissen, 1930).[55] Studies also exist, moreover, in which organisms withdrew in fear from "familiar objects in an unfamiliar guise." These were objects that could never have been associated with painful stimulation in their previous experience because the animals had been reared under known conditions at the Yerkes Primate Laboratory. Festinger (1957)[56] has, also, found people withdrawing from information dissonant with their strong held beliefs, plans, or commitments.

It is no easy matter to characterize properly what is essential in that glibly called "novelty." I believe, however, that we can say that novelty resides within the organism's informational interaction with its environment. I have termed this essence "incongruity" (Hunt, 1963a),[57] Berlyne (1960)[58] has written of the "collative variables" underlying "arousal potential"; Festinger (1957)[59] has talked of "dissonance"; Hebb (1949)[60] has written of the stage of development in cortical organization; and Munsinger & Kesson (1964)[61] are using the term "uncertainty." Whatever this essence is called, too much of it gives rise to withdrawal and gestures commonly connoting fear. Too little appears to be associated with boredom. That novelty that is attractive appears to be an optimum of discrepancy in this relationship between the informational input of the moment and the information already stored in the cerebrum from previous encounters with similar situations.

Once interest in novelty appears, it is an important source of motivation. Perhaps it is the chief source of motivation for cognitive learning. Interest in novelty appears to motivate the improvement of locomotor skills, for the novel objects "needing" examination or manipulation are typically out of reach. It appears to motivate imitation of unfamiliar verbal phones and unfamiliar gestures and even of fairly complex actions. Imitated vocalizing of unfamiliar phones and vocal patterns appears to be exceedingly important in the acquisition of language. The notion that all infants vocalize all the phones of all languages (Allport, 1924)[62] has long been hard to believe. The social side of language acquisition appears to be more than the mere reinforcing with approval or notice of those vocal patterns characteristic of the parents' language. If the interest in novelty provides an intrinsic motivational basis for (imitatively) vocalizing phones that have never been a part of the infant's vocal repertoire, then we have a believable explanation for the fact that most of the first pseudo-words are approximations of adult vocalizations that have occurred repeatedly in connection with novel and exciting events. Repetition of encounters with a given class of events may be presumed gradually to establish central processes representative of that class of event, that is, *images*, if you will. Imitation of the novel phones verbalized by adults in association with the class of events may provide the infant with a vocalization that can serve him as a sign of his image. Later, reinforcement, partially based on approval-disapproval and partially based on growing cognitive differentiation, may lead gradually to images and phonemic combinations that are sufficiently like those of the people taking care of an infant to permit communication.

Once language is acquired, the human child comes into basically the same existential situation in which all of us find ourselves. He then has two major sources of informational input: first, the original one of perceiving objects and events and, second, the new one of learning about them through the language of others. One of his major intellectual tasks is to make what he learns about the "real world" through the communications of others jibe with what he learns about it directly through his own receptors. This is a creative task of no mean proportion, and it is not unlike the task with which mature men of science are continuously concerned. This is one of George Kelly's (1955)[63] major points.

The considerations already outlined in connection with my suggestions concerning repeated encounters with a given class of stimulus change and "recognition" show again the basis for the principle that "the more a child has seen and heard, the more he wants to see and hear" and do. If an infant has encountered a wide variety of changes in circumstances during his earliest days, and if he has encountered them repeatedly enough to become attached to them through recognition, and if he has had ample opportunity to act upon them and to manipulate them, he will become, I believe, ready to be intrigued by novel variations in an ample range of objects, situations, and personal models.

The fact that too much novelty or incongruity can be frightening and too little can be boring, however, creates a problem for those who would stimulate cognitive development. They must provide for encounters with materials, objects, and models that have the proper degree of that incongruity (Hunt, 1963a).[64] This is one aspect of what I have termed the "problem of the match" (Hunt, 1961b, pp. 267ff.).[65]

Third Suggestion for the Stimulation of Early Cognitive Learning.

Consideration of the problem of the match brings me to my third concrete suggestion for stimulating cognitive learning in the very young. I must confess that I have borrowed this suggestion from Montessori (1909; see also Fisher, 1912).[66] The first portion of this suggestion is that careful observation be made of what it is in the way of objects, situations, and models for imitation that interests the infant. Once it is clear what objects and models are of interest, then I suggest providing each infant with an ample variety of them and with an opportunity to choose spontaneously the ones that intrigue him at a given time. This latter suggestion assumes, of course, that the infant is already comfortable, that he feels safe, and that he is satisfied so far as homeostatic needs are concerned. I really feel that we do not have to worry too much about gratifying the sex appetite of a child under three years of age.

When I wrote *Intelligence and Experience* (1961b),[67] this problem of providing a proper match between the materials with which a child is confronted by teachers and what he already has in his storage loomed large because of our tremendous ignorance of the intricacies involved. This ignorance is a major challenge for investigation; in the meantime, however, as Jan Smedslund pointed out to me in a conversation in Boulder last summer, Montessori long ago provided a practical solution. She based her system of education on intrinsic motivation, but she called it "spontaneous learning." She provided young children with a wide variety of materials, graded in difficulty and roughly calculated to be the range of materials that would provide a proper match for children of ages three to six if they were given opportunity for choice. She also gave each of the children in her school an opportunity to occupy himself or herself with those materials of his or her own individual choice. To do this, she broke the lock-step in the educational process. A Montessori school was socially so structured that the children were obviously expected to occupy themselves with the materials provided. Moreover, by having together within a single room children ranging in age from three to six years, she provided a graded series of models for the younger children and an opportunity for some of the older children to learn by teaching the younger ones how to do various things. You will be interested to know that a substantial proportion of the slum children in Montessori's school began reading and writing before they were five years old. In the Casa di Bambini, which Montessori founded in 1907 in the basement of a slum apartment-house in Rome, the teacher was the apartment-house superintendent's 16-year-old daughter who had been trained by Montessori. You will also be interested to know that the old nursery school bugaboo that children have very brief spans of attention did not hold. Dorothy Canfield Fisher (1912)[68]—the novelist who spent the winter of 1910–1911 at the original Casa di Bambini—has written that it was common to see a three-year-old continuously occupied with such a mundane task as buttoning and un-buttoning for two or more hours at a stretch.

Montessori's contributions to the education of the very young were discussed with excitement in America until the time of World War I. Thereafter the discussion ended almost completely. I suspect that this occurred because Montessori's theoretical views were so dissonant with what became about then the dominant views of American psychologists and American educators. Her theory that cognitive capacity could be modified by proper education was dissonant with the dominant and widely-prevailing notions of "fixed intelligence" and "predetermined development." These notions were implicit in the doctrine of a constant IQ. Her notion of spontaneous learning was sharply dissonant with the doctrine that all behavior is extrinsically motivated by painful stimulation, or homeostatic need, or sex. Moreover, the importance she attributed to sensory training was dissonant with what became the prevailing presumption that it is the observable motor response that counts. We need to reexamine her contributions in the light of the theoretical picture that has been emerging since World War II. I am grateful to Jan Smedslund for calling her contributions to my attention.

My discourse has skipped roughly half of the second year and all of the third year of life, because interest in novelty typically makes its earliest appearance toward the end of the first year or early in the second. (Montessori's schools took children only at three years of age or older.) I suspect that the basic principle involved in stimulating cognitive learning is fairly constant once the interest in novelty appears. On the other hand, I would not be surprised if it were precisely during this period between 18 months and three years of age that lower-class families typically most hamper the kind of cognitive learning that is later required for successful performance in school and in our increasingly technological culture. Let me explain briefly.

During the first year, the life of an infant in a family crowded together in one room—as Oscar Lewis (1961)[69] has described such living in his *Children of Sanchez* and as I have observed it in the slums of New York—

probably provides a fairly rich variety of input. On the other hand, once an infant begins to use his new-found locomotor and linguistic skills, his circumstances in a lower-class setting probably become anything but conducive to appropriate cognitive learning. Using his new locomotor skills gets him in the way of problem-beset adults and, all too likely, may bring punishment which can be avoided only by staying out of their way. This in turn deprives the infant of the opportunity to hear and imitate the verbal phones that provides the basis for spoken language. If a slum child should be lucky enough to acquire the "learning set" that things have names and to begin his repetitive questioning about "what's that?", he is not only unlikely to get answers but also likely to get his ears cuffed for asking such silly questions. Moreover, in the slum setting of lower-class family life, the models that an infant has to imitate are all too often likely to result in the acquisition of sensorimotor organizations and attitudes that interfere with rather than facilitate the kinds of cognitive learning that enable a child to succeed in school and in a technological culture such as ours. How long such interference with development can last without resulting in a permanent reduction in cognitive potential remains an unsolved problem. It is likely, however, that day-care centers and nursery schools prepared to face such children with situations, materials, and models that are not too incongruous with the schemata and attitudes that they have already acquired, can counteract much of the detrimental effect of lower-class life. Such preschool experience during the second and third, and possibly even during the fourth, years of life can perhaps serve well as an antidote to this kind of cultural deprivation (see Hunt, 1964).[70]

SUMMARY

I have limited my discussion to the implications, for the stimulation of early cognitive learning, of the epigenesis of intrinsic motivation that I believe I can see taking place during preverbal development. I have identified three stages of intrinsic motivation that are separated by two major "reversal transformations." In the first of these, repeated encounters with patterns of change in perceptual input lead to recognition that I now believe to be a source of pleasure and a basis for cathexis or for affectional attachment. The second consists in a transition from an interest in the familiar to an interest in the novel. During the first few months, when the child is responsive chiefly to changes in the character and intensity of ongoing stimulation, I suspect it is most important to provide for repeated encounters with as wide a variety as possible of changes in receptor input. It may also be important to provide for sequential arrangements of these inputs that will provide a basis for a coordination of all combinations of the ready-made reflexive sensorimotor systems. As the infant becomes attached to objects, people, and situations by way of the hypothetical joys of new-found recognition, it is probably most important to provide opportunities for him to utilize his own repertoire of intentional activities to retain or elicit or manipulate the objects, people, and situations, again in as wide a variety as is feasible. Once interest in novelty appears, I suspect it is most important to give the child access to a variety of graded materials for manipulation and coping and to a variety of graded models for imitation. With what little we now know of what I call the "problem of the match," I suspect it is important to follow Montessori's principle of trusting to a considerable degree in the spontaneous interest of the individual infant instead of attempting to regiment his learning process in any lock-step method of preschool education.

REFERENCES

1. J. McV. Hunt, *Intelligence and Experience* (New York: Ronald Press, 1961).
2. W. Johannsen, *Über Erblichkeit in populationen und in reinen Linien* (Jena: Gustav Fisher, 1903).
3. S. Freud, "Three Contributions to the Theory of Sex" (1905), in A. A. Brill (tr. and ed.), *The Basic Writings of Sigmund Freud* (New York: Modern Library, 1938).
4. J. McV. Hunt, "The Effects of Infant Feeding Frustration Upon Adult Hoarding in the Albine Rat," *Journal of Abnormal Social Psychology*, 36 (1946), pp. 338-360.
5. D.O. Hebb, "The Effects of Early Experience on Problem-Solving at Maturity," *American Psychology*, 2 (1947), pp. 306-307.
6. W. R. Thompson and W. Heron, "The Effects of Restraining Early Experience on the Problem-Solving Capacity of Dogs," *Canadian Journal of Psychology*, 8, (1964), pp. 17-31.
7. D.O. Hebb, *Organization of Behavior* (New York: Wiley, 1964).
8. D.O. Hebb and K. Williams, "A Method of Rating Animal Intelligence," *Journal of Genetic Psychology*, 34 (1946), pp. 59-65.
9. D. G. Forgays, and Janet W. Forgays, "The Nature of the Effect of Free Environmental Experience in the Rat," *Journal of Comparative and Physiological Psychology*, 45 (1952), pp, 32-328; R. H. Furgus, "The Effect of Early Perceptual Learning on the Behavioral Organization of Adult Rats," *Journal of Comparative and Physiological Psychology*, 47 (1954), pp. 331-336; B. Hymovitch, "The Effects of Experimental Variations on Problem-Solvings in the Rat," *Journal of Comparative and Physiological Psychology*, 45 (1952), pp. 313-321.
10. Hebb, "Effects of Early Experience."
11. Thompson and Heron, "Effects of Restraining Early Experience."
12. K. H. Pribram, "A Review of Theory in Psychological Psychology," *Annual Review of Psychology*, 11 (1960), pp. 1-40.
13. Hebb, *Organization of Behavior*.
14. R. A. Spitz, "Hospitalism: An Inquiry into the Genesis of Psychiatric Conditions in Early Childhood," *Psychoanalytic Study of the Child*, 1 (1945), pp. 54-74; idem. "Hospitalism: A Follow-up Report," *Psychoanalytic Study of the Child*, 2 (1946), pp. 113-117.
15. S.R. Pinneau, "The Infantile Disorders of Hospitalism and Anaclitic Depression," *Psychological Bulletin*, 52 (1955), pp. 429-459.
16. W. Dennis, "Causes of Retardation Among Institutional Children: Iran," *Journal of Genetic Psychology*, 96 (1960), pp. 47-59.
17. *Ibid.*, p. 58.
18. Thompson and Heron, "Effects of Restraining Early Experience."
19. W. Goldfarb, "Emotional and Intellectual Consequences of Psychologic Deprivation in Infancy: A Re-evaluation," pp. 105-119, in P. Hoch and J. Zubin (eds.), *Psychopathology of Childhood* (New York: Grune and Stratton, 1955).

20. V. H. Denenberg, "The Interactive Effects of Infantile and Adult Shock Levels Upon Learning," *Psychological Reports*, 5 (1959), pp. 357–364; idem. "The Effects of Early Experience," Gh. 6, in E. S. E. Hafez (ed.), *The Behavior of Domestic Animals* (London: Balliere, Tindall, and Cox, 1962); Denenberg and G. G. Karas, "Interactive Effects of Age and Duration of Infantile Experience on Adult Learning," *Psychological Reports*, 7 (1960), pp. 313–322; Denenberg, J. R. C. Morton, N. S. Kline, and L. J. Grota, "Effects of Duration of Infantile Stimulation Upon Emotionality," *Canadian Journal of Psychology*, 16 (1962), pp. 72–76; S. Levine, "A Further Study of Infantile Handling and Adult Avoidance Learning," *Journal of Personality*, 27 (1956), pp. 70–80; idem. "Infantile Experience and Consummatory Behavior in Adulthood," *Journal of Comparative and Physiological Psychology*, 50 (1957), pp. 609–612; idem, "Effects of Early Deprivation and Delayed Weaning on Avoidance Learning in the Albino Rat," *Archives of Neurology and Psychiatry*, 79 (1958), pp. 211–213; idem, "The Effects of Differential Infantile Stimulation on Emotionality at Weaning," *Canadian Journal of Psychology*, 13 (1959), pp. 243–247.

21. K. H. Brookshire, R. A. Littman, and C. N. Stewart, "Residua of Shocktrauma in the White Rat: A Three-Factor Theory," *Psychological Monographs*, 75 (1961), p. 514; K. H. Brookshire, "An Experimental Analysis of the Effects of Infantile Shock-trauma," *Dissertation Abstracts*, 19 (1958), p. 180; V. H. Denenberg, "The Interactive Effects of Infantile and Adult Shock Levels upon Learning," *Psychological Reports*, 5 (1959), pp. 357–364; Denenberg and R. W. Bell, "Critical Periods for the Effects of Infantile Experience on Adult Learning," *Science*, 131 (1960), pp. 227–228; Denenberg and Karas, "Interactive Effects," S. Levine, "Infantile Handling"; idem, "Effects of Early Deprivation"; S. Levine, J. A. Chevalier, and S. J. Korchin, "The Effects of Early Shock and Handling on Later Avoidance Learning," *Journal of Personality* 24 (1956), pp. 475–493.

22. G. Lindzey, D. T. Lykken, and H. D. Winston, "Infantile Trauma, Genetic Factors, and Adult Temperament," *Journal of Abnormal Social Psychology*, 61 (1960), pp. 7–14

23. S. Levine, "Effects of Differential Infantile Stimulation."

24. A. A. Salama and J. McV. Hunt, "Fixation in the Rat as a Function of Infantile Shocking, Handling, and Gentling," *Journal of Genetic Psychology*, 105 (1964) pp. 131–162.

25. J. McV. Hunt, "Motivation Inherent in Information Processing and Action," in O. J. Harvey (ed.), *Motivation and Social Organization: The Cognitive Factors* (New York: Ronald Press, 1963).

26. G. Razran, "The Observable Unconscious and the Inferable Conscious in Current Society Psychophysiology; Interoceptive Conditioning, Semantic Conditioning, and the Orienting Reflex," *Psychological Review*, 68 (1961), pp. 81–147.

27. W. Dennis, "Causes of Retardation Among Institutional Children: Iran," *Journal of Genetic Psychology*, 96 (1970), pp. 47–59; W. Dennis and Marsena G. Dennis, "The Effect of Cradling Practice Upon the Onset of Walking in Hopi Children," *Journal of Genetic Psychology*, 56 (1940), pp. 77–86.

28. Cf. D. W. Fiske and S. R. Maddi, *Functions of Varied Experience* (Homewood, Ill,: Dorsey Press, 1961).

29. J. Piaget, *The Origins of Intelligence in Children*, 1936 (trans. Margaret Cook) (New York: International Universities Press, 1952).

30. A. Wolf, "The Dynamics of the Selective Inhibition of Specific Functions in Neurosis: A Preliminary Report," *Psychosomatic Medicine*, 5 (1943), pp. 27–38. Reprinted in S. S. Tomkins (ed.), *Contemporary Psychopathology*, Ch. 31 (Cambridge: Harvard University Press, 1943).

31. E. F. Gauron and W. C. Becker, "The Effects of Early Sensory Deprivation on Adult Rat Behavior Under Competition Stress: An Attempt at Replication of a

Study by Alexander Wolf," *Journal of Comparative and Physiological Psychology,* 52 (1959). pp. 689-693.

32. S. O. Brattgård, "The Importance of Adequate Stimulation for the Chemical Composition of Retinal Ganglion Cells During Post-natal Development," *Acta Radiologica* (Stockholm, 1952).

33. A. H. Riesen, "The Development of Visual Perception in Man and Chimpanzee," *Science,* 106 (1947), pp. 107-108; A. H. Riesen, "Plasticity of Behavior: Psychological Aspects," pp. 425-450, in H. F. Harlow and C. N. Woolsey (eds.), *Biological and Biochemical Bases of Behavior* (Madison: University of Wisconsin Press, 1958); idem, "Stimulation as a Requirement for Growth and Function in Behavioral Development," in D. W. Fiske and S. R. Maddi (eds.), *Functions of Varied Experience* (Homewood, Ill.: Dorsey Press, 1961).

34. Brattgård, "Importance of Adequate Stimulation."

35. H. Hydén, "Biochemical Changes in Glial Cells and Nerve Cells at Varying Activity," pp. 64-89, in F. Brucke (ed.), *Proceedings of the 4th International Congress of Biochemistry, III, Biochemistry of the Central Nervous System* (London: Pergamon Press, 1959).

36. Riesen, "Development of Visual Perception."

37. Piaget, *Origins of Intelligence.*

38. J. M. Baldwin, *Mental Development in the Child and in the Race* (New York: Macmillan, 1895); K. Buhler, *Die Giestige Entwicklung des Kindes* (Jena: Fischer, 1918); idem, "Displeasure and Pleasure in Relation to Activity," Ch. 14, in M. L. Reymert (ed.), *Feelings and Emotions: the Wittenberg Symposium* (Worcester, Mass.: Clark University Press, 1928); I. Hendrick, "The Discussion on the 'Instinct to Master,' " *Psychoanalytic Quarterly,* 12 (1943), pp. 561-565; B. Mittelman,: Motility in Infants, Children, and Adults," *Psychoanalytic Study of the Child,* 9 (1954), pp. 142-177.

39. F. Froebel, *The Education of Man* (trans., W. T. Harris) (New York: Appleton, 1887).

40. J. Dewey, *The School and Society* (Chicago: University of Chicago Press, Phoenix Books, P3. 1960).

41. Maria Montessori, *The Montessori Method* (New York: Frederick A. Stokes, 1912).

42. Piaget, *Origins of Intelligence.*

43. J. McV. Hunt, "Piaget's Observations as a Source of Hypotheses Concerning Motivation," *Merrill-Palmer Quarterly,* 9 (1963), pp. 253-275.

44. Anna Freud and Dorthy Burlingham, *Infants Without Families* (New York: International Universities Press, 1944).

45. Hebb, *Organization of Behavior.*

46. Piaget, *Origins of Intelligence.*

47. W. Dennis, and Marsena G. Dennis, "Infant Development Under Conditions of Restricted Practice and Minimum Social Stimulation," *Genetic Psychology Monographs,* 23 (1941), pp. 149-155; also as: "Development Under Controlled Environmental Conditions," III-one, in W. Dennis (ed.), *Readings in Child Psychology* (New York: Prentice-Hall, 1951).

48. G. A. Miller, E. H. Galanter, and K. H. Pribram, *Plans and the Structure of Behavior* (New York: Holt, 1960).

49. Piaget, *Origins of Intelligence:* Piaget, *The Construction of Reality in the Child,* 1937 (trans. Margaret Cook) (New York: Basic Books, 1954).

50. N. E. Miller and J. Dollard, *Social Learning and Imitation* (New Haven, Conn,: Yale University Press, 1941).

51. See E. B. Titchener, *A Text-book of Psychology* (New York: Macmillan, 1926), p. 425.

52. Hebb. *Organization of Behavior,* p. 224.

53. Piaget, *Orgins of Intelligence.*

54. W. N. Dember, R. W. Earl, and N. Paradise, "Response by Rats to Differential Stimulus Complexity," *Journal of Comparative and Physiological Psychology,* 50 (1957), pp. 514–518; D. O. Hebb, and Helen Mahut, "Motivation et Recherche du Changement Perceptif Chez le Rat et Chez l'Homme," *Journal de Psychologie Normale et Pathologique,* 48 (1955), pp. 209–220; K. Montgomery, "A Test of Two Explanations of Spontaneous Alternation," *Journal of Comparative and Physiological Psychology,* 45 (1952), pp. 287–293; idem, "Exploratory Behavior as a Function of 'Similarity' of Stimulus Situations," *Journal of Comparative and Physiological Psychology,* 46 (1953), pp. 129–133.

55. H. W. Nissen, "A Study of Exploratory Behavior in the White Rat by Means of the Obstruction Method," *Journal of Genetic Psychology,* 37 (1930), pp. 361–376.

56. L. Festinger, *A Theory of Cognitive Dissonance* (Evanston, Ill.: Row, Peterson, 1957).

57. Hunt, "Motivation Inherent in Information Processing."

58. D. E. Berlyne, *Conflict, Arousal, and Curiosity* (New York: McGraw-Hill, 1960).

59. Festinger, "Theory of Cognitive Dissonance."

60. Hebb, *Organization of Behavior.*

61. H. Munsinger and W. Kessen, "Uncertainty, Structure and Preference," *Psychological Monographs,* 78 (1964), p. 586.

62. F. H. Allport, *Social Psychology* (Boston: Houghton Mifflin, 1924).

63. G. A. Kelly, *A Psychology of Personal Constructs* (New York: Norton, 1955).

64. Hunt, "Motivation Inherent in Information Processing."

65. J. McV. Hunt, *Intelligence and Experience,* p. 267 ff.

66. Montessori, *Montessori Method;* Dorothy Canfield Fisher, *A Montessori Mother* (New York: Holt, 1912).

67. Hunt, *Intelligence and Experience.*

68. Fisher, *Montessori Mother.*

69. O. Lewis, *The Children of Sanchez* (New York: Random House, 1961).

70. J. McV. Hunt, "The Psychological Basis for Using Pre-School Enrichment as an Antidote for Cultural Deprivation," *Merrill-Palmer Quarterly,* 10 (1964), pp. 209–248.

5. The Act of Discovery

Maimonides, in his *Guide for the Perplexed*[1], speaks of four forms of perfection that men might seek. The first and lowest form is perfection in the acquisition of worldly goods. The great philosopher dismisses such perfection on the ground that the possessions one acquires bear no meaningful relation to the possessor: "A great king may one morning find that there is no difference between him and the lowest person." A second perfection is of the body, its conformation and skills. Its failing is that it does not reflect on what is uniquely human about man: "he could [in any case] not be as strong as a mule." Moral perfection is the third, "the highest degree of excellency in man's character." Of this perfection Maimonides says: "Imagine a person being alone, and having no connection whatever with any other person; all his good moral principles are at rest, they are not required and give man no perfection whatever. These principles are only necessary and useful when man comes in contact with others." "The fourth kind of perfection is the true perfection of man; the possession of the highest intellectual faculties. . . ." In justification of his assertion, this extraordinary Spanish-Judaic philosopher urges: "Examine the first three kinds of perfection; you will find that if you possess them, they are not your property, but the property of others. . . . But the last kind of perfection is exclusively yours; no one else owns any part of it."

It is a conjecture much like that of Maimonides that leads me to examine the act of discovery in man's intellectual life. For if man's intellectual excellence is the most his own among his perfections, it is also the case that the most uniquely personal of all that he knows is that which he has discovered for himself. What difference does it make, then, that we encourage discovery in the learning of the young? Does it, as Maimonides would say, create a special and unique relation between knowledge possessed and the possessor? And what may such a unique relation do for a man—or for a child, if you will, for our concern is with the education of the young?

The immediate occasion for my concern with discovery—and I do not restrict discovery to the act of finding out something that before was unknown to mankind, but rather include all forms of obtaining knowledge for oneself by the use of one's own mind—the immediate occasion is the work of the various new curriculum projects that have grown up in America during the last six or seven years. For whether one speaks to mathematicians or physicists or historians, one encounters repeatedly an

From Jerome S. Bruner, "The Act of Discovery," *Harvard Educational Review*, Vol. 31 (1961), pp. 21-32. Copyright © 1961 by President and Fellows of Harvard College.

[1]Maimonides, *Guide for the Perplexed* (New York: Dover Publications, 1956).

expression of faith in the powerful effects that come from permitting the student to put things together for himself, to be his own discoverer.

First, let it be clear what the act of discovery entails. It is rarely, on the frontier of knowledge or elsewhere, that new facts are "discovered" in the sense of being encountered as Newton suggested in the form of islands of truth in an uncharted sea of ignorance. Or if they appear to be discovered in this way, it is almost always thanks to some happy hypotheses about where to navigate. Discovery, like surprise, favors the well prepared mind. In playing bridge, one is surprised by a hand with no honors in it at all and also by hands that are all in one suit. Yet all hands in bridge are equiprobable: one must know to be surprised. So too in discovery. The history of science is studded with examples of men "finding out" something and not knowing it. I shall operate on the assumption that discovery, whether by a schoolboy going in on his own or by a scientist cultivating the growing edge of his field, is in its essence a matter of rearranging or transforming evidence in such a way that one is enabled to go beyond the evidence so reassembled to additional new insights. It may well be that an additional fact or shred of evidence makes this larger transformation of evidence possible. But it is often not even dependent on new information.

It goes without saying that, left to himself, the child will go about discovering things for himself within limits. It also goes without saying that there are certain forms of child rearing, certain home atmospheres that lead some children to be their own discoverers more than other children. These are both topics of great interest, but I shall not be discussing them. Rather, I should like to confine myself to the consideration of discovery and "finding-out-for-oneself" within an educational setting—specifically the school. Our aim as teachers is to give our student as firm a grasp of a subject as we can, and to make him as autonomous and self-propelled a thinker as we can—one who will go along on his own after formal schooling has ended. I shall return in the end to the question of the kind of classroom and the style of teaching that encourages an attitude of wanting to discover. For purposes of orienting the discussion, however, I would like to make an overly simplified distinction between teaching that takes place in the *expository mode* and teaching that utilizes the *hypothetical mode*. In the former, the decisions concerning the mode and pace and style of exposition are principally determined by the teacher as expositor; the student is the listener. If I can put the matter in terms of structural linguistics, the speaker has a quite different set of decisions to make than the listener: the former has a wide choice of alternatives for structuring, he is anticipating paragraph content while the listener is still intent on the words, he is manipulating the content of the material by various transformations, while the listener is quite unaware of these internal manipulations. In the hypothetical mode, the teacher and the student are in a more cooperative position with respect to what in linguistics would be called "speaker's decisions." The student is not a bench-bound listener, but is taking a part in the formulation and at times may play the principal role in it. He will be aware of alternatives and may even have an "as if" attitude toward these and, as he receives information he may evaluate it as it comes. One cannot describe the process in either mode with great precision as to detail, but I think the foregoing may serve to illustrate what is meant.

Consider now what benefit might be derived from the experience of learning through discoveries that one makes for oneself. I should like to discuss these under four headings: (1) The increase in intellectual potency, (2) the shift from extrinsic to intrinsic rewards, (3) learning the heuristics of discovering, and (4) the aid to memory processing.

1. *Intellectual Potency.* If you will permit me, I would like to consider the difference between subjects in a highly constrained psychological experiment involving a two-choice apparatus. In order to win chips, they must depress a key either on the right or the left side of the machine. A pattern of payoff is designed such that, say, they will be paid off on the right side 70 per cent of the time, on the left 30 per cent, although this detail is not important. What is important is that the payoff sequence is arranged at random, and there is no pattern. I should like to contrast the behavior of subjects who think that there *is* some pattern to be found in the sequence—who think that regularities are discoverable—in contrast to subjects who think that things are happening quite by *chance*. The former group adopts what is called an "event-matching" strategy in which the number of responses given to each side is roughly equal to the proportion of times it pays off: in the present case R70:L30. The group that believes there is no pattern very soon reverts to a much more primitive strategy wherein *all* responses are allocated to the side that has the greater payoff. A little arithmetic will show you that the lazy all-and-none strategy pays off more if indeed the environment is random: namely, they win seventy per cent of the time. The event-matching subjects win about 70% on the 70% payoff side (or 49% of the time there) and 30% of the time on the side that pays off 30% of the time (another 9% for a total take-home wage of 58% in return for their labors of decision). But the world is not always or not even frequently random, and if one analyzes carefully what the event-matchers are doing, it turns out that they are trying out hypotheses one after the other, all of them containing a term such that they distribute bets on the two sides with a frequency to match the actual occurrence of events. If it should turn out that there is a pattern to be discovered, their payoff would become 100%. The other group would go on at the middling rate of 70%.

What has this to do with the subject at hand? For the person to search out and find regularities and relationships in his environment, he must be armed with an expectancy that there will be something to find and, once aroused by expectancy, he must devise ways of searching and finding. One of the chief enemies of such expectancy is the assumption that there is nothing one can find in the environment by way of regularity or relationship. In the experiment just cited, subjects often fall into a habitual attitude that there is either nothing to be found or that they can find a pattern by looking. There is an important sequel in behavior to the two attitudes, and to this I should like to turn now.

We have been conducting a series of experimental studies on a group of some seventy school children over the last four years. The studies have led us to distinguish an interesting dimension of cognitive activity that can be described as ranging from *episodic empiricism* at one end to *cumulative constructionism* at the other. The two attitudes in the choice experiments just cited are illustrative of the extremes of the dimension. I might mention some other illustrations. One of the experiments employs the game of Twenty Questions. A child—in this case he is between 10 and 12—is told that a car has gone off the road and hit a tree. He is to ask questions that can be answered by "yes" or "no" to discover the cause of the accident. After completing the problem, the same task is given him again, though he is told that the accident had a different cause this time. In all, the procedure is repeated four times. Children enjoy playing the game. They also differ quite markedly in the approach or strategy they bring to the task. There are various elements in the strategies employed. In the first place, one may distinguish clearly between two types of questions asked: the one is designed for locating constraints in the problem, constraints that will eventually give shape to an hypothesis; the other is the hypothesis as question. It is the difference between, "Was there anything wrong with the driver?" and "Was the driver rushing to the doctor's office for an appointment and the car got out of control?" There are children who precede hypotheses with efforts to locate constraint and there are those who, to use our local slang, are "pot-shotters," who string out hypotheses non-cumulatively one after the other. A second element of strategy is its connectivity of information gathering: the extent to which questions asked utilize or ignore or violate information previously obtained. The questions asked by children tend to be organized in cycles, each cycle of questions usually being given over to the pursuit of some particular notion. Both within cycles and between cycles one can discern a marked difference on the connectivity of the child's performance. Needless to say, children who employ constraint location as a technique preliminary to the formulation of hypotheses tend to be far more connected in their harvesting of information. Persistence is another feature of strategy, a characteristic compounded of what appears to be two components: a sheer doggedness component, and a persistence that stems from the sequential organization that a child brings to the task. Doggedness is probably just animal spirits or the need for achievement—what has come to be called *n-ach*. Organized persistence is a maneuver for protecting our fragile cognitive apparatus from overload. The child who has flooded himself with disorganized information from unconnected hypotheses will become discouraged and confused sooner than the child who has shown a certain cunning in his strategy of getting information—a cunning whose principal component is the recognition that the value of information is not simply in getting it but in being able to carry it. The persistence of the organized child stems from his knowledge of how to organize questions in cycles, how to summarize things to himself, and the like.

Episodic empiricism is illustrated by information gathering that is unbound by prior constraints, that lacks connectivity, and that is deficient in organizational persistence. The opposite extreme is illustrated by an approach that is characterized by constraint sensitivity, by connective maneuvers, and by organized persistence. Brute persistence seems to be one of those gifts from the gods that make people more exaggeratedly what they are.[2]

Before returning to the issue of discovery and its role in the development of thinking, let me say a word more about the ways in which information may get transformed when the problem solver has actively processed it. There is first of all a pragmatic question: what does it take to get information processed into a form best designed to fit some future use? Take an experiment by Zajonc[3] as a case in point. He gives groups of subjects information of a controlled kind, some groups being told that their task is to transmit the information to others, others that it is merely to be kept in mind. In general, he finds more differentiation and organization of the information received with the intention of being transmitted than there is for information received passively. An active set leads to a transformation related to a task to be performed. The risk, to be sure, is in possible overspecialization of information processing that may lead to such a high degree of specific organization that information is lost for general use.

I would urge now in the spirit of an hypothesis that emphasis upon discovery in learning has precisely the effect upon the learner of leading him to be a constructionist, to organize what he is encountering in a manner not only designed to discover regularity and relatedness, but also to avoid the kind of information drift that fails to keep account of the uses to which information might have to be put. It is, if you will, a necessary condition for learning the variety of techniques of problem solving, of transforming information for better use, indeed for learning how to go about the very task of learning. Practice in discovering for oneself teaches one to acquire information in a way that makes that information more readily viable in problem solving. So goes the hypothesis. It in still in need of testing. But is an hypothesis of such important human implications that we cannot afford not to test it—and testing will have to be in the schools.

2. *Intrinsic and Extrinsic Motives.* Much of the problem in leading a child to effective cognitive activity is to free him from the immediate control of environmental rewards and punishments. That is to say, learning that starts in response to the rewards of parental or teacher approval or the avoidance of failure can too readily develop a pattern in which the child is seeking cues as to how to conform to what is expected of him. We know from studies of children who tend to be early over-achievers in school that they are likely to be seekers after the "right way to do it" and that their capacity for transforming their learning into viable thought structures tends to be lower than children merely achieving at levels predicted by intelligence tests. Our tests on such children show them to be lower in analytic ability than those who are not conspicuous in over-achievement.[4] As we shall see later, they develop rote abilities and depend

---

[2]I should also remark in passing that the two extremes also characterize concept attainment strategies as reported in *A Study of Thinking* by J. S. Bruner *et al.* (New York: J. Wiley, 1956). Successive scanning illustrates well what is meant here by episodic empiricism; conservative focussing is an example of cumulative constructionism.

[3]R. B. Zajonc (personal communication, 1957).

[4]J. S. Bruner and A. J. Caron, "Cognition, Anxiety, and Achievement in the Preadolescent," *Journal of Educational Psychology* (in press).

upon being able to "give back" what is expected rather than to make it into something that relates to the rest of their cognitive life. As Maimonides would say, their learning is not their own.

The hypothesis that I would propose here is that to the degree that one is able to approach learning as a task of discovering something rather than "learning about" it, to that degree will there be a tendency for the child to carry out his learning activities with the autonomy of self-reward or, more properly by reward that is discovery itself.

To those of you familiar with the battles of the last half-century in the field of motivation, the above hypothesis will be recognized as controversial. For the classic view of motivation in learning has been, until very recently, couched in terms of a theory of drives and reinforcement: that learning occurred by virtue of the fact that a response produced by a stimulus was followed by the reduction in a primary drive state. The doctrine is greatly extended by the idea of secondary reinforcement: any state associated even remotely with the reduction of a primary drive could also have the effect of producing learning. There has recently appeared a most searching and important criticism of this position, written by Professor Robert White,[5] reviewing the evidence of recently published animal studies, of work in the field of psychoanalysis, and of research on the development of cognitive processes in children. Professor White comes to the conclusion, quite rightly I think, that the drive-reduction model of learning runs counter to too many important phenomena of learning and development to be either regarded as general in its applicability or even correct in its general approach. Let me summarize some of his principal conclusions and explore their applicability to the hypothesis stated above.

I now propose that we gather the various kinds of behavior just mentioned, all of which have to do with effective interaction with the environment, under the general heading of competence. According to Webster, competence means fitness or ability, and the suggested synonyms include capability, capacity, efficiency, proficiency, and skill. It is therefore a suitable word to describe such things as grasping and exploring, crawling and walking, attention and perception, language and thinking, manipulating and changing the surroundings, all of which promote an effective—a competent—interaction with the environment. It is true of course, that maturation plays a part in all these developments, but this part is heavily overshadowed by learning in all the more complex accomplishments like speech or skilled manipulation. I shall argue that it is necessary to make competence a motivational concept; there is *competence motivation* as well as competence in its more familiar sense of achieved capacity. The behavior that leads to the building up of effective grasping, handling, and letting go of objects, to take one example, is not random behavior that is produced by an overflow of energy. It is directed, selective, and persistent, and it continues not because it serves primary drives, which indeed it cannot serve until it is almost perfected, but because it satisfies an intrinsic need to deal with the environment.[6]

I am suggesting that there are forms of activity that serve to enlist and

[5]R. W. White, "Motivation Reconsidered: The Concept of Competence," *Psychological Review*, LXVI (1959), 297–333.

[6]Ibid., pp. 317–18.

develop the competence motive, that serve to make it the driving force behind behavior. I should like to add to White's general premise that the *exercise* of competence motives has the effect of strengthening the degree to which they gain control over behavior and thereby reduce the effects of extrinsic rewards or drive gratification.

The brilliant Russian psychologist Vigotsky[7] characterizes the growth of thought processes as starting with a dialogue of speech and gesture between child and parent; autonomous thinking begins at the stage when the child is first able to internalize these conversations and "run them off" himself. This is a typical sequence in the development of competence. So too in instruction. The narrative of teaching is of the order of the conversation. The next move in the development of competence is the internalization of the narrative and its "rules of generation" so that the child is now capable of running off the narrative on his own. The hypothetical mode in teaching by encouraging the child to participate in "speaker's decisions" speeds this process along. Once internalization has occurred, the child is in a vastly improved position from several obvious points of view—notably that he is able to go beyond the information he has been given to generate additional ideas that can either be checked immediately from experience or can, at least, be used as a basis for formulating reasonable hypotheses. But over and beyond that, the child is now in a position to experience success and failure not as reward and punishment, but as information. For when the task is his own rather than a matter of matching environmental demands, he becomes his own pay-master in a certain measure. Seeking to gain control over his environment, he can now treat success as indicating that he is on the right track, failure as indicating he is on the wrong one.

In the end, this development has the effect of freeing learning from immediate stimulus control. When learning in the short run leads only to pellets of this or that rather than to mastery in the long run, then behavior can be readily "shaped" by extrinsic rewards. When behavior becomes more long-range and competence-oriented, it comes under the control of more complex cognitive structures, plans and the like, and operates more from the inside out. It is interesting that even Pavlov, whose early account of the learning process was based entirely on a notion of stimulus control of behavior through the conditioning mechanism in which, through contiguity a new conditioned stimulus was substituted for an old unconditioned stimulus by the mechanism of stimulus substitution, that even Pavlov recognized his account as insufficient to deal with higher forms of learning. To supplement the account, he introduced the idea of the "second signalling system," with central importance placed on symbolic systems such as language in mediating and giving shape to mental life. Or as Luria[8] has put it, "the first signal system [is] concerned with directly perceived stimuli, the second with systems of verbal elaboration." Luria, commenting on the importance of the transition from first to second signal system, says: "It would be mistaken to suppose that verbal intercourse

[7] L. S. Vigotsky, *Thinking and Speech* (Moscow, 1934).

[8] A. L. Luria, "The Directive Function of Speech in Development and Dissolution," *Word* XV (1959), 341–464.

with adults merely changes the contents of the child's conscious activity without changing its form. .... The word has a basic function not only because it indicates a corresponding object in the external world, but also because it abstracts, isolates the necessary signal, generalizes perceived signals and relates them to certain categories; it is this systematization of direct experience that makes the role of the word in the formation of mental processes so exceptionally important."[9, 10]

It is interesting that the final rejection of the universality of the doctrine of reinforcement in direct conditioning came from some of Pavlov's own students. Ivanov-Smolensky[11] and Krasnogorsky[12] published papers showing the manner in which symbolized linguistic messages could take over the place of the unconditioned stimulus and of the unconditioned response (gratification of hunger) in children. In all instances, they speak of these as *replacements* of lower, first-system mental or neural processes by higher order or second-system controls. A strange irony, then, that Russian psychology that gave us the notion of the conditioned response and the assumption that higher order activities are built up out of colligations or structurings of such primitive units, rejected this notion while much of American learning psychology has stayed until quite recently within the early Pavlovian fold (see, for example, a recent article by Spence[13] in the *Harvard Educational Review* or Skinner's treatment of language[14] and the attacks that have been made upon it by linguists such as Chomsky[15] who have become concerned with the relation of language and cognitive activity). What is the more interesting is that Russian pedagogical theory has become deeply influenced by this new trend and is now placing much stress upon the importance of building up a more active symbolical approach to problem solving among children.

To sum up the matter of the control of learning, then, I am proposing that the degree to which competence or mastery motives come to control behavior, to that degree the role of reinforcement or "extrinsic pleasure" wanes in shaping behavior. The child comes to manipulate his environment more actively and achieves his gratification from coping with problems. Symbolic modes of representing and transforming the environment arise and the importance of stimulus-response-reward sequences declines. To use the metaphor that David Riesman developed in a quite different context, mental life moves from a state of outer-directedness

---

[9]*Ibid.*, p. 12.

[10]For an elaboration of the view expressed by Luria, the reader is referred to the forthcoming translation of L. S. Vigotsky's 1934 book being published by John Wiley and Sons and the Technology Press.

[11]A. G. Ivanov-Smolensky, "On the Study of the Joint Functioning of the First and Second Signal Systems of the Cortex of the Brain," *Journal of Higher Nervous Activity*, I (1951), 55–66.

[12]N. D. Krasnogorsky, *Studies of Higher Nervous Activity in Animals and in Man*, Vol. I (Moscow, 1954).

[13]K. W. Spence, "The Relation of Learning Theory to the Technique of Education," *Harvard Educational Review*, XXIX (1959), 84–95.

[14]B. F. Skinner, *Verbal Behavior* (New York: Appleton-Century-Crofts, 1957).

[15]N. Chomsky, *Syntactic Structure* (The Hague, The Netherlands: Mouton & Co., 1957).

in which the fortuity of stimuli and reinforcement are crucial to a state of inner-directedness in which the growth and maintenance of mastery become central and dominant.

3. *Learning the Heuristics of Discovery*   Lincoln Steffens,[16] reflecting in his *Autobiography* on his under graduate education at Berkeley, comments that his schooling was overly specialized on learning about the known and that too little attention was given to the task of finding out about what was not known. But how does one train a student in the techniques of discovery? Again I would like to offer some hypotheses. There are many ways of coming to the arts of inquiry. One of them is by careful study of its formalization in logic, statisitcs, mathematics, and the like. If a person is going to pursue inquiry as a way of life, particularly in the sciences, certainly such study is essential. Yet, whoever has taught kindergarten and the early primary grades or has had graduate students working with him on their theses—I choose the two extremes for they are both periods of intense inquiry—knows that an understanding of the formal aspect of inquiry is not sufficient. There appear to be, rather, a series of activities and attitudes, some directly related to a particular subject and some of them fairly generalized, that go with inquiry and research. These have to do with the *process* of trying to find out something and while they provide no guarantee that the *product* will be any *great* discovery, their absence is likely to lead to awkwardness or aridity or confusion. How difficult it is to describe these matters—the heuristics of inquiry. There is one set of attitudes or ways of doing that has to do with sensing the relevance of variables— how to avoid getting stuck with edge effects and getting instead to the big sources of variance. Partly this gift comes from intuitive familiarity with a range of phenomena, sheer "knowing the stuff." But it also comes out of a sense of what things among an ensemble of things, "smell right" in the sense of being of the right order of magnitude or scope or severity.

The English philosopher Weldon describes problem solving in an interesting and picturesque way. He distinguishes between difficulties, puzzles, and problems. We solve a problem or make a discovery when we impose a puzzle form on to a difficulty that converts it into a problem that can be solved in such a way that it gets us where we want to be. That is to say, we recast the difficulty into a form that we know how to work with, then work it. Much of what we speak of as discovery consists of knowing how to impose what kind of form on various kinds of difficulties. A small part but a crucial part of discovery of the highest order is to invent and develop models or "puzzle forms" that can be imposed on difficulties with good effect. It is in this area that the truly powerful mind shines. But it is interesting to what degree perfectly ordinary people can, given the benefit of instruction, construct quite interesting and what, a century ago, would have been considered greatly original models.

Now to the hypothesis. It is my hunch that it is only through the exercise of problem solving and the effort of discovery that one learns the working heuristic of discovery, and the more one has practice, the more likely is one to generalize what one has learned into a style of problem solving or

[16]L. Steffens, *Autobiography of Lincoln Steffens* (New York: Harcourt, Brace, 1931).

inquiry that serves for any kind of task one may encounter—or almost any kind of task. I think the matter is self-evident, but what is unclear is what kinds of training and teaching produce the best effects. How do we teach a child to, say, cut his losses but at the same time be persistent in trying out an idea; to risk forming an early hunch without at the same time formulating one *so* early and with so little evidence as to be stuck with it waiting for appropriate evidence to materialize; to pose good testable guesses that are neither too brittle nor too sinuously incorrigible; etc., etc. Practice in inquiry, in trying to figure out things for oneself is indeed what is needed, but in what form? Of only one thing I am convinced. I have never seen anybody improve in the art and technique of inquiry by any means other than engaging in inquiry.

4. *Conservation of Memory.* I should like to take what some psychologists might consider a rather drastic view of the memory process. It is a view that in large measure derives from the work of my colleague, Professor George Miller.[17] Its first premise is that the principal problem of human memory is not storage, but retrieval. In spite of the biological unlikeliness of it, we seem to be able to store a huge quantity of information—perhaps not a full tape recording, though at times it seems we even do that, but a great sufficiency of impressions. We may infer this from the fact that recognition (i.e., recall with the aid of maximum prompts) is so extraordinarily good in human beings—particularly in comparison with spontaneous recall where, so to speak, we must get out stored information without external aids or prompts. The key to retrieval is organization or, in even simpler terms, knowing where to find information and how to get there.

Let me illustrate the point with a simple experiment. We present pairs of words to twelve-year-old children. One group is simply told to remember the pairs, that they will be asked to repeat them later. Another is told to remember them by producing a word or idea that will tie the pair together in a way that will make sense to them. A third group is given the mediators used by the second group when presented with the pairs to aid them in tying the pairs into working units. The work pairs include such juxtapositions as "chair-forest," "sidewalk-square," and the like. One can distinguish three styles of mediators and children can be scaled in terms of their relative preference for each: *generic mediation* in which a pair is tied together by a superordinate idea: "chair and forest are both made of wood"; *thematic mediation* in which the two terms are inbedded in a theme or little story: "the lost child sat on a chair in the middle of the forest"; and *part-whole mediation* where "chairs are made from trees in the forest" is typical. Now, the chief result, as you would all predict, is that children who provide their own mediators do best—indeed, one time through a set of thirty pairs, they recover up to 95% of the second words when presented with the first ones of the pairs, whereas the uninstructed children reach a maximum of less than 50% recovered. Interestingly enough, children do best in recovering materials tied together by the form of mediator they most often use.

[17] G. A. Miller, "The Magical Number Seven, Plus or Minus Two," *Psychological Review,* LXIII (1956), 81-97.

One can cite a myriad of findings to indicate that any organization of information that reduces the aggregate complexity of material by imbedding it into a cognitive structure a person has constructed will make that material more accessible for retrieval. In short, we may say that the process of memory looked at from the retrieval side, is also a process of problem solving: how can material be "placed" in memory so that it can be got on demand?

We can take as a point of departure the example of the children who developed their own technique for relating the members of each word pair. You will recall that they did better than the children who were given by exposition the mediators they had developed. Let me suggest that in general material that is organized in terms of a person's own interests and cognitive structures is material that has the best chance of being accessible in memory. That is to say, it is more likely to be placed along routes that are connected to one's own ways of intellectual travel.

In sum, the very attitudes and activities that characterize "figuring out" or "discovering" things for oneself also seems to have the effect of making material more readily accessible in memory.

REFERENCES

Bruner, J. S. et al. *A Study of Thinking.* New York: John Wiley & Sons, Inc., 1956.

Bruner, J. S., and Caron, A. J. "Cognition, Anxiety and Achievement in the Preadolescent." *Journal of Educational Psychology* (in press).

Chomsky, N. *Syntactic Structure.* The Hague, Netherlands: Mouton & Co., 1957.

Ivanov-Smolensky, A. G. "On the Study of the Joint Functioning of the First and Second Signal Systems of the Cortex of the Brain." *Journal of Higher Nervous Activity*, 1 (1951), pp. 56–66.

Krasnogorsky, N. D. *Studies of Higher Nervous Activity in Animals and Man.* Vol. 1, Moscow, 1954.

Luria, A. L. "The Directive Function of Speech in Development and Dissolution." *Word*, 55 (1959): 341–464.

Maimonides. *Guide for the Perplexed.* New York: Dover Publications, Inc., 1956.

Miller, G. A. "The Magical Number Seven, Plus or Minus Two." *Psychological Review*, 43 (1956), pp. 81–97.

Skinner, B. F. *Verbal Behavior.* New York: Appleton-Century-Crofts, 1957.

Spence, K. W. "The Relation of Learning Theory to the Technique of Education." *Harvard Educational Review*, 29 (1959), pp. 84–95.

Steffens, L. *Autobiography of Lincoln Steffens.* New York: Harcourt Brace Jovanovich, Inc., 1931.

Vigotsky, L. S. *Thinking and Speech.* Moscow, 1934: also New York: John Wiley & Sons, Inc., 1962.

White, R. W. "Motivation Reconsidered: The Concept of Competence." *Psychological Review*, 46 (1959), pp. 297–333.

ROBBIE CASE

6. Piaget's Theory of Child Development and Its Implications

Should the elementary school curriculum be overhauled? Should formal instruction in reading be delayed until the third grade? Is didactic pedagogy at all suited to the natural reasoning processes of young children? Are conventional IQ tests invalid?

Questions such as these are not new in education. What *is* relatively new is the extent to which educators are basing their answers on the work of Swiss psychologist Jean Piaget. The purpose of this article is to summarize Piaget's research and theory, and to take a critical look at its implications for education.

PHILOSOPHICAL FOUNDATIONS

In order to put Piaget's work in perspective, it is worthwhile to point out that it stems from a very different philosophic position from the work of many American psychologists. The latter, particularly the behaviorists, draw heavily upon the philosophy of the British empiricists, Locke and Hume. Both Locke and Hume were concerned with formulating ideas about the way in which man comes to acquire knowledge of the world. They both came to a conclusion that, although somewhat heretical at the time, seems almost commonplace now: Man acquires his knowledge of the world not from God or from logic but from the impressions he receives through his various sense organs. At birth, man is essentially a "blank slate," but as sensations are etched into this slate, he acquires knowledge of the world. The process by which this knowledge is acquired is essentially that of association: the association of one set of sensations or stimuli with another.

By contrast, the work of Piaget was based on the writings of the German philosopher, Immanuel Kant. Although Kant was impressed by much of what Locke and Hume asserted, he decided that their conceptualization of the knowing process was incomplete.

One of the main dimensions of human knowledge on which Kant focused was its organization. He concluded that, while it is true that human beings cannot acquire any knowledge of the world *without* their sense organs, it is impossible to explain the universal organizational properties of their knowledge by assuming their sense organs to be the *only* source of this knowledge. All human beings have certain basic notions—of space, for

From Robbie Case, "Piaget's Theory of Child Development and Its Implications" *Phi Delta Kappan*, Vol. LV-1 (September 1973), pp. 20-25. © 1973 by Phi Delta Kappa, Inc.

example, and of time—which they do not simply "receive" from their senses but which they in a way possess already, and which they use to give order and meaning to what they *do* receive. Consider the simple fact that objects have a permanence independent of our own sensations. For Kant this truth could not simply be "etched in" to our minds by sensation, since it refers to something which must by definition always lie *beyond* our sensation. Rather than being a perceivable fact, then, it is a precondition which is necessary for what *is* perceived to have any meaning, or coherent organization. The human mind does not accept the registration of total chaos, as a blank slate might. In effect, it *demands* that the world be organized, and it has the inherent capacity to make that demand come true.

When Piaget began his pioneering studies, it was with this basic philosophic perspective. Like Kant, he assumed that human beings are not blank slates which passively receive the world; rather, that they actively structure it. Like Kant, he assumed that the structure of man's knowledge depends on certain universal notions which he is never explicitly taught: notions concerning space, time, causality, the permanence of objects, and so on. What Piaget became interested in was the *development* and *origin* of these basic notions. As he himself described it, what he became interested in was *genetic epistemology*.

Perhaps because the notions Piaget was interested in *were* so very basic, and were so "taken for granted" by adults all over the world, the results of his investigations were often quite surprising.

EXPERIMENTAL FINDINGS AND THEORY

The Sensorimotor Stage

From the first days of life, the infant exhibits basic reflexes when confronted by certain stimuli. If a nipple is placed in his mouth, he will suck; if something enters his hand, he will grasp; if a shape moves into his field of vision, he will track it. But his appreciation of causality, or of the permanence of objects, does not appear to be as inborn as these basic reflexes. In fact, it does not appear to be really *finely* developed until he is about two years of age.

Consider the following simple facts. If an interesting object enters his field of vision, even the youngest infant will track it. However, if it goes out of his field of vision repeatedly and then immediately returns, he will not wait for it: His glance will move to other things. Time does not appear to be represented the same way for a child as it is for an adult. When something is out of sight, it is out of mind.

When he is somewhat older, the infant's glance *will* linger in a situation such as that mentioned above. In other situations, however, he will still act as though that which is not immediately present does not exist. For example: Hold a rattle out to a six-month-old child. Then, as he starts to reach out, conceal it behind something he could easily move, such as a handkerchief. All his signs of intention will vanish and he will not try to retrieve it. In fact, he may not try to retrieve it even if it is only *partially* hidden.

When one thinks about it carefully, one can appreciate that a half-hidden object does not look exactly the same as one that is completely in view. How is the child to know it is not "half-made," as it were? When one thinks about it carefully, one can appreciate that a covered object is not present to sensation at all. How is the child to know it has not been completely *un*made? Piaget's interpretation is that this is exactly how infants do see the world—things are made and unmade, and a half-hidden object is only half an object.

Consider another example. There is a stage in the first year of life when a baby will make no attempt to rotate a baby bottle that is presented to him bottom first instead of nipple first. Once again, how is he supposed to know that they are the same object? The bottom certainly doesn't look like the top. The knowledge that an object looks different at different times but is actually a constant thing seems to be one that the infant has to *develop*. In short, the world as we see it is not something that is automatically *given* to the infant by sensation at all; it is something that he has to construct.

In constructing his world, the small child seems to follow a definite series of steps, or successive approximations, to the world we know. When he is just beginning to toddle, one can hide his favorite toy under a bright red handkerchief (in his full view) and he will remove the handkerchief with great glee. Aha, you say, he has learned that an inanimate object continues to stay where it was put. But has he? After you have played this game a few times, place the favorite toy, again in full sight, under a yellow handkerchief. Then watch as he looks under the red one again and appears baffled that the toy is not there. What he appears to have learned is only a first approximation—that when someone causes something to disappear, it will always continue to exist under a red handkerchief.

Piaget invented a number of these sorts of "trick" situations, and he found that it was not until about the age of 18 months to 2 years that the child ceased to be fooled by any of them. Piaget's inference was that it is not until this time that the child has a really strong intuitive notion of the fact that objects have a permanence independent of his perception and that cause and effect can operate independently of his willing them.

How does the child acquire this knowledge? If you watch an infant, you will note that he is continually exploring things with his mouth, his hands, his eyes, and so on. At first these explorations occur independently of each other; later they are coordinated; and finally they are extended to include shaking, throwing, and other actions. Such exploration and testing may not be too easy on parents, but the indications are that it is universal.

For Piaget, this activity is the key mechanism by which an organized view of the world is constructed. An action, even if it is a reflex, is represented in the brain by some sort of plan. You could call it a program. You could call it a neural impulse: the firing of some cells in the brain. It doesn't matter. Piaget calls it a *scheme*. Consider what happens when the child looks at his bottle or a matchbox. The visual configuration of the top activates something in the brain, called a *schema* by Piaget, and the child then acts on the object himself by manipulating it. Presto! A brand new visual configuration appears. Furthermore, when he manipulates the bottle again the first configuration reappears.

In Piaget's terminology, the first schema, or the representation in the brain of the top of the box, is assimilated by (or actually incorporated into) the scheme representing the child's action. Then the reciprocal event occurs: The second schema or visual pattern is assimilated by the same action scheme. As this happens time and again, a compound schema is built up, composed of all the various ways the matchbox can look (all the various schemata) and bound together, as it were, by all the ways it can be acted upon (the schemes). Thus the top of the box is no longer a floating, isolated pattern. It becomes part of a series of patterns, which are intimately connect by virtue of the fact that any one can be produced from any other by simply acting on it. It becomes part of a coordinated whole. Because Piaget sees the product of the child's first two years of life as the result of this sensorimotor integration, he labels this first phase of the child's development the sensorimotor stage.

Preconceptual and Intuitive Thought

The toddler now uses the achievements of the first stage of his life as building blocks to reduce the chaos of the world even further. Now that objects are perceived as entities, and reflexes are integrated into coordinated movements, they can be given names. A little later they can be grouped together in different ways and the whole group can be named.

However, once again, none of these accomplishments occurs overnight. To begin with, the child's language reflects that his psychological units are still objects very different from adult units, which tend to be concepts. At first he seems very uncertain as to the difference between particular objects (for example, his brother), and whole classes of objects (for example, boys). He is not always sure if objects are actually in the same group. When he does build rules about general categories, they tend (as with the rules built in the sensorimotor stage) to be only first approximations to the ones used by adults. They tend to focus on only one attribute of a class and then not necessarily on the adult one. We are all familiar with the child who delights his parents by labeling a dog as "doggie," and who goes on to label a cow as doggie, a cat as doggie, and maybe even his younger brother as a doggie too. By degrees, of course, the child's organization and classification of the world becomes more refined. By the age of 5 or 6, although he cannot yet answer such tricky questions as whether there are more red roses or more roses in a flower bowl, he does appreciate that all the flowers are roses, and that some are red and some are white.

According to Piaget, the mechanism at work is very similar to that in the first stage. By forming things into classes and dividing them again, by calling a certain pattern a cow at one time and an animal at another, the child's mental activity begins to tie together the separate labels and the separate groups into an organized hierarchical framework. At first, during the preconceptual stage, a moving object is gradually tied together with other similar movings things until they all may be called cows. Then, in the intuitive stage, cows are tied together with cats and put into the category of animals, and the whole classification system is bound together as a whole.

In short, between the second and seventh year of his life, the child builds on objects to form concepts and on concepts to form classes of concepts. He does this by grouping things together, regrouping them, naming them, and continuing to explore. By the age of 7 or 8, he is capable of making some remarkably sophisticated observations about the world. His thinking begins to take on quite a logical character. However, it still depends heavily on interacting with the concrete world and it is still different from adult thought in many interesting respects.

Concrete Operations

The building blocks are now not just individual objects or people but classes of objects or people. Not only does a lump of Plasticine remain in existence when hidden but it remains Plasticine, able to be differentiated from other similar objects such as mud by certain properties, and itself containing subcategories depending, say, on whether or not it will harden overnight.

Once more, by acting on the world, the child begins to reduce the remaining chaos. He begins to extract higher-order features of groups that do not change, even though the groups change drastically. For example, having learned by the age of 5 or 6 to classify objects as long or short, heavy or light, and so on, and to relate perceptual properties of objects by using categories like more and less, he begins to appreciate that there are such higher-order categories as length and amount, which remain constant even though the perceptual input (on which the classification is orginally made) may change drastically.

Probably the most famous of Piaget's experiments concerns just this sort of achievement. Take your bright-eyed little 5-year-old daughter who has just learned to count. Have her count out five beads in one row, then five in another row right beside it, and ask her if there are the same number in each row. She will tell you—perhaps proudly—that there are. However, spread out one row a little farther so it looks longer and ask her if there are still the same number in each row. Again, perhaps proudly, she will tell you that there are not, that there are more beads in the long row of five than in the short row of five. What we see once more is that her first understanding is only an approximation of the adult one and that it is based more on changing sensations.

By age 7 she will no longer make this mistake. However, her understanding will not yet be complete; once again it will proceed in definite steps. If we take two balls of Plasticine that she agrees are equal in size, and roll one into a sausage, she will not think that the long one has more Plasticine than the short one, but she *will* still think that the long one weighs more.

Although the kind of activity taking place is no longer one of sensorimotor manipulation, or of grouping and naming, Piaget sees the mechanism by which these higher-order adult constancies are introduced as essentially the same as the mechanism operating in the first two stages. The child learns that although one can always transfer two arrays of five into states where they appear different, the number you get by counting each array will still be five. Furthermore, you can always conduct the reciprocal operation: You can always transform them back into a state where they *are* in one-to-one correspondence. Once again, then, the various possible perceptual configurations of "five" all get tied together into an organized whole, connected by the internalized operations, the mental schemes. The result is that one label can eventually be applied to any array of the same number, no matter how different they look.

Formal Operations

With such higher-order concepts of the properties of objects as number, quantity, and weight, with a good intuitive grasp of causality, and with an understanding of the various possible ways things can be transformed, the child is ready to begin creating an order that is more formal. He is ready to begin relating things—for example, such concepts as mass and number—in terms of invariants which are of a higher order still, such as scientific laws. In addition, his activity in noting the things that actually happen in the world and in producing changes appears to enable him to begin thinking about what *might* happen and to envision all the changes that are possible. It enables him to reason without visual props. This in turn enables him to deduce an appropriate method for scientific procedure.

Consider the following problem: A spinning wheel has holes of various sizes in it and marbles of various sizes on it. A child is asked to figure out why some marbles fall off before others and then to test to see if he is correct.

The child who is in the concrete stage can classify the holes quite accurately and can even cross-classify them. He can see that there are big and small holes and that in both categories there are some near the center and some near the edge. He also has an intuitive notion of causality. However, he appears restricted to noting what actually occurs. If you ask why the big one fell off first, he will say, "Because it's bigger." Then, if you arrange them so that a small one falls off first, he will sometimes say, "Because it's smaller," without being overly upset by the contradiction. If you ask him to *prove* that big ones fall off first, he will not always bother to keep other things constant.

For Piaget, this child has not internalized a system in which *any* relevant attribute may vary and in which many different combinations of possibilities can all produce the same result. The child sees a big marble in a small hole near the edge and concludes that it fell off so soon because it was big. He does not imagine that one could put a small marble in a small hole near the edge and that it might fall off too, so he does not see the need to control other factors before he draws a conclusion about size. In short, although he has an internalized classification system, it is still bound to the concrete things he sees before him. The organization of his knowledge is not yet complex enough to represent conditions of the world accurately which are not before him.

In describing the sequence of stages, I have been referring with confidence to *the* child rather than to *some* children. This is because a remarkable uniformity has been found in the things children can and cannot do (the knowledge they have and don't have) and in the order in which they learn to do them. The exact age at which an individual child may begin to appreciate that weight does not change if nothing is added or subtracted may vary, but it never occurs before he learns that objects have a permanence or after he learns that all other things must be equal in a scientific experiment. Within substages the same is true; a child will always learn the conditions under which weight remains constant before he learns the conditions under which displaced volume remains constant and after he learns the conditions under which number and amount remain constant. We may thus talk about *the* child, since in these most basic interactions with the world and in the constructions of reality, all children achieve an identical series of accomplishments in an identical order.

What Piaget has described, then, is a series of stages through which all children develop. What he has postulated is that the process which propels them through these stages is a highly active one: At each stage the child starts with a world that is ordered in some respects and chaotic in others. And at each level, by acting on the world, by executing transformations, by reversing these transformations, and so on, he builds some further element of order into it. He constructs something that remains unchanged in the face of change—a coordinated whole.

I would now like to turn to the influence Piaget's theory has had, or is having, on education.

EDUCATIONAL APPLICATIONS AND INFLUENCES

Basis for the Content of New Curricula

One of the first applications of Piaget's theory, dating back almost a decade, was to suggest the content for new curricula. The reasoning of the curriculum developers probably went something like this: If these are the stages of development through which a child passes, if the abilities he acquires are really the crucial ones from a cognitive viewpoint, and if one of our jobs as educators is to assist in intellectual development, then maybe we should start providing some assistance to the child in precisely the processes and achievements which Piaget has concentrated on. Furthermore, since one stage appears to be built on the prior stage and to incorporate its achievements, maybe we should start this assistance at an early age. Whether or not this has been the precise reasoning, a number of different curricula have been developed, all aimed at providing activities to assist the preschool or elementary school child in representing number, space, and time, or to help him in classifying the world around him. Curricula have also been developed for elementary and high school students to better prepare them to understand formal and experimental reasoning in science. Particular attention has been paid to making these programs suitable for disadvantaged children. It is felt that such children may benefit more than others from programs aimed not at specific rote skills or the acquisition of factual knowledge but at broader cognitive development.

Exciting as it may seem on the surface, however, the attempt to make Piaget's stages the basis for new curriculum content is not one which, in my opinion, should be accepted uncritically. When one sees how painfully inadequate (by adult standards) is the knowledge of some children, there is a great temptation to rush out and prove that one is a really good teacher: that one can teach the child what he doesn't know or, at least, "help him in his attempts to teach himself." There is an equally strong pull to take something new and exciting and clearly intellectual and, because it *is* all these things, put it in the classroom. But, even if we assume that intellectual development is important—which I *do* assume—I submit that this extension of Piagetian theory into classroom practice can be justified only on the basis of one of two further assumptions: that children would not achieve the stages of development unless they had our help or that (if they *could* achieve the stages without our help) they could not achieve them as early.

Let us consider these assumptions separately. There is some evidence to suggest that not all adults reach the stage of formal operations. Estimates of adults who do not reach this stage vary between about 30 and 90%. The people trying to teach formal operational skills would seem, then, to be on the right track. Assuming that these skills are important and that 50% of the people in the world never achieve them, here is a definite task in which the schools might help.

But what about concrete operational activity and the insights about the world that result from it? Here the evidence (literally, from around the world) is very different. Children appear to acquire these insights and skills on their own almost universally. Why, then, should we expend effort and money teaching them these skills in the classroom?

The only possible justification I can see is the second assumption: that for some reason children should learn these things a little earlier. But this assumption cannot be accepted simply on faith. What reasons are there for rushing a child toward a goal he will reach in a year or so anyway? The only reason I can think of is that the skills in question are somehow necessary for success in the *other* things that the school must teach and that the child who is missing them will therefore be handicapped. Yet, although I stand to be corrected, I know of no evidence to indicate that this is the case or that any conventional elementary school subject cannot be taught until children have reached the stage of concrete operations. I have seen studies quoted which suggest that children often learn to perform certain kinds of arithmetic problems at the same time as they learn to solve certain concrete operational problems, but this is obviously not the same thing.

A crucial study would be to take a group of children who were low in general development, to accelerate or broaden their development with a Piaget-based curriculum, and to show not only that they could *now* learn the required material or generalize it to the required variety of situations, but also that they could do so with less effort than a group for whom the same amount of time had been spent teaching the specific lower-order subject skills prerequisite to mastering the later material. Until such a study is done, I see no reason to support the investment of money in Piagetian elementary school curricula other than in the hope that they *might* help the children and might be fun. But similar reasoning could support the abolition of curricula completely.

Basis for New Assessment Procedures

A second school-related use to which Piaget has been put has been the development of a new intelligence scale. So far, the results have correlated well with those obtained on regular intelligence scales. The Piagetian items, although they probably can be influenced by specially enriching experiences, are said by those developing them to have the advantage of being linked to a theory of intelligence, which normal IQ tests are not. Also, they are said to draw on experience which varies less widely from subculture to subculture; they do not appear to depend on linguistic sophistication, for example, or on any particular knowledge unique to middle-class North Americans.

The attempt to construct and validate an intelligence scale based on Piaget's tests seems to me to be a basically worthwhile one. The only comment I would offer is that any decision as to which sort of test should actually be used in a school should depend on which sort of test proves to be the most useful. This means that criteria other than those of academic or developmental psychologists have to be invoked. Is the test any better at predicting school success? Does it arouse any less hostility in the community at large? Does it provide any more clues as to what help should be given to a child whose poor school performance is associated with a low IQ, and so on?

Justification for a "Readiness" Approach

A third educational influence I feel Piaget is having is that of providing people who believe in "readiness" with some additional ammunition for their arguments. This influence is not so easy to demonstrate as the first two I mentioned. I cannot point to particular teachers or particular programs and say, "There. They are doing that because they believe in readiness, and one of the reasons they believe in readiness is clearly Jean Piaget's work." Yet in the discussions I have had with teachers and have seen in the literature on Piaget's discussions with teachers, his developmental findings are often cited in precisely this connection.

The argument generally goes something like this: The stages of intellectual development have been discovered across a wide variety of tasks. Furthermore, they have always emerged in a definite order; the consolidation of activity and knowledge at one stage is clearly a prerequisite for the progression to activity and knowledge at the next. Since the base of these stages *is* so broad, since one stage *is* the prerequisite for the next, and finally, since the child must actively restructure his world at each stage *for himself*, one should therefore not try to lead the child too much. The best that a school can hope to do is to offer an environment that maximizes readiness-related experience; then, when the child appears to be ready, the teacher can introduce him to those activities that will produce the desired learning. "We can get more mileage from five minutes of teaching at this time than from five hours of teaching before he is ready" is the kind of argument put forward by proponents of readiness.

However, once again, arguments using Piaget to support a laissez faire approach should not be accepted uncritically. Ironically, one can uncover exactly the same unsupported assumption in them as is present in the arguments of those who advocate acceleration. That the achievements of one stage normally depend on massive general experience is probably true. That the achievements of one stage are prerequisite for those of the next stage may also be true. One can even assert the opposite of that which is claimed by those who have developed Piagetian curricula: that the school cannot provide a program which is much superior to normal general experience from an intellectual point of view. However, even if one assumes all three of these propositions, it does not follow that one should avoid teaching a child some specific subject (for example, reading) until he had reached a certain developmental stage—unless one also assumes that some general level of intellectual development is vital to achievement in this subject. And, as I have mentioned already, there is really no strong evidence either way on this point.

Given the pressures inherent in our present system—the stigma and frustration, for example, that are attached to not being able to read until grade five—it would seem that the greatest short-term payoff for our children would be to adopt a chain of reasoning something like this: If some children do not appear "ready" to profit from our current teaching methods, let us not stigmatize them by waiting four years to teach them. Let us find out what specific skills they can be taught so that they *will* be able to profit from our methods. Either that or change the methods.

Justification for Activity-Learning and Self-Discovery Approaches

A fourth use to which Piaget's theory has been put is similar to the third, in that it is not easy to demonstrate and also represents an attempt to justify a teaching method in which—perhaps for other reasons—people already believe. Since early in the century, "progressive" educators have believed that children should learn from their own spontaneous activity, that they should discover facts about the world for themselves, and that education should not be some tight little ticky-tacky compartment set off from the rest of children's experience. Renewed life has been added to this philosophy recently, with student unrest, with liberal criticism of our mechanized, uncreative way of life, with the advent of open plan schools, and so on. One of the bodies of evidence to which people interested in alternative education have turned has been the work of Jean Piaget.

Their reasoning has been roughly as follows: Piaget has shown that the child's own activity is what is responsible for his intellectual development, that he has to rediscover what the adult world already knows. It is therefore a mistake to make him enter a classroom, sit down in one of five rows of eight desks per row, and absorb facts for 15 years, as though he were a blank slate. In so doing, conventional education, like conventional psychology, is employing an understanding of human knowledge that has not evolved since the time of Locke and Hume. What we should be doing is encouraging activity or discovery learning.

The only comment I would make on this point is that one must be very careful about what one means by "activity" and "discovery," and one must be very precise in one's thinking about goals, before one can come to a decision as to whether Piaget's work is even relevant to this argument. Piaget's point, as has been stressed by Vinh Bang (his colleague most closely connected with education), is that when school children do learn something that really becomes a part of their view of the world or their way of thinking, it is by internalized activity. In the early years this activity must have a concrete base, but, nevertheless, it is still internalized, i.e., thinking. This would certainly imply that if one's goal was to produce such learning, one should not merely talk to young children or have them recite rules. However, this probably happens (even in traditional schools) much less often than liberal educators think. Teachers have got the message that rote learning is not the most desirable kind. Rote learning is not at issue.

What is at issue is whether, by setting tasks for children, especially tasks that are done at desks and in which the goal is not to discover something but to demonstrate or apply it, one can really bring about this sort of "constructive" mental activity—whether one can get the child to re-discover what one has just told him and to make it a part of himself. What is at issue is not the *nature* of thought, which would certainly appear to be active, but whether children can genuinely be stimulated to think without being left on their own, taken to the zoo, told to choose a project, or asked to discover a principle. My suspicion is that they *can* be stimulated to think and that this is what good traditional schools have always attempted to do. However, what is needed to answer this sort of question is a Piaget-type study about concepts that are taught in school rather than concepts that are never taught in school.

Even if this type of study were conducted, however, the implications for education would not be automatic. Let us suppose it was discovered that a proper mix of didactic instruction and interaction with concrete props produced a greater amount of mental activity and a greater depth of conceptual understanding than an activity or discovery method. This finding could still not be used as sufficient evidence to argue that traditional methods are more desirable than progressive ones. A question of desirability like this—like the one about IQ tests—simply cannot be answered purely on the basis of psychological investigations. All that can be shown is that A does or does not produce X, not whether X is or is not desirable. It could well be, for example, that although a discovery method turned out to be inferior at eliciting scientific understanding, it might nevertheless be more desirable than a lecture method from other view-points—perhaps motivation, recall after 30 years, training in independent work, absence of anxiety, sense of controlling one's own destiny, and so on. And these other standpoints might well be more important to parents, students, and teachers alike than scientific understanding.

Questions of desirability do not depend only on empirical facts about their consequences. They also depend on value judgments about the desirability of those consequences. And one simply cannot ask psychology—or, for that matter, science—to make these value judgments for one.

SUMMARY

The research and theory of Jean Piaget takes as its point of departure the philosophy of Immanuel Kant—in particular, Kant's proposition that some knowledge of the world is universal and inborn in the human species and not stamped in by sensation. Piaget has shown that, while a certain kind of knowledge is indeed universal, it is not present at birth but is, rather, constructed in a series of stages over the course of the first 16 years of human life. Piaget has also theorized that the mental process through which these stages are achieved is a highly active one, with origins in the first reflexes that the human infant exhibits.

Since one of the universal functions of education is to ensure that the younger generation does not lose the knowledge and perspective that the older generation went to so much trouble to acquire, it would be hard to argue that any theory related to the nature of that knowledge or the processes by which it is acquired could be dismissed as irrelevant. However, what I have attempted to show is that most of the current "applications" of Piaget's work actually go a good deal beyond what he has established empirically, or even what he has theorized. At a deeper level, most of them depend for their justification on an additional set of assumptions, which are either untested as yet, or inherently untestable.

7. Piaget and Montessori

In recent years there has been a renaissance of American interest in the work of two Europeans, Jean Piaget and Maria Montessori. Although the reasons for this rebirth of interest are many and varied, two reasons appear beyond dispute. First of all, both Piaget and Montessori have observed hitherto unexpected and unknown facets of child thought and behavior. Secondly, and in this lies their impact, both of these innovators have derived the general laws and principles regarding child thought and behavior which were implicit in their observations. In the case of Piaget, these observations led to a new philosophy of knowledge while in the case of Montessori, they led to a new philosophy of education.

Unfortunately, it is not possible, in a presentation such as this one, to do any sort of justice to the contributions of these two innovators. Under the circumstances, all that I would like to do is to describe, and to illustrate with research data, three original ideas about child thought and behavior which Piaget and Montessori arrived at independently but share in common. Before turning to those ideas, however, it seems appropriate, by way of introduction, to note some of the parallels and divergences in the Piagetian and Montessorian approaches to child study.

PARALLELS AND DIVERGENCES

Among the many parallels between the work of Piaget and Montessori, one of the most pervasive is the predominantly biological orientation which they take towards the thought and behavior of the child. This is not surprising in view of their backgrounds. Piaget, for example, was publishing papers in biology while still in his teens and took his doctorate in biology at the University of Lausanne. Likewise, Montessori was trained as a physician (she was, it will be recalled, the first woman in Italy to receive a medical degree) and engaged in and published medical research (cf. Standing, 1957). This shared biological orientation is important because both these workers see mental growth as an extension of biological growth and as governed by the same principles and laws.

In addition to, and perhaps because of, this shared biological orientation, both Piaget and Montessori emphasize the normative aspects of child behavior and development as opposed to the aspects of individual difference. Piaget, for example, has been concerned with identifying those mental structures which, if they hold true for the individual, also hold true

From David Elkind, "Piaget and Montessori," *Harvard Educational Review*, Vol. 37 (1967), pp. 535-545. Copyright © 1967 by the President and Fellows of Harvard College.

for the species. Likewise, Montessori has been concerned with those needs and abilities that are common to all children such as the "sensitive periods" and the "explosions" into exploration. This is not to say that Piaget and Montessori in any way deny or minimize the importance of individual differences; far from it. What they do argue is that an understanding of normal development is a necessary starting point for a full understanding of differences between individuals.

The last parallel in the approaches of Piaget and Montessori which I would like to mention is of a more personal nature. Both of these workers manifest what might be called a *genius for empathy with the child*. When reading Piaget or Montessori, one often has the uncanny feeling that they are somehow able to get inside the child and know exactly what he is thinking and feeling and why he is doing what he is doing at any given moment. It is this genius for empathy with the child which, or so it seems to me, gives their observations and insights—even without the buttressing of systematic research—the solid ring of truth.

Despite these parallels, Piaget and Montessori also diverge in significant ways in their approaches to the child. For Piaget, the study of the child is really a means to an end rather than an end in itself. He is not so much concerned with children *qua* children as he is with using the study of the child to answer questions about the nature and origin of knowledge. Please do not misunderstand; Piaget is in no way callous towards the child and has given not a little of his considerable energies and administrative talents to national and international endeavors on the part of children. He has not, however, concerned himself with child-rearing practices, nor—at least until recently and only with reluctance—has he dealt with educational issues (e.g. Piaget, 1964). There is only so much any one person can do, and Piaget sees his contribution primarily in the area of logic and epistemology and only secondarily in the area of child psychology and education.

Montessori, on the other hand, was from the very outset of her career directly concerned with the welfare of the child. Much of her long and productive life was devoted to the training of teachers, the education of parents, and the liberation of the child from a pedagogy which she believed was as detrimental to his mental growth as poor diet was to his physical growth. Montessori, then, was dedicated to improving the lot of the child in very concrete ways.

The other major divergences between these two innovators stem more or less directly from this central difference in approach. Piaget is primarily concerned with theory while Montessori's commitment was to practice. Moreover, Piaget sees his work as being in opposition to "arm chair" epistemology and views himself as the "man in the middle," between the arch empiricists and the arch nativists. Montessori, in contrast, saw herself in opposition to traditional Herbartian pedagogy, which she regarded as medieval in its total disregard for the rights and needs of the child.

CONVERGING IDEAS

I hope that I will be excused if I focus upon Montessori's ideas rather than her methods, for that is where the convergence of Piaget and Montessori is greatest and where the available research is most relevant. Definitive research with respect to the effectiveness of Montessori's methods seems, insofar as I have been able to determine, yet to be completed.

Nature and Nurture

It would be easy, but unfair and incorrect, to contrast Piaget and Montessori with those who seem to take a strong environmentalist position with respect to mental development. Even if we start with writers at the extreme end of the environmentalist camp such as Watson (1928) or more recently, at least apparently, Bruner (1960), it would be a misrepresentation to say that they deny the role of nature in development. The real issue is not one of either nature or nurture but rather one of the character of their interaction. One of the innovations of Piaget and Montessori lies, then, not so much in their championing of the role of nature as in the original way in which they have conceived the character of nature-nurture interaction.

As was mentioned earlier, both Piaget and Montessori see mental growth as an extension of physical growth, and it is in the elaboration of this idea that they have made their unique contribution to the problem of nature-nurture interaction. Their position means, in the first place, that the environment provides nourishment for the growth of mental structures just as it does for the growth of physical organs. It means in addition, and this has been stressed particularly by Montessori, that some forms of environmental nourishment are more beneficial than others for sustaining mental growth just as some foods are more beneficial than others for sustaining physical growth. The "prepared environment" in the Montessori school is designed to provide the best possible nourishment for mental growth.

The relation between nature and nurture in mental growth is, however, not as one-sided as that. Not only does the child utilize environmental stimuli to nourish his own growth, but growth must adapt and modify itself in accordance with the particular environment within which it takes place. Of the many possible languages a child can learn, he learns the one to which he is exposed. The same holds true for his concepts and percepts which are, in part at least, determined by the social and physical milieu in which he grows up. Both Piaget and Montessori recognize and take account of this directive role which the environment plays in the determination of mental content. Indeed, the beauty of the Montessori materials (such as sandpaper letters, number rods, form and weight inset boards) lies in the fact that they simultaneously provide the child with nourishment for the growth of mental capacities and with relevant educational content. In short, for both Piaget and Montessori, nature interacts in a dual way with nurture. As far as mental capacities are concerned, the environment serves as nourishment for the growth of mental structures or abilities whose pattern of development follows a course which is laid down in the genes. Insofar as the content of thought is concerned, nurture plays a more directive role and determines the particular language, concepts, percepts, and values that the child will acquire.

What evidence do we have for this conception of the dual character of nature-nurture interaction? With respect to the environment as a provider of nourishment for an inner-directed pattern of structural development, there is considerable evidence[1] from Piaget-related research. In a study by Hyde (1959) for example, children of different nationalities—British, Arab, Indian, and Somali—were given a battery of Piaget-type number and quantity tasks. Regardless of nationality and language, these children gave the same responses as Piaget had attained with Swiss children. More recently, Goodnow and Bethon (1966) found little difference between Chinese and American children with respect to the age at which they manifested concrete reasoning. These cross-cultural findings suggest that children can utilize whatever stimuli are available in their immediate environs to foster their mental growth just as children all over the world can utilize quite different diets to realize their physical growth.

At the same time, there is also considerable evidence with respect to the directive role which environmental stimulation plays with respect to the content of thought. In a cross-cultural study by Lambert and Klineberg (1967) for example, there were differences even at the six-year-old level in response to the question "What are you?" Most American children thought of themselves primarily as "a boy" or as "a girl" while Bantu youngsters usually described themselves in terms of race. Furthermore, Lebanese children, frequently responded to the question in kinship terms and gave responses such as "the nephew of Ali." This study amply illustrates the role of the physical and social environment in shaping the child's self-concept.

For both Piaget and Montessori, then, nature-nurture interaction has a dual character. In the case of mental capacities, nature plays the directive role and nurture is subservient, while just the reverse is true with respect to the content of thought. It is in their emphasis upon the dual character of nature-nurture interaction that Piaget and Montessori have made their signal contribution to this age-old problem.

Capacity and Learning

Within experimental psychology, the child is generally viewed as a naive organism. That is to say, a child is one who is lacking in experience although his capacity to learn is no different from that of the adult. If differences between children and adults exist, then they reside in the fact that adults have had more opportunity and time to profit from experience than have children. For both Piaget and Montessori, however, the child is a *young* organism which means that his needs and capacities are quite different from those of the adult. This issue can be put more directly by saying that for the experimental psychologist capacity is determined by learning, whereas for the developmental psychologist learning is determined by capacity or development.

[1]For a more complete summary of this evidence see J. H. Flavell, *The Developmental Psychology of Jean Piaget* (New York: Van Nostrand, 1963).

To make this point concrete, let me use a crude but useful analogy. Over the past ten years, we have seen several "generations" of computers. The early computers were relatively slow and quite limited in the amount of information which they could store. The most recent computers, on the other hand, are extremely fast and have enormous memories. Even the earliest computers, however, could handle some of the programs that the highspeed computers can. On the other hand, no matter how many programs were run on the early computers, their capacity was not altered but remained fixed by the limits of their hardware. To be sure, by ingenious programing, these early computers were able to do some extraordinary things, but their limitations in terms of hardware persisted.

As you have anticipated, the several generations of computers can be likened to the several stages in the development of intelligence. Just as the hardware of the computer determines its memory and speed, so the mental structures at any given level of development determine the limits of the child's learning. Likewise, just as the number of programs run on a computer leaves its speed and memory unaltered, so does the number of problems a child has solved or the number of concepts attained not change his problem-solving or concept-learning capacities. Furthermore, just as we can, with elaborate programing, get the computer to do things it was not intended to do, so we can with specialized training get children to learn things which seem beyond their ken. Such training does not, however, change their capacity to learn any more than an ingenious computer program alters the speed or memory of the computer. This is what Piaget and Montessori have in mind by the notion that capacity determines learning and not the reverse.

This idea is frequently misunderstood by many advocates of Piaget and Montessori. Indeed, and here we must be frank, much of the acceptance of Piaget and Montessori in America today seems to be based on the promise which their ideas hold out for accelerating growth. Nothing, however, could be further from their own beliefs and intentions. Piaget was recently quoted as saying, "Probably the organization of operations has an optimal time. . . . for example, we know that it takes nine to twelve months before babies develop the notion that an object is still there even when a screen is placed in front of it. Now kittens go through the same stages as children, all the same substages, but they do it in three months—so they are six months ahead of babies. Is this an advantage or isn't it? We can certainly see our answer in one sense. The kitten is not going to go much further. The child has taken longer, but he is capable of going further, so it seems to me that the nine months probably were not for nothing" (Jennings, 1967, p. 82). In the same vein, Montessori wrote, "We must not, therefore, set ourselves the educational problem of seeking means whereby to organize the internal personality of the child and develop his characteristics: the sole problem is that of offering the child the necessary nourishment" (Montessori, 1964, p. 70).

The view that capacity determines what will be learned has been supported in a negative way by the failure of many experiments designed to train children on Piaget-type reasoning tasks[2] (e.g., Greco, 1959; Smedslund, 1959; Wohlwill, 1959; 1960). In addition, however, there is also evidence of a positive sort which substantiates the role of capacity in the determination of what is learned. In one of our studies, for example, we demonstrated that while six-, seven-, and eight-year-old children could all improve their perceptual performance as a result of training, it was also true that the oldest children made the most improvement with the least training (Elkind, Koegler, and Go, 1962). We have, moreover, recently shown (Elkind, Van Doorninck, and Schwarz, 1967) that there are some perceptual concepts—such as setting or background—which kindergarten children cannot attain but which are easily acquired by second-grade youngsters. In the same vein, we have also demonstrated that there are marked differences in the conceptual strategies[3] employed by children and adolescents and that these strategies limit the kinds of concepts which elementary-school children can attain (Elkind, 1966; Elkind, Barocas, and Johnsen, forthcoming; Elkind, Barocas, and Rosenthal, forthcoming). Similar findings have been reported by Weir (1964) and by Peel (1960).

There is, then, evidence that capacity does determine what is learned and how it is learned. Such findings do not deny that children "learn to learn" or that at any age they can learn techniques which enable them to use their abilities more effectively. All that such studies argue is that development sets limits as to what can be learned at any particular point in the child's life. These studies are in keeping with the positions of Piaget and Montessori. As we have seen, neither of these innovators advocates the acceleration of mental growth. What they do emphasize is the necessity of providing the child with the settings and stimuli which will free any given child to realize his capacities at his own time and pace. Such a standpoint is quite different from one which advocates the acceleration of mental growth.

Cognitive Needs and Repetitive Behavior

One of the features of cognitive growth which Piaget and Montessori observed and to which they both attached considerable importance, is the frequently repetitive character of behaviors associated with emerging mental abilities. Piaget and Montessori are almost unique in this regard since within both psychology and education repetitive behavior is often described pejoratively as "rote learning" or "perseveration." Indeed, the

[2]Most of these tasks deal with conservation or the child's ability to deduce permanence despite apparent change. For example, the child might be "shown" two equal quantities of colored water in identical containers one of which is emptied into two smaller containers before his eyes. Since the child has no way of measuring the equality of the liquid in the large container and that in the two smaller containers, he must—if he can—*deduce* the equality on the basis of their prior equality and his awareness that pouring does not change amount.

[3]In a problem-solving task, for example, once a child sets up an hypothesis, he continues to maintain it even when the information he receives clearly indicates that it is wrong. The adolescent, on the other hand, immediately gives up an hypothesis that is contradicted by the data and proceeds to try out a different one.

popular view is that repetition is bad and should be avoided in our dealings with children.

What both Piaget and Montessori have recognized, however, is the very great role which repetitive behavior plays in mental growth. In his classic work on the origins of intelligence in infants, Piaget (1952a) illustrated in remarkable detail the role which primary, secondary, and tertiary circular reactions play in the construction of intellectual schemas. Likewise at a later age, Piaget (1952b) has pointed out the adaptive significance of children's repetitive "Why?" questions. Such questions, which often seem stupid or annoying to adults, are in fact the manifestation of the child's efforts at differentiating between psychological and physical causality, i.e., between intentional or motivated events and events which are a consequence of natural law.

Montessori has likewise recognized the inner significance of repetitive behavior in what she calls the "polarization of attention." Here is a striking example with which, I am sure, many of you are familiar:

I watched the child intently without disturbing her at first, and began to count how many times she repeated the exercise; then, seeing that she was continuing for a long time, I picked up the little arm chair in which she was seated and placed chair and child upon the table; the little creature hastily caught up her case of insets, laid it across the arms of the chair and gathering the cylinders into her lap, set to work again. Then I called upon the children to sing; they sang, but the little girl continued undisturbed, repeating her exercise even after the short song had come to an end. I counted forty-four repetitions; when at last she ceased, it was quite independently of any surrounding stimuli which might have distracted her, and she looked around with a satisfied air, almost as if awakening from a refreshing nap. (Montessori, 1964, pp. 67–68)

The role of repetitive behavior in intellectual development is not extraordinary when we view mental growth as analogous to physical growth. Repetitive behavior is the bench mark of maturing physical abilities. The infant who is learning to walk constantly pulls himself into an erect position. Later as a toddler he begins pulling and dropping everything within reach. Such behavior does not derive from an innate perversity or drive towards destruction but rather out of a need to practice the ability to hold and to let go. What the child is doing in such situations is practicing or perfecting emerging motor abilities. Mental abilities are realized in the same way. In the course of being constituted, intellectual abilities seek to exercise themselves on whatever stimuli are available. The four-year-old who is constantly comparing the size of his portions with those of his siblings is not being selfish or paranoid. On the contrary, he is spontaneously exercising his capacity to make quantitative comparisons. The Montessori child who repeatedly buttons and unbuttons or replaces inserts into their proper holes is likewise exercising emerging mental abilities. Piaget and Montessori see such repetitive behaviors as having tremendous value for the child and as essential to the full realization of the child's intelligence.

Although there is not a great deal of research evidence relevant to the role of repetition in mental growth, I would like to cite some findings from one of our studies which points in this direction. In this study (Elkind and Weiss, 1967), we showed kindergarten-, first-, second-, and third-grade children a card with eighteen pictures pasted upon it in the shape of a triangle. The children's task was simply to name every picture on the card. The kindergarten children named the pictures according to the triangular pattern in which the pictures were pasted. That is to say, they began at the apex and worked around the three sides of the triangle. This same triangular pattern of exploration was employed by third-grade children and to some extent by second-grade children. First-grade children and some second-grade youngsters, however, did a peculiar thing. *They read the pictures across the triangle from top to bottom and from left to right.*

Why did the first-grade children read the pictures in this clearly inefficient way? The answer, it seems to me, lies in the fact that these children were in the process of learning the top to bottom and left to right swing which is essential in reading English. Because they had not entirely mastered this swing, they spontaneously practiced it even where it was inappropriate. Viewed in this way, their behavior was far from being stupid, and the same can be said for older slow-reading children who read the pictures in the same manner as the first-graders.

These findings thus support the arguments of Piaget and Montessori regarding the adaptive significance of repetitive behavior in children. Repetitive behavior in the child is frequently the outward manifestation of an emerging cognitive ability and the need to realize that ability through action. It was the genius of Piaget and Montessori which saw, in such repetitive behaviors as sucking and putting insets into holes, not stupidity, but rather, intelligence unfolding.

SUMMARY AND CONCLUSIONS

In this paper I have tried to describe and illustrate with research data, three original ideas about child thought and behavior which Piaget and Montessori arrived at independently but which they share in common. The first idea is that nature and nurture interact in a dual way. With respect to the growth of abilities, nature provides the pattern and the time schedule of its unfolding while nurture provides the nourishment for the realization of this pattern. When we turn to the content of thought, however, just the reverse is true; nurture determines what will be learned while nature provides the prerequisite capacities. A second idea has to do with capacity and learning. For both Piaget and Montessori, capacity sets the limits for learning and capacity changes at its own rate and according to its own time schedule. Finally, the third idea is that repetitive behavior is the external manifestation of cognitive growth and expresses the need of emerging cognitive abilities to realize themselves through action.

The recent acceptance of Piagetian and Montessorian concepts in this country is gratifying and long overdue. It would be a great loss if within a few years these ideas were once again shelved because they failed to accomplish that which they were never designed to achieve. To avoid that eventuality, we need to try and accept Piaget and Montessori on their own terms and not force their ideas into our existing conceptual frameworks, or distort them for our own pragmatic purposes. Only in this way can we hope to gain lasting benefit from the outstanding contributions which Piaget and Montessori have made to the study of the child.

REFERENCES

Bruner, J. S. *The process of education.* Cambridge, Mass.: Harvard Univer. Press, 1960.

Elkind, D., Barocas, R. B., & Johnsen, P. H. Concept production in children and adolescents. *J. Exp. Child Psychol.,* (forthcoming).

Elkind, D., Barocas, R. B., & Rosenthal, R. Concept production in slow and average readers, *J. Educ. Psychol.,* (forthcoming).

Elkind, D., Koegler, R. R., & Go, Elsie. Effects of perceptual training at three age levels. *Science,* 1962, 137, 755-756.

Elkind, D., Van Doorninck, W. & Schwarz, Cynthia. Perceptual activity and concept attainment. *Child Develpm.,* (forthcoming).

Elkind, D. & Weiss, Jutta. Studies in perceptual development III: perceptual exploration. *Child Develpm.,* 1967, 38, 553-561.

Goodnow, Jacqueline J. & Bethon, G. Piaget's tasks: the effects of schooling and intelligence. *Child Develpm.,* 1966, 37, 573-582.

Greco, P. L'apprentissage dans une situation à structure opératoire concrète: les inversions successives de l'ordre lineaire pare des rotations de 180°. In J. Piaget (Ed.), *Études d'epistemologie genetique.* Vol. 8. Paris: Presses Universitaires de France, 1959, 68-182.

Hyde, D. M. An investigation of Piaget's theories of the development of the concept of number. Unpublished doctoral dissertation, Univer. of London, 1959.

Jennings, F. G. Jean Piaget: notes on learning. *Saturday Rev.,* May 20, 1967, p. 82.

Lambert, W. E. & Klineberg, O. *Children's view of foreign peoples.* New York: Appleton-Century-Crofts, 1967.

Montessori, Maria. *Spontaneous activity in education.* Cambridge, Mass.: Robert Bentley Inc., 1964.

Peel, E. A. *The pupil's thinking.* London: Oldhourne Press, 1960.

Piaget, J. *The origins of intelligence in children.* New York: International Universities Press, 1952 (a).

Piaget, J. *The language and thought of the child.* London: Routledge & Kegan Paul, 1952 (b).

Piaget, J. Development and learning. In R. E. Ripple & V. N. Rockcastle (Eds.), *Piaget rediscovered.* Ithaca, N.Y.: Sch. of Educ., Cornell Univer., 1964.

Smedslund, J. Apprentissage des notions de la conservation et de la transitivité du poids. In J. Piaget (Ed.), *Études d'epistemologie genetique.* Vol. 9. Paris: Presses Universitaires de France, 1959, 85-124.

Standing, E. M. *Maria Montessori.* Fresno: Academy Library Guild, 1957.

Watson, J. B. *Psychological care of infant and child.* New York: Norton, 1928.

Weir, M. W. Developmental changes in problem solving strategies. *Psychol. Rev.,* 1964, 71, 473-490.

Wohlwill, J. F. Un essai l'apprentissage dans le domaine de la conservation du nombre. In J. Piaget (Ed.), *Études d'epistemologie genetique.* Vol. 9. Paris: Presses Universitaries de France, 1959, 125-135.

Wohlwill, J. F. A study of the development of the number concept by scalogram analysis. *J. Genet. Psychol.,* 1960, 97, 345-377.

SIDNEY W. BIJOU

8. Behavior Analysis Applied to Early Childhood Education

Fifty years from now it is both possible and likely that educators will claim that preschool is the most important single educational experience in the life of a child. It is currently accepted, almost without exception, that the preschool years constitute one of the most important stages of human development. It would follow that, when a truly effective approach to teaching in the preschool years is achieved, the preschool period should be the most significant and influential in a child's life. If one accepts this line of reasoning, the problems of preschool education should be considered in light of the most reliable knowledge of human behavior and development—in other words, in light of the concepts, principles, and methodology of behavior analysis.

The application of behavioral principles to preschool education is by no means a recent innovation. It is, in fact, as old as the original behavioristic brand of functionalism. At the turn of the century Patty Smith Hill, a follower of John Dewey, John B. Watson, and Edward L. Thorndike, contended that the kindergarten curriculum should develop from the subject matter of the school, the developmental status of the children, and the history and future potentialities of society.[1] She maintained, further, that the method of teaching should be based on "habit" training, very much in the mode of Watson.[2] The present day behavioral approach to preschool education is clearly manifested in the work of many, including Donald Bushell; Barbara Etzel, Nancy Bybel, Karen Busby, Lois Dixon, and Joseph Spradlin; Todd Risley, Nancy Reynolds, and Betty Hart; and Carolyn Thompson.[3] The theoretical underpinning of the work of these investigators relies heavily not on Watson but on B. F. Skinner, who integrated Thorndike's theory of trial-and-error learning and Pavlov's concept of classical conditioning into a system for the understanding of human behavior.[4]

The behavioral influence can be seen in other approaches to preschool education, among them, the Bereiter-Engelmann structured program, the early training project known as DARCEE (Demonstration and Research Center for Early Childhood), and the Tucson early educational model.[5] This chapter focuses on the behavioral approach to preschool education as it affects the philosophy or the goals of teaching, the methods used in teaching or the means of achieving preschool goals, and the support needed by teachers to perform their jobs to the extent of their training.

From *Early Childhood Education* by Bernard Spodek and Herbert J. Walberg et al. Berkeley: McCutchan Publishing Corporation. © 1977. Reprinted by permission of the Publisher.

PHILOSOPHY OF PRESCHOOL EDUCATION: THE GOALS OF TEACHING

Everyone—parent, older sibling, relative, friend, or teacher—who helps a young child learn has some kind of philosophy of education. For parents and older siblings (really parent aides), the goals are implicit or "natural" to the practices of the family and consist of helping the child to learn self-care skills and to achieve the beginnings of social, cognitive, and moral behavior. For relatives and friends, the goals are also implicit and "natural" to practices of the extended family and the neighborhood, practices that lead to the achievement of certain broader social and recreational abilities and knowledge. The goals of preschool teachers are, on the other hand, explicit. They have some kind of child development rationale, and they are linked to educational materials and methods and form a curriculum that focuses primarily on the child's verbal abilities and knowledge and on his social-emotional needs.

Preschool Goals Are Value Judgments

Regardless of the teacher, the setting, and the degree of explicitness, the goals of teaching are value judgments about what the behavior of a child should be; they are by no means conclusions drawn directly from research, whether it be educational, sociological, psychiatric, or psychological.[6] The goals for preschool education are based on ideological or philosophical conceptions of the child, the society, and the role of preschool education in that society. Those who should be responsible for selecting goals are parents, teachers, school administrators, members of boards of education, and governmental officials. Experts in early childhood education serve, or should serve primarily as resource persons who provide the decision makers with information on human development, learning, adjustment, and instructional process, the workings and future directions of society, the benefits and risks of particular educational practices, methods of evaluating educational programs, and the principles of the decision-making process itself.

Advice from professional educators about preschool goals has been divergent, conflicting, and confusing. There are those who hold that the goals should depend entirely on the psychological needs of the child. At the same time others maintain that the needs of society should be the sole determining factor. Educators who espouse child-centered goals generally hold that a child is born with built-in, self-actualizing tendencies and that one should leave the child to his own devices in discovering his naturally constructive nature. Such educators support unstructured teaching programs, and present-day advocates of something akin to Froebelian doctrine include the Piagetians, with their hypothetical cognitive structures and processes evolving through predetermined stages;[7] the neo-Freudians, with their concepts of the development of the components of personality structure (id, ego, and superego and the evolution of the sense of trust, autonomy, and initiative);[8] and the Gesellians, with their notions about the growth of the mind, manifested to motor, social, adaptive, and language development.[9] Cognitive structures, the components of personality structure, and parallel divisions of the mind are hypothetical internal causal entities, inferred from behavior and preconceptions about the original nature of man. They exist only in the behavior of the theorists, that is to say, in their writings and lectures. When the theories that they espouse lose their credibility, nursery school goals based upon such theories also become meaningless because the hypothetical terms and relationships upon which they depend become nonfunctional when it is demonstrated that preschool goals and the means of achieving them can be stated in terms of observable behavior.

Educators who hold that preschool goals must be based not on the needs of the child but on the needs of society contend that a child is naturally unsocial or antisocial and that if he is not given a structured school situation, such as occurs with the Bereiter-Engelmann program,[10] he fails to acquire behaviors essential for societal living. This rationalization carries over from the days when parents used children, as soon as they were physically able, to augment the economic resources of the family. In the preindustrial period, prior to the delegation of education to a social agency, children automatically joined their parents in helping the family to survive, a practice that constituted a most important part of the offsprings' education and training. With the onset of the industrial age and the establishment of community schools, the pressing of children into large-scale farm operations and factories proved hazardous to children. Ultimately there were laws forbidding such practices. This broader social view of the goals of education coincides with the belief held by certain religious groups that a child is sinful by nature.

It is my contention that any acceptable philosophy of preschool education must take into account both the developmental status of the child and the characteristics of his society. This position is not derived from a pragmatic attempt to make the best of both worlds. It relies, instead, on the natural science assumption that a child develops, or changes progressively, as a consequence of interactions with the environment and therefore that *the development of a child cannot ever be considered separately from the specific events that constitute his environment.* The behavior displayed by a child entering nursery school is the result of interaction between his own unique biological makeup (including natural bodily changes or biological maturation) and specific events encountered since the day he was born. By the time he finishes nursery school, his behavior is a function of his unique biological makeup and interactions among specific events not only in his home but also in the nursery school and the immediate community. These streams of interactions make the child the "personality" that he is at any stage in his development.

The goals of the preschool, like the goals of any school, should help the child develop behaviors that relate to his current environment and to situations he can expect in his life. Behaviors should, moreover, aim at enhancing the development of both child and society, at helping each to grow stronger and to survive. Although "enhancing the strength and the survival possibilities of a society" has a somewhat lofty sound, it actually ranges from simply managing one's own affairs to spearheading innovations that could benefit society as a whole. Helping a child derive satisfaction from living and developing and at the same time preparing him to participate and to contribute to the welfare of society are compatible goals.

Goals based on a child's current interactions with the environment should be compatible with practices in both the home and the community. As for goals based on home practices, the question that confronts us is: How effective are current parent programs, first, in conveying to the nursery school staff the practices of the home and, second, in helping the staff integrate the practices of home and school? Goals based on practices in the immediate community are achieved mainly through direct contact with institutions of community living such as shopping centers, power plants, and bus terminals, in conjunction with discussions about how they function.

Preschool goals based on future situations should include behaviors that will help a child cope with the practices of the kindergarten or first grade he is likely to attend and with the social activities that probably foreshadow changes in his culture. Several semibehavioral preschool programs focus on just such goals. "In most of the programs of early childhood education, goals are stated in terms of the behaviors necessary for success in later schooling. These might be cognitive skills as in the DARCEE program, or academic skills as in the Bereiter-Englemann-Becker-program, or a combination of social skills necessary for the role of student and academic skills as in the Behavior Analysis program."[11] It is obvious that goals of this sort are desirable, but they should constitute only a part of the objectives of preschool education.

Preschool goals relating to preparing a child for probable future changes in society are more difficult to attain than those geared to his current situation because knowledge about teaching problem-solving behavior is limited and the nature of future events is uncertain. Preschool programs should, nevertheless, include goals pertaining to the teaching of problem-solving techniques, at least to the extent of our present knowledge. They should also include activities that have implications for life in the future, such as space exploration, developments in electronics, and concern about food supply and distribution, energy shortages, ecology, and international relationships.

Behaviorally Oriented Preschool Goals

Those responsible for selecting goals for a preschool program traditionally make collective decisions based on the objectives of preschools already in operation (especially demonstration schools), on the literature available on early childhood education, on family and community considerations, on economic factors, and on consultation with educators and other professionals. If a behavior analyst were to advise such a group, he would recommend a set of goals that would emphasize the furthering of individuality and of problem-solving ability through the development of abilities and knowledge, the extension of motivations, and the enhancement of self-management skills. The specific items under each of the following headings are not viewed as immutable but as alterable in light of further research. The items do indicate change in society, where it is (its image), and where it is probably heading.

Development of Abilities and Knowledge

Ability and knowledge goals imply that the child will be taught how to do things and how to acquire information about objects, people, occurrences, and himself, that is, his self-concept.[12] These goals fall into ten subclasses. The first four pertain to behavior primarily in relation to self; the last six, to behavior mainly in relation to society. The subclasses are listed as:

1. Body management and control, including manual dexterity and locomotor skills.
2. Physical health and safety.
3. Self-care, including dressing, undressing, and toilet training.
4. Recreation and play.
5. Social behavior, including all forms of communication.
6. Aesthetic knowledge and abilities in relation to art, crafts, music, and literature.
7. Everyday mechanical skills.
8. Knowledge of community services (for example, transportation, sanitation, fire fighting).
9. Preacademic and academic subjects.
10. Methods and content of science.

Extension of Motivations

In technical behavioral terms the extension of motives, in the form of attitudes, interests, and values, involves replacing appetitive and aversive contingencies with positive, conditioned reinforcers; specific, generalized, extrinsic, and intrinsic. In psychoanalytic terms, the objective is to change behavior motivated by id forces to behavior motivated by ego and superego impulses. Goals in the behavioral sense include:

1. Preservation and extension of moral values in keeping with the family moral code and the moral code of the classroom as a subculture.
2. Preservation and extension of ecological (natural) reinforcers, and, by definition, preservation and extension of exploratory behavior.
3. Development of positive attitudes toward and interests in people as individuals and as groups.
4. Positive attitudes toward and interests in attending school and in the activities of school and community.

Enhancement of Self-management Skills

This third category of objectives refers to the acquisition of self-management skills in the broadest sense. These skills are usually deemed desirable because they are said to enhance innovative behavior, self-control, and problem-solving ability. They consist of the beginning stages of:

1. Personal self-management techniques including the development of desirable "personal habits," "moral habits," and "work habits," as well as the ability to concentrate on the subject at hand and work independently and systematically (development of autonomy).
2. Problem solving (thinking) and decision-making skills, including creative and innovative behavior.

TEACHING METHODS: MEANS OF ACHIEVING GOALS

From the dawn of human culture there have been highly effective teachers who achieve their effectiveness "on their own" or through the specific contingencies that constitute their personal histories. With the advent of an applied science of human behavior, competent teachers can be trained to be even more effective, and less competent teachers can be trained to perform their job adequately.

The notion that a teacher can be trained leads one to question learning models offered in teacher training. One example is the *experience* model, which emphasizes exposing a child to a great variety of stimulating experiences. Then there is the *doing* model, which encourages all sorts of activity, especially exploratory behavior. Another example is the *trial-and-error* model, which affords a child opportunities to interact with objects and people in order to learn from "feedback," that is, the consequences of his actions. One final example is the *open situation* model, which provides a child with physical and social environments that encourage desirable behavior to evolve naturally.

Each of these models is inadequate because each stresses only a single aspect of learning. In the experience model it is the material to be learned or the task to be performed that is emphasized. In the doing model the behavioral component receives most of the attention. In the trial-and-error model it is the consequences of the behavior that are paramount. In the open situation model the setting for learning is stressed.

There is another model, based on modern behavior theory, that brings together all four components, and teaching is defined as the arrangement of the components in a way that facilitates learning.[13] The selection and sequencing of the material or procedure, and the techniques used for presentation (for example, priming, modeling, fading, and rule giving), require actual experience. The behavioral aspect enters into the shaping of behavior or the development of motor and verbal abilities and skills. The consequences of behavior relate to the management of reinforcing contingencies, including their proper selection and use in developing personal traits (for example, autonomy) and new reinforcers (new interests). And, finally, it is the setting or contextual component that allows control of the entire situation to promote educationally desirable behavior throughout a school day.

A child is, of course, perfectly capable of learning without a teacher and should be given ample opportunity and encouraged to do so. But the learning of many abilities and much knowledge does require a teacher because the reinforcement contingencies involved do not ordinarily occur naturally (as in concept formation), or because the contingencies are too remote to influence appropriate behavior (as in learning to avoid poisonous plants).

Applied Behavior Analysis Teaching Strategy

Applied behavior analysis teaching strategy, which is always directed to an individual child, has been described in the educational literature in many different ways. The strategy, it seems, consists of five basic phases: specifying or clarifying the goals of teaching in observable terms; beginning instruction at the child's level of competence; arranging the teaching situation (materials, procedures, instructions, setting, and contingencies) to facilitate learning in directions that enhance the individuality of a child; monitoring progress and altering materials and procedures to advance learning; and following practices that generalize, elaborate, and maintain the behaviors acquired.

It has already been stated that the goals of preschool teaching are, or should be, established by a representative group of people, with parents having a clear and strong voice. The goals should stem from their understanding of the child, of the society, and of the role of preschool education in that society. The teacher's main function then becomes the division of each general goal into logical subdivisions and subgoals that are appropriate for each child and that heighten each child's individuality.

To begin a teaching program at a child's level of competence, the teacher must first assess the child's preinstructional behavior (competencies) in relevant areas, that is, the teacher makes an educational diagnosis. Criterion-referenced tests, which provide information on social and cognitive repertories, are more useful in making the diagnosis than norm-referenced tests, which yield data on mental age, social age, intelligence, or grade achievement.[14]

The teacher plans and selects those materials, activities, and situations that, under most conditions, will lead to reaching the preestablished goal. When planning art experiences, for example, three kinds of art activities must be considered: those that allow freedom to combine elements, those that deal with the development of skills and discriminations, and those that are craft-oriented. The teacher should use techniques that encourage original productions stemming from the child's personal history and encourage him to interact with the materials, her instructions, and the reinforcers.[15]

Keeping samples of productions, such as handwriting and artwork, and of records that show each child's social behaviors, such as initiating conversation with a peer, provides the teacher with a systematic account of progress. Based on this data, the teacher can reevaluate the programming of material, the physical setting, the instructions, and the effectiveness of the reinforcers.

Lastly, the teacher incorporates into daily teaching plans those activities that generalize, elaborate, and maintain the abilities and knowledge that the child has acquired: This can be done in the school setting by posing problems and questions in contexts that differ from the learning situation and by reinforcing instances of related learned behaviors that occur "spontaneously," but are not arranged by the teacher. The teacher can also work with the mother and demonstrate how to help a child generalize, elaborate, and maintain school-learned behavior at home.

Behavior acquired in a learning situation generalizes to other situations, or, stated more precisely, learned behavior automatically comes under the control of stimuli similar to those in the learning situation. But effective teaching, whether by teachers or parents, increases the probability of generalization, mainly through practices that strengthen learned behaviors. For example, contingencies can be arranged that teach cooperative behavior in the preschool during group activities, recess, snack time, and art class. There are similar opportunities at home while playing, cleaning up, eating, and performing chores. The elaborating of learned behavior actually refers to the arranging of contingencies so as to transform learned behavior into more complex forms: extending walking to hopping, skipping, and jumping; expanding one-word sentences to phrases and longer sentences.

Maintaining learned behavior, often referred to as improving memory or retention, consists of arranging reinforcing contingencies so that learned behavior preserves its strength. Once a child is taught to remove his coat and hang it up, he should be encouraged by a pleasant remark, or a pat on the back so tht he will continue this practice whenever he enters the house. The key principle underlying this aspect of applied behavioral analysis teaching strategy is to distribute reinforcement on a schedule that will keep the behavior vigorous, starting with frequent reinforcement and gradually reducing the frequency.

Applying Behavioral Teaching Strategy to Preschool Situations

The effectiveness of the application of the behavior strategy to teaching specific objectives ultimately depends upon the teacher's dedication to achieving curriculum goals and her skill in applying behavior principles to develop the individuality of each child in her class. It is agreed almost unanimously that the teacher is the most important factor in any teaching situation since she is the one who has direct contact with the child. Research has shown, however, that the correlation between teacher characteristics and pupil accomplishment and achievement is close to zero. This astonishing fact calls for new ways of conceptualizing the teacher and the teaching process.[16] A measure of effectiveness that should be explored is how well a teacher applies principles of behavior and development. If she is skillful, continually rearranging the teaching situation to suit the child's progress as recorded in objective terms, there should be a substantial positive relationship between her teaching behavior and pupil achievement and school attitudes.

Development of Abilities and Knowledge

Teaching both the abilities and the knowledge required to deal with the ten behavior subgroups mentioned earlier involves the effective management of reinforcing contingencies. The key procedure for teaching ability categories is differential reinforcement of successive approximations to the form of the goal response. Working with a young child faced with the task of learning how to draw a circle, the teacher reinforces him first as he learns more efficient ways of holding the pencil, and then of drawing curved lines that more closely approximate those of a circle, until he eventually draws an acceptable circle. This procedure is referred to as response differentiation or shaping.[17] To say that the key principle in teaching abilities and skills involves reinforcing successive changes in response form does not imply that the occasion (discriminative stimulus or cue) and context (setting factor) can be ignored. An ability is always taught in relation to some situation (the ability to draw is taught in relation to a pencil or crayon and a sheet of paper) and a favorable context (a quiet and relaxed setting) for performing that task.

The fundamental procedure for teaching knowledge categories is discrimination training or differential reinforcement on the basis of an occasion (discriminative stimulus or cue). Sometimes the occasion for differential reinforcement is the action of a person, such as extending the hand to greet someone; sometimes it is one or several aspects of two stimulus complexes, such as teaching a child to discriminate between an apple and an orange; sometimes it is abstraction, such as teaching "in-front-of" spatial relations and other concepts.[18] The form of knowledge behavior, which ranges from a simple pointing response to a complex verbal structure (interactional chain), and the setting factors for learning are also factors to be considered in the teaching of knowledge.

There is an additional significant and essential point about the teaching of abilities and knowledge. *The achievement of the other two categories of goals—motivations and self-management skills—depends to a large extent on techniques used to teach the abilities and knowledge categories.* In other words, abilities and knowledge taught according to the principles described here serve to extend and elaborate motives and to strengthen self-control and self-management skills.

Extension of Motivations

Procedures that the teacher uses in teaching abilities and knowledge can make the activity, the situation, and even the teacher distasteful to a child. Even though a student responds as required and the teacher works diligently at presenting, explaining, repeating, and reviewing, teaching procedures might rouse little enthusiasm for learning. It is possible, however, for teaching procedures to rouse enthusiasm for the activity, the situation, and the teacher, and, ultimately, for learning.

Teaching designed to extend moral values and positive attitudes toward peers and adults, school and school activities, and ecological (natural) reinforcers involves the skillful management of positive reinforcers in ways that establish new positive conditioned reinforcers for a child.[19] The extension of moral values depends largely on clearly specifying the behaviors classified as "good" and applying positive contingencies when they occur and on specifying "bad" behaviors and applying either no contingencies at all or techniques of self-control, including mild reprimands, when they take place.[20]

The teaching of positive attitudes toward peers and adults, both as individuals and as members of groups, involves pairing the activities of peers and adults with social or physical stimuli (including activities) that are meaningful (functional) for a child. Since most children enter nursery school with positive attitudes toward their peers, the teacher, and aides, training for a child with negative attitudes is usually categorized as remedial.

To teach positive attitudes toward attending school, reinforcers must be paired with coming to school. The first step in planning the program is an assessment of the child's attendance record. "Liking for school" might be evaluated by the rate and regularity of school attendance, crying (frequency and duration) or smiling upon arrival at school, the parents' report of the child's eagerness (or reluctance) to go to school, or whether the opportunity to attend school could be used to reinforce other low frequency behavior in the home, such as eating breakfast, putting away pajamas, or helping to make the bed. The desired goal for a child who cries each time he comes to school would, of course, be to have him arrive at school in a "good," that is, cheerful and eager, frame of mind.

The principle involved in developing a child's interests in nonpreferred school activities is the establishing of intrinsic reinforcers that come from participation in the activity. The conditioned reinforcing properties of school activities can be assessed when a child first enters school by measuring the time spent at a given task without prompts, primes, or reinforcement from the teacher, or by recording choice or preference when the child is given an opportunity to select an activity. Then there is a need to provide social or other contrived reinforcers to responses to school tasks. Finally there is a need to fade these response contingencies on a percentage reinforcement schedule, that is, on a schedule that starts with 100 percent pairing and is gradually reduced to some value such as 30 percent, so that the activity itself, and in some cases its products, develops conditioned reinforcement properties. For example, performing an activity such as painting "art" products that are viewed with approval by the teacher, the teacher's aide, and parents will, after such training, become automatically reinforcing providing approval is functionally reinforcing for the child. To maintain this behavior, occasional social reinforcers are also required.

The strengthening of ecological (natural) reinforcers requires opportunities for the child to engage in exploratory behavior in physical environments highly responsive to his overtures at times when he is alert, rested, has no need for food, drink, toileting, and the like, that is, when he is free from appetitive and aversive stimulations.[21] It also involves using ecological reinforcers, whenever possible, in the teaching of any school subject. In teaching rhythms, for example, it is simple to arrange conditions so that the sounds the child produces are exciting and naturally reinforcing.

Enhancement of Self-management Skills.

The enhancement of self-management skills includes the development of personal "habits" (self-control) and problem-solving abilities (thinking). The teaching of these behaviors relies heavily on a teacher's ability to impart self-management techniques, for they help a child to respond in ways that increase the probability that he will seek positive reinforcers and avoid aversive stimuli in the future.

In teaching of personal (self-control) techniques, contingencies must be arranged that strengthen desirable work and play "habits," such as concentrating on the task at hand, working independently for reasonable periods or proceeding with a task in an orderly and systematic manner. At the heart of teaching these behaviors is the artful use of increasing and decreasing interval and ratio schedules of reinforcement.[22] A decreasing ratio reinforcement schedule can be used to teach a child to work steadily on ever-larger blocks of arithmetic problems on a single sheet of paper. At the beginning of training, he might be reinforced for doing one or two problems on a page. Shortly, he would be reinforced for doing three, then four, and so on. The rapidity with which he reaches the set goal of doing, say, six problems on a page without assistance, depends on previous training and the teacher's ability to reinforce and sustain ever-longer interactional chains.

The goal of teaching problem solving and thinking, including creative behavior, is to help a child learn how to cope with any situation—personal, social, physical, or biological—for which he does not have an immediate response that is likely to result in an appropriate reinforcer. Unfortunately, limited information from research makes problem solving a difficult subject to teach at the preschool level. Only recently has this behavior been cast in terms of observable objectives and methods of achieving them.[23] It is recognized, however, that the teaching of problem solving includes helping a child to develop a rich repertoire of abilities and knowledge; developing positive attitudes and motivations for solving problems; providing a wide variety of opportunities to engage in problem-solving behavior; giving guidance, through prompts, primes, and reinforcement support, in approaching problems and in acquiring techniques that rearrange the external environment and individual behavior (for example, concentrating and recalling) in making the solution response more probable; and withdrawing or fading guidance and support in such a way that reinforcers generate from the problem-solving behavior itself, that is, problem solving itself becomes intrinsically reinforcing. It should be apparent from this list that all preschool goals described here interrelate and augment each other.

The systematic teaching of problem solving and creative behavior as presented here is practically nonexistent in the typical preschool. Currently attempts at teaching these skills consist mainly of providing a child with unstructured situations in the hope that he can achieve these complex goals "naturally," or of merely exposing him to situations that are said to generate creativity, originality, and exploratory behavior.[24]

NOTES

1. Patty Smith Hill, "Kindergartens of Yesterday, and Tomorrow," *Journal of the National Education Association* 1 (No. 4, 1916): 294–297.

2. John B. Watson, *Psychology from the Standpoint of a Behaviorist* (Philadelphia: J. B. Lippincott Co., 1929).

3. Donald Bushell, "The Behavior Analysis Classroom," in *Early Childhood Education*, ed. Bernard Spodek (Englewood Cliffs, N.J.: Prentice-Hall, 1973), 163–175; Barbara C. Etzel et al., "Experimentally Demonstrated Advantages of 'Errorless, (Programmed) Learning Procedures in Children's Learning: Assessment, Cue Relevance, Generalization, and Retention," symposium presented at the meeting of the Society for Research in Child Development, Philadelphia, March 29-April 1, 1973; Todd R. Risley, Nancy Reynolds, and Betty Hart, "The Disadvantaged: Behavior Modification with Disadvantaged Preschool Children," in *Behavior Modification: The Human Effort*, ed. R. H. Bradfield (San Rafael, Calif.: Dimensions Publishing Co., 1970), 123–157: Carolyn L. Thomson, "Skills for Young Children," unpublished manuscript, Edna A. Hill Child Development Preschool Laboratories. Department of Human Development, University of Kansas, 1972.

4. B. Frederic Skinner, *Science and Human Behavior* (New York: Macmillan Co., 1953).

5. Carl Bereiter and Siegfried Engelmann, *Teaching the Disadvantaged Child in the Preschool* (Englewood Cliffs, N.J.: Prentice-Hall, 1966): Rupert A. Klaus and Susan W. Gray, *The Early Training Project for Disadvantaged Children: A Report after Five Years*, Monograph No. 120, *Monographs of the Society for Research in Child Development* 33 (No. 4, 1968). Marie M. Hughes, Ralph J. Wetzel, and Ronald W. Henderson, "The Tucson Early Education Model," in Spodek, *Early Childhood Education*, 230–248.

6. Lilian G. Katz, "Where Is Early Childhood Education Going?" unpublished manuscript, College of Education Curriculum Laboratory, University of Illinois, Urbana, 1973; Spodek, *Early Childhood Education*.

7. Lawrence Kohlberg and Rochelle Mayer, "Development as the Aim of Education" *Harvard Educational Review* 42 (November 1972): 449–496.

8. Erik Erikson, *Childhood and Society*, 2d ed. (New York: W. W. Norton & Co., 1963).

9. Vivian E. Todd and Helen Hefferman, *The Years before School: Guiding Preschool Children*, 2d ed. (London: Collier-Macmillan, 1970).

10. Bereiter and Engelmann, *Teaching the Disadvantaged Child in the Preschool*.

11. Spodek, *Early Childhood Education*, 69.

12. Sidney W. Bijou, *Childhood Development: The Basic Stage of Early Childhood* (Englewood Cliffs, N.J.: Prentice-Hall, 1976).

13. B. Frederic Skinner, *The Technology of Teaching* (Englewood Cliffs, N.J.: Prentice-Hall, 1968).

14. Robert A. Glaser, "A Criterion-Referenced Test," in *Criterion-Referenced Measurement: An Introduction*, ed. W. James Popham (Englewood Cliffs, N.J.: Educational Technology Publications, 1971), 41–51.

15. Thomson, "Skills for Young Children."

16. Bernard Spodek, "Staff Requirements in Early Childhood Education," in *Early Childhood Education*, ed. Ira J. Gordon, Seventy-first Yearbook of the National Society for the Study of Education, Part II (Chicago: University of Chicago Press, 1972), 347.

17. Sidney W. Bijou and Donald M. Baer, *Child Development: A Systematic and Empirical Theory*. Vol. I (Englewood Cliffs, N.J.: Prentice-Hall, 1961).

18. Lois S. Dixon, Joseph E. Spradlin, and Barbara C. Etzel, "A Study of Stimulus Control Procedures to Teach an "In-Front" Spatial Discrimination," presentation at the meeting of the Society for Research in Child Development, Philadelphia, March 29-April 1, 1973.

19. Bijou and Baer, *Child Development: A Systematic and Empirical Theory; id., Child Development: The Universal Stage of Infancy*. Vol. II (Englewood Cliffs, N.J.: Prentice-Hall, 1965).

20. Skinner, *Science and Human Behavior;* Bijou, *Child Development: Basic Stage of Early Childhood.*

21. Bijou, *Child Development: Basic Stage of Early Childhood.*

22. Bijou and Baer, *Child Development*, Vols. I and II.

23. Joseph A. Parsons, "Development and Maintenance of Arithmetic Problem-Solving Behavior in Preschool Children," unpublished dissertation, University of Illinois, Urbana-Champaign, 1973).

24. Ellis D. Evans, *Contemporary Influences in Early Childhood Education* (New York: Holt, Rinehart and Winston, 1971), Chap. 5.

Content Areas Part II
in Early Childhood

MOTOR DEVELOPMENT IN
EARLY CHILDHOOD

Motor movement has often been referred to as the child's first way of learning about his environment. Because motor development is easily observable and has an immediate impact on objects and people in the child's world, it is often used to measure the child's level of achievement. Even before his birth, the child's movements *in utero* are used to determine his age and well-being. After birth, reflex actions like sucking and thrusting and early responses to perceptual stimulation like noise and pain are used as indications of neonatal competence. Later, more complex motor actions like drawing and perceiving shape are useful in determining the child's educational level. Viewed within this context, the role that motor development plays in other areas of growth is crucial. How motor skills develop and how they influence and are influenced by the environment are the focus of this chapter.

Several of the articles deal directly with a particular skill area of motor development. White, Castle, and Held discuss the fine motor ontogeny of visually directed reaching and grasping during the first six months of life. Although essentially designed as a normative study, this article also examines the role of the environment in accelerating or delaying fine and visual-motor responses. The central focus of Vernon's article is visual perceptual growth, detailing how children develop the capacity to attend, select, and perceive rapidly and accurately. He provides numerous research findings on the growth of perception in young children and relates these findings to the formation of concept development, particularly the concepts of space, form, shape, depth, and function. Just as Vernon's work suggests the interdependency of perception and thought, Kaplan-Sanoff's article analyzes the contribution of gross, fine, and visual-motor skills to social and intellectual growth. By tracing early motor development from the reflex actions of the neonate to the thoughtful, purposeful responses of the young child, she offers a framework by which to view the relationship between major motor milestones and social and cognitive concepts.

In a more practical vein, Stecher's article illustrates how educators can use gross motor movement as a vehicle for teaching specific concepts to children. She suggests topics that can be explored through nonverbal and physical modes of expression and offers techniques and comments for helping children move in uninhibited, fluid ways. Examining the efficacy of active motor play in young children's learning, Moffitt presents a set of parallels between motor play and cognitive activity; in addition, she lays the groundwork for testing some of the propositions about play and cognition. In conclusion, all of these authors suggest that by observing what a child does motorically with materials, we can gain valuable insight into his way of thinking and feeling about himself and the world around him.

BURTON L. WHITE, PETER CASTLE,
and RICHARD HELD

9. Observations on the Development of Visually Directed Reaching

The prehensory abilities of man and other primates have long been regarded as one of the most significant evolutionary developments peculiar to this vertebrate group (2, 17). In man, the development of prehension is linked phylogenetically with the assumption of erect posture (thus freeing the forelimbs from the service of locomotion), the highly refined development of binocular vision, and the possession of an opposable thumb, among other specializations. One important accompaniment of the development of prehension is man's unique capacity to make and utilize tools. Considering the acknowledged importance of these developments in phylogeny, it is surprising how little is presently known about the ontogeny of prehension in man. The research to be presented here is focused on the behavioral ontogenesis of this vital function in the human infant during the first six months of life.

The detailed analysis of the development of a sensorimotor function such as prehension inevitably raises a classic theoretical problem. The human infant is born with a diversified reflex repertoire, and neuromuscular growth is rapid and complex. In addition, however, he begins immediately to interact with his postnatal environment. Thus we face the complex task of distinguishing, to the extent that is possible, between those contributions made to this development by maturation or autogenous neurological growth and those which are critically dependent upon experience or some kind of informative contact with the environment. Previous work in the area of prehension has been variously oriented in regard to these polar alternatives, and it is important to note that the positions taken with regard to this theoretical problem have resulted in the gathering of selected kinds of data: namely, those kinds deemed relevant by each particular investigator to the support of his point of view on the development of prehension. Our own point of view is focused primarily around the role that certain kinds of experience have been shown to play in the growth and maintenance of sensorimotor coordinations (11). Consequently, we have focused our attention on gathering detailed longitudinal data of a kind that would aid us in eventually testing specific hypotheses about the contributions of such experience to the development of prehension.

From Burton L. White, Peter Castle, and Richard Held, "Observations on the Development of Visually Directed Reaching," *Child Development*, Vol. 35 (1964), pp. 349-364. Reprinted with permission of The Society for Research in Child Development, Inc. © Society for Research in Child Development, Inc., 1964.

Halverson (7) studied the reaching performance of infants, beginning only after the onset of what we have come to consider a rather advanced stage in the development of prehension (16 weeks). Gesell (5) used the response to single presentations of a dangling ring and a rattle as items in his developmental testing procedures. These tests were designed to be used with subjects as young as 4 weeks of age, but prehension was of only peripheral concern to Gesell. Both of these workers subscribed to the theoretical position, championed by Gesell, that most if not all of early growth, including the development of prehension, is almost exclusively a function of progressive neuromuscular maturation: an "unfolding" process. This view undoubtedly contributed to their neglect of the possible significance of the role of input from the sensory environment and to their stress on normative level of performance per se, rather than the relation between a level of performance and its behavioral antecedents.

Piaget (20) made a number of original observations on the development of prehension, including the earliest stages of the process, which are prior to 3 months of age. His data are somewhat limited since his subject group consisted only of his own three children. And, as with Gesell, Piaget's interest in prehension was peripheral to another concern, namely, the sensorimotor origins of intelligence. Piaget's theoretical approach differs considerably from that of Gesell, being concerned primarily with the cognitive aspects of development. His work is focused on the adaptive growth of intelligence or the capacity of the child to structure internally the results of his own actions. As a result, he has formulated a theoretical point of view that centers around the interaction of the child with his environment, an approach similar to our own. This interaction is seen by Piaget as giving rise to mental structures (schemas) which in turn alter the way in which the child will both perceive and respond to the environment subsequently. This point of view avoids the oversimplified dichotomy of maturation versus learning by conceptualizing development as an interaction process. Without the aliment provided by the environment schemas cannot develop, while without the existence of schemas the environment cannot be structured and thus come to "exist" for the child.

Some primitive sensorimotor schemas are, of course, present at birth, the grasp reflex and visual-motor pursuit being two that are particularly relevant to prehension. Both Gesell and Piaget describe the observable development of the subsequent coordination between vision and directed arm and hand movements, part of which is clearly dependent on some kind of practice or experience. Gesell, however, contented himself with a vague acknowledgment of the probable role of experience in development, whereas Piaget attempted to determine in a loose but experimental fashion the role of specific kinds of experiences and structured his theorizing explicitly around the details of the interaction process.

Piaget takes the position that informative contact with the environment plays an important role in the development of spatial coordination and, in particular, prehension. The work of Held and his collaborators (11, 13, 14, 15, 16) on the development and maintenance of plastic sensorimotor systems in higher mammals, including human adults, has led to a similar point of view. These laboratory studies have addressed themselves to the question of which specific kinds of contact with the environment are required for the maintenance and development of accurate sensorimotor abilities such as hand-eye coordination. This work constitutes a more rigorous experimental approach to some of the same kinds of problems that Piaget has dealt with on the basis of his extensive observations and seems likely to be relevant to the ontogeny of prehension in particular.

It was with this general framework in mind that we undertook the study of prehension. In studies of animal development (21, 22) the technique of selective deprivation of environmental contact has been successfully used to factor out critical determinants. Since human infants obviously cannot be deliberately deprived, other experimental strategies must be employed. One approach would be to enrich in selective fashion the environment of a relatively deprived group of infants, such as might be found in an institutional setting. The rate of development of such a group could then be compared with that of a similar group not receiving such enrichment. Under such conditions the differences might well be small and consequently the techniques of observation and measurement should be as precise and as sensitive as possible to detect systematic differences. Consequently, our first task was to determine in detail the normal sequence of behaviors relevant to prehension spanning the first six months of life. At the end of this time, visually-directed prehension is well developed. This preliminary information would enable us to devise sensitive and accurate scales for the measurement of prehension. We could then proceed with an examination of the role of contact with the environment in the development of this capacity. In addition, we felt that a detailed normative study of prehension was an important goal in its own right and one that would help fill an important gap in the study of human growth. It should be noted, however, that the results of this study can only be considered normative for subject groups such as ours.

METHOD

Subjects

Our subjects were 34 infants born and reared in an institution because of inadequate family conditions. These infants were selected from a larger group after a detailed evaluation of their medical histories[1] and those of their mothers along with relevant data on other family members whenever available. All infants included in the study were judged physically normal.

---

[1]Infants' daily records were screened under the supervision of Drs. P. Wolff and L. Crowell for signs and abnormality using standard medical criteria. Mothers' records were examined for possible genetic pathology and serious complications during pregnancy or delivery.

Procedure

For testing, infants were brought to a secluded nursery room where lighting, temperature, and furnishings were constant from day to day. After diapering, the infant was placed in the supine position on the examination crib. We used a standard hospital crib whose sides were kept lowered to 6 inches above the surface of the mattress in order to facilitate observation.

Our procedure consisted of 10 minutes of observation of spontaneous behavior (pretest) during which the observers remained out of view. This period was then followed by a 10-minute standardized test session during which stimulus objects were used to elicit visual pursuit, prehensory, and grasping responses. For the purposes of this report, the prehension-eliciting procedure is most germane. On the basis of several months of pilot work we selected a fringed, multicolored paper party toy as the stimulus object (Figure 1) since it seemed to produce the greatest number of responses in tests of a large number of objects. This object combines a complex contour field with highly contrasting orange, red, and yellow hues. We suspect that these qualities underlie the effectiveness of this stimulus. This speculation is consistent with the findings in the field of visual preferences of human infants (1, 4). The infant's view of the object consists of a red and orange display, circular in form, with a diameter of about 1½ inches. He sees a dark red core, 1 inch square, surrounded by a very irregular outline. Two feathers, one red and one yellow, protrude 1 inch from the sides. We presented the object to the supine infant at three positions for 30 seconds each. Presentations were initiated when the infant's arms were resting on the crib surface. The infant's attention is elicited by bringing the stimulus into the infant's line of sight at a distance of about 12 inches and shaking it until the infant fixates it. The infant's head is then led to the appropriate test posture (45° left, 45° right, or midline) by moving the stimulus in the necessary direction while maintaining the infant's attention with renewed shaking of the stimulus when necessary. The object is then brought quickly to within 5 inches of the bridge of the nose and held in a stationary position. Infants over 2½ months of age do not require as much cajoling and the stimulus may be placed at 5 inches immediately. This entire procedure takes no more than 10 seconds with most infants, but occasionally it takes much more time and effort to get young subjects to respond appropriately. The order of presentation was changed from test to test. In certain cases it was necessary to vary the position of the object to determine whether a response was accurately oriented or not. All data were collected by the authors. No infant was tested if he was either ill, drowsy, asleep, or obviously distressed (3, 23). On the average, each infant was tested at weekly intervals. Generally, two observers were present during testing. However, both testing and recording could be handled by a single person.

RESULTS

The Normative Sequence

We found that under our test conditions infants exhibit a relatively orderly developmental sequence which culminates in visually-directed reaching.

FIGURE 1 Stimulus object.

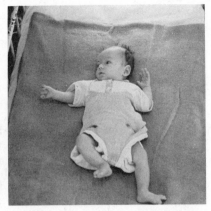

FIGURE 2 Tonic neck reflex position.

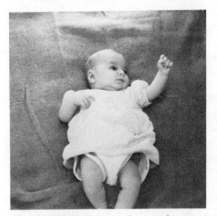

FIGURE 3 Hand regard.

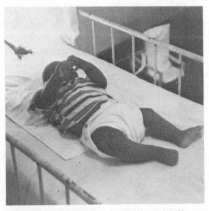

FIGURE 4 Hands clasped at midline.

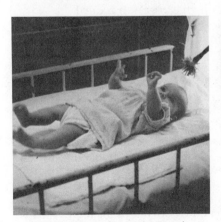

FIGURE 5 Both hands raised.

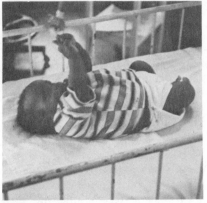

FIGURE 6 Oriented hands clasped at midline.

The following outline, based upon a frequency analysis, describes briefly the spontaneous behaviors and test responses characteristic for each half month interval from 1 through 5 months.

1. *1 to 1½ Months.*

Pretest observations. The infant lies in the tonic neck reflex position so that his head is fully turned to the side (Figure 2). The hand towards which the eyes are oriented is often in the center of the visual field, but the eyes neither converge on it nor do they adjust to variations in its position. The infant maintains one direction of gaze for prolonged periods. The infant can be made to track a moving object with his head and eyes over an arc of 180° given the proper stimulus conditions. We have obtained reliable responses using a 7½ inch bright red circle against a 14 by 12 inch flat white background as a stimulus. This target is brought into the line of sight of the supine infant at a distance of 12 to 36 inches from the bridge of his nose. Optimal distance at this age is about 24 inches. Attention is elicited by low amplitude, rapid oscillation of the stimulus in the peripheral portion of the visual field. The same motion in the foveal area is ineffective in initiating fixation. Visual pursuit is then induced by moving the target at an approximate speed of 12 inches per second in a semicircular path above the infant's head and in front of his eyes. At this age, pursuit consists of a series of jerky fixations of the red circle which bring its image to the foveal area. As the target continues to move across the field, there is a lag in the following response of the eye until the image again falls on the peripheral region of the retina. At this point, the infant responds with a rapid recentralizing of the image. If the target does not continue its motion or is moving too slowly, and therefore remains in the foveal range for more than a few seconds, the infant's gaze drifts off. We have called this level of response "peripheral pursuit."

Retinoscopic studies (8) indicate that infants have not yet developed flexible accommodative capacities at this age: their focal distance when attending to stimuli between 6 and 16 inches appears to be fixed at about 9 inches. Visual stimuli closer than 7 inches are rarely fixated.

Test responses. In view of the foregoing retinoscopic finding, it is not surprising that the test object fails to elicit the infant's attention. Since the infant's fixed focal distance to near stimuli is approximately 9 inches, the test object at 5 inches produces a badly blurred image on the retina. Usually, however, the infant looks away from the stimulus at this time. When he does attend to the object, he is considerably farsighted (at least three diopters) according to retinoscopic responses. It is clear then that, during this age period, the stimulus is not as effective as it is for older infants whose accommodative capacities are more advanced. This ineffectiveness is probably attributable in large part to loss of the complexity of patterning of the retinal image caused by poor focusing. Occasionally, a brief glance may be directed at the stimulus when it is presented on the side favored by the tonic neck reflex. Presentations on the other side are most always ineffective, since they are generally outside of the infant's field of view, as a result of the tonic neck reflex.

2. *1½ to 2 Months.*

Pretest observations. The tonic neck reflex is typically present. The infant's eyes occasionally converge on and fixate his own hand (usually the extended hand in the preferred tonic neck reflex posture, Figure 3). The direction of gaze now shifts occasionally to various parts of the visual surround. The responses to the retinoscope indicate that the infant now has the capacity to focus a clear image on the retina when the stimulus is 6 inches above the bridge of the nose. Often, at this age, a new form of visual pursuit is seen. Attention may be elicited in the foveal region using the previously described technique, and tracking is continuous over wide sectors (up to 90°) of the stimulus path. During these periods the response seems to anticipate the motion of the stimulus rather than lagging behind as in the peripheral pursuit. We have called this behavior "central" pursuit. This finding is in agreement with Gesell's observations (6).

Test responses. The infant glances at the test object in all presentations. However, sustained fixations are only present on the side of the favored tonic neck reflex. At best, fixation lasts only 5 to 10 seconds. Fixation is judged according to Ling's criteria (18). As Wolff has noted (23), shifts in activity level occur during these periods. At this time such shifts do not follow immediately upon fixation of the object, but appear gradually. Whether the infant becomes more or less active depends on his initial level of behavior. If an infant is alert and inactive, he usually becomes active; whereas if he is active, he becomes less so as he directs his gaze at the stimulus. The latter phenomenon is more common.

3. *2 to 2½ Months.*

Pretest observations. The tonic neck reflex is still typically present although the head is now only half turned (45°) to the side. In contrast to the previous stages, the infant may shift his gaze rapidly from one part of his surround to another and he rotates his head with comparative ease and rapidity. He now shows a good deal of interest in the examiner. The hand in view in the tonic neck reflex posture is now the object of his attention much of the time that he is awake and alert. The viewed hand may be on the crib surface or held aloft. His eyes now occasionally converge on objects as near as 5 inches from his eyes and central pursuit is usually present. For the first time it is possible to elicit central pursuit of the test object placed as near as 5 inches and moving with a velocity of about 12 inches per second.

Test response. Typically, the infant exhibits immediate and prolonged interest in the stimulus, fixates the object, his activity level shifts, and he makes a swift accurate swipe with the near hand. Usually the object is struck but there is no attempt to grasp since the hand is typically fisted. The probability of a swipe response is greater when the test object is presented on the side of the commonly viewed hand which is the hand extended in the favored tonic neck reflex position.

4. *2½ to 3 Months.*

Pretest observations. The tonic neck reflex is often present though less frequently than in earlier periods. The head is often near the midline position, and the limbs are usually symmetrically placed. Sustained hand regard continues to be very common. Sustained convergence upon objects as near as 3 inches from the eyes can now be elicited. The infant is more active than at earlier ages. According to retinoscopic examinations, the infant's accommodative capacities are fast approaching adult standards. They differ from the adult in that there is a slightly smaller range of accurate function (5 to 20 inches) and a slower rate of adaptation to the changing stimulus distances.

Test responses. All presentations of the test object result in immediate fixation and an abrupt decrease in activity. Side presentations elicit either swiping behavior as described in the previous age range or else the infant raises the near hand to within an inch or so of the object (unilateral hand raising) and glances repeatedly from object to hand and back (alternating glances).

5. *3 to 3½ Months.*

Pretest observations. The tonic neck reflex is now rare, and the head is mostly at the midline position. Sustained hand regard is very common, and bilateral arm activity is more frequent than in previous months, with hands clasped together over the midline often present. Occasionally, the glance is directed towards the hands as they approach each other or during their mutual tactual exploration. The infant's accommodative performance is now indistinguishable from that of an adult.

Test responses. The typical response to a side presentation is one or both hands raised with alternating glances from the stimulus to the hand nearest the object. The middle presentation is more likely to elicit bilateral activity such as hands over the midline and clasped (Figure 4), or both hands up (Figure 5), or one hand up and the other to the midline where it clutches the clothing. Here too, alternation of glance from hand to object is common.

6. *3½ to 4 Months.*

Pretest observations. The tonic neck reflex is now absent. Occasional sustained hand regard continues. Hands clasped over the midline is common, and visual monitoring of their approach and subsequent interplay is usually present.

Test responses. The responses are similar to the previous group with bilateral responses predominating. Hands to the midline and clasped is a favored response at this time even to a side presentation. It is now sometimes combined with a turning of the torso towards the test object (torso orienting).

7. *4 to 4½ Months.*

Pretest observations. Sustained hand regard is now less common, although examination of hands clasped at the midline is sometimes present. The infant is much more active. The feet are often elevated, and the body is occasionally rotated to the side.

Test responses. Bilateral responses such as hands to midline, both hands up, or one hand up and the other to the midline are now the most common responses to all presentations. These responses are usually accompanied by several alternating glances from the stimulus to one or both hands and back to the stimulus. Torso orientation to the side presentation is now common. At times, the clasped hands are raised and oriented towards the stimulus (Figure 6). Occasionally, one hand will be raised, looked at, and brought slowly to the stimulus while the glance shifts from hand to object repeatedly. When the hand encounters the object it is fumbled at and crudely grasped. This pattern has been described by Piaget (20). Towards the end of this stage, opening of the hand in anticipation of contact with the object is seen.

8. *4½ to 5 Months.*

Pretest observations. At this age pretest findings are no different from those obtained during the previous stage.

Test responses. The last stage of this sequence is signified by the appearance of what we call top level reaching.[2] This response is a rapid lifting of one hand from out of the visual field to the object. As the hand approaches the object, it opens in anticipation of contact. Hands to the midline with alternating glances and Piaget-type responses are still more likely than top level reaching, but within the next few weeks they drop out rather quickly.

The chronology of 10 response patterns is presented in Table 1. This chronology focuses on the test responses seen most consistently in our subject groups. The columns "Observed In" and "N" indicate that some of the responses are now shown by all subjects. Although 34 subjects were tested, the group size for each response is considerably smaller for several reasons. First, infants were not available for study for a uniform period of time. All of our subjects were born at the maternity section of the hospital. Usually they were transferred to the children's section at 1 month of age where they remained until they were placed in private homes. Aside from neonatal screening procedures, all tests and observations were performed at the children's section. Some infants arrived from maternity at 1 month of age and stayed through the next 5 or 6 months. Others arrived at the same age and left after a few weeks, and still others arrived as late as 3 months of age, etc. Since we were concerned with the time of emergence of the new forms of behavior, we were obliged to exclude a large number of data because we could not be sure that a late-arriving infant would not have shown the response had we been able to test him earlier.

Another factor which guided us in the analysis of our test protocols was the ease of detection of responses. Each of the 10 items listed is relatively easy to pick out of the diverse behaviors shown by infants and therefore can serve as a developmental index. At times, the presence of a response was questionable. Such data were excluded from the analysis. It is likely therefore that the correct median dates are actually a few days earlier than those charted. A single clear instance of a response was considered sufficient for inclusion in the "observed" column, although multiple instances were by far more common. Another relevant consideration is the limiting effect of weekly testing. Although more frequent testing would

---

[2]Halverson (7) has described the gradual refinement of visually directed reaching from this point on. Subsequent developments, however, concern modifications of the trajectory and posture of the hand rather than new categories of prehensile response.

TABLE 1. Chronology of Responses

Response	Observed In	N	Median and Range of Dates of First Occurrence
Swipes at object	13	13	(2:5)
Unilateral hand raising	15	15	(2:17)
Both hands raised	16	18	(2:21)
Alternating glances (hand and object)	18	19	(2:27)
Hands to midline and clasp	15	15	(3:3)
One hand raised with alternating glances, other hand to midline clutching dress	11	19	(3:8)
Torso oriented towards object	15	18	(3:15)
Hands to midline and clasp and oriented towards object	14	19	(4:3)
Piaget-type reach	12	18	(4:10)
Top level reach	14	14	(4:24)

Timeline axis: 2m, 3m, 4m, 5m, 6m

have resulted in more accurate data, we felt the added exposure to test conditions might introduce practice effects into our subject groups.

Summary of the Normative Sequence

In summary, then, given the proper object in the proper location and provided that the state of the subject is suitable, our subjects first exhibited object-oriented arm movements at about 2 months of age. The swiping behavior of this stage, though accurate, is not accompanied by attempts at grasping the object; the hand remains fisted throughout the response. From 3 to 4 months of age unilateral arm approaches decrease in favor of bilateral patterns, with hands to the midline and clasped the most common response. Unilateral responses reappear at about 4 months, but the hand is no longer fisted and is not typically brought directly to the object. Rather, the open hand is raised to the vicinity of the object and then brought closer to it as the infant shifts his glance repeatedly from hand to object until the object is crudely grasped. Finally, just prior to 5 months of age, infants begin to reach for and successfully grasp the test object in one quick, direct motion of the hand from out of the visual field.

An Analysis of the Normative Sequence

When one examines the course of development of prehension, it becomes apparent that a number of relatively distinct sensorimotor systems contribute to its growth. These include the visual-motor systems of eye-arm and eye-hand, as well as the tactual-motor system of the hands. These systems seem to develop at different times, partly as a result of varying histories of exposure, and may remain in relative isolation from one another. During the development of prehension these various systems gradually become coordinated into a complex superordinate system which integrates their separate capacities.

During stages 1 and 2 (1 to 2 months), the infant displays several response capacities that are relevant to the ontogeny of prehension. The jerky but coordinated head and eye movements which are seen in *peripheral* visual pursuit are one such capacity. This form of pursuit is an innate coordination since it is present at birth (19). However, another form of pursuit is seen during the second month. The smooth tracking response present in *central* visual pursuit is a more highly refined visual-motor coordination. The path now followed by the eyes appears to anticipate, and thus predict, the future position of a moving target. Whether this response is in fact predictive at this early age remains to be conclusively determined. But this growing capacity of the infant to localize and follow with both his eyes and head is clearly an important prerequisite for the development of visually directed prehension. It should be noted that motion seems to be the stimulus property critical for eliciting attention during this stage.

Arm movements show little organized development at this stage and are limited in the variety of positions that they can assume, in large part because of the influence of the tonic neck reflex. The grasp reflex is present and can be elicited if the palm of the hand encounters a suitable object. But neither of these capacities is yet integrated with the more highly developed visual-motor tracking capacity. Infants of this age do not readily attend to near objects, namely those less than 9 inches distant. Thus, it is not surprising that objects which the infant is able to explore tactually, including his own hands, are not yet visually significant. At this stage, the tactual-motor capacities of the hands remain isolated from the visual-motor ones of the eye and head.

During stages 3 and 4 (2 to 3 months), the isolation of response capacities begins to break down, in part because the infant's eyes can now readily converge and focus on objects that are potentially within his reach. Central pursuit can be elicited from as near as 5 inches. One important consequence of this is that the infant now spends a good deal of time looking at his own hands. In addition, visual interest, sustained fixation, and related shifts in activity level are now readily elicited by a static presentation of the proper stimulus object. This indicates a growing capacity for focusing attention which is no longer exclusively dependent on motion.

In keeping with the above developments, it is at this stage that we see swiping, the first prehensory behavior. The appearance of this behavior indicates the development of a new visual-motor localizing capacity, one which now coordinates not only movements of the eyes and head but also those of the arms. Swiping is highly accurate, although it occasionally overshoots the target. It does not include any attempt at visually controlled grasping. Such grasping would indicate anticipation of contact with the object and is not seen at this stage. Instead, grasping is exclusively a tactually-directed pattern, which remains to be integrated into the growing visual-motor organization of prehension.

The next prehensory response, which develops soon after swiping, is that of raising a hand to within an inch or so of the stationary object followed by a series of alternating glances from object to hand and back. The crude but direct swiping response has been replaced by a more refined behavior. The visual-motor systems of eye-object and eye-hand are now juxtaposed by the infant and seem to be successively compared with each other in some way. This is the kind of behavior that Piaget refers to as the mutual assimilation and accommodation of sensorimotor schemas (24).

During stages 5 and 6 (3 to 4 months), the infant exhibits mutual grasping, a new pattern of spontaneous behavior. This pattern, in which the hands begin to contact and manipulate each other, is particularly important for tactual-motor development. In addition, the visual monitoring of this pattern results in the linking of vision and touch by means of a double feedback system. For the eyes not only see what the hands feel, namely each other, but each hand simultaneously touches and is being actively touched.

In keeping with these developments, hands to midline and clasped is now seen as a test response. This is a tactual-motor response pattern during which the infant fixates the object while the hands grasp each other at the midline. Grasping is thus coming to be related to the now highly developed visual-motor coordination of the head and eyes. At this time, however, grasping is not yet directed towards the external object but remains centered on the tactual interaction of the infant's own hands.

During stages 7 and 8 (4 to 5 months), the infant finally succeeds in integrating the various patterns of response that have developed and coordinating them via their intersection at the object. Thus, alternating glances now become combined with the slow moving of the hand directly to the object which is fumbled at and slowly grasped. The visual-motor schemas of eye-hand and eye-object have now become integrated with the tactual-motor schema of the hand, resulting in the beginnings of visually directed grasping. This pattern has been described by Piaget (20). It is not until the attainment of the highest level of reaching at the end of this stage, however, that one sees the complete integration of the anticipatory grasp into a rapid and direct reach from out of the visual field. Here all the isolated or semi-isolated components of prehensory development come together in the attainment of adult-like reaching just prior to 5 months of age.

The Role of Contact with the Environment

Having made a preliminary analysis of the normative sequence of behaviors, we may proceed to a detailed consideration of the question that originally motivated this study. How can we test for the contribution made by conditions of exposure to the development of prehension? At what stages of growth and in what manner can experimental techniques be applied? Our findings, examined in the light of these questions, yield a projected program of experimental investigation.

Experimental research with both human adults (10, 11, 12, 13, 14, 16) and with animals (15, 21) has strikingly demonstrated the importance of motility for the development and maintenance of visual-motor capacities. This work has shown that the variations in visual stimulation that result from self-produced movements constitute a source of information to the growing nervous system that is required for the proper development of function. Two factors are critical for providing this information. They are certain natural movements of the organism and the presence of stable objects in the environment that can provide sources of visual stimulation that will vary as a consequence of these movements. Deprivation studies with higher infra-human mammals have shown that, in the absence of either one of these factors, vision does not develop normally (15, 21). No comparable systematic studies of the importance of such factors in the development of human infants are available. However, the complementarity of results between studies of adult rearrangement and of neonatal deprivation in animals (13) leads to specific suggestions as to the conditions of exposure essential for the development of the infant's coordination. For example, in the special case of eye-hand coordination, the work of our laboratory indicates the importance of visual feedback from certain components of motion of the arm, as well as from grosser movements of the body, as in locomotion. How shall we test the applicability of these findings to the development of the human infant? Obviously, we cannot experimentally deprive human infants, but the subjects of the present study are already being reared under conditions that seem to us deficient for optimal development. Thus, we are able to study the effects of systematic additions to the environments of our subjects. Moreover, since our research emphasis is on the importance of the exposure history of the human infant, the fact that our subjects are born and reared under uniform conditions is a distinct advantage. It assures us that previous and current extra-experimental exposure will not be a major source of variability as it might well be under conditions of home-rearing.

The everyday surroundings of our subjects are bland and relatively featureless compared to the average home environment. Moreover, the infants almost always lie in the supine posture which, in comparison to the prone position, is much less conducive to head and trunk motility.

Furthermore, the crib matresses have become hollowed out to the point where gross body movements are restricted. We plan to provide a group of these infants with enriched visual surrounds designed to elicit visual-motor responses. In addition, we will place these infants in the prone position for brief periods each day and use plywood supports to flatten the mattress surfaces. These changes should result in significantly greater motility in the presence of stable visible objects. We will assess the effects of such procedures by comparing the sensorimotor capacities of our experimental group with those of a control group reared under currently existing conditions.

We recognize that any effects which may result from the exposure of infants to enriched sensory environments are contingent upon the state of maturation of their neuromuscular mechanisms. We do not, for example, expect visually-directed reaching within the first six weeks of life, when the infant's hands are generally kept fisted and objects within reaching distance are inappropriate for sustained visual fixation. On the other hand, it is quite likely that some aspects of the development of prehension are critically dependent upon prior sensorimotor experience.

A preliminary study has confirmed our suspicion that the onset of sustained hand regard is in part a function of the alternative visual objects present in the infant's environment. For example, under the normal hospital routine where alternative visual objects are at a minimum, the control group of infants began sustained hand viewing at about 2 months of age. In contrast, a pilot group whose cribs were equipped with a variety of objects for viewing failed to exhibit sustained hand regard until 3 months of age. The reason for this marked delay appeared to be the presence of a small mirror placed some 7 inches above the infant's eyes. Invariably, within a week after being placed in the experimental cribs, each infant began to spend most of his waking time staring at his reflection in the mirror. This stimulus virtually monopolized the infants' visual exploratory efforts. This average delay of one month in the appearance of sustained hand regard seems to be clear evidence of the relevance of the visual surround for its development. Since the time of onset can be significantly delayed by a procedure which diverts the infant's attention from his hands, perhaps other procedures designed to direct the infant's attention towards his hands will result in the advanced onset of sustained hand regard. However, the normal hospital environment may already constitute the optimal condition for directing the child's attention to his hands, since there is virtually nothing else for him to look at. If so, our control group should not be considered deprived with respect to the visual requirements underlying the onset of this particular behavior.

Once sustained hand regard appears, swiping at the test object inevitably follows within a few days. On the average, our infants first exhibited swiping responses at 2 months and 3 days of age. We have called this behavior swiping rather than reaching since the hand is kept fisted, thereby precluding successful grasping of the object. Swiping, like visual motor pursuit and fixation, seems to be a stimulus-bound response. This means that the presence of stimuli appropriately designated and located guarantees repeated responses from the infants. The latter half of the path of the swiping response is often viewed by our infants. Moreover, this path is curved rather than direct and entails a rotation of the hand. Precisely this kind of experience has been found necessary for the compensation of errors in reaching caused by the wearing of prism-goggles by human adults (9). We therefore plan to provide our infants with stimulus objects suitably designed to elicit such responses as soon as sustained hand regard appears. We suspect that the increased occurrence of these rotational arm movements, and the feedback stimulation that results, may facilitate the acquisition of eye-hand coordinations in infants. We cannot, however, expect visually-directed prehension to occur at 2½ months of age, even though it seems that we can elicit repeated swiping behavior almost at will. The missing element is the grasp, which is precluded by an innate reflex which keeps the hands fisted, or partially so, until at least 3 months of age.

As the tonic neck reflex drops out at about 3 months of age, the arms are released from their asymmetric posture and tend to move in more similar paths. The inevitable consequences of this development is the mutual discovery of the hands at some point near the middle of the infant's chest. This pattern is initially nonvisual. It is usually several weeks before the infant begins to look at this tactual interplay of his hands. He then spends a great deal of time watching their mutual approach and departure as well as their contacts. Piaget has suggested (20) that this pattern may be conducive to the onset of visually directed prehension of external objects. We have found that this is sometimes the case, but, just as often, infants who exhibit this behavior early are either late in top level reaching or arrive at this stage at about the median age of the group. The prolonged observation of one hand approaching and grasping the other is a virtually innate guarantee of the visual-motor integration of the arm approach and the grasp. On the other hand, since swiping, which appears six weeks earlier, guarantees frequent contact of the hand with the prehensory object, and tactual exploration and the grasp reflex often result in closure, it seems reasonable to assume that integrated prehensory responses would develop through the introduction of suitable external objects at this earlier time. Perhaps it is the absence of such objects that accounts for the 81-day average gap between the onset of swiping responses and the attainment of successful visually-directed reaching seen in our subject group.

In addition to the study of prehension, we plan similar tests of the role of exposure in the development of prerequisite behaviors such as accommodation, convergence, and visual motor pursuit.

References

1. Berlyne, D. The influence of the albedo and complexity of stimuli on visual fixation in the human infant. *Brit. J. Psychol.*, 1958, 49, 315–318.

2. Darwin, C. *The descent of man.* Modern Library, 1871.

3. Escalona, S. The study of individual differences and the problems of state. *J. Amer. Acad. Child Psychiat.*, 1962, 1, 11–37.

4. Fantz, R. L. A method for studying depth perception in infants under six months of age. *Psychol. Rec.*, 1961, 11, 27–32.

5. Gesell, A., & Amatruda, C. *Developmental diagnosis*. Hoeber, 1941.

6. Gesell, A., Ilg, F. L., & Bullis, G. F. *Vision: its development in infant and child*. Hoeber, 1949.

7. Halverson, H. M. An experimental study of prehension in infants by means of systematic cinema records. *Genet. Psychol. Monogr.*, 1932, 10, 110–286.

8. Haynes, H. Retinoscopic studies of human infants. Unpublished manuscript.

9. Hein, A. Typical and atypical feedback in learning a new coordination. Paper read at Eastern Psychol. Ass., Atlantic City, April, 1959.

10. Held, R. Shifts in binaural localization after prolonged exposures to atypical combinations of stimuli. *Amer. J. Psychol.*, 1955, 68, 526–548.

11. Held, R. Exposure-history as a factor in maintaining stability of perception and coordination. *J. nerv. ment. Dis.*, 1961, 132, 26–32.

12. Held, R. Adaptation to rearrangement and visual-spatial aftereffects. *Psychol. Beiträge*, 1962, 6, 439–450.

13. Held, R., & Bossom, J. Neonatal deprivation and adult rearrangement: complementary techniques for analyzing plastic sensory-motor coordinations. *J. comp. physiol. Psychol.*, 1961, 54, 33–37.

14. Held, R., & Hein, A. Adaptation of disarranged hand-eye coordinations contingent upon reafferent stimulation. *Percept. mot. Skills*, 1958, 8, 87–90.

15. Held, R., & Hein, A. Movement-produced stimulation in the development of visually-guided behavior. *J. comp. physiol. Psychol.*, 1963, 56, 872–876.

16. Held, R., & Schlank, M. Adaptation to optically-increased distance of the hand from the eye by reafferent stimulation. *Amer. J. Psychol.*, 1959, 72, 603–605.

17. Jones, F. W. *Arboreal man*, London: E. Arnold, 1916.

18. Ling, B. A genetic study of sustained visual fixation and associated behavior in the human infant from birth to six months. *J. genet. Psychol.*, 1942, 61, 227–277.

19. Peiper, A. *Die Eigenart der Kindlichen Hirntätigkeit*. (2nd ed.) Leipzig: Thieme, 1956.

20. Piaget, J. *The origins of intelligence in children*. (2nd ed.) International Universities Press, 1952.

21. Riesen, A. H. Plasticity of behavior: psychological series. In H. Harlow and C. Woolsey (Eds.), *Biological and biochemical bases of behavior*. Univer. of Wisconsin Press, 1958. Pp. 425–450.

22. Riesen, A. H. Stimulation as a requirement for growth and function in behavioral development. In D. W. Fiske and S. R. Maddi (Eds.), *Functions of varied experience*. Dorsey Press, 1961. Pp. 57–80.

23. Wolff, P. H. Observations on newborn infants. *Psychosom. Med.*, 1959, 21, 110–118.

24. Wolff, P. H. The developmental psychologies of Jean Piaget and psychoanalysis, *Psychol. Issues*, 1960, 2, 1–181.

MARGOT KAPLAN-SANOFF
10. Motor Development: A Broader Context

In recent years, doctors, educators, and parents have emphasized the importance of major milestones, like sitting and walking, to the young child's growth. This emphasis had led to the view of motor development as a mere taxonomy of physical skills, as if walking in and of itself is the goal of development. Although helpful in alerting parents to possible developmental delays, this tendency to focus exclusively on achievement of motor milestones obscures the influence of motor development on other areas of growth. There is, indeed, a subtle, intimate relationship between motor acts and the social and cognitive growth of the child:

The development of gross motor abilities is important both as an index of the maturation of the central nervous system and because of its psychological meaning as the very first manifestation of the infant's control of his body in relation to the environment . . . the infant's gradually developing motor abilities—to sit without support, to hold his head upright, to change his position by rolling from back to stomach, or to pull to a standing position—are also the earliest evidences of the infant's attempt to become a self-sufficient, autonomous being. From a psychological perspective, these early developments reflect the infant's capacity to counter the forces of gravity, to bring himself into a position where he can see objects from different perspectives, and to control his relationship to objects through standing and reaching.[1]

Although psychologists have alluded to the relationship between motor acts and cognitive and social growth, few have fully elucidated these connections. The first part of this essay seeks to clarify these associations by tracing the motor development of the newborn from reflex movement to intelligent action, from isolated hand movements to purposeful, directed manipulation of objects. Secondly, this essay explores the child's emotional and intellectual accomplishments that are related to his growing motor abilities.

In the first few weeks of life, the neonate appears ill equipped to deal with the complexity of his environment. Although he can see, hear, and suck at birth (Klaus and Kennel, 1976), these activities are all involuntary. They are elicited primarily by external environmental stimulation like sound, movement, and light. Their importance however should not be underestimated, for these reflex actions are necessary to sustain life as the infant shifts from uterine to external environment. The rooting reflex, for example, whereby the infant reflexively turns his head towards a source of

---

[1]L. Yarrow and F. Pedersen, "The Interplay Between Cognition and Motivation in Infancy," in *Origins of Intelligence: Infancy and Early Childhood* ed. Michael Lewis (New York: Plenum Press, 1976), p. 390.

stimulation touching his cheek, allows the newborn to reach for the nipple as he comes in contact with the breast. Many reflex movements like the tonic neck, crawling, and walking reflexes provide the groundwork for, and are later incorporated into, voluntary movement patterns (Cratty, 1970). The reflex actions of the newborn, however, exist not solely for survival or for motoric development but also for enhancing the child's knowledge of how his world operates.

Piaget (1952) was the first to recognize the cognitive component in early motor development. He views the newborn's early movements as a way of organizing experiences in the environment. He categorizes these movements into six reflexive schema: grasping, looking, listening, sucking, vocalizing, and moving arms and legs. Because the child at this point is incapable of voluntary movement, his reflexive schema develop from stimulation provided by his environment. In Piagetian terms, reflexive schema are nourished by the environment. Thus light provides the nourishment, the aliment, for the looking schema, just as sounds are the aliment for the newborn's listening schema. Each schema grows as the child absorbs more experiences from the environment. As Piaget states, the child changes from "looking for the sake of looking" to "looking in order to see". By assimilating information about his surroundings, the infant begins to formulate his first primary classifications about the world. For example, the differences experienced between sucking a breast and his own hand lead the infant to adjust or accommodate his sucking schema to include nutritional and nonnutritional categories. And while staring intently into his mother's face, the infant absorbs and delineates those criteria that make up a human face. Indeed, it has been shown that the ability to distinguish those characteristics that comprise a face develops within the first month of life (Fantz, 1963). Gradually, these six primary reflexes become altered through assimilation of information and accommodation of schema to form simple motor repertoires called *primary circular reactions*. In the course of seeking aliment from the environment, the infant may, for example, notice his hand as it crosses his field of vision. Unaware that this interesting image is indeed part of his own body, the infant attempts to reinstate the event by calling into play all of his developing voluntary actions. As he kicks, gurgles, and eventually waves his hands, the novel object—his hand—reappears. This simple circular reaction—the sight of his hand stimulating the infant to recreate the event—promotes a major motor milestone: hand regard. But more importantly, it represents the beginning stages of object permanence—knowing an object continues to exist when it is no longer in sight. And it also helps the infant to differentiate the boundaries of his own body from the external environment.

With further maturation and experience, the infant moves from interest in his own body to a fascination with the consequences of his behavior on objects. Continuing the example of the hand-waving schema, Piaget discusses the infant who, while waving his arms, accidentally causes a mobile hung over his crib to move. In trying to make this interesting sight last, the child again runs through his repertoire of behaviors—bouncing, vocalizing, and waving his hands until the mobile moves again. Having established a connection between hand waving and the movement of the toy, the child begins to vary his movements, waving faster, slower, harder in order to observe their effects on the mobile. These actions, called *secondary circular reactions*, are still not truly intentional since the goal of moving the mobile is discovered by chance. Yet once having moved the mobile, the child's actions in trying to replicate the event become purposeful. This stage in a child's motoric development can be seen as the threshold between involuntary and voluntary actions. Piaget also refers to the infant's growing ability to recognize objects and to express that recognition of how objects work through motor acts. Perhaps the earliest example of this concept of motor recognition of objects is the child who, having learned through experience that a bottle is to be sucked, begins rooting and sucking as soon as the bottle comes into view. It's as if he is saying, "I know what to do with that bottle. I can suck on it."

Finally, in the later part of the first year of life, the infant begins to coordinate various schema, looking and grasping for example, to achieve guided, intentional activity. Motor manipulations become centrally mediated and directed towards some kind of adjustment to, or coping with, the environment. From primitive, uncoordinated reaching for objects purely as aliment for the grasping schema, the infant now reaches accurately for objects, crawls to get desired toys, and even develops a new schema of throwing—combining grasping, looking, waving, and releasing as he hurls toys out of his crib and playpen.

Thus, many of the accomplishments during this sensorimotor period occur because the child is developing voluntary control of reflex actions and is learning to coordinate motorically, for example, reaching precisely for a toy and bringing it to his mouth. This coordination provides him with some basis for responding to the environment and, through his play with objects, he learns to combine simple schema into more complex ones to achieve desired goals.

The Piagetian concept of "intelligence-as-action" links the simple sensorimotor adjustments of the infant with the later social and cognitive skills of the preschool child. As the child gains more control over his fine motor skills—effectively grasping objects and bringing them into his field of vision—he is increasingly able to obtain feedback from his environment. The intricate manipulations of a ten-month-old child as he twists, turns, mouths, shakes, and fingers a new object attest to his tactile curiosity. This early sensory exploration helps him to discover both the properties and the various functions of different objects. He learns that a blanket can be clutched and pulled towards him, whereas a bell can be shaken and made to ring. As distinguished from mere reaching for objects as aliment, these secondary circular reactions have as their goal the manipulation of objects to obtain responses from them. Doing something to an object and observing the consequences of that action clearly enhances the child's emerging sense of mastery and competence—an understanding that he can have an impact on his environment.

The infant's growing proficiency in the visual-motor domain also contributes to his sense of purpose and intention. His visual orientation to novel objects is perhaps the earliest manifestation of goal-directedness, for example, his concentrated and intense staring at a new toy or at the changing facial expressions of an adult. This visual examination is soon followed by attempts to secure interesting objects and to explore them (Yarrow and Pedersen, 1976).

Obtaining this feedback about objects underlies the complex process of problem solving. As motor actions become more goal-directed, the child is able to persist in reaching for an object in the face of environmental difficulties. Whereas a year-old child might be unable to get an object when it is placed behind a barrier like a pillow or even an adult's arm, a somewhat older child can reach effortlessly around the obstacle to grasp the object. Similarly, when unable to secure a toy placed too far away from him, the younger child usually cries for help or diverts his attention elsewhere; a slightly older child, on the other hand, begins to explore how to use tools as an extension of his hand to reach for distant objects. He learns to pull a blanket to obtain a favorite toy placed on the blanket; he tugs at the string of a pull toy to get the toy at the end of the string (See *Bayley Scales of Infant Development,* 1969, referring to the red ring activities; also see Gordon's 1970 work on infant activities).

Adeptness in obtaining objects and manipulating them allows the child substantially to broaden his base of experience. He is no longer dependent upon gaining information through chance encounters with the environment; rather, he can actively investigate a wide range of previously inaccessible objects. By subjecting these objects to a repertoire of motor acts—shaking, mouthing, and pulling—the child abstracts data about those objects: their texture, weight, function, and so on. He acts on objects to learn their properties and then he categorizes them in his schematic representation of the world. Encountering a new puzzle, for example, the young child may begin to explore it by sucking on the individual pieces, throwing them, and finally banging on the puzzle so that a piece fits into its designated spot. Repeated trials help the child to formulate a concept of puzzles: They are nonnutritional; in fact, they are completely unappealing to suck on. However, the pieces are exciting to manipulate and bang, and the specific pieces belong in certain spaces based on shape, color, and size. With each new object encountered, the child repeats this exploratory procedure until his schema for objects are quite sophisticated, involving criteria for spatial orientation, temporal relations, and functional discriminations: Balls are for throwing, pillows are for sleeping, stairs are for climbing. Through the expansion and modification of his schema, the child imposes cognitive classifications upon his world, rendering it much more accessible and comprehensible.

Gross motor accomplishments, like holding up the head, turning over, sitting, and walking provide the child with exciting new shifts in his perspective. No longer confined to one visual field, the more mobile child can perceive new dimensions in his environment. Inanimate objects, like chairs and candy dishes, and animate objects, like mother's body and a barking dog, look very different from the vantage of standing on one's own two feet rather than creeping along the floor. Just as sitting allows the child to see more, crawling and walking greatly expand the child's environment, providing a wider range of objects to be grasped and explored. It is interesting to note that the critical period for competence development as postulated by Burton White (White and Watts, 1973) begins at about eight months with the child's growing locomotor abilities.

The child's active motoric exploration is not only useful for gathering information about events in the environment, but is also responsible for helping the child become familiar with his own body. Regarding his hand and playing with his toes facilitate the child's understanding of how far his body extends into space, while clasping his hands and transferring objects from one hand to the other build his sense of laterality, the internal awareness that there are two sides to his body—right and left. Thus a child who can reach for and grasp a block in one hand and a cracker in the other demonstrates his ability to use his body effectively to manipulate the environment and control it. The infant also learns to use his image of his body and his sense of body space as a point of reference from which to organize and interpret sensory data. Spreading his arms wide, the young child graphically shows that he is "so big," his body expressing his understanding of his relation to the world.

Although it may be difficult to see a direct correlation between an infant's specific motor act and the cognitive implications of that act, one cannot deny the more general relationship between increased motoric competence and the child's growing intellectual awareness within the first two years of life. As his fine motor and visual-perceptual skills allow for more active and sustained interaction with objects, his feelings of mastery and influence over the environment are also enhanced. His actions become more goal-directed, and it is this defined sense of purpose that underlies Piaget's conception of true intellectual thought. The infant gradually begins to act with intent, setting his goal of securing a desired toy regardless of environmental barriers. Initially, the child attempts to attain his goal through trial-and-error learning—hitting the barrier and perhaps kicking it before discovering the solution of reaching around it. It is this persistence in motor acts that leads to effective means of solving problems and the insightful behavior characteristic of mature thought.

Early motor development contributes not only to the child's growing cognitive competence but also to his social abilities. This social dimension in motor skills is most apparent in the bond between mother and infant. Although theorists disagree over the extent to which a neonate responds to and recognizes his mother (Bowlby, 1969; Freud, 1960; Klaus and Kennel, 1970), recent research using split-screen photography offers fascinating data on the relationship between the gestures and speech of the mother and her newborn's movements (Brazelton, 1977). Although barely perceptible to an observer without benefit of stop-frame camera action, the infant can be seen moving his body in response to his mother's movements, posturing and arching to the intonations of her speech and to the random motions of her body. This "dance," or synchrony of body movements, is the first step in an extensive process of separation and individuation in which the infant formulates the boundaries of his own body and develops a primary attachment to his mother.[2]

Mahler (1975) offers a detailed review of this process, but what is most important to the present discussion is how the child's developing motor skills help him first to merge with and attach to his mother through synchrony and then slowly to separate from her and become an individual in his own right. Mahler refers to those first, tentative steps of separating as "hatching out," literally breaking away in a bodily sense from the close, dependent relationship with mother. The infant pushes away from her body with his arms, trunk, and legs, and, as soon as his motor ability permits, he slides down from his mother's lap. This separation, once effected, increases in distance and duration over the life of the child (Rheingold and Eckerman, 1970) and becomes even more apparent when the child begins to crawl. Now he can take a more active role in determining his closeness and distance to mother. He is not longer dependent on her to take him from room to room with her. Rather he can follow her, maintaining a distance that allows him some measure of independence while still remaining within close proximity to her. One often sees seven-to-ten-month-old infants crawling rapidly towards their mother after a period of intense independent exploration. Mothers who provide that mixture of optimal proximity to their children while encouraging them to explore on their own serve as a secure "home base" for their infants. At the same time, they actively promote independent motor skills in their children. Thus, motor growth does not simply evolve through maturation but is influenced by the child's interaction with adults and objects in the environment (Yarrow and Pedersen, 1976).

It is significant to note that Mahler bases her delineation of the subphases of individuation upon the child's emerging motor proficiency. Upright locomotion marks the beginning of the "practicing subphase proper," a time when the child invests considerable energy into practicing and testing out the functions of his own body while continuing to move farther away from his mother. Most children during this phase seem impervious to scrapes and falls; their overwhelming confidence in their motor abilities plays an important role in promoting a positive self-concept. The practicing period can be seen as a time when the child is developing a sense of trust in himself and in his environment, while also building a degree of autonomy in his actions and relations with others (Erikson, 1950).

Ideally, the child's awareness of his separation from mother should coincide with the development of independent locomotion. Children who are precocious in their motor development and who separate early from their mothers may become aware of their own separateness much before their independent functioning has provided them with a means of coping

---

[2]Although most of the research cited makes specific reference to the child's biological mother, the formation of an attachment is also quite possible between a father and his child or a primary caregiver and a child. This essay uses the term *mother* in a broad sense to convey that person who is primarily responsible for the child and his care.

with this awareness (Mahler, 1975). Although their motor development has progressed to support autonomous movement, their social and cognitive skills are not yet as advanced; they therefore often experience frustration and anger at being unable to control the situation imposed by their separation from mother. Thus the relationship between emerging motor skills and social awareness is a complex one, affected by maturation as well as environmental factors.

Yet even before the child is aware that mother is indeed a separate person who comes and goes independently of his actions, he must have some notion that people continue to exist when they are no longer in sight. Attainment of this concept of person permanence is facilitated by the child's ability to search actively for his mother when she leaves his field of vision. Crawling after her fleeting image, the child gradually learns that she remains the same person and continues to function in her role as mother even though he cannot always see her. Just as the fine and visual-motor skills necessary for hand regard help the child to develop the idea that objects continue to exist when out of sight, so the gross motor ability to follow mother independently enables the infant to establish a concept of person permanence.

Mastering a wide range of motor skills also affects the child's social development with respect to the objects in his environment. With increased proficiency, he can selectively interact with the objects around him rather than merely adapt passively to them (Riggs, 1978). He can actively reach for and secure a vast array of stimulating new objects, and he can competently manipulate and play with them. These feelings of self-confidence are deeply rooted in his early motor behavior. Not only can he maneuver his body in and out of things, but he can also explore new, and often forbidden, objects with ease. Children often use these newly found toys to initiate social contacts with adults, holding out their prize to an adult in an attempt to communicate (Uzgiris, 1967). The child's offer of a newly acquired toy as an invitation to play functions in much the same way as the earlier milestone of motor recognition; it expresses motorically what the child cannot express verbally: "Come use this toy with me."

Although motor development alone is not responsible for the total creation of the child's self-concept and social relationships with others, motor skills can be seen to enhance directly healthy emotional development through attachment, separation, and individuation. Clearly, the responsiveness and sensitivity of the mother or primary caregiver has a vital impact on the child's social development, his sense of well-being, and basic trust. Yet without the means to separate voluntarily from mother and to retrieve desired toys, the child's social and emotional growth might be severely impaired (See Mahler's case studies, 1975). Teachers of young handicapped children must often compensate for this lack of autonomous locomotion with ingenious devices and techniques to encourage the children to become independent and confident in their social skills.

Given the complex nature of the relationship between motor development and social and cognitive growth, it is of utmost importance that young children not be pushed to perform motor skills before they are maturationally or psychologically prepared to accomplish those tasks. Adult teaching or help may actually hinder to a certain extent the gross motor development of infants. When helped and supported to achieve a position that he cannot reach or maintain on his own, the child is forced to spend a lot of time in the same position without his being able to change the situation (Pikler, 1972). This situation both disrupts the normal ontogeny of skill development, focusing attention away from other, more appropriate learning tasks, and leads to feelings of helplessness and passivity. However, there are means by which adults can facilitate the child's motor development that also enhance intellectual and emotional growth. A complete discussion of materials and curriculum ideas is not within the scope of this essay; however, there are some general principles to consider. White's research on fine motor control highlights the importance of an enriched environment for the child's motor development (White, Castle, and Held, 1964). Hunt (1966) suggests that the child's surroundings be full of inviting and challenging toys to explore, toys that do something and provide direct feedback to the child when he manipulates them. A push toy like the "popcorn pusher," which makes noise and moves various parts when pushed at different speeds over different surfaces, is an excellent example of a toy that focuses the child's attention on the consequences of his motor actions on objects in the environment. White's later work (1975) discusses the role of adults in fostering motor skills. He views adults as "designers" of the child's environment, planners who create a physical space that allows for free, spontaneous movement without the frustration of barriers or the fear of danger. Adults also function as "consultants" for the child's independent activities, acting as resource people who offer support and encouragement while providing new material to help the child with his problem solving. White does not advocate completely "baby-proofing" the environment, but he offers practical suggestions for ways to restrict hazards while fostering independent locomotion and exploration.

In conclusion, the achievement of motor milestones by the young child should not be considered as a goal in and of itself. Rather, key motor accomplishments should be seen as guidelines for the far less visible development of social and cognitive concepts. As we have seen, learning to walk is not an isolated skill to be checked off on a developmental chart, but an integral component in the process of separating from mother and becoming an independent person. Walking also changes the child's visual perspective on his environment, greatly expanding his horizon of objects to be discovered, manipulated, and categorized. The passive lap baby is now an active explorer, capable of inventing ingenious ways of getting into things previously out of reach. This development, in turn, adds a new dimension to his relationship with his mother, affecting his sense of self-confidence and trust. Clearly, one cannot equate a specific motor skill to a complementary social or cognitive accomplishment; each child's development is differentially affected by his maturational level and his relationship to people and objects in his environment. Yet, it is possible to trace the consequences of motor growth to advances in the social and cognitive domain. It is the outcome of this subtle, yet complex relationship in each child that must be considered as he attains new motor milestones.

REFERENCES

Bayley, N. *Bayley Scales of Infant Development.* New York: Psychological Corporation, 1969.

Bowlby, J. *Attachment and Loss.* Vol. 1, *Attachment.* New York: Basic Books, Inc. Publishers, 1969.

Brazelton, T. B. "Keynote address." Proceedings from November 1977, National Association for the Education of Young Children Conference. Chicago.

Cratty, B. *Perceptual and Motor Development in Infants and Children.* New York: Macmillan Publishing Co., Inc., 1970.

Erikson, E. *Childhood and Society.* New York: Penguin Books, 1950.

Fantz, R. L. "Pattern Vision in Newborn Infants." *Science* 140 (1963): 296–297.

Freud, S. *The Ego and the Id.* New York: N. W. Norton and Co., Inc., 1960.

Gordon, I. *Baby Learning Through Baby Play.* New York: St. Martin's Press, Inc., 1970.

*Hunt, J. M. "The Epigenesis of Intrinsic Motivation and Early Cognitive Growth." In *Current Research in Motivation,* edited by Ralph H. Haber, pp. 355–370. New York: Holt, Rinehart and Winston, 1966.

Klaus, M. and Kennel, J. *Maternal-Infant Bonding.* St. Louis: The C. V. Mosby Company, 1976.

Mahler, M. *The Psychological Birth of the Human Infant,* New York: Basic Books, Inc., Publishers, 1975.

Piaget, J. *The Origins of Intelligence in Children,* New York: International Universities Press, Inc., 1952.

Pikler, E. "Data on Gross Motor Development of the Infant." *Early Child Development and Care* 1 (1972): 297–309.

Rheingold, H., and Eckerman, C. "The Infant Separates from His Mother." *Science* 168 (1970): 78–83.

Riggs, M. L. "Children Involved in Purposeful Activity." Proceedings from August 1978, National Association for the Education of Young Children Conference. New York.

Uzgiris, I. "Ordinality in the Development of Schemas Relating to Objects." In *Exceptional Infant,* edited by Jerome Hellmuth, pp. 315–334. Vol. 1. Special Child Publications, 1967.

White, B. *The First Three Years of Life.* Englewood Cliffs, N. J.: Prentice-Hall. Inc., 1975.

*White, B.; Castle, P.; and Held, R. "Observations on the Development of Visually-Directed Reaching." *Child Development* 35 (1964): 349–364.

White, B. and Watts, J. *Experience and Environment: Major Influences on the Development of the Young Child.* Englewood Cliffs, N. J.: Prentice-Hall, Inc., 1973.

Yarrow, L. and Pedersen, F. "The Interplay Between Cognition and Motivation in Infancy." *In Origins of Intelligence: Infancy and Early Childhood.* edited by Michael Lewis. New York: Plenum Press, 1976.

11. Perception in Relation to Cognition

I

It has been customary for psychologists to allocate sensory perception and other cognitive processes such as learning and thinking to different categories, and to discuss them more or less in isolation from each other. There may be a certain justification for this procedure for adults, whose perceptual processes are well developed and stabilized, and therefore not often in need of modification through learning and reasoning. But even for adults the author has argued that perception of everyday life situations is to a considerable extent a function of cognitive inference from schematized knowledge about the nature of the situation perceived (Vernon, 1957). However, there is little doubt that the percepts of children, even if initially a function of the immediate sensory data and of innate perceptual tendencies such as those postulated by the gestalt psychologists, are modified and adapted in the light of acquired information by thought processes and by learning through experience.

Yet, unfortunately, little experimental study has been devoted to the development of perception and understanding of the environment. Extensive studies have been made of reflex and conditioned responses to isolated sensory stimuli, of the perception of simple shapes, and of the formation of concepts of shape, number, etc. But to adapt appropriately to the environment the child requires much more than the capacity to perceive and react to such relatively isolated and abstract stimuli. Most important of all, he must acquire some understanding of the nature of objects in the environment, recognizing and identifying them from their appearance and behavior, knowing what they can do and what he can do with them. Such an understanding implies a considerable amount of knowledge which must be acquired by experience and remembered afterwards; acquisition is therefore dependent upon the cognitive processes of learning and memory, supplemented increasingly by reasoning about the physical environment and the forces which operate in it. If this knowledge were stored in a random and heterogeneous manner, it could not be utilized rapidly and effectively. Thus it has been postulated (Piaget, 1952, 1955; Vernon, 1955) that perceptions and memories of perceptions and of reactions to them become coordinated in "schemes" with which similar memories are organized, together with the relevant knowledge which has been acquired in relation to these percepts. Whenever a perceptual situation is encountered, especially one difficult to perceive or understand, it will be referred to the relevant scheme. Thus the perceiver is enabled to elucidate the situation, recognize its significant features, and react appropriately. In general, the more frequently a particular situation has been encountered, the greater the expectation of its recurrence, and the easier and more rapid the operation of the appropriate scheme and the recognition and subsequent reaction.

Thus the processes of perceptual learning and of the development of schemes are vital to the young child if he is to be able to adapt himself to his environment. Certain perceptions may be innate, for instance, of light and shade, color and form; certain types of perceptual response may develop through maturation alone, for instance, the specific response of smiling at a smiling human face (Spitz and Wolf, 1946; Ambrose, 1961), and the recoil from a sudden drop in the ground (Walk and Gibson, 1961). But it cannot be supposed that there is an innate capacity to perceive, comprehend, and utilize all the objects which confront the child; such knowledge must be learned. Though in recent years there has been considerable study and discussion of perceptual learning, these have been devoted largely to the perceptual learning of adults, in whom it tends to be relatively specific to the particular situations presented. But children must acquire general and organized knowledge about the nature of the environment as a whole. They must also develop the capacity to attend and select, and to perceive rapidly and accurately, dependent in part on maturation but also assisted by learning. This learning, it may be supposed, is guided and reinforced by the consequences of actions stimulated by perception. That is to say, if children find that actions based upon what they have perceived are successful, then the perceptions are stabilized in that form; but if not, they are repeated and corrected.

Understandably, it is less easy to obtain accurate evidence about the actual perceptual experience of children than to study their overt behavior. Thus the nature of their perceptions must be inferred from their spontaneous actions or from their responses to perceptual material. In infants, we must utilize mainly inferences from spontaneous behavior, and for these we are largely dependent upon the work of Piaget. It must be noted, however, that it is difficult to validate these inferences. Thus our knowledge of the nature of perception in infancy is both incomplete and to some extent speculative. Even when, with rather older children, it is possible to introduce experimental techniques of study, the children's reactions may be affected by other than cognitive factors, for instance, motivational states. Verbal reports of what has been perceived afford additional data from the age of about a year and upwards, but again are not wholly reliable until later childhood.

However, in spite of these difficulties it is worth considering the data which have been obtained concerning the manner in which children's perceptions develop as they gain increasing facility and increasing knowledge. There appear to be two main characteristics of perception in infancy and early childhood: in the first place, it is vague and diffuse, lacking in accurate observation of detail and selection of what to us seem to be the significant aspects of the situation; and second, the child is relatively unable to make inferences from his immediate sensory perceptions of the nature of objects and of the environment because he lacks the knowledge to guide him. These two characteristics are interdependent: there is a close relationship between the inability to perceive accurately and discriminatively and to direct attention appropriately (as suggested by Piaget, 1961), on the one hand, and the partial and incomplete knowledge which the child has obtained of his environment on the other hand. Thus it may be that inability to direct attention appropriately to the significant features of the environment is caused at least in part by an incapacity to understand the nature of the situation and to perceive its significant features.

II

It appears from the observations made by Piaget of the development of his three children in infancy that some understanding of the nature of solid objects and of their location in space emerges toward the end of the first year of life. This is preceded, however, by the coordination of simple sensory data into sensorimotor "schemata" (Piaget, 1952), since the infant cannot begin to realize the nature of objects until he can combine together the visual impressions of their shape and the tactile and kinesthetic impressions obtained by touching and handling them. The first stage of coordination is attained when the infant reaches for, grasps, and handles objects toward which his gaze has been directed (Gesell et al., 1949; Piaget, 1952); this occurs at about the third to the fourth month. Whereas at first these actions seem to appear when something chances to touch his hand, at 5 to 6 months the infant deliberately reaches for near objects which attract his attention, and examines and manipulates them. Especially if the object is new and unfamiliar, he uses a variety of actions to discover its nature; he feels it, explores its contour, balances it, strikes it, and hits it against other things. If it is slippery and slips from his hand, he picks it up again. He also turns it round in space and views it from different angles. In this way he learns that the same object in different spatial positions may produce different visual impressions, but that its identity is maintained whatever its spatial orientation. This is not fully grasped until the latter part of the first year. Before the age of 7 to 8 months the infant does not recognize and reach for his bottle when it is presented to him with the nipple turned away from him (Piaget, 1955), but thereafter he reaches or cries for it even if only a small part of it is visible to him.

Perhaps the most important stage in understanding the nature of objects is the realization of their continuous and permanent existence. At 6 to 7 months an infant may look for something which he has just dropped, but only for a short time while he continues to want to play with it. Or he may cry for it as he sees it disappearing. But at 8 to 9 months he may deliberately search for something which is no longer in view. Whereas before this a hidden object may seem to have vanished altogether, thereafter he conceives of its continuing existence, and tries to find it, although not necessarily in the right place. Indeed, there seems to be a tendency to conceive of objects as associated with particular spatial surroundings, and this stage may continue for some time. Thus one child, who had been playing with her sister downstairs, subsequently went upstairs to look for her in the bedroom in which she had earlier been lying ill (Piaget, 1955). However, there can be little doubt that from the age of about a year the child realizes and remembers the existence of particular objects, and may ask for them when he wants them.

How does the young child identify objects? By the mental age of 2 years he is expected to be able to identify four out of the six objects presented to him in the Terman-Merrill test (Terman and Merrill, 1937), namely, a button, a thimble, a miniature toy cat, an engine, and a spoon. Presumably, therefore, he may be able to identify the actual objects, not in miniature, at an earlier age. Since he can identify objects in any spatial orientation, it seems unlikely that identification is based upon any single isolated visual cue. What is most probable is that young children at first perceive the more immediately obvious and noticeable characteristics, including outline shape, and that these percepts are coordinated to form a general impression which is remembered. It is doubtful to what extent shape alone functions in identification; possibly it is more important in some cases than in others, as for instance the spherical shape of a ball. We know from the findings of Gellermann (1933) that even children of 2 years can distinguish and remember simple shapes such as those of a triangle and a cross. (It should be noted that this is something more than discrimination between shapes, which Ling [1941] showed to begin at 6 months.) But Werner (1948) quotes Knoblauch (1934) as finding that subnormal children of 5 to 7 years (presumably equivalent in ability to much younger normal children) matched shapes on the basis of blackness and solidity rather than on shape characteristics such as circularity and angularity. This seems to suggest that younger children may not notice shape characteristics as such unless forced to do so by the experimental conditions. Indeed, O'Connor and Hermelin (1963) found that imbecile adults of a mental age of about 5 years were less able than were normal children of the same mental age to recognize previously presented shapes visually, but in touch recognition the imbeciles were superior to the normal children. One must infer, therefore, that the visual perception of shape was the more highly developed capacity.

Again, in identifying ordinary objects, children may be influenced by the activities of the objects, and particularly by their movements, which seem to attract attention readily. Thus such things as animals may well be characterized and identified by their movements. At an early age children become interested in the use and function of objects. Piaget (1952) noted that infants of 10 to 11 months were constantly trying to find what they could do with objects, letting them fall, throwing them, sliding them along, floating them on water. This indicates that the child was beginning to link his perceptions of objects with his actions in relation to them, and their practical significance to him.

III

During his second year the child's perceptions and memories of particular single objects are supplemented and to some extent superseded by the development of concepts, in which the salient characteristics of similar objects are schematized into categories, each of which can be designated by a name. From this period onward, verbalization plays an increasingly important part in many perceptions. At first, however, names may be used for single objects only. Thus Liublinskaya (1957) noted that at 12 to 14 months the word "cup" might be used for a small pink cup, but not for a large white one. Welch (1940) tried to teach children of 12 to 26 months to give the names chair, ball, etc., as class names to groups of different examples of these objects. Though the children learned to apply the names appropriately to several of the objects, they could not use them as class names for whole groups.

But at about the same time the child often begins to use names for classes of objects quite spontaneously, though often incorrectly. Thus the name "dog" may be given to a variety of animals, and the name "auntie" to a number of different adult females. Brown (1958) has pointed out that in fact children tend to use the names which they most commonly hear uttered by adults. Sometimes these refer to single objects, sometimes to classes of objects. It is only gradually that children learn to apply the names correctly, either to single objects or to classes, as the case may be.

However, there seems little doubt that the child also has to learn gradually to differentiate the significant aspects of objects and then to generalize them, classifying them according to the correct schematic categories. It appears likely that in general some form of multiple classification takes place at first, in terms of a number of what appear to the child to be related characteristics of appearance and behavior. Thus Reichard et al. (1944) found that with the Goldstein test of sorting objects into groups, children aged 4 to 5 years tended to sort in an idiosyncratic manner into categories based upon incidental and nonessential likenesses which seemed obvious to them but not to other people. Up to 8 and 9 years they sorted according to the function and use of the objects, and only after that by means of abstract generalization. It seems probable, therefore, that although schematic classification of objects and situations is of great value to the child in enabling him to identify and react appropriately to new and unfamiliar objects by assimilating them to already existent categories, the categories he employs may be of his own construction, and, from the adult point of view, quite illogical and unsystematic. Again, children may attach too much weight to particular cues, and too little to a balanced representation of all the significant features. Thus Vurpillot and Brault (1959) found that children to 5 to 6 years paid relatively more attention to single identifying cues in viewing miniature objects, whereas older children were more concerned with all the principal characteristics of the objects.

Although during their second and third years children may give incorrect names to the objects they perceive, there is evidence to show that the use of language is of considerable value to them in assisting correct identification. Luria and Yodovich (1959) studied a pair of twins of 5 years, who, although they could communicate with each other, could neither utter nor understand normal speech. They could identify objects only in terms of their practical use, that is to say, by finding out what could be done with them, but they did not understand what they were from verbal descriptions. Nor could they group similar objects together. Liublinskaya (1957) found that normal children of 1 to 2½ years could identify and recognize a butterfly by the pattern of stripes on its wings only when it was labeled with the word "Stripes." Cantor (1955) showed that children of 3 to 5 years could recognize faces more correctly when they had learned to attach names to them than when they had merely been shown them. O'Connor and Hermelin (1961) found that imbeciles of mental ages of 4 to 6 years were better able to recognize pictures of real objects from among others when the names of the former had previously been spoken to them than when they had seen the pictures without naming them. It appeared that the naming had impressed the pictures on their minds. Another illustration of the value of naming was given by Werner (1948) with two boys, aged 4 to 6 years, who were building with different-shaped bricks. One boy kept a store of the bricks and handed them to the other to do the building; in order to facilitate this procedure, they invented an elaborate system of names, "Big Miller," "Little Miller," etc., for the different shapes of brick.

IV

We have already noted that the perceptions of younger children generally tend to be relatively global and diffuse, and that they do not perceive detail accurately. As they grow older, they are better able to analyze perceptual material and differentiate its parts, and subsequently to reorganize these percepts in such a manner as to select and emphasize the relevant aspects of the situation, and to ignore the relatively unimportant. This differentiation and reorganization undoubtedly depend in part on the cognitive structuring of experience, and the ability to think out what is important and what irrelevant. Thus Ames et al. (1953) found that children of 2 years tended to perceive the Rorschach inkblots as wholes, naming them as if they actually represented objects rather than being vaguely similar in form. But after 3 years of age the children began to perceive the major details within the whole, and to attempt some organization of them. However, there was still a good deal of pure invention, and accurate appreciation of form did not appear until a later age.

There have been many studies of the perception of simple and complex forms which have indicated that children may perceive shapes as such before they are able to grasp their interrelations. This is apparent in studies of the Bender Visual Motor Gestalt Test (Bender, 1938), and also in the study of Gesell and Ames (1946). In the latter, children were given a figure to copy which consisted of two crosses contained in a rectangle. The "Union Jack" is shown in Figure 1. They reproduced the crosses separately before they could combine them.

The gradual development of perceptual organization is also illustrated by children's responses to pictures (Vernon, 1940; Amen, 1941). The

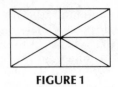

FIGURE 1

youngest children tend to enumerate the people and objects depicted in a complex picture, slightly older children to describe their overt activities. Still later, some interpretation is given of the meanings of the activities, and last of all the feelings and intentions of the people in the pictures are mentioned. There is some disagreement about the ages at which these types of response appear. But at least until 5 years there is a strong tendency to introduce irrelevant and unimportant details. The younger children, according to Amen, tended to concentrate on one particular part of the picture, that which they found the most interesting even if it was not actually the most important, and to ignore the rest.

Piaget (1961) discussed the manner in which direct and immediate perception of shape is extended and corrected by perceptual activity, in which the exploration and comparison of all aspects of complex figures continue until their relation is accurately perceived and fully understood. Children up to the age of 5 and 6 years, when shown complex figures such as the visual illusions, tend to let their eyes wander at random over the whole field of view (even outside the figure), or else to remain fixated on particular salient points of the figures, ignoring the remainder. Thus they perceive many illusions, such as the Müller-Lyer, to a greater extent than do older children and adults who, given time to do so, compare the parts of the figure systematically with each other and thus to some extent dispel the illusion. They apply their intelligence in directing their perceptual activities, reorganizing their percepts in accordance with cognitive schemes based upon general ideas about the nature of form and its relation to its spatial surroundings.

V

The influence of cognitive processes is apparent in the development of perception not only of objects and forms, but also of their surroundings and their disposition in space, including distance from the observer and from each other. It is probable that some perception of distance of objects from the self begins at an early age. Thus Walk and Gibson (1961) found that infants at 6 to 7 months discriminated between a checkered surface immediately below a sheet of glass and a similar surface 4 feet below; they would crawl across the former but not the latter. Although there is some doubt about the basis of this perception of distance, it seems clear that it was immediate and direct, without cognitive inference.

Nevertheless even in the first year of life infants, according to Piaget (1955), begin to develop spatial schemata. In early infancy there may be different sensorimotor "spaces": a "mouth space" for what the infant can suck and chew; a "visual space" for things followed by the eyes; a "tactile space" for things he can touch and grasp. As he realizes that the objects located in these "spaces" are the same, the infant coordinates the separate "spaces" into a single spatial schema. The next important development is the realization that objects moving about in space retain their identity although the sizes of the images they project on the retina grow smaller or larger as the objects recede from him or advance toward him. Thus the child develops an appreciation of size constancy with near objects. Judgment of distance is checked and refined, first by the movements of reaching and grasping, later, when the child is able to crawl and walk, by movement of the whole body. During the second year, the child begins to show interest in the spatial relations of objects to each other, for instance, by throwing them and searching for the different positions in which they have fallen. Topological relations, of inside and outside, above and below, are also of great interest to him. Gradually he learns to visualize spatial relations, so that at about 1½ years, for instance, he can envisage how to reach an object the direct path to which is blocked; thus he runs immediately to the further side of the sofa to retrieve a ball which has rolled underneath it. However, this perception of space relations operates almost entirely with near objects. The child's verbalized ideas about space become increasingly exact at about 2½ to 3 years, and he becomes interested in far distances also at 3 to 3½ years (Ames and Learned, 1948). But even then he is not at all clear about the fact that far distant objects may really be much larger than they appear. Thus Piaget (1951) noted that a child of 5 years seemed to think that a distant lake and houses actually became much larger as he approached them.

We know that in adult perception of space and judgment of distance many different types of data are utilized, particularly when the primary binocular data afforded by disparity of the retinal images and convergent eye movements are lacking. Adults can judge the distances of objects in monocular vision, and beyond the distance at which binocular cues are functional; the infant may not. Adults can utilize cues given by the gradual diminution of size in linear perspective, and of brightness, color, and surface detail in aerial perspective. They are able to coordinate these data and make fairly accurate judgments of distance even in quite difficult circumstances. Children are less adept. Thus Denis-Prinzhorn (1960) required children of 5 to 7 years to bisect the distance between two objects, one at a distance of 34 cm, the other at 200 cm. She found that, whereas adults could perform this task with fair accuracy, the children consistently underestimated the further half. This she attributed to a tendency in younger children to underestimate the expansion of far distant space by comparison with nearer space. So also Lambercier (1946a) showed that they underestimate the size of further objects by comparison with nearer objects. The greater the distance, the greater the underestimation (Zeigler and Leibowitz, 1957). Also in making such size judgments children are less well able than are adults to utilize cues to distance given by a series of objects spaced out between the near and the far one (Lambercier, 1946b).

Older children and adults may also use their spatial schemata to enable them to perceive three-dimensionality indirectly, in pictures. But Hudson

(1960) found that children of 6 years tended to perceive outline drawings and even a photograph showing distance effects as flat, whereas children of 12 years perceived the three-dimensionality. However, this seems to have been to a considerable extent a result of their education, since culturally isolated adult laborers who had received little education also tended to see the drawings as flat.

We noted that children begin at an early age to perceive in a rather vague manner the relative positions and distances of objects in space. However, it is some time before they are able to visualize these and conceive such relations correctly. This fact was demonstrated in an experiment by Piaget and Inhelder (1956), in which they showed children a model layout consisting of a miniature landscape with a road, a stream, two houses, trees, and a small hill. There was an identical model rotated through 180° alongside it. A doll was placed in various positions in the first model, and the children were asked to place another doll in the same position in the rotated model. At 3 to 4 years they put it in a similar position of proximity to a single object near a house or in a field but without any regard to its exact spatial relation with the model as a whole; at 4 years, some regard was paid to position relative to two or three features of the model. At 5 to 5½ years, the children seemed to realize that the second model had been rotated, but were uncertain about the effects of this and often needed several attempts before placing the doll correctly. Only at about 7 years and upwards could they grasp the nature of the whole spatial layout and visualize exactly where to place the doll. In further experiments children were required to arrange a number of objects on a board in positions corresponding to those of similar objects in a model layout. This they were unable to do with any sort of accuracy before about 7 years, and trial-and-error procedures persisted until a later age.

Both in these tasks and in another similar one, it was clear that children had considerable difficulty in envisaging any aspect of certain objects or groups of objects other than that which they perceived at that moment. Although the child acquires in infancy a knowledge of the changes in shape of objects which he rotates in his hands, apparently he is much slower to understand the similar phenomenon which occurs when his orientation to a large object or a group of objects is changed. Thus Piaget (1951) reported that a child of 4½ years thought that a mountain had really changed its shape when he saw it from a new place. Again, Piaget and Inhelder (1956) presented to children a model of a group of mountains, and a collection of pictures painted in the same colors as the model, showing it from different aspects. The children were asked to select the picture which represented what the mountains would look like when seen from different viewpoints. Children of 4 to 6½ years always selected the same picture, that which showed the mountains from the point of view from which they themselves were looking. At a later age, they began to realize that there are other and different aspects, but these were not accurately judged until the age of about 9 years.

Although it is perhaps not possible to determine from these data the extent to which direct spatial perception in ordinary life depends on the development of coordinated spatial schemata, it does seem probable that they play an increasingly important part, especially in circumstances in which the perceptual data are to some extent diminished. That judgments of distance can be improved even in adult life was shown by E. J. Gibson et al. (1955), who taught adults to make absolute judgments of long distances by dividing these up into halves, quarters, etc., and estimating each length separately. This highly intellectualized procedure enabled them to judge quite different absolute distances better, though it had no effect on their accuracy in comparing distances. It seems probable that in somewhat the same way children learn to make more accurate absolute judgments, by themselves moving to and fro across them; or with long distances, by traveling over them.

VI

We noted that one of the characteristics of the global perception of young children was the failure to isolate the parts within the whole, and objects from their surroundings. This remains apparent in the immediate perception even of adults, as in the case of visual illusions. But through the cognitive processes of perceptual activity they may correct and refine their immediate perceptions, and thus obtain a more veridical understanding of the nature of the environment. This is particularly apparent in judgments of movement and of the speed of movement. Even adults are likely to make mistaken judgments, and, for instance, to perceive larger and brighter objects as moving more slowly than smaller and dimmer ones; or movement as being more rapid across a heterogeneous than across a homogeneous background (Brown, 1931). But they may correct these judgments through their knowledge that speed is a function solely of the distance moved in a given time. The young child, however, depends on his immediate perceptions, and does not correct judgments in this way. According to Piaget (1946), he tends to say that the speed of movement of an object is greater than that of another only if he perceives the first to pass the second. If two objects arrive at the same point at the same moment, they are judged to be moving at the same speed no matter where they started nor what path they took. If one arrives before the other, it is judged to have moved more quickly. These errors may arise because the earliest perceptions of movement are of objects moving away from himself, which thus have a uniform starting point. But his perceptions continue to be dominated by a single aspect of the situation, the finishing point. It requires the control of thought processes to correct and refine these early perceptions.

VII

We may conclude from this discussion that the simplest primary perceptions of sensory stimuli and of forms and their relation to their spatial surroundings are modified from infancy upward in the light of their association with other cognitive data, and in particular through the acquisition of knowledge about the nature of objects and of the environment. Thus percepts, after the first few months of life, do not exist in isolation, but are related across sensory modes; they are integrated with memories of previous similar perceptual experiences, and of reactions to these, into schematic categories of associated percepts. The categories are further refined and restructured through the development of relevant ideas by intelligent reasoning. Thus eventually the older child and adult attend to and become aware of, not so much the immediate and obvious aspects of the present situation, as those characteristics which are significant with regard to its underlying meaning, and which can be used to predict the course of action most likely to be successful for adaptation of behavior to the total situation. In the course of this development, accuracy of discrimination and rapidity of perception increase, to some extent through maturation alone, though probably also through learning. Maturation, and certainly also learning, enable the child to analyze the perceptual situation and extract its important features. But these improved capacities would be of far less value to the child if he were not constantly employed in gauging the significance to himself of the perceptual situation and in relating it to his ideas and actions.

That the ability to analyze the perceptual situation actively and differentiate its parts may show important individual differences has recently been studied by Witkin et al. (1962). These authors demonstrated that such differences may exist in children from 8 years upward; indeed, they consider that the differences may appear even earlier in life, though this has not yet been established. The analytical capacity, which they term "field independence," appears in the performance of various perceptual tasks in which the person has to differentiate certain aspects of the field and make judgments of them, ignoring any interference from the remainder of the field; and also in a high degree of structuring in the Rorschach inkblot responses. It is correlated with performance on the WISC Picture Completion, Object Assembly, and Block Design tests, but not with any of the WISC verbal tests. However, this lack of relationship may be due to the fact that adequate tests of differentiation and analysis of verbal material were not utilized. "Field independence" seems to arise notably in children of independent personality, who are sufficiently self-reliant to treat their social and physical environment objectively, to understand its essential nature, and to utilize it actively and effectively for the satisfaction of their needs. It may have a constitutional basis, but is also considerably affected by the personality of the mother and her manner of bringing up her children. We may therefore conclude that the capacity to apply the cognitive processes generally in an active appraisal and understanding of the nature of the environment is a fundamental personality characteristic of great importance in the perceptual development of children.

BIBLIOGRAPHY

Ambrose, J. A. (1961), The Development of the Smiling Response in Early Infancy. *Determinants of Infant Behaviour*, Foss, B. M. (Ed.). London: Methuen.

Amen, E. A. (1941), Individual Differences in Apperceptive Reaction: A Study of the Response of Pre-School Children to Pictures. *Genetic Psychology Monographs*, 23:319.

Ames, L. B. et al. (1953), Development of Perception in the Young Child as Observed in Response to the Rorschach Test Blots. *Journal of Genetic Psychology*, 82:183.

—— & Learned, J. (1948), The Development of Verbalized Space in the Young Child. *Journal of Genetic Psychology*, 72:63.

Bender, L. (1938), *A Visual Motor Gestalt Test and Its Clinical Use*. New York: American Orthopsychiatric Association.

Brown, J. F. (1931), The Visual Perception of Velocity, *Psychol. Forschung*, 14:199.

Brown, R. (1958), How Shall a Thing be Called? *Psychological Review*, 65:14.

Cantor, G. N. (1955), Effects of Three Types of Pre-Training on Discrimination Learning in Pre-School Children. *Journal of Experimental Psychology*, 49:339.

Denis-Prinzhorn, M. (1960), Perception des Distances et Constance des Grandeurs (étude génétique). *Archives de Psychologie*, 37:181.

Gellerman, L. W. (1933), Form Discrimination in Chimpanzees and Two-Year-Old Children. *Journal of Genetic Psychology*, 42:3.

Gesell, A. & Ames, L. B. (1946), The Development of Directionality in Drawing. *Journal of Genetic Psychology*, 68:45.

——, Ilg, F. L. & Bullis, G. E. (1949), *Vision: Its Development in Infant and Child*. New York: Harper.

Gibson, E. J. et al. (1955). The Effect of Prior Training with a Scale of Distance on Absolute and Relative Judgments of Distance over Ground. *Journal of Experimental Psychology*, 50:97.

Hudson, W. (1960), Pictorial Depth Perception in Sub-Cultural Groups in Africa. *Journal of Social Psychology*, 52:183.

Knoblauch, E. (1934), Vergleichende Untersuchungen zur Optischen Auffassung hochgradig schwachsinniger und normaler Kinder. *Zeitschrift Angew. Psychol.*, 47.

Lambercier, M. (1946a), La Constance des Grandeurs en Comparaisons Sériales. *Archives de Psychologie*, 31:78.

——(1946b), Le Configuration en Profondeur dans la Constance des Grandeurs. *Archives de Psychologie*, 31:287.

Ling, B. C. (1941), Form Discrimination as a Learning Cue in Infants. *Comparative Psychological Monographs*, 17 (2).

Liublinskaya, A. A. (1957), The Development of Children's Speech and Thought. *Psychology in the Soviet Union*, Simon, B. (Ed.). London: Routledge and Kegan Paul.

Luria, A. R. & Yudovich, F. I. (1959), *Speech and the Development of Mental Processes in the Child*. London: Staples.

O'Connor, R. & Hermelin, B. (1961), Like and Cross Modality Recognition in Subnormal Children. *Quarterly Journal of Experimental Psychology*, 13:48.

—— & —— (1963), *Speech and Thought in Severe Subnormality*. London: Pergamon.

Piaget, J. (1946), *Les Notions de Mouvement et de la Vitesse chez l'Enfant*. Paris: Presses Universitaires de France.

——(1951), *Play, Dreams and Imitation in Childhood*, London: Heinemann.

——(1952), *The Origins of Intelligence in Children*. New York: International Universities Press.

——(1955), *The Child's Construction of Reality*. London: Routledge and Kegan Paul.

————(1961), *Les Mécanismes Perceptifs*. Paris: Presses Universitaires de France.

———— & Inhelder, B. (1956), *The Child's Conception of Space*. London: Routledge and Kegan Paul.

Reichard, S. et al. (1944), The Development of Concept Formation in Children. *American Journal of Orthopsychiatry*, 14:156.

Spitz, R. A. & Wolf, K. M. (1946), The Smiling Response: A Contribution to the Ontogenesis of Social Relations. *Genetic Psychology Monographs*, 34:57.

Terman, L. M. & Merrill, M. A. (1937), *Measuring Intelligence*. London: Harrap.

Vernon, M. D. (1940), The Relation of Cognition and Phantasy in Children. *British Journal of Psychology*, 30:273.

————(1955), The Functions of Schemata in Perceiving. *Psychological Review*, 62:180.

————(1957), Cognitive Inferences in Perceptual Activity. *British Journal of Psychology*, 48:35.

Vurpillot, E. & Brault, H. (1959), Etude Expérimentale sur la Formation des Schèmes Empiriques. *L'Année Psychologique*, 59:381.

Walk, R. D. & Gibson, E. J. (1961), A Comparative and Analytical Study of Visual Depth Perception. *Psychological Monographs*, 75(15).

Welch, L. (1940), The Genetic Development of the Associational Structures of Abstract Thinking. *Journal of Genetic Psychology*, 56:175.

Werner, H. (1948), *Comparative Psychology of Mental Development*. New York: International Universities Press, second edition.

Witkin, H. A. et al. (1962), *Psychological Differentiation: Studies of Development*. New York: Wiley.

Zeigler, H. P. & Leibowitz, H. (1957), Apparent Visual Size as a Function of Distance for Children and Adults. *American Journal of Psychology*, 70:106.

MARY W. MOFFITT

12. Play as a Medium for Learning

Play activities provide for "information-seeking" behavior. We have known for a long time that play is a powerful inner force through which a child reaches out to interact with his environment involving movement and different sensory modes. He seems to learn more when he can move around, handle, and manipulate objects. Through such sensory-motor activities, he learns much about the properties of matter and finds ways to adapt to a complex environment through experiences related to cause and

From Mary W. Moffitt, "Play as a Medium for Learning," *Journal of Health, Physical Education, Recreation* (June 1972), pp. 45–47. Reprinted with permission.

effect. Children who are prevented from having a wide range of sensory-motor experiences in these early years, due to illness, overprotection, or other reasons, are not likely to develop certain kinds of percepto-cognitive information in the same way later on.

The schematic drawing below is an attempt to show the relationship of different play activities to perceptual-motor development and cognitive development that are necessary for success in academic subjects.

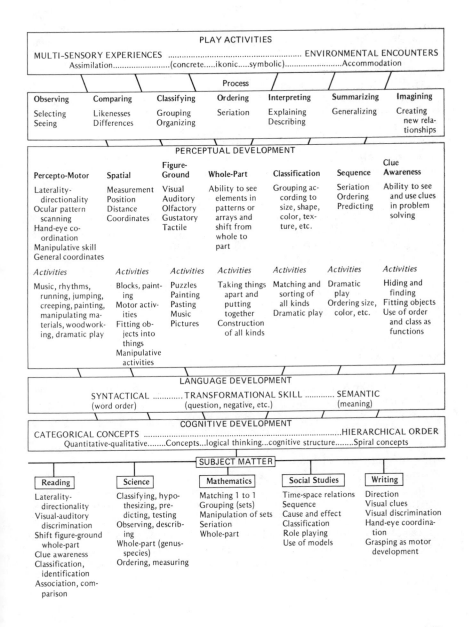

Both Bruner and Piaget have expressed the point of view that multi-sensory experiences obtained through environmental encounters with the concrete, three-dimensional world are important. It is through sensory experiences that children build a repertoire of "referents" that can be used for interpretation of new experiences. These referents form a basis for classifying information and the child indicates this by saying, "It is like . . ."

The many aspects of sensory experiences are processed through observing, comparing, classifying, ordering, interpreting, summarizing, and imagining. Each of these processes is an integral part of the way a child acts upon the stimuli he receives. As a child develops his language and is able to speak about what he sees, hears, feels, tastes, and smells, he extracts meaning from his experiences, which in turn helps him to build his cognitive structure in various ways.

As one can see from the schematic drawing, there is a circular relationship of the parts that make up the whole. Each is dependent upon other parts. Play activities provide the momentum through which a child can make a more balanced thrust toward maturation. It has been recognized for a long time that there is a close relationship between perceptual development and school achievement. If a person selects any one of the subject areas and asks the question, "What does a child need for success in this area?" he is struck by the fact that all of the above mentioned activities are basic to learning to read and write, for understanding science, social studies, and other areas.

An attempt will be made to describe in more detail the specifics of percepto-cognitive development and the activities that may be important in each area as shown on the schematic representation.

PERCEPTO-MOTOR SKILLS

Body Image

Laterality is an internal realization that the body has spatially oriented parts such as a right and left side, a front and a back, which must be coordinated. A child must sense that he is an object in space and that he takes up a certain amount of space. The body may be used to measure space as a child finds out where he can reach, step, jump, and what he can get into, through, and around. Neuromuscular control is promoted as a child assumes various positions and when he propels his body through space in different ways. *Directionality* is an external referent by which the child learns to use the horizontal and vertical coordinates in the environment for relating himself to other objects in space. His eye must accommodate to space at various focal points such as near, mid, and far areas. Some children have trouble adjusting to the illusion of size related to distances. The airplane which is seen as large on the ground is explained to be "shrinking" when seen as a tiny object in the sky.

128

Motor Patterns

Running, jumping, skipping, creeping, throwing, and the like require balance, control, and muscular strength. Bones and muscles grow according to usage. The muscles are arranged in pairs and must be used to develop reciprocal action that is necessary for efficient movement. Many movements are dependent on *hand-eye-cordination*. All kinds of manipulative skills involve the extension of the body through the use of tools. Certain occular patterns are a part of hand-eye coordination. Both eye focus and eye following are important. Where does the child look? Does the eye follow the hand in a rhythmic fashion? Many activities such as painting, pushing a small truck along the floor, steering a bicycle, bouncing, throwing, and rolling a ball provide for near focus and eye following patterns.

PERCEPTION OF SPACE

Measurement

A child must acquire spatial accommodations for objects in relation to other objects in a variety of ways. Comparative forms require a referent when differentiation is made for how long, how high, how deep, and the like.

Position

Up, down, above, under, aside, below, in the middle are but a few of the words that are used to designate position of objects in relation to other objects. A child needs to learn how to organize objects and himself in space by the positions so designated.

FIGURE-GROUND

Figure-ground

Figure-ground is a term applied to the way a child selects a certain stimulus from a complex background by ignoring all other stimuli. Perception of form, texture, smell, and taste is dependent upon what a child picks out to attend to. Some parts will stand out as "figural" and details noted while the background will tend to fall back and lack clarity. Ability to concentrate is related to how long a child can attend to a specific configuration.

Configuration

A child needs to have a clear image or a basic configuration of an object if he is to make some differentiation of it from among other materials. Special problems may arise in figure-ground differentiation when items are embedded in extraneous detail or only partial figures are shown. Children are often asked to select a particular item from a picture with many other details. If a child does not understand how to use certain clues or he lacks a clear image of the object, the task may cause some difficulty for him. There is some relationship between motor development and figure-ground differentiation because it has been found that children score poorly on figure-ground if their motor development is poor. Language disorders may arise, too, from inability to hear sounds distinctly which is another form of figure-ground differentiation.

Symbolization

A child needs to have some experience with concrete objects if he is to fully recognize their symbolization. Some children have difficulty in recognizing specific symbols due to inexperience in handling, seeing, or hearing. Painting is an activity that is particularly useful for learning symbolization. Through painting and drawing, a child may learn that he can represent the three-dimensional world through line and form and thus develop his own symbols. Clay is another medium that may be used for this purpose. When a child makes his own symbols, he can better accept the symbols of mathematics and those used to represent sounds for reading.

WHOLE-PART LEARNING

Learning to see the parts or elements that make up the whole is related to reading and other academic skills. Young children tend to see the whole rather than the parts although some children may see some small detail. Piaget speaks of this tendency as "centration" or, in other words, the child tends to become fixed on one element within the whole. On the other hand, if two shapes are similar but differ only on interior detail, the child may fail to see the interior detail as part of the whole pattern.

Reading, for instance, requires the skill of looking at individual letters and then at the word as a whole. Some children learn to identify words by configuration or shape of the word while others look at the elements or individual letters and then at the whole word. There are many activities that are related to whole-part learning. Construction of all kinds such as block building, woodworking, collage, painting are some of the activities that require the child to assemble or note discrete parts that make up the larger whole. Taking apart and putting together provide opportunities for learning to look at sequence and order of parts as they relate to each other.

CLASSIFICATION-SERIATION

Classification and seriation are cognitive processes that result from a child's ability to perceive the attributes of various kinds of materials and organize them in some class or category. Many concepts in science and mathematics are dependent upon the ability to place objects in various kinds of categories or put them in ordered arrangements. Activities for matching and sorting of a wide variety of objects for size, shape, texture and the like are essential and involve perceptual acuity.

LANGUAGE DEVELOPMENT

Language and thought are closely allied. As children work and play they learn to talk about the attributes of objects and describe what they are perceiving. The English language, of course, has its own word order and the child learns to transform the syntax in various ways. Actual experience provides for ideas associated with the experience and helps to build meaning for the words he hears and learns to use.

COGNITIVE DEVELOPMENT

Basically, cognitive development is composed of ideas or concepts. These may be both quantitative (many, more, few, numerical, etc.) and qualitative (warm, cold, rough, smooth, etc.). As children build concepts about their world, they build on past experiences and understandings. Bruner speaks about learning as "continual deepening of one's understanding . . . that comes from learning to use ideas in progressively more complex forms."[1] Learning proceeds in a spiral order. A child can learn something new because he has a schema into which the new information may be fitted.

The schematic drawing attempts to show the relationship of processes, perceptual intake, language and cognitive development in a circular fashion as indicated by the lines. Each part is related to the other.

ACADEMIC SUBJECTS

It should be noted that the skills for academic learnings are the same as those that are found in the schema under perceptual development. It is important, therefore, to provide the kinds of activities that are important for the development of perceptual skills. It has been noted that if a child does not succeed in learning to read, for instance, he is referred to the remedial teacher who frequently has to work with perceptual deficiencies before the child can progress with the task of reading.

[1] Jerome Bruner, *The Process of Education* (Cambridge, Massachusetts: Harvard Press, 1966), p. 13.

It is apparent that many of the activities that are called "play" are directly related to the development of various kinds of skills that children need for achieving success in academic subjects. Nothing has been found to take the place of play, and we eliminate these activities at our peril. Furthermore, play is a medium for sustaining interest and mental energy when a child becomes involved in working with materials and pursuing his ideas.

Play activities should be planned to provide for optimal learning conditions. This means that materials should be well selected and strategically placed for good use. Adequate amounts should be provided so that children may work without the frustration of waiting too long for turns. Time for play is essential. This does not mean that children will work at academic work and then have ten minutes of "free play"; it means that teaching becomes a process of diagnosing the needs of children and planning for individual progress in a total program.

Children need and respond to activities that contribute to both perceptual and conceptual learning. This demands that the environment present challenge to children. When there is no challenge, attention deteriorates or fluctuates with the result that learning may be affected.

MIRIAM B. STECHER

13. Concept Learning Through Movement Improvisation: The Teacher's Role as Catalyst

Young children learn and express their learning in many nonverbal ways. Movement is said to be the core of all learning, yet we make so little use of it in the classroom. Although most very young children enjoy moving rhythmically at "music time," and spontaneous dance-like movement frequently occurs during free play, few teachers have tried to tune in to these kinesthetic experiences to develop any important relevant learnings.

The following suggestions present an approach to teaching concepts which are fundamental to music and movement and which are related to the young child's life experiences. They represent only one aspect of a broad approach[1] to develop an aesthetic and productive awareness of

[1]Further described in a larger work by the author and Hugh McElheny on the Musical Arts in the Early Childhood Curriculum.

Reprinted by permission from Young Children, Vol. 25, No. 3 (Jan. 1970), pp. 143-153. Copyright © 1970, National Association for the Education of Young Children, 1834 Connecticut Avenue, N.W., Washington, DC 20009.

sound, song and movement as media for the child's own inventive expression, both verbal and nonverbal.

Although these ideas are listed in a developmental sequence, they are definitely *not* step-by-step lesson plans. What will happen in each classroom must depend on the responses received. The teacher must relate to *those* responses. It is through such interaction that meaningful experiences can occur. It is only through meaningful experiences that learning can occur. These can be repeated again and again for new variations, which will always present themselves if the teacher can learn to recognize and accept even tentative offerings as just that—as possible beginnings.

The first week of the school year, a group of five-year-old children were asked to show some ways to "make a motion" (a line from a song they had just sung). At first, the children were too shy to volunteer or even accept a turn. They merely shook their heads negatively, perhaps not understanding what was expected. Since nothing was offered, the teacher spontaneously used the only movement then apparent—the simple and natural movement of the head in the act of refusing.

TEACHER: "Miguel, your way to say 'No' is a motion. Isn't it? How did you use your head? Was it like this?"
(She imitated the tense, rapid gesture he had used. Some children laughed and joined in the head-shaking.)
TEACHER: "But Sabrina's motion to say 'No' was not like Miguel's. It was different. Was it like this?"
(She imitated the slow, stolid certainty of Sabrina, adding a long drawn-out sound of "N-o-o" as accompaniment.)
TEACHER: "Which one was slow and which one was fast? Let's try them again."
(They did, adding a sharp sound of "NoNoNo" to Miguel's.)
TEACHER: "Maybe we can find more ways to say 'No.' Not just with our heads. Find a slow or a fast way with hands."

Once the children had experienced that many movements were acceptable and that slower and faster were ways to vary them, the group relaxed and became enjoyably involved in the search. They discovered and contributed:

FRANCIS: "You can say 'No' with your hand like a cop."
(He held his arm high, as if stopping traffic.)
WILLIAM: "You can say 'No' to a baby like this, 'Uh, Uh'."
(He wagged a finger in the air.)
TEACHER: "How about 'Yes' motions?"
MARIA: "They go up and down, like this, 'Uh, Huh'."

The teacher's role is a dual one: a catalyst for action and a stabilizer for focusing attention on the problem to be solved. She does not demonstrate or teach "how," although she is a co-participant at times. She invites exploration by means of provocative and open-ended questions. She encourages deeper involvement by her comments on the variety of responses rather than by restrictive directions. She uses them to strengthen the children's body awareness, sense awareness and concept understanding. Her parallel objective is to spur self-directed creativity. The following are offered as useful catalytic spurs.

INVITATION TO FURTHER INVOLVEMENT

With Music

Invite participation in the pleasure of the physical experience. (Play clearly rhythmic music in short sequences and obviously different tempo.)

"This music makes me feel like moving. Does it make you want to move? Let's move with it."

If the teacher participates, she should avoid using patterned or stylized dance movement which the children would imitate but can herself imitate or enlarge upon different children's responses (i.e., first as they do it and then repeating it on another level of space: higher, lower, wider, etc.)

"Move how the music sounds to you—the way it makes you feel. Then if you want to, you can try somebody else's way."

We are asking the children to respond spontaneously to the music, rather than to dance or move "in time." Accuracy of rhythm develops after frequent experiences of moving in free and then in focused response.

"Let's stop when the music stops. Maybe the next part will be different. . . . Is it?" (The teacher is now directing attention to the music itself—listening with specific focus. The change, when it comes, must be obvious rather than subtle, i.e., much slower or faster, much louder or softer, different rhythm, etc.)

To be able to stop (as well as start) in response to signals (in this case the music) is the first step in self-control prerequisite for group movement experience to develop further. To stop anything is not easy for young children. To stop pleasurable activity like rhythmic movement is especially difficult. Providing a focus such as *listening for the anticipated change* in the music is a pleasurable challenge and also aids in developing self-controls and listening skills.

"Use your whole self to show how this music sounds to you."

This is a more meaningful request than "Do what the music tells you." It allows alternatives. It frees timid children from fears of not knowing "how," or being "wrong." There is not "wrong." There is only "not listening."

Some children will relate to the over-all dramatic quality. ("That's spooky—I'm a ghost." "That's space music." "That's a storm, I'm thunder—c-r-a-s-h.") Other children will hear the beat or rhythm of the melody and merely march about. A few will not be listening at all, but will use the opportunity for haphazard or perhaps popular style dance movement. A few might prefer to watch. We want to reach all of them.

RELAXATION AND BODY AWARENESS

Between selections, ask the children to lie down and close their eyes "to hear better." This is also an opportunity to relax, to catch the breath and cool off after energetic movement. Test how "loose" they can make themselves. To do so, gently lift their arms. They should be limp. If not, wobble them slightly, bend them gently at the joints and let them slide back to the floor *gently*. Do the same with the legs. Roll the head slowly from side to side. If there is space, gently roll the child completely over. Some five-year-old children can do this for each other. If the teacher's voice is kept to a whisper and her touch is warmly supportive, even the tense children will begin to trust the experience and relax fully. Demonstrate it on a rag doll first. In fact, some teachers like to refer to this complete relaxation as "sleepy ragdoll." Barbara Mettler, in her book *Materials of Dance as a Creative Art Activity*, points out " . . . movement has meaning only in relation to *no movement* . . . (the child) must learn to experience deeply . . . the motionlessness of complete relaxation." Valuable as a contrast to a period of vigorous activity, it prepares the children for slow or sustained movement which is usually more difficult to achieve.

Without Music

Encourage body awareness through freely exploring and then identifying movement in verbal and nonverbal terms. (The nonverbal experience must come first.)

"Let's walk."
"Let's walk another way." (On tiptoe, on heels, on outside of foot.)
"When we walk, what part of us must move?"
"Can you stay in the same place and move your whole self but not your feet?" (Everyone explores at the same time.)
"What's moving?" (Some children will call out, i.e., hands, head, shoulders, etc. Others will demonstrate nonverbally.)

Look for and select only a few movements for demonstration and imitation; those that are obviously different. It is better not to set a precedent of having everyone demonstrate for several reasons; it leaves little time for developments and it is difficult for young children to wait long for turns. The emphasis here is on experiencing the discovery that variations are possible and valued by the teacher.

135

"Can we move around the room without our feet? Everybody try to find a way. Try to come to me, but don't use your feet for walking." (Children are likely to roll, crawl, drag, rock.)
"What did you do?" (A chance to find language to describe movement after moving.)
"Look at all those different ways to move!" (Indicating there is no one right answer.)
"I wonder how else we can do it?" (Indicating there is more to be discovered, though not necessarily on the same day.)

Individual differences are admired for being just that—other effortful ways of responding to a challenge, rather than in judgmental terms of "good" or "right" or "beautiful." Movement is a medium for learning and expression that does not depend on such evaluation for encouragement to develop further.

AVOIDING INHIBITIONS

The very young child's free response to rhythmic sound or music is spontaneous and unself-conscious rhythmic movement. When he is deeply absorbed, his movements seem better coordinated than usual and naturally graceful even when they are also vigorous and abandoned. Unless something occurs to influence the response, the experience is obviously emotionally expressive and satisfying.

The spontaneous reactions of others can be negative and inhibiting or positive and strengthening.

Inhibition may begin with the unexpected reaction of an observer who makes the child self-conscious. The laughter of peers, parents or teachers, whether in amusement or delight, can bring sudden and painful embarrassment. The child becomes aware that when he is spontaneously, freely responsive, he may be exposing himself to the possible risk of ridicule from others (who are less free). The child then tends to become guarded, distorting his original movements as if to indicate that he, too, agrees that they are laughable. He may become clown-like and he, too, joins in laughing at others.

Another negative influence is an adult's interference with many specific directives. Although meant to expand the child's capabilities, in actuality, they restrict them by too much control. Equally, to limit movement experiences to the learning of "steps" or techniques is inappropriate for this young age. It tends to make the child constrained, imitative and overly concerned with the critical judgments of others. It dilutes and distorts the original joyous impulse to movement, to react feelingly to mood or music, a gift with which most of us are born and then have "educated out of us"[2] by well-meaning teachers and parents. Worse, it can diminish the sense of self-worth, one of our prime concerns. The child thinks: "This is what you have to know or else you can't really dance" and surrenders the beauty and

[2]Sheehy, Emma. *Children Discover Music and Dance.*

satisfaction of his own intuitive response. What a damaging mistake! Some will themselves grow up to be teachers, holding on to and fostering this inhibiting misconception, thus continuing the negative influence on the creative growth of another generation of children.

COMMUNICATING MOVEMENT RESPONSES THROUGH LANGUAGE

To Aid in Clarifying Concepts

"Let's find lots of ways to move only our arms."
"Johnny's way is up and down—like reaching!"
"Daniel's way is up and down, too, but it's different from Johnny's. Is it pushing? Punching?"
"Who found a way that's not up and down?"
"Can we try it with you? What shall we call it?"
"Let's say those words to help us move together. Make them fit." ("Open-close," "in-out," etc.)

Such chanting provides a simple, rhythmic accompaniment that supports and describes the movement.

Mouth sounds—the whole gamut of the wonderful inventory of children's "sound effects" are legitimate and relevant here. Often they are as appropriate as any composed music (i.e., "Zing around and f-r-r-p" to describe and support a wide whirl and a sudden stop). Whenever possible, pick up a child's imaginative use of language and substitute it for yours.

A CLASSROOM EXPERIENCE

The kindergarten was exploring the concept of *lightness* and *looseness* through movement experience with tension and relaxation.

TEACHER: "Hug yourself real hard. Harder. That's very tight! Let go! That's not tight at all now, is it?"
KATY: "It's loose."
TEACHER: "Do it with your hands. Can you make a fist like this? Make it so tight that I can't open it." *(She tried to pry open Peter's fist.)*
PETE: "It's like a knot in my shoelace."
TONY: "B-o-i-i-n-g!" *(He fell down and remained there limp.)*
TEACHER: *"What's that?"*
TONY: *"The knot busted."*

Both teacher and children were delighted with the image and together proceeded to develop it, first with isolated parts of the body, then the whole body, and finally "tying up" with a partner. At a signal (a glissando on the piano) all shouted "Boing!" then, falling suddenly, they lay quietly and limply loose. Later, when the teacher wished them to relax again after vigorous galloping, she asked them to lie down and "be loose like a busted shoelace."

When the teacher accepts and uses the children's vocabulary and imagery as well as their movement discoveries, there is always an upsurge of interest and enthusiasm and an apparent growth in self-esteem. The children also become more amenable to accepting the limits of one focus of attention when set by the teacher in her effort to make challenges more interesting.

Frequent opportunities to experience concepts as pairs of opposites can clarify their meanings through revealing their special relatedness. However, in offering a contrast, i.e., to moving "fast," try asking the children to move "not a bit fast" (rather than asking for "slow"). This will allow them to explore, compare and perceive the movements (or sounds) as *relative to each other* (opposite poles on a continuum of speed). Moreover, it enables the young child to make his own perceptual connections—to experience that flash of insight which makes learning a joy. We deprive him of this opportunity when we continually make these connections for him. This is learning through discovery—in this case, discovery through movement.

TEACHER: "Let's use our backs and shoulders with this music." *(Play quick and staccato sounds.)*
   "How does it feel?"
MEG: "It's like laughing but not with your mouth."
TONY: "It's like shivering."
TEACHER: "Now can we move them *not a bit* like that?"
(Play a clear contrast—a soft, slow waltz or "soft shoe" dance music.)
   "How does that feel?"
TONY: "Now the sun came out."

Such attempts at communicating verbally after nonverbal movement responses to music encourage imagination in thinking and using language. The teacher's use of her own imagery can further stimulate the imagination of the children and the fuller and more self-controlled involvement of the total body. However, since it is meant to evoke kinesthetic sense memory, it must be based on the *real* experience of the children; at least with concepts with which they are already somewhat familiar. Since clarity of conceptual understanding is also a goal, it is important that the imagery used will really clarify rather than confuse or diffuse the young child's effort.

For example, exhortations to move "light as a feather" will yield no appreciable difference in response unless and until the children have had recent experience with the airiness of feathers. Children who have never been to the sea cannot identify with what it is like to be "rocked by the waves." To "tiptoe like an elf" is altogether meaningless for today's children who deal with much more colorful fantasy characters. Teachers need to check periodically on their favorite clichés and substitute the imagery meaningful for the children they are teaching at the time. Build on immediate experience. For example, children can explore and immediately know the floatingness of paper streamers or large silky scarves. They can experience rocking while sitting in a hoop, and tiptoe "like you want to surprise somebody." Ask them *then* what it feels like and develop the responses into a dramatic sequence: the hoops can become boats, the scarves can become waves, the tiptoe experience might become "fog creeping in."

Focusing with Music as the Catalyst

Help the movement become more self-controlled, after the group has had many experiences of hearing and responding freely to a variety of music.

"Don't start to move too soon when this music begins. Wait until you hear how it sounds to you. Close your eyes. It helps us to listen better."
"What kind of sounds can we listen for? Faster or—, softer or —?" *(Providing a specific focus for listening.) "What do you hear?"*
"Listen to this music. When you feel it deep inside you, tap it with your fingers, bounce it in your knees. Feel it in your shoulders and your back. Now put it in your feet and let it take you all around the room."
"Some of you are really moving with that music. You look like you really feel it."
Let's look at how different some of your ways are." (A few at a time can demonstrate.)
"How are they different? Heavier? Lighter?"
"Is her's round and round like his? Up and down?"
"Can you try it sideways sometimes? Backwards and not bump anybody else?"
"How else can you do it? Robert's going zig-zag!"

Always the asking of *how else can you do it?* implies that inventiveness is never-ending and that all children are potential inventors.

PERCEIVING CONTRASTS AND CONNECTIONS

Awareness of likeness and difference.

"Is this music like the other record we just played?"
"How is it different?"
"Show that you hear it's different. Use your whole self to show how it's different. Stop when it stops."
"Now, is this music that's playing, the same or different?"
"Did you hear it before?"

To aid the young child's awareness of differences in tempo, dynamics and tone color, play two *short* selections of marked contrast to make the difference obvious. For example, follow a segment of rousing Dixieland Band sound with a bit of the sinuous peacefulness of an Indian Saga either sung or played on the flute. Then return to the first music. (Avoid a *very* fast or *very* slow tempo; they are too difficult for very young children to cope with.) By controlling the sequence of what is played in this way, the contrast itself evokes awareness and inventiveness naturally. The improvisations become more appropriate, freer of stereotypes, more rhythmic, more dance-like.

EXTENDING CREATIVE RESPONSE

Encourage individual and cooperative creative productivity and aesthetic awareness.

"Look around at all the different ways to move to that music."
"Do you see anybody moving in the same way the music sounds to you?"
"Move near that person when the music gets softer." (If necessary, use volume controls.) "Move away when the music gets louder." (Or vice-versa.)
"Decide together when to go away from each other and when to come back." (Take a moment for the "partners" to talk about it.)
"Listen for a place in the music to help you decide." (Use familiar music here.)
"Find a new way to move with this music with your partner."
"Listen for a place in the music to change back to your first way." (Developing awareness of phrasing.) "And back again to your second way."
"That's how some people can begin to make a dance, their very own dance that has parts to it." (Awareness of form.)

The above comments are intended to indicate to the child that creative dance (organized movement originating from the child's own explorations with improvisation) is as worthy of recognition and development as his other forms of organized expression—stories, paintings, block-building, etc.

THE TEACHER AS CATALYST

Although it would certainly be better for the teacher to have had some pleasurable movement experience herself, it is not a prerequisite. She need not be a dancer, nor consider herself inadequate because she cannot "teach" dance. Obviously, the teaching of dance as a skill is not involved in the foregoing paragraphs. In fact, expertise, or special knowledge of a particular technique of dance, can sometimes narrow the view of a classroom teacher so that she finds it difficult to be open to the fresh innovations of young children. Such a teacher tends to think in terms of training the body instead of recognizing the opportunities to make relevant use of the authentic grace of young children deeply involved in natural movement.

If little children do not need to be taught "how to" dance, what *do* they need from teachers? Most important, they need the supportive encouragement to pursue their own style so that what Maslow calls "peak experiences" become possible.[3] If it is the spontaneous evolvement of a small group, the arrangement and protection of space and a nod of awareness that something worthwhile is happening, may be all that is required. At other group times, it may be a genuine expression of admiration that there can be so many different ways to express ideas and feelings through movement. This allows each child to "hold on to the integrity of his own personal response."[4] It recognizes that there can be no specific right or wrong response in movement. There can only be *your* way and *his* way and *her* way and responses that are like these or different from them.

Although the use of movement experience as described here indicates how it can be useful in developing language skills, it would be a mistake if this were regarded as its primary purpose. Non-verbal experience has its own values as communication. The teacher must remain sensitively aware of the possibility of too much verbalizing. While words can evoke and inspire, they can also distract, dilute or distort a deep experience.

The teacher should, therefore, make it clear that the children can respond spontaneously and feelingly and that their individual responses will be acceptable. This is ego strengthening. It gives the children (and the teacher) courage to adventure on new paths to constructive creativity without fear of getting lost (being wrong). There are many ways to the top of the mountain and we want to keep all of them open. The most memorable are not always the straight paths but those that interweave and spiral around each other; from playful pleasure in movement to learning through movement, from learning through pleasure to pleasure in learning.

SELECTED READING LIST

Mettler, Barbara. *Materials of Dance as a Creative Art Activity.* Tucson: Mettler Studios.

Rowen, Betty. *Learning Through Movement.* New York: Teachers College Press.

Sheehy, Emma. *Children Discover Music and Dance.* New York: Teachers College Press.

SELECTED RECORD LIST FOR MOVEMENT

Capital: *Listen, Move and Dance.* (Vols. 1 & 2; classics, modern & electronic music).

Bowmar: *Classroom Concert; Children's Rhythms in Symphony; Pictures and Patterns* (a wide variety of good, short selections and teaching suggestions).

[3]Abraham Maslow. Music education and peak experience. *Music Educators Journal,* Feb. 1968.

[4]As expressed by Helen Lanfer, Music Education Specialist.

UNICEF: *Album II, 1959* (ethnic music from Africa, Japan, Brazil, Israel & Turkey).

FOLKWAYS: *Sounds of New Music* (avant garde); *1, 2, 3 and a Zing, Zing, Zing* (street chants and music improvisations): *I'll Sing a Song and You Sing a Song* (rhythmic tunes): *American Indian Dances (authentic music)*.

RCA Victor: Michael Herman's Folk Dance Series (omit directions).

Tikva: *Dance with the Sabras.* (exciting Israeli dances).

For more suggestions, catalogues may be obtained from Children's Music Center, 5373 West Pico Blvd., Los Angeles, Calif.

SOCIAL DEVELOPMENT IN EARLY CHILDHOOD

Social development represents the broadest area of child development, encompassing such concepts as self-image, sex-role differentiation, socialization, and prosocial skills. Yet rather than exploring each concept as a separate component in child growth, it is perhaps more compelling to view social development as a unique combination of skills that lead children to feel a sense of mastery and control over their daily lives. This development of human competence involves skills that help children deal effectively with the people, objects, and events in their environment. In this chapter, the authors address the issue of how children become competent adults; they examine what kinds of early experiences promote feelings of mastery over the environment, and they offer suggestions for how to structure experiences to foster the growth of competence in young children.

Ainsworth and Bell's work focuses on the growth of infant competence, correlating maternal-infant attachment with infant exploration, psychomotor development, and the attainment of object permanence. And looking at slightly older children, Baumrind describes how child-rearing practices and different types of parenting styles relate to the development of what she calls "instrumental competence." Her article analyzes how the socialization process affects boys and girls differently in the growth of socially responsible and independent behavior.

Yet children learn social competence not only from parent-child interactions but also from self-discovery, peer interaction, and environmental feedback. One of the first aspects of self-concept which children learn is their gender identity—"I am a boy/girl." Kohlberg and Ullian's work explores how and why children attain their knowledge of gender identity and their stereotypic attitudes on sex-role differentiation.

Although the primary means of fostering competence have traditionally been in the home, the schools have also attempted to build social skills. Kohlberg looks at how schools have tried to instill social and moral conduct; he cites unsuccessful attempts at preaching virtues, and he examines the current approaches to moral education. His research demonstrates the vital role that teacher-child interactions also play in the development of competence. Yet when dealing with the daily misbehavior of children, teachers are confronted by a confusing and often contradictory array of techniques for disciplining children. The article by Glickman and Wolfgang offers a coherent look at these diverse methods of controlling child behavior by outlining the major theoretical models and suggesting specific approaches to discipline that derive from those models. Their work also examines the implications of each discipline technique for the growth of competence in children.

As Almy eloquently argues in her article, self-initiated play is an important vehicle for the development of competence in children; through play, children try out new ways of coping with their environment. But if toys and play are so crucial to the growth of competence, what happens to children who are unable to play? Wolfgang's work on passive and aggressive children formulates specific principles of intervention that provide structure for these children within a free play situation. His article also provides an extensive list of materials and play themes to use in helping children play constructively and competently.

MARY D. SALTER AINSWORTH and
SILVIA M. BELL

14. Mother–Infant Interaction and the Development of Competence

Competence in infancy may be defined in three major ways, and in each case it is illuminating to consider the neonate as well as the older infant. First, competence may be defined in terms of cognitive abilities and motor skills. In these terms an infant, especially a neonate, must be assessed as incompetent and helpless, both absolutely and when compared with an older child or an adult. At the beginning, for example, he cannot reach out and grasp an object that interests him. He becomes more competent later when he can do so, and his competence in this regard can increase as his speed, precision, and control increases. This definition of competence is obviously useful when one is concerned with a child's development towards adult ability. On the other hand, it tends to minimize the effectiveness of an infant's behaviour and to neglect the extent to which it is preadapted to perform vital biological functions.

The second definition implies age- or stage-relevant assessment. An infant is competent to the extent that he functions well in the various situations that an infant normally encounters. As a neonate his competence rests on the adequacy of patterns of reflex activity (reflex schemata, or fixed action patterns), and hence upon the integrity of his neural, muscular, and sensory equipment. A competent neonate thus, for example, sucks well and cries lustily; a relatively incompetent one might suck or cry weakly. This view gives an infant his due as an infant, and also takes into account the fact that much of his competence rests, particularly at the beginning, upon the efficiency of his preadapted equipment. According to this view competence is most appropriately assessed relative to age peers. This is, of course, the core of the age-scale principle of assessing intelligence; it has been a useful principle. Its chief shortcoming, as applied to infancy, is that a baby's preadapted behaviours cannot be effective in performing the functions for which they were selected (in an evolutionary sense) should his environment depart unduly from the environment to which they were originally adapted. Thus it matters little how well a baby cries or roots or sucks if no one heeds the signal of his crying, and no one picks him up and makes a nutritive nipple available enough that he can find it and suck it.

A third view of competence views neonatal patterns as adapted to an environment that contains an accessible mother figure whose responsive reciprocal behaviour is to a substantial extent under the control of the

From Mary D. Salter Ainsworth and Silvia M. Bell, "Mother–Infant Interaction and the Development of Competence," in Kevin Connolly and Jerome Bruner, *The Growth of Competence*, 1974, pp. 97–118, omitting references to earlier chapters in the book. Reprinted with permission of Developmental Sciences Trust.

144

infant's behaviour. This implies that at first an infant's competence rests, in most essential respects, upon the co-operation of his mother figure. This defines an infant's competence as his effectiveness. An infant is competent to the extent that he can, through his own activity, control the effect that his environment will have on him. This definition includes such matters as controlling when and how he is fed and control of his proximity to companions, as well as control of the continuation or recurrence of interesting sights and sounds or control of reaching out and grasping an interesting object.

This definition of competence implies a competent mother–infant pair—an infant who is competent in his pre-adapted function (as in our second definition) and a mother who is competent in the reciprocal role to which the infant's behaviour is pre-adapted. The infant in such a competent pair is effective in getting what he wants, at least in part, because he can influence the behaviour of a responsive mother. It is our hypothesis that this fosters the further growth of the competence of the infant both in absolute terms and in terms of increasing skill in enlisting the cooperation of others.

According to this view, an infant who is initially relatively incompetent in the sense of inefficient function may, when paired with a mother highy responsive to the signals implicit in his behaviour, gradually increase his effectiveness in dealing with his environment, both physical and social. On the other hand, an infant, competent enough in his pre-adapted behaviours, may be ineffective in getting what he wants, if paired with a mother unresponsive to his signals. As a pair, this couple is relatively incompetent. The infant himself, although competent in his initial functioning, is ineffective. Such initial ineffectiveness tends to hamper the further development of his sensorimotor and social skills, and hence adversely affects the development of competence relative to his more favoured age-peers. Finally, of course, an initially malfunctioning infant may be paired with an unresponsive mother; this is the condition with the poorest prognosis for the development of infant competence. In the ultimate biological terms of survival this third view of competence is the crucial one.

Furthermore, one facet of competence, important throughout the entire life span, is social competence—the ability of the person to elicit the cooperation of others. According to our third definition of competence, maternal responsiveness provides the conditions for a normally functioning infant to influence what happens to him by influencing the behaviour of his mother. This, we believe, fosters a general "sense of competence" (White, 1963), and a sense of competence—or confidence—influences the development of increased competence in other realms, whether viewed in age-relevant or in absolute terms.

CRYING, COMMUNICATION, MATERNAL RESPONSIVENESS AND SOCIAL COMPETENCE

Central to social competence is effective communication. So let us begin by considering communication in mother–infant interaction to which

Richards (1974) attributes primary significance. Perhaps the most important contributions an infant makes to mother–infant interaction are his signalling behaviours, especially crying, through which he can attract his mother from a distance into closer proximity. Although to a sensitive mother an infant's entire behavioural repertoire may have signalling value, it can scarcely perform this function if she is not close enough to perceive his other signals hence the special significance of crying as a signal.

These early signals at first imply no intent to communicate. It seems unlikely that communication can become fully intentional until Stage 4 of the sensorimotor period (Piaget, 1936) or until there is a shift from fixed-action patterns to goal-corrected behaviour (Bowlby, 1969)—that is, not until the last three or four months of the first year. Nevertheless, long before an infant can intentionally seek to influence the behaviour of his companions, he does in fact exert a measure of control through the expressive, signalling quality of his behaviour. Through interaction with them his signalling behaviour may become increasingly differentiated and effective in influencing their response to him.

Elsewhere (Bell and Ainsworth, 1972) we have presented findings pertinent to the argument that the responsiveness of a mother figure to infant signals promotes the development of infant communication and hence the development of social competence. These findings emerged from a short-term longitudinal study of the development of infant–mother attachment in the first year of life. The subjects were 26 infant–mother pairs from white, middle-class, Baltimore families. They were observed in their own homes at intervals of three weeks, each visit lasting approximately four hours. The raw data are in the form of detailed narrative reports. A variety of coding, rating, and classificatory procedures have been used in the data analysis.

The signalling behaviour that concerned us in the above mentioned analysis was crying. Each instance of crying that occured in the course of a home visit was coded. Among the particulars coded were: the duration of the cry, whether the mother responded to it or ignored it, and, if she responded to it, how long she delayed before responding. We were interested in ascertaining whether a mother's responsiveness was associated with a change in the incidence and duration of infant crying in the course of the first year. We were also interested in teasing out the direction of effects—a difficult matter in a naturalistic study which must use correlational procedures.

First, a word about our procedures. Our infant crying measures included fussing as well as crying, and very brief cries as well as full-blown, prolonged crying. There were two measures of infant crying: (a) the frequency of crying episodes per waking hour, and (b) the total duration of crying in minutes per waking hour. The two measures of maternal responsiveness that are relevant to this report are: (a) the number of crying episodes that a mother altogether ignored, and (b) the duration of maternal unresponsiveness—the length of time in minutes per waking hour that a baby cried without or before an intervention by the mother.

The first step in our analysis was to examine the stability of infant crying throughout the first year and to compare it with the stability of maternal responsiveness to crying over the same period. Do infants who cry relatively frequently at the beginning continue to cry relatively frequently throughout the first year? Are there constitutional differences in irritability that make some infants cry more than others both at first and throughout the first year? Our findings suggested that there is not stability in infant crying until the very end of the first year, and therefore no support for the view that babies who cry more than others at the end of the first year do so because they are constitutionally irritable.

Mothers were found to be substantially more stable in their responsiveness to infant crying than infants in their tendency to cry. Their responsiveness in each quarter-year was significantly related to their responsiveness in the previous quarter. This stability was particularly striking in regard to the duration measure, the length of time a baby cried without or before maternal intervention. The first and second quarters, as well as the third quarter, were significantly correlated with the fourth quarter.

The second step was to consider the intercorrelations between infant crying and maternal responsiveness. Table 1 shows the correlation between the number of crying episodes ignored by the mother and the frequency of infant crying episodes. There are three parts of the table upon which to focus. The first is the diagonal, which gives the correlation of maternal behaviour and infant behaviour in the same quarter. The second is the six-celled lower left portion of the matrix, which shows the correlation of maternal behaviour in each quarter with infant behaviour in subsequent quarters. The third part is the six-celled upper right portion of the matrix which gives the correlation of crying in each quarter with maternal ignoring in subsequent quarters.

Let us first consider the information on the diagonal. Here it was necessary to introduce a correction for the confounding of measures. The confounding consists in the fact that the number of crying episodes (within a quarter) includes those that the mother ignored as well as those to which she responded. The correction consisted of excluding from the infant measure those episodes that the mother ignored. After this correction is made it is evident that the extent to which a mother ignores crying and the frequency with which an infant cries are not significantly related either

TABLE 1. Episodes of Crying Ignored by the Mother and Frequency of Crying*

| Frequency of Crying | Episodes Ignored by the Mother | | | |
	First Quarter	Second Quarter	Third Quarter	Fourth Quarter
First quarter	−0.04	0.34	0.48†	0.21
Second quarter	0.56†	0.35	0.32	0.29
Third quarter	0.21	0.39†	0.42†	0.40†
Fourth quarter	0.20	0.36	0.52‡	0.45†

*The figures in italics have been corrected to avoid confounding.
†p 0.05.
‡p 0.01.

within the first or within the second quarter. Within each of the third and fourth quarters, however, babies who cry more frequently have mothers who more frequently ignore their crying.

The lower left portion of the matrix shows that from the beginning of the first year maternal ignoring in each quarter correlates significantly with infant crying in the subsequent quarter. (A correction was not necessary here, because the frequency with which a baby cries in one quarter is not confounded with the number of episodes which his mother ignores in another quarter.) Thus tiny babies do not respond immediately to maternal ignoring by crying more frequently, but from the end of the third month onward they tend to be more insistent in their crying as a result of the past history of mother's ignoring tactics. Finally, the upper right hand portion of the matrix suggests that there is no consistent tendency for an infant's crying in one quarter to be associated with maternal ignoring in the following quarter, until the fourth quarter.

These findings, together with the findings on stability, summarized earlier, suggest that maternal ignoring increases the likelihood that a baby will cry relatively more frequently from the second quarter onward, whereas the frequency of *his* crying has no consistent influence on the number of episodes his mother will be likely subsequently to ignore.

Table 2 shows a comparable analysis of the relation between the duration of maternal unresponsiveness and the duration of infant crying. For intra-quarter comparisons, those shown on the diagonal, there was again a correction for confounding since the duration of an infant's crying includes both the time during which his mother was unresponsive and the time he continued to cry after she intervened. The corrected measure deals only with the time he cried after she intervened. When this measure is used, it may be seen that babies whose mothers are unresponsive in the first quarter do not cry more (after intervention) than those whose mothers are responsive. But within each of the second, third and fourth quarters, babies with unresponsive mothers do cry more.

For inter-quarter comparisons there is no confounding of measures and hence no correction. The lower left portion of the matrix shows that babies

TABLE 2. Duration of Mother's Unresponsiveness to Crying and Duration of Crying*

| Duration of Crying | Mother's Unresponsiveness | | | |
	First Quarter	Second Quarter	Third Quarter	Fourth Quarter
First quarter	0.19	0.37	0.12	0.41†
Second quarter	0.45†	0.67‡	0.51‡	0.69‡
Third quarter	0.40†	0.42†	0.39†	0.52‡
Fourth quarter	0.32	0.65‡	0.51‡	0.61‡

*The figures in italics have been corrected to avoid confounding.
†p 0.05.
‡p 0.01.

whose mothers were unresponsive in the first quarter tend to cry more in subsequent quarters, and that, generally, maternal unresponsiveness in one quarter is associated with longer duration of crying in subsequent quarters. The upper right-hand cells differ, however, from those of the previous table. It appears that by the second half of the first year infants who persistently cry for long periods tend to make mothers more than ever reluctant to respond. This suggests that a vicious spiral may have been established. Mothers who are unresponsive to the crying of their tiny infants have babies who cry more later on, which in turn further discourages the mother from responding promptly, and results in relatively increased infant crying.

These findings are of considerable interest in themselves, perhaps especially since they fail to confirm the common belief that to respond promptly to a baby's cry will strengthen his tendency to cry on subsequent occasions. But let us consider the findings within the context of the various concepts of competence. Even though crying may be age-appropriate at the beginning of the first year, substantially diminished crying is appropriate towards the end of the first year and later. It is evident that maternal unresponsiveness to crying does not diminish it. On the contrary, it tends to prolong this primitive form of signalling up to at least the end of the first year. If, however, an infant's competence is viewed as depending on his mother's cooperativeness, one might argue that a one-year-old (albeit to a lesser extent than a neonate) still must be able to signal effectively if he is to be deemed competent. What has happened to the signalling behaviour of infants whose mothers have been relatively responsive?

This question led us to assess infant communication in the fourth quarter of the first year. A seven-point rating scale was constructed, which took into consideration facial expression, gesture, and non-crying vocalizations. At the positive pole of the scale was a wide variety of subtle yet clear modes of communication (as described by the observer in his narrative report, and without taking into account maternal response to the communication). At the negative pole was a limited variety in modes of signalling, and signals that were difficult to "read". (The seven-point scale was subsequently collapsed into a three-point scale, in the interests of obtaining good inter-rater agreement, but the poles retained this definition.) Table 3 shows the relationship between our ratings of communication and infant crying on the one hand and maternal responsiveness on the other. It may be seen that there are substantial negative correlations between infant communication and the frequency and duration of crying. Babies who cried little had a wider range of differentiated modes of communication than did babies who cried much. Furthermore, it is clear that those mothers who were responsive to infant crying, ignoring few episodes and responding with little delay, have infants who have more variety, subtlety and clarity of non-crying communication.

It is not suggested that this relationship is entirely attributable to maternal responsiveness to crying. There is good reason to believe that those mothers in our sample who are relatively responsive to crying are also responsive to a wide range of other infant signals. We assessed such responsiveness by a rating scale designed to measure a mother's sensitivity-

TABLE 3. Infant Communication in the Fourth Quarter, Crying and Maternal Responsiveness

	Fourth Quarter Infant Communication
Duration of crying	−0.71*
Frequency of crying	−0.65*
Mother's unresponsiveness	−0.63*
Episodes ignored by mother	−0.54*

*P 0.01.

insensitivity to infant signals. (The rating scale is reproduced in Ainsworth *et al.*, 1974.) Sensitivity–insensitivity ratings have significant negative correlations with maternal ignoring of crying episodes ($r = -0.41$; $p < 0.05$) and with duration of maternal unresponsiveness to crying ($r = -0.58$; $p < 0.01$. It therefore seems likely that it is a mother's responsiveness to non-crying signals as well as to the more obvious and urgent crying signals that facilitates the development of a differentiated repertoire of non-crying modes of communication. Thus maternal responsiveness to signals supports the development of a variety of communicative behaviours which are easy to read and hence are likely to influence the behaviour of others in a more differentiated way than an infant can through merely crying.

COMPETENCE IN DIRECT DEALING WITH THE PHYSICAL ENVIRONMENT

Important though social competence may be, one can further ask about the manner in which mother–infant interaction may influence those aspects of cognitive development that imply a direct interaction with the physical environment and the gaining of control over it—rather than the indirect control gained through influencing the behaviour of others. There seem to be at least three important ways in which mother-infant interaction might influence the development of an infant's competence in direct interaction with his physical environment and the objects in it.

First, it seems reasonable to suppose that maternal behaviour might facilitate the development of abilities directly pertinent to an infant's dealings with his physical environment. Thus, for example, in the course of being held by his mother, his adjustment of posture to the shifts of position occasioned by her movements might well accelerate the acquisition of control over head and trunk musculature, which in turn would accelerate the development of locomotion, and consequent exploration and manipulation of his physical environment. Similarly, it has been suggested (Piaget, 1937, 1954) that the mother, in the course of interacting with him, is the one object who can serve as "aliment" simultaneously to many of the infant's schemata, and thus promotes their inter-coordination and his general development. It can be further argued (Bell, 1971) that the mother's initiative in introducing her child to stimulating conditions through play has an increasingly important role in the course of cognitive development from the end of the first year of life onwards.

Second, even when she is not in interaction with him, a mother may substantially influence the kind of experience an infant can have with his environment. For example, she may provide interesting objects for him to see when he is lying in his crib rather than a barren visual surround; she may tuck him up so his hands are not free, or leave him free to use his hands. When he has become mobile, she may give him freedom to explore interesting facets of his environment, or she may confine him in a playpen.

Third, a baby's experience with his mother may have an indirect effect on his dealings with the rest of his world through affecting his confidence. This confidence has at least two noteworthy aspects—confidence in her and confidence in himself. Trust in her may well be a necessary condition for him to venture forth to explore the world, this will be discussed later. Confidence in himself may also be affected by his experience with her, through fostering a "sense of competence". It seems reasonable to suppose that the more consistently an infant has experienced effective control of what happens to him as a consequence of his own activity, the more likely he is to approach a new object or new situation with the expectation that he can control its effect on him. Thus it seems likely that an infant whose mother's responsiveness has given him frequent experiences of affecting what happens to him (through affecting her behaviour) would have influenced his confidence in his own ability to act effectively on his environment.

When attempting to ascertain the effect of maternal behaviour on the development of an infant's competence it is very difficult to sort out those particular aspects of her behaviour that may have been responsible for any specific effect that might be attributed to her. Despite this difficulty, there are a few findings from our investigation of the development of infant–mother attachment and related studies which suggest generally that maternal behaviour can influence the development of infant competence.

Maternal Behaviour and Intelligence

The first of these findings relates to infant intelligence as measured by the Griffiths (1954) Scale. Whether or not such measures predict later I.Q. at least they may be accepted as valid assessments of developmental level in infancy, and as such may be considered overall measures of the level of competence achieved by an infant. In the course of our longitudinal study of the development of infant–mother attachment, the Griffiths test was administered at intervals of approximately nine weeks during the first year. The measure that concerns us here is the mean "General Quotient" for the tests undertaken in the fourth quarter-year.

The analysis of the relationship between maternal behaviour and infant intelligence is a reworking of the correlational matrix presented by Stayton et al. (1971), which was concerned with the relationship of infant obedience and infant I.Q. The correlation matrix is shown in Table 4. The first three variables were measured by nine-point rating scales. Maternal sensitivity-

TABLE 4. Intercorrelations Between Maternal Variables and Infant I.Q.

Variables	1	2	3	4	5	6
1. Sensitivity–insensitivity	. . .					
2. Acceptance–rejection	0.91†	. . .				
3. Cooperation–interference	0.87†	0.88†	. . .			
4. Frequency of verbal commands	−0.14	−0.05	−0.35	. . .		
5. Frequency of physical interventions	−0.44*	−0.38	−0.59†	0.62†	. . .	
6. Floor freedom	0.07	0.00	0.10	−0.03	0.07	. . .
7. Infant I.Q.	0.46*	0.45*	0.44*	0.06	0.06	0.46*

*p 0.05.
†p 0.01.

insensitivity to infant signals was mentioned earlier. This and the two other variables, acceptance–rejection and cooperation–interference, were described briefly by Stayton *et al.* The frequency of mother's verbal commands and the frequency of her physical interventions in lieu of, or to reinforce commands were derived from coding and refer to the mean number of such behaviours per visit. Floor freedom refers to the degree to which a baby was permitted to be free on the floor during his waking hours; two groups were distinguished, those given relatively much and those given relatively little floor freedom. It may be seen that four of the six maternal variables have a significant, moderate, positive relationship with infant I.Q.—floor freedom and the three rated variables.

Table 5 shows the results of a stepwise regression using these six maternal variables, with infant I.Q. as the criterion variable. Although all three rated variables (sensitivity–insensitivity, acceptance–rejection, and cooperation–interference) were significantly related to infant I.Q. they were so highly correlated with each other that the addition of a second or third to the regression equation effected little or no increase in the multiple correlation coefficient. However, when floor freedom was added to the first of the rated variables, maternal sensitivity–insensitivity, the R was raised to 0.63. The addition of two other variables raised the multiple correlation coefficient to 0.70, and the addition of the last two variables effected no further increase.

TABLE 5. Stepwise Multiple Regression: Infant I.Q. as Criterion Variable

Step Number	Variable Entered	R with I.Q.
1	Sensitivity–insensitivity	0.46
2	Floor Freedom	0.63
3	Frequency of physical interventions	0.67
4	Cooperation–interference	0.70
5	Acceptance–rejection	0.70
6	Frequency of verbal commands	0.70

The correlation matrix in Table 4 was not originally assembled with the prediction of infant I.Q. in mind, and obviously omits a number of variables that ought to be included in such an analysis, for example, parents' education and occupation, stimulating nature of physical environment provided in the home, and parental encouragement of the acquisition of verbal and motor skills. Nevertheless the findings of the stepwise regression analysis are suggestive. Mothers who both are sensitive to infant signals *and* permit their babies freedom of movement to explore the world on their own account tend to have babies who are relatively accelerated in psychomotor development, whereas mothers who are insensitive to signals *and* who limit their infants' opportunity to interact with their physical environment tend to have babies who are relatively retarded in development.

The contribution of floor freedom to the development of competence seems obvious. The contributions of maternal sensitivity to signals is perhaps less immediately apparent. It suggests that the behaviour characteristic of the sensitive mother has, as Piaget proposed, a facilitating effect on the development of the infant's ability to deal with his physical environment. It also fits the hypothesis, advanced earlier, that a baby whose signals are responded to promptly and appropriately builds up a sense of competence—a confidence that he can through his own activity control what happens to him—and this confidence carries over into his transactions with his physical environment.

Substantial confirmation of these findings comes from two sources. First, Beckwith (1971) studied twenty-four adopted infants living in middle-class families, in order to control possible confoundings of genetic effects and maternal behaviour. She used two composite measures of maternal behaviour derived from time-sampled observations during home visits. One measure was "stimulation" which combined scores on verbal and physical contact; another was a measure of restrictiveness of exploration. A highly significant relationship was found between these measures and Cattell intelligence scores. Low maternal verbal and physical contact plus high maternal restrictiveness of exploration significantly lowered I.Q.

Second, one of us (S.M.B.), in the course of a longitudinal study of thirty-three black socio-economically underprivileged children, obtained findings of the relation between the quality of the infant–mother attachment, floor freedom and I.Q. which closely parallel those outlined above. The children in this study were tested repeatedly during the first two years of life on several measures of cognitive development, the Griffiths Scale and two tests of the object concept. In addition they were observed in free play and in interaction with their mothers for a two-hour period subsequent to each testing. An informal interview was also conducted with the mother in each session for the purpose of evaluating the stimulating potential of the home environment, parental education, and other pertinent factors. The findings relevant to the concern of this paper are presented in Table 6 and show the correlation between I.Q. at two age levels, some of the variables assessed in interview, and a measure of the observed quality of the infant–mother attachment relationship.

At both eight and eleven months, floor freedom and a harmonious

TABLE 6. Correlation of I.Q. at Two Age Levels with: Stimulating Potential of the Environment, Quality of the Infant-Mother Attachment, and Several Variables of Maternal Care

	I.Q. Eight Months	I.Q. Eleven Months
Stimulating potential of environment: eight months		
Floor freedom	0.61†	0.34†
Toys	0.43†	0.13
Amount of play	0.14	0.04
Stimulating potential of environment: eleven months		
Floor freedom	0.56†	0.57†
Toys	0.45†	0.41†
Amount of play	0.21	0.34*
Quality of infant-mother attachment	0.55†	0.46†
Maternal variables		
Verbal stimulation	0.18	0.23
Frequency of punishment	−0.24	−0.34*
Education	0.16	0.08

*P 0.05.
†P 0.01.

infant-mother attachment relationship were found to be highly correlated with I.Q. Availability of toys also showed a significant, but lower, correlation with I.Q. at both age levels. Amount of time that adults or other children spent in playing with the baby was positively correlated with I.Q. towards the end of the first year. Frequency of punishment was negatively and moderately correlated with development at eleven months. Parental education, in contrast, was not significantly correlated with infant I.Q. at either eight or eleven months.

This table presents only a part of the total matrix of variables reported by Bell (1971). The larger matrix was subjected to a factor analysis, with Varimax rotation. The first factor, which accounted for 52% of the variance, was defined primarily by high loadings on the cognitive tests, including I.Q., at the two age levels, the quality of the infant-mother attachment relationship, and floor freedom. Availability of toys at eleven months loaded primarily, but only moderately, on this factor. Since the quality of the infant-mother attachment relationship, observed in this study, is largely a function of the degree of maternal sensitivity characteristic of the transactions between mother and infant (Bell, 1970) the findings corroborate the conclusions of Ainsworth's and Beckwith's studies discussed above.

The Use of the Mother as a Secure Base from Which to Explore

We have often emphasized one significant outcome of infant-mother attachment, namely, that an infant can use his mother as a secure base from which to explore his world (Ainsworth, 1967; Ainsworth and Bell, 1970; Ainsworth *et al.*, 1971; Salter, 1940). The fact that a baby has become attached to his mother does not mean that he constantly seeks to be in contact, close proximity, or even in interaction with her. On the contrary, he may leave her often on his own initiative and may move about, interested in investigating his surroundings and the objects and other people in it. He keeps track of his mother's whereabouts, however, and tends to return to her briefly from time to time before moving off again. He may go out of sight in the course of his explorations, showing no sign of fear, presumably because he knows where his mother is and expects her to remain accessible to him. But should his mother get up to leave the room, he may well abandon his explorations and scuttle after her, or perhaps merely gravitate to where she now is. It is her presence that provides him with a secure base from which to explore.

The secure-base phenomenon may be viewed within the context of Bowlby's (1969) control-systems model of attachment behaviour. There are at least two systems of behaviour that are in dynamic balance with each other, attachment behaviour that promotes proximity to an attachment figure and exploratory behaviour (including locomotion, manipulation, visual investigation, and exploratory play) that promotes acquisition of knowledge of the environment and adaptation to environmental variations. The balance is tipped towards exploration by complex, novel, or changing features of the environment, provided that these are not so sudden, intense, or strange as to provoke alarm. The balance is tipped towards proximity seeking by a number of conditions, both intra-organismic and environmental. Important among the environmental conditions that heightens a child's attachment behaviour are alarm and threatened or actual separation from the attachment figure. Obviously, if attachment behaviour were constantly activated at a high level a child's development would be greatly hampered for he would not be attracted away from his attachment figure to explore his world. Perhaps not so obviously, if his exploratory behaviour constantly overrode his attachment behaviour then his survival would be threatened, unless his mother were constantly vigilant to retrieve him from danger.

An optimum balance between exploratory and attachment behaviour would seem to be a favourable condition for cognitive development and thus, for the development of competence. It is by no means easy to study the attachment–exploration balance, however. Our first attempt to do so prompted us to devise a strange-situation procedure (Ainsworth and Wittig, 1969). When observing a baby at home it was not clear whether it was his mother who was providing the secure base for his exploration of his whole familiar home environment. In an unfamiliar laboratory situation, however, it was intended to tip the balance towards exploration by providing an attractive display of toys at a distance from the mother. If a baby left his mother to explore the toys when she was present and ceased to explore when she was absent, it could be inferred that her presence provided security for his exploration. A majority of one-year-olds, both in our longitudinal sample and in Bell's (1970) project, did in fact behave as our hypothesis predicted they would (Ainsworth and Bell, 1970). There were striking individual differences, however, especially (a) in the extent to which attachment behaviour replaced exploratory behaviour during the brief separation episodes of the strange situation and in the reunion episodes that followed, and (b) in the intensity and quality of attachment behaviour in the reunion episodes.

Babies were classified into three groups chiefly in terms of their attachment behaviour in the reunion episodes (Ainsworth *et al.*, 1971). Group A infants tended neither to maintain contact with the mother nor to seek proximity to her even in the reunion episodes following brief separation, but rather conspicuously avoided proximity to her and interaction with her. Group B infants' attachment behaviour was heightened by separation; in the reunion episodes they actively sought to be near the mother, to gain and to maintain contact with her, or, at least to establish interaction with her. The attachment behaviour of Group C infants was also heightened by separation but was of highly ambivalent quality.

In an attempt to throw light upon these individual differences, assessments were made of the behaviour of mother and infant at home. Maternal behaviour was rated on four nine-point rating scales; sensitivity-insensitivity to infant signals, acceptance–rejection, and cooperation-interference, which were mentioned earlier, and also accessibility-ignoring. Whereas all the mothers of Group B infants were above the median on each of four scales, the mothers of both Group A and Group C infants were below the median on all scales. Group A mothers were especially rejecting, whereas Group C mothers were not, although they were either strongly interfering or very inaccessible.

In regard to infant behaviour we tackled the difficult job of assessing attachment–exploration balance as it appeared in behaviour in the familiar home environment. In advance of this analysis symmetrical findings were expected, with a majority showing a smooth balance between attachment and exploratory behaviour but with some having the balance tipped towards exploratory behaviour with less than average attachment behaviour, and others having the balance tipped towards attachment behaviour with less than average exploratory behaviour. The findings (reported by Ainsworth *et al.*, 1971) did not turn out precisely according to expectation. It seemed to be not so much the quantitative ratio of exploratory to attachment behaviour that was significant as the smoothness of the transition from one to the other, and the quality of the attachment behaviour when it was activated.

The strange-situation classification showed remarkable congruence with the classification of attachment–exploration balance at home. At home all but one of the thirteen Group B babies showed at least a fairly smooth kind of transition between exploratory and attachment behaviour. They were not especially clingy; they enjoyed physical contact with their mothers when it occured, but they were content to be put down and to move off into independent activity. They tended to follow their mothers about in a casual way, but tended not to be distressed by minor everyday situations in the familiar home environment. Three infants (two A and one B) did seem to have the balance tipped towards exploratory behaviour with relatively infrequent attachment behaviour. But the remaining eight subjects (four A and four C) seemed not so much to show below average exploratory behaviour as disturbances in the infant–mother attachment relationship. Their attachment behaviour was ambivalent, and they were more insecure than the average, crying relatively frequently, and especially prone to separation anxiety.

One of us (S.M.B.) is currently studying the quality of investigative behaviour and exploratory play, and its relation to maternal behaviour and to the quality of the infant–mother attachment relationship. In the course of studying the cognitive development of black underprivileged children mentioned earlier (Bell, 1971), infants were observed with their mothers in a free-play situation for a two-hour period several times in the first three years of life. Each session was subsequently coded for infant exploration and for maternal behaviour. The coding of infant exploration consisted of: (a) noting all the behaviours shown by the child and all the toys explored in the course of the session, and (b) ascertaining the number of different schemata exhibited and the cognitive level of the play. The coding of maternal behaviour referred primarily to: (a) the qualitative and quantitative engagement of the mother with the toys and the child during his exploration, and (b) the quality and quantity of her transactions with him unrelated to his exploration. The analysis of these data is still underway but results obtained for the last quarter of the first year indicated that there is a substantial relationship between an infant's competence and his mother's behaviour. Infants who had frequent harmonious transactions with their mother in the course of the play session, and whose mothers were generally responsive to their initiations of interaction (whether directly related to exploration or not), tended to explore more toys and, more important, to display more behavioural schemata in the course of play. In addition, infants who experienced frequent prolonged periods of play with their mother, or main caretaker, outside the observed play session, explored more toys and displayed a greater number of schemata and a more advanced level of play in the play session itself, than did infants whose mother figures did not characteristically spend time playing with them. The findings of this study suggest that variety of exploration and level of behavioural repertoire are associated with the general quality of the infant–mother relationship and also with the amount of time that a child spends in play and in one-to-one interaction with a significant attachment figure.

Mother–Infant Interaction and the Development of the Concept of the Object

One of us (Bell, 1970) compared the development of the concept of inanimate objects as permanent with the development of the concept of persons as permanent objects. A scale of object permanence was developed, based on Piaget's (1937) detailed observations, and a parallel scale of person permanence. The subjects were thirty-three infants of white, middle-class families who were tested on these two scales three times between the ages of 8½ and eleven months. Attention was directed towards the horizontal decalage between the two measures of development of the object concept.

The hypothesis was that infants who had enjoyed relatively harmonious interaction with their mothers in the course of the first year would be accelerated in person permanence in contrast with the concept of permanence of inanimate objects, while the reverse would hold for infants who had experienced relatively disharmonious interaction. The assessment of the degree of harmony of mother–infant interaction was indirect; the strange-situation technique was used to classify the infants, and as reported above, it is clear that Group B infants have more harmonious mother–infant interaction than do either Group A or Group C infants.

Twenty-four of the thirty-three infants in this sample could be classified in Group B in regard to strange-situation behaviour. Twenty-three of these had a positive decalage, being more advanced in the development of person permanence than in the development of the concept of the permanence of inanimate objects. One of them showed no decalage. None of the babies classified in either Group A or in Group C had a positive decalage. Four Group A babies showed a negative decalage, and one no decalage. Three Group C babies showed a negative decalage, and one no decalage. It was concluded that babies who have had a harmonious interaction with mothers sensitive to their signals, and who have developed an attachment relationship of normal quality, tend to develop person permanence in advance of inanimate-object permanence.

Once the relationship between the type of decalage and quality of attachment had been established, it was of interest to determine if those babies who had a positive decalage differed from the others in terms of the maximum level of the object concept they had achieved. For this analysis the negative and no decalage groups were combined. Figure 1 shows the mean scores on person permanence and object permanence at 8½ and eleven months. At both ages it may be seen that the person-permanence scores of the positive decalage group are significantly in advance of the object-permanence scores of the negative and no decalage group. At 8½ months the positive decalage group was facile in coping with the visible displacements of persons, and thus had nearly reached stage 6 in person permanence, although they were just beginning stage 5 in object permanence. The negative and no decalage group was significantly better in object permanence, and had scarcely begun to search for hidden persons, and hence were at the beginning of stage 4 in person permanence. By eleven months the majority of babies in the sample had begun to cope with invisible displacements of inanimate objects and thus had entered stage 6. Babies in the positive decalage group had also completed the higher substages of stage 6 in regard to person permanence, and thus had acquired an ability to handle complex invisible displacements of one type of object. About half of the babies were retested at 13½ months. Of these, a significantly higher number in the positive decalage group had completed the object-permanence scale than in the negative-no decalage group (Fisher, $p > 0.01$). In addition, the rate of development with respect to both object and person permanence was found to be significantly faster for the positive decalage group (Fisher, $p < 0.05$). This study indicated that the environmental circumstances that affect the quality of an infant's attachment to his mother—namely, maternal characteristics of perceptiveness, appropriate-

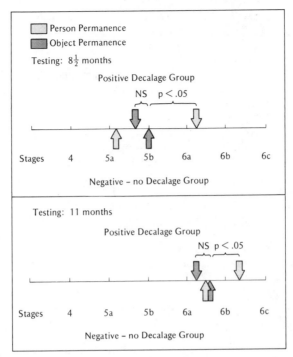

FIGURE 1. Mean scores on object and person permanence for the positive and negative–no decalage groups at 8½ and eleven months.

ness and contingency of responding subsumed under the label "sensitivity" —affect also an important aspect of cognitive development in the first two years of life.

Continuing with her work in this area, Bell undertook a study to evaluate the importance of the mother–infant relationship in affecting cognitive development, relative to ethnic and socio-economic factors. One aspect of the project (Bell, 1971), which was outlined in an earlier section of this chapter, aimed to study black under-privileged infants using procedures similar to those utilized in the (1970) study of white, middle-class infants. The results of the second study directly parallel those obtained in the first. There was a perfect correspondence between type of decalage and quality of infant–mother attachment; only those infants who had a positive decalage had had a harmonious relationship with the mother. Those infants who had a positive decalage were significantly more advanced in the development of the object concept than were the negative–no decalage group.

In addition, a comparison of the middle-class and socio-economically deprived samples revealed no differences in the level of the object concept at eight months, but significant differences in the level of both object and person permanence at eleven months, differences which favoured the middle-class sample (t significant at 0.01 level for both tests). But when the decalage subgroups were compared across socio-economic level, there were no differences in the level of the object concept at either eight or eleven months for those infants who had a positive decalage and had experienced a harmonious relationship with the mother. On the other hand, those infants in the low socio-economic sample who had experienced a disharmonious relationship with the mother were significantly inferior to the middle-class infants who had experienced disharmony. These findings suggest that, whereas the environmental conditions associated with socio-economic deprivation have a detrimental effect on cognitive development, a harmonious infant–mother relationship can act as a buffer protecting a child from their detrimental effect, and, in fact, is the single most important factor alleviating socio-economic disadvantage.

SUMMARY

Several sets of evidence have been offered to support the hypothesis that cognitive and social development are intimately interrelated, and that mother–infant interaction influences both. A mother's prompt responsiveness to her baby's signals tends to foster the development of varied and clear modes of communication and thus the development of one facet of social competence. Sensitive maternal responsiveness to infant signals, especially when combined with giving a baby freedom to explore his physical environment, facilitates the overall development of competence as measured by a general intelligence quotient. The quality of mother–infant interaction affects both the quality of a baby's attachment relationship with his mother and at least one important specific aspect of cognitive development, the development of the concept of the object. The balance between exploratory and attachment behaviour has been considered, and it has been suggested that the significance of this is not so much quantitative as qualitative. That is, the significant individual differences lie not so much in the relative quantities of attachment and exploratory behaviour as in the quality of each and the smoothness of the transition from one to the other. Evidence has been presented that the quality of mother–infant interaction influences the quality of the infant's attachment relationship to his mother, and that it also influences the level and quality of exploratory behaviour and play. These findings from one set of related studies have accomplished little more than demonstrating a relationship between mother–infant interaction and the development of competence. Further research is presently under way to yield more detailed knowledge of which specific aspects of the mother–infant relationship interact with other variables, both environmental and organismic, to affect the development of specific aspects of competence.

ACKNOWLEDGMENTS

This paper has been prepared while one author's (M.D.S.A.) research was supported by the Grant Foundation and the others' (S.M.B.) by the Office of Child Development (grant number OCD-CB-49) but acknowledgments are due also to the agencies which supported the earlier research upon which the paper is based, grant number 62–244 of the Foundations' Fund for Research in Psychiatry, USPHS grant number R01 01712, and grant number OEG-3-70-0036 of the Office of Education. We acknowledge with gratitude Donelda J. Stayton, our colleague in much of this research, whose study of infant obedience formed the basis for the analysis of the relationship of maternal variables to infant I.Q. in one of the samples, and Inge Bretherton who initiated and carried through that analysis. We also thank the many other research colleagues and student assistants who helped to collect and to analyse the data summarized in this paper, in particular Carolyn Bates whose enthusiasm and dedication were invaluable in enlisting and maintaining the cooperation of S.M.B.'s sample.

REFERENCES

Ainsworth, M. D. S. 1967. *Infancy in Uganda: infant care and the growth of love.* Johns Hopkins University Press, Baltimore.

Ainsworth, M. D. S. and Bell, S. M. 1970. Attachment, exploration, and separation: illustrated by the behavior of one-year-olds in a strange situation. *Child Dev.*, **41**, 49–67.

Ainsworth, M. D. S., Bell, S. M. V. and Stayton, D. J. 1971. Individual differences in strange-situation behaviour of one-year-olds. In H. R. Schaffer (Ed.), *The origins of human social relations.* Academic Press, London.

Ainsworth, M. D. S., Bell, S. M. V. and Stayton, D. J. 1974. Infant–mother attachment and social development: socialization as a product of reciprocal responsiveness to signals. In M. P. M. Richards (Ed.), *The integration of a child into a social world.* Cambridge University Press, Cambridge.

Ainsworth, M. D. S. and Wittig, B. A. 1969. Attachment and exploratory behavior of one-year-olds in a strange situation. In B. M. Foss (Ed.) *Determinants of infant behaviour IV.* Methuen, London.

Beckwith, L. 1971. Relationships between attributes of mothers and their infants' I.Q. scores. *Child Dev.*, 42, 1083–1097.

Bell, S. M. 1970. The development of the concept of object as related to infant–mother attachment. *Child Dev.*, 41, 291–311.

Bell, S. M. 1971. Early cognitive development and its relationship to infant–mother attachment: A study of disadvantaged Negro infants. Report prepared for the U.S. Office of Education, Project No. 00542.

Bell, S. M. and Ainsworth, M. D. S. 1972. Infant crying and maternal responsiveness. *Child Dev.*, 43, 1171–1190.

Bowlby, J. 1969. *Attachment and loss,* Vol. 1. *Attachment.* Hogarth Press, London; Basic Books, New York.

Griffiths, R. 1954. *The abilities of babies.* University of London Press, London.

Piaget, J. 1936. *The origins of intelligence in children,* 2nd ed. International Universities Press, New York, 1952.

Piaget, J. 1937. *The construction of reality in the child.* Basic Books, New York, 1954.

Piaget, J. 1954. *Les relations entre l'affectivité et l'intelligence dans le développement mental de l'enfant.* Centre de Documentation Universitaire, Paris.

Richards, M. P. M. 1974. The development of psychological communication in the first year of life. In K. Connolly and J. Bruner (Eds.), *The growth of competence.* Academic Press, New York.

Salter, M. D. 1940. *An evaluation of adjustment based upon the concept of security*. University of Toronto Studies, Child Development Series, No. 18. University of Toronto Press, Toronto.

Stayton, D. J., Hogan, R. and Ainsworth, M. D. S. 1971. Infant obedience and maternal behavior: the origins of socialization reconsidered. *Child. Dev.*, 42, 1057–1069.

White, R. W. 1963. *Ego and reality in psychoanalytic theory*. International Universities Press, New York.

DIANA BAUMRIND

15. Socialization and Instrumental Competence in Young Children

For the past 10 years I have been studying parent-child relations, focusing upon the effects of parental authority on the behavior of pre-school children. In three separate but related studies, data on children were obtained from three months of observation in the nursery school and in a special testing situation; data on parents were obtained during two home observations, followed by an interview with each parent.

In the first study, three groups of nursery school children were identified in order that the childrearing practices of their parents could be contrasted. The findings of that study (Baumrind, 1967) can be summarized as follows:

1. Parents of the children who were the most self-reliant, self-controlled, explorative and content were themselves controlling and demanding; but they were also warm, rational and receptive to the child's communication. This unique combination of high control and positive encouragement of the child's autonomous and independent strivings can be called *authoritative* parental behavior.

2. Parents of children who, relative to the others, were discontent, withdrawn and distrustful, were themselves detached and controlling, and somewhat less warm than other parents. These may be called *authoritarian* parents.

3. Parents of the least self-reliant, explorative and self-controlled children

Reprinted by permission from *Young Children*, Vol. 26, No. 2 (Dec. 1970), pp. 104–119. Copyright © 1970, National Association for the Education of Young Children, 1834 Connecticut Avenue, N.W., Washington, DC 20009.

162

were themselves noncontrolling, nondemanding, and relatively warm. These can be called *permissive* parents.

A second study, of an additional 95 nursery school children and their parents also supported the position that "authoritative control can achieve responsible conformity with group standards without loss of individual autonomy or self-assertiveness (Baumrind, 1966, p. 905)." In a third investigation (Baumrind, 1971), patterns of parental authority were defined so that they would differ from each other as did the authoritarian, authoritative, and permissive combinations which emerged from the first study.

PATTERNS OF PARENTAL AUTHORITY

Each of these three authority patterns is described in detail below, followed by the subpatterns that have emerged empirically from my most recent study. The capitalized items refer to specific clusters obtained in the analysis of the parent behavior ratings.

The *authoritarian* parent[1] attempts:

to shape, control and evaluate the behavior and attitudes of the child in accordance with a set standard of conduct, usually an absolute standard, theologically motivated and formulated by a higher authority. She values obedience as a virtue and favors punitive, forceful measures to curb self-will at points where the child's actions or beliefs conflict with what she thinks is right conduct. She believes in inculcating such instrumental values as respect for authority, respect for work, and respect for the preservation of order and traditional structure. She does not encourage verbal give and take, believing that the child should accept her word for what is right (Baumrind, 1968, p. 261).

Two subpatterns in our newest study correspond to this description; they differ only in the degree of acceptance shown the child. One subpattern identifies families who were Authoritarian but Not Rejecting. They were high in Firm Enforcement, low in Encourages Independence and Individuality, low in Passive-Acceptance, and low in Promotes Nonconformity. The second subpattern contained families who met all the criteria for the first subpattern except that they scored high on the cluster called Rejecting.

The *authoritative* parent, by contrast with the above, attempts:

to direct the child's activities but in a rational, issue-oriented manner. She encourages verbal give and take, and shares with the child the reasoning behind her policy. She values both expressive and instrumental attributes, both autonomous self-will and disciplined conformity. Therefore, she exerts firm control at points of parent-child divergence, but does not hem the child in with restrictions. She

[1]In order to avoid confusion, when I speak of the parent I will use the pronoun "she," and when I speak of the child, I will use the pronoun "he," although, unless otherwise specified, the statement applies to both sexes equally.

recognizes her own special rights as an adult, but also the child's individual interests and special ways. The authoritative parent affirms the child's present qualities, but also sets standards for future conduct. She uses reason as well as power to achieve her objectives. She does not base her decisions on group consensus or the individual child's desires; but also, does not regard herself as infallible or divinely inspired (Baumrind, 1968, p. 261).

Two subpatterns corresponded to this description, differing only in the parents' attitudes towards normative values. One subpattern contained families who were Authoritative and Conforming. Like the Authoritarian parents described above, these parents had high scores in Firm Enforcement and low scores in Passive-Acceptance. However, they also had high scores in Encourages Independence and Individuality. The second subpattern contained parents who met the criteria for the first subpattern, but who also scored high in Promotes Nonconformity.

The *permissive* parent attempts:

to behave in a nonpunitive, acceptant and affirmative manner towards the child's impulses, desires, and actions. She consults with him about policy decisions and gives explanations for family rules. She makes few demands for household responsibility and orderly behavior. She presents herself to the child as a resource for him to use as he wishes, not as an active agent responsible for shaping or altering his ongoing or future behavior. She allows the child to regulate his own activities as much as possible, avoids the exercise of control, and does not encourage him to obey externally-defined standards. She attempts to use reason but not overt power to accomplish her ends (Baumrind, 1968, p. 256).

We were able to locate three subpatterns reflecting different facets of this prototypic permissiveness. One subpattern, called Nonconforming, typified families who were nonconforming but who were not extremely lax in discipline and who did demand high performance in some areas. The second subpattern, called Permissive, contained families who were characterized by lax discipline and few demands, but who did not stress nonconformity. The third subpattern contained families who were both nonconforming and lax in their discipline and demands; hence, they are referred to as Permissive-Nonconforming.

INSTRUMENTAL COMPETENCE

Instrumental Competence refers to behavior which is socially responsible and independent. Behavior which is friendly rather than hostile to peers, cooperative rather than resistive with adults, achievement, rather than nonachievement-oriented, dominant rather than submissive, and purposive rather than aimless, is here defined as instrumentally competent. Middle-class parents clearly value instrumentally competent behavior. When such parents were asked to rank those attributes that they valued and devalued in children, the most valued ones were assertiveness, friendliness, independence and obedience, and those least valued were aggression, avoidance and dependency (Emmerich & Smoller, 1964). Note that the positively valued attributes promote successful achievement in United States society and, in fact, probably have survival value for the individual in any subculture or society.

There are people who feel that, even in the United States, those qualities which define instrumental competence are losing their survival value in favor of qualities which may be called *Expressive Competence.* The author does not agree. Proponents of competence defined in terms of expressive, rather than instrumental, attributes value feelings more than reason, good thoughts more than effective actions, "being" more than "doing" or "becoming," spontaneity more than planfulness, and relating intimately to others more than working effectively with others. At present, however, there is no evidence that emphasis on expressive competence, at the expense of instrumental competence, fits people to function effectively over the long run as members of any community. This is not to say that expressive competence is not essential for effective functioning in work as well as in love, and for both men and women. Man, like other animals, experiences and gains valid information about reality by means of both noncognitive and cognitive processes. Affectivity deepens man's knowledge of his environment; tenderness and receptivity enhance the character and effectiveness of any human being. But instrumental competence is and will continue to be an essential component of self-esteem and self-fulfillment.

One subdimension of instrumental competence, here designated *Responsible vs. Irresponsible,* pertains to the following three facets of behavior, each of which is related to the others:

a. *Achievement-oriented vs. Not Achievement-oriented.* This attribute refers to the willingness to persevere when frustration is encountered, to set one's own goals high; and to meet the demands of others in a cognitive situation versus withdrawal when faced with frustration and unwillingness to comply with the teaching or testing instructions of an examiner or teacher. Among older children, achievement-orientation becomes subject to autogenic motivation and is more closely related to measures of independence than to measures of social responsibility. But in the young child, measures of cognitive motivation are highly correlated with willingness to cooperate with adults, especially for boys. Thus, in my study, resistiveness towards adults was highly negatively correlated with achievement-oriented behavior for boys, but not for girls. Other investigators (Crandall, Orleans, Preston & Rabson, 1958; Haggard, 1969) have also found that compliance with adult values and demands characterize young children who display high achievement efforts.

b. *Friendly vs. Hostile Behavior Towards Peers.* This refers to nurturant, kind, altruistic behavior displayed toward agemates as opposed to bullying, insulting, selfish behavior.

c. *Cooperative vs. Resistive Behavior Towards Adults.* This refers to trustworthy, responsible, facilitative behavior as opposed to devious, impetuous obstructive actions.

A second dimension of child social behavior can be designated *Inde-*

165

pendent vs. Suggestible. It pertains to the following three related facets of behavior:

a. *Domineering vs. Tractable Behavior.* This attribute consists of bold, aggressive, demanding behavior as opposed to timid, nonintrusive, undemanding behavior.
b. *Dominant vs. Submissive Behavior.* This category refers to individual initiative and leadership in contrast suggestible, following behavior.
c. *Purposive vs. Aimless Behavior.* This refers to confident, charismatic, self-propelled activity versus disoriented, normative, goalless behavior.

The present review is limited to a discussion of instrumental competence and associated antecedent parental practices and is most applicable to the behavior of young children rather than adolescents. Several ancillary topics will be mentioned, but not discussed in depth, including:

The relation of IQ to instrumental competence. My own work and that of others indicate that, in our present society, children with high IQs are most likely to be achievement-oriented and self-motivated. The correlations between IQ and measures of purposiveness, dominance, achievement-orientation and independence are very high even by ages three and four.

The relation of moral development and conscience to instrumental competence. This area of research, exemplified by some of the work of Aronfreed, Kohlberg, Mussen, and Piaget, is of special importance with older age groups and will be covered tangentially when the antecedents of social responsibility are explored.

The relation of will to instrumental competence. This topic, which overlaps with the previous one, has received very little direct attention during the past 30 years. In the present review, this area is discussed to some extent along with antecedents of independence.

The antecedents of creative or scientific genius. Socialization practices which lead to competence are not the same as those associated with the development of high creativity or scientific genius. Most studies, such as those by Roe (1952) and Eiduson (1962), suggest that men of genius are frequently reared differently from other superior individuals. It has been found, for example, that as children men of genius often had little contact with their fathers, or their fathers died when they were young; they often led lonely, although cognitively enriched, existences. Such rearing cannot be recommended, however, since it is unlikely that the effects on most children, even those with superior ability, will be to produce genius or highly effective functioning.

The development of instrumental competence in disadvantaged families. The assumption cannot be made that the same factors relate to competence in disadvantaged families as in advantaged families. The effect of a single parental characteristic is altered substantially by the pattern of variables of which it is a part. Similarly, the effect of a given pattern of parental variables may be altered by the larger social context in which the family operates. The relations discussed here are most relevant for white middle-class families and may not always hold for disadvantaged families.

DEVELOPMENT OF INSTRUMENTAL INCOMPETENCE IN GIRLS

Rapid social changes are taking place in the United States which are providing equal opportunity for socially disadvantaged groups. If a socially disadvantaged group is one whose members are discouraged from fully developing their potentialities for achieving status and leadership in economic, academic and political affairs, women qualify as such a group.

There is little evidence that women are biologically inferior to men in intellectual endowment, academic potential, social responsibility or capacity for independence. Constitutional differences in certain areas may exist, but they do not directly generate sex differences in areas such as those mentioned. The only cognitive functions in which females have been shown consistently to perform less well than males are spatial relations and visualization. We really do not know to what extent the clearly inferior position women occupy in United States society today should be attributed to constitutional factors. The evidence, however, is overwhelming that socialization experiences contribute greatly to a condition of instrumental *incompetence* among women. It follows that if these conditions were altered, women could more nearly fulfill their occupational and intellectual potential. The interested reader should refer to Maccoby's excellent "Classified Summary of Research in Sex Differences" (1966, pp. 323–351).

Few women enter scientific fields and very few of these achieve eminence. According to the President's Commission on the Status of Women in 1963, the proportion of women to men obtaining advanced degrees is actually dropping. Yet there is little convincing evidence that females are constitutionally incapable of contributing significantly to science. Girls obtain better grades in elementary school than boys, and perform equally to boys on standard achievement tests, including tests of mathematical reasoning. By the high school years, however, boys score considerably higher than girls on the mathematical portion of the Scholastic Aptitude Test (Rossi, 1969). It is interesting to note that a high positive relation between IQ and later occupational levels holds for males, but does not hold for females (Terman & Oden, 1947). According to one study of physics students, girls have more scholastic aptitude and understanding of science and scientific processes than boys (Walberg, 1969). As Rossi has argued:

If we want more women to enter science, not only as teachers of science but as scientists, some quite basic changes must take place in the way girls are reared. If girls are to develop the analytic and mathematical abilities science requires, parents and teachers must encourage them in independence and self-reliance instead of pleasing feminine submission; stimulate and reward girls' efforts to satisfy their curiosity about the world as they do those of boys; encourage in girls not unthinking conformity but alert intelligence that asks why and rejects the easy answers [Rossi, 1969, p. 483].

Femininity and being female is socially devalued. Both sexes rate men as more worthwhile than women (e.g., McKee & Sherriffs, 1957). While boys of all ages show a strong preference for masculine roles, girls do not show a similar preference for feminine roles, and indeed, at certain ages, many girls as well as boys show a strong preference for masculine roles (Brown, 1958). In general, both men and women express a preference for having male children (Dinitz, Dynes, & Clarke, 1954). Masculine status is so to be preferred to feminine status that girls may adopt tomboy attributes and be admired for doing so, but boys who adopt feminine attributes are despised as sissies. Feminine identification in males (excluding feminine qualities such as tenderness, expressiveness and playfulness) is clearly related to maladjustment. But even in females, intense feminine identification may more strongly characterize maladjusted than adjusted women (Heilbrun, 1965). Concern about population control will only further accelerate the devaluation of household activities performed by women, and decrease the self-esteem of women solely engaged in such activities.

Intellectual achievement and self-assertive independent strivings in women are equated with loss of femininity by men and women alike. Women, as well as men, oppose the idea of placing women in high-status jobs (Keniston & Keniston, 1964). One researcher (Horner, 1969) thinks that women's higher test anxiety reflects the conflict between women's motivation to achieve and their motivation to fail. She feels that women and girls who are motivated to fail feel ambivalent about success because intellectual achievement is equated with loss of femininity by socializing agents and eventually by the female herself.

Generally, parents have higher achievement expectations for boys than they do for girls. Boys are more frequently expected to go to college and to have careers (Aberle & Naegele, 1952). The pressure towards responsibility, obedience and nurturance for girls, and towards achievement and independence for boys which characterizes United States society also characterizes other societies, thus further reinforcing the effect of differential expectations for boys and girls (Barry, Bacon, & Child, 1957). In the United States, girls of nursery school age are not less achievement-oriented or independent than boys. By adolescence, however, most girls are highly aware of, and concerned about, social disapproval for so-called masculine pursuits. They move toward conformity with societal expectations that, relative to males, they should be nonachievement-oriented and dependent.

Girls and women consistently show a greater need for affiliation than do boys and men. The greater nurturance toward peers and cooperation with adults shown by girls is demonstrable as early as the preschool years. In general, females are more suggestible, conforming and likely to rely on others for guidance and support. Thus, females are particularly susceptible to social influences, and these influences generally define femininity to include such attributes as social responsibility, supportiveness, submissiveness and low achievement striving.

There are complex and subtle differences in the behavior of boys and girls from birth onward, and in the treatment of boys and girls by their caretaking adults. These differential treatments are sometimes difficult to identify because, when the observer knows the sex of the parent or child, an automatic adjustment is made which tends to standardize judgments about the two sexes. By the time boys enter nursery school, they are more resistant to adult authority and aggressive with peers. Thus, a major socialization task for preschool boys consists of developing social responsibility. While preschool girls (in my investigations) are neither lacking in achievement-orientation nor in independence, the focal socialization task for them seems to consist of maintaining purposive, dominant and independent behavior. Without active intervention by socializing agents, the cultural stereotype is likely to augment girls' already well-developed sense of cooperation with authority and eventually discourage their independent strivings towards achievement and eminence. As will be noted later, there is reason to believe that the socialization practices which facilitate the development of instrumental competence in *both* girls and boys have the following attributes: a) they place a premium on self-assertiveness but not on anticonformity, b) they emphasize high achievement and self-control but not social conformity, c) they occur within a context of firm discipline and rationality with neither excessive restrictiveness nor overacceptance.

SOCIALIZATION PRACTICES RELATED TO RESPONSIBLE VS. IRRESPONSIBLE BEHAVIOR

The reader will recall that I have defined Responsible vs. Irresponsible Behavior in terms of: a) Friendliness vs. Hostility Towards Peers, b) Cooperation vs. Resistance Towards Adults, and c) High vs. Low Achievement Orientation. Socialization seems to have a clearer impact upon the development of social responsibility in boys than in girls, probably because girls vary less in this particular attribute. In my own work, parents who were authoritative and relatively conforming, as compared with parents who were permissive or authoritarian, tended to have children who were more friendly, cooperative and achievement-oriented. This was especially true for boys. Nonconformity in parents was not necessarily associated with resistant and hostile behavior in children. Neither did firm control and high maturity-demands produce rebellious-ness. In fact, it has generally been found that close supervision, high demands for obedience and personal neatness, and pressure upon the child to share in household responsibilities are associated with responsible behavior rather than with chronic rebelliousness. The condition most conducive to antisocial aggression, because it most effectively rewards such behavior, is probably one in which the parent is punitive and arbitrary in his demands, but inconsistent in responding to the child's disobedience.

Findings from several studies suggest that parental demands provoke rebelliousness only when the parent both restricts autonomy of action and does not use rational methods of control. For example, Pikas (1961), in a survey of 656 Swedish adolescents, showed that differences in the child's acceptance of parental authority depended upon the reason for the parental directive. Authority based on rational concern for the child's welfare was accepted well by the child, but arbitrary, domineering or exploitative authority was rejected. Pikas' results are supported by Middleton and Snell (1963) who found that discipline regarded by the child as either very strict or very permissive was associated with rebellion against the parent's political views. Finally, Elder (1963), working with adolescents' reports concerning their parents, found that conformity to parental rules typified subjects who saw their parents as having ultimate control (but who gave the child leeway in making decisions) and who also provided explanations for rules.

Several generalizations and hypotheses can be drawn from this literature and from the results of my own work concerning the relations of specific parental practices to the development of social responsibility in young children. The following list is based on the assumption that it is more meaningful to talk about the effects of *patterns* of parental authority than to talk about the effects of single parental variables.

1. *The modelling of socially responsible behavior facilitates the development of social responsibility in young children, and more so if the model is seen by the child as having control over desired resources and as being concerned with the child's welfare.*

The adult who subordinates his impulses enough to conform with social regulations and is himself charitable and generous will have his example followed by the child. The adult who is self-indulgent and lacking in charity will have his example followed even if he should preach generous, cooperative behavior. Studies by Mischel and Liebert (1966) and by Rosenhan, Frederick, and Burrowes (1968) suggest that models who behave self-indulgently produce similar behavior in children and these effects are even more extensive than direct reward for self-indulgent behavior. Further, when the adult preaches what he does not practice, the child is more likely to do what the adult practices. This is true even when the model preaches unfriendly or uncooperative behavior but behaves towards the child in an opposite manner. To the extent that the model for socially responsible behavior is perceived as having high social status (Bandura, Ross & Ross, 1963), the model will be most effective in inducing responsible behavior.

In our studies, both authoritative and authoritarian parents demanded socially responsible behavior and also differentially rewarded it. As compared to authoritative parents, however, authoritarian parents permitted their own needs to take precedence over those of the child, became inaccessible when displeased, assumed a stance of personal infallibility, and in other ways showed themselves often to be more concerned with their own ideas than with the child's welfare. Thus, they did not exemplify prosocial behavior, although they did preach it. Authoritative parents, on the other hand, both preached and practiced prosocial behavior and their children were significantly more responsible than the children of authoritarian parents. In this regard, it is interesting that nonconforming parents who were highly individualistic and professed anticonforming ideas had children who were more socially responsible than otherwise. The boys were achievement-oriented and the girls were notably cooperative. These parents were themselves rather pacific, gentle people who were highly responsive to the child's needs even at the cost of their own; thus, they modelled but did not preach prosocial behavior.

2. *Firm enforcement policies, in which desired behavior is positively reinforced and deviant behavior is negatively reinforced, facilitate the development of socially responsible behavior, provided that the parent desires that the child behave in a responsible manner.*

The use of reinforcement techniques serves to establish the potency of the reinforcing agent and, in the mind of the young child, to legitimate his authority. The use of negative sanctions can be a clear statement to the child that rules are there to be followed and that to disobey is to break a known rule. Among other things, punishment provides the child with information. As Spence (1966) found, nonreaction by adults is sometimes interpreted by children as signifying a correct response. Siegel and Kohn (1959) found that nonreaction by an adult when the child was behaving aggressively resulted in an increased incidence of such acts. By virtue of his or her role as an authority, the sheer presence of parents when the child misbehaves cannot help but affect the future occurrence of such behavior. Disapproval should reduce such actions, while approval or nonreaction to such behavior should increase them.

In our studies, permissive parents avoided the use of negative sanctions, did not demand mannerly behavior or reward self-help, did not enforce their directives by exerting force or influence, avoided confrontation when the child disobeyed, and did not choose to or did not know how to use reinforcement techniques. Their sons, by comparison with the sons of authoritative parents, were clearly lacking in prosocial and achievement-oriented behavior.

3. *Nonrejecting parents are more potent models and reinforcing agents than rejecting parents; thus, nonrejection should be associated with socially responsible behavior in children, provided that the parents value and reinforce such behavior.*

It should be noted that this hypothesis refers to nonrejecting parents and is not stated in terms of passive-acceptance. Thus, it is expected that nonrejecting parental behavior, but not unconditionally acceptant behavior, is associated with socially responsible behavior in children. As Bronfenbrenner pointed out about adolescents, "It is the presence of rejection rather than the lack of a high degree of warmth which is inimical to the development of responsibility in both sexes (1961, p. 254)." As already indicated, in our study authoritarian parents were more rejecting and punitive, and less devoted to the child's welfare than were authoritative parents; their sons were also less socially responsible.

4. *Parents who are fair, and who use reason to legitimate their directives are more potent models and reinforcing agents than parents who do not encourage independence or verbal exchange.*

Let us consider the interacting effects of punishment and the use of reasoning on the behavior of children. From research it appears that an accompanying verbal rationale nullifies the special effectiveness of immediate punishment, and also of relatively intense punishment (Parke, 1969). Thus, by symbolically reinstating the deviant act, explaining the reason for punishment, and telling the child exactly what he should do, the parent obviates the need for intense or instantaneous punishment. Immediate, intense punishment may have undesirable side effects, in that the child is conditioned through fear to avoid deviant behavior, and is not helped to control himself consciously and willfully. Also, instantaneous, intense punishment produces high anxiety which may interfere with performance, and in addition may increase the likelihood that the child will avoid the noxious agent. This reduces that agent's future effectiveness as a model or reinforcing agent. Finally, achieving behavioral conformity by conditioning fails to provide the child with information about cause and effect relations which he can then transfer to similar situations. This is not to say that use of reasoning alone, without negative sanctions, is as effective as the use of both. Negative sanctions give operational meaning to the consequences signified by reasons, and to rules themselves.

Authoritarian parents, as compared to authoritative parents, are relatively unsuccessful in producing socially responsible behavior. According to this hypothesis, the reason is that authoritarian parents fail to encourage verbal exchange and infrequently accompany punishment with reasons rather than that they use negative sanctions and are firm disciplinarians.

SOCIALIZATION PRACTICES RELATED TO INDEPENDENT VS. SUGGESTIBLE BEHAVIOR

The reader will recall that Independent vs. Suggestible Behavior was defined with reference to: a) Domineering vs. Tractable Behavior, b) Dominance vs. Submission, c) Purposive vs. Aimless Activity, and d) Independence vs. Suggestibility. Parent behavior seems to have a clearer effect upon the development of independence in girls than in boys, probably because preschool boys vary less in independence.

In my own work, independence in girls was clearly associated with authoritative upbringing (whether conforming or nonconforming). For boys, nonconforming parent behavior and, to a lesser extent, authoritative upbringing were associated with independence. By independence we do not mean anticonformity. "Pure anticonformity, like pure conformity, is pure dependence behavior (Willis, 1968, p. 263)." Anticonforming behavior, like negativistic behavior, consists of doing anything but what is prescribed by social norms. Independence is the ability to disregard known standards of conduct or normative expectations in making decisions. Nonconformity in parents may not be associated in my study with independence in girls (although it was in boys) because females are especially susceptible to normative expectations. One can hypothesize that girls must be trained to act independently of these expectations, rather than to conform or to anticonform to them.

It was once assumed that firm control and high maturity demands lead to passivity and dependence in young children. The preponderance of evidence contradicts this. Rather, it would appear that many children react to parental power by resisting, rather than by being cowed. The same parent variables which increase the probability that the child will use the parent as a model should increase the likelihood that firm control will result in assertive behavior. For example, the controlling parent who is warm, understanding and supportive of autonomy should generate less passivity (as well as less rebelliousness) than the controlling parent who is cold and restrictive. This should be the case because of the kinds of behavior reinforced, the traits modelled and the relative effectiveness of the parent as a model.

Several generalizations and hypotheses can be offered concerning the relations between parental practices and the development of independence in young children:

1. *Early environmental stimulation facilitates the development of independence in young children.*

It took the knowledge gained from compensatory programs for culturally disadvantaged children to counteract the erroneous counsel from some experts to avoid too much stimulation of the young child. Those Head Start programs which succeed best (Hunt, 1968) are those characterized by stress on the development of cognitive skills, linguistic ability, motivational concern for achievement, and rudimentary numerical skills. There is reason to believe that middle-class children also profit from such early stimulation and enrichment of the environment. Fowler (1962) pointed out, even prior to the development of compensatory programs, that concern about the dangers of premature cognitive training and an overemphasis on personality development had delayed inordinately the recognition that the ability to talk, read and compute increases the child's self-respect and independent functioning.

Avoidance of anxiety and self-assertion are reciprocally inhibiting responses to threat or frustration. Girls, in particular, are shielded from stress and overstimulation, which probably serves to increase preferences for avoidant rather than offensive responses to aggression or threat. By exposing a child to stress or to physical, social and intellectual demands, he or she becomes more resistant to stress and learns that offensive reactions to aggression and frustration are frequently rewarding. In our studies, as the hypothesis would predict, parents who provided the most enriched environment, namely the nonconforming and the authoritative parents, had the most dominant and purposive children. These parents, by comparison with the others studied, set high standards of excellence, invoked cognitive insight, provided an intellectually stimulating atmosphere, were themselves rated as being differentiated and individualistic, and made high educational demands upon the child.

2. *Parental passive-acceptance and overprotection inhibits the development of independence.*

Passive-acceptant and overprotective parents shield children from stress and, for the reasons discussed above, inhibit the development of assertiveness and frustration tolerance. Also, parental anxiety about stress to which the child is exposed may serve to increase the child's anxiety. Further, willingness to rescue the child offers him an easy alternative to self-mastery. Demanding and nonprotective parents, by contrast, permit the child to extricate himself from stressful situations and place a high value on tolerance of frustration and courage.

According to many investigators (e.g., McClelland, Atkinson, Clark, & Lowell, 1953), healthy infants are by inclination explorative, curious and stress-seeking. Infantile feelings of pleasure, originally experienced after mild changes in sensory stimulation, become associated with these early efforts at independent mastery. The child anticipates pleasure upon achieving a higher level of skill, and the pleasure derived from successfully performing a somewhat risky task encourages him to seek out such tasks.

Rosen and D'Andrade (1959) found that high achievement motivation, a motivation akin to stress-seeking, was facilitated both by high maternal warmth when the child pleased the parent and high maternal hostility and rejection when the child was displeasing. Hoffman, et al., (1960), found that mothers of achieving boys were more coercive than those who performed poorly, and it has also been found (Crandall, Dewey, Katkovsky, & Preston, 1964) that mothers of achieving girls were relatively non-nurturant. Kagan and Moss (1962) reported that achieving adult women had mothers who in early childhood were unaffectionate, "pushy," and not protective. Also, Baumrind and Black (1967) found paternal punitiveness to be associated positively with independence in girls. Finally, in my most recent study, there were indications for girls that parental nonacceptance was positively related to independence. That is, the most independent girls had parents who were either not passive-acceptant or who were rejecting.

Authoritarian control and permissive noncontrol both may shield the child from the opportunity to engage in vigorous interaction with people. Demands which cannot be met, refusals to help, and unrealistically high standards may curb commerce with the environment. Placing few demands on the child, suppression of conflict, and low standards may under-stimulate him. In either case, he fails to achieve the knowledge and experience required to desensitize him to the anxiety associated with nonconformity.

3. *Self-assertiveness and self-confidence in the parent, expressed by an individual style and by the moderate use of power-oriented techniques of discipline, will be associated with independence in the young child.*

The self-assertive, self-confident parent provides a model of similar behavior for the child. Also, the parent who uses power-oriented rather than love-oriented techniques of discipline achieves compliance through means other than guilt. Power-oriented techniques can achieve behavioral conformity without premature internalization by the child of parental standards. It may be that the child is, in fact, more free to formulate his own standards of conduct if techniques of discipline are used which stimulate resistiveness or anger rather than fear or guilt. The use of techniques which do not stimulate conformity through guilt may be especially important for girls. The belief in one's own power and the assumption of responsibility for one's own intellectual successes and failures are important predictors of independent effort and intellectual achievement (Crandall, Katkovsky, & Crandall, 1965). This sense of self-responsibility in children seems to be associated with power-oriented techniques of discipline and with critical attitudes on the part of the adult towards the child, provided that the parent is also concerned with developing the child's autonomy and encourages independent and individual behavior.

In my study, both the authoritative and the nonconforming parents were self-confident, clear as well as flexible in their childrearing attitudes, and willing to express angry feelings openly. Together with relatively firm enforcement and nonrejection, these indices signified patterns of parental authority in which guilt-producing techniques of discipline were avoided. The sons of nonconforming parents and the daughters of authoritative parents were both extremely independent.

4. *Firm control can be associated with independence in the child,*

174

provided that the control is not restrictive of the child's opportunities to experiment and to make decisions within the limits defined.

There is no logical reason why parents' enforcing directives and making demands cannot be accompanied by regard for the child's opinions, willingness to gratify his wishes, and instruction in the effective use of power. A policy of firm enforcement may be used as a means by which the child can achieve a high level of instrumental competence and eventual independence. The controlling, demanding parent can train the child to tolerate increasingly intense and prolonged frustration; to broaden his base of adult support to include neighbors, teachers and others; to assess critically his own successes and failures and to take responsibility for both; to develop standards of moral conduct; and to relinquish the special privileges of childhood in return for the rights of adolescence.

It is important to distinguish between the effects on the child of restrictive control and firm control. *Restrictive control* refers to the use of extensive proscriptions and prescriptions, covering many areas of the child's life; they limit his autonomy to try out his skills in these areas. By *firm control* is meant firm enforcement of rules, effective resistance against the child's demands, and guidance of the child by regime and intervention. Firm control does not imply large numbers of rules or intrusive direction of the child's activities.

Becker (1964) has summarized the effects on child behavior of restrictiveness vs. permissiveness and warmth vs. hostility. He reported that warm-*restrictive* parents tended to have passive, well-socialized children. This author (Baumrind, 1967) found, however, that warm-*controlling* (by contrast with warm-*restrictive*) parents were not paired with passive children, but rather with responsible, assertive, self-reliant children. Parents of these children enforced directives and resisted the child's demands, but were not restrictive. Early control, unlike restrictiveness, apparently does not lead to "fearful, dependent and submissive behaviors, a dulling of intellectual striving, and inhibited hostility," as Becker indicated was true of restrictive parents (1964, p. 197).

5. *Substantial reliance upon reinforcement techniques to obtain behavioral conformity, unaccompanied by use of reason, should lead to dependent behavior.*

To the extent that the parent uses verbal cues judiciously, she increases the child's ability to discriminate, differentiate, and generalize. According to Luria (1960) and Vygotsky (1962), the child's ability to "order" his own behavior is based upon verbal instruction from the adult which, when heeded and obeyed, permits eventual *cognitive* control by the child of his own behavior. Thus, when the adult legitimizes power, labels actions clearly as praiseworthy or changeworthy, explains her rules and encourages vigorous verbal give and take, obedience is not likely to be achieved at the cost of passive dependence. Otherwise, it may well be.

It is self-defeating to attempt to shape, by extrinsic reinforcement, behavior which by its nature is autogenic. As already mentioned, the healthy infant is explorative and curious, and seems to enjoy mild stress. Although independent mastery can be accelerated if the parent broadens the child's experiences and makes certain reasonable demands upon him, the parent must take care not to substitute extrinsic reward and social approval for the intrinsic pleasure associated with mastery of the environment. Perhaps the unwillingness of the authoritative parents in my study to rely solely upon reinforcement techniques contributed substantially to the relatively purposive, dominant behavior shown by their children, especially by their daughters.

6. *Parental values which stress individuality, self-expression, initiative, divergent thinking and aggressiveness will facilitate the development of independence in the child, provided that these qualities in the parent are not accompanied by lax and inconsistent discipline and unwillingness to make demands upon the child.*

It is important that adults use their power in a functional rather than an interpersonal context. The emphasis should be on the task to be done and the rule to be followed rather than upon the special status of the powerful adult. By focusing upon the task to be accomplished, the adult's actions can serve as an example for the child rather than as a suppressor of his independence. Firm discipline for both boys and girls must be in the service of training for achievement and independence, if such discipline is not to facilitate the development of an overconforming, passive life style.

In our study, independence was clearly a function of nonconforming but nonindulgent parental attitudes and behaviors, for boys. For girls, however, nonconforming parental patterns were associated with independence only when the parents were also authoritative. The parents in these groups tended to encourage their children to ask for, even to demand, what they desired. They themselves acquiesced in the face of such demands provided that the demands were not at variance with parental policy. Thus, the children of these parents were positively reinforced for autonomous self-expression. In contrast to these results, the authoritarian parents did not value willfulness in the child, and the permissive parents were clearly ambivalent about rewarding such behavior. Further, the permissive parents did not differentiate between mature or praiseworthy demands by the child and regressive or deviant demands. These permissive parents instead would accede to the child's demands until patience was exhausted; punishment, sometimes very harsh, would then ensue.

SUMMARY

Girls in western society are in many ways systematically socialized for instrumental incompetence. The affiliative and cooperative orientation of girls increases their receptivity to the influence of socializing agents. This influence, in turn, is often used by socializing agents to inculcate passivity, dependence, conformity and sociability in the young females at the expense of independent pursuit of success and scholarship. In my studies, parents designated as authoritative had the most achievement-oriented and independent daughters. However, permissive parents whose control was lax, who did not inhibit tomboy behavior, and who did not seek to produce sex-role conformity in girls had daughters who were nearly as achievement-oriented and independent.

The following adult practices and attitudes seem to facilitate the development of socially responsible and independent behavior in both boys and girls.

1. Modelling by the adult of behavior which is both socially responsible and self-assertive, especially if the adult is seen as powerful by the child and as eager to use the material and interpersonal resources over which he has control on the child's behalf.
2. Firm enforcement policies in which the adult makes effective use of reinforcement principles in order to reward socially responsible behavior, but in which demands are accompanied by explanations, and sanctions are accompanied by reasons consistent with a set of principles followed in practice as well as preached by the parent.
3. Nonrejecting but not overprotective or passive-acceptant parental attitudes in which the parent's interest in the child is abiding, and, in the preschool years, intense; but where approval is conditional upon the child's behavior.
4. High demands for achievement, and for conformity with parental policy, accompanied by receptivity to the child's rational demands and willingness to offer the child wide latitude for independent judgment.
5. Providing the child with a complex and stimulating environment offering challenge and excitement as well as security and rest, where divergent as well as convergent thinking is encouraged.

These practices and attitudes do not reflect a happy compromise between authoritarian and permissive practices. Rather, they reflect a synthesis and balancing of strongly opposing forces of tradition and innovation, divergence and convergence, accommodation and assimilation, cooperation and autonomous expression, tolerance and principled intractability.

REFERENCES

Aberle, D. F. & Naegele, K. D. Middle-class fathers' occupational role and attitudes toward children. *American J. Orthopsychiatry.* 1952, 22, 366–378.

Bandura, A., Ross, D. & Ross, S. A. A comparative test of the status envy, social power, and the secondary-reinforcement theories of identificatory learning. *J. abnorm. soc. psychol.*, 1963, 67, 527–534.

Barry, H., Bacon, M. K. & Child, E. L. A cross-cultural survey of some sex differences in socialization. *J. abnorm. soc. psychol.*, 1957, 55, 327–332.

Baumrind, D. Effects of authoritative parental control on child behavior. *Child Develpm.*, 1966, 37, 887–907.

———. Child care practices anteceding three patterns of preschool behavior. *Genetic psychol. Monogr.*, 1967, 75, 43–88.

———. Authoritarian vs. authoritative parental control. *Adolescence*, 1968, 3, 255–272.

———. Current patterns of parental authority. *Developmental psychol. Monogr.*, 1971, 4 (I), 1–103.

————, & Black, A. E. Socialization practices associated with dimensions of competence in preschool boys and girls. *Child Develpm.* 1967, 38, 291–327.

Becker, W. C. Consequences of different kinds of parental discipline. In M. L. Hoffman & L. W. Hoffman (eds.), *Review of Child Development Research.* Vol. 1. New York: Russell Sage Foundation, 1964, 169–208.

Bronfenbrenner, U. Some familiar antecedents of responsibility and leadership in adolescents. In L. Petrullo & B. M. Bass (eds.), *Leadership and interpersonal behavior.* New York: Holt, Rinehart & Winston, 1961, 239–271.

Brown, D. Sex role development in a changing culture. *Psychol. Bull.,* 1958, 55, 232–242.

Crandall, V., Dewey, R., Katkovsky, W. & Preston, A. Parents' attitudes and behaviors and grade school children's academic achievements. *J. genet. psychol.,* 1964, 104, 53–66.

————, Katkovsky, W. & Crandall, V. J. Children's beliefs in their own control of reinforcements in intellectual-academic achievement situations. *Child Develpm.,* 1965, 36, 91–109.

————, Orleans, S., Preston, A. & Rabson, A. The development of social compliance in young children. *Child Develpm.,* 1958, 29, 429–443.

Dinitz, S., Dynes, R. R. & Clarke, A. C. Preference for male or female children: Traditional or affectional. *Marriage and Family Living,* 1954, 16, 128–130.

Eiduson, B. T. *Scientists, their psychological world.* New York: Basic Books, 1962.

Elder, G. H. Parental power legitimation and its effect on the adolescent. *Sociometry,* 1963, 26, 50–65.

Emmerich, W. & Smoller, F. The role patterning of parental norms. *Sociometry,* 1964, 27, 382–390.

Fowler, W. Cognitive learning in infancy and early childhood. *Psychol. Bull.,* 1962, 59, 116–152.

Haggard, E. A. Socialization, personality, and academic achievement in gifted children. In B. C. Rosen, H. J. Crockett & C. Z. Nunn (eds.), *Achievement in American society.* Cambridge, Mass.: Schenkman Publishing, 1969, 85–94.

Heilbrun, A. B. Sex differences in identification learning. *J. genet. psychol.,* 1965, 106, 185–193.

Hoffman, L., Rosen, S. & Lippit, R. Parental coerciveness, child autonomy, and child's role at school. *Sociometry,* 1960, 23, 15–22.

Horner, M. Fail: Bright women. *Psychology Today,* 1969, 3 (6).

Hunt, J. McV. Toward the prevention of incompetence. In J. W. Carter, Jr. (ed.), *Research Contributions from Psychology to Community Mental Health.* New York: Behavioral Publications, 1968.

Kagan, J. & Moss, H. A. *Birth to Maturity: A Study in Psychological Development.* New York: John Wiley, 1962.

Keniston, E. & Keniston, K. An American anachronism: the image of women and work. *Am. Scholar,* 1964, 33, 355–375.

Luria, A. R. Experimental analysis of the development of voluntary action in children. In *The Central Nervous System and Behavior.* Bethesda, Md.: U.S. Department of Health, Education, & Welfare, National Institutes of Health, 1960, 529–535.

Maccoby, E. E. (ed.). *The Development of Sex Differences.* Stanford, Calif.: Stanford University Press, 1966.

McClelland, D., Atkinson, J., Clark, R. & Lowell, E. *The Achievement Motive.* New York: Appleton-Century-Crofts, 1953.

McKee, J. P. & Sherriffs, A. C. The differential evaluation of males and females. *J. Pers.,* 1957, 25, 356–371.

Middleton, R. & Snell, P. Political expression of adolescent rebellion. *Am. J. Sociol.*, 1963, 68, 527–535.

Mischel, W. & Liebert, R. M. Effects of discrepancies between observed and imposed reward criteria on their acquisition and transmission. *J. Pers. & soc. Psychol.*, 1966, 3, 45–53.

Parke, R. D. Some effects of punishment on children's behavior. *Young Children*, 1969, 24, 225–240.

Pikas, A. Children's attitudes toward rational versus inhibiting parental authority. *J. abnorm. soc. Psychol.*, 1961, 62, 315–321.

Roe, A. *The Making of a Scientist.* New York: Dodd, Mead, 1952.

Rosen, B. C. & D'Andrade, R. The psychological origins of achievement motivation. *Sociometry*, 1959, 22, 185–218.

Rosenhan, D. L., Frederick, F. & Burrowes, A. Preaching and Practicing: effects of channel discrepancy on norm internalization. *Child Develpm.*, 1968, 39, 291–302.

Rossi, A. Women in science: why so few? In B. C. Rosen, H. J. Crockett, & C. Z. Nunn (eds.), *Achievement in American Society.* Cambridge, Mass.: Schenkman Publishing, 1969, 470–486.

Siegel, A. E. & Kohn, L. G. Permissiveness, permission, and aggression: the effects of adult presence or absence on aggression in children's play. *Child Develpm.*, 1959, 36, 131–141.

Spence, J. T. Verbal-discrimination performance as a function of instruction and verbal reinforcement combination in normal and retarded children. *Child Develpm.*, 1966, 37, 269–281.

Terman, L. M. & Oden, H. H. *The Gifted Child Grows Up.* Stanford, Calif.: Stanford University Press, 1947.

Vygotsky, L. S. *Thought and Language.* Cambridge, Mass.: M.I.T. Press, 1962.

Walberg, H. J. Physics, femininity, and creativity. *Develpml. Psychol.*, 1969, 1, 47–54.

Willis, R. H. Conformity, independence, and anticonformity. In L. S. Wrightsman, Jr. (ed.), *Contemporary Issues in Social Psychology.* Belmont, Calif.: Brooks/Cole Publishing, 1968, 258–272.

LAWRENCE KOHLBERG
DOROTHY ZELNICKER ULLIAN

16. Stages in the Development of Psychosexual Concepts and Attitudes

In 1966, a cognitive-developmental analysis of children's sex-role concepts and attitudes was reported (1). The first part of this chapter essentially summarizes that theory and data. The first real study based on this approach since that time is reported in the second part of this chapter.

Basically, the original approach was simple: to study the development of sex-role concepts at face value rather than as indicators of something underlying them, such as identification, masculinity, or personality characteristics. Concepts of sex roles, whatever else they may be, are concepts, and so should undergo the transformations with development that Piaget (2) found in the development of conceptualizing physical objects.

As concepts change in development, so do the attitudes associated with them. Most research on children's psychosexuality formerly focused on either sex differences in behavior, on attitudes, or on measures of masculinity/femininity. The significance of these parameters is not clear. In some cultural settings or for some individuals, a given sex difference might be extremely significant, but for others, it is not. Much research utilized an implicit value that needed questioning: that it was good or mentally healthy for boys to be masculine and for girls to be feminine. This seemed to be a cultural stereotype rather than a scientific notion. Data, except in extreme circumstances, showed no empirical relationship between objective measures of masculinity/femininity and measures of mental health and adjustment.

To search for something meaningful in this area, it would seem that one should start with what was important to the child itself. Not all elements of sex differences or masculinity/femininity are significant for the child; however, one factor clearly is: its gender identity—the sheer fact that it is a boy or a girl. If you doubt that, imagine your reaction if your gender were suddenly transformed. Actually such a transformation has happened to children against their will. The subjects studied by Money and Hampson (3) were hermaphrodites, hormonally of one sex but with some or all of the external genital characteristics of the opposite sex. At various points in childhood, gender was reassigned. One would imagine that this was traumatic and damaging, but if reassignment occured before age 2 to 4, it had little effect on later sexual adjustment. For gender reassignment to have psychological meaning, the child must have cognitively developed a conception of its own gender identity, an identity that can be at variance with its biological gender. These findings suggest that the growing cognitive constancy or irreversibility of gender identity in early childhood is the bedrock of later sexual and sex-role attitudes. Although the significance of gender identity is not solely its influence on the child's later life, it is the most salient category to which the child assigns itself. In fact, it is the only basic general category or role to which it does assign itself. The other basic category of self-identity for the child is that of child as opposed to adult. Unlike gender, however, age identity is not fixed; children know they will become adults. Perhaps only race can be considered a comparable category to children and then only under some conditions.

Because gender is the only fixed general category into which the child can sort itself and others, it takes on tremendous importance in organizing the child's social perceptions and actions. Therefore the first question we studied was that of the actual development of basic gender identity. Absent in the first year or two of life, by age 6, children's gender identities were found to be fixed and were organizing foci for their social interactions. It seemed to me that the development of the child's physical gender-identity category must coincide in time with the development of the other basic physical categories studied by Piaget. If this were the case, gender identity would not become a perceptually or logically unshakeable category until the child reached concrete operations and conservation. This was easy to demonstrate: we simply asked with appropriate illustrations whether a girl could turn into a boy if she wished to, by wearing a boy's haircut or a boy's clothes. Not until age 6 or 7 were most children quite certain that a girl could not be a boy regardless of changes in appearance or behavior. Long before, by age 3, a child will label itself correctly and will label the gender of others with partial accuracy. By age 4, children label gender correctly and show some awareness that gender cannot change. For example, Johnny, who is 4½ years old, points out gender constancy to younger Jimmy, who is just reaching age 4. Here is the conversation:

OLDER JOHNNY: I'm going to be an airplane builder when I grow up.
YOUNGER JIMMY: When I grow up, I'll be a mommy.
OLDER JOHNNY: No, you can't be a mommy, you have to be a daddy.
YOUNGER JIMMY: No, I'm going to be a mommy.
OLDER JOHNNY: No, you're not a girl; you can't be a mommy.

Although constancy of gender identity starts to appear at age 4, it does not have a clear logical basis, nor is it linked to genital differences until about age 6 to 7.

So far we have talked about the growth of a single concept, gender and gender identity. We believed that developmental changes in the cognitive structure of this concept will be reflected in developmental changes in the attitudes more usually studied in young children. The first was the so-called attitude of masculinity/femininity assessed by various tests of preference for sex-typed objects and activities. Not surprisingly, as a boy becomes sure he is immutably a boy and that boys like certain activities and girls like others, he will come to prefer boy-things. By age 6 to 7, when children reach the ceiling on gender identity, they also reach a ceiling on these tests, making 80 to 100% same-sex choices on them. This is not a response to cultural training or reward any more than the development of constancy of gender identity is. Rather, it is to be explained in terms of two tendencies. The first is the belief that the child has little choice about sex-typed activities and roles. When our 4-year-old Jimmy abandons the belief that he can be a mother, he also abandons the belief that he can be a nurse or a secretary, or can wear girls' clothes or play with feminine dolls. At age 6 to 7 a child equates the "is" of its sex identity with social value: "You can't be a girl, so you don't want to, you can't be a nurse, so you don't want to, and it's no good to be a nurse." The second tendency is the natural tendency to like oneself, think well of oneself and of that which is connected to the self or is like the self. If other boys are like the self, you like them more than you like girls. A 4-year-old boy expressed a preference for a male babysitter. Asked why, his 7-year-old brother intervened to say, "because he's a boy himself." Actually this consistent or categorical tendency to prefer males because one is a male requires the conceptual growth reflected in the ability to perform concrete operations and to maintain fixed logical classes. For boys less than 5 years old it only applies to peers. By age 6 to 7 it applies to both fathers and strange adults. Doll-play measures of preference and imitation for the father over the mother cross over to same-sex preference at age 6. So do measures of preferential dependency toward strange adult males over females. Thus what is often called father identification, as well as what is called masculinity of values, grows with and out of the cognitive growth of the child's gender identity.

Now that the child has organized its identity and its attitudes and values around its gender identity, we must ask what these attitudes and values are. We enter into the attributes children assign to male and female roles, and the issues of the superiority of one to the other. Here we find almost as much cognitive-developmental regularity as we did for gender identity. By age 6 almost all boys see males as more powerful, aggressive, authoritative, and smarter than females. In part, this is also the old tendency of the boy to attribute value to what is like himself. This is not all, however, because most girls of the same age agree with him. Cross-cultural studies suggest that these stereotypes are universal. In our work, we found that father-absent black boys developed the same stereotypes of a father at the same age as did father-present black and white boys. How do we explain this? By returning to the notion that for the young child sex-linked roles and attributes are linked to body attributes. Because males are perceived as physically bigger, stronger, and more active than females, they are also thought to have certain psychological attributes; physical strength and energy are equated with intelligence, aggression, and dominance. This tendency to derive psychological attributes and values from physical attributes is compounded by the child's categorical view of sex-role assignments. Boys cannot be nurses, girls cannot be soldiers. Roles we believe that both sexes can play, but are more commonly played by males, are categorically assigned to the male sex; roles from doctor to policeman to President.

In summary, we see that the 6-year-old boy is a full-fledged male chauvinist, much more so than his parents, and he is that way regardless of how he is brought up in a society that fosters role differentiation. Fortunately, later phases of cognitive growth qualify, moderate, or undo this male chauvinism.

At age 6, the physical concepts of sex role have completed their course of cognitive growth. The next phase of cognitive growth in sex-role concepts takes place because the child redefines roles in terms of their place in a moral order called society, rather than in terms of their physical characteristics. It would seem that there are definite stages in sex-role cognitions, stages to be found in any culture and occurring because of general cognitive transformations in the child's perception of its social world. These stages are not biologically innate, like libidinal stages, nor are they cultural age grades. Rather, they are the result of interaction between universal cognitive and social tendencies in the child with the universals in its social world; the universals that in any culture, involve body differences between the categories of males and females. These categories constitute a pivotal focus of social organization. For the child, stages in the development of its psychosexual concepts represent an organizing focus in the development of its attitudes toward love, work, and parenthood: the main themes of adult life.

The study about to be described was designed to examine the nature of sex-typed concepts at various ages and to identify some of the dimensions on which change occurs. The basic task was to discover the qualitative changes in attitudes that occur with increasing age.

One may view statements on sex roles in two ways. First, one might ask, "How does the subject describe the male and female roles as he perceives them?" And second, "What are the subject's conceptions of what a male and female ought to be like?" The first component we refer to as the *descriptive*, for it refers only to perceptions of male and female differences, and the second is referred to as the *prescriptive*, for it pertains to the issue of how men and women ought to be, as opposed to how they are perceived. Based on this distinction, one might further ask how these components of sex typing are related to each other in the process of development. What is the relationship of the descriptive to the prescriptive factor; of what "is" to what "ought to be"?

On the basis of preliminary data, we can suggest the following changes that occur in the development of sex typing: At the earliest level, sex-role differences are based on observable physical criteria, such as size, strength, and material status. What one wants to be at this stage is limited by the physical characteristics associated with one's gender identity. A conventional level of development follows in which differences in sex roles define social duties. Males and females are seen as occupying a particular role within a larger social system. At this stage, what one wants to be in terms of roles is largely defined by conformity to existing sex roles. At the third level, sex-role characteristics are personally chosen from a conception of what one wants to be. The choice is based on a need for mutuality and equality of individuals in sexual relationships. In the remainder of this chapter, our findings with regard to these levels of cognitive development will be discussed.

Seventy boys and girls were given an extensive interview asking what they perceived as salient sex-role characteristics, why such sex-role characteristics existed, and whether one sex might have more valuable characteristics than the other. In addition, they were asked how extensively and why sex-typed characteristics ought to be expressed or conformed to by males and females. Subjects were selected at 2-year intervals between the ages of 6 and 18. The findings reported here are based on a preliminary analysis of two randomly selected interviews with male subjects in the first and the fifth grades. It was our impression that the two males in each of these subgroups were representative of their group as a whole. Since the data on females were unavailable at the time of writing, they are not included.

Let us now turn to our first-grade subjects. With regard to the descriptive aspect of sex typing, the most important characteristic of our 6-year-old boys is the equation of sex roles with the possession of specific physical characteristics. This group of subjects showed a consistent orientation to physical, external features in differentiating between males and females. For the 6-year-old child, male and female identities are defined by such things as size, strength, depth of voice, skin characteristics, ornaments, and clothes. For example, a 6-year-old boy is asked:

WHAT ARE LADIES LIKE?

Ladies have long hair and men don't.

HOW ELSE ARE THEY DIFFERENT FROM MEN?

They wear lipstick and men don't.

In accord with this physical emphasis, mental or psychological differences between the sexes were confused with the physical attributes of men and women. A boy is asked why girls seem to get hurt more easily than boys. He responds:

Because the boys have a little tougher skin.

Later he is asked why he thinks boys are smarter than girls, and he responds:

Because they have a bigger brain, I guess.

Thus physical characteristics are also assumed either to cause or to be identical with a variety of sex-linked social and psychological attributes, such as competence, power, or nurturance. In this way, strength is equated with energy, so that males are seen as capable of more difficult physical and mental labor. A 6-year-old boy illustrates this point when he observes that:

Women can't do as much as men, like I said, that is why men are smarter. . . . Men, they learn harder, because their job is harder.

WHO SHOULD HAVE A HARDER JOB?

The man. Because the woman wouldn't be that strong to do a hard job. She wouldn't be able to build.

WHAT ABOUT A SMART JOB?

The man. He is smarter because he works, he can be a fireman, a policeman, and a worker.

Similar conclusions are reached in the context of family roles. When asked who would be the boss in the family, a student answers:

The man. Because if the man wasn't and the lady was, then the lady wouldn't know what to do so very often.

WHY?

Because the man is smarter. he works harder and he plays harder.

This equation of psychological differences with physical differences and activity differences leads to a belief in male superiority because strength, energy, intelligence, and working for money are all equated.

Let us now turn to the 6-year-old's *conception of sex identity*. Here we see that deviations from any of the usual external signs of one's sex (such as clothing or hair style) are perceived as a possible change in one's real or perceived basic gender identity. As a result, others will think they are of the opposite sex and consequently will see them as funny, bizarre, or distorted:

SHOULD A BOY EVER WEAR A GIRL'S NECKLACE?

No, because it would look funny and everyone would say he was a girl.

Because social role differences between males and females are believed to be tied to their biological or physical identities, only men can play typically male roles, and only women can play typically female roles. Like 6-year-olds, we think that boys cannot become mothers because of their bodily characteristics and gender identities. Unlike 6-year-olds, we do think that boys can become nurses or secretaries, or engage in other stereotypically feminine roles. This is because we see the role of the nurse as a function, not as a set of physical characteristics and activities. In contrast, when a 6-year-old boy is asked whether a male could be a nurse, he responds:

He could still be in the hospital because the doctor is almost like a nurse. He could wear the stuff, but he would still be called a doctor.

WHY?

Because he is still a boy and doctors are supposed to be boys.

The differences between doctors and nurses is not in their function but in their gender identity and the uniforms they wear.

Turning to the prescriptive aspect of sex typing, we find that 6-year-old boys derive what males and females *should be* from what they are; that is, from their physical attributes and gender identity. All observed differences between the sexes ought to be maintained because they are necessary to the basic gender identity of each sex. Earlier we referred to the boy who thought that women are different from men because "they have long hair and wear lipstick." When asked, "Is it alright for a man to wear lipstick?" he answered, "No, they should have men not wearing lipstick and ladies wearing lipstick because they are different from each other." Clearly, any change from the customary attributes of one's sex is perceived as a violation of one's biological or physical nature and hence as "dumb," "funny," or "weird."

There are two major characteristics that distinguish the sex-role concepts of fifth-graders from those of the first-graders. First, psychological distinctions between males and females are seen as deriving from differences in wishes or intentions, rather than from physical differences. Asked who is more active, a boy replies:

Boys are more active.

WHY?

Well, they might be active because they like to play sports and that. And a lot of girls like to play sports.

Second, differences between males and females are seen in terms of the differences in the social roles they play. Fifth-graders are aware of differences in social roles and define sex differences in terms of social roles instead of relying on physical or biological characteristics. Whereas first-graders conceive of roles as classes of activities and physical characteristics, fifth-graders see roles as defined by social or shared expectations and norms. The fifth-grader sees these differences in role expectations as due to the social function of the role, its function for other people or society. How do these two characteristics—definition of sex differences in terms of psychological intention and definition of sex differences in terms of social roles—relate to one another? Primarily in that the fifth-grader's intentions and wishes are dictated by social roles they are expected to play in the future. A boy answers the following question:

HOW COME GIRLS LIKE TO STAY HOME AND DO THE HOUSEKEEPING?

I don't know, maybe they like to do what their mother does. Because they are going to be a mother.

Psychological sex differences also derive from society's definition of different roles for men and women. One boy was asked:

WHO IS SMARTER, IN GENERAL, MEN OR WOMEN?

Men, because they have to do a lot of things, like thinking. They have to work at their jobs. They have to think a lot and they have to work and they have to figure things out.

In terms of sex-role identity, we recall that first-graders saw what we now call social sex roles as fixed by one's gender identity and saw deviations from these physicalistic roles as distortions of identity. In contrast, fifth-graders are aware that some social sex roles are chosen, rather than prescribed. A fifth-grader tells us that if a boy wants to become a nurse, "it is okay because they can do what they want." While it is believed that social sex roles are chosen, the limits of individual choice are determined by an awareness of social expectation. The fifth-grader goes on to say:

But I still think a boy should become a doctor because I think a doctor's job is mostly for men, not for women.

Awareness of social roles implies awareness of social prescriptions or expectations. Role differences between the sexes are seen by the fifth-graders as expected or prescribed. In this sense, then, fifth-graders' sex-role identities are determined by what they ought to be, whereas for first-graders, what they ought to be is determined by what they are. As a subject is asked whether it would be right or wrong for a woman to ask the man to stay home with the children, he responds:

Wrong, because I think the woman should take care of them. Because the woman is usually the one to take care of them.

Although sex roles are socially prescriptive at this age, they are not prescriptive in the moral sense. There is no standard or moral principle behind sex-role prescriptions or for justifying sex-role differences. While in the first-grade, sex-role prescription derives from the physical "is," now it derives from the social "is," from the way things usually are or are expected to be. A fifth-grade boy tells us:

Men should act like men and ladies like ladies. They should act like they should. Take care of things, and that. You do what most women usually do.

If moral reasons for sex-role differences cannot be given beyond "that's what is supposed to be," neither can functional reasons for sex-role differences be given. Although these children are aware of social role functions divided by sex, they have no conception of the basis on which such sex-linked roles are assigned.

The data presented here indicate the importance of examining the reasoning from which sex-typed judgments are derived. Although the content of sex-typed responses at all ages seems to conform to social stereotypes of masculinity and femininity, it is apparent that the mode of thinking about sex roles may indicate a particular developmental level. For example, subjects at each developmental level felt that women should be soft and gentle. However, when asked why they felt so, variations in reasoning became evident. The youngest group of subjects based their judgments on physical differences between men and women. Thus women should be softer than men because their skin is softer or their bones are smaller. Older subjects, on the other hand, conceptualized female gentleness in terms of the need to conform to social or familial expectations.

187

Women should be softer because "mothers are supposed to be that way." A college student also prescribed softness as a characteristic for women, but this standard derived from an autonomous value system with universal applicability. Thus he felt not only that women should be soft and gentle but that it was a positive attribute for members of either sex.

This content–structure distinction implies that, though the content of sex-typed responses may suggest increasing conformity to social norms, there are differing bases for these responses. The data presented here support the view that changes in thinking about sex roles do, indeed, follow age-developmental trends.

REFERENCES

1. Kohlberg, L., in Maccoby, E. E. (ed.), *Development of Sex Differences*, Stanford University Press, Stanford, Calif., 1966.

2. Piaget, J., *The Construction of Reality in the Child*, Basic Books, New York, 1954.

3. Money, J., J. G. Hampson, and J. L. Hampson, *AMA Arch. Neurol. Psychiatr.* 77:333, 1957.

LAWRENCE KOHLBERG

17. Moral Education in the Schools: A Developmental View

For many contemporary educators and social scientists, the term "moral education" has an archaic ring, the ring of the last vestiges of the Puritan tradition in the modern school. This archaic ring, however, does not arise from any intrinsic opposition between the statement of educational aims and methods in moral terms and their statement in psychological terms. In fact, it was just this opposition which the great pioneers of the social psychology of education denied in such works as John Dewey's *Moral Principles in Education*[1] and Emile Durkheim's *Moral Education*.[2] Both of these works attempted to define moral education in terms of a broader consideration of social development and social functions than was implied by conventional opinion on the topic, but both recognized that an ultimate

From Lawrence Kohlberg, "Moral Education in the Schools: A Developmental View," *School Review*, Vol. 74, No. 1 (1966; published by The University of Chicago Press), pp. 1–30. © 1966 by The University of Chicago.

statement of the social aims and processes of education must be a statement couched in moral terms.

Unfortunately, the educational psychologists and philosophers who followed Dewey's trail retained his concern about a broad phrasing of the goals of education in terms of the child's social traits and values (e.g., co-operation, social adjustment, "democraticness," mental health) without retaining Dewey's awareness that intelligent thought about these traits and values required the concepts dealt with by moral philosophers and psychologists. More recently, however, thoughtful educators and psychologists have become acutely aware of the inadequacies of dealing with moral issues under cover of mental-health or group-adjustment labels. We have become aware, on the one hand, that these mental-health labels are not really scientific and value-neutral terms; they are ways of making value judgments about children in terms of social norms and acting accordingly. On the other hand, we have come to recognize that mental-health and social-adjustment terms do not really allow us to define the norms and values that are most basic as ideals for our children. The barbarities of the socially conforming members of the Nazi system and the other-directed hollow men growing up in our own affluent society have made us acutely aware of the fact that adjustment to the group is no substitute for moral maturity.

It is apparent, then, that the problems of moral education cannot be successfully considered in the "value-neutral" terms of personality development and adjustment. In this paper, I shall attempt to deal with some of the value issues involved in moral education but will approach these issues from the standpoint of research findings. I believe that a number of recent research facts offer some guide through the problems of moral education when these facts are considered from Dewey's general perspective as to the relationship between fact and value in education.

I. RESEARCH FINDINGS ON THE DEVELOPMENT OF MORAL CHARACTER RELEVANT TO MORAL EDUCATION IN THE SCHOOLS

One of the major reasons why the social functions of the school have not been phrased in moral-education terms has been the fact that conventional didactic ethical instruction in the school has little influence upon moral character as usually conceived. This conclusion seemed clearly indicated by Hartshorne and May's findings that character-education classes and religious-instruction programs had no influence on moral conduct, as the latter was objectively measured by experimental tests of "honesty" (cheating, lying, stealing) and "service" (giving up objects for others' welfare).[3] The small amount of recent research on conventional didactic moral education provides us with no reason to question these earlier findings. Almost every year a professional religious educator or community-service educator takes a course with me and attempts to evaluate the effect of his program upon moral character. While each starts by thinking his program is different from those evaluated by Hartshorne and May, none comes away with any more positive evidence than did these earlier workers.

While recent research does not lead us to question Hartshorne and May's findings as to the ineffectiveness of conventional, formal moral education, it does lead us to a more positive view as to the possibility of effective school moral education of some new sort. In particular, recent research leads us to question the two most common interpretations of the Hartshorne and May findings: the interpretation that moral behavior is purely a matter of immediate situational forces and rewards and the interpretation that moral character is a matter of deep emotions fixed in earliest childhood in the home. Instead, recent research suggests that the major consistencies of moral character represent the slowly developing formation of more or less cognitive principles of moral judgment and decision and of related ego abilities.

The first interpretation of the Hartshorne and May findings mentioned was essentially that of these authors themselves. Their conclusions were much more nihilistic than the mere conclusion that conventional moral-education classes were ineffective and essentially implied that there was no such thing as "moral character" or "conscience" to be educated anyway. Hartshorne and May found that the most influential factors determining resistance to temptation to cheat or disobey were situational factors rather than a fixed, individual moral-character trait of honesty. The first finding leading to this conclusion was that of the low predictability of cheating in one situation for cheating in another. A second finding was that children were not divisible into two groups, "cheaters" and "honest children." Children's cheating scores were distributed in bell-curve fashion around an average score of moderate cheating. A third finding was the importance of the expediency aspect of the decision to cheat, that is, the tendency to cheat depends upon the degree of risk of detection and the effort required to cheat. Children who cheated in more risky situations also cheated in less risky situations. Thus, non-cheaters appeared to be primarily more cautious rather than more honest than cheaters. A fourth finding was that even when honest behavior was not dictated by concern about punishment or detection, it was largely determined by immediate situational factors of group approval and example (as opposed to being determined by internal moral values). Some classrooms showed a high tendency to cheat, while other seemingly identically composed classrooms in the same school showed little tendency to cheat. A fifth finding was that moral knowledge had little apparent influence on moral conduct, since the correlations between verbal tests of moral knowledge and experimental tests of moral conduct were low ($r = 34$). A sixth apparent finding was that where moral values did seem to be related to conduct, these values were somewhat specific to the child's social class or group. Rather than being a universal ideal, honesty was more characteristic of the middle class and seemed less relevant to the lower-class child.

Taken at their face value, these findings suggested that moral education inside or outside the school could have no lasting effect. The moral educator, whether in the home or in the school, could create a situation in which the child would not cheat, but this would not lead to the formation of a general tendency not to cheat when the child entered a new situation. Carried to its logical conclusion, this interpretation of the findings suggested that "honesty" was just an external value judgment of the child's act which leads to no understanding or prediction of his character. It suggested that concepts of good or bad conduct were psychologically irrelevant and that moral conduct must be understood, like other conduct, in terms of the child's needs, his group's values, and the demands of the situation. "While from the standpoint of society, behavior is either 'good' or 'bad,' from the standpoint of the individual it always has some positive value. It represents the best solution for his conflicting drives that he has been able to formulate."[4] This line of thought was extended to the view that moral terms are sociologically as well as psychologically irrelevant. From the standpoint of society, behavior is not clearly good or bad either, since there are a multiplicity of standards that can be used in judging the morality of an action. As sociologists have pointed out, delinquent actions may be motivated by the need to "do right" or conform to standards, to both the standards of the delinquent gang and the great American standard of success.[5]

A second interpretation of the Hartshorne and May findings was somewhat less nihilistic. This interpretation was that suggested by psychoanalytic and neopsychoanalytic theories of personality.[6] In this interpretation, moral instruction in the school was ineffective because moral character is formed in the home by early parental influences. Moral character, so conceived, is not a matter of fixed moral virtues, like honesty, but of deep emotional tendencies and defenses—of love as opposed to hate for others, of guilt as opposed to fear, of self-esteem and trust as opposed to feelings of inadequacy and distrust. Because these tendencies are basically affective, they are not consistently displayed in verbal or behavioral test situations, but they do define personality types. These types, and their characteristic affective responses, can be defined at the deeper levels tapped by personality projective tests, but they are also related to other people's judgments of the child's moral character. This point of view toward moral character was mostly clearly developed and empirically supported in the writing and research of Robert Havighurst and his colleagues.[7]

While both the "situational" and the "psychoanalytic" interpretations of moral-character research have some validity, recent research findings support a different and more developmental conception of moral character with more positive implications for moral education.[8] While a specific act of "misconduct," such as cheating, is largely determined by situational factors, acts of misconduct are also clearly related to two general aspects of the child's personality development. The first general aspect of the child's development is often termed "ego strength" and represents a set of inter-related ego abilities, including the intelligent prediction of consequences, the tendency to choose the greater remote reward over the lesser immediate reward, the ability to maintain stable focused attention, and a number of other traits. All these abilities are found to predict (or correlate with) the child's behavior on experimental tests of honesty, teacher's ratings of moral character, and children's resistance to delinquent behavior.[9]

The second general aspect of personality that determines moral conduct is the level of development of the child's moral judgments or moral concepts. Level of moral judgment is quite a different matter from the knowledge of, and assent to, conventional moral clichés studied by Hartshorne and May. If one asks a child, "It is very bad to cheat?" or "Would you ever cheat?" a child who cheats a lot in reality is somewhat more likely to give the conforming answer than is the child who does not cheat in reality.[10] This is because the same desire to "look good" on a spelling test by cheating impels him to "look good" on the moral-attitude test by lying. If, instead, one probes the reasons for the moral choices of the child, as Piaget and I have done,[11] one finds something quite different. As an example, we present the child with a series of moral dilemmas, such as whether a boy should tell his father a confidence about a brother's misdeed. In reply, Danny, age ten, said: "In one way, it would be right to tell on his brother or his father might get mad at him and spank him. In another way, it would be right to keep quiet or his brother might beat him up." Obviously, whether Danny decides it is right to maintain authority or right to maintain peer "loyalty" is of little interest compared to the fact that his decision will be based on his anticipation of who can hit harder. It seems likely that Danny will not cheat if he anticipates punishment but that he has no particular moral reasons for not cheating if he can get away with it. When asked, the only reason he gave for not cheating was that "you might get caught," and his teacher rated him high on a dishonesty rating form.

Danny's response, however, is not a unique aspect of a unique personality. It represents a major aspect of a consistent stage of development of moral judgment, a stage in which moral judgments are based on considerations of punishment and obedience. It is the first of the following six stages found in the development of moral judgment:[12]

LEVEL I—PREMORAL

Stage 1.—Obedience and punishment orientation. Egocentric deference to superior power or prestige, or a trouble-avoiding set. Objective responsibility.

Stage 2.—Naively egoistic orientation. Right action is that instrumentally satisfying the self's needs and occasionally other's. Awareness of relativism of value to each actor's needs and perspective. Naive egalitarianism and orientation to exchange and reciprocity.

LEVEL II—CONVENTIONAL ROLE CONFORMITY

Stage 3.—Good-boy orientation. Orientation to approval and to pleasing and helping others. Conformity to stereotypical images of majority or natural role behavior, and judgment of intentions.

Stage 4.—Authority and social-order-maintaining orientation. Orientation to "doing duty" and to showing respect for authority and maintaining the given social order for its own sake. Regard for earned expectations of others.

LEVEL III—SELF-ACCEPTED MORAL PRINCIPLES

Stage 5.—Contractual legalistic orientation. Recognition of an arbitrary element or starting point in rules or expectations for the sake of agreement.

Duty defined in terms of contract, general avoidance of violation of the will or rights of others, and majority will and welfare.

Stage 6—Conscience or principle orientation. Orientation not only to actually ordained social rules but to principles of choice involving appeal to logical universality and consistency. Orientation to conscience as a directing agent and to mutual respect and trust.

Each of these stages is defined by twenty-five basic aspects of moral values. Danny's responses primarily illustrated the motivation aspect of stage 1, the fact that moral motives are defined in terms of punishment. The motivation for moral action at each stage, and examples illustrating them, are as follows:

Stage 1.—Obey rules to avoid punishment. Danny, age ten: (Should Joe tell on his older brother to his father?) "In one way it would be right to tell on his brother or his father might get mad at him and spank him. In another way it would be right to keep quiet or his brother might beat him up."

Stage 2.—Conform to obtain rewards, have favors returned, and so on. Jimmy, age thirteen: (Should Joe tell on his older brother to his father?) "I think he should keep quiet. He might want to go someplace like that, and if he squeals on Alex, Alex might squeal on him."

Stage 3.—Conform to avoid disapproval, dislike by others. Andy, age sixteen: (Should Joe keep quiet about what his brother did?) "If my father finds out later, he won't trust me. My brother wouldn't either, but I wouldn't have a *conscience* that he (my brother) didn't." "I try to do things for my parents; they've always done things for me. I try to do everything my mother says; I try to please her. Like she wants me to be a doctor, and I want to, too, and she's helping me to get up there."

Stage 4.—Conform to avoid censure by legitimate authorities and resultant guilt. Previous example also indicative of this.

Stage 5.—Conform to maintain the respect of the impartial spectator judging in terms of community welfare or to maintain a relation of mutual respect. Bob, age sixteen: "His brother thought he could trust him. His brother wouldn't think much of him if he told like that."

Stage 6.—Conform to avoid self-condemnation. Bill, age sixteen: (Should the husband steal the expensive black-market drug needed to save his wife's life?) "Lawfully no, but morally speaking I think I would have done it. It would be awfully hard to live with myself afterward, knowing that I could have done something which would have saved her life and yet didn't for fear of punishment to myself."

While motivation is one of the twenty-five aspects of morality defining the stages, many of the aspects are more cognitive. An example is the aspect of "The Basis of Moral Worth of Human Life," which is defined for each stage as follows:

Stage 1.—The value of a human life is confused with the value of physical objects and is based on the social status or physical attributes of its possessor. Tommy, age ten: (Why should the druggist give the drug to the dying woman when her husband couldn't pay for it?) "If someone important is in a plane and is allergic to heights and the stewardess won't give him medicine because she's only got enough for one and she's got a sick one, a friend, in back, they'd probably put the stewardess in a lady's jail because she didn't help the important one."

(Is it better to save the life of one important person or a lot of unimportant people?) "All the people that aren't important because one man just has one house, maybe a lot of furniture, but a whole bunch of people have an awful lot of furniture and some of these poor people might have a lot of money and it doesn't look it."

Stage 2.—The value of a human life is seen as instrumental to the satisfaction of the needs of its possessor or of other persons. Tommy, age thirteen: (Should the doctor "mercy kill" a fatally ill woman requesting death because of her pain?) "Maybe it would be good to put her out of her pain, she'd be better off that way. But the husband wouldn't want it, it's not like an animal. If a pet dies you can get along without it–it isn't something you really need. Well, you can get a new wife, but it's not really the same."

Stage 3.—The value of a human life is based on the empathy and affection of family members and others toward its possessor. Andy, age sixteen: (Should the doctor "mercy kill" a fatally ill woman requesting death because of her pain?) "No, he shouldn't. The husband loves her and wants to see her. He wouldn't want her to die sooner, he loves her too much."

Stage 4.—Life is conceived as sacred in terms of its place in a categorical moral or religious order of rights and duties. John, age sixteen: (Should the doctor "mercy kill" the woman?) "The doctor wouldn't have the right to take a life, no human has the right. He can't create life, he shouldn't destroy it."

Stage 5.—Life is valued both in terms of its relation to community welfare and in terms of life being a universal human right.

Stage 6.—Belief in the sacredness of human life as representing a universal human value of respect for the individual. Steve, age sixteen: (Should the husband steal the expensive drug to save his wife?) "By the law of society he was wrong but by the law of nature or of God the druggist was wrong and the husband was justified. Human life is above financial gain. Regardless of who was dying, if it was a total stranger, man has a duty to save him from dying."

We have spoken of our six types of moral judgment as stages. By this we mean more than the fact that they are age-related. First, a stage concept implies sequence, it implies that each child must go step by step through each of the kinds of moral judgment outlined. It is, of course, possible for a child to stop (become "fixated") at any level of development, but if he continues to move upward he must move in this stepwise fashion. While the findings are not completely analyzed on this issue, a longitudinal study of the same boys studied at ages ten, thirteen, sixteen, and nineteen suggests that this is the case. Second, a stage concept implies universality of sequence under varying cultural conditions. It implies that moral development is not merely a matter of learning the verbal values or rules of the child's culture but reflects something more universal in development which would occur in any culture. In order to examine this assumption, the same moral-judgment method was used with boys aged ten, thirteen, and sixteen in a Taiwanese city, in a Malaysian (Atayal) aboriginal tribal village, and in a Turkish village, as well as in America. The results for Taiwan and for America are presented in Figure 1.

Figure 1 indicates much the same age trends in both the Taiwanese and the American boys. It is evident that in both groups the first two types decrease with age, the next two increase until age thirteen and then stabilize, and the last two continue to increase from age thirteen to age sixteen. In general, the cross-cultural studies suggest a similar sequence of development in all cultures, although they suggest that the last two stages of moral thought do not develop clearly in preliterate village or tribal communities.

In the third place, the stage concept implies personality consistency. We said that there was little consistency to honest behavior as such. There is, however, a high degree of consistency, a "g-factor" of moral stage, from one verbal moral situation to the next.[13]

In order to consider the relevance of these moral-judgment stages for our conceptions of moral character, we must consider a little further their

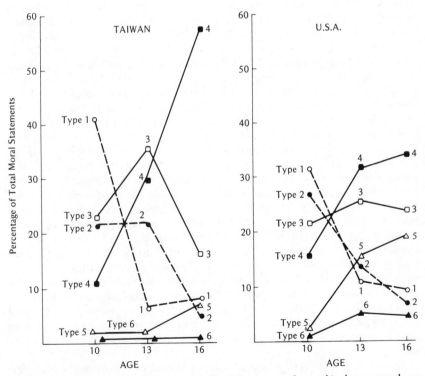

FIGURE 1 Mean per cent of use of each of six stages of moral judgment at three ages in Taiwan and the United States.

relationship to moral conduct. We have already noted that verbal agreement to moral conventions does not generally predict to moral behavior. We noted that when Hartshorne and May measured the child's "knowledge" of the society's moral conventions (as opposed to his response to moral-attitude tests, assessing strength of verbal assent to these convictions), slightly better predictions were obtained; tests of moral knowledge correlated with experimental tests of cheating in the low 30's, about as well as a single cheating test correlates with another. These tests of moral knowledge require somewhat more cognitive understanding of cultural moral prescriptions than do verbal moral-attitude tests, and they are somewhat more age developmental. Our tests of moral judgment, which are more genuinely developmental and reflective of basic cognitive structuring of values than moral-knowledge tests are still better predictors of moral conduct, however, if moral conduct is conceived in developmental terms.

In referring to a definition of moral conduct, in developmental terms, we refer to the implications of the fact found by Hartshorne and May and corroborated by more recent investigations[14]—the fact that such behaviors as honesty (resistance to cheating) do not increase with age during the elementary school years.[15] In contrast, we saw that moral judgment and values were developing in sequential fashion during these years. For the majority of these elementary school years, however, the child has not developed any clear or internal moral values or principles that condemn cheating, so it is not surprising that cheating behavior does not decline in these years. While most elementary school children are aware of, and concerned about, the harm done others by acts of aggression or theft,[16] their only reason for not cheating is their fear of being caught and punished. Even at older ages, teachers give children few moral or mature reasons to think cheating is bad. Sixth-grade children tell us their teachers tell them not to cheat because they will get punished (stage 1) "or because the person you copied from might have it wrong and so it won't do you any good" (stage 2, expediency). In these years, then, resistance to cheating is not so much a matter of internal moral principles as of the situational and expediency factors stressed by Hartshorne and May. With regard to the type of cheating test situation used by Hartshorne and May, the critical issue for the subject's moral judgment is that of trust, what the experimenter or the teacher expects and what he has the right to expect. The experimenter explicitly leaves the subject unsupervised in a situation where he ordinarily expects supervision. This abandonment of control or authority is interpreted in varying ways. A very high degree of cheating in such a situation seems to primarily reflect a naïve abandon to the surface impression that the experimenter doesn't care. A lesser degree of cheating seems to reflect the child's belief that the experimenter doesn't care very much about his not cheating or he wouldn't leave him unsupervised and that a little cheating isn't too bad anyhow, so long as it is not too obvious and excessive or more than the others do.

In one study of sixth graders[17] almost all (80 per cent) of the children cheated somewhat. The majority of children at the premoral level of moral judgment (stages 1 and 2) cheated a great deal, and the majority of the children at the conventional level of moral judgment (stages 3 and 4) cheated a slight or moderate amount.[18] In contrast, adolescents at the level of moral principle (stages 5 and 6) do interpret the opportunity to cheat as involving issues of maintaining trust, contract, social agreement, and equality of reward for equal effort and ability. The one sixth grader in the Kohlberg study at this level did not cheat at all.[19] Among a group of college students also studied, only one of nine principled-level subjects cheated on an experimental test while about one-half of the twenty-six conventional-level subjects did so. (There were no premoral-level subjects in this group.)

Cheating, then, is not a good indicator of moral character until the child has developed in adolescence a set of inner moral principles that prohibit it. By that time, cheating behavior may reflect a lack of full development of moral values (i.e., a failure to reach the level of moral principles) or a discrepancy between action and moral values (a discrepancy due to a variety of possible deficits in ego strength or ego abilities).

More generally, then, there is some meaning to "moral character" as an aim of moral education if moral character is conceived in developmental terms rather than as a set of fixed conventional traits of honesty, responsibility, etc.

Hartshorne and May's critique is justified insofar as it is a critique of a tendency of teachers to respond to isolated acts of deviance as indicating the child's bad or dishonest character. Specific acts of conformity or deviance in themselves reflect primarily situational wishes and fears rather than the presence or absence of conscience or moral character. Nevertheless, there is evidence that repeated misconduct tends to indicate general deficits or retardation of general moral-judgment capacities, or related guilt capacities, and the lack of internal ego control rather than simply situational values or emotional conflicts. While everyday judgments of moral character and worth are often psychologically erroneous, they do correlate with important consistencies in personality and development, which are positive from almost any viewpoint.

In addition to giving new meaning to notions of moral character, recent research also suggests that it may be possible to stimulate the development of moral character in the school. We said that there has been no recent research evidence to suggest revision of Hartshorne and May's finding that convention moral- and religious-education classes had no direct influence on moral conduct as usually conceived. (More recently, ongoing research by Jacob Kounin also suggests that the teacher's use of various techniques of punishment and reward for misconduct has no relationship to the amount and type of misconduct that occurs in the classroom.) These negative results have usually been interpreted as indicating that only the home can have any real effect in moral teaching, because only the home teaching involves the intense and continuing emotional relationships necessary for moral teaching or for induction of potential guilt feelings for wrongdoing. In fact, the failure of conventional moral education in the school is probably not the result of the powerlessness of the school to influence the child's character but the result of the inadequacy of prevalent American conceptions of character education. These conceptions usually center on the training of good "habits" of honesty, responsibility, etc., through preaching, example, punishment, and reward. This conception of character education appears to be just as ineffective in the home as it is in the school. Extensive research on parental practices has found no positive or consistent relationships between earliness and amount of parental demands or training in good habits (obedience, caring for property, performing chores, neatness, or avoidance of cheating) and their children's actual obedience, responsibility and honesty. Amount of use of praise, of deprivation of physical rewards, or of physical punishment is also not found to relate consistently or positively to measures of moral character.[20]

There are, of course, a number of unique influences of the home on the development of character which the school cannot reproduce. These are not matters of specific moral training, however, but of the emotional climate in which the child develops. The only parent-attitude variables consistently found to relate to children's moral character are not "moral training" variables but variables of parental warmth.[21] These emotional-climate variables, however, only account for a very small percentage of the differences between children in moral development or moral character. Many of the environmental influences important in moral development are more cognitive in nature than either the "good habits" or the "early emotions" views have suggested. In part, this cognitive influence is meant in a relatively conventional mental-age or I.Q. sense. Intelligence quotient correlates well with maturity of moral judgment (31 to 53 at varying ages) and almost equally well with behavioral measures of honesty. At the kindergarten level, the capacity to make judgments of good or bad in terms of standards rather than in terms of punishment and egoistic interests is a capacity almost completely determined by cognitive development on Piaget tests of cognition.[22]

We have discussed the influence of general intellectual advance upon the development of moral judgment. In addition, advances in a number of aspects of social concepts customarily thought of as part of the social-studies curriculum are correlated with advance in moral judgment. Children in the original Kohlberg study were asked to say how much and why various occupations (such as judge, policeman, soldier, artist, senator) were respected by most people, an apparent question of comprehension of social fact and function. Responses to this task could be scored in a fashion similar to the moral-judgment questions, and individual children's levels were similar on the two tasks.

This task pointed up the fact that some of the difficulties in moral development of lower-class children are largely cognitive in nature. Sociologists and social critics like Paul Goodman and Edgar Friedenberg have stressed the notion that the school not only transmits middle-class moral values at the expense of lower-class moral values but that there is a certain fundamental "immorality" or inauthenticity" about these middle-class values to the lower-class child in comparison with lower-class values. While sociologists are correct in stressing class-linked value systems, they are not correct in postulating class-based differences in *basic moral* values. The lower-class parent and the middle-class parent show little difference in the rank order of moral values desired for their children; for example, both put honesty at the top of the list.[23] In the Kohlberg studies of moral ideology middle-class and working-class children (matched for I.Q.) differed considerably. These differences, however, were developmental in nature. At one age, middle-class and working-class children differed in one way, at another in a different way. At all ages, however, the middle-class children tended to be somewhat in advance of the working-class children. The differences, then, were not due to the fact that the middle-class children heavily favored some one type of thought, which could be seen as corresponding to the prevailing middle-class pattern. Instead, middle-class and working-class children seemed to move faster and farther.

This finding becomes intelligible when it is recalled that the institutions with moral authority (law, government, family, the work order) and the basic moral rules are the same regardless of the individual's particular position in society. The child's position in society does to a large extent, however, determine his interpretation of these institutions and rules. Law and the government are perceived quite differently by the child if he feels a sense of understanding and potential participation in the social order than if he does not.[24]

The slower development of moral judgment of the working-class boys seemed largely accountable for by two factors, lesser understanding of the broader social order and lesser sense of participation in it. Both factors showed up especially in the social-concept task conceiving occupations but were apparent in their moral judgments as well. It seems likely that social-studies programs in the school could have considerably more positive effect upon these class-differentiating aspects of moral development than is true at present.

Our discussion of social class stressed opportunities for social participation and role-taking as factors stimulating moral development. Perhaps a clearer example of the importance of social participation in moral development is the finding that children with extensive peer-group participation advance considerably more quickly through the Kohlberg stages of moral judgment than children who are isolated from such participation (with both groups equated for social class and I.Q.). This clearly suggests the relevance and potential of the classroom peer group for moral education. In pointing to the effects of extra-familial determinants upon moral development, we have focused primarily on their influence upon development of moral judgment. However, these same determinants lead to more mature moral behavior as well, as indicated by teachers' ratings and experimental measures of honesty and of moral autonomy.[25]

II. A DEVELOPMENTAL CONCEPTION OF THE AIMS AND NATURE OF MORAL EDUCATION

The facts, then, suggest the possibilities of useful planning of the moral-education component of schooling. Such planning raises more fundamental value issues, however, the issues as to the legitimate aims and methods of moral education in the American public schools. The writer would start by arguing that there are no basic value problems raised by the assertion that the school *should* be consciously concerned about moral education, since all schools necessarily are constantly involved in moral education. The teacher is constantly and unavoidably moralizing to children, about rules and values and about his students' behavior toward each other. Since such moralizing is unavoidable, it seems logical that it be done in terms of conscious formulated goals of moral development. As it stands, liberal teachers do not want to indoctrinate children with their own private moral values. Since the classroom social situation requires moralizing by the teacher, he ordinarily tends to limit and focus his moralizing toward the necessities of classroom management, that is, upon the immediate and relatively trivial behaviors that are disrupting to him or to the other children. Exposure to the diversity of moral views of teachers is undoubtedly one of the enlightening experiences of growing up, but the present system of thoughtlessness as to which of the teacher's moral attitudes or views he communicates to children and which he does not leaves much to be desired. Many teachers would be most mortified and surprised to know what their students perceive to be their moral values and concerns. My seven-year-old son told me one day that he was one of the good boys in school, but he didn't know whether he really wanted to be. I asked him what the differences between the good and bad boys were, and he said the bad boys talked in class and didn't put books away neatly, so they got yelled at. Not only is it highly dubious that his teacher's moralizing was stimulating his or any of the children's moral development, but it is almost inevitable that this be the case in an educational system in which teachers have no explicit or thought-out conception of the aims and methods of moral education and simply focus upon immediate classroom-management concerns in their moralizing.

The value problems of moral education, then, do not arise concerning the necessity of engaging in moral education in the school, since this is already being done every day. The value problems arise, however, concerning the formulation of the aims and content of such education. At its extreme, such a formulation of aims suggests a conception of moral education as the imposition of a state-determined set of values, first by the bureaucrats upon the teachers, and then by the teachers upon the children. This is the system of "character education" employed in Russia, as described by U. Bronfenbrenner.[26] In Russia, the entire classroom process is explicitly defined as "character education," that is, as making good socialist citizens, and the teacher appears to have an extremely strong influence upon children's moral standards. This influence rests in part upon the fact that the teacher is perceived as "the priest of society," as the agent of the all-powerful state, and can readily enlist the parents as agents of discipline to enforce school values and demands. In part, however, it rests upon the fact that the teacher systematically uses the peer group as an agent of moral indoctrination and moral sanction. The classroom is divided into co-operating groups in competition with one another. If a member of one of the groups is guilty of misconduct, the teacher downgrades or sanctions the whole group, and the group in turn punishes the individual miscreant. This is, of course, an extremely effective form of social control if not of moral development.

In our view, there is a third alternative to a state moral-indoctrination system and to the current American system of moralizing by individual teachers and principles when children deviate from minor administrative regulations or engage in behavior personally annoying to the teacher. This alternative is to take the stimulation of the development of the individual child's moral judgment and character as a goal of moral education, rather than taking as its goal either administrative convenience or state-defined values. The attractiveness of defining the goal of moral education as the stimulation of development rather than as teaching fixed virtues is that it means aiding the child to take the next step in a direction toward which he is already tending, rather than imposing an alien pattern upon him. An example of the difference may be given in terms of the use of the peer group. In Russia the peer-group structure is created by the teacher (i.e., he divides the classroom into groups), and the peer group is then manipulated by punishments and rewards so as to impose the teacher's or the school's values upon its deviant members. If one took the stimulation of the moral development of the individual child as a goal, one would consider the role of the peer group in quite a different way. In the previous section we discussed the fact that classroom isolates were slower in development of moral judgment than were integrates. This suggests that inclusion of the social isolates in the classroom peer group might have considerable influence on their moral development, though not necessarily an influence of immediate conformity to teacher or school demands.

The implementation of this goal would involve various methods to encourage inclusion of isolates such as are under investigation in a research project at the University of Michigan conducted by Ronald Lippett. Some of these methods involve creating a classroom atmosphere encouraging participation rather than attempting to directly influence sociometric integrates to include isolates. Some of these methods involve more direct appeal to integrated members of sociometric groups, but an appeal to the implementation of already existing social and moral values held by these children rather than an effort to impose the teacher's values upon them by reward or punishment. The process raises many valuable issues potentially stimulating the moral development of the integrates as well, since they must cope with the fact that, "Well, we were finally nice to him and look what he did." These issues involve the opportunity for the teacher to play a different and perhaps more stimulating and open role as a "moral guide" than that involved in supporting conformity to school rules and teacher demands.

A definition of the aims of moral education as the stimulation of natural development is most clear-cut in the area of moral judgment, where there appears to be considerable regularity of sequence and direction in development in various cultures. Because of this regularity, it is possible to define the maturity of a child's moral judgment without considering its content (the particular action judged) and without considering whether it agrees with our own particular moral judgments or values or those of the American middle-class culture as a whole. In fact, the sign of the child's moral maturity is his ability to make moral judgments and formulate moral principles of his own, rather than his ability to conform to moral judgments of the adults around him.[27]

How in general, then, may moral maturity as an aim of education be defined? One general answer starts from the conception of maturity in moral judgment and then considers conduct in terms of its correspondence to such judgment. Maturity levels are most clearly apparent in moral judgment. Furthermore, the general direction of maturity of moral judgment is a direction of greater morality. Each of the Kohlberg stages of moral judgment represents a step toward a more genuinely or distinctly moral judgment. We do not mean by this that a more mature judgment is more moral in the sense of showing closer conformity to the conventional standards of a given community. We mean that a more mature judgment more closely corresponds to genuine moral judgments as these have been defined by philosophers. While philosophers have been unable to agree upon any ultimate principle of the good that would define "correct" moral judgments, most philosophers agree upon the characteristics that make a judgment a genuine moral judgment.[28] Moral judgments are judgments about the good and the right of action. Not all judgments of "good" or "right" are moral judgments, however; many are judgments of esthetic, technological, or prudential goodness or rightness. Unlike judgments of prudence or esthetics, moral judgments tend to be universal, inclusive, consistent, and to be grounded on objective, impersonal, or ideal grounds.[29] "She's really great, she's beautiful and a good dancer"; "the right way to make a Martini is five to one"—these are statements about the good and right that are not moral judgments since they lack these characteristics: If we say, "Martinis should be made five to one," we are making an esthetic judgment, and we are not prepared to say that we want everyone to make them that way, that they are good in terms of some impersonal ideal standard shared by others, and that we and others should make five-to-one Martinis whether they wish to or not. In a similar fashion, when Danny answered our "moral should" question, "Should Joe tell on his older brother?" in stage 1 terms of the probabilities of getting beaten up by his father and by his brother, he did not answer with a moral judgment that is universal (applies to all brothers in that situation and ought to be agreed upon by all people thinking about the situation) or that has any impersonal or ideal grounds. In contrast, the stage 6 statements quoted earlier not only specifically use moral words, such as "morally right" and "duty," but use them in a moral way; for example, "regardless of who it was" and "by the law of nature or of God" imply universality; "morally, I would do it in spite of fear of punishment" implies impersonality and ideality of obligation, etc. Thus the value judgments of lower-level subjects about moral matters are not moral responses in the same sense in which the value judgments of high-level subjects about esthetic or morally neutral matters are not normal. The genuinely moral judgment just discussed is what we mean by "judgments of principle" and "to become morally adult is to learn to make decisions of principle; it is to learn to use 'ought' sentences verified by reference to a standard or set of principles which we have by our own decision accepted and made our own."[30]

How can the teacher go about stimulating the development of moral judgment? We have already rejected the notion of a set curriculum of instruction and exhortation in the conventional moral virtues, a conception killed by Hartshorne and May's demonstration of ineffectiveness. Dewey[31] pointed to the inadequacy of such a conception long ago and traced it to the fact that it assumed a divorce between moral education and intellectual education on the one side, and a divorce between education and real life on the other. To put Dewey's critique more bluntly, both conventional character-education classes or preaching and conventional moralizing by teachers about petty school routines are essentially "Mickey Mouse" stuff in relationship to the real need for moral stimulation of the child. To be more than "Mickey Mouse," a teacher's moralizings must be cognitively novel and challenging to the child, and they must be related to matters of obvious, real importance and seriousness.

It is not always necessary that these matters be ones of the immediate and real-life issues of the classroom. I have found that my hypothetical and remote but obviously morally real and challenging conflict situations are of intense interest to almost all adolescents and lead to lengthy debate among them. They are involving because the adult right answer is not obviously at hand to discourage the child's own moral thought, as so often is the case. The child will listen to what the teacher says about moral matters only if the child first feels a genuine sense of uncertainty as to the right answer to the situation in question. The pat little stories in school readers in which virtue always triumphs or in which everyone is really nice are unlikely to have any value in the stimulation of moral development. Only the presentation of genuine and difficult moral conflicts can have this effect.

It is obvious, however, that discussion of such more remote but important moral conflicts as are involved in the situations we have used are only a supplement to the discussion of the more immediate "real-life" issues of classroom life. The most serious and vital value issues represented by school life are not moral values per se but are intellectual in nature. As Dewey points out in discussing moral education, the serious business of the school is, and should be, intellectual. The principle values and virtues the teacher attends to are intellectual. However, the teacher may attend to these values and virtues either with awareness of their broader place in moral development or without such awareness. If such awareness is not present, the teacher will simply transmit the competitive-achievement values that dominate our society. He will train the child to think that getting a good mark is an absolute good and then suddenly shift gears and denounce cheating without wondering why the child should think cheating is bad when getting a good mark is the most important value. If the teacher has a greater awareness of the moral dimensions of education, his teaching of the intellectual aspects of the curriculum will illustrate the values of truth integrity, and trust in intellectual affairs and intellectual learning in such a way as to carry over to behaviors like cheating.

We have mentioned that to stimulate development of moral communication by the teacher should involve issues of genuine moral conflict to the child and represent new cognitive elements. There is also an important problem of match between the teacher's level and the child's involved in effective moral communication. Conventional moral education never has had much influence on children's moral judgment because it has disregarded this problem of developmental match. It has usually involved a set of adult moral cliches that are meaningless to the child because they are too abstract, mixed up with a patronizing "talking down" to the child in concrete terms beneath his level. In fact, the developmental level of moral-education verbalizations must be matched to the developmental level of the child if they are to have an effect. Ideally, such education should aim at communicating primarily at a level one stage above the child's own and secondarily at the child's own level. Experimental demonstration of this principle is provided in a study by E. Turiel.[32] Turiel ascertained the moral level of sixth graders on the Kohlberg stages, matched them for I.Q., and divided them into three experimental groups (and a fourth control group). All the groups (except the controls) were then exposed to short role-playing and discussion sessions with the experimenter centered on hypothetical conflict situations similar to those used in the Kohlberg tests. For one experimental group, the experimenter presented a discussion using moral judgments and reasons *one level above* the child's own. For a second group, the experimenter used moral judgments *two levels above* the child's own. For the third group, the experimenter used moral judgments *one level below* the child's own. All the children were then retested on the original test situations as well as on the situations discussed with the experimenter. Only the children who were exposed to moral judgments one level above their own showed any appreciable absorption of the experimenter's moral judgments. The children exposed to judgments one level below their own showed some absorption (more than those exposed to judgments two levels above) but not nearly as much as those exposed to one level above. Thus, while children are able to understand moralizing that is talking down beneath their level, they do not seem to accept it nearly as much as if it is comprehensible but somewhat above their level. It is obvious that the teacher's implementation of this principle must start by his careful listening to the moral judgments and ideas actually expressed by individual children.

So far, we have talked about the development of moral judgment as an aim of moral education. The sheer ability to make genuinely moral judgments is only one portion of moral character, however. The remainder is the ability to apply these judgmental capacities to the actual guidance and criticism of action. Thus, in addition to stimulating the development of general moral judgment capacities, a developmental moral education would stimulate the child's application of his own moral judgments (not the teacher's) to his actions. The effort to force a child to agree that an act of cheating was very bad when he does not really believe it (as in the case of the author of the school-newspaper article) will only be effective in encouraging morally immature tendencies toward expedient outward compliance. In contrast, a more difficult but more valid approach involves getting the child to examine the pros and cons of his conduct in his own terms (as well as introducing more developmentally advanced considerations).[33]

In general, however, the problem of insuring correspondence between developing moral judgments and the child's action is not primarily a problem of eliciting moral self-criticism from the child. One aspect of the problem is the development of the ego abilities involved in the non-moral or cognitive tasks upon which the classroom centers. As an example, an experimental measure of high stability of attention (low reaction-time variability) in a simple monotonous task has been found to clearly predict to resistance to cheating in Hartshorne and May's tests (r = .68).[34] The encouragement of these attentional ego capacities is not a task of moral education as such but of general programming of classroom learning activities.

Another aspect of the encouragement of correspondence between the child's moral values and his behavior is more difficult and fundamental. In order to encourage the application of his values to his behavior, we need to make sure that the kinds of behavior demands we make have some match to his already existing moral values. Two major types of mismatch occur. One type, which we have already mentioned, occurs when teachers concentrate on trivial classroom routines, thus moralizing issues that have no moral meaning outside the classroom. If the teacher insists on behavioral conformity to these demands and shows no moral concerns for matters of greater relevance to the child's (and the society's) basic moral values, the child will simply assume that his moral values have no relevance to his conduct in the classroom. It is obvious that the teacher must exert some influence toward conformity to trivial classroom rules, but there are two things he can do to minimize this sort of mismatch. The first is to insure that he does communicate some of his values with regard to broader and more genuinely moral issues. The second is to treat administrative demands as such and to distinguish them from basic moral demands involving moral judgment of the child's worth and moral sanctions. This does not imply that no demands should be treated as moral demands but that the teacher should clearly distinguish his own attitudes and reactions toward moral demands from his more general conformity demands. The second form of mismatch between the teacher's moral demands and the child's moral values arises from the fact that the teacher feels that certain behavioral demands are genuine moral demands, but the child has not yet developed any moral values that require these behaviors. We gave as an example the fact that resistance to cheating on tests does not derive from anything like moral values in young children aged five to seven, whereas resistance to theft and aggression do correspond to more spontaneous and internal moral values at this age. Given this fact, it does not seem wise to treat cheating as a genuine moral issue among young children, while it may be with older children. In general, the teacher should encourage the child to develop moral values relevant to such behavior as cheating but should not treat the behavior as a moral demand in the absence of such values.

It is clear, then, that a developmental conception of moral education does not imply the imposition of a curriculum upon the teacher. It does demand that the individual teacher achieve some clarity in his general conceptions of the aims and nature of moral development. In addition, it implies that he achieve clarity as to the aspects of moral development he should encourage in children of a given developmental level and as to appropriate methods of moral communication with these children. Most important, it implies that the teacher starts to listen carefully to the child in moral communications. It implies that he becomes concerned about the child's moral judgments (and the relation of the child's behavior to these judgments) rather than about the conformity of the child's behavior or judgments to the teacher's own.

NOTES

1. J. Dewey, *Moral Principles in Education* (Boston: Houghton Mifflin Co., 1911).

2. E. Durkheim, *Moral Education* (Glencoe, Ill.: Free Press, 1961; originally published in 1925).

3. H. Hartshorne and M. A. May, *Studies in the Nature of Character* (3 vols.; New York: Macmillan Co., 1928-30).

4. I. M. Josselyn, *Psychosocial Development of Children* (New York: Family Service Association, 1948).

5. It is evident that the cheating behavior so extensively studied by Hartshorne and May does not represent a conflict between unsocialized base instinctual impulses and moral norms. The motive to cheat is the motive to succeed and do well. The motive to resist cheating is also the motive to achieve and be approved of, but defined in more long-range or "internal" terms. Moral character, then, is not a matter of "good" and "bad" motives or a "good" or "bad" personality as such. These facts, found by Hartshorne and May, have not yet been fully absorbed by some clinical approaches to children's moral character. If a child deviates a little he is normal; if he deviates conspicuously, he is believed to be "emotionally disturbed," i.e., to have mixed good and bad motives; if he deviated regularly or wildly, he is all bad (a "psychopathic" or "sadistic" personality).

6. E.g., S. Freud. *Civilization and Its Discontents* (London: Hogarth Press, 1955; originally published in 1930); E. Fromm, *Man for Himself* (New York: Rinehart, 1949); and K. Horney, *The Neurotic Personality of Our Time* (New York: W. W. Norton & Co., 1937).

7. R. J. Havighurst and H. Taba, *Adolescent Character and Personality* (New York: John Wiley & Sons, 1949); and R. F. Peck and R. J. Havighurst, *The Psychology of Character Development* (New York: John Wiley & Sons, 1960).

8. L. Kohlberg, "Moral Development and Identification," in H. Stevenson (ed.), *Child Psychology* (Chicago: University of Chicago Press, 1963); "The Development of Children's Orientations toward a Moral Order: I. Sequence in the Development of Moral Thought," *Vita Humana*, VI (1963), 11-33; and "The Development of Moral Character and Ideology," in M. Hoffman and L. Hoffman (eds.), *Review of Child Development Research* (New York: Russell Sage Foundation, 1964).

9. Kohlberg, "The Development of Moral Character and Ideology," *op. cit.* These factors are also stressed in the works of Peck and Havighurst, *op. cit.*, who found extremely high correlations between ratings of moral character and ratings of ego strength.

10. L. Kohlberg, "The Development of Children's Orientations toward a Moral Order: II. Social Experience, Social Conduct, and the Development of Moral Thought," *Vita Humana*, Vol. IX (1966).

11. J. Piaget, *The Moral Judgment of the Child* (Glencoe, Ill.: Free Press, 1948; originally published in 1932); Kohlberg, "The Development of Children's Orientations toward a Moral Order: I," *op. cit.*

12. Kohlberg; *ibid.*

13. L. Kohlberg, "Stage and Sequence: The Developmental Approach to Moralization," in M. Hoffman (ed.), *Moral Processes* (Chicago: Aldine Press, 1966).

14. Kohlberg, "The Development of Moral Character and Ideology," *op. cit.*

15. This has sometimes been viewed as consistent with the psychoanalytic view that character is fixed at an early age in the home. In fact, this does not seem to be true, as there is little predictability from early moral conduct to later adolescent moral conduct *(ibid.).*

16. R. Krebs, "The Development of Moral Judgment in Young Children" (Master's thesis, Committee on Human Development, University of Chicago, 1965).

17. Kohlberg, "The Development of Children's Orientations toward a Moral Order: II," *op. cit.*

18. The attitude of this latter group is probably well expressed by the following anonymous student article in a British school paper written after a siege of experimental studies of honesty: "The next test reminded me of the eleven plus exam. I had great fun doing these but they are sure to think I am barmy. But then they made a fatal mistake; they actually gave us our own papers to mark. We saw our mistakes in time and saved the day by changing the answers."

19. Kohlberg, "The Development of Children's Orientations toward a Moral Order: II," *op. cit.*

20. Findings reviewed in Kohlberg, "Moral Development and Identification," *op. cit.,* and "The Development of Moral Character and Ideology," *op. cit.*

21. See n. 20, above.

22. Krebs, *op. cit.*

23. M. Kohn, "Social Class and Parental Values," *American Journal of Sociology,* LXIV (1959), 337–51.

24. The effect of such a sense of participation upon development of moral judgments related to the law is suggested by the following responses of sixteen-year-olds to the question, "Should someone obey a law if he doesn't think it is a good law?" A lower-class boy replies, "Yes, a law is a law and you can't do nothing about it. You have to obey it, you should. That's what it's there for." For him the law is simply a constraining thing that is there. The very fact that he has no hand in it, that "you can't do nothing about it," means that it should be obeyed (stage 1).

A lower-middle-class boy replies, "Laws are made for people to obey and if everyone would start breaking them. . . . Well, if you owned a store and there were no laws, everybody would just come in and not have to pay." Here laws are seen not as arbitrary commands but as a unitary system, as the basis of the social order. The role or perspective taken is that of a storekeeper, of someone with a stake in the order (stage 4).

An upper-middle-class boy replies, "The law's the law but I think people themselves can tell what's right or wrong. I suppose the laws are made by many different groups of people with different ideas. But if you don't believe in a law, you should try to get it changed, you shouldn't disobey it." Here the laws are seen as the product of various legitimate ideological and interest groups varying in their beliefs as to the best decision in policy matters. The role of law-obeyer is seen from the perspective of the democratic policy-maker (stage 5).

25. Kohlberg, "The Development of Children's Orientations toward a Moral Order: II," *op. cit.*

26. "Soviet Methods of Character Education: Some Implications for Research, *American Psychologist,* XVII (1962), 550–65.

27. A research indication of this comes from the Kohlberg study. After individual moral-judgment interviews, the children in the study were subjected to pressure from an adult and from disagreeing peers to change their views on the questions. While maturity of moral judgment predicted to moral behaviors involving conformity to authority (e.g., cheating), it predicted better to behaviors involving maintaining one's own moral views in the face of pressure from

authorities (r= .44). Among college students, not only were principled subjects much less likely to cheat, but they were much more likely to engage in an act of moral courage or resistance when an authoritative experimenter ordered them to inflict pain upon another subject (Kohlberg, "The Development of Children's Orientations toward a Moral Order: II," *op. cit.*).

28. R. M. Hare, *The Language of Morals* (New York: Oxford University Press, 1952); I. Kant, *Fundamental Principles of the Metaphysics of Morals*, trans. T. K. Abbott (New York: Liberal Arts Press, 1949); and H. Sidgwick, *Methods of Ethics* (London: Macmillan, 1901).

29. L. Kohlberg, "The Development of Modes of Moral Thinking and Choice in the Years Ten to Sixteen" (Ph.D. dissertation, University of Chicago, 1958).

30. Hare, *op. cit.*

31. *Op. cit.*

32. "An Experimental Analysis of Developmental Stages in the Child's Moral Judgment," *Journal of Personality and Social Psychology*, 1966 (in press).

33. This is actually more valuable for acts of good conduct than for acts of bad conduct. We expect children to justify defensively acts of misconduct. If we take the trouble to find out, however, we will often be surprised that the acts of good conduct we praise are valued by the child himself for immature reasons and that we are really rewarding "selfish" rather than moral values. In such cases it is relatively easy to foster the application of developmentally more advanced values in the child's repertoire to his own behavior.

34. P. Grim, L. Kohlberg, and S. White, "Some Relationships between Conscience and Attentional Processes," *Child Development*, Vol. XXXVII (1966) (in press).

CARL D. GLICKMAN
CHARLES H. WOLFGANG

18. Dealing with Student Misbehavior: An Eclectic Review

There are many teachers today who find themselves locked into an isolated, volatile classroom. Under pressure of court decisions, mass media, and a wide array of social change, the teacher confronts a group of children from diverse ethnic and cultural populations who are seething with fears and prejudices they developed in the outside world.

Because of his or her training, educational strategies, and beliefs, the

From Carl D. Glickman and Charles H. Wolfgang, "Dealing with Student Misbehavior: An Eclectic Review," *Journal of Teacher Education*, Vol. 30, No. 3 (May/June 1979), pp. 7–13. © 1979 American Association of Colleges for Teacher Education.

teacher may be committed to operating a classroom that falls pedagogically and stylistically between one that is open and informal and one that is structured. With the existing climate of fear and hostility, however, students do not adapt readily to the teacher's particular style. Learning is thwarted.

Barth (1977, p. 491) aptly describes the teacher's plight:

(they) cannot afford the tidy luxury of running classrooms which comply with an ideology. For them the question is not which banner to wave or which model has the most to offer children and adults, but rather, "When . . . method A doesn't work for Johnny, what can I try next? B? C? or D?"

Teachers must live with harsh realities. If students do not adjust to a particular approach, teachers must adapt by drawing from a spectrum of strategies.

What are these strategies? Where are they derived? How might they be used?

Answers to these questions may help equip the educator with ways to interact successfully with the wide varieties of student behavior.

TEACHER-CHILD INTERACTION

Popular educational literature contains a rash of teacher-child interaction programs and models under the jargon of contingency management, reality therapy, teacher effectiveness training and supportive discipline. There are also the old standbys like behavior modification, now known as behavior analysis.

Many of these strategies are based on psychological theories that have been formulated in the last 20 or 30 years. The popular teacher-child interaction models may be classified into three ideological camps: the non-interventionists, interactionalists, and the behaviorists.

Non-interventionists

Proponents of this approach have an abiding faith in the child as master of his/her own destiny.

The child above all is a rational being who is constantly striving *inwardly* to perfect himself *outwardly*. The function of the teacher is to provide a facilitating environment for a child to give feelings free expression. The teacher then verbally reflects the child's emotions.

This view is evident in the writings of Rogers (1969), Axline (1947), Moustakas (1971), and Gordon (1975).

Moustakas (p. 33) expressed this point as:

Personal interaction between teacher and child means that differences in children are recognized and valued . . . Relations must be such that the child is free to recognize, express, actualize, and experience his own uniqueness. Teachers help to make this possible when they show they deeply care for the child, respect his individuality, and accept the child's being without qualification.

The non-interventionists believe in a supportive, facilitating environment where the teacher is present to accept and empathize with the child in his or her inner struggle.

Interactionalists

This theory of teacher-child behavior views the child as developing not from an inward unfolding or from conditioning by outside forces, but from simultaneous pushes and pulls from within and without.

The child must be made aware of behaviors that enhance or detract from the functioning of society. The teacher's role is to be constantly interacting with the child. A modicum of leeway must be allowed to a circumscribed point. Upon transgressing acceptable boundaries, a child comes into conflict with the teacher. The teacher then takes command and either unilaterally or jointly forces a resolution.

This theoretical view is broadly evident in the writings of Berne (1966), Harris (1969), Dreikurs (1972), and Glasser (1969).

Dreikurs (p. 71) observes:

Conflicts cannot be resolved without shared responsibility, without full participation in decision making of all the participants in a conflict. Democracy does not mean that everybody can do as he pleases. It requires leadership to integrate and to win mutual consent.

The interactionalist theory of coping with child behavior is based on the teacher's ability to be a clarifier, boundary delineator, and finally an enforcer. These theorists believe that the child should take responsibility for his/her actions but needs the active involvement of a firm, though kind, teacher. The child and/or teacher may decide on the remedy. Regardless of action, a solution acceptable to all must result.

Behaviorists

These theorists hold to the assumption that a child develops according to environmental conditions. It is only with the implementation of a logical system of conditioning for the child that rationality of behavior can be assured.

Skinner (1971) put it this way:

An experimental analysis shifts the determination of behavior from autonomous man to the environment—an environment responsible both for the evolution of the species and for the repertoire acquired by each member . . . It is the autonomous inner man who is abolished and that is a step forward.

The teacher is the controller of the environment. His or her task is to select the appropriate conditioners to insure the proper learning behavior in the classroom. Conditioners come in the form of material and verbal rewards, direct commands, and physical contact.

Examples of behaviorist theory are evident in the writings of Dobson (1970), Homme (1973), Blackham and Silberman (1975), Siegfried and Therese Englemann (1969), and Axelrod (1977).

Axelrod (p. 158) echoes the behaviorist's point of view by saying:

By accepting a position as a teacher, a person has not only a right but an "obligation" to modify student behavior. Children enter the schools without the necessary social and academic skills to function independently and productively in adult society . . . Teachers who do not bring about suitable changes in student behavior are failing to live up to the responsibilities of their profession.

With the behaviorist, there is no recognition of the inner emotions and rationality of the child. There are no second thoughts in the teacher taking command over a child's actions. The teacher makes immediate use of directive techniques to channel the child into constructive actions. To keep a child learning efficiently, misbehavior is dealt with by selective reinforcement until the desired behavior is obtained.

MERGING OF THOUGHT

Each of the three ideological models rests upon a particular set of assumptions, ideas, and parameters. These, in turn, determine the teacher's strategies of dealing with children on a daily basis.

Unfortunately for most teachers who must face the emergent realities of daily classroom interaction, it is quite possible that none of these models will meet their needs totally.

What help is the non-interventionist's belief in the child's "freedom to express his feelings" when the teacher finds the sixth-grader ready to strike a peer with a dangerous object?

How can one use an interactional strategy of developing a joint commitment with a student who angrily refuses to speak?

Or within the behaviorist framework of ignoring misbehavior and reinforcing positive behavior, what is the teacher to do with the young child suffering anxiety and screaming in fear?

Redl's criticism expressed in 1944 (p. 259) might still hold true today:

All sides have pitched "belief" versus "belief" leaving the classroom teacher alone on the job in the process. Well, then, why the heck don't we forget about our theoretical disputes or convictional competitions and get together on the job?

What Redl was suggesting is an eclectic position that would take best from each of the current theories and procedures.

A CONTINUUM OF POWER

The key concepts of the three theoretical positions can be placed along a continuum of power between child and teacher. At one end (large C, little t)

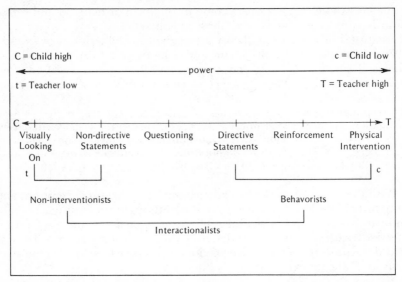

FIGURE 1. Continuum of power between child and teacher and placement of key concepts of the three theoretical positions.

the child has the most control of his/her behavior. At the other end, (little c, large T) the teacher subsumes the child's power.

At the child-centered end of the continuum, the non-interventionists use minimal teacher power. The teacher uses an empathic glance, physical presence, and reflective questions—supportive and accepting behavior towards the child to maximize the chances of a child working through his or her misbehavior.

The interactionalists have the teacher move in more boldly by drawing attention to the behavior through non-directive questions and statements. They strive for an "all win" solution, where the teacher and child attempt to find an integrative answer to the deviant behavior. They employ some of the centralist techniques of the non-interventionists and behaviorists, but are on guard against any unilateral control of behavior.

On the teacher-centered end of the continuum, the behaviorists have the teacher take control. The child corrects his or her behavior as a result of commands, explicit teacher modeling, rewards, and/or being physically restrained or moved away. In all techniques, the behaviorist looks for a tangible, immediate way to correct misbehavior.

Using this continuum of power as a framework, it is interesting to see how the strategies of popular approaches to discipline fit in; to trace the differences within the same ideological camps and thus multiply the possible tools of use for the classroom teacher.

Our attempt is to provide maximum knowledge with the minimum of words and any particular approach that sparks the reader's interest should be pursued through the original source.

A NON-JUDGMENTAL APPROACH

Non-interventionists are fixed at the child-centered end of the continuum.

Basic to these writers is the ability to establish a nonjudgmental relationship with each child. The teacher helps the child through sensitive listening and watching. The teacher accepts the child as trustworthy and does not evaluate or analyze the child's behavior. The teacher supports the child by simply glancing and making his/her visual presence felt.

After observing and listening to the child, the teacher may reflect the child's emotions through non-directive questions that facilitate the child's understanding of his action. Axline (1947, p. 156) gave this example:

When Malcolm picks up a vicious-looking stick and raises it to strike George, the teacher can effectively stop the blow if she remarks, "Malcolm is angry enough to try to use violence to settle the argument." Malcolm puts down the weapon and resorts once more to words.

If the child persists in annoying behavior, all the authors agree on confronting the child. Axline (p. 155) suggests a non-directive statement to the child, with an either/or alternative:

Bob is feeling tough today. He thinks if he uses force, he can get to the head of the line. But our rules, Bob, say that you will either take your turn fairly or get out of the line.

Rogers (pp. 18–141) discussed the use of the encounter group as a vehicle for giving the student feedback on how his or her behavior is affecting others. Moustakas (pp. 22–26) wrote of the teacher expressing disagreement with the child's action, yet unequivocally allowing the child to also disagree. In his opinion, the confrontation should continue until a joint resolution of *feeling,* (not necessarily the issue) is made.

Gordon (p. 39) amplifies the non-interventionists' position by more clearly delineating the teacher's role by first assessing the problem. "It is *imperative* that teachers be able to distinguish between those problems students have in their lives that cause *them* a problem . . . and those that have a tangible and concrete effect on the teacher by interfering with the teacher's needs."

If the problem (daydreaming, or refusing to work with other children, for example) does not have a tangible effect on others, the teacher should not use judgmental language such as lecturing, praising, or probing. Rather, the teacher should begin a four-step process with passive listening. Step two, if needed, would be acknowledgement through such gestural responses as head nodding to indicate the teacher is listening. Step three would be to encourage the child to make an expression of feelings and/or ideas through such "door opener" questions as "Do you want to talk more about it?" The final step is active listening in which the teacher periodically "mirrors" the child with non-directive statements.

THE CHILD: "I don't want to work with Marcia; she is a stuck-up snob."
TEACHER: "At times you feel that Marcia doesn't like you."

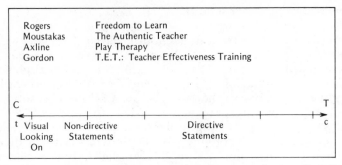

FIGURE 2. Non-interventionists and their approaches to discipline.

It is through this technique that the child will eventually solve his/her own problems.

The process can be used also with the entire class if the problems involve others.

If the problem is a teacher "owned" problem (a student scratching a desk, for example, or a student who repeatedly arrives late and disturbs the class), Gordon advocates "I" messages as the proper tool.

The teacher expresses the problem to the child or class with a message which describes the behavior, states its tangible or concrete effects, plus the teacher's feelings. Each "I" message begins with "when."

"When you have your feet in the aisle (description of behavior), I'm apt to trip over them (tangible effect) and I'm afraid I'll fall and get hurt (feelings)."

Once the teacher has given an "I" message, she/he moves back into "active listening" (non-directive statements) allowing the child or class to freely express feelings and perceptions. The child or class thus can enter a problem process involving these six steps:

1. Defining the problem.
2. Generating possible solutions.
3. Evaluating the solutions.
4. Deciding which solution is best.
5. Determining how to implement the decision.
6. Assessing how well the solution solved the problem.

Rogers, Axline, and Moustakas place particular stress on the non-judgmental climate. Gordon suggests specific steps to achieve it. All share a total belief in the child as capable, rational, and the controller of his/her own destiny.

POWER-SHARING THEORY

The interactionalists believe in the sharing of power between student and teacher.

214

They analyze the causes of both teacher and student behavior, with the goal being a joint resolution satisfactory to both. Unlike the non-interventionists, they feel the misbehaving child must be helped through selective questioning, directive statements, a system or plan of action. Interactionalists are concerned with the psychological "feeling" level of behavior as the cause of deviance in antisocial behavior. They neither accept the child as capable of resolution as the non-interventionists do, nor do they view the teacher as responsible for imposing correct behavior as the behaviorists do.

Raths, Harmin, and Simon; Berne; Harris; and others place great stress on analyzing verbal messages to clarify inner values and various mental states. Dreikurs and Cassel and Glasser focus on particular plans of action after joint analysis.

Raths, Harmin, and Simon (1966, p. 11) use value clarification questions so the student will become "less apathetic, confused, and irrational and (act) in ways that are more positive, purposeful, and enthusiastic." The basic strategy is to respond to a student with questions so he or she might consider what he has chosen, what he prizes, and/or what he is doing. The following are sample questions under the value area:

1. "Where do you suppose you got that idea?" (choosing freely).
2. "What else did you consider?" (choosing from alternatives).
3. "What do these terms mean to you?" (choosing thoughtfully and reflectively).
4. "Are you glad you feel that way?" (prizing and cherishing).
5. "Are you willing to stand up to be counted?" (affirming).
6. "Have you made plans to do more than you already have done?" (acting upon choices).
7. "Has it been worth the time and effort?" (repeating).

Raths, Harmin, and Simon do not put their clarification techniques in an immediate situation of misbehavior. But a teacher could draw upon the strategies in a follow-up conference with a misbehaving student. For example, Jimmy tears Fred's jacket after being called mother_____.

The teacher might call the two together and probe with:

1. Where did you get the idea to tear his jacket?
2. What else did you consider doing?
3. Has it been worth the time and effort?

The belief is that value questions will stimulate the student to clarify his/her thinking and thus allow him to act in a rational manner.

Freed, Berne, and Harris provide a system that allows for the coding of messages between child and teacher. The basic tenant of *I'm O.K., You're O.K.* is that messages should support a child's and adult's acceptance of each other.

For example, a student knocks paints to the floor in a display of frustration. The student may be acting as a child looking for a parent to acknowledge his inadequacy.

The teacher may decide to affirm this by using parent messages such as:

1. Who made this mess?
2. See this mess you made, because you're not careful.

The teacher might give egocentric child messages:

1. Why is it that I always have to clean up your mess?
2. I'm so mad, I'm not giving you any more paint.

If the teacher believes the child is adequate, the response should be one which states, in essence, let's get on with doing something about this mess.

Learning to code messages between student and teacher provides a framework of common language to establish mutual wavelengths that are affirming of each other. Afterwards, the teacher and student should be able to signal each other when verbal and non-verbal messages are creating feelings of inadequacy.

Dreikurs sees misbehavior as only a discouraged child trying to find his/her place. The child acts on the faulty logic that misbehavior will provide the social acceptance desired.

His procedures in responding to children is for the teacher to: observe the behavior, and be sensitive to his/her own feelings. From these observations and feelings, the teacher should attempt to determine what *goal* is motivating the child's behavior.

Dreikurs classifies children's misbehavior in terms of four goals: Attention-getting, Power, Revenge, Inadequacy. The teacher can determine which goal the child possesses through observation, questioning, and the child's impact on him or herself.

In counseling the child, the teacher may confront the child with questions:

1. Could it be that you want special attention? (attention).
2. You want your own way and hope to be boss? (power).
3. You want to hurt others as much as you feel hurt by them? (revenge).
4. You want to be left alone? (inadequacy).

As a response to each one of the child's motivational goals, the teacher attempts to find realistic ways that the child can behave in a socially acceptable manner.

Glasser, as a part of reality therapy, asks the teacher to reflect on his or her own behavior.

The first step is to determine whether a student's misbehavior is due to such factors as irrelevant classroom experiences, unreasonable expectations, or teacher negativity. If such instances have occurred and the teacher has corrected them, the problem must be analyzed as student-caused.

Glasser also advocates a written agreement, signed by the student, on a plan to abide by the rules. The technique can also be used with an entire class.

Glasser's next step would be partial isolation in an area of the room

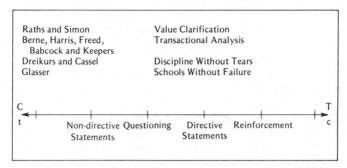

FIGURE 3. Interactionalists and their approaches in discipline.

where a disruptive student can hear and partially see what is happening. This isolation should not be considered as punishment, but simply an opportunity to let the child have time to get himself under control.

If the child continues to be disruptive, he or she could be removed to the school office with the principal repeating quiet correction. The principal must assure the child that he will not be punished and allow him to be as comfortable as possible.

If these steps failed, Glasser would remove the child from school to the home to return on a "Tolerance Day" or trial basis. The last resort would be suspension or expulsion.

Glasser bases his teacher-student interactions on commitment to carry out an agreed-upon plan that is relevant and will help the student. The teacher's role is to aid in the development of the plan, commitment, and to follow through with enforcement. Once a student makes a commitment, "no excuse is acceptable for not following through" (p. 23).

The interactionalists have in common a belief in the rational process when shared *between* student and teacher. They agree on the need to analyze verbal and non-verbal behavior for the inner meaning. They differ in the extent of focusing on self-analysis and categorization versus planning and implementing specific treatment.

MOLDING BEHAVIOR

The behaviorists believe the teacher should be the molder of behavior.

Whether admitted or not, they argue that adults shape a child's learning. Rather than leaving such an influence to chance, one should be systematic about insuring that students act in an acceptable manner.

Unlike the non-interventionists and the interactionalists, they are concerned with behavior itself—not any deeper emotional levels.

Homme, Axelrod, and Blackham and Silberman take a scientific approach to conditioning through reinforcement. Dobson and, to some extent, Englemann move to the farthest end of the Power Continuum by using physical force and the fear of punishment to mold behavior.

Positive reinforcement, according to Blackham and Silberman (pp. 144-151), can be derived from four options:

1. Token Reinforcement. A tangible item that has value in that it can be exchanged for materials of a reinforcing event.
2. Social Reinforcement. The use of teacher attention, approval, and praise after desirable student behavior.
3. Primary Reinforcement. A tangible item that satisifies a biologically based need. The use of sweets, popcorn, cereal, or a drink after appropriate behavior.
4. Contingency Management. Providing a self-satisfying behavior after displaying correct actions. For example, after Sue Ann completes her chronically neglected mathematics assignments, she can read the "Teen" magazines that she enjoys.

Homme includes all four types as usable for contingency contracting a student's performance. He suggests a series of rewards (longer recess time, for example) for correct behavior. His concept of contingency contracting is based on ways of *increasing* desirable behavior.

Axelrod (pp. 20–40) proposes four main strategies, not in any order, for *decreasing* deviance in student behavior:

1. *Reinforcing Desired Behavior* by, for example, rewarding the frequently moving child when he or she sits still.
2. *Ignore the Misbehavior* by pursuing classroom routine. (Axelrod warns that the misbehavior will increase at first but then will decline.)
3. *Punishment* by making the consequences of misbehavior not worth its doing. Marks could be kept for a child's misbehavior, for example, with detention or less play time for a specified number of marks. Or the teacher could point at the student and shout "No" each time he/she misbehaved.
4. *Enforced Time Out* for a designated time in an absolutely bare room devoid of all interests.

Axelrod, Homme, and Blackham and Silberman urge a positive approach to conditioning that is based on scientific recording and analysis of student actions. They do not espouse the use of physical intervention as Englemann and Dobson do.

Englemann views misbehavior within the context of deprivation. When the student is not behaving correctly, he/she is not learning and in many cases is keeping other students from learning. Since a teacher's job, in his opinion, is to concentrate on learning, he proposes that the teacher needs to interact quickly and forcefully to get the child back on track. His strategy (pp. 61–80) is to:

1. Tell the child how to act.
2. Repeat the rules.
3. Compliment those who are quiet.
4. Remove the disruptive student to an isolated area.
5. If the student still misbehaves, put your hands over his mouth and say, "Be quiet in class."

6. Repeat the action, standing over the deviant until the student is quiet; then move back to teaching.
7. Finally, reward the student in the form of tokens or praise when he/she continues to be quiet.

Englemann, adamant about dealing with misbehavior, wrote (p. 77):

If the child does not stand up on command, forcefully stand him up. From time to time remind him, "When I say, 'stand up,' you stand up." If he turns his head away . . . forcefully turn his head back.

Dobson transfers Englemann's physical intervention from a single misbehaving child to an entire classroom. He provides a rationale for solving discipline problems by suggesting that they should not happen in the first place (pp. 96–106). Misbehavior occurs, he says, because the teacher does not initially take the offensive.

1. *Rules.* On the first day of class, the teacher should explain the rules of the class in a stern manner.
2. *Intimidation.* The rules should be backed up with a challenge ". . . if you choose to challenge me I have 1,000 ways to make you miserable."
3. *Example.* When a child misbehaves in the first few days, accept it as a challenge and demonstrate to all students the consequences by punishing the child severely.

Dobson believes that by November the strict enforcer will have proven that he or she is "tougher, wiser, and braver than they are" (p. 99). The result, in his opinion, is a comfortable, secure, and productive classroom.

The behaviorists, although split on the use of physical intervention versus reinforcement, agree with having a child conform to a teacher's or adult's standard of behavior.

They are directly opposite from the non-interventionists who value a non-judgmental relationship with students. The interactionalists' position of sharing power is negated by the behaviorists' techniques that give unilateral power to the teacher.

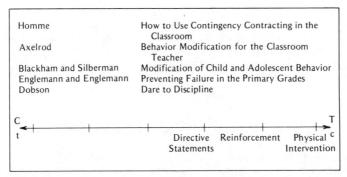

FIGURE 4. Behaviorists and their approaches to discipline.

CONCLUSIONS

By pulling together the techniques and strategies used by the authors and their models, we have a collection of teacher behaviors that can be used as a composite resource.

The teacher can determine:

1. The type of individual that is desirable in the classroom and the larger society, and
2. The particular needs of the child in becoming such an individual.

Within this context, the teacher can judge the congruency of practices already being used and then determine if revisions or new strategies are needed.

In simplified terms:

If we wish children to express themselves freely and work out their own difficulties, we largely use nonintrusive techniques of visually looking on, listening, and verbally reflecting back the child's emotional state;

If we wish children to clarify their behavior in terms of consequences with others, we largely use interactional techniques of questioning; "I" messages; categorizing the content of messages (Parent, Child, Adult); value discussion; sorting out motives (attention-getting, power, revenge, and inadequacy); and mutual contracting;

If we wish children to learn appropriate behavior as determined by the teacher, we largely use behaviors and strategies of contingency contracting, various reinforcement schedules, commanding, punishing, and isolating.

Each of the above techniques raises a host of questions.

1. What techniques best help to develop an adult who will function rationally in a wider society?
2. At what age can rational techniques work?
3. What are the legal rights of a child under each of these systems?
4. Which system is most appropriate for those children with gross social, physical, or mental differences?
5. In today's age of individualization, is an individual approach needed for each child?

The answers are not easily found. It is the teacher who must decide. Many alternatives exist. The teacher must select those that are most acceptable to oneself and the needs of the children under one's guidance.

REFERENCES

Axelrod, S. *Behavior modification for the classroom teacher*. New York: McGraw-Hill, 1977.

Axline, V. M. *Play therapy*. Boston: Houghton-Mifflin, 1947.

Babcock, D. & Keepers, T. *Raising kids O.K.* New York: Grove Press, 1976.

Barth, R. *Beyond open education*. Phi Delta Kappan, February 1977.

Berne, E. *Games people play*. New York: Grove Press, 1966.

Blackham, G. & Silberman, A. *Modification of child and adolescent behavior* (2nd ed.). Belmont, Calif.: Wadsworth, 1975.

Dobson, J. *Dare to discipline.* Wheaton, Ill.: Tyndale House, 1970.

Dreikurs, R. & Cassel, P. *Discipline without tears.* New York: Hawthorne, 1972.

Englemann, S. & Englemann, T. *Preventing failure in the primary grades.* New York: Simon and Schuster, 1969.

Freed, A. M. *TA for kids: and grown-ups, too.* Los Angeles, Calif.: Jalmar Press, 1973.

Glasser, W. *Schools without failure.* New York: Harper & Row, 1969.

Gordon, T. *T.E.T.: Teacher effectiveness training.* New York: Peter H. Wyden, 1975.

Harris, T. A. *I'm OK—You're OK: A practical guide to transactional analysis.* New York: Harper and Row, 1969.

Homme, L. *How to use contingency contracting in the classroom.* Champaign, Ill.: Research Press, 1970.

Moustakas, C. *The authentic teacher.* Cambridge, Mass.: Doyle, 1972.

Raths, L. E., Harmin, M., & Simon, S. B. *Values and teaching: Working with values in the classroom.* Columbus, Ohio: Merrill, 1966.

Redl, F., & Wineman, D. *When we deal with children: Selected writings.* New York: Free Press, 1972.

Rogers, C. R. *Freedom to learn: A view of what education might become.* Columbus, Ohio: Merrill, 1969.

Skinner, B. F. *Beyond freedom and dignity.* New York: Bantom, 1972.

MILLIE ALMY

19. Spontaneous Play: An Avenue for Intellectual Development

Early child education has just been rediscovered. Psychologists interested in learning and cognition, linguists, mathematicians, physicists, economists, anthropologists and representatives of other scholarly disciplines are beginning to recognize that a child's experience in the years before he is six may influence not only his attitudes toward intellectual ideas, but his actual abilities for grasping them.

This is no new idea to the nursery educator and one might anticipate

Reprinted by permission from *Young Children,* Vol. 22, No. 5 (May 1967), pp. 265–277. Copyright © 1967, National Association for the Education of Young Children, 1834 Connecticut Avenue, N.W., Washington, DC 20009.

that she would welcome new support for it. She has appreciated such support. Unfortunately, however, attempts to explore cooperatively the implications of the idea that children really learn in nursery school have often come to nothing or ended in mutual distrust. Many different factors contribute to this state of affairs, but perhaps most crucial has been a lack of mutual understanding of the nature and function of play in the cognitive life of the young child.

Nursery educators, since the very beginning of the nursery school movement, have regarded play as an inherent right of the child (Omwake, 1963). Moreover they have long identified the child's play with experimentation that offers unlimited opportunities for learning (Johnson, 1928; Goldsmith, 1946). In this regard, they are in complete accord with their colleagues in other professions, though the latter may more recently have given up the layman's notion that play is merely "nonconstructive and unrealistic behavior" (Mussen, Conger & Kagan, 1963, p. 269).

Suppose, however, that the nursery educator and her colleague visit a typical nursery school classroom together. The activity is kaleidoscopic, as children flow out of one small group and into another. Domestic themes merge with transportation themes as the husbands from the housekeeping corner become the truck drivers delivering cement to the construction workers in the block corner. This is play. It represents "important learning" for the nursery educator. Her colleague is baffled. He sees no apparent beginning, no apparent end, little "structure," and surprisingly little teacher participation. What he had in mind is quite different: equipment more obviously designed to teach specific concepts, teacher-directed games to stimulate language and thought, and less or none of the same kind of activity he observes in his own children's play at home. At this point collaboration often ceases. The nursery educator is horrified at her colleague's notion of "play." He is unconvinced of the validity of her notion of "learning."

Progress can only be made when a clearer differentiation is made between two forms of play, both important to intellectual development, both holding legitimate places in the nursery school curriculum, but each having certain specific characteristics. The first form of play, the one so highly valued by the nursery educator, is activity that is self-initiated by the child. It is lacking in structure, other than that given it by his interests and his imagination. The second form is adult-prescribed activity, initiated and directed by the nature of the equipment (Omwake, 1963).

Traditionally (if an institution with something less than 50 years of existence can properly be said to have a tradition), the greater portion of the nursery school day has been allotted to play of the first kind. Even during so-called "work" periods, when many children painted or made things at the carpentry bench or built with blocks, strong elements of spontaneous play were usually present. During the years when emotional and social development received primary emphasis in most nursery schools, this type of play predominated. But a combination of circumstances has recently begun to call into question the proper balance between the two forms of play.

The new proponents of the importance of early learning do not discount the importance of the child's spontaneous inclination toward play. They would indeed capitalize on it. O.K. Moore, for example, avers that his "prepared learning environment" simply shapes the investigative, manipulative, repetitive behavior characteristic of the normal child's play into the responses involved in learning to read. J. McV. Hunt (1961), in *Intelligence and Experience*, a volume that devotes many pages to Piaget's views on the function of play in intellectual development, makes a general proposal for "governing the encounters" young children have with their environments. He specifies that these encounters should be enthusiastically relished by the child since they are to be "matched" to his developing abilities, providing enough challenge to be interesting but not so much as to be frustrating. Not surprisingly, Hunt and others with similar concerns for the early intellectual experience of young children have been much attracted to the Montessori method since its apparatus is designed to pattern the child's play toward the eventual development of specific and basic concepts. The possibilities for intervention in the child's play in order to give it particular meaning have also been given impetus in revised curricula for elementary schools. J. S. Bruner's (1961) much quoted hypothesis that "any subject can be taught effectively in some intellectually honest form to any child at any stage of development" has added weight to the notion that at least some elements of the fundamental ideas of the disciplines should be taught in the kindergarten, and perhaps also in nursery school.

What does this mean for the nursery school curriculum? Is spontaneous, free-flowing, self-initiated play to be replaced by structured play where the cognitive culmination can be clearly foreseen (by the adult at least) from the outset? Perhaps—if nursery educators and their colleagues fail to appraise adequately the cognitive elements in spontaneous play, and if nursery teachers continue, as some have in recent years, to abdicate their responsibility for nurturing these elements.

Those who must make decisions as to what constitutes a proper balance between structured and spontaneous play can find little to guide them in either psychological or educational research. There is substantial evidence that both children and animals, deprived of opportunities for play, fail to learn as effectively as those who have freedom to manipulate and explore. But the issue here is a different one. Should the nursery school, an educational institution, assume responsibility for an activity that healthy children are going to initiate and carry on regardless of whether they happen to be enrolled in a nursery school? What justification, if any, can be found for the deliberate inclusion of such activity?

For possible answers to these questions we turn, initially, to a reexamination of some of the tenets of psychoanalytic theory that have in one way or another profoundly influenced the thinking of nursery school educators at least since the early 1940s. Next we look to the theory and experiments of Piaget, whose ideas about the nature of intellectual development are only now beginning to permeate American psychology and education. Finally, we also give brief consideration to some current research in cognitive development.

PSYCHOANALYTIC VIEWS OF PLAY

One has only to put on the spectacles provided by psychoanalytic theory to see in the spontaneous play of young children some of the most elementary human emotions laid bare. Love and hostility, anxiety and aggression, sympathy and jealousy are all there together with a great variety of fantasies and defensive maneuvers. But play, as some of the earliest psychoanalytic studies of children clearly indicated, reflects much more than emotion alone. Its emotional, physiological and intellectual aspects are interwoven and only logically separable. "In actual experience they are closely associated, developing together . . . almost from the beginning and growing the one out of the other as well as reacting the one upon the other" (Griffiths, 1935, p. 269).

The cohesiveness is perhaps nowhere better illustrated than in the work of Susan Isaacs (1930, 1933) who, as one of the first to conduct a nursery school based on a psychoanalytic theory of development, entitled the first volume of her observations *Intellectual Growth in Young Children* and the second, *Social Development in Young Children*. Anna Freud, long concerned with the ramification of psychoanalytic theory for education, observes that the thinking of the young child is often brilliant (he arrives at solutions to problems that may amaze the adult), but it is not solidly based (A. Freud, 1946, pp. 179–180). It is bound neither to logic nor to reality. This is nowhere more apparent than in spontaneous play. In a somewhat similar vein, Lili Peller (1952) notes that play is largely wishful thinking. Accordingly, solving a problem through play appears the opposite of intellectual problem solving. Nevertheless, play and reasoning have several common elements. Neither has direct and immediate consequences in the outer world. In both, certain elements of reality are selected and varied. Both are far quicker than is direct action in reality. Isaacs (1950, p. 104) identifies an "as if" orientation in both play and reasoning. One play or thinks *as if* the world were ordered in a certain way. Such an orientation serves to overcome the obstacles of space and time. Peller (1954) also comments that play like reasoning is precipitated by an experience that is not satisfactorily completed. Play provides the opportunity not only to savor whatever pleasurable aspects the experience had and in various ways to work out compensations for its hurts, but also to understand it.

From such a view of spontaneous play, one might well conclude that it provides a setting for the exercise of certain of the abilities involved in thinking and reasoning. It is as though at this period the child, freed from the handicaps eventually to be imposed by logic and some of the realities of space and time, could try out incipient intellectual powers.

Clearly, however, play in the usual nursery school setting does place any number of reality-based limitations on the child. A doll-carriage may serve equally as cradle, shopping cart or delivery van, but it will not go through an opening that is too narrow for it. A block construction can be the Empire State Building, or a satellite on its launching pad, but it will not stand unless it is properly balanced. Each such instance constitutes a challenge, to which the child can respond in various ways. With emotion clearly in the foreground, he may cry or kick or leave the scene. More playfully, he will incorporate the physical realities into his fantasy. The carriage changes its destination, the Empire State blows down, the satellite blasts off prematurely or play retreats while reasoning comes to the foreground and a problem is solved. A new gate is constructed. The blocks are rearranged.

Anna Freud (1963) underlines the importance of achievement of these sorts where the child solves a problem independently of adult praise and approval. It represents the capacity the child has for deriving pleasure from task completion and problem solution. This aspect of the child's development, although for a time rather neglected in psychoanalytic theory, has long been recognized by Anna Freud and has figured prominently in the formulations of psychoanalytical ego psychology. In a recent monograph, R. W. White (1963), reviewing the history of psychoanalytic and specifically its ego psychology, also cites more academically oriented research in child and animal psychology dealing with manipulative behavior, curiosity and explorative play. He proposes the incorporation into the psychoanalytic theory of development of a new motive, *effectance* or the active tendency to influence the environment.

The theoretical issues involved are of little interest here. What is relevant is the fact that psychoanalytic theory has for so long regarded the young child's spontaneous play as a reflection not only of his emotional conflicts, but also of his developing intellectual competence. Despite this, it appears that many nursery schools (there are notable exceptions), including both those acknowledging a psychoanalytic orientation and those influenced less directly by the general infiltration of psychoanalytic thought into child psychology, have been so pervasively and persistently preoccupied with the emotional aspects of play as to neglect its intellectual connotations.

The symptoms of such preoccupation are varied. One is the teacher's assertion that the children "learn through their play," an assertion accompanied by an inability to describe that learning in any terms other than those having to do with emotional or social adjustment. To say that the children are "forming concepts" in their play is not enough. One needs to know what concepts are revealed and at what level of adequacy.

A second symptom of preoccupation with the emotional is apparent lack of involvement of the teacher in the intellectual life of the child. She is an observer who intervenes to arbitrate disputes and to comfort the frustrated. But she seldom rearranges the environment to confront the child with a possiblity for reducing his frustration by solving a problem. She sometimes notes the intellectual confusions his play reveals (they become part of her repertoire of amusing incidents) but she feels no particular responsibility for providing experience in play or elsewhere to correct misconceptions.

A third indication of disregard of the intellectual is the striking similarity (in some instances one could say identity) of materials and equipment, and indeed of much of the play itself, from one classroom to another, whether the children are three-year-olds, four-year-olds or five-year-olds.

Perhaps what is lacking here is a clear sense of developmental direction. "The playing child," says Erikson (1959, p. 85), "advances forward to new stages of real mastery." The advance proceeds along two fronts, one related to association with peers, the other to the use of toys and equipment. Along both, the child, in a sense, moves out of himself to confront reality more effectively.

At first, the nursery school child treats other children as things. Gradually he learns "what potential play content can be admitted only to fantasy, and only to play by and with oneself, and what content can be shared with others" (Erikson, 1959, p. 85). This is an essential step toward the intelligent grasp of ideas other than one's own. The child also makes intellectual progress as he uses toys and equipment. "If the first use of the thing world is successful and guided properly, the pleasure of mastering toy things becomes associated with the mastery of conflicts which were projected on them and with the prestige gained through such mastery" (Erikson, 1959, p. 85).

The goal, of course, is not the mere mastery of toys but the understanding of the larger physical and social environment, and one's place in it. For the three- or four-year-old child's nursery school teacher to see his becoming a five- or six-year-old through his play, and to help him to become so, need not be to push or pressure him, but rather to nurture basic abilities as they are developing. That this is no easy task is readily granted. Children do not all progress in the same fashion nor at the same rate. What may be an intriguing challenge to one child, offers real threat to another. Furthermore, most nursery school teachers, with the possible exception of those whose professional education is very recent, have very hazy notions about cognitive advances they might reasonably expect to observe and to promote during the nursery school years. Their uncertainty reflects, in part, the research available to teachers. This literature is considerably better at describing the nature of the concepts children of these ages are likely to have than it is at delineating the processes involved in their formation. Despite its inadequacies, however, a considerable body of research literature dealing with cognitive processes in young children is now accumulating. Some of it has direct relevance to the place of play in the child's intellectual development. Much has been stimulated by the theories and investigations of Jean Piaget.

PIAGET'S VIEWS

Perhaps no single investigator in the world has given more attention to cognition in children than has Piaget. His volume, *Play, Dreams and Imitation in Childhood* (1962), describes the evolution of the child's thought as revealed in his play from infancy through the period of early childhood. Its illustrations are drawn from his observations of his own three children. Another volume, *The Early Growth of Logic in the Child* (Inhelder & Piaget, 1964), includes "experiments with children as young as two years, and deals with the development of the ability to classify objects on the basis of their similarities, and to arrange them in order on the basis of some attribute on which they differ." Piaget has also investigated children's concepts of space, geometry, number, quantity, time and velocity, but in these areas he has included relatively few subjects younger than five.

Piaget's theory of the development of intelligence encompasses the infant's sucking, looking and grasping and the adolescent's ability to deal with abstract logical propositions, and attempts to describe the evolution of the latter from the former.

As the child grows and his experience increases, one might say that he mentally stores more and more information, and constructs new and more effective ways of retrieving and applying it. In infancy, information is stored in patterns-of-action (schemas). The baby "knows" his environment through what he can do with it. By the time he is established in elementary school he has an array of relatively stable concepts with which to apprehend his world. Such stability comes only as the child's perceptions and actions and the information he derives therefrom are adapted to the ways others perceive and act. Thinking becomes less egocentric and more socialized.

Piaget describes the adaptive processes involved as consisting on the one hand of *accommodation,* in which the child's behavior, or more specifically his thinking, conforms to fit the outer reality, and on the other hand of *assimilation,* in which the child integrates the information thus gained into his already existing systems of meaning. The two processes are reciprocal though at any given point in development they may or may not be in equilibrium. For example, most children make a kind of verbal accommodation in learning to count to five considerably before the counting experience becomes sufficiently well assimilated for them to have a stable concept of fiveness. Piaget identifies instances in which accomodation is ascendant over assimilation as instances of imitation. Conversely when assimilation takes priority the child is seen as playing. Obviously in spontaneous play as here defined, imitation is not ruled out. Children imitate adults, other children, animals, even machines. But the predominant process in most of spontaneous play seems to be assimilation. "Play constitutes the extreme pole of assimilation of reality to the ego while at the same time it has something of the creative imagination which will be the motor of all future thought and even of reason" (Piaget, 1962, p. 162).

PLAY REFLECTS CHILD'S PROGRESS

Although, as Piaget indicates, there is no reason to think that the child believes in everything he plays (we are reminded of the child who proposed that he and his playmate "pretend we are not playing pretend"), the content of the play and extent of its egocentricity reveals something of the child's progress toward more socialized thought. To view that progress as Piaget does, one needs to contrast the thinking of an average four-year-old with his brother or sister who has reached the age of seven.[1] Typically, the latter is not only more objective, that is, less inclined to be able to view the world only from the limits of his own perspective, but is also more conceptual in his thinking. Where the younger child tends to be taken in by

[1]When Piaget attributes a particular way of thinking to a specific age level, he refers to the age at which three-quarters of the children in his studies thought in this fashion. Some of them would have reached that mode of thinking by six, some as early as five. The ages he reports are also specific to Geneva, Switzerland. (Piaget, 1964.)

the appearance of things—he will think, for example, that there is more to drink when the water from one vessel is poured into two smaller ones—the older one is not deceived by such transformations. Where the older child can mentally manipulate the relationships between two or more variables (think "operationally" in Piaget's terms), the younger child tends to focus on the first one and then another.

The growing awareness that objects have many properties, that they can be viewed along different dimensions, and that they can be classified in a variety of ways is, Piaget believes, a product of the child's activity with them. Through manipulation—touching, lifting, holding, arranging, sorting and so on—the child begins to take note of similarities among the objects he encounters. In like fashion he comes to pay attention to differences in objects that are alike in some respects and differ in others. Eventually, just as he can sort an array of objects into collections that have one or more similar attributes, such as form, color and weight, he can order them on the basis of their differences, arranging them from smallest to largest, darkest to lightest, softest to hardest, and so on. In these activities, Piaget sees the origins of truly conceptual thinking. Such thought implies the existence of a system whereby the individual can identify the defining attributes of a concept and the extent to which a particular instance of the concept may vary and still be included in the class, and at the same time deal with the intricacies of inclusion in more than one class.

At first glance, the ability to arrange experience in logical categories seems far removed from spontaneous self-initiated play as here described. Would it not more likely be a product of structured, teacher-arranged play? Clearly, the latter kind of play contributes. But Piaget seems to suggest that structured play may not be sufficient, particularly for the younger children. The reason lies in the necessity for the child to take in reality in his own egocentric and affect-laden way before he can adapt to the system of logical thought that characterizes adult thinking. Piaget (1962, p. 166) states his convictions thus.

Why is there assimilation of reality to the ego instead of immediate assimilation of the universe to experimental and logical thought? It is simply because in early childhood this thought has not yet been constructed, and during development it is inadequate to supply the needs of daily life.

According to Piaget, the construction of logical thought depends not only on the child's activity with material things, but also on his social collaboration with other children. Characteristically, the preschool child has difficulty in conceiving a point of view different from his own. But interaction with his peers in the social give-and-take of spontaneous play confronts him with the necessity of accommodating himself to their ideas. Presumably, since these ideas are not so strikingly different from his own as may be those of the adults, adaptation is more readily made to their thought than to the thought of the older person. ". . . doing things in social collaboration, in a group effort . . . leads to a critical frame of mind, where children must communicate with each other. This is an essential factor in intellectual development" (Piaget, 1964, p. 4).

Clearly, Piaget's theoretical formulations regarding the function of play in the intellectual life of the child can be used to support the contention that spontaneous play has a legitimate place in the nursery school and kindergarten curriculum. Unfortunately, neither Piaget nor others who are espousing or testing his theories have carried on the experimental work necessary to reveal the intricate relationships between the intellectual experience the child has during this period and his later conceptual development. Most of the experimentation that has been done so far deals with various possibilities for facilitating the transition from the intuitive, perceptually dominated thought of the preschool period, to the logical, "operational" thinking of the older child. Such a transition is manifested in the ability to "conserve." The child who has made such a transition no longer insists that the quantity of a ball of clay changes as it is elongated, or that there are "more" blocks when they are spread over a large area than when they are bunched together. Several studies (Almy, 1966, pp. 40–48) have revealed the difficulties involved when short-term training procedures are used in an attempt to accelerate the child's progress toward his transition. On the other hand, some of the work, notably that of Smedslund, suggests that procedures that lead a child to question the adequacy of his own responses and consequently re-think them may be more effective. Progress, accordingly, comes only as the child experiences some dissatisfaction with what he already knows. From this one might argue that spontaneous play provides not only a good means for practicing and thus consolidating or assimilating what one knows, but also for confronting or accommodating to situations that may challenge and potentially revise that knowledge.

It is Piaget's view that the child's response to instruction from without is always relative to whatever internal construction he has already developed (Flavell, 1963, p. 406). Such a view supports the idea that the curriculum should provide some balance between adult prescribed experiences that are intended for all the children, and those that are oriented to the individual child.

INDIVIDUALITY IN COGNITION

While some investigators are concerned with tracing the steps in intellectual development that seem to be common to the majority of children, others attempt to isolate the factors that make for individual differences in cognitive activity. For example, one group (Kagan, Moss & Sigel, 1963) has identified certain stable cognitive preferences or "styles" among individuals of adequate intelligence that can be traced back to the nursery school years. Some children tend to analyze and seek out details in scanning their environment. Others tend to respond to the field as a whole. Grossly, the analytic children appear to be less impulsive, less hyperkinetic, more apt to become absorbed in tasks and to be oblivious to distraction than their equally intelligent but nonanalytic peers. In a group of adults studied from infancy these differences seemed to be as apparent in spontaneous play in the nursery school as they were in their responses to assigned cognitive tasks in later years. Interestingly, the differences are much greater for boys than for girls.

229

Cognitive "style" represents a dimension of child behavior of which nursery educators have likely long had an intuitive but vague awareness. Many view it as a personality variable or emotional response, not necessarily identified with the way the child copes intellectually.

Further information on individuality in cognitive development can also be anticipated as more reports come in from work currently in progress with children from disadvantaged homes. Most of the investigations so far have pointed up their deficits in perceptual learning and in the acquisition of concepts.

Hunt (1961), drawing in part on Piaget, has proposed that a better match between children's cognitive organization and the educational experiences provided might serve to improve their cognitive functioning. Factors similar to those subsumed under "cognitive style" may need to be taken into account in the matching process.

Another manifestation of individuality in cognition receiving considerable attention of late is often labeled "creativity." The term means different things to different investigators. Nor is it certain how many of these meanings are shared by the nursery educator, who has long been ostensibly concerned with its nurture. Nonetheless it seems clear that connections may be found between certain aspects of spontaneous play, and performance on some of the cognitive tasks that are currently being used to appraise creative thinking (or potential for it.). Nina Lieberman (1964), for example, found some association between teachers' ratings of the "playfulness" of kindergarten children, and the "divergent thinking" factors of "ideational fluency," "spontaneous flexibility" and "originality" as measured on cognitive tasks derived from work by Guilford and Torrance.

A great number of other studies dealing with various aspects of cognition in children of nursery school and kindergarten age might be included here. Some provide information directly relevant to early childhood, and implicity to children's play. Other studies are so specific to a given theoretical issue and a given experimental condition that any generalizations must await further experimentation in more naturalistic settings. Obviously there is also great need for further investigation of children's cognitive activity during spontaneous play. To what extent does it reflect fantasy, and to what extent is there evidence of learning through encounters with the physical environment and with one's peers? Despite the lack of completely definitive answers to these and related questions, the available theory and research clearly support the idea that spontaneous play can contribute importantly to the young child's developing intelligence. What then are the implications for the curriculum?

UNDERSTANDING AND SUPPORTING SPONTANEOUS PLAY IN THE NURSERY SCHOOL

We start with the assumption that the nursery school, serving as a specially prepared educational environment, and under the direction of teachers who have had special professional training, should provide something more as a setting for spontaneous play than does a typical home setting. This "something more" is a function of the teacher's ability to analyze or diagnose cognitive functioning as it is revealed in play, and in the light of that analysis, to make further provisions for the children's development both in their play and in other aspects of the curriculum.

The analysis here proposed is not intended to supersede the appraisal of emotional, personality or adjustment factors that skilled nursery school teachers have always made, but rather to underline the importance of another dimension of that appraisal.

Teachers have long studied children's spontaneous play for evidence of their motivation, their ways of coping with anxiety, their developing concepts of themselves. No less important, to some extent interwoven, and yet to some extent separable is evidence regarding the children's curiosity, their interest in investigation, in problem solving, and in mastery. The extent to which children manifest such motivation reflects in part the history of their experiences in their family, and the kinds of pressure, encouragement and defeat they have known there. But it is also a product of the expectations for and support of the learning they encounter in the nursery school.

Similarly, the concepts the child reveals in his play reflect not merely the information he has gained outside school, but also in school. Teachers might well watch and listen to spontaneous play not only for evidence as to what information the children have, but also how it is organized and categorized. What attributes or properties do the children notice as they encounter objects and materials? How effectively do they label these and other experiences? What kinds of relationships enter into their awareness? What kinds of reasoning are revealed in their play? Do they proceed from one particular instance to another particular instance, picking up some similar elements, or are they beginning to weigh situations more deductively? What kinds of interferences and generalizations can they make? What sorts of contradictions do they notice? To what extent do they see situations only from their own point of view, and to what extent can they stand, as it were, in another's place?

These are the kinds of questions that teachers need to consider if they are to appraise the cognitive levels at which each of the children is functioning, and if they are to provide experience to further cognitive development. Obviously whatever information can be gleaned from spontaneous play will serve to supplement what is known from the child's functioning in other parts of the curriculum.

Such dimensions in intellectual behavior as cognitive style and playfulness can also be appraised in the child's spontaneous play. What implications these may have for the child's further instruction, either in the nursery school or later, are by no means clear. Perhaps they represent orientations toward learning that had best be respected throughout schooling. Or perhaps it is possible to encourage children to shift orientations according to the tasks at hand.

In general, such analysis or diagnosis as has been proposed here is for the teacher's own and rather immediate use in planning for individual children and for the group as a whole. Closer attention to both the level of the child's cognitive functioning and the apparent content of this thought should provide the teacher with many possibilities for stimulating further thought and providing him with further information.

The content of many of the activities typically provided in the nursery school curriculum might well reflect this analysis. The trips that are arranged for all or for part of the group, the visitors that are invited to share experiences with the children, the books and pictures, the natural science observations and experiments that are introduced can all be chosen not simply because children of these ages have tended to enjoy them, but because they offer appropriate possibilities for extending or strengthening the knowledge of these particular children. In like fashion some of the teacher's cues as to the kinds of structured games, puzzles and so on to be provided can come from her expanded knowledge of the children's cognitive abilities as revealed in their spontaneous play.

So far as the balance between spontaneous and more structured play is concerned, it seems likely that the more the teacher knows about the ways in which each child functions, the more apt she will become in maintaining an appropriate balance. Erikson's (1959, p. 83) observation that some elementary school children learn more readily from directed instruction, others from guided play, is somewhat supported by the investigations of cognitive style, and may have relevance for nursery school children as well. But to limit the play of the younger child solely to that structured by the adult would not only run counter to the child's typical way of life, but would be to deny him the important opportunities to initiate and test his own ideas and schemes in spontaneous play. Further, play at this stage of development is not simply an avenue for moving ahead in the acquisition of knowledge and skills. It serves equally as a place where past experience is confronted (sometimes over and over) and eventually consolidated.

Because there are these uniquely personal dimensions to the child's spontaneous play, one might question whether it is appropriate for the teacher to intervene in it at all. But children normally do look to the teacher for some help, particularly in keeping their behavior within acceptable bounds. She must at least step in when the play seems to be leading toward physical harm or the destruction of valued property. Beyond this, the amount and kind of direct intervention seems to be largely a matter of the teacher's artistry and sensitivity. Less directly, the teacher can set the stage for the child's play, and accordingly open new cognitive possibilities for it. Rearranging materials and equipment and introducing those with which the children are not familiar are obvious means to this end. Creating opportunities for children to associate with different playmates may also be appropriate.

If there is to be a continuous appraisal of play and the way it serves the development of each child's powers, teachers cannot be responsible for many children. The task demands keen awareness of each child, what he does and how he thinks today, where he was yesterday and where he may go tomorrow. In a sense nothing that has been suggested here goes beyond what some nursery school teachers have done intuitively, if not always with explicit consciousness, for years. Today there is available enough information about cognition in play that one can hope that nursery teachers will become truly articulate about what they do and how the children respond. There is also need for much more study and research into the nature of play, and what it means in the life of the young child.

REFERENCES

Almy, Millie. *Young Children's Thinking.* New York, Teachers College Press, 1966.

Bruner, Jerome S. *The Process of Education.* New York, Random House, 1961.

———. "The Course of Cognitive Growth." *Amer. Psychol.* 1964, Vol. 19, pp. 1-15.

Erikson, Erik H. *Identity and the Life Cycle.* New York, International Universities Press, 1959.

Flavell, John H. *The Developmental Psychology of Jean Piaget.* Princeton, N.J., D. Van Nostrand Co., Inc., 1963.

Freud, Anna. *The Ego and the Mechanism of Defense.* New York, International Universities Press, 1952.

———. "The Concept of Developmental Lines." In Eissler, Freud, Hartmann and Kris (eds.), *Psychoanalytic Study of the Child.* Vol. 18, New York, International Universities Press, 1963, pp. 245-265.

Goldsmith, Cornelia. "Good Education for Our Young Children—What Is It?" *Good Education For Young Children.* New York, NACE & NANE, pp. 5-12.

Griffiths, Ruth. *A Study of Imagination in Early Childhood and Its Function in Mental Development.* London, Trench, Trucker & Co. Ltd., 1935.

Hunt, J. McV. *Intelligence and Experience.* New York, The Ronald Press Co., 1961.

Inhelder, Barbel, & Piaget, Jean. *The Early Growth of Logic in the Child.* New York, Harper & Row, 1964.

Isaacs, Susan. *Intellectual Growth in Children.* London, Routledge & Kegan Paul Ltd., 1950 (6th ed.).

———. *Social Development in Young Children.* London, G. Routledge & Sons, Ltd., 1933.

Johnson, Harriet. *Children in the Nursery School.* New York, The John Day Co., 1928.

Kagan, J., Moss, H. A., & Sigel, I. E. "Psychological Significance of Styles of Conceptualization in Basic Cognitive Processes in Children." Wright, J. C., & Kagan, J. (eds.), *Monog. Soc., Res. Ch. Dvlpt.* Vol. 28, No. 2, 1963.

Lieberman, Josefa N. "Playfulness and Divergent Thinking: an Investigation of Their Relationship at the Kindergarten Level." Unpublished doctoral thesis, Columbia University, 1964.

Moore, Omar K. *Early Reading and Writing.* (Film)

Mussen, Paul H., Conger, John J., & Kagan, Jerome. *Child Development and Personality.* New York, Harper & Row, 1963 (2nd ed.).

Omwake, Eveline. "The Child's Estate." In A. M. Solnit and S. A. Provence (eds.), *Modern Perspectives in Child Development.* New York, International Universities Press, 1963, pp. 277-594.

Peller, Lili E. "Models of Children's Play," *Mental Hygiene,* 1952, Vol. 36, pp. 66-83.

———. "Libidinal Phases, Ego Development and Play." In Eissler, Freud, Hartmann and Kris (eds.), *Psychoanalytic Study of the Child,* Vol. 9, New York, International Universities Press, 1954. pp. 178-198.

Piaget, Jean. "Cognitive Development in Children." The Piaget papers in R. E. Ripple and V. N. Rockcastle (eds.). *Piaget Rediscovered: a Report on the Conference on Cognitive Study and Curriculum Development*. Ithaca, School of Education, Cornell University, Mar. 1964, pp. 6–48.

————. *Play, Dreams and Imitation in Childhood*. New York, W. W. Norton, 1962.

White, Robert W. "Ego and Reality in Psychoanalytic Theory." *Psychological Issues*. 1963, Vol. 3, No. 3.

CHARLES H. WOLFGANG

20. Teaching Preschool Children to Play

During the 60's, with the establishment of compensatory Head Start programs for preschool children from economically deprived areas, the traditional nursery school curriculum based on expressive play began to come under fire (Beilin, 1972; Bereiter and Englemann, 1966). New programs were sought—particularly those based on skill development—with the hope they would prepare children for formal schooling and such vital skills as reading.

Also during this time, the fields of psychology and education (Singer, 1973) focused on play as a subject for scholarly research. Out of this new wave of research came the benchmark work of Sara Smilansky (*The Effects of Sociodramatic Play on Disadvantaged Preschool Children*, 1968). Smilansky's work demonstrated that the children who live in "deprived" settings did not engage in high levels of symbolic play. Heretofore, symbolic play had been regarded by the developmental theorists (Bühler, 1930; Peller, 1959; Piaget, 1962; Curry, 1971) to be an ontogenous stage through which all children living in highly linguistic societies must pass. Additionally, Smilansky (1968) reported that non-symbolic playing children failed to "play the game" of formal schooling and acquire such basic skills as reading in the elementary grades.

A direct parallel can be drawn between symbolic play and reading; i.e., each activity involves representation (Vygotsky, 1962; Piaget, 1962; Kamii, 1972; Weikart, 1970). The child in play takes an object or toy and through

From Charles H. Wolfgang, "Teaching Preschool Children to Play," in QUEST: *Learning How to Play*, ed. D. Siedentop, NAPECW-NCPEAM, Monograph 26 (Summer 1976), pp. 117–126. Reprinted with permission.

his actions signifies or gives meaning to the objects. The block "flown" through the air with accompanying motor sounds *represents* an airplane. In reading the child must bring forward mentally an image to give meaning to the external written signifier, thus C-A-T equals a four-legged animal with a tail and whiskers. Therefore, in the area of representational knowledge (Kamii, 1972) the symbols that dominate the age period for two to seven appear to be the precursors for written signifiers in reading (Piaget, 1962; Vygotsky, 1962; Weikart, 1970).

It is somewhat startling to discover that the important element of symbolic play is lacking in the development of children who are socioeconomically deprived. This information raises such questions as "How can we as teachers facilitate the symbolic play of preschool children?" and "Will this increased play performance effect later school success?" There have been in recent years a number of research efforts to answer these questions (Melragon, 1973; Rosen, 1976; Sears, 1972) but, as yet, there is no orderly sequential intervention program to be found in the literature. It is the purpose of this paper to outline a program of play intervention based on known child development principles and theory. Our program of intervention will accept the premise that through the use of appropriate materials and teacher intervention we can *recapitulate* and take the non-players through earlier play forms and stages until they are able to do high forms of expressive play, i.e., sociodramatic. Our techniques are an expanded version of an intervention program used with autistic children (Mahler, 1970). However, our non-players, who are generally found in all normal classrooms should not be considered pathological, nor should the techniques proposed be considered as "play therapy," but simply as play facilitation with normal, non-playing children.

Such non-players are described by Smilansky (1968) and Krown (1974) as:

1. Aimless, lethargic, and sometimes impulsive.
2. Difficult to arouse and give pleasure.
3. Able to move objects and toys with some hint of play but movement is repetitive and stereotyped.
4. Afraid to tackle new tasks.
5. Drifting to small structured materials, rather than bulding with blocks, doing carpentry, or anything that requires self-assertion.
6. Perceiving the world as if in a fog, with everything lacking order, or clarity.
7. Perceiving objects lacking names.
8. Unable to accept physical comfort or, conversely, are clinging.

Our general purpose in a program of play intervention is to reactivate such "shut off" children and help them to acquire the ability to creatively use their world.

DEFINING PLAY

There are many varied forms of play (Hartley, 1952; Herron & Sutton-Smith, 1971) that support the development of young children but for the purpose of this discussion we will confine our focus to the area of symbolic play. With the ability to hold objects mentally permanent and to perform simple problem-solving (Piaget, 1952) the young child (near the end of the second year of life) is able to take objects, or even with the use of his own body, to express story-like forms of fantasy play. When two or more children join in this fantasy play and enact dramatic sequences, such as portraying doctors, firemen, policemen, the play becomes true sociodramatic play. If we look closely at such role play we find (1) the children are make-believing in regard to actions and situations, (2) that social interaction is occurring, (3) the children are using social communication, (4) that they are imitating roles, (5) that they are make-believing with regard to objects, and finally, (6) that they are able to persist in and sustain social activity (Smilansky, 1968). To perform such high level of symbolic play the child is challenged in many growth dimensions that facilitate his over-all development, particularly in the cognitive areas.

The following are a few learning possibilities that can be generated from theme play, and one can see that the traditional subjects of science, math, geography, and social studies concepts are embedded in such play.

Themes around Stores and Restaurants:

a. Different stores and their purposes (classifying, conceptualizing).
b. Money, goods, colors, labeling, signs and symbols (counting, categorizing).
c. Drive-in, sit-down eating places, foods.
d. People who work: salesmen, customers, waitresses, cooks (appropriate interactions, exchange of services involving language, math, memory, etc.).

Themes around Firemen:

a. Going to a fire: relaying information, preparations, maps, directionality.
b. At: equipment needed—ropes for hoses, ladders, water, pumping, hoists, protection.
c. Other helpers: police, ambulance—functions and roles.
d. People involved in fire: safety, problem solving, escape, fear, care of injured, saving one's treasures.
e. After fire: clean-up of equipment, rebuilding structures (Anker, et al., 1974).

Out of these dramatic themes the observer can also classify such cognitive strategies as:

1. Measurement: In relation to height, width, length, depth, weight, time, comparisons, spatial relationships.
2. Quantity: In relation to amounts (a lot, a few, many, some, more, less) counting, ordering, fractions, whole/part, sets.
3. Categorizing and Classifying: With regard to similarities and differences (by color, shape, size, feel, taste, sex, age, function, pairs, sets).

4. Sequencing or Seriation: Of amounts (few to many, tall to short), of events (cooking experiences, growth and development of plants and animals), of time (before, after, yesterday, tomorrow, school routines), of stories (sequencing events).
5. Process of Change: Chemical changes (dissolving, mixing substances, effects of water, oxidation, heat, cold on various substances); physical changes (due to force, gravity, magnetism, pressure, electricity); temporal changes (day, night, seasons); biological changes (body changes, growth, decay, birth, death).
6. Adaptation: In reaction to problem solving, experimenting, finding alternative solutions, memory, flexibility in thinking and actions (Anker, *et al.*, 1974).

The above concepts are not taught as a static curriculum, but evolve out of the child's dynamic play use of his preschool world, and thus we see that dramatic play is an essential ingredient for learning in the early years.

PRINCIPLES OF INTERVENTION

The teacher is armed with two tools to facilitate symbolic play, (1) the structure or lack of structure of play objects and materials, and (2) the form and amount of structure she/he provides by her/his own behavior.

Objects

Objects normally placed into a preschool play environment may be viewed as if they were on a continuum with regard to the amount of structure embedded in them and the difficulty which they present to preschoolers who are attempting to use them.

On the structured side we may place more convergent items such as Montessori materials (1965), puzzles, and sorting boards. Then becoming less structured, Lego, with the use of unit blocks, and scissors with variety of papers and materials. At the opposite or "open" end of the materials continuum we may place materials including water play, sand play, finger painting, easel painting; less fluid materials such as clay or playdough, and even crayons with papers. The most structured materials can generally be used only convergently as they maintain their own form, while the fluids lack shape and are constantly transforming. There are many children that either refuse to use fluid materials (refusing to finger paint) or there are other children who, when they do get involved with fluids, simply lose control and use the materials destructively. The general line of intervention will be to have the non-players spend much of their beginning school day and play period in the structured materials (much as Montessori did with her street children) (Montessori, 1965) and then with teacher intervention we will be able to gradually lead these non-players into dynamic fluids where we can help them gain a freedom to act but with control. (See Figure 1)

237

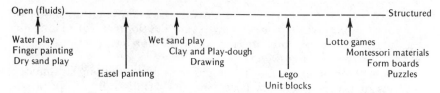

FIGURE 1. Materials continuum.

The third classification of play materials falls under a general heading called symbolic objects or toys. These are the miniature life-toys of people, animals, house furniture, that children use in isolated dramatic play on the floor or at tables, a form of play material known as microcosmic (Erikson, 1950). Also under this heading may be placed the items referred to as macrocosmic to be used in the larger life space (Erikson, 1950) that support sociodramatic play. This would include child-size furniture, eating utensils, clothing, and a wide array of props needed for role play (See "Have you ever thought of a prop box?" Bender, 1971).

With an awareness of the structure-to-fluid continuum, and symbolic toys both Micro and Macro, the teacher must prepare a well-balanced environment to support social play. One cannot overstate the importance of the room arrangement; just as a well-organized airport can support rapid movement of many people or a well-planned restaurant supports comfortable dining, the organization of materials is a prerequisite for successful play. Each play center can be viewed as a social sponge that, when organized properly, will absorb more and more children with the increased potential for being used in creative ways (Kritchevsky, 1969).

Teacher Behavior

The teacher's actions can also be viewed as a structure continuum. The most structured form would be physical intervention and modelling. The teacher by her/his own behavior demonstrates an action to which she/he requires the child to imitate. Again, this is much like the convergent structured form of modelling used by Montessori teachers (Montessori, 1965). Becoming less structured we may consider the teacher's direction. "You are a fireman, Tommy, pick up the hose (rope) and spray the fire with water!" Moving down the continuum, she/he may use verbal questioning, "What equipment do fire trucks need? What will happen to the people now that they are hurt?" The last form of verbal intervention would be verbal nondirective statements. "I see we have two firemen, and the owner of the house," or "The customer is sitting at the table waiting for the waiter." On the most extreme open-end of the teacher behavior continuum we may simply place "visual-looking on" as a non-participant observer (Robinson, 1971). This visual investment, although the least intrusive, must still be considered a structure. The actions the teacher responds to visually will be used more often by the children than those that do not receive her attention. The importance of this visual attention

Fluids

water play toys, bubble set
finger painting materials
clay on wooden clay board
sand and sand toys
sand or water table with
—aluminum or plastic measuring cups
—hand water pump, siphon, hose, funnels
—sand tools
—can and sifter set
—washable, unbreakable
small family figures and animals
—balances
—boats
—scoops
—double easels with non-spill paint pots and smocks
—felt tip markers, colored chalk, wax crayons

Structured

inlay puzzles, matching games
hammer, nails and soft wood with work bench
unit blocks
giant blocks
play planks
scissors, variety of paper, paste
paper punch, felt pieces
bits of cloth, bits of wood
yarn, styrofoam, pipe cleaners
typewriter
manipulatives (strings and beads, sewing basket, chunky nuts, pegboard, lacing boards)
Lego, multi-fit, Octons, toymakers, tinkerboys
Sorting boards and box for shape, color, and size
Simple card games
Dominoes and number boards or games
Stand up mirrors

Symbolic

Micro

—washable, unbreakable doll that can be dressed and undressed
—assorted floor blocks with small family figures
—farm and zoo animal sets to include
—puppets
—aggressive vs. tame animals (lion vs. sheep)
—animal families
—wooden vehicles
—table blocks
—open top doll house including furniture and people

Macro

—housekeeping equipment of all kinds including cooking, laundry, etc.
—costume box for "dress-up" clothes
—toy luggage
—steering wheel
—ride-a-stick horse
—sheet or blanket for play tent
—large cartons for making stores, houses, stations and for climbing into
—rocking chair
—large cuddly toy animals
—dolls of all types
—doctor equipment
—plastic food
—balance scales
—cash register and play money
—variety of hats
—toy telephones

FIGURE 2. Fluid, Structured, and Symbolic Materials.[1]

[1]The list is provided to give examples; many other materials may and should be added to the list by the teacher.

can be assessed when one notes that after the teacher withdraws her "looking" from the play area, the play disintegrates and at times will degenerate into aggressive behavior. The teacher radiates, by her/his visual looking, a sense of security and control among preschool children and she and her co-teachers must use "looking" to literally "cover" the play space with their presence. Thus, through coordinated movements all areas in the play space will fall under at least one teacher's "safety and control." With the teacher presence as the catalyst, preschoolers will develop sufficient trust to produce high levels of creative play.

In general, the line of movement for the teacher in working with non-players is to use much structure initially and as the children become more productive the teacher gradually moves to "visual" support and as a non-participant observer.

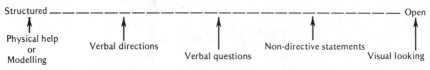

FIGURE 3. Teacher behavior continuum.

DEVELOPMENTAL PLAY INTERVENTION

Phase 1. Reestablishing a body level of trust.

Goal: To develop an empathic relationship between non-player and teacher.

Procedure: A teacher cannot be told how to be empathic, but must use her/his own personality and warmth to win the child's affection. Ultimately she/he will relate to the child physically by first getting him to take her/his hand and then finally being able to cuddle on her/his lap.

Comments: Normally non-players relate physically to others with a range of extremes; either totally rejecting a physical advance, or constantly clinging, or responding to physical affection as if they were a "wet noodle" (Krown, 1974; Mahler, 1970). (We are attempting to reestablish a basic level of trust that normally develops in the first year of life at the very basic body level.)

Phase II. Learning to be the "cause" on others and helping to establish a growing awareness of self.

Goal: To teach the child to imitate and become aware of body parts.

Procedure: The teacher brings the child onto her/his lap while sitting in front of a large standing mirror. She/he initiates a game of facial and body imitation through the mirror. It might be necessary to establish teacher-child eye contact with use of small pieces of candy (say M & M's) by "flying" the candy through the air landing in the teacher's mouth and then a second in the child's. With the attainment of the child's attention the teacher plays (1) I will imitate you, (2) You imitate me, and then, finally (3) again, I will imitate you. As a part of this imitative mirror the teacher should play body referencing games of "Show me my mouth, show me your mouth, show me my nose, show me your nose." The teacher should feel free to enrich this imitative play with a wide array of such games that are a part of teacher and pre-school "lore." (such as peek-a-boo play)

Comments: During the second half of the first year of life, the child learns to imitate. This is the precursor for imitation seen in symbolic play, as a lap baby doing such facial play with mother as peek-a-boo play (Piaget, 1962; Spitz, 1965; McFarland, 1971; Mahler, 1970). In infancy, mother serves as a mirror and the child acquires an awareness that his actions can have a cause on others. It is also this play, such as placing one finger in mother's mouth and the other in his, that the child discovers his own body self. Through mirroring we are attempting to recapitulate this phase.

Phase III.   Learning to be the cause on objects.

Goal: To develop the ability to use fluids freely but with control.

Procedures: The teacher brings the child onto her lap in front of a table prepared with finger paint. She/he models (most extreme form of teacher structure) for the child by (1) moving through the paint with a small object (say a piece of wood) in each hand, (2) then, smears with one finger, and then (3) finally smears totally with both hands. As she/he models these lead-in activities, she/he requires the child to place her/his hands on top of the teacher's hands to feel her free movements. Next, the child is encouraged to repeat the above actions until he/she becomes free to smear in the paint with his hands, but with control. If the media begins to "take over on the child" the teacher inhibits his/her actions and repeats the lead-in activity. With the newly developed freedom the child can produce symbols in the fluid material which should now be saved as creative products. The teacher may continue to introduce the beginning player to a wide array of similar fluids such as easel painting, water play, sand play, and clay modelling, with the teacher providing "lead-in" activities through modelling.

Comments: The child in the first two years of life develops a gradual awareness of the "joy of being the cause." (Bühler, 1930) Fluids are able to show the immediate actions of the child (such as in finger painting) and give the child immediate feedback. These early years are also the period that the child begins to gain control (Spitz, 1957) over his/her own actions. Fluids lacking structure enable the preschooler to practice active control by pitting himself against such materials (Hartley, 1952). (See film, *This is Robert, Part I*, Stone, L. J., New York University, 1942.)

Phase IV.   Acquiring the ability to symbolize in the microcosmic.

Goal: To have the child play out symbolically short dramatic themes with miniature toys.

Procedures: In the space arranged to support symbolic play with miniature life toys (microcosmic) the teacher and the child seat themselves on the floor or at a table with a wide assortment of miniature items that either reflect the child's home setting, or a social activity such as a garage with toy autos and supportive props. The teacher enacts with the toy models (most extreme form as structured teacher behavior) a dramatic play sequence with a theme having a beginning and ending lasting two to three minutes. The child is then asked to "retell" the story with the object by imitating the teacher's dramatization.

The teacher supports the play by telling the child, if need be, just what to do, and physically helping the beginning player. Slowly the teacher moves to being less intrusive providing verbal questions, then non-directive statements, and finally simply visually "looking-on" as the child enacts his own "stories." If the child seems unable to elaborate a symbolic drama the teacher may immediately repeat the mirroring described in Phase II and then bringing the child quickly back to the miniature toys. Such mirroring activity can be repetitively used anytime through the school day when the child appears to retreat into a general state of passivity, or becomes too aggressive; thereby restating a sense in the child of being the cause.

Comments: Because of the child's strong attachment to primary adults, he desired to be like and do like adults do. We therefore see during the second and third year of life the young toddler imitating in play dramatic sequences reflecting his own life experiences (Piaget, 1962; Peller, 1959; Erikson, 1950).

Phase V. Acquiring the ability to symbolize in the macrocosmic.

Goal: To have the child play with others to produce sociodramatic play.

Procedure: With a well designed "dress-up" corner (See Kritchevsky, 1973) the teacher will bring together two excellent social dramatic players with one "non-player." The teacher may read a story or show a film about people involved in roles such as doctor, nurse, fireman, etc. Or, the children as a member of the class may visit a hospital or fire station, where they may view the daily activities of these adults. From this experience base, and after introducing new props (say fireman's hats and hoses) the children are requested to play "fireman." The teacher helps the children define their roles and she joins in as an active member with the "star" players while the "non-player" watches her action. After playing out a short drama, the teacher then requests that the "non-player" takes over the role that was played by the teacher. The teacher continues to support the play of the "non-player" with verbal directions ("Lay down and pretend you are a sleeping fireman, and when the alarm rings, you jump up and put on your hat, and get on the fire engine"), then less intrusively with verbal questions ("What will happen to the injured man?"), then non-directive statements ("I see that all the firemen are now on the fire engine ready to leave."), and finally, she/he will retreat to a position of "looking on" as a nonparticipant observer. With many such attempts at a variety of roles the child gradually becomes an active social player. Again, mirroring activities such as described in Phase II and used in Phase IV can be initiated by the teacher when the child becomes passively nonproductive or overly excited or aggressive.

Comment: With the attainment of the ability to play sociodramatic play the child has acquired the age appropriate form of preschool play. It is with this vehicle of social dramatic play that young children become able to integrate the cognitive capacities needed for later social activities such as formal schooling. Through role-playing the child acquires the ability to follow social rules that enable him to move from a generally egocentric preschooler to a comparative "worker" committed to industry and acquiring his/her cultural tools (Erikson, 1950; Smilanksy, 1968).

Doctor	Electrician	Railway engineer
Nurse	Teacher	Cowboy
Post office worker and mail person	Police officer	Beautician
	Grocer	Cook
Ship captain	Astronaut	Farmer
Bus driver	Pilot	Milkman
Gas station attendant		

FIGURE 4. Suggested roles and themes.

SUMMARY

Our sequential program of play intervention involves an attempt to recapitulate, with the non-playing child, various earlier stages of play, and finally to develop the ability to do age appropriate social-dramatic play. The teacher must have an awareness of the structure or lack of structure of the play material, and through intervening with her own behavior, leads children through a series of activities which "reactivates" the nonplayers, helping them to relate to others, developing an awareness that their actions can be the cause on the world of others and materials, and finally move from initiation to symbolic play first in miniature life and then the larger life space of social dramatic play.

Because of the limited space the phases and activities are presented here in an abbreviated outline form, and should not be followed as a recipe but should serve instead as a *directional sign* pointing the way toward growth experiences for children. Ultimately it is the teacher's own play potential of warmth and empathy that will serve as the true catalyst and facilitator of play, and she/he must be free to experiment, alter, and enrich the above activities to fit her/his own personality and the needs of her/his particular maturing child.

References

Anker, Dorothy, Jackie Foster, Joan McLane, Joyce Sobel, and Bernice Weissbourd. "Teaching Children as They Play." *Young Children*. Washington, D.C.: NAEYC, May, 1974.

Beilin, H. "The Status and Future of Preschool Compensatory Education." In J. Stanley (ed.) *Preschool Programs for the Disadvantaged*. Baltimore: The Johns Hopkins Press, 1972, 165–181.

Bender, Judith. "Have You Ever Thought of a Prop Box?" *Young Children*. Washington, D.C.: NAEYC, January, 1971.

Bereiter, C. and Englemann, S. E. *Teaching Disadvantaged Children*. Englewood Cliffs, New Jersey: Prentice-Hall, 1966.

Bühler, K. *The Mental Development of the Child*. New York: Harcourt, 1930.

Curry, N. "Consideration of Current Basic Issues on Play." In *Play: The Child*

Strives Toward Self-Realization (ed.). Georgianna Engstrom. Washington, D.C.: NAEYC, 1971.

Erikson, E. H. *Childhood and Society*. New York: Norton, 1950.

Hartley, R. E., Lawrence K. Frank and Robert M. Goldenson. *Understanding Children's Play*. New York: Columbia University Press, 1952.

Herron, R. E., and Brian Sutton-Smith (eds.) *Child's Play*. New York: John Wiley, 1971.

Kamii, C. "An Application of Piaget's Theory to the Conceptualization of Preschool Curriculum." In *The Preschool-in Action*. (ed.) Ronald K. Parker. Boston: Allyn and Bacon, Inc., 1972.

Kritchevsky, S., Elizabeth Prescott and Lee Walling. *Planning Environments for Young Children: Physical Space*. Washington, D.C.: NAEYC, 1969.

Krown, S. *Threes and Fours Go to School*. Englewood Cliffs, New Jersey: Prentice-Hall, Inc., 1974.

Mahler, M. *On Human Symbiosis and the Vicissitudes of Individuation*. New York: International University Press, Inc., 1970.

McFarland, M. B. "The First Year of Life." In *Play: The Child Strives Toward Self-Realization* (ed.) Georgianna Engstrom. Washington, D.C.: NAEYC, 1971.

McIragon, Betty. "A Comparison of the Sociodramatic Play of Low Socioeconomic Status Black Second Grade Children and Low Socioeconomic Status Black Kindergarten Children," unpublished Ph.D. dissertation, The Ohio State University, 1973.

Montessori, M. *Dr. Montessori's Own Handbook*. New York: Schocken Books, 1965.

Peller, L. "Libidinal phases, ego development and play." In *Psychoanalytic Study of the Child*. Vol. 9. New York: International University Press, 1959.

Piaget, J. *The Origins of Intelligence in Children*. New York: International Universities Press, Inc., 1952.

Piaget, J. *Play, Dreams and Imitation in Childhood*. New York: Norton, 1962.

Rosen, Catherine Elkin. "The Effects of Sociodramatic Play on Problem Solving Behavior Among Culturally Disadvantaged Preschool Children." In press, 1976.

Robinson, Helen F. "The Decline of Play in Urban Kindergartens." *Young Children*. Washington, D.C.: NAEYC, 1971.

Smilansky, Sara. *The Effects of Sociodramatic Play on Disadvantaged Preschool Children*. New York: John Wiley and Sons, 1968.

LANGUAGE DEVELOPMENT IN EARLY CHILDHOOD

Even more so than in other areas of child development, the role of language learning in children cannot be reduced to any single function. Although linguists and philosophers have debated the question whether language precedes thought or thought precedes language, no one doubts the critical role that language plays in cognition. Indeed, language serves as the structure for thought, helping the child to organize and interpret information about the world. Language also serves to define social relationships; a large part of social interaction is based on verbal communication. Finally, language functions to control behavior, suggesting its importance to both emotional and moral development.

The articles in this chapter focus, in part, on the various roles that language plays in the life of the growing child. Berko Gleason details the function of very early language by examining how adults talk to children and how, in turn, children address adults and other children. She discusses the almost universal characteristics of Baby Talk as a language uniquely designed for teaching. When the child enters the preschool years, the function of language changes from one of teaching vocabulary and grammar to one of controlling behavior by showing the child how to carry on a conversation and how to behave. Castle's article extends the idea of language as a means of socialization, offering both theoretical discussion and practical suggestions for how language can be used as an alternative to physical punishment in disciplining even young children.

Although Hess and Shipman acknowledge the importance of language in socializing groups of people, their work emphasizes the cognitive implications of communication, particularly in the mother-child relationship. They postulate that the structure of the family shapes the child's language and that language, in turn, shapes the child's thoughts and problem-solving abilities. The article by the Sparlings is more practical in its approach, proposing that children's early art can be used as a vehicle to talk to children about the way things look and about how they feel.

Finally, the last two articles in this section deal with the role of language as a means for both verbal and written expression. Wolfgang provides a theoretical framework for viewing young children's literature and Elkind suggests what children need to be successful readers. It is not surprising that Elkind's criteria—a language-rich environment, attachment to adults who model and reward speaking and reading, and logical thinking—all speak to the early role of language as a means of teaching vocabulary, socializing behavior, and structuring thought.

JEAN BERKO GLEASON
21. Code Switching in Children's Language

Somewhere along the road to language acquisition children must gain control over not only a vast vocabulary and a complicated grammar, but a variety of styles of speaking to different people under differing circumstances. The code for addressing a policeman who has just stopped you for speeding is not the same as the code for addressing either little babies or old friends; and anyone studying adult language who restricts himself to one or another of these situations would obviously have only a part of the picture of the complexity and variety that exists in adult language. Paradoxically, until recent times, those of us who have studied child language have restricted ourselves to samples of the child's language to us, the interviewer, or to the child's mother or teacher, and we have assumed that that was it: child language. Whether children, like adults, have control of several codes, and vary their speech in accordance with the situation they are in or the person they are addressing has become an area of increasing interest to a number of researchers in the past few years. In order to investigate code switching in children's language, it is necessary to observe the same child in a number of different speech situations.

This article is a preliminary report on a study that Elliot Mishler and I conducted. The findings are observational, rather than quantitative; and it is my hope that experiments with hard data and statistically meaningful results will follow.

In order to investigate the child's emerging control of different styles or codes, we began with the study of the natural conversations that occur in families with several children; this enabled us to study the way that parents alter their style in speaking to children of different ages and sexes, and it put the children in a natural position to direct their language to a variety of addressees: their parents, ourselves, other children, and babies.

Our basic data were collected from five similarly constituted families who have children attending a private school in Cambridge, Massachusetts. Each of these families has at least three children: a first- or second-grader; a preschool child aged 4 or 5; and an even younger child under the age of 3. All of these families are well-educated and upper middle-class. Most of the data were taped in the families' homes in two 1-hour sessions by Sara Harkness, a doctoral candidate in social anthropology at Harvard, or by myself and Elliot Mishler, head of the Laboratory of Social Psychiatry at the Harvard Medical School. In addition to these tapes we have recorded one other family whose children attend public school in another community. Finally, I made extensive recordings of

From Jean Berko Gleason, "Code Switching in Children's Language," in *Cognitive Development and the Acquisition of Language*, ed. T. Moore (Academic Press, 1973), pp. 159–167. Reprinted with permission.

the 4-year-old son of one of the five families in several different settings: in his own home with his parents; outdoors with his younger and older brothers; at my home talking to me and playing with my 8-year-old daughter, Cindy; and at his nursery school with his friends and teachers. For this one 4-year-old, at least, I have captured a broad variety of speech situations and the stylistic variations that attend them.

ADULT LANGUAGE TO CHILDREN

Since we were observing families, it was inevitable that our sample contain a great deal of language to children from adults, and we examined this adult language for evidence of stylistic variation. Since this adult language is the basic input to the child, some understanding of it is prerequisite to understanding the full significance of the children's productions. It is important to know, for instance, which codes are the children's own, passed on by the peer group, and which codes are passed to the child by adults. Therefore, before discussing the children's language some description of the salient features of the adult codes is in order.

The adults use baby-talk style in talking to the babies. The features of this style have been well reported by others but, briefly, we can say they raised the fundamental frequency of their voices, used simple short sentences with concrete nouns, diminutives, and terms of endearment, expanded the children's utterances, and in general performed the linguistic operations that constitute baby-talk style. There was a lot of individual variation in the extent to which all of these features might be employed. One mother, for instance, spoke in a normal voice to her husband, a high voice to her 4-year-old, a slightly raised voice to her 8-year-old, and when she talked to her baby she fairly squeaked. Fathers and mothers did not talk in exactly the same way to the babies, and there seemed to be some sex differences, as well, in how the babies were addressed. Some of the boy babies were addressed, especially by their fathers, in a sort of hail-baby-well-met style: While turning them upside down or engaged in similar play, the fathers said things like "Come here, you little nut!" or "Hey fruitcake!" Baby girls were dealt with more gently, both physically and verbally.

Adults used a quite different style to the children who were no longer babies, although there were some common features—the use of endearments, for instance. Both children and babies might be called "sweetie" or have their names played with—one baby was called "funny bunny," for instance, and in a different family a 5-year-old girl was called "Huffy Muffy," so this kind of rhyming play is not uncommon. Otherwise, once the little children's language was comprehensive, expansion and similar devices dropped out while other features assumed salience. Several of these features might be sketched here.

The language addressed to the children we saw who were between the ages of 4 and 8 was basically a language of socialization, and it was a very controlling language in so far as it told the child what to do, what to think, and how to feel.

Although the language was not rich in actual imperatives, the implied imperatives abounded; a mother might say to a child: "Do you want to take your own plate off the table, sweetie?" when the child really had no options in the matter. We saw a lot of dinner-table interaction because we were hoping to get samples of the father's speech as well, and this talk contained many instructions on sitting up, not throwing forks, and generally, how to behave.

The parents typically spelled out explicitly the dangers of situations: a mother might place the food in front of a child while saying, "hot, hot!" One does not give boiling hot food to a little baby, and hostesses do not say, "hot, hot!" as they serve their dinner guests, so this is a special situation. A hostess might, of course, say, "Watch out for this dish—it's just out of the oven."

In their conversations with the children of this age, parents typically supplied the entire context. If they asked a question, they included with it the answer. We have, for instance, the following: a father comes to pick up his son at nursery school and says: "Where's your lunchbox? I bet it's inside." or the following conversation between a mother and her 5-year-old son:

MOTHER: How was school today? Did you go to assembly?
SON: Yes.
MOTHER: Did the preschoolers go to assembly?
SON: Yes.
MOTHER: Did you stay for the whole assembly or just part of it?

The child really does not have to do anything but say yes or no—the mother is providing the whole conversation herself, and, undoubtedly, in the process, teaching him how to make a conversation and what kind of responses are expected of him.

Another feature of this adult to child language was that the adults frequently exaggerated their responses, almost beyond reason, or reacted in the way they thought the child ought to feel. For instance, the following:

A child in nursery schools fills a bucket with a hose. The teacher says: "Hey, wow, that's almost full to the *top!*"

A child shows his mother some old toys that he has just been given by another child. The mother whoops with joy.

A child shows his father a simple model he has made. The father says: "Hey, that's *really* something, isn't it?"

A child tells a neighbor he has been to the circus. The neighbor says: "Boy! That must have been fun."

Since full buckets, old toys, simple models, and even the circus do not really impress adults that much, they must be telling the child how *he* ought to feel.

These are only a few of the special features of the language of socialization.

The transition from this directive socializing language to the colloquial style used by adult familiars is not easily accomplished. Quite to the contrary, parents often persist in addressing their 8-year-olds as if they were 4, much to the dismay of the children. From what we have seen, it is actually because of signals from the child, often very explicit and angry signals, that the adult ceases to address him as if he were very little. Mothers, for instance, typically spell out all the dangers of the situation to young children, as I have said. At some point the child begins to act quite disgusted with what the parents say. When the mother tells him to be careful crossing the street, he says something like, "O.K., O.K., I *know* how to cross the street." This angry negative feedback to her utterances in the language of socialization eventually teaches her to address him in a different style, and perhaps only mention that traffic is very heavy that day. Of course some parents never do seem to understand the angry signals and continue telling their children to wear their rubbers until they are 35.

THE CHILDREN'S LANGUAGE

The children in our sample ranged in age from infancy to 8 years. By and large we were not primarily looking for evidence of code switching or stylistic variation in the children under 4. These children were included in the sample because we wanted to get examples of the adults and older children talking to them for evidence of baby-talk style. Some things did seem readily evident from observing the very young children and talking to their parents, however. The first is that even the tiniest children make some distinctions. The basic, earliest variation is simply between talking and not talking. Very small children will frequently talk or jabber nonsense to their own parents or siblings, but fall silent in the presence of strangers. When the parent tries to get the baby to say, "Hi," or "Bye-bye," to the interviewer, the baby stares blankly; and the mother says, "I don't know what's wrong. He really can talk. He says bye-bye all the time." The baby remains silent. After the interviewer leaves, surrounded once more by familiar faces, the baby suddenly springs to life and says a resounding "Bye-bye!" So the first variation is between speech and silence.

Another, more obviously stylistic variation we have seen in the language of the children under 4 as well as those over 4, has been the selective use of whining, by which I mean a repetitive, insistent, singsong demand or complaint, and not crying, which is very difficult for little children to inhibit. The whining basically occurs to parents and parent figures, and a child may abruptly switch to a whine at the sight of his parent, when he has previously been talking to someone else in a quite normal tone. In the nursery school I visited, for instance, one child was talking with his friends when his father arrived. At the sight of his father, he abruptly altered his tone and began to whine, "Pick me up" at him.

In listening to the tapes of the children's speech, we had in mind the generally recognized kinds of language style that linguists talk about. Baby-talk style, peer-group colloquial style, and a more formal style for talking to older people and strangers seemed to be three kinds of codes that all adults have and that we might expect to see emerging in the children as they grow older. We thought that the interviewers or other strange adults would bring out the formal style; that the other children of about the same age—close siblings and the many friends who appeared—would bring out the colloquial style; and that baby-talk style would begin to emerge in the language of these children when they talked to the babies in their families.

We did not originally count on the presence of the language of socialization, but it soon became evident that it was there in many cases where children were talking to somewhat younger children. Part of a conversation between my 8-year-old daughter, Cindy, and the 4-year-old I was studying went as follows. She wanted to give him some of her toys, and she said, "Would you like to have some for you at your house?" When he agreed, she said, "Now you just carry them home, and don't run." She then helped him across the street to his house, and when they got there said, "Ricky, you want to show your mother? You want to show your mother that you got these?"

He said, "Yeah. For me." And she replied, "You share them." We have many other instances of older children talking to younger children this way.

We have no real instances of these children using typical adult formal style, probably in part at least because we, as interviewers, were familiar to them and part of their own community. We failed to be formidable strangers, and the parents addressed us in familiar ways as well, so there was very little in the way of formal greetings and farewells, or politeness formulas. Only in one family did we get anything like formal language, and this was the one family outside our Cambridge private school sample that Elliot Mishler and I visited together. In this family, our language and the language of the family proved far more formal. The mother, for example, said to us after we had come in "Have a seat. It's the best one in the house." We had brought some small toys for the children in the family, and the first-grade boy approached Dr. Mishler somewhat later and said, "Thank you for bringing the presents" in a very formal way, with pauses between the words, careful enunciation, and a flat, affectless tone. The other families treated us in a far more colloquial way.

While it was not marked by adult formal features, the children's language to us had its own characteristics. Ricky, the 4-year-old, who said to his father things like "I wanna be up on your shoulder" *fourteen times* in a row, gave me the following explanation of the tooth fairy:

Uh, well, you see, if your teeth come out, the teeth come back and by, uh, a fairy. And, you see, the teeth that came out you have to put under your pillow, and then the fairy comes and takes 'em, you see, and he leaves a little money or a little candy.

This language is far more narrative and far more didactic than anything he directed at either his parents or other children. This is clearly different speech.

The style the children employed in talking to one another was markedly different from their style to adults or to babies, especially in those cases where they were playing together. This peer-group style included a very rich use of expressive words like "yukk" and "blech," and of sound effects. Our tapes are full of bangs, sirens, airplane noises, animal sounds, and explosions. There are some sex differences, since the boys played more violent games and accompanied them with appropriate sounds, but the girls made a lot of noises as well.

The children playing together often launched into chants, rhymes, television commercials, theme songs of favorite shows, and animal acts. They frequently took off from what they were saying into dramatic play involving changing their voices and pretending they were other people or other creatures. This peer-group language was very different from the language directed at adults. Other features of this child-to-child language that might be mentioned are the very frequent use of first names, as in adult–child language, but no endearments, even in those cases where a somewhat older child was speaking to a somewhat younger one as if she were a parent, as I mentioned before. Finally, there was a striking amount of copying behavior in the children's utterances; many instances of one child saying just what another child has said, without any change in emphasis or structure. For instance, the following example from the nursery school:

SUE: Well, don't you want to see the raspberries?
MALCOLM: How 'bout you pick some for me and I'll eat them?
ERIC: Yeah, and how 'bout pick some for me and I'll eat them?

The third child adds *yeah, and* to the second child's statement and then repeats it. An adult would not have repeated *and I'll eat them* under the same circumstances, although he might have said, "How 'bout picking some for *me*?" Eric's repetition is quite flat—the intonation contours are the same as Malcolm's, and there is no shift of emphasis. He is really not varying the statement so much as echoing it. Where an adult says just what another adult has said, his intention is usually mockery, but for the children, imitation of this sort is very common, and passes unremarked.

The children's language to the babies in the families was also examined for evidence of baby-talk style. While most of the features of peer group code appeared in the language of the entire 4- to 8-year-old sample, there were age differences in the ability to use baby-talk style. The older children were in control of the basic features of baby-talk style—their sentences to the babies were short and repetitive, and uttered in a kind of singing style. In one family I asked an 8-year-old to ask his 2-year-old brother to take a glass to the kitchen. He said:

"Here, Joey, take this to the kitchen. Take it to the kitchen." (Baby-talk intonation, higher voice.)

A little while later, I asked him to ask his 4-year-old brother to take a glass to the kitchen. This time he said:

"Hey, Rick, take this to the kitchen, please." (Normal intonation). This is clear evidence of code switching in the language of this 8-year-old child.

On the other end of the spectrum, the 4-year-old, Ricky, whom I followed about, did not use baby-talk style to his 2-year-old brother. He typically did not use either a special intonation or repetition. He said to the baby: "Do you know what color your shoes are?" in just the same way he said: "What's the name of the book, Anthony?" to his brother; and "I don't think he know how to climb up" to his father.

Somewhere in between no baby-talk style and full baby-talk style lies slightly inappropriate baby-talk style, which we saw particularly in some 5- and 6-year-old girls. Unlike the 4-year-olds, 5- and 6-year-old children made clear efforts to adjust their language to suit the babies they addressed. We have the following conversation:

2-YEAR-OLD: Dead bug!
6-YEAR-OLD: That ant!
2-YEAR-OLD: That bug!
6-YEAR-OLD: Hey, Susie, that's ant; that's not bug, that ant!

The 6-year-old is here obviously trying to accommodate the baby sister by talking in what she regards as "her language," but she misses the cues when she says "That's ant." Good baby sentences would be either "That ant," as the child says, or "That a ant," but a copula without an article in "That's ant" doesn't ring true.

Listening to these children begin to use baby-talk style and then use it fluently by the time they are 7 or 8 makes it clear that knowing how to talk to babies is not something you keep with you from having been a baby; you have to learn it again. The young children in the sample who were still completing their knowledge of regular English syntax were in no position to play with it. They made their sentences the only way they knew how, grinding them out with laborious intensity at times, looking neither to the baby left nor formal right.

The observations we have made thus far are in their preliminary stages, based on only five families, all from the same socioeconomic background and geographical region. The similarities among these families were, however, so great as to make us feel confident that they are generally occurring features, at least in upper middle-class homes. From what we have seen, it seems clear that children are not faced with a vast undifferentiated body of English from which they must make some order as best they can. The parents in these families talked in a very consistent and predictable style to their babies, a style which other researchers have described; and we have found that parents and other adults use a separate style for talking to growing children. This style is different from the informal or colloquial style that teenagers or old friends use to one another, and serves special functions: It is the language of socialization. While baby-talk style is concerned with learning the language, with establishing communication, the language of socialization is filled with social rules. The mother's questions contain answers and in this way show how to make a conversation. The adult emphasizes and exaggerates his own reactions, points up relationships, names feelings, controls and directs the child, and in many ways makes explicit his own world view. The language directed at young children is a teaching language. It tells about the world, and must, because of its special features, be recognized as a separate code.

The original aim of this study was to see if, indeed, children talk in different ways to different people. The answer is yes; infants are selective about whom they talk to at all. Four-year-olds may whine at their mothers, engage in intricate verbal play with their peers, and reserve their narrative, discursive tales for their grown-up friends. By the time they are 8, children have added to the foregoing some of the politeness routines of formal adult speech, baby-talk style, and the ability to talk to younger children in the language of socialization. The details of the emergence of these codes are yet to be elaborated.

ROBERT D. HESS and VIRGINIA C. SHIPMAN

22. Early Experience and the Socialization of Cognitive Modes in Children

THE PROBLEM

One of the questions arising from the contemporary concern with the education of culturally disadvantaged children is how we should conceptualize the effects of such deprivation upon the cognitive faculties of the child. The outcome is well known: children from deprived backgrounds score well below middle-class children on standard individual and group measures of intelligence (a gap that increases with age); they come to school without the skills necessary for coping with first grade curricula; their language development, both written and spoken, is relatively poor; auditory and visual discrimination skills are not well developed; in scholastic achievement they are retarded an average of 2 years by grade 6 and almost 3 years by grade 8; they are more likely to drop out of school before completing a secondary education; and even when they have adequate ability are less likely to go to college (Deutsch, 1963; Deutsch & Brown, 1964; Eells, Davis, Havighurst, Herriels, & Tyler 1951; John, 1963; Kennedy, Van de Riet, & White, 1963; Lesser, 1964).

For many years the central theoretical issues in this field dealt with the origin of these effects, argued in terms of the relative contribution of genetic as compared with environmental factors. Current interest in

From Robert D. Hess and Virginia C. Shipman, "Early Experience and the Socialization of Cognitive Modes in Children," *Child Development*, Vol. 36 (1965), pp. 869–886. Reprinted by permission of The Society for Research in Child Development, Inc. Copyright © 1965 by the Society for Research in Child Development, Inc.

the effects of cultural deprivation ignores this classic debate; the more basic problem is to understand how cultural experience is translated into cognitive behavior and academic achievement (Bernstein, 1961; Hess, 1964).

The focus of concern is no longer upon the question of whether social and cultural disadvantage depress academic ability, but has shifted to a study of the mechanisms of exchange that mediate between the individual and his environment. The thrust of research and theory is toward conceptualizing social class as a discrete array of experiences and patterns of experience that can be examined in relation to the effects they have upon the emerging cognitive equipment of the young child. In short, the question this paper presents is this: what *is* cultural deprivation, and how does it act to shape and depress the resources of the human mind?

The arguments we wish to present here are these: first, that the behavior which leads to social, educational, and economic poverty is socialized in early childhood—that is, it is learned; second, that the central quality involved in the effects of cultural deprivation is a lack of cognitive meaning in the mother-child communication system; and, third, that the growth of cognitive processes is fostered in family control systems which offer and permit a wide range of alternatives of action and thought and that such growth is constricted by systems of control which offer predetermined solutions and few alternatives for consideration and choice.

In this paper we will argue that the structure of the social system and the structure of the family shape communication and language and that language shapes thought and cognitive styles of problem-solving. In the deprived-family context this means that the nature of the control system which relates parent to child restricts the number and kind of alternatives for action and thought that are opened to the child; such constriction precludes a tendency for the child to reflect, to consider and choose among alternatives for speech and action. It develops modes for dealing with stimuli and with problems which are impulsive rather than reflective, which deal with the immediate rather than the future, and which are disconnected rather than sequential.

This position draws from the work of Basil Bernstein (1961) of the University of London. In his view, language structures and conditions what the child learns and how he learns, setting limits within which future learning may take place. He identifies two forms of communication codes or styles of verbal behavior: *restricted* and *elaborated*. Restricted codes are stereotyped, limited, and condensed, lacking in specificity and the exactness needed for precise conceptualization and differentiation. Sentences are short, simple, often unfinished; there is little use of subordinate clauses for elaborating the content of the sentence; it is a language of implicit meaning, easily understood and commonly shared. It is the language form often used in impersonal situations when the intent is to promote solidarity or reduce tension. Restricted codes are nonspecific clichés, statements, or observations about events made in general terms that will be readily understood. The basic quality of this mode is to limit the range and detail of concept and information involved.

Elaborated codes, however, are those in which communication is individualized and the message is specific to a particular situation, topic, and person. It is more particular, more differentiated, and more precise. It permits expression of a wider and more complex range of thought, tending toward discrimination among cognitive and affective content.

The effects of early experience with these codes are not only upon the communication modes and cognitive structure—they also establish potential patterns of relation with the external world. It is one of the dynamic features of Bernstein's work that he views language as social behavior. As such, language is used by participants of a social network to elaborate and express social and other interpersonal relations and, in turn, is shaped and determined by these relations.

The interlacing of social interaction and language is illustrated by the distinction between two types of family control. One is oriented toward control by *status* appeal or ascribed role norms. The second is oriented toward *persons*. Families differ in the degree to which they utilize each of these types of regulatory appeal. In status- (position-) oriented families, behavior tends to be regulated in terms of role expectations. There is little opportunity for the unique characteristics of the child to influence the decision-making process or the interaction between parent and child. In these families, the internal or personal states of the children are not influential as a basis for decision. Norms of behavior are stressed with such imperatives as, "You must do this because I say so," or Girls don't act like that," or other statements which rely on the status of the participants or a behavior norm for justification (Bernstein, 1964).

In the family, as in other social structures, control is exercised in part through status appeals. The feature that distinguishes among families is the extent to which the status-based control maneuvers are modified by orientation toward persons. In a person-oriented appeal system, the unique characteristics of the child modify status demands and are taken into account in interaction. The decisions of this type of family are individualized and less frequently related to status or role ascriptions. Behavior is justified in terms of feelings, preference, personal and unique reactions, and subjective states. This philosophy not only permits but demands an elaborated linguistic code and a wide range of linguistic and behavioral alternatives in interpersonal interaction. Status-oriented families may be regulated by less individuated commands, messages, and responses. Indeed, by its nature, the status-oriented family will rely more heavily on a restricted code. The verbal exchange is inherent in the structure—regulates it and is regulated by it.

These distinctions may be clarified by two examples of mother-child communication using these two types of codes. Assume that the emotional climate of two homes is approximately the same; the significant difference between them is in style of communication employed. A child is playing noisily in the kitchen with an assortment of pots and pans when the telephone rings. In one home the mother says, "Be quiet," or "Shut up," or issues any one of several other short, preemptory commands. In the other home the mothers says, "Would you keep quiet a minute? I want to talk on the phone." The question our study poses is this: what inner response is elicited in the child, what is the effect upon his developing cognitive network of concepts and meaning in each of these two situations? In one instance the child is asked for a simple mental response. He is asked to attend to an uncomplicated message and to make a conditioned response (to comply); he is not called upon to reflect or to make mental discriminations. In the other example the child is required to follow two or three ideas. He is asked to relate his behavior to a time dimension; he must think of his behavior in relation to its effect upon another person. He must perform a more complicated task to follow the communication of his mother in that his relationship to her is mediated in part through concepts and shared ideas; his mind is stimulated or exercised (in an elementary fashion) by a more elaborate and complex verbal communication initiated by the mother. As objects of these two divergent communication styles, repeated in various ways, in similar situations and circumstances during the preschool years, these two imaginary children would be expected to develop significantly different verbal facility and cognitive equipment by the time they enter the public-school system.

A person-oriented family allows the child to achieve the behavior rules (role requirements) by presenting them in a specific context for the child and by emphasizing the consequences of alternative actions. Status-oriented families present the rules in an assigned manner, where compliance is the *only* rule-following possibility. In these situations the role of power in the interaction is more obvious, and, indeed, coercion and defiance are likely interactional possibilities. From another perspective, status-oriented families use a more rigid learning and teaching model in which compliance, rather than rationale, is stressed.

A central dimension through which we look at maternal behavior is to inquire what responses are elicited and permitted by styles of communication and interaction. There are two axes of the child's behavior in which we have a particular interest. One of these is represented by an *assertive, initiatory* approach to learning, as contrasted with a *passive, compliant* mode of engagement; the other deals with the tendency to reach solutions impulsively or hastily as distinguished from a tendency to *reflect*, to compare alternatives, and to choose among available options.

These styles of cognitive behavior are related, in our hypotheses, to the dimensions of maternal linguistic codes and types of family control systems. A status-oriented statement, for example, tends to offer a set of regulations and rules for conduct and interaction that is based on arbitary decisions rather than upon logical consequences which result from selection of one or another alternatives. Elaborated and person-oriented statements lend themselves more easily to styles of cognitive approach that involve reflection and reflective comparison. Status-oriented statements tend to be restrictive of thought. Take our simple example of the two children and the telephone. The verbal categoric command to "Be quiet" cuts off thought and offers little opportunity to relate the information conveyed in the command to the context in which it occurred. The more elaborated message, "Would you be quiet a minute? I want to talk on the phone" gives the child a rationale for relating his behavior to a wider set of considerations. In effect, he has been given a *why* for this mother's request and, by this example, possibly becomes more likely to *ask* why in another situation. It may be through this type of verbal interaction that the child learns to look for action sequences in his own and others' behavior. Perhaps through these more intent-oriented statements the child comes to see the world as others see it and learns to take the role of others in viewing himself and his actions. The child comes to see the world as a set of possibilities from which he can make a personal selection. He learns to role play with an element of personal flexibility, not by role-conforming rigidity.

RESEARCH PLAN

For our project a research group of 163 Negro mothers and their 4-year-old children was selected from four different social status levels: Group A came from college-educated professional, executive, and managerial occupational levels; Group B came from skilled blue-collar occupational levels, with not more than high-school education; Group C came from unskilled or semiskilled occupational levels, with predominantly elementary-school education; Group D from unskilled or semiskilled occupational levels, with fathers absent and families supported by public assistance.

These mothers were interviewed twice in their homes and brought to the university for testing and for an interaction session between mother and child in which the mother was taught three simple tasks by the staff member and then asked to teach these tasks to the child.

One of these tasks was to sort or group a number of plastic toys by color and by function; a second task was sort eight blocks by two characteristics simultaneously; the third task required the mother and child to work together to copy five designs on a toy called an Etch-a-Sketch. A description of various aspects of the project and some preliminary results have been presented in several papers (Brophy, Hess, & Shipman, 1965, Jackson, Hess & Shipman, 1965; Meyer, Shipman, & Hess, 1964; Olim, Hess, & Shipman, 1965; Shipman & Hess, 1965).

RESULTS

The data in this paper are organized to show social-status differences among the four groups in the dimensions of behavior described above to indicate something of the maternal teaching styles that are emerging and to offer examples of relations between maternal and child behavior that are congruent with the general lines of argument we have laid out.

Social-Status Differences

Verbal Codes: Restricted Versus Elaborated

One of the most striking and obvious differences between the environments provided by the mothers of the research group was in their pat-

257

terns of language use. In our testing sessions, the most obvious social-class variations were in the total amount of verbal output in response to questions and tasks asking for verbal response. For example, as Table 1 shows, mothers from the middle-class gave protocols that were consistently longer in language productivity than did mothers from the other three groups.

Taking three different types of questions that called for free response on the part of the mothers and counting the number of lines of type-script of the protocols, the tally for middle-class mothers was approximately 82 contrasted with an average of roughly 49 for mothers from the three other groups.

These differences in verbal products indicate the extent to which the maternal environments of children in different social-class groups tend to be mediated by verbal cue and thus offer (or fail to offer) opportunities for labeling, for identifying objects and feelings and adult models who can demonstrate the usefulness of language as a tool for dealing with interpersonal interaction and for ordering stimuli in the environment.

In addition to this gross disparity in verbal output there were differences in the quality of language used by mothers in the various status groups. One approach to the analysis of language used by these mothers was an examination of their responses to the following task: They were shown the Lion Card of the Children's Apperception Test and asked to tell their child a story relating to the card. This card is a picture of a lion sitting on a chair holding a pipe in his hand. Beside him is a cane. In the corner is a mouse peering out of a hole. The lion appears to be deep in thought. These protocols were the source of language samples which were summarized in nine scales (Table 2), two of which we wish to describe here.

The first scale dealt with the mother's tendency to use abstract words. The index derived was a proportion of abstract noun and verb types to total number of noun and verb types. Words were defined as abstract when the name of the object is thought of apart from the cases in which it is actually realized. For example, in the sentence, "The lion is an *animal*," "animal" is an abstract word. However, in the sentence, "This animal in the picture is sitting on his throne," "animal" is not an abstract noun.

In our research group, middle-class mothers achieved an abstraction score of 5.6; the score for skilled work levels was 4.9; the score for the unskilled group was 3.7; for recipients of Aid to Dependent Children (ADC), 1.8.

TABLE 1. Mean Number of Typed Lines in Three Data-Gathering Situations

	Upper Middle N = 40	Upper Lower N = 40	Lower Lower N = 36	ADC N = 36
School situations	34.68	22.80	18.86	18.64
Mastery situations	28.45	18.70	15.94	17.75
CAT card	18.72	9.62	12.39	12.24
Total	81.85	51.12	47.19	48.63

**TABLE 2. Social Status Differences in Language Usage
(Scores are the Means for Each Group)**

Scale	Social Status			
	Upper Middle N = 40	Upper Lower N = 42	Lower Lower N = 40	ADC N = 41
Mean sentence length[a]	11.39	8.74	9.66	8.23
Adjective range[b]	31.99	28.32	28.37	30.49
Adverb range[c]	11.14	9.40	8.70	8.20
Verb elaboration[d]	.59	.52	.47	.44
Complex verb preference[e]	63.25	59.12	50.85	51.73
Syntactic structure elaboration[f]	8.89	6.90	8.07	6.46
Stimulus utilization	5.82	4.81	4.87	5.36
Introduced content	3.75	2.62	2.45	2.34
Abstraction[g]	5.60	4.89	3.71	1.75

[a]Average number of words per sentence.
[b]Proportion of uncommon adjective types to total nouns, expressed as a percentage.
[c]Proportion of uncommon adverb types to total verbs, adjectives, and adverbs, expressed as a percentage.
[d]Average number of complex verb types per sentence.
[e]Proportion of complex verb types to all verb types, simple and complex.
[f]Average number of weighted complex syntactic structures per 100 words.
[g]Proportion of abstract nouns and verbs (excluding repetitions) to total nouns and verbs (excluding repetitions), expressed as a percentage.

The second scale dealt with the mother's tendency to use complex syntactic structures such as coordinate and subordinate clauses, unusual infinitive phrases (e.g., "To drive well, you must be alert"), infinitive clauses (e.g., "What to do next was the lion's problem"), and participial phrases (e.g., "Continuing the story, the lion . . ."). The index of structural elaboration derived was a proportion of these complex syntactic structures, weighted in accordance with their complexity and with the degree to which they are strung together to form still more complicated structures (e.g., clauses within clauses), to the total number of sentences.

In the research group, mothers from the middle class had a structure elaboration index of 8.89; the score for ADC mothers was 6.46. The use of complex grammatical forms and elaboration of these forms into complex clauses and sentences provides a highly elaborated code with which to manipulate the environment symbolically. This type of code encourages the child to recognize the possibilities and subtleties inherent in language not only for communication but also for carrying on high-level cognitive procedures.

Control Systems: Person Versus Status Orientation

Our data on the mothers' use of status- as contrasted with person-oriented statements comes from maternal responses to questions inquiring what the mother would do in order to deal with several different hypothetical situations at school in which the child had broken the rules of the school, had failed to achieve, or had been wronged by a teacher or classmate. The results of this tally are shown in Table 3.

As is clear from these means, the greatest differences between status groups is in the tendency to utilize person-oriented statements. These differences are even greater if seen as a ratio of person-to-status type responses.

The orientation of the mothers to these different types of control is seen not only in prohibitive or reparative situations but in their instructions to their children in preparing them for new experiences. The data on this point come from answers to the question: "Suppose your child were starting to school tomorrow for the first time. What would you tell him? How would you prepare him for school?"

One mother, who was person-oriented and used elaborated verbal codes, replied as follows:

"First of all, I would remind her that she was going to school to learn, that her teacher would take my place, and that she would be expected to follow instructions. Also that time was to be spent mostly in the classroom with other children, and that any questions or any problems that she might have she could consult with her teacher for assistance."

"Anything else?"

"No, anything else would probably be confusing for her at her particular age."

In terms of promoting educability, what did this mother do in her response? First, she was informative; she presented the school situation as comparable to one already familiar to the child; second, she offered reassurance and support to help the child deal with anxiety; third, she described the school situation as one that involves a personal relationship between the child and the teacher; and, fourth, she presented the classroom situation as one in which the child was to learn.

TABLE 3. Person-Oriented and Status-Oriented Units on School Situation Protocols (Mothers)

A. Mean Number					
Social Class	Person-Oriented		Status-Oriented		P/S Ratio	N
Upper middle	9.52	(1–19)	7.50	(0–19)	1.27	40
Upper lower	6.20	(0–20)	7.32	(2–17)	0.85	40
Lower lower	4.66	(0–15)	7.34	(2–17)	0.63	35
ADC	3.59	(0–16)	8.15	(3–29)	0.44	34

B. Mean Per Cent			
Social Class	Person-Oriented	Status-Oriented	N
Upper middle	36.92	27.78	40
Upper lower	31.65	36.92	40
Lower lower	26.43	40.69	35
ADC	20.85	51.09	34

A second mother responded as follows to this question: "Well, John, it's time to go to school now. You must know how to behave. The first day at school you should be a good boy and should do just what the teacher tells you to do."

In contrast to the first mother, what did this mother do? First, she defined the role of the child as passive and compliant; second, the central issues she presented were those dealing with authority and the institution, rather than with learning; third, the relationship and roles she portrayed were sketched in terms of status and role expectations rather than in personal terms; and, fourth, her message was general, restricted, and vague, lacking information about how to deal with the problems of school except by passive compliance.

A more detailed analysis of the mothers' responses to this question grouped their statements as *imperative* or *instructive* (Table 4). An imperative statement was defined as an unqualified injunction or command, such as, "Mind the teacher and do what she tells you to do," or "The first thing you have to do is be on time," or "Be nice and do not fight." An instructive statement offers information or commands which carry a rationale or justification for the rule to be observed. Examples: "If you are tardy or if you stay away from school, your marks will go down"; or "I would tell him about the importance of minding the teacher. The teacher needs his full cooperation. She will have so many children that she won't be able to pamper any youngster."

Status Differences in Concept Utilization

One of the measures of cognitive style used with both mothers and children in the research group was the S's mode of classificatory behavior. For the adult version, (Kagan, Moss & Sigel, 1963) S is required to make 12 consecutive sorts of MAPS figures placed in a prearranged random order on a large cardboard. After each sort she was asked to give her reason for putting certain figures together. This task was intended to reveal her typical or preferred manner of grouping stimuli and the

TABLE 4. Information Mothers Would Give to Child on His First Day at School

Social Status	Imperative	Instructive	Support	Preparation	Other	N
			% of Total Statements			
Upper middle	14.9	8.7	30.2	8.6	37.6	39
Upper lower	48.2	4.6	13.8	3.8	29.6	41
Lower lower	44.4	1.7	13.1	1.2	39.6	36
ADC	46.6	3.2	17.1	1.3	31.8	37
		% of Mothers Using Category				
Upper middle	48.7	38.5	76.9	33.3	87.2	
Upper lower	85.4	17.1	39.0	19.5	70.7	
Lower lower	75.0	5.6	36.1	8.3	77.8	
ADC	86.5	16.2	43.2	8.1	86.5	

level of abstraction that she uses in perceiving and ordering objects in the environment. Responses fell into four categories: descriptive part-whole, descriptive global, relational-contextual, and categorical-inferential. A descriptive response is a direct reference to physical attributes present in the stimuli, such as size, shape, or posture. Examples: "They're all children," or "They are all lying down," or "They are all men." The subject may also choose to use only a part of the figure—"They both have hats on." In a relational-contextual response, any one stimulus gets its meaning from a relation with other stimuli. Examples: "Doctor and nurse," or "Wife is cooking dinner for her husband," or "This guy looks like he shot this other guy." In categorical-inferential responses, sorts are based on nonobservable characteristics of the stimulus for which each stimulus is an independent representative of the total class. Examples: "All of these people work for a living" or "These are all handicapped people."

As may be seen in Table 5, relational responses were most frequently offered; categorical-inferential were next most common, and descriptive most infrequent. The distribution of responses of our status groups showed that the middle-class group was higher on descriptive and categorical; low-status groups were higher on relational. The greater use of relational categories by the working-class mothers is especially significant. Response times for relational sorts are usually shorter, indicating less reflection and evaluating of alternative hypotheses. Such responses also indicate relatively low attention to external stimuli details (Kagan, 1964). Relational responses are often subjective, reflecting a tendency to relate objects to personal concerns in contrast with the descriptive and categorical responses which tend to be objective and detached, more general, and more abstract. Categorical responses, in particular, represent thought processes that are more orderly and complex in organizing stimuli, suggesting more efficient strategies of information processing.

The most striking finding from the data obtained from the children's Sigel Sorting Task was the decreasing use of the cognitive style dimensions and increasing nonverbal responses with decrease in social-status level. As may be seen in the tables showing children's performance on the Sigel Sorting Task (Tables 6 and 7), although most upper middle-class children and a majority of the upper lower-class children use re-

TABLE 5. Mean Responses to Adult Sigel Sorting Task (Maps)

	Social Status			
Category	Upper Middle N = 40	Upper Lower N = 42	Lower Lower N = 39	ADC N = 41
Total descriptive	3.18	2.19	2.18	2.59
Descriptive part-whole	1.65	1.33	1.31	1.49
Descriptive global	1.52	0.86	0.87	1.10
Relational-contextual	5.52	6.79	7.38	6.73
Categorical-inferential	3.30	3.00	2.23	2.66

lational and descriptive global responses, there is no extensive use of any of the other cognitive style dimensions by the two lower lower-class groups. In looking at particular categories one may note the relative absence of descriptive part-whole responses for other than the middle-class group and the large rise in nonverbal responses below the middle-class level. These results would seem to reflect the relatively undeveloped verbal and conceptual ability of children from homes with restricted range of verbal and conceptual content.

Relational and descriptive global responses have been considered the most immature and would be hypothesized to occur most frequently in preschool children. Relational responses are often subjective, using idiosyncratic and irrelevant cues; descriptive global responses, often referring to sex and occupational roles, are somewhat more dependent upon experience. On the other hand, descriptive part-whole responses have been shown to increase with age and would be expected to be used less frequently. However, these descriptive part-whole responses, which are correlated with favorable prognostic signs for educability (such as

TABLE 6. Children's Responses to Sigel Sorting Task (Means)

	Social Status			
Category	Upper Middle N = 40	Upper Lower N = 42	Lower Lower N = 39	ADC N = 41
Descriptive part-whole	2.25	0.71	0.20	0.34
Descriptive global	2.80	2.29	1.51	0.98
Relational-contextual	3.18	2.31	1.18	1.02
Categorical-inferential	2.02	1.36	1.18	0.61
Nonscorable verbal responses	5.75	6.31	6.64	7.24
Nonverbal	3.00	6.41	7.08	8.76
No sort	1.00	0.62	2.21	1.05

TABLE 7. Percentage of Four-Year-Old Children Responding in Each of the Categories

	Social Status			
Category	Upper Middle N = 40	Upper Lower N = 42	Lower Lower N = 39	ADC N = 41
Descriptive part-whole	40.0	28.6	18.0	14.6
Descriptive global	70.0	54.8	53.8	31.7
Total descriptive	80.0	66.7	59.0	39.0
Relational-contextual	77.5	66.7	41.0	43.9
Categorical-inferential	52.5	45.2	30.8	24.4
Nonscorable verbal	85.0	88.1	92.3	85.4
Nonverbal	52.5	66.7	82.0	87.8
No sort	12.5	7.1	25.6	19.5

attentiveness, control and learning ability), were almost totally absent from all but the upper middle-class group. Kagan (1964) has described two fundamental cognitive dispositions involved in producing such analytic concepts: the tendency to reflect over alternative solutions that are simultaneously available and the tendency to analyze a visual stimulus into component parts. Both behaviors require a delayed discrimination response. One may describe the impairment noted for culturally disadvantaged children as arising from differences in opportunities for developing these reflective attitudes.

The mothers' use of relational responses were significantly correlated with their children's use of nonscorable and nonverbal responses on the Sigel task and with poor performance on the 8-Block and Etch-a-Sketch tasks. The mothers' inability or disinclination to take an abstract attitude on the Sigel task was correlated with ineffectual teaching on the 8-Block task and inability to plan and control the Etch-a-Sketch situation. Since relational responses have been found (Kagan, Moss & Sigel, 1963) to be correlated with impulsivity, tendencies for nonverbal rather than verbal teaching, mother-domination, and limited sequencing and discrimination might be expected and would be predicted to result in limited categorizing ability and impaired verbal skills in the child.

Analysis of Maternal Teaching Styles

These differences among the status groups and among mothers within the groups appear in slightly different form in the teaching sessions in which the mothers and children engaged. There were large differences among the status groups in the ability of the mothers to teach and the children to learn. This is illustated by the performance scores on the sorting tasks.

Let us describe the interaction between the mother and child in one of the structured teaching situations. The wide range of individual differences in linguistic and interactional styles of these mothers may be illustrated by excerpts from recordings. The task of the mother is to teach the child how to group or sort a small number of toys.

The first mother outlines the task for the child, gives sufficient help and explanation to permit the child to proceed on her own. She says:

"All right, Susan, this board is the place where we put the little toys; first of all you're supposed to learn how to place them according to color. Can you do that? The things that are all the same color you can put in one section; in the second section you put another group of colors, and in the third section you put the last group of colors. Can you do that? Or would you like to see me do it first?"

Child: "I want to do it."

This mother has given explicit information about the task and what is expected of the child; she has offered support and help of various kinds; and she has made it clear that she impelled the child to perform.

A second mother's style offers less clarity and precision. She says in introducing the same task:

"Now, I'll take them all off the board; now you put them all back on the board. What are these?"

Child: "A truck."

"All right, just put them right here; put the other one right here; all right put the other one there."

This mother must rely more on nonverbal communication in her commands; she does not define the task for the child; the child is not provided with ideas or information that she can grasp in attempting to solve the problem; neither is she told what to expect or what the task is, even in general terms.

A third mother is even less explicit. She introduces the task as follows: "I've got some chairs and cars, do you want to play the game?" Child does not respond. Mother continues: "O.K. What's this?"

CHILD: "A wagon?"
MOTHER: "Hm?"
CHILD: "A wagon?"
MOTHER: "This is not a wagon. What's this?"

The conversation continues with this sort of exchange for several pages. Here again, the child is not provided with the essential information he needs to solve or to understand the problem. There is clearly some impelling on the part of the mother for the child to perform, but the child has not been told what he is to do. There were marked social-class differences in the ability of the children to learn from their mothers in the teaching sessions.

Each teaching session was concluded with an assessment by a staff member of the extent to which the child had learned the concepts taught by the mother. His achievement was scored in two ways: first, the ability to correctly place or sort the objects and, second, the ability to verbalize the principle on which the sorting or grouping was made.

Children from middle-class homes were well above children from working-class homes in performance on these sorting tasks, particularly in offering verbal explanations as to the basis for making the sort (Tables 8 and 9). Over 60 per cent of middle-class children placed the objects correctly on all tasks; the performance of working-class children ranged as low as 29 per cent correct. Approximately 40 per cent of these middle-class children who were successful were able to verbalize the sorting principle; working-class children were less able to explain the sorting principle, ranging downward from the middle-class level to one task on which no child was able to verbalize correctly the basis of his sorting behavior. These differences clearly paralleled the relative abilities and teaching skills of the mothers from differing social-status groups.

The difference among the four status levels was apparent not only on these sorting and verbal skills but also in the mother's ability to regulate her own behavior and her child's in performing tasks which require planning or care rather than verbal or conceptual skill. These differences were revealed by the mother-child performance on the Etch-a-Sketch task. An Etch-a-Sketch toy is a small, flat box with a screen on which lines can be drawn by a device within the box. The marker is

TABLE 8. Differences Among Status Groups in Children's Performance in Teaching Situations (Toy Sort Task)

Social Status	Placed Correctly (%)	Verbalized Correctly (%)		N
A. Identity sort (cars, spoons, chairs):				
Upper middle	61.5	28.2	45.8[a]	39
Upper lower	65.0	20.0	30.8	40
Lower lower	68.4	29.0	42.3	38
ADC	66.7	30.8	46.2	39
B. Color sort (red, green, yellow):				
Upper middle	69.2	28.2	40.7[a]	39
Upper lower	67.5	15.0	22.2	40
Lower lower	57.9	13.2	22.7	38
ADC	33.3	5.1	15.4	39

[a]Per cent of those who placed object correctly.

TABLE 9. Differences Among Status Groups in Children's Performance in Teaching Situations (8-Block Task)

Social Status	Placed Correctly (%)	One-Dimension Verbalized (%)		Both Verbalized (%)		N
A. Short O:						
Upper middle	75.0	57.5	57.5[a]	25.0	33.3[a]	40
Upper lower	51.2	39.0	43.2	2.4	4.8	41
Lower lower	50.0	29.0	33.3	15.8	31.6	38
ADC	43.6	20.5	22.2	2.6	5.9	39
B. Tall X:						
Upper middle	60.0	62.5	64.1[a]	27.5	45.8[a]	40
Upper lower	48.8	39.0	42.1	17.1	35.0	41
Lower lower	34.2	23.7	26.5	7.9	23.1	38
ADC	28.2	18.0	20.0	0.0	0.0	39

[a]Per cent of those who placed object correctly.

controlled by two knobs: one for horizontal movement, one for vertical. The mother is assigned one knob, the child the other. The mother is shown several designs which are to be reproduced. Together they attempt to copy the design models. The mother decides when their product is a satisfactory copy of the original. The products are scored by measuring deviations from the original designs.

These sessions were recorded, and the nonverbal interaction was described by an observer. Some of the most relevant results were these: middle-class mothers and children performed better on the task (14.6 points) than mother and children from the other groups (9.2; 8.3; 9.5; [Table 10]). Mothers of the three lower-status groups were relatively persistent, rejecting more complete figures than the middle-class mothers; mothers from the middle class praised the child's efforts more than did other mothers but gave just as much criticism; the child's cooperation as rated by the observer was as good or better in low-status groups as in middle-class pairs (Table 11), there was little difference between the groups in affect expressed to the child by the mother (Brophy et al., 1965).

In these data, as in other not presented here, the mothers of the four status groups differed relatively little, on the average, in the affective elements of their interaction with their children. The gross differences appeared in the verbal and cognitive environments that they presented.

Against this background I would like to return for a moment to the problem of the meaning, or, perhaps more correctly, the lack of meaning in cultural deprivation. One of the features of the behavior of the working-class mothers and children is a tendency to act without taking sufficient time for reflection and planning. In a sense one might call this impulsive behavior—not by acting out unconscious or forbidden impulses, but in a type of activity in which a particular act seems not to be related to the act that preceded it or to its consequences. In this sense it lacks meaning; it is not sufficiently related to the context in which it occurs, to the motivations of the participants, or to the goals

TABLE 10. Performance on Etch-a-Sketch Task (Means)

	Social Status			
	Upper Middle N = 40	Upper Lower N = 42	Lower Lower N = 40	ADC N = 41
Total score (range 0–40)	14.6	9.2	8.3	9.5
Average number of attempts	12.7	17.2	12.2	15.1
Complete figures rejected	2.3	3.6	3.5	3.4
Child's total score	5.9	4.0	3.4	4.0
Child's contribution to total score (per cent)	40.4	43.5	41.0	42.1

TABLE 11. Mother-Child Interaction on Etch-a-Sketch Task (Means)

	Social Status			
	Upper Middle N = 40	Upper Lower N = 41	Lower Lower N = 39	ADC N = 39
Praises child	4.6	6.9	7.2	7.5
Criticizes child	6.4	5.5	6.4	5.9
Overall acceptance of child	2.2	3.2	3.4	3.6
Child's cooperation	5.6	5.3	4.5	5.1
Level of affection shown to child	4.8	5.4	5.2	5.8

[a]Ratings made by observer; low number indicates more of the quality rated.

of the task. This behavior may be verbal or motor; it shows itself in several ways. On the Etch-a-Sketch task, for example, the mother may silently watch a child make an error and then punish him. Another mother will anticipate the error, will warn the child that he is about to reach a decision point; she will prepare him by verbal and nonverbal cues to be careful, to look ahead, and to avoid the mistake. He is encouraged to reflect, to anticipate the consequences of his action, and in this way to avoid error. A problem-solving approach requires reflection and the ability to weight decisions, to choose among alternatives. The effect of restricted speech and of status orientation is to foreclose the need for reflective weighing of alternatives and consequences; the use of an elaborated code, with its orientation to persons and to consequences (including future), tends to produce cognitive styles more easily adapted to problem-solving and reflection.

The objective of our study is to discover how teaching styles of the mothers induce and shape learning styles and information-processing strategies in the children. The picture that is beginning to emerge is that the meaning of deprivation is a deprivation of meaning—a cognitive environment in which behavior is controlled by status rules rather than by attention to the individual characteristics of a specific situation and one in which behavior is not mediated by verbal cues or by teaching that relates events to one another and the present to the future. This environment produces a child who relates to authority rather than to rationale, who, although often compliant, is not reflective in his behavior, and for whom the consequences of an act are largely considered in terms of immediate punishment or reward rather than future effects and long-range goals.

When the data are more complete, a more detailed analysis of the findings will enable us to examine the effect of maternal cognitive environments in terms of individual mother-child transactions, rather than in gross categories of social class. This analysis will not only help us to understand how social-class environment is mediated through the interaction between mother and child but will give more precise information about the effects of individual maternal environments on the cognitive growth of the young child.

REFERENCES

Bernstein, B. Social class and linguistic development: a theory of social learning. In A. H. Halsey, Jean Floud, & C. A. Anderson (Eds.), *Education, economy, and society.* Glencoe, Ill.: Free Pr., 1961.

Bernstein, B. Family role systems, communication, and socialization. Paper presented at Conf. on Develpm. of Cross-National Res. on the Education of Children and Adolescents, Univer. of Chicago, February, 1964.

Brophy, J., Hess, R. D., & Shipman, Virginia. Effects of social class and level of aspiration on performance in a structured mother-child interaction. Paper presented at Biennial Meeting of Soc. Res. Child Develpm., Minneapolis, Minn., March, 1965.

Deutsch, M. The disadvantaged child and the learning process. In A. H. Passow (Ed.), *Education in depressed areas.* New York: Columbia Univer. T.C., 1963. Pp. 163–180.

Deutsch, M., & Brown, B. Social influences in Negro-white intelligence differences. *J. soc. Issues*, 1964, **20** (2), 24–35.

Eells, K., Davis, Allison, Havighurst, R. J., Herrick, V. E., & Tyler, R. W. *Intelligence and cultural differences.* Chicago: Univer. of Chicago Pr., 1951.

Hess, R. D., Educability and rehabilitation: the future of the welfare class. *Marr. fam. Lvg*, 1964, **26**, 422–429.

Jackson, J. D., Hess, R. D., & Shipman, Virginia. Communication styles in teachers: an experiment. Paper presented at Amer. Educ. and Res. Ass., Chicago, February, 1965.

John, Vera. The intellectual development of slum children: some preliminary findings. *Amer. J. Orthopsychiat.*, 1963, **33**, 813–822.

Kagan, J., Moss, H. A., & Sigel, I. E. Psychological significance of styles of conceptualization. *Monogr. Soc. Res. Child Develpm.*, 1963, **28**, No. 2.

Kagan, J. Information processing in the child: significance of analytic and reflective attitudes. *Psychol. Monogr.*, 1964, **78**, No. 1 (Whole No. 578).

Kennedy, W. A., Van de Riet, V., & White, J. C., Jr. A normative sample of intelligence and achievement of Negro elementary school children in the southeastern United States. *Monogr. Soc. Res. Child Develpm.*, 1963, **28**, No. 6.

Lesser, G. Mental abilities of children in different social and cultural groups. New York: Cooperative Research Project No. 1635, 1964.

Meyer, Roberta, Shipman, Virginia, & Hess, R. D. Family structure and social class in the socialization of curiosity in urban preschool children. Paper presented at APA meeting in Los Angeles, Calif. September, 1964.

Olim, E. G., Hess, R. D., & Shipman, Virginia. Relationship between mothers' language styles and cognitive styles of urban preschool children. Paper presented at Biennial Meeting of Soc. Res. Child Develpm., Minneapolis, Minn., March, 1965.

Shipman, Virginia, & Hess, R. D. Social class and sex differences in the utilization of language and the consequences for cognitive development. Paper presented at Midwest. Psychol. Ass., Chicago, April, 1965.

JOSEPH J. SPARLING and MARILYN C. SPARLING
23. How to Talk to a Scribbler

A young child draws wiggly-looking marks on paper (or on less approved places) and derives much joy and satisfaction from the experience. These marking or scribbling experiences can be the child's first steps in visual self-expression. Understandably, we adults want to clear the way for "first

Reprinted by permission from *Young Children*, Vol. 28, No. 6 (Aug. 1973), pp. 333–341. Copyright © 1973, National Association for the Education of Young Children, 1834 Connecticut Avenue, N.W., Washington, DC 20009.

steps" of any kind and to lend a helping hand if possible. One way to help the scribbler is by offering an occasional, well-chosen comment as the child finishes a scribble.

But just how many sensible things can one say about a scribble? The random markings of a one- or two-year-old can tax the imagination of the most resourceful adult. Even the more controlled scribbles of a three- or four-year-old do not present an easy topic of conversation between adults and children. Yet the beginner in art needs encouragement in the form of verbal approval and respect. He benefits also from language which stimulates him to be aware of the creative process and product, and of his own thoughts and feelings. The gaining of new names or labels for things give the child a way of recalling and reusing an experience, and skill in concept formation has been shown to be linked to the acquisition of language, particularly to labeling (Kendler & Kendler, 1961). Adults might well view language stimulation as helping the child to gain some of the basic equipment needed to grow toward more mature forms of thought.

What principles can guide an adult who wants to improve his or her communication with scribblers? First, communication must be geared to the developmental level of the scribbler. Comments which are appropriate for a child who scribbles without control are hardly adequate for a child who has gained good control of his crayon. Second, comments must relate specifically to what each child has done. Most of us as adults have been guilty at one time or another of not really looking at what a child has done or not noticing what type of experience he has had. When this happens our responses are often stereotyped phrases which do not provide rich language stimulation. These two principles ("gear to the developmental level" and "be specific") are the source of the positive suggestions and examples in this article.

THE VERY FIRST SCRIBBLES[1]

Since the young child does not have a high degree of control over his motions, the first drawings are usually little more than a few random marks. The physical process of scribbling is fascinating to the young child, while the marks which are made are of less interest to him. In talking about the very first scribbles, an adult can mention (1) the child's movements, (2) the way the scribble looks and (3) the way the child probably felt as he made the drawing. There are, of course, many things which could be said under these three headings, but in each of the following sections only one or two samples are provided. Hopefully, these will stimulate the reader to think of many other possible choices. The best remarks are simple and to the point. In each exchange with a young child, usually no more than one or two individual comments are appropriate, and there are many instances when the adult may wisely remain silent.

[1]This is the first of three levels of scribbling, each a little more advanced than the previous level (Lowenfeld & Brittain, 1964, p. 95).

Talking About Movement

Commenting about movement emphasizes the actual physical process, the act of creating, and helps the child to be more aware of his own movements. The development of motor coordination is a major task of the child during the scribbling period. Thus, comments such as this one are appropriate and make sense to the child: "Look how fast your hand is jumping back and forth!" One could mention instead, something positive about how big or small a child's movements are, or how light or hard he is pressing with his crayon.

Talking About the Way Things Look

Comments which center on the visual features of his work help the child to be more aware of the various kinds of things he has spontaneously created. An appropriate comment here might be: "You've made some little dots and a long curvy line." Besides describing some of the actual marks, one could talk about the placement of the marks on the paper or about the colors used.

It may be helpful at times to point to that aspect of the child's work to which a comment refers. For example, when talking about a particular line in the child's drawing, it is appropriate to touch or trace it with a finger. This helps to guarantee that the child understands what the adult is referring to.

Talking About Feelings

By providing language models, an adult can help children to be more conscious of the way they feel during and after creation and can lead children to independently verbalize these feelings. Clues to a child's feelings can be "read" in his facial and body expressions, and noted in his preferences for certain activities, colors or ways of working. Comments such as "You worked a long time on your painting—you must have enjoyed it very much," help the child realize that what he is doing and what he is feeling are understood and valued.

THE MORE CONTROLLED SCRIBBLES

After many experiences, a child will gradually develop visual and motor control over his scribbles. As with the very first scribbles, comments can be made regarding movement, the visual aspects and feelings. Most children will begin to spend a little longer time on their work now, and will be more interested in the actual marks they have made. Again, one or two comments are adequate. Sometimes, however, several comments and questions may be effectively used if a child seems particularly responsive.

271

Talking About Movement

Comments about developing motor control and increasing ability to devise a variety of movements are now of special significance to children. They will be able to keep their marks more on the paper, and to repeat certain movements, such as up and down and circular scribbles (de Francesco, 1958, p. 251). Comments such as "See how you make your hand go around and around—like a merry-go-round!" can focus attention on these newly acquired skills.

Talking About the Way Things Look

Adults can strengthen a child's self-confidence and stimulate his thinking by encouraging him to look more carefully at what he has done. Comments and labels can help a child realize that he has made a certain mark many times or that he has created a great variety of lines and closed shapes. One specific comment might be: "See how well you've drawn a small circle right inside this big one. That's hard to do." Other appropriate comments concerning the visual features of a child's work might refer to contrasting colors and values, comparisons or descriptions of different lines or shapes, and the relationship of various marks to each other.

Talking About Feelings

The scribbler who is gaining fine motor control develops feelings of pride which are the topic of some important adult comments. This pride is seen in the child's satisfaction over his increasing skills and growing ability to control his movements and markings. A comment such as this focuses attention on feelings that go with new accomplishments: "It's exciting to find new ways to use a crayon!"

THE SCRIBBLES CHILDREN NAME

One day the child will discover for himself that the various lines and shapes he has drawn "look like" something he has seen around him. A person will often be identified first, and the child may call his drawing *a man* or *my mommy* (Lowenfeld & Brittain, 1964, pp. 116–117). This new development (of relating marks on paper to things in the visual world) usually stimulates the child to show and talk to others about his work. At this point a rich opportunity for communication exists.

Unfortunately for the adult, these named scribbles will not look much different from earlier markings. Children will further confuse us by rapidly changing the ideas and meanings that they read into their pictures. Thus a particular shape may at one time be called a ball, five minutes later a sun, and perhaps the next day a flower. For these reasons, adults are rather presumptuous if they attempt to guess or name a shape in a child's art work. Adults need to listen carefully to the child's comments and capitalize on the meaning *to the child* at that moment. Whatever the statement by a child about his picture (and some statements may be not at all what the adults expect), we can do no more or less than to accept these meanings which are personal to the child and respond to them sincerely.

The following suggestions to adults are divided into two categories: (1) how to respond to a child who initiates a conversation, and (2) what to say when a child is reluctant to discuss his work.

When Children Make Comments

Some children are ready to name or comment about their work without any questioning from adults. When the child does offer some comment about his work, the adult then has a clue to the child's thinking and can ask a leading question to help expand the child's thinking even further (Lowenfeld & Brittain, 1964, p. 102).

These leading questions should include both aesthetic and personal ideas. If a child says "See my big man," the adult could stimulate awareness of aesthetics by asking about the colors, shapes or repetition of lines. To encourage awareness of the personal aspects, the adult could ask about the child's relationship to the man (as a Daddy) or the child's thoughts about the man. For example: "Your man is so big he fills up the whole paper! Is he someone that you know?"

Such comments and questions help carry the child's thoughts in the direction *he* initiated and are therefore likely to have meaning for him. But the child must feel free also to disregard adult comments and questions and adults must willingly accept rebuffs at their attempts to stimulate discussion.

When Children Are Reluctant to Comment

Sometimes a child may hesitate to talk about his work. At such times, an adult might encourage conversation by asking questions such as: "That looks like fun. Would you like to tell me about some of the things you've made?"

Sometimes a child may appear confused by a request such as "I'd like to know more about your drawing." This probably means that the child is still at an earlier scribbling level and has not yet begun to name his markings. At other times, a child may simply be unwilling to enter a conversation. In either case, the adult should then make a positive comment to the child such as "I'm glad you're having fun drawing," or "You're making lots of nice lines go all around your paper." Comments such as these offer reassurance that the adult understands and respects the child's way of working and does not intend to try to force him to comment. Everyone has the right to at times enjoy his own private world. With continual support and through many opportunities to create, more children will gradually want to talk about their work. The adult can then respond to that need and strengthen it through appropriate questions and comments.

WHAT IF A CHILD DOESN'T SCRIBBLE?

A few children will be inhibited in their visual self-expression, or will seem reluctant to scribble. In such situations an adult may want to initiate some special stimulation. Motivational techniques such as this may be of some help:

> Let's try drawing together today. We can pick out some special paper and a crayon to use. Oh, you chose a bright red crayon. That's a beautiful color! Now, I'm going to let my crayon move all around my paper. Like this. It feels good to move it all around. Sometimes I like to close my eyes when I draw. Then I just let my hand move anywhere it wants to. Let's try it together now. Want to close our eyes? Okay. Now open them. Wow! Look at all the things we made. I like the way your lines go around and around . . . You might like to draw again sometime.

This approach provides encouragement and approval for the creative act itself. This procedure is generally to be used with a single child but might prove effective at times with a small group of children. The adult should praise even the smallest effort and should keep trying a little each day. It takes a while for a child to build up courage and confidence, especially when the child has had a bad experience before or is fearful of trying anything new or different. If the adult is unable to get the child to participate, he should let the child go on to something he likes and give a positive statement such as "I enjoyed sitting down with you. Maybe we can do something special again tomorrow." Through such stimulation, we hope to gradually involve even the most reluctant scribbler in satisfying motor activities.

WHEN NOT TO TALK AND WHAT NOT TO SAY

Children need to gain satisfaction from their work without constant adult approval. Thus, comments and questions need not be given every time a child does something. In fact, adults should look for appropriate opportunities to be silent and should frequently remain away from children while they are working.

Some children hum to themselves as they scribble. This is a natural response to the rhythm of the scribbling activity. Usually it is an indication of involvement in the experience, and so the child should be left to himself at this time.

Other children stare off into space as they scribble contentedly. This, too, is reasonable since the motor activity predominates, especially in the first two levels of scribbling. At such a time children are not usually interested in the actual marks they are making. It is the process of scribbling itself which is immensely satisfying. During this occurrence nothing needs to be said and the adult can leave the child alone to finish at his own pace.

When a child is fully involved in his activity, it is best not to interrupt him with a comment. When the child puts down his crayon or brush, looks up, or otherwise takes his attention from his work, the time is ripe for communication. The adult can then show interest in the child and his work by making a thoughtful, sincere comment. Additional respect can be shown by using the child's name when talking to him. Of importance to many children is actual physical contact. So, when speaking, a thoughtful adult may put a hand on the child's shoulder, sit or kneel to his level, and direct all attention for a moment to the child and his work.

Comments and questions, to be appropriate and effective, must be open-ended and help to heighten the sensitivity of each child to what he is doing or has done. Therefore, adults should avoid questions such as "What are you drawing?" "Is this a house?" or "What's this?" This type of question puts the child on the spot, leaving no room for varied interpretations and often closing the door on creativity and further exploration.

Instead of asking a child what he is making, one might comment first on the nice bright red color used and then ask if he or she would like to tell about something special in the painting. This approach emphasizes the importance of a positive initial statement to let the child know that the adult accepts what the child is doing and finds meaning in some part of the child's creation. The follow-up question is then an expression of genuine interest and is worded in such a way that the child can choose freely whether or not to respond.

CONCLUSION

Why all this fuss about talking to a scribbler? Hopefully, the kinds of conversations suggested here will result in young children who are more enthusiastic about expressing themselves through art and who are motivated to continue and expand their art activity. In addition, the general awareness that is built up through language is the catalyst which enables the young child to translate art experiences into art concepts. This general awareness is the forerunner of a critical awareness the child will need if he is to reach later stages in his development where he must *evaluate* his own work and the work of others by applying aesthetic concepts.

Clearly, the comments given here cannot be picked up and used verbatim by other adults. These sample comments can act only as a stimulus to the thinking of others. Communication is an important matter, and anyone who reaches out to another human being must be ready to expend effort in the process. Parents, teachers and day care workers cannot expect to "turn on" a scribbler with a casual glance at his work and a stock or pat phrase.

The thoughtlessness of this approach was pointed out in an eye-opening classroom experience. Smiling at a child's drawing, a teacher said "That's nice." With painful honesty, the little girl replied "Oh, Mrs. Merrill, you say that to everybody!"

REFERENCES

Bland, J. C. *Art of the Young Child.* New York: Simon & Schuster, 1969.
de Francesco, I. L. *Art Education, Its Means and Ends.* New York: Harper & Bros., 1958.
Kellogg, R. & O'Dell, S. *The Psychology of Children's Art.* San Diego: CRM-Random House, 1967.
Kendler, H. H. & Kendler, T. S. Effect of verbalization on discrimination reversal shifts in children. *Science,* 1961, 134, 1619–1620.
Lowenfeld, V. & Brittain, W. L. *Creative and Mental Growth.* New York: Macmillan, 1964.

KATHRYN CASTLE

24. A Language Model for Moral Development

Teachers who are concerned with the positive growth and development of young children are constantly struggling with the question of how to communicate with a child in ways that will not only enhance the child's self-esteem but also help the child learn how to get along with others. Behavior problems and conflicts among children occur in every classroom. It is through these conflicts that the child learns that other people have different points of view about things. Through these conflicts, children learn that others often have feelings different from their own. Children learn the importance of sharing resources and taking turns. They learn how to express their angry feelings with words rather than with fists. A warm, accepting teacher who uses verbal reasoning and encourages verbal communication can provide a positive atmosphere in which children can learn better how to work and play together.

Discipline without repression is a major concern of most classroom teachers. Teachers want to know how to discipline in positive ways that will eliminate problem behavior but will also preserve the child's self-esteem and help the child view the teacher as a positive influence in settling disputes. There are a variety of ways, some more positive than others, in which teachers can communicate with children when handling discipline problems. One way is the teacher's assuming an authoritarian role by verbally commanding children to behave in certain ways. An authoritarian role is one in which the teacher asserts her power of author-

With permission from Kathryn Castle.

ity over children to get them to do what she wants. For example, an authoritarian teacher may use such statements as, "Sit down, shut your mouth, and listen to me," "Stop that because I said so!" or "No fighting or I will spank you!"

These examples represent commands from a higher authority but provide little explanation for why a child should or should not do something other than because the boss is commanding it or because he fears physical punishment. Little appeal is made to cognitive processing. A child does not have to think about his response. Consequently, the child acts without much thought. These authoritarian statements may be quite effective in producing immediate results; however, they may also generate such adverse side effects as anger and hostility.

For teachers who do not wish to communicate with children in an authoritarian way, there is an alternative: the authoritative role. The authoritative teacher provides children with viable reasons for changing their behavior in addition to providing choices. For example, an authoritative teacher may say, "Please stop talking so that others may hear the story" or "You may either find a book to read or get a game to play, but you may not fight in the classroom." These examples of authoritative statements provide verbal reasons why the child must change his behavior. These statements encourage the child to think about his alternatives and provide some information to help make a decision. This form of communication provides a rationale for behavior in addition to offering a choice among alternatives.

The authoritative teacher, according to Katz (1973), combines both warmth and strength—conformity and explanation—and, in addition, treats children's opinions and feelings as valid. Baumrind (1970) investigated the roles of both the authoritarian and authoritative parent. She defined the role of the authoritarian parent as (1) appealing to a higher authority in controlling the child's behavior, (2) using force and punishment to get children to behave correctly, and (3) discouraging verbal give-and-take with the child. On the other hand, the role of the authoritative parent involves reasoning with the child, encouraging verbal give-and-take, and accepting the child's individual interests. The authoritative parent encourages independent behavior. He or she exerts firm control but combines this with warmth and acceptance of the child's communication. Baumrind (1967) found that of the children she studied, those who were discontented, withdrawn, and distrustful had parents best described as authoritarian. The children who were the most self-reliant, self-controlled, explorative, and contented had parents best described as authoritative.

Whether parent or teacher, the authoritative adult is warm and accepting of the child and sets and enforces clear-cut limits to behavior. The authoritative adult consistently uses reasoning as a discipline technique to explain the need for behavioral limits and to communicate with the child. Reasoning with the child as a discipline technique has been termed *induction* (Hoffman, 1970). The use of induction means giving verbal explanations or reasons for requiring a child to change his behavior. Examples provided by Hoffman (1970) include pointing out the harmful consequences of the child's behavior for himself or others ("It hurts Rachel when you pinch her"); providing the child with a reason to stop his behavior ("If you break your toy airplane, you won't have one to play with later"); and giving the child a choice or alternative to his behavior ("You can clean up your materials now and then go outside to play, or you can clean up your materials later and miss the movie"). These techniques do not make use of physical punishment; rather, they involve a verbal attempt to convince the child that he should change his behavior. These techniques appeal less to the child's fear of punishment and more to his cognitive comprehension.

Hess and Shipman (1965) maintain that the child's development of cognitive processes is enhanced when families offer and permit a wide range of alternatives of action and thought; such growth is hampered when families offer the child predetermined solutions and few alternatives for consideration and choice. They argue that the structure of the family shapes communication and language and that language shapes thought and cognitive styles of problem solving. They discuss two basic types of family control: One is oriented toward control by appealing to the status of authority; the other is oriented toward persons. Person-oriented messages appeal to reflection and reflective comparisons and provide the child with a rationale for his behavior. Status-oriented messages imply power and compliance and arbitrary decisions rather than decisions based on logical consequences. Hess and Shipman conclude that the use of an elaborated linguistic code with its more complex grammatical structure and its orientation to persons and consequences facilitates the development of problem solving and the ability to take the role of others. For example, a mother using an elaborated code to give directions to a child will say, "Go get the scissors in the top drawer of the nightstand in the bedroom and please bring them to me so that I can cut your hair." A mother using a more restricted linguistic code will merely command, "Get the scissors." The first example is more grammatically complex, provides much more information, and gives the child a reason for the request.

Although the subjects of the Hess and Shipman study were mothers, the implications of the study apply equally to teachers and to all those adults who interact with children. Teachers provide language models for young children. Through verbal communications, teachers can stimulate cognitive processing in children. Teachers can provide verbal opportunities for children to be given choices that prompt them to think through available alternatives.

By what Hoffman (1970) describes as other-oriented induction, the teacher can verbally point out to a child the consequences of the child's actions as they affect another person, animal, object, or event ("When you scribble in your textbook, others will not be able to read the stories"). Hoffman gives several examples of other-oriented induction, such as explaining the nature of the consequences of the child's act ("If you jump on the toy it will break"); pointing out the relevant needs or desires of others ("Please listen to George. He is trying to tell you he doesn't like sand thrown in his face"); and explaining the motives underlying the

278

other person's behavior toward the child ("Nancy didn't mean to bump you. She slipped and fell against you by accident"). To these categories, the present author would also add (1) providing the child with rational alternatives ("You may play with the ball as long as you don't throw it at anyone, or you may play with the truck") and (2) explaining the function of objects ("Chairs are for sitting in, not standing on").

Other-oriented induction is a tool that teachers can use in their verbal interactions with children to stimulate thinking, decision making, and independence in actions. The teacher who uses other-oriented induction statements is able to deal with short-term behavior problems while providing long-term language examples and cognitive constructs that the child may recall in future situations. When the child is given a rationale for his behavior, he can carry this cognitive and verbal handle into other situations, such as those involving peer conflict. He has a cognitive and language model that he can recall and utilize in dealing with others.

INDUCTION COMPARED TO OTHER APPROACHES

Young children tend to imitate and model the verbal expressions of their parents and teachers. The parroting by children of comments such as, "Shut up!" and "Do what I say or I'll knock your head off!" tend to return to haunt adults. A teacher who uses other-oriented induction statements can constructively take advantage of the child's verbal modeling of such statements in the settling of peer disputes in a verbal, nonphysical manner. For example, the young child who is just learning to express his emotions in words rather than in actions may model such statements as, "I don't like it when you hit me. It hurts my feelings" or, "You took Joan's puzzle. Now she is sad because she doesn't have anything to play with" or, "You can either stop teasing Mark and play the game with us, or you can go somewhere else."

Besides providing a cognitive and language model, there are many other advantages to using other-oriented induction in the classroom. For example, although punishment suppresses problem behavior and does produce immediate results, its effects tend to be of short duration, and it is often accompanied by adverse side effects such as the "ripple effect." When one child is being punished, similar feelings of "bad me" and hostility are produced in children nearby who witness the example of the punished child. In addition, the adult who administers the punishment may become an aversive stimulus to the child: The child may withdraw from or avoid that adult. This is especially a problem in the classroom because children will often tune out a punishing teacher. In this situation it is difficult for the child to learn from an adult who is perceived as an aversive stimulus.

High-intensity punishment can also hinder learning and performance by creating high levels of anxiety. In addition, punishment without a rationale appeals more to emotional reactions than to cognitive processing. It often hinders communication and positive interactions between child and adult by creating anger and hostility. The adult who spanks a child for hitting another child may serve as an aggressive model to the child by demonstrating that when one is angry, one hits. And finally, once punishment is used, greater and greater intensities of that punishment will be required in the future to suppress the behavior, because the child tends to habituate to the original intensity level.

Another basic approach to discipline and an alternative to physical punishment has been termed *love withdrawal*. An adult who uses love withdrawal in communicating with a child poses no physical threat to the child but threatens to stop loving the child unless the child does as the adult wishes (Hoffman, 1970). Love withdrawal can be even more emotionally harmful to the child than punishment because it threatens the loss of love or possible separation. Examples of love-withdrawal techniques include ignoring the child, refusing to speak or listen to the child, stating a dislike for the child, and isolating or threatening to leave the child. Love withdrawal tends to be more effective when used by a nurturant parent. Sears, Maccoby, and Levin (1957) found that love withdrawal is only effective when the parent expresses enough affection in the first place to show the child he has something to lose.

Love withdrawal tends to appeal to the child's sense of guilt and may produce so much anxiety that the child is motivated to cease his problem behavior. Another disadvantage of using love withdrawal is the length of time it seems to last to the child. Whereas physical punishment may be over with quickly and provide relief for the child's feelings of guilt, love withdrawal may seem to go on forever. The young child who has not developed a proper sense of time may not be able to comprehend that there will eventually be an end to the adult's attitude and may therefore become even more anxious. Love withdrawal may also produce a child hungry for adult approval. The child may become so anxious about losing adult affection and approval that he will go to extremes to get it, for example, cheating in school in order to get good marks.

ADVANTAGES OF INDUCTION AS A COMMUNICATION TOOL

As a rational and humane alternative to punishment and love withdrawal, the use of induction to communicate with children provides many advantages while minimizing the disadvantages. The production of anxiety and hostility are at a minimum. The adult using induction is not physically punishing the child nor is he or she perceived as an aversive stimulus or an aggressive model. Children are not made anxious by the threat or actual loss of love or affection from important adults. To the child, induction presents an adult who is rational and nonarbitrary. Other-oriented induction tends to focus the child's attention on the effects of his behavior on others rather than on adults as punishing agents. Even if the young child may not entirely comprehend the rationale, he is stimulated to think about his actions and their effects on others. The emphasis of other-oriented induction is on the building of long-term internal controls rather than on dependence on external restrictions. Because the adult using induction is showing respect for the child's ability to make decisions and control his own behavior, the child's development of self-esteem is enhanced.

Another good reason for using induction is its link with cognitive and moral development. According to Piaget (1932) and Kohlberg (1969), moral development is highly related to cognitive development. The child must be able to reason if he is to make moral decisions. Induction stimulates and facilitates the child's ability to reason and therefore facilitates his moral reasoning and decision making.

The research studies on induction have, for the most part, been in the area of child-rearing and deal with the use of induction by the parent rather than by the teacher. Hoffman (1970) provides an excellent summary of the importance of other-oriented induction for the child's moral and social development by citing child-rearing research that indicates that parental use of induction is associated with advanced moral development. There appears to be a positive relationship between the mother's use of other-oriented induction and the child's level of moral development. In fact, induction, especially other-oriented induction, is the type of parental discipline most conducive to moral development according to Hoffman's review.

In a recent study relating family structure to cognitive development in young children, Sigel and McGillicuddy-DeLisi (1979) indicate that children whose parents use "distancing strategies" evidenced better problem-solving abilities than those whose parents did not. Distancing strategies, much like induction, encourage a child's imagination and ability to infer. For example, when a child refuses to share, a parent using distancing may say, "How will your friend feel with nothing to play with?" In this example, the child is encouraged to imagine being the other child or to take another's point of view. This technique is an example of other-oriented induction because it encourages the child to consider the consequences of his actions as they affect another person.

Ginott (1965) discusses rational ways of conversing and dealing with children in order to preserve their self-esteem. He maintains that children need a rational and clear definition of acceptable and unacceptable behavior. Ginott says that parents should state the limits of behavior clearly and firmly and then provide the child with examples of acceptable alternative behaviors. Ginott also stresses that limits are accepted more willingly when, for example, they point out the function of an object. "Pillows are for leaning against" is less antagonistic and provides more information than "Don't throw that pillow!" Although Ginott does not call the first statement induction, it does fulfill the requirements of an induction technique while stressing the importance of respecting the child as a person.

In his description of the rational management of children, Hauck (1972) emphasizes the use of "logical consequences" in communicating with children. Hauck suggests that parents should put the responsibility for the child's behavior on the child. The parent should explain and point out the consequences of the child's behavior and then allow the child to learn by dealing with the resulting consequences. The child sees for himself that certain consequences will follow certain behaviors. Hauck's idea of logical consequences is also an induction method in the sense that the adult explains the consequences of a child's behavior and encourages the child to think through his actions and their effects on others.

From the child-rearing research, it appears that induction has many advantages over other discipline techniques such as physical punishment and love withdrawal. The use of induction effectively deals with behavior while providing important information to the child, thus stimulating his cognitive, social, and moral development. It appears to be a technique that can be used constructively by both parents and teachers, and it should be especially beneficial for the classroom because it minimizes the production of anxiety and hostility. Rather than being perceived as an aversive stimulus, the teacher who uses induction will appear as a rational adult who is there to aid and guide the child by pointing out the consequences of his actions and thus facilitate the child's ability to take another person's point of view. Induction will also stimulate the child's language development through the introduction of new concepts and new relationships. The benefit to the overall classroom atmosphere will be to minimize the use of physical aggression and maximize the use of verbal expression in settling conflicts.

SUGGESTIONS FOR USING OTHER-ORIENTED INDUCTION IN THE CLASSROOM

Other-oriented induction is a verbal communication tool that can be learned with a little effort. However, like any discipline technique, it implies an underlying attitude about adult-child relationships. Adults who use the technique tend to believe in a positive, rational, nonpunitive approach to child guidance. They also tend to respect the integrity of the child and believe that children should be encouraged to discover their own solutions to their own problems.

Teachers who wish to begin using other-oriented induction in their classrooms may feel somewhat awkward at first if they attempt to memorize specific statements or parrot the phrases of those who use the strategy. The use of other-oriented induction will be more natural for those teachers who attempt to understand the approach and who sincerely believe that children are capable of making decisions about their own learning. Teachers who trust children to become independent learners and who respect the individuality of the child will find other-oriented induction a valuable tool. Some classroom situations in which other-oriented induction may be beneficial follow:

1. Other-oriented induction is most appropriate for the child who has a difficult time making decisions and choosing activities. To help this child get started, the teacher may give the child a limited number of alternatives at first and then increase the number as the child becomes better able to choose for himself. The teacher may say, "This morning you may either work at the art table or choose a puzzle." As a result, the child is encouraged to think about the two alternatives and make an

individual choice. When the child has experienced some success in making a choice between two alternatives, the teacher adds a third alternative. The teacher gradually adds several alternatives in helping the child become a successful decision maker.

2. A teacher can use other-oriented induction to redirect behavior into constructive activities. For example, the teacher may say, "I know you like to run, but our rules say no running in the classroom because you might fall and hurt yourself or someone else. So you may walk to the block area to play, or you may play this game with the group." In this example, the teacher respects and accepts the child's *desire* to run, but reminds the child that the *behavior* of running in the classroom is against the rules. In addition, he or she provides a reason for the rule, thus encouraging the child to take another's point of view. The teacher firmly enforces the limits without damaging the child's self-esteem by yelling at the child or using physical punishment. As an alternative, the teacher rechannels the child's behavior by offering a choice between two alternatives. She or he provides an opportunity for the child to change his behavior in addition to an opportunity to experience the power of making a decision about his actions.

3. Disputes may be settled with other-oriented induction. For example, the teacher may encounter two children who are arguing about which one gets to play with the one available doll. The teacher may say, "I can see that both of you want to play with the doll. So you may both play with the doll together without fighting, or you may take turns playing with the doll for ten minutes each. You decide." In this example, the teacher again accepts each child's desire to play with the doll. Because there is only one doll and two children, the teacher provides a choice of two alternatives. As a result, the children are encouraged to make a choice and settle their own dispute. The teacher offers them the opportunity to work out a mutual agreement on their own. In this particular situation, if the children decide to play with the doll for ten minutes each, it would be helpful to provide them with a kitchen timer that can be easily set and will remind them when it is time to take turns.

Another example of settling a dispute with other-oriented induction presents itself when one child knocks down the tower that another child is attempting to build. The teacher may say, "I know you like to knock things down, but Mark has worked very hard to build this tower, and it hurts his feelings when you knock it down. You can build your own tower and knock it down, or you can play outside." The teacher accepts the child's desire to knock down the tower but not the child's action of knocking it down. The teacher points out to the child the consequences of his actions as they affect Mark whose feelings are hurt. This is an appeal to the child's ability to empathize with another and encourages the child to look at the situation from Mark's point of view. The teacher also provides the child with a choice of what to do next. The child is then responsible for rechanneling his own behavior.

4. Other-oriented induction can be used by the teacher in pointing out

the needs or desires or motivations of others. For example, the teacher may say, "Please stop telling ghost stories to Eric. He does not like to hear about ghosts because it gives him scary feelings." In this situation, the teacher points out the desire of Eric not to hear ghost stories and encourages the taking of Eric's point of view. At the same time, the teacher provides a reason to stop the undesired behavior of telling ghost stories to Eric.

In pointing out another's motivation, the teacher may say to several children, "Alice sits quietly in the corner all alone because she feels unliked. Calling her names will only make her feel worse." Here the teacher provides an explanation for Alice's antisocial behavior while giving a reason for the children to stop their behavior of teasing Alice.

5. A teacher may use other-oriented induction to introduce new vocabulary words and concepts and to explain the functions of objects. For example, "Tables are for sitting at, not crawling under"; "Blocks are for building, not for throwing"; "Pencils are for writing and drawing, not for poking others." In addition to encouraging them to change their behavior, the teacher uses these examples to teach the children about various concepts and the purposes for certain objects. This is a good example of changing undesired behavior while simultaneously stimulating cognitive processing.

6. A teacher may use other-oriented induction to encourage problem solving. For example, a teacher may say, "When you push and hit someone, it hurts him. Find a way to show how you feel without pushing or hitting"; "James is sad today because he has no one to play with. Let's think of some ways to help James"; "We have five musical instruments and ten children. Let's discover how we can give everyone a turn." These examples can be the initiators of creative discussions for discovering solutions to everyday problems. In addition to encouraging children's logical thought processes and verbal expression, these situations help children take responsibility for solving their own problems and creating a classroom where their individual needs and desires are taken into consideration. Beginning problem solving with everyday experiences can help transfer to more abstract situations, such as scientific and mathematical activities.

Teachers who use other-oriented induction supply information, give explanations, and provide rational alternatives to children. Children benefit with gains in cognitive and moral development and become more independent learners. But perhaps even more important than these benefits is the resulting positive classroom atmosphere in which children feel good about themselves and their ability to make rational decisions.

REFERENCES

Baumrind, Diana. "Child Care Practices Anteceding Three Patterns of Preschool Behavior." *Genetic Psychology Monograph* 75 (1967): 43–88.

*_____. "Socialization and Instrumental Competence in Young Children." *Young Children* 26 (1970): 104-119.

Ginott, Haim G. *Between Parent and Child.* New York: Avon Books, 1965.

Hauck, Paul. *The Rational Management of Children.* New York: Libra Publishers Inc., 2nd ed. 1972.

*Hess, Robert D., and Shipman, Virginia C. "Early Experience and the Socialization of Cognitive Modes in Children." *Child Development* 36 (1965): 869-886.

Hoffman, Martin L. "Moral Development." In *Carmichael's Manual of Child Psychology.* Vol. 2, edited by P. Mussen, 261-359. New York: John Wiley & Sons, Inc., 1970.

*Katz, Lilian. "Perspectives on Early Childhood Education." *Educational Forum* 37 (1973): 393-398.

Kohlberg, Lawrence. "Stage and Sequence: The Cognitive Developmental Approach to Socialization." In *Handbook of Socialization Theory and Research,* edited by D. A. Goslin. Skokie, Ill.: Rand McNally & Company, Inc., 1969, 347-480.

Piaget, Jean. *The Moral Judgement of the Child.* New York: Harcourt Brace Jovanovich, Inc., 1932.

Sears, Robert R.; Maccoby, Eleanor E.; and Levin, Harry. *Patterns of Child Rearing.* New York: Harper & Row, 1957.

Siegel, Irving, and McGillicuddy-DeLisi, Ann. "Research Links Parental Beliefs to Learning in Young Children." *Review of Research in ETS Developments.* Vol. 25, edited by M. Churchill (1979): 4-5.

CHARLES H. WOLFGANG

25. Psychological Theory and Young Children's Literature

One of my first adventures in the world of young children occurred during my student-teaching experience with three-year-olds. A young child riding a tricycle came peddling along and, mine being a new face, he stopped and smiled broadly. Pleased to be acknowledged, I said, "Hi, my name is Mr. Wolfgang." The child's face changed from a radiant smile to an expression of total fear. He jumped from his tricycle and ran to the opposite end of the playground shouting, "Woof, Woof." This was immediately picked up by the remainder of the class, and I became the object of fearful play to a group of fifteen three-year-olds. Such behavior suggests that the young child understands his world and emotionally

With permission from Charles H. Wolfgang.

responds to that understanding quite differently from the way adults respond to the world around them.

As educators, we now have a vast bulk of psychological knowledge and child-development theory to help us gain an understanding of what emotional and intellectual processes are occurring within children. We are just beginning to translate this theory into educational practice to help teachers make appropriate choices of experiences and curricula for young children. It will be my purpose in this paper to attempt to provide a theoretical framework, or construct, based on known child-development theory for use in viewing the subject of literature for preschool children. This attempt will view this subject from within the child, with his cognitive and emotional growth used as the basis for judgments, rather than discuss it by the more traditional division of literature into categories of fiction, nonfiction, and fairy tales.

To begin this process, it is necessary to return to the child's cries of "Woof, Woof" and to gain an understanding of why the child responded in this way both from his intellectual and emotional position.

Piaget, the Swiss psychologist, has provided us a wealth of information on the intellectual or cognitive capacities of children. He demonstrates that not only is the child's thinking quantitatively different from ours but also qualitatively different. In other words, children, because of their limited experiences, have not stored up large amounts of information, and they use the information that they possess much differently from the way adults use theirs.

For example, if a young child is playing with a paper, waving it before his face and feeling the air move, he thinks, understandably, "Moving paper causes wind to blow." Later, when the child finds himself outside just before a storm in the midst of a swirling wind and swaying trees, he generalizes from past experience and thinks, "Moving trees cause wind to blow." It is with these same limited cognitive capacities that the child attempts to comprehend the content of stories and books read to him. Consequently, we may present literature to the child that is misunderstood or simply incomprehensible at his particular stage of development.

Piaget has given us a logico-mathematical model (1958, 1926, 1952) for viewing the mind as it integrates and stores new information to be used for problem solving. The preschool years, ages 2-7, are identified as the Preoperational Period. This period is characterized by the type of thinking in the examples of "Woof, Woof" and "Moving paper causes wind to blow." The ages from 7 to 11 are called the Concrete Operational Period and are characterized by mature forms of reason similar to those used by adults. The difference between these two stages must be described.

In a logico-mathematical framework, the mind receives new information and stores it by a process of classification with the information that the mind already possesses. The young child, seeing a horse or cow, shouts, "Doggie, Doggie." A four-legged animal in the young child's understanding is classified in a broad concept under the term, "Dog." The child has not developed a fine discrimination and a subclassification system for four-legged animals to include cows, horses, and so on.

An example from Piaget might develop this classification idea further. Piaget was walking with his four-year-old daughter Jacqueline, when they came upon a man with a pronounced body deformity. Jacqueline questioned his appearance, and Piaget explained it as an illness, On a later walk, they discovered the man was missing from his usual spot, and Jacqueline was told that the man was at home with the flu. Days later they were told that the man was now well, and upon hearing this, Jacqueline stated, "He now no longer has the deformity." Jacqueline, as a preoperative thinker, had not built up in her mind a hierarchical classification pattern in order to deal effectively with this type of informational input.

When this information in our mind is organized, it becomes hierarchically patterned into subclasses in much the same way that all matter can be subdivided into animate and inanimate groupings and all animate beings can be further subdivided into plants and animals.

Jacqueline's sense of "illness" can be intellectually organized:

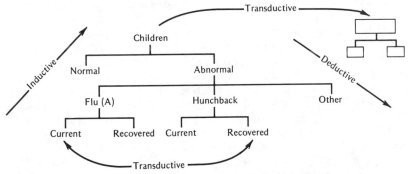

FIGURE 1 Operational thinking.

Adults, as well as children in the concrete operational stage (ages 7–11), have developed these mental hierarchical (logico–mathematical) patterns in their minds. Thus, the more mature thinkers can reason (operationally), with a mobility of thought which moves from a particular or lower subclass to a general or higher classification (inductive thinking) and then from a general classification to a particular subclass (deductive). The preschooler, as a preoperational thinker, has not built up this relationship or classification system and therefore thinks transductively— from a particular to a particular (Jacqueline identifying "illness" and the child thinking, "Moving trees cause wind to blow")—or from a general classification to a general classification, that is, all men are "Daddies." Thus, we gain an understanding of the child's comprehension when he shouted, "Woof, Woof."

It is with this limited intellectual foundation that the young child attempts to understand the children's literature that he hears. Because of the preschooler's transductive reasoning, the child's thinking is centered. The child centers on one dominant feature, not being able to consider a second or third feature of the problem. If, for example, two equal balls of clay are shown to the preschooler, and then one is rolled into a sausage, the preoperational thinker will declare that the sausage now has more clay, because it appears long (and, therefore, larger). The child is centered only on length. Again, the child cannot comprehend change or transformation between states. In the children's story, *The Ugly Duckling*, the protagonist is transformed into a beautiful swan. The preschooler cannot intellectually follow this movement. Imagine how difficult it is for a two- or three-year-old simply to pour his milk from a large container to a small glass. Intellectually the child must decenter to take in two reference points while pouring the liquid. The milk, as it pours, would be a classic example of transformation. We might think that the young child who spills lacks fine motor control, when in actual fact such a task is an intellectually challenging one.

With this basic understanding of the thought processes, how shall we view the content of children's literature and its concomitant role in emotional development?

I can recall watching an amateur magician presenting his act to a group of four-year-olds. He made objects appear, disappear, or transform but was disappointed that the children did not laugh or appear very excited by his magical talents. For the young transductive thinker, whose thoughts are centered and cannot comprehend dynamic change, the entire child's world appears magical. With a limited sense of causality, things appear and disappear with little reason or rhythm. In fact, it is children in middle childhood (concrete operational period) who love magic acts, because they have just gained a reality-based understanding of their world and can be amused by this sudden contradiction to reality.

The young preschooler's world, then, appears magical and is largely fantasy-based. The child can see no reason why animals and objects that move, such as a car, should not talk or have feelings just as he does. The dominant activity of the preoperational child is fantasy play. The child eating his cereal pretends the corn flakes are "boats" and "sails" them across the bowl. The child takes a pencil and ignores or does not understand its reality use and makes it in play a "robot."

If we look closely at the content of children's literature, we will find that it is this fantasy, simply written down with words and pictures. Fantasy, as it appears both in children's literature and his own play, helps the child integrate his world both emotionally and intellectually.

How can the transductive thinker comprehend why his loving mother takes him to a strange man with a white uniform called a "Doctor," one who injects him with a needle? After all, the child is told by Mother not to touch the bread knife; when he does, mother gives him a slight slap on the backside. He reasons, "Failing to do what mother says brings physical punishment." Likewise, at the grocery, mother tells the child, "Don't run. You will fall and get hurt." He runs, falls, and does get hurt. Again, he reasons, "Failing to do what mother says brings physical pain." For the transductive thinker, each of the three incidents, including the inoculation by the doctor, is generalized as imminent punishment (Piaget, 1965) for "naughtiness." Conversely, these years are at times full of joy and happiness, but these states are punctuated with fearful encounters beyond the child's ability to comprehend. It is fantasy that provides an escape valve.

288

The child who feels frustrated when he is told that he cannot have ice cream until after dinner retreats to his sandbox and in fantasy makes "hundreds" of ice cream cones, while casting triumphant looks at the unaware mother. Fantasy, especially as it is seen in play and the expressive arts, allows the child emotionally and intellectually to digest reality experiences that are far beyond the transductive thinker's ability to handle in one swoop. The child re-acts the larger experience over and over as he bites off pieces of the larger reality experience until he can finally understand encounters, such as that with the "Doctor," and can emotionally accept the experience. This is much the same as adults retelling the details of their hospital experience to all who will listen until it finally becomes "old hat." (Erikson, 1963; Griffiths, 1945; Isaacs, 1972; Peller, 1954; Piaget, 1951; Vygotsky, 1962; Wolfgang, 1977).

LITERATURE FOR PRESCHOOL CHILDREN

Now that we have a general understanding of the thought processes of young chldren and the role of fantasy, how should we approach preschool children with the literary experience? It might be helpful to classify children's stories into two large categories: those with primary content and those with secondary content.

Primary content stories deal with deeply positive or negative emotional content without dealing with the objective realities we would find in secondary content stories. *Peter Rabbit* (1908) by Beatrix Potter focuses upon the young child's fear of separation and loss. There is no need for the young child to have a reality understanding of the habits and ways of rabbits as a concept to enjoy the story. The rabbits, as such, merely serve as vehicles for presenting the deeper meaning. With such primary content stories, the child "hears" the story at the deeper subliminal level of thinking. These deeper thoughts are fantasy-based and dreamlike in nature and usually contain an affective dimension, either pleasurable or unpleasurable.

In *Peter Rabbit* we see the emotional concern over loss, a concern that originally develops during infancy. We also see imminent punishment when Peter has an upset stomach for "failing to do as Mother said." Preschool children demand to have this story read repetitively. Each time, the child "hears" the story at the deeper level until he gains ascendance over the fear of loss and pushes it out of his mind. The great bulk of literature for young children falls into the primary content classification, fairy tales being the most extreme of this subjective literature.

Secondary content literature for children deals with reality experiential themes containing a limited hidden meaning. This literature focuses upon the type of secondary thinking that we use daily to solve such reality problems as baking a cake, repairing a chair, or telling someone how to find a street address. *Mr. Small, the Fireman* (1934) by Lois Lenski is an example of secondary content literature. Mr. Small deals with the realities of a fireman's role in life.

It would be incorrect to place all stories in an either/or classification of primary subjective content or secondary objective content. It is better to place the content of a story along a continuum between these two extremes with some stories blending the two classifications as illustrated by Figure 2. *Peter's Chair* (1967) by Ezra Keats has a story content that might be placed evenly between the two extremes. The story definitely deals with a deeper message, the concern of a maturing child's loss of possession to a younger sibling, but this message is conveyed through a reality objective incident of a type that can and does happen to children. As stated earlier, fairy tales are the extreme form of primary content, whereas concept books are considered the most extreme form in the secondary objective category. The bulk of the stories read to young preschoolers have fantasy-based primary content, but the reality secondary content books should be presented with greater frequency as illustrated in Figure 3 as the child moves into the elementary years and conceptual thinking.

FIGURE 2 Content continuum.

Primary Content Literature

Generally, primary content books with their hidden emotional meanings should be shared in a one adult-one child relationship that permits the child to cuddle or touch the adult for purposes of emotional refueling. The story will and should gradually build to where the emotional excitement or conflict reaches an apex and then is quickly and positively resolved. We caution against the recent "reality" books that do not resolve

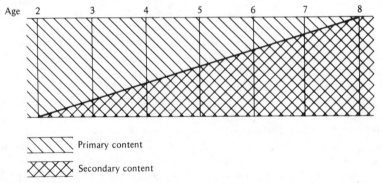

FIGURE 3 The movement from primary (fantasy) to secondary (reality) understanding in children's literature.

290

the conflicts they present and leave the child emotionally flooded. Such stories destroy the basic faith of childhood and present no hope for the future. Again, we caution, as Bettleheim has done in his book *The Meaning of Enchantment* (1976), against confronting the child's fears at the the secondary thought level. I believe it does a disservice to the child to ask blatantly, after reading *Peter Rabbit*, "Can you remember when you got lost at the department store?" or "can you remember when you were punished for not listening to mother?" The child cannot deal with these concerns at the reality secondary level, and such intrusive questions, charged with the idea of imminent punishment, simply manage to flood preschoolers emotionally and make them feel guilty. These primary content stories merely need to be shared with one child or a small group with little need for follow-up, but the child should be permitted to thumb through the book repetitively until it is no longer meaningful or of value for him.

Secondary Content Literature

Preschoolers moving toward operational or reality-based thinking will spend much of their time actively searching their world for what is animate and inanimate and attempting to further define themselves. A three-year-old boy standing in the preschool wearing a man's hat and a woman's skirt and clutching a baby bottle characterizes the pivotal point in his life. The bottle symbolizes the infancy that he must give up, while he experiments with the roles that he is and is not. When children do imaginative play and dress up as firemen, doctors, and nurses or engage in other forms of role play, they are representing their interpretation and transductive understanding of their world and themselves. The cognitive capacity to represent develops further with the ability to do reality problem solving. Literature, and eventually reading, is one of the highest forms of representation, where, as in play, one object stands for or represents another (Piaget, 1951).

In play and the expressive arts, the child takes toys, objects, and materials and performs make-believe play called *symbolizing*. These symbols, such as pretending a pencil is a "flute," are private and idiosyncratic to the child's own fantasy-based primary transductive thinking. The highest and most abstract form of representation is words and especially written words, the capacity for which develops normally during the operational period of thinking in the elementary years.

Written words are called *signs* by Piaget (1951) and are arbitrarily selected and socially agreed upon. If we ask everyone to draw the *symbol* for cat, every symbolic picture will be somewhat different because each comes from his or her internal primary subjective thought. If we ask everyone to make the English written *sign* for cat, everyone will write c–a–t, which represents a four-legged animal with whiskers and tail, differing from all other classifications of animals or objects. These written concepts, as the highest form of representation, have not been developed by the preschooler; therefore symbols will dominate his representational activities between ages 3 and 7, while an understanding of written signs in reading will not begin to blossom until the beginning of middle childhood. In fact, it is exposure to children's literature or written stories that helps children make this transition.

Librarians and teachers, using literature having secondary content (reality stories) with preschool children, should have the child begin with an experience and then have him or her represent that experience first at the symbolic level through play and expressive art and later at the written word or sign level (Weikart, 1971). For example, children are taken to the fire station and experience climbing on the equipment, blowing the whistle, and squirting the hose. Such experiences are too large for children to digest intellectually or emotionally in one swoop. They return to the classroom or library with the need to re-represent this experience through symbolic expression. Children will require time, space, equipment, and encouragement to paint the experience and form symbols with clay, wood, or scraps of materials and will finally play out the experience with small fire station toys and puppets or with dress-up play. During the time that the child is rerepresenting the fireman experience at the symbolic level, literature can begin to bridge the experience into operational thinking and written signs (Weikart, 1971; Hirsch, 1974).

Stories about firemen and related aspects will help the children consolidate, integrate, and expand their thoughts about their world. Stories and literature ask them to decenter and take into consideration many dimensions and relationships around the topic of firefighters. Stories will require that the children mentally reverse the incidents so they can be relived in book form, giving order and sequence to the happenings (Brearly, 1969). Finally, the children will gain greater definition of themselves and gain greater insight into others by projecting themselves in symbolic role play and then in story content.

Children are also helped in vocabulary development by having stories read out loud to them—a process called *verbal encoding* by Piaget. The preschooler, who has been to the fire station and has squirted the hose and who then returns to the classroom or library and plays at "squirting the hose" in symbolic dress-up play, has the motor-meaning of "hose." But, as the child looks through the pictures in a book about firefighters, he or she points to the hose and says, "This is the squirter." The word "squirter" is a motor action word that indicates that the child has the concept and that the teacher or librarian may directly provide the correct sign or word, thus helping the child to encode verbally this concept (Vygotsky, 1962; Weikart, 1971).

Verbal encoding, or the learning of new words with their conceptual meanings, occurs very rarely when adults merely provide the correct words. Most verbal encoding of concepts occurs incidentally through children's direct experience in conversation with others or through hearing the correct concept words read to them by adults. Therefore, this incidental verbal encoding helps the child integrate images, ideas, and words and helps bring the child to a concrete operational level of reasoning.

It is with the help of repetitive experiences and of experiences that symbolize that re-experiencing and of the re-reading of literature that the child is aided in integrating and expanding upon his newly acquired knowledge. Thus, you will find the child wanting to write the sign "firetruck" on the side of his make-believe firetruck made out of packing boxes, or you will find the child adding signs like "Danger! Keep out!" to the play space (Isaacs, 1972). Later, the same child will want to point these written signs out while reading the story books. What we see is a natural transition to reading. Indeed, symbolizing experiences in art forms and play are a precursor of success with later reading signs (Vygotsky, 1962; Weikart, 1971).

For those adults using secondary reality literature with preschool children, the sequence of presentation should be experience, rerepresentation in expressive symbols, integration through stories, and the repetition of this sequence with another expanded experience building on the original one. These forms of experiences, with literature bridging the gap between symbol and sign, will also facilitate the child's intellectual and emotional development (Wolfgang, 1977).

It has been my purpose to apply child development to literature for preschool children. With an understanding of the transductive thinking based in fantasy and the gradual movement to operational or concept reality thinking beginning with middle childhood, we may classify children's literature along a primary to secondary continuum. The preschooler with his limited intellect is rooted in a fantasy perception of his world that he uses to replay, re-experience, and rerepresent until he can intellectually understand and emotionally accept a larger experience. The content of children's literature, in order to be meaningful to the child, will follow this same progress, that is, from fantasy to reality or from primary content to reality content.

References

Bettelheim, Bruno. *The Uses of Enchantment: The Meaning and Importance of Fairy Tales.* New York: Alfred A. Knopf, Inc., 1976.

Brearly, Molly. *Fundamentals in the First School.* London: Basil Blackwell, 1969.

Erikson, Erik H. *Childhood and Society.* New York: W. W. Norton & Co., Inc., 1963.

Griffiths, Ruth. *A Study of Imagination in Early Childhood.* London: Kegan Paul, Trench, Trubner and Co., Ltd., 1945.

Hirsch, Elisabeth S. *The Block Book.* Washington, D.C.: National Association for the Education of Young Children, 1974.

Isaacs, Susan. *Intellectual Growth in Young Children.* New York: Shocken Books, Inc., 1972.

Isaacs, Susan. *Social Development in Young Children.* New York: Schocken Books, Inc., 1972.

Keats, Ezra Jack. *Peter's Chair.* New York: Harper & Row, Publishers, Inc., 1967.

Lenski, Lois. *Fireman Small.* Philadelphia: J. B. Lippincott Company, 1934.

Peller, Lilli. "Libidinal Phases, Ego Development and Play." *Psychoanalytic*

Study of the Child. Vol. IX. New York: International Universities Press, Inc., 1954.

Phillips, J. L. *The Origins of Intellect: Piaget's Theory.* San Francisco: W. H. Freeman & Company Publishers, 1969.

Piaget, Jean. *The Growth of Logical Thinking from Childhood to Adolescence.* Translated by A. Parsons and S. Seagrin. New York: Basic Books, Inc., Publishers, 1958.

Piaget, Jean. *The Language and Thought of the Child.* Translated by M. Gabain. London: Routledge and Kegan Paul, Ltd., 1926.

Piaget, Jean. *The Moral Judgement of the Child.* Translated by Marjorie Gabain. New York: First Free Press, 1965.

Piaget, Jean. *The Origins of Intelligence in Children.* Translated by M. Cook. New York: International Universities Press, Inc., 1952.

Piaget, Jean. *Play, Dreams and Imitation in Childhood.* Translated by C. Cattegno and F. M. Hodgson. New York: W. W. Norton & Co., Inc., 1951.

Potter, Beatrix. *Peter Rabbit.* New York: Frederick Warne & Co., Inc., 1908.

Vygotsky, Lev Semenovich. *Thought and Language.* Translated by E. Hanfmann and G. Vakar. Cambridge, Mass.: The M.I.T. Press, 1962.

Weikart, David *et al. The Cognitively Oriented Curriculum.* Washington, D.C.: National Association for the Education of Young Children, 1971.

Wolfgang, Charles H. *Helping Aggressive and Passive Preschoolers Through Play.* Columbus, Ohio: Charles E. Merrill Publishing Company, 1977.

DAVID ELKIND

26. We Can Teach Reading Better

Can we do a better job of teaching children to read? Yes, I believe we can if we take into consideration how their minds develop. To illustrate this point, I'd first like to discuss beginning reading and the child's concept of letters and then move on to how children who are more advanced readers use their accumulated storehouse of knowledge to give meaning to the printed word.

A basic error in much beginning reading instruction centers about the concept of the letter, which is, in many ways, the basic unit of reading. To the adult, the letter appears as a discrete object which is a conventional representation of one or more sounds. But the letter as adults see it is not the letter known to the beginning reader.

As Piaget points out, children and adults see the world in different

From David Elkind, "We Can Teach Reading Better," *Today's Education,* Vol. 64, No. 4 (1975), pp. 34–38. With permission from David Elkind and *Today's Education.*

ways. The well-known "conservation" experiments are a case in point. Most adults are amazed to discover that young children believe that changing the shape of a piece of clay will change the *amount*.

This amazement suggests that most adults assume that children see the world in much the same way they do. They make this assumption because they are unable to recall or reconstruct the course of their own cognitive growth. This phenomenon, the loss of awareness of their own part in the construction of reality, is what Piaget means by *externalization*.

In general, externalization serves a useful adaptive purpose and allows the individual to operate more effectively in the environment. *Externalization* only becomes a problem when we try to teach the young, that is, when we try to present material that we have already mastered. In that case, we as adults, who have conceptualized and externalized many facets of the world, have trouble appreciating the difficulties children encounter in their attempts at making sense out of their world.

From the child's point of view, the concept of the letter poses many of the same problems as concepts of number, space, and time. Before the age of six or seven, most children lack a true unit or number concept because they cannot coordinate two dimensions or relationships simultaneously. Such coordinations are basic to the construction of a unit concept because a unit is, by definition, both like every other unit and different from it in its order of enumeration.

In many ways, children's problems in understanding the concept of a letter are even more difficult than those they encounter in constructing the concept of a number. Like numbers, letters have an ordinal property, which is their position in the alphabet. And letters also have a cardinal property, which is their name (A, B, C, etc.) and which each letter shares with all other letters of the same name (all B's are B and so on).

Letters are even more complicated than numbers because, in addition to their ordinal and cardinal properties, they also have phonic contextual properties. One letter can stand for one or more sounds and one sound can be represented by different letters. Hence, to understand phonics, a child must be able to perform logical operations on letters and sounds to understand all their possible combinations.

Many different kinds of evidence support this logical analysis of the difficulties in early reading. Written languages that are more regularly phonetic than English are apparently much easier to learn to read than is English. In these alphabets such as Japanese, the logical difficulties are removed because one and the same element always has one and the same sound regardless of its position or phonetic context.

In addition to this cultural evidence, various collaborators and I have published a body of research which also points to the logical difficulties inherent in beginning reading. We have shown that reading achievement and logical ability are highly correlated; that average readers are superior in logical ability to slow readers of comparable overall intelligence; and that training children in logical skills has a significant positive effect upon some aspects of reading achievement.

All these findings are consistent with the view that the letter is a complex logical construction that requires the ability to reason, which Piaget attributes to the appearance of *concrete operations* for its full elaboration. To test this hypothesis in still another way, a collaborator and I have begun, in the last few years, to look at the cognitive competencies of children who read early, that is, children who read before they enter kindergarten. One of our hypotheses was that if reading involves concrete operations, which are usually attained at age six to seven, then early readers should show these abilities at an early age. In addition to assessing children's cognitive abilities, we were also interested in the personal-social characteristics of these children and in the educational-emotional climate that prevails in their homes.

We have now completed two studies of early readers, one with 16 early readers and another with 38. In both studies, the early readers were matched with a control group of non-early-reading children on such things as age, sex, IQ, and socioeconomic status. All the children were given a large battery of achievement and intelligence tests as well as personality and creativity tests. In addition, their parents were interviewed. In both studies, we found that early reading children were superior to non-early-reading children on Piagetian measures of conservation. They were also better on certain psycholinguistic measures, such as sound blending.

It is important to emphasize, however, that cognitive construction of a letter is only one of the requirements for successful reading. Our parent interview data suggest that a rich background of early experience with spoken and written language provided by homes where books and magazines are plentiful and where parents frequently read to the children is also important for successful reading. In addition, social motivation to please significant adults appears to be a necessary, if not a sufficient, factor in giving zest to the dull and unrewarding process of learning to read.

In talking about cognitive development and early reading, it is therefore important to avoid the two extremes that are sometimes advocated when cognitive "readiness" is discussed. One extreme is the effort to train children of preschool age in cognitive abilities they have not yet attained. I have seen no evidence that such early intervention has any lasting effectiveness. But the alternative extreme, allowing children to learn in their own time and in their own way, is also unwarranted. Children need instruction in learning to read, but only after they have demonstrated the requisite cognitive abilities.

In summary, there appear to me to be at least four requirements for successful beginning reading: a language-rich environment, attachment to adults who model and reward reading behavior, attainment of concrete operations, and an instructional program. All other things being equal, namely, that the children in question are of at least average intellectual ability and are free of serious emotional or physical handicaps, the presence of these four characteristics should ensure that most children will learn to read with reasonable ease and considerable enjoyment.

Let us now turn to advanced reading and the construction of meaning. It has already been suggested that the intellectual processes involved in beginning reading are analogous to those involved in concept formulation. A child who is learning to read has to coordinate similarities and differences and construct concepts of letters which are both like every other letter in that they represent sounds but different in the specific sounds they stand for.

Concept formation also involves inferential processes, and these can be observed in beginning reading as well. Many errors in beginning reading, such as reading *where* for *when*, are inferential errors rather than discrimination errors. The child is inferring the whole from observing the part (the *wh*). Such inferential errors are high-level cognitive errors inasmuch as the child is doing what more advanced and accomplished readers do. These processes should be encouraged by temporarily sacrificing accuracy for fluency. Experience indicates that once children are fluent readers, they can always correct for accuracy, but an overconcern with accuracy can retard fluent reading.

When concept formation and inferential aspects of reading have become automatized and children can recognize printed words with ease and rapidity, they enter the phase of rapid silent reading. In silent reading, the major cognitive task is no longer concept formation and inference but rather interpretation, the construction of meaning. In constructing meanings, children have to relate representations—in this case, printed words—with their own concepts and ideas. Success in interpretation, or comprehension, depends upon a different set of characteristics than learning to read, and these are described below.

VISUAL INDEPENDENCE

Rapid silent reading and comprehension require, at the very outset, that the visual verbal system become independent of the sensory motor system. Rapid reading involves fewer motor fixations and wider visual segments of scanning, and this in turn means less motor involvement and more conceptual inferential activity. In effect, in rapid silent reading, the brain does more work and the eyes do less. We have some recent evidence that supports the importance of visual independence in advanced reading.

In one study we found that while tactile discrimination of sandpaper letters was positively related to reading achievement among beginning readers, it was negatively correlated with reading achievement among advanced readers. Apparently, motoric identification and discrimination of letters, as advocated by Fernald and Montessori, is beneficial in the beginning phases of learning to read, but the coordination of visual and motor processes has to be given up if more rapid reading is to develop.

Put more concretely, it is helpful for beginning readers to use their fingers as markers to direct attention and exploration of printed matter. But once they become advanced readers, using a finger as a marker would impede reading. Rapid reading requires a certain independence from the tactile motor system.

Some recent data on perceptual exploration and memory demonstrate this growth of visual independence in another way. Children at different age levels (from age four through age eight) were shown large cards upon which were pasted 16 pictures of familiar objects. On one card, the pictures were pasted in an upright position whereas on another, the same pictures were pasted at 180 degrees from their normal position.

At each age level, half the children viewed the cards with the pictures upright, while the other half viewed the cards with the pictures at 180 degrees to the upright. Each child had two tasks: to name each of the figures on the cards and then to recall as many of the figures as possible once the cards were turned over.

Among young children (age four to five), there was a significant difference in recall scores in favor of the figures rotated 180 degrees. This difference, however, diminishes as children grow older and disappears at about the age of eight or nine. A similar pattern appears to hold true for children with limited hearing, who use finger spelling and vocalization in communication. These data suggest that in young children the motoric system is still tied to the visual system. In identifying the 180-degree figures, these children may implicitly try to "right" the figures, which produces increased motoric involvement.

Our hypothesis is that the increased motoric involvement and attendant heightened attention account for the superior memory for upside-down figures in young children. Among older children, in whom identification can occur without implicit motoric "righting," this attentional advantage for upside-down figures is no longer present.

There is thus some direct as well as indirect evidence that rapid, silent reading involves the attainment of considerable visual independence from the tactile motor system. Apparently this occurs even among children with limited hearing who use finger spelling as well as vocalization to communicate. Indeed, among older deaf children, the rapidity with which they finger spell and read finger spelling is very much like rapid reading. Visual independence amounts to a kind of automatization of the visual aspect of reading in which the visual scanning process is relatively independent of tactile motor input.

MEANING CONSTRUCTION

A second prerequisite to advanced silent reading is facility in meaning construction. From a cognitive development point of view, reading comprehension is not a passive process of decoding written symbols. On the contrary, it must be regarded as a constructive activity analgous to creative writing.

The point is that meaning is not inherent in written or spoken words but rather that the words are given meaning by readers or listeners who interpret them within their own storehouse of knowledge. Silent readers give meaning to the words they read by relating these to the conceptual system they have constructed in the course of their development. The richness of meaning they derive from their reading will depend both upon the quality of the material they are reading and the breadth and depth of their conceptual understanding. Satisfaction in reading often derives, in part at least, from the degree of fit between the material being read and the conceptual level of the reader.

A recent doctoral dissertation supports this position. The author chose 33 books that had won Newbery awards for excellence. She then determined how frequently each had been checked out over the preceding three-year period in a number of libraries. On the basis of these data, she selected the five most frequently chosen books and the five least frequently chosen books from her original list. She then analyzed the books from the standpoint of their congruence with the conceptual systems of the age group for which they were written. She found that the five most frequently chosen books were congruent with the cognitive level of the children for whom they were written, while this was not true for the five least chosen books. Apparently, other things being equal, children prefer stories which have meaning within their own cognitive organization.

Comprehension, or the construction of meanings, is also helped by the children's own efforts at giving meaning to (i.e., representing) their own experiences. The more opportunity children have to experience the effort and satisfaction of representing their own thoughts verbally and otherwise, the better prepared they will be for interpreting the representations of others.

In contemporary education, teachers often do not leave time for the children to write creatively or otherwise. But I believe that the more children write, the more they will get from their reading. Writing and reading are reciprocal processes of meaning construction which mutually reinforce one another.

Receptive Discipline

A third prequisite to effective silent reading seems at first to be a contradiction to what has just been said about the readers being an active participant in the process. This prerequisite is that the reader have a receptive attitude, a willingness to respond to the representations of others. Good readers, like good listeners, have to be simultaneously passive (receptive to the representations of others) and active (interpreting those representations within their own conceptual framework).

Many young people are poor readers for the same reason that they are poor listeners: They are more interested in representing their own thoughts and ideas than they are in interpreting the thoughts and ideas of others. They lack what might be called receptive discipline.

Young people demonstrate receptive discipline when they attend fully to the representations of others and resist following their own free associations and tangents. Many so-called slow readers have problems with receptive discipline and not with rapid reading.

Receptive discipline is not innate and can be facilitated and taught. Text material that is of interest to readers and at their level of competence facilitates a receptive attitude. Another way to encourage receptive discipline is to have goals for nonrecreational reading. When young people (or adults for that matter) know that they will have to present what they have read to a group, they are likely to be more attentive than if this were not so.

These are but a few examples of techniques that might be employed to encourage receptive discipline. Whatever techniques are used to instill it, receptive discipline seems to be an important ingredient for successful reading comprehension.

COGNITIVE DEVELOPMENT IN EARLY CHILDHOOD

In studying cognitive development, one must consider both the processes of learning (ordering, classifying, inferring) and the observable products of that learning (facts and concepts). American education has, for the most part, been built on the concerns of the latter domain, emphasizing rote learning, drill, and memorization of facts and figures. The cognitive developmental theories of Jean Piaget, however, have caused psychologists and educators to reexamine the appropriateness of such a singular approach, particularly in the education of young children. All of the articles in this chapter deal with the conflict between process and product learning. Although Levitt addresses the larger question of how children acquire and utilize knowledge to solve problems, the other authors focus their attention on specific areas of learning in science and mathematics.

Levitt's article provides a concise comparison between process or developmental learning and product or stimulus-response learning. She explores the vital role of motivation in cognition, contrasting Bereiter's assumptions of child learning with Piaget's. Estvan's article explores the use of inquiry skills to help children think critically and solve problems. He proposes a set of goals for teaching inquiry and offers suggestions for teaching and evaluating inquiry behavior in young children.

Neuman begins his article by comparing the traditional school science curriculum with its focus on particular facts and concepts to a more science-related, process-oriented technique he calls *sciencing*. Neuman believes that sciencing facilitates the development of process skills like inferring and communicating, skills that form the basis for all intellectual development. His practical suggestions make it clear that teachers need not be scientists themselves to encourage children to observe and explore the world around them.

The last article in this chapter challenges the widespread use of product techniques like workbooks and number rods to teach mathematical concepts. Kamii and DeVries discuss the nature of number and provide principles for process approaches to the teaching of numerical concepts. Although educators must examine both process and product strategies when determining how and what to teach young children in the cognitive domain, the work of these authors underscores the vital importance of process learning to early childhood education.

EDITH LEVITT

27. Views of Cognition in Children: "Process" vs. "Product" Approach

The field of psychology currently offers the educator two contrasting views of cognition in children. The first—the "process" approach—is represented by Piaget's theory of cognitive development and by information-processing theory. The second—the "product" approach—is represented by SR (stimulus-response) theory, one long dominant in psychology. SR theory appears to have marked limitations as a base for education, the most serious being its focus on products of cognitive function, as opposed to underlying processes. On the other hand, the process approach has as a central goal the inference and investigation of these processes: hence, it could lead to helpful insights for the educator.

A practical example will help point up the difference between these two views of cognition. Suppose a psychologist presents a child with some familiar task, such as copying a block design, and then sets out to evaluate his performance. With the "product" approach, he would focus on the child's product, whether in terms of its correctness or in terms of other characteristics. But with the "process" approach, he would attempt to infer mediational processes as well, by considering qualitative aspects of performance. Cognitive processes that might be of interest could include: (a) the child's analysis of the model into its components, (b) intervening processes contributing to its reproduction, and (c) a rechecking of the model by the child to confirm accuracy of response. It should be immediately apparent that the process approach to cognition is the more complex of the two methods and, by the same token, the more difficult to apply.

Information-processing theory first became prominent in the field of psychology about 10 years ago, while general interest in Piaget's theory, at least in the United States, is somewhat more recent. Up to that time, psychology had been dominated largely by SR theory, which holds that human behavior can be interpreted entirely in terms of stimulus-response associations, and that learning consists of the building up of such associations.

Classical SR theorists had sought to apply the methods of the physical sciences to their work; thus, they limited themselves to objectively verifiable data. In turn, this meant a focus on terminal, or stimulus-response, aspects of behavior. Intervening, or central, cognitive processes were dismissed as unimportant and relegated to a so-called "mysterious black box" whose contents could never be known. Later SR theorists have at-

Reprinted by permission from *Young Children*, Vol. 23, No. 4 (Mar. 1968), pp. 225–232.

tempted to incorporate these central processes into their framework by postulating additional links in the SR chain; however, according to Hunt (1963), this has left the essential SR interpretation of cognition intact, that is, it is still seen as an elaborate but static "switchboard" housed within a relatively passive organism.

INTRINSIC MOTIVATION IGNORED

SR theorists have also been concerned with motivational factors underlying cognitive function—particularly learning. But here, too, their interpretation has had a passive connotation. Learning is said to be reinforced as a consequence of various external factors; these are viewed as related to drive reduction and/or avoidance of unpleasant stimuli. Thus, no allowance is made for intrinsic motivation, or the attraction to an activity for its own sake.

It is only natural that the field of education, dependent as it is on psychology for its theoretical underpinnings, should show the impact of the SR orientation. While such an orientation is seldom explicitly expressed, one or another of its aspects seems to pervade much of education today. One such program which might be regarded as a logical embodiment of SR theory will serve to illustrate this point. This program, considered a controversial one, is directed by Bereiter at the University of Illinois.

Bereiter works with disadvantaged preschool children, and sees as his principal goal the acceleration of learning in areas crucial to academic achievement. He describes this program as run in a "highly task-oriented no-nonsense" manner. Children work in small groups for three 20-minute periods daily devoted to instruction in language, reading and arithmetic. Bereiter is particularly concerned with the language problems of disadvantaged children. His basic technique for teaching language is based on "pattern drill," modeled after methods for teaching foreign languages. Children are first presented with "basic statement patterns" and then are taught to answer fundamental questions about those patterns. As an example, the concepts of "big" and "little" are taught in the following ways: by repetition (e.g., "This block is big."), by location of concept (e.g., "Show me the block that is big."), and by verbal statement (e.g., Teacher: "Tell me about the block." Child: "The block is big."). Bereiter has also adapted the pattern drill method for teaching reading and arithmetic.

Children in Bereiter's program are motivated for learning and for socially acceptable behavior chiefly through a system of external rewards and punishments. Examples of external rewards are cookies or an approving handshake from the teacher, while examples of punishment are withholding of cookies and isolation from the group.

The assumption that Bereiter has an SR orientation is supported by four major aspects of his program.

● The main focus of the program is on the behavioral, or product, aspects of cognition.

- Learning appears to be equated with establishing specific SR associations.
- The learner is relegated to a passive role, exemplified by Bereiter's statement that the child has to "learn to be taught."
- Motivation for learning is viewed as depending on extrinsic factors.

While SR principles reviewed above have been most logically implemented in programs such as Bereiter's, one or the other of them is evident in most educational settings today, the most pervasive being the focus on terminal rather than mediational aspects of learning. It is against this background that the process approach to cognition in children and its implications for education will now be considered.

Piaget's theory and information-processing theory, designated here as representing the process view, have some broad features in common. Because of semantic differences these might not always be immediately apparent; however, they emerge upon closer scrutiny. Thus, both theories center on mediational processes. Too, both stress the essential role of these processes in the individual's organization of incoming information, and in his generally efficient conduct of transactions with the environment. Such an individual is described as actively engaged in the regulation of these processes. He does this through selecting and activating out of a large repertoire of possible "mental operations" or "strategies" those most appropriate to the situation at hand. (Such judgments are viewed as occurring on an automatic rather than purposeful level.) These mental operations, or strategies, are seen as gradually evolving in young children in an autogenous (i.e., self-taught) manner. The precise way this comes about is unclear and has excited considerable curiosity and interest in developmental theorists.

Piaget, the first representative of the process theories to be considered, has long been concerned with cognitive development in children and more particularly with the structures that underlie that development. His method of research involves structured clinical interviews with children during which their knowledge of a given concept is probed; hence it contrasts with more controlled methods of child study.

Piaget's theoretical system includes the following broad postulates:

- Intellectual development—or the structure of knowledge—proceeds in an orderly way through four main stages. These are: a sensori-motor stage which lasts up to age 18 months to two years; a preoperational stage lasting to about age seven; a stage of concrete operations lasting to age 11 or 12; and the stage of formal operations which dominates cognitive function thereafter.
- The central component in the structure of knowledge is the operation. Piaget defines an operation as an "internalized action," an action that can be mentally manipulated. Thus, he stresses the primacy of action, or manipulation, as a base for cognition, in contrast to those who see language in this role. Operational children are those who have acquired various broad concepts exemplified by conservation, or a grasp of sameness in an entity despite variations in its form.

- Cognitive development takes place through continuous interaction with the environment. This interaction consists of two complementary processes: the first is the child's accommodation, or adaptation, to the environment; the second his assimilation, or internal organization, of the information resulting from that accommodation.
- Cognitive growth hinges particularly on a process of "equilibrium," of self-regulation, by the child. This occurs when he perceives a mismatch between beliefs which relate to the same concept and then strives to reconcile them as a means of regaining equilibrium.

UTILIZING PIAGET'S THEORY

Here is an example of the way Piaget's theory is utilized in studying cognitive processes in children. It deals with the child's development of equilibration in relation to a particular concept—in this case, the conservation of quantity. The child is initially presented with two tall glasses, both containing water. The contents of one of them is then emptied into a shallow bowl and he is asked to compare the amount of water in each. At the lowest level, the nonconserving child will focus on the most salient dimension—namely, the tallness of the glass—and assert that it contains the greater amount of water. Subsequently, his attention may be drawn to the width of the shallow bowl, and this time he will assert that it contains more water than the glass. In these instances, he is able to reason with regard to only one aspect of each container at a time, e.g., he focuses either on the tallness of the glass or else on its narrowness. At a later stage, the child is able to take both aspects into account and see that they counteract each other; thus, he is finally able to grasp the notion that the amount of water remains the same even when the shape of the container is changed. He has then achieved equilibration with regard to the concept of conservation.

The second major process theory to be considered is information-processing. As its name suggests, information-processing theory is based on the notion that there is an analogy between the mental operations of human beings and the operations carried out by an electronic computer. Quite soon after information-processing theory made its appearance in the field of psychology, it began to attract a good deal of interest and has continued to do so ever since. This is reflected in the stream of relevant publications, probably numbering in the thousands at this point, which have been appearing in the literature. By now, the influence of the information-processing concept appears to have filtered into all the important branches of psychology. Frick (1959) has commented in this connection that this concept has led to a "general reorientation in thinking" in the field of psychology. Hebb (1960) has described information-processing theory as a "powerful contender for the center of the stage" in psychology.

Information-processing theory has had a particular impact on the field of child psychology. This is indicated in a variety of ways. Two leading figures, J. McV. Hunt (1961) and Bruner (1966), have incorporated information-processing theory—along with Piaget's concepts—into their own work. Thus, they not only have been influenced by the process approach, but also may themselves be regarded as representative of it. Information-processing theory is beginning to be utilized as a base for research on cognitive function in children, as exemplified by studies of Hochberg (1966) and Kagan (1966). A summary statement by Kagan and Wright (1963) at a conference on children's cognition is also pertinent here: they note that all papers presented emphasized the "information-producing behavior" typical of children.

MAN AS "COMMUNICATION CHANNEL"

Information-processing theory can be summed up briefly in the following terms. The human being, like the computer, may be viewed as a "commmunication channel." As such, he is equipped with two essential features: first, he has a capacity for storing information (roughly equivalent to memory); secondly, he possesses a repertoire of so-called "strategies," or response patterns, which are used to process, or act on, both stored and incoming information. Human information processing is viewed as taking place in an orderly sequence of steps. First, incoming information is identified and decoded; next, it is related to already available information and either recoded for storage and ultimate retrieval, or used as a basis for a program, or plan, for producing an appropriate output. Each of these steps presumably requires a distinctive set of strategies.

Here is a concrete example of information processing based on an experience of the writer's. (This will be an example of processing incoming, as opposed to stored, information.) Suppose you saw a vaguely puzzling figure coming towards you on the street. It would probably set off an exploratory strategy in which you would focus on selected cues in the figure, such as proportions, general outline, etc., which have previously provided relevant information in identifying such figures. This might lead to the formulation of a tentative percept: namely, a tall woman, dressed in black, with a disproportionately small face. The percept would then be matched against an appropriate category of previously stored information pertaining to human figures, and would be rejected as incompatible with it. You might then revert to the use of the exploratory strategy, this time searching specifically in the incongruous area, namely the tiny face; whereupon you might note that what you had assumed to be the rounded outline of a chin actually was a horizontal line. You might then formulate a new percept which included the upper half of a normal face, and a lower half covered by a black scarf which in turn blended into a black coat. This percept would again be checked against the appropriate category and, since it was now compatible with it, would be considered confirmed. This example serves to illustrate the perceiver's active, self-regulating role in the processing of incoming information.

The above example also suggests an intrinsic interest in a highly casual encounter with the environment on the part of the perceiver. This dovetails with Berlyne's (1960) notion that intrinsic motivation is an essential element in information processing. According to Berlyne, there is both an initial attraction to the novel and the complex for their own sakes, and a pull towards extracting meaning from them.

It can be seen that, despite a difference in terminology, Piaget's theory and the information-processing concept have important features in common. These common features, indicated below, form a neat contrast with corresponding aspects of SR theory. This contrast may be summed up as follows:

- The process theories see the individual as active in the selection and regulation of his mental processes, whereas SR theory sees him as relatively passive in this regard.
- The process theories focus on inferred mediational processes, while SR theory focuses on behavioral responses in cognition.
- The process theories consider that learning includes the mastery of certain central processes, termed operations or strategies, while SR theory regards learning as essentially the building up of associations.
- The process theories stress the role of intrinsic motivation, including the pull towards the resolution of incongruity: SR theory, on the other hand, views motivation as dependent on extrinsic factors.

If it were granted that the process approach is a more sophisticated and more valid concept of cognitive function than SR theory, what implications does this hold for education?

First and foremost, there would be a critical reassessment of the role of SR theory in education, and particularly of the product approach to learning derived from it. Secondly, as a complementary move, there would be a comprehensive reorientation towards the process approach to learning, on both an experimental and empirical level, as a base for education.

Sporadic indications of such a reorientation can be seen in the literature even at this time. One comes from the field of psychological assessment. Limitations of intelligence tests as measures of cognitive function have been apparent for some time (Bayley, 1949; Cronbach, 1960). As a consequence, increased weight has recently been placed on supplementing quantitative data on test performance with clinical impression. Some workers (Haeussermann, 1958; Taylor, 1959; Luria, 1966) concerned with assessment of deviant children have gone a step further and urged that assessment is best undertaken on a qualitative basis alone. In advocating the use of this method, these authors in essence argue for a process approach to evaluation, as opposed to a product approach.

An increased focus on process aspects of learning is also suggested by the revival of interest in naturalistic child research, notably in classroom settings (MacKinnon, 1959; Levin, 1965; Bruner et al., 1966). Such research generally undertakes an open-ended scrutiny of the ongoing teaching-learning process as a means for generating useful hypotheses that can then be more rigorously tested. Another body of research, that of

Piaget and his colleagues, centering as it does on the structured clinical interview, can also be broadly subsumed under the naturalistic category.

The influence of a process orientation is also seen in the increasing number of experimental studies dealing with inferred mediational processes in children. One group of researchers (Smedslund, 1964; Beilin, 1965; Almy *et al.*, 1966) has been concerned with experimental verification of Piaget's concepts under more controlled conditions than he himself has employed. Others (Olson, 1966; Holmes, 1960; Anisfeld, 1966; Mosher, 1962) have utilized information-processing theory as a base for a wide variety of studies. Additional broad research areas can also be regarded as dealing in one way or another with inferred mediational variables in children's cognition. These are exemplified by Witkin's (1960) study on cognitive style, Goss' (1957) study on verbal mediation and Cantor's (1963) study on a cognitive component of curiosity.

Again, it is relevant to note a statement made by Melton (1967) in summing up a recent conference on individual differences in learning. Melton stressed the participants' belief that individual differences in learning can most profitably be framed in terms of "process variables." These variables may be regarded as encompassing the mental operations, or strategies, discussed in the present paper.

If the process orientation towards cognition in children continues to gain momentum, it may have a far-reaching impact on their education. Ultimately it could lead to a systematic program of study centering on major process variables in children's cognition and on their practical implications for the educator. Appropriate goals of such a program include the following:

1. Further development and experimental investigation of presently available theoretical constructs (exemplified by Piaget's system and information processing theory.)
2. Longitudinal research, both naturalistic and controlled, on these variables, and on the developmental stages at which they characteristically emerge.
3. A logical analysis of findings leading to the formulation of a taxonomy of salient process variables in children's cognition.
4. Development of relevant assessment methods.
5. Development of relevant educational methodology.
6. Development of specialized methods for approximating such goals with handicapped children.

REFERENCES

Almy, Millie, *et al. Young Children's Thinking.* New York: Teachers College Press, 1966.

Anisfeld, M. The child's knowledge of English pluralization rules. In *Project Literacy Reports*, No. 7, Cornell Univ., 1966.

Bayley, N. Consistency and variability in growth of intelligence from birth to 18 years. *J. genet. Psychol.*, 1949, 75, 165–196.

Beilin, H. Learning and operational convergence in logical thought development. *J. exp. child Psychol.*, 1965, 2, 317–339.

Bereiter, C., Engelmann, S., Osborn, Jean, & Reidford, P. A. An academically oriented pre-school for culturally deprived children. In F. Hechinger (Ed.), *Pre-School Education Today*. Garden City, N.Y.: Doubleday, 1966.

Berlyne, D. E. *Conflict, Arousal and Curiosity*. New York: McGraw-Hill, 1960.

Bruner, J. S., Olver, Rose R., Greenfield, Patricia M., *et al. Studies in Cognitive Growth*. New York: John Wiley, 1966.

Caney, Janice E., & Goss, A. E. The role of mediating verbal responses in the conceptual sorting behavior of children. *J. genet. Psychol.*, 1957, 90, 69–74.

Cantor, G. N., Cantor, Joan H., & Ditrichs, R. Observing behavior in pre-school children as a function of stimulus complexity. *Child Developm.*, 1963, 34, 683–689.

Cronbach, L. J. *Essentials of Psychological Testing*. New York: Harper & Row, 1960.

Frick, F. C. Information theory. In S. Koch (Ed.). *Psychology: A Study of Science*, Vol. II. New York: McGraw-Hill, 1959, pp. 611–634.

Haeussermann, Else. *Developmental Potential of Preschool Children*. New York: Grune & Stratton, 1958.

Hebb, D. O. The American Revolution. *Amer. Psychol.*, 1960, 15, 735–745.

Hochberg, J. Perceptual "chunking" and storage in reading words. In *Project Literacy Reports*, No. 7, Cornell Univ., 1966.

Holmes, J. A. The substrata-factor theory of reading: some experimental evidence. In J. A. Figurel (Ed.), *New Frontiers in Reading*. New York: Scholastic Magazines, 1960.

Hunt, J. McV. *Intelligence and Experience*. New York: John Wiley, 1961.

————. Motivation inherent in information processing and action. In O. J. Harvey (Ed.), *Motivation and Social Interaction: Cognitive Determinants*. New York: Ronald, 1963.

Kagan, J. Developmental studies in reflection and analysis. In Aline H. Kidd & Jeanne L. Rivoire (Eds.), *Perceptual Development in Children*. New York: International Universities Press, 1966. pp. 487–522.

Kagan, J., & Wright, J. C. (Eds.), Basic cognitive processes in children. *Monogr. Soc. Res. Child Dev.*, 1963, 28 (Serial No. 86).

Levin, H. Studies of various aspects of reading. In *Project Literacy Reports*, No. 5, Cornell Univ., 1965.

Luria, A. R. *Higher Cortical Functions in Man*. New York: Basic Books, 1966.

MacKinnon, A. R. *How Do Children Learn to Read?* Vancouver: Copp Clark, 1959.

Melton, A. W. Individual differences and theoretical process variables: general comments on the conference. In R. M. Gagne (Ed.), *Learning and Individual Differences*. Columbus, Ohio: Charles F. Merrill, 1967.

Mosher, F. A. Strategies in the acquisition and use of information. Unpublished doctoral dissertation, Harvard Univ., 1962.

Olson, D. R. On conceptual strategies. In J. S. Bruner, Rose R. Olver, Patricia M. Greenfield, *et al. Studies in Cognitive Growth*. New York: John Wiley, 1966.

Piaget, J. The general problems of the psychobiological development of the child. In J. M. Tanner & Bärbel Inhelder (Eds.), *Discussions on Child Development*. New York: International Universities Press, 1960, pp. 3–27.

Smedslund, J. Concrete reasoning: a study of intellectual development. *Monogr. Soc. Res. Child Dev.*, 1964, 29 (Serial No. 93).

Taylor, Edith Meyer. *Psychological Appraisal of Children with Cerebral Defects*. Cambridge: Harvard Univ. Press, 1959.

Witkin, H. A., Dyk, R. B., Fattuson, H. F., Goodenough, D. R., & Karp, S. A. *Psychological Differentiation: Studies of Development*. New York: John Wiley, 1962.

FRANK J. ESTVAN

28. Teaching the Very Young: Procedures for Developing Inquiry Skills

Growing recognition of the importance of the first five years in shaping human development has renewed concern about the nature of the goals and procedures to be used in early childhood education. Some, for example, view these programs as an early start in the race to college. Others promote enrichment to make up for limitations in the background of culturally deprived children. The current interest in inquiry raises the question of the place of discovery methods in early childhood education.

Growing insights about human behavior shed some light on the purposes and methods appropriate for teaching the very young. One of these principles is that behavior is whole; it follows that educational goals for the early-age child, as for the teen-age child, must include a broad spectrum of ideas, feelings, and skills. Another principle is that development is continuous. Accordingly, any curriculum plan must begin at the beginning and provide for systematic development of behavior until a desired level of achievement is reached.

The decisions early childhood educators make, therefore, rarely are simple choices such as between social-emotional as opposed to intellectual goals or between "play" in contrast with highly structured methods and materials. Nowhere is this better demonstrated than in programs which attempt to help young children develop the power to think critically, to solve problems, to "learn how to learn."

CHILDREN AND INQUIRY

The child goes forth each day and, as Walt Whitman pointed out some years ago, becomes a part of the things he looks upon, and they become a part of him. Today's child goes forth into a much larger world, the product of family mobility, travel, television. To complicate matters, much more is going on in his world, and more of it impinges upon him at one time. As a result, a five-year-old last year may have known that Johnson was President, but when asked the President's first name replied "Howard!" He may wonder, too, in view of the antics on TV, whether a political party is the same as a birthday party.

Inquiry is a way of satisfying curiosities. The method is essentially one of raising questions and seeking answers.[1] These processes are not unknown to the young, for it is common observation that children are "full

From Frank J. Estvan, "Teaching the Very Young: Procedures for Developing Inquiry Skills," *Phi Delta Kappa* (March 1969). © 1969, Phi Delta Kappa, Inc. Reprinted by permission.

of questions" and that they are "always getting into everything." Unfortunately, the modern world makes little provision for being understood by young minds; neither do adults always have the time or skill to help children understand what they see and hear.

Teachers of the very young are in a unique position, for they can use the child's question as the organizing center for activities which help him learn the beginnings of inquiry skills. Such efforts will be effective to the degree that the teacher gives careful consideration to all the elements involved in instruction: goals, methods and materials, and evaluation.

GOALS FOR TEACHING INQUIRY

All the various types of goals bearing on the various kinds of inquiry are suitable for nursery-kindergarten children, provided that they are appropriately defined. As is true for any age group, young children of the same age differ greatly; they are not at the same point in the development of any form of behavior. Studies of the social perceptions of three- and four-year-old children indicate that they are well beyond the zero point in the formation of many basic concepts. Three or more years of living in varied home environments, furthermore, have produced marked differences that are related to sex, race, social status, and age.[2] In view of this great variability and the rapid developments that occur between three and six years of age, inquiry goals should be designated in terms of levels to meet each child's requirements.

Cognitive objectives deal with knowledge and understanding. A basic step in learning to conduct inquiry is to acquire a meaningful grasp of terms involved, for these are the concepts with which the child must deal. For a series of activities focusing on the question, "What makes flowers grow?," instructional objectives for a three-year-old, stated in behavioral terms, might be: The child *recognizes* basic vocabulary related to plants (seed, roots, bud, "to water a plant"). For a more mature child, the emphasis would be on a higher level of understanding: The child *uses* correctly basic terms related to plants.

Affective objectives, the feeling component of behavior, might center on the child's interest in discovering answers for himself and his persistence in the face of frustration. Behavior indicating an early step in the development of a commitment to inquiry would be: The child asks the teacher to read a book that will provide him with the needed information. (His own efforts to come close enough to birds in the play area in order to note their color and other characteristics proved unsuccessful.)

For a more mature child, the goal would be for him to take steps to find his own answers: The child leafs through old magazines or pictures books looking for illustrations that give him the answer to his question. (Viz., different kinds of birds.) Hopefully, young children will ascend to higher levels of determination as they acquire more experience in facing obstacles and enjoying success. Instead of simply terminating inquiry, behavioral goals for a very young child might be: The child repeats his procedures when his first attempt fails. For a child who has had considerable experience in coping with difficulties and is beyond this point, an instructional goal could be: The child tries another approach when his first method proves unsuccessful.

Psychomotor objectives include all the skills involved in the inquiry process: formulating a question, collecting information, working with data, and confirming findings. An attainable goal for the very young child who stands mute before the teacher with an object in his arms or tugs at her sleeve, would be: The child verbalizes a question that is understood after some clarification by the teacher. For the more verbal child, a higher goal can be set: The child asks a clear, direct question. Another objective might deal with the scope of the question. Stated behaviorally, a beginning level would be: The child asks one question about an object or event. Some children will be able to reach the following goal by the time they have finished kindergarten: The child asks a series of related questions about the phenomenon under observation.

Objectives for data-collecting skills can be expressed in terms of the number of senses involved and the child's ability to participate in experiments. For the child whose first exploratory move is to put an object in his mouth, a reasonable goal would be: The child uses a limited but increasing number of senses to obtain data. (He squeezes, pokes, pounds, shakes, lifts, drops.) With greater maturity the goal might be: The child uses all appropriate senses in finding out about the nature of an object. (A ghetto child might look at grass, chew it, stroke his hand over the turf to feel its texture, bend down close to the earth and smell it, and run on a lawn in his bare feet.)

Four levels in ability to participate in an investigation are listed below in ascending order of difficulty to indicate the range of data-collecting behaviors involved:

- The child *attends* to what the teacher is doing as she performs a demonstration.
- The child *reports* accurately the series of steps involved in an experiment performed by the teacher or classmates.
- The child *follows* the teacher's directions step by step as he performs an experiment.
- The child *plans* his own experiment for finding an answer to his question. (E.g., he suggests that a dish of snow be placed in various locations, including the refrigerator, to test the hypothesis that "snow melts when it is brought inside.")

Skill objectives for dealing with information include both the ability to differentiate and to synthesize data. Goals for analyzing skills can be based on the number of items involved: The child discriminates between two objects which differ in size or color or shape. A higher level goal is: The child detects the middle or median position among three objects which differ in some respect. For the synthesizing of data a low level behavioral goal is: The child classifies objects in terms of their functions. (A bed, pillows, and covers are for sleeping.) Given proper guidance and experience, the child should gradually be able to note relational generalizations as in the following goal: The child forms simple cause-and-effect associations. (Dark clouds often bring rain.)

Very young children take a significant step forward in their development of inquiry skills when they check results to confirm their findings instead of being satisfied with the manipulative aspects of their experience or of asking the teacher if they are "right." Two levels of behavioral goals which represent growth in this skill are:

● The child repeats his procedures to see if he gets the same results.
● The child compares his product with the real thing, a model, or picture.

TEACHING INQUIRY BEHAVIOR

The nature of inquiry processes dictates the tasks of the teacher: to help the child formulate questions that are important and meaningful to him and to aid him in his quest for answers.

Several conditions must be met if the child of five or below is to raise questions. The most important is to establish a classroom climate that is open to his queries. The child must be made to feel comfortable in voicing questions. He should have the assurance that his teacher and classmates will listen with respect to his wonderings, and that there is always the possibility that some of them will be acted upon. More than encouragement is required—the child should feel rewarded for initiating thoughtful questions.

The nursery-kindergarten teacher must also stimulate curiosities in areas that are not commonly available to the child. She must provide a wealth of wide-ranging experiences—indoors and outdoors, in school and in the community—that involve concrete, pictorial, printed media calling for manipulative, dramatic, creative, investigative activities. These should be introduced gradually so that there is always something fresh and new to capture the child's imagination but never so much as to overwhelm him.

The way the teacher structures school experiences influences the kind of questions that are evoked. A child-structured situation, such as a "free" period, makes it possible for the child to pursue his own interests and get answers on his own. A teacher-structured experience, such as a story or a rhythms period, is more suitable for provoking new areas of interest. Between these two lies the semi-structured situation, such as show-and-tell and "juice" periods, in which the activity is designated by the teacher but the content and trend of the discussions are largely the children's.

The teacher will stimulate a broader range of questions if the child has opportunities for experiencing a variety of ways of working. There are times when he should work alone, seeking guidance from the teacher when he needs help. Because interests are contagious—one individual's enthusiasms may produce a snowballing effect on others—the child should also participate with his peers in small-group projects and total-class activities. Since attention time is a function of interest (a young child can concentrate for 15 minutes or longer *if he is interested*), the scheduling of these various types of working arrangements should be flexible.

How the teacher deals with the child's questions will determine the kind of inquiry skills he develops. The great majority of his questions are direct, explicit requests for information: Why does it get dark at night? Who runs the train? How does the fireman know where the fire is? If the teacher readily supplies the information, the nursery child's customary reaction is to terminate his present explorations and turn to something else.[3] In such a transaction the child is learning to use human resources as a means of getting "instant" answers to his questions, but he is not learning how to discover answers by himself.

The basic canon, therefore, for helping children learn inquiry skills is: Don't tell—ask! *The teacher's questioning is the basic technique for guiding the very young child through the inquiry process.* Her questions perform two primary functions: that of focalizing the child's attention and directing his inquiry.

"Focalization" is the act of concentrating on an object or event so that it stands apart from the general stream of impressions which constantly bombard the individual. If the young child does not discriminate between the phenomenon to be studied and other stimuli, he cannot even begin to come to grips with it. Such discrimination is also necessary because of the way children perceive their world. The young child is highly selective in his perceptions; the teacher's questions can direct his attention to other important elements in the situation. Those elements which he does perceive are regarded globally and are differentiated only to the degree that is necessary for the circumstances; the teacher's questioning can lead him to note important details. The child also tends to perceive these elements in isolation; the teacher's questioning can lead him to see how these parts are related to constitute a whole.

The nature of the questioning employed by the teacher provides the child with clues as to the kind of thinking and procedures required to find answers. Replication of some of Piaget's work on the additive composition of classes suggests that children's ability to deal with the logical relationship between "some" and "all" (e.g., the sub-class "brown beads" to the total-class "beads") is related to the types of questions asked by the experimenter.[4] The order of questioning is important, too. Children find questions about the structure or external appearance of objects to be easier than those having to do with their function or how they work. Children also seem to deal more easily with differences than with likenesses, for in most cases the former are based on physical realities whereas the latter require them to engage in more abstract conceptualization. (A saw and a hammer are different because one is used to cut wood and the other to pound nails; they are similar in that both are tools.)

Lastly, the teacher's questioning can offer leads to the young child as to the kind of investigation that is needed. "Is it better to _____ or _____?" suggests that the child carry on an experiment. "Are big packages heavier than smaller packages?" identifies for the child the size-weight variables which he can put to test. "How can we fix this?" presents the child with a problem-solving situation. "I wonder how we can find out?'' encourages the child to plan a method of procedure for discovering a solution.

There is no pattern of teacher questioning that can be used for all children for all questions. In a sequence of teacher-pupil interaction (consisting of a child-initiated question, the teacher's response, and the child's reaction to her response), the form, content, and function of both the nursery child's and the teacher's comments may be combined in innumerable ways.[5] Because children are different and thinking complex, the teaching of inquiry skills is a highly individual and personal matter which cannot be reduced to a simple formula.

EVALUATING INQUIRY BEHAVIOR

Decisions about every phase of instruction rest upon feedback gained from evaluation. The teacher's diagnosis of where the child is in his development will help her set up goals representing higher levels of achievement *for him*. If she has determined that the child can keep in mind one question that he is to ask on a field trip, she might decide that he is now ready to learn how to report the information back to the others. As learning experiences unfold, the teacher will evaluate the child's reactions to the various activities and related materials which were selected to bring about the desired learning. Does he appear to be sufficiently familiar with the situation to be able to cope with it, or is it so strange that he does not seem to know where to begin? Often it is simply a case of whether he understands the question or whether she should rephrase it. In terms of her evaluation, she may modify the goal, provide alternative learning experiences, or help him over a hurdle which is impeding his progress. On completion of a sequence of experiences, the teacher must evaluate to see whether or not the child has achieved the goals set up for the unit. Not only is she interested in knowing whether the child found an answer to his question, "Where does the store get the things it sells?," but if in the process of finding out he has grown in ability to carry on inquiry— to give a clear, concise report of his findings, for example.

Observation is the primary means of obtaining evidence of the progress being made by very young children toward the goals of instruction. By stating objectives in behavioral terms, as in the illustrations above, the teacher knows what to look for. Anecdotal recording of these observations over a period of time is probably the most common technique employed in early childhood education. Other techniques become more feasible as the presence of teacher aides, student teachers, high school future teacher club members, and cooperating parents grows and the use of instructional technology becomes widespread. An audio-tape recording can be made of several children discussing a large picture to find out "what is wrong"; a portable video-tape recorder can be used to record how a child of four or five goes about building an airport out of wooden blocks or tries to make a mechanical toy "work."

Regardless of which techniques are used to obtain evidence, the data must be summarized periodically. Rating scales and checklists are convenient forms for making such notations when the items reflect the specific goals of the program, and they are scaled according to degrees of proficiency so that growth can be noted. Explanatory or interpretive comments add to the usefulness of such ratings, and judgments about the adequacy of a child's progress will be more reliable if the results are viewed in terms of all the informaton contained in the child's cumulative folder.

SUMMARY

The development of inquiry behavior is one of the most important functions of early childhood education. As in all instructional programs, the approach must be diagnostic and individualized. The child works best on questions which are important to him and geared to his level of development. He must have sufficient time to explore, create, and discover answers by himself, but this does not mean leaving him to his own devices. The teacher must intervene to direct the child's random (sometimes destructive) behavior into more inquiry-oriented channels, to assist him when frustration begins to mount. The primary means by which the teacher helps the child is by setting up a stimulating environment and by guiding his explorations through questioning procedures. Throughout, the teacher evaluates the child's behavior to determine the suitability of goals and teaching techniques as well as the progress he is making. The identification of specific goals, provision of appropriate learning experiences, and continuous evaluation are, of course, the prime requisites for effective teaching of any kind of behavior.

REFERENCES

[1]For a discussion of the nature of inquiry and types of skills involved see Frank J. Estvan, *Social Studies in a Changing World: Curriculum and Instruction.* New York: Harcourt, Brace & World, 1968.

[2]Frank J. Estvan, "The Social Perception of Nursery School Children," *Elementary School Journal*, April, 1966, pp. 377–85. Also by the same author, "The Relationship of Nursery School Children's Social Perception to Sex, Race, Social Status, and Age," *Journal of Genetic Psychology*, 1965, pp. 295–308.

[3]Dorothy Haupt, "Teacher-Child Interaction: A Study of the Relationships Between Child-Initiated Questions and Nursery School Teacher Behaviors." Unpublished Doctoral Dissertation, Wayne State University, College of Education, 1965.

[4]Eileen Thomas, "The Effect of Procedure on Piaget's Theory of Additive Composition of Classes." Unpublished Master's Thesis, Wayne State University, College of Education, 1964.

[5]Haupt, *op. cit.*

29. Sciencing for Young Children

If you are interested in some novel activities for preschool and kinder-garten children or in a variety of exciting and meaningful ways to stimulate their interests and curiosity, then you should know about sciencing. If you want to involve three- to seven-year-old children in a series of activities that are designed to promote their intellectual growth and increase their potential for success in school, then you should provide children with the opportunity to do some sciencing.

Note that I didn't say teach the children science; I said let them do sciencing. Science instruction is typically designed to teach the facts, concepts and generalization of science and occasionally to use the investigative activities of the scientist to carry out simple experiments. The emphasis is on the facts; the "what" of science (the products of the scientists). Little emphasis is placed on the *activities* of the scientist; "how" he finds out (the processes of science). Significantly however, it is the process activities that are realistic and appropriate for young children, not the factual content material. Therefore I have found it preferable to avoid the term science entirely when I speak of science-related, process-oriented activities that are appropriate for young children. Instead, I use the term sciencing. This "label" seems to provide a clearer and more accurate way of denoting the kinds of activities I have in mind.

WHAT IS SCIENCING?

Basically, children who are engaged in sciencing are given a chance to observe and manipulate a variety of man-made and natural objects in ways that help them to recognize similarities, differences and relationships among the objects and phenomena. They sniff, look at, listen to, feel, pinch and if possible taste a variety of materials in order to develop and extend their ability to make careful and accurate observations. They are encouraged to extend their thinking beyond what is observed directly and make inferences about the compositions of or relationships among certain objects. They group and regroup objects into classification schemes of their own choosing—schemes that make sense to them. At all times the children are encouraged to discuss what they are doing or what they have done with teachers and peers in order to clarify their thinking, share their findings and compare their results with others. Thus a child who is sciencing involves himself in activities that are, except for the level of sophistication, quite similar to those of the practicing scientist. The

Reprinted by permission from *Young Children*, Vol. 27, No. 4 (April 1972), pp. 215–226. Copyright © 1972, National Association for the Education of Young Children, 1834 Connecticut Avenue, N.W., Washington, DC 20009.

child experiences *how* a scientist makes discoveries and *how* to process simple sensory information.

SCIENCING IS APPROPRIATE FOR PRESCHOOLERS

The more I observe preschool children and read about the observations of others, the more convinced I become that sciencing is an appropriate activity for young children. It is one of the significant ways in which classroom activities can fit the special needs and abilities of children in the three- to seven-year age group. For instance, despite the high interest some factual knowledge holds for children (including preschoolers), these young children are basically unable to deal with words alone—with abstract concepts. Three-, four- and five-year-olds are perception bound. They are able to deal best with the here and now. They easily center all of their attention on one prominent dimension or attribute of an object or event and are unable to make mental reversals. They frequently see only what they choose to see and ignore all else. They don't appear to be at all concerned with adult logic and are often totally and blithely unconcerned with obvious discrepancies in their explanations or descriptions of a particular event or series of events. Therefore it seems quite fruitless to stress the "what" of science for children who are unprepared intellectually to fully or even partly comprehend science knowledge—even very simple and basic knowledge.

On the other hand it is quite realistic for preschool children to participate in activities that are basically open-ended, free-wheeling and based on the manipulation of a variety of materials in a variety of ways. Thus, in planning sciencing activities, one must recognize the nature of the preschool and primary level child and plan activities that are realistic, useful and amenable to individual pursuit. Lock-step lessons where all children are performing exactly the same tasks, making the same observations or coming up with the same findings are the antithesis of what we can or should be expecting of young children who are sciencing. By its very nature, sciencing is made up of a variety of activities in which children are allowed to make their *own observations*, draw their *own inferences*, sort objects into classification schemes of their *own choosing* and share findings that *they feel* are important. The teacher structures the situation only in terms of the types of materials provided, types of suggestions offered and types of limitations placed on what can or cannot be done with safety for the individual or the group. Despite the intellectual limitations and developmental immaturity of preschool and kindergarten children, sciencing can and does coincide with their abilities and makes demands on the children that are realistic and attainable.

BASIC CONSIDERATIONS

The activities of sciencing are divided into three very general categories. First, there is what I call "formal sciencing" which takes place as a planned group activity and is marked by a certain amount of structure (structure in this phase of sciencing is the result of limitations inherent in the equipment and materials provided for the children). Second, there is "informal sciencing" which is a completely open-ended and generally individualized phase of the total sciencing program. Finally, there is "incidental sciencing" which, as its name implies, is carried out when a motivating incident occurs and is highly flexible in degree of group participation.

Before describing the three categories in more detail and suggesting some possible activities, let us consider the role of the teacher in sciencing. If sciencing is to be successful—that is if it is to be a unique and valuable experience for the child, the following tenets should be understood and followed:

1. The teacher must plan activities in ways that will provide children with maximum opportunities to discover concepts and relationships for themselves. This, can be done only if a child has his *own* materials with which to work and is given sufficient freedom to manipulate his materials in a variety of ways over a period of time.
2. The teacher must accept and live by the principle that *no* concept, relationship, or skill can be considered so important that a child is made to sense failure because he has been unable to grasp or perform it.
3. The teacher must plan activities that stress the development of process skills (the "how" of science) such as observing, inferring, classifying and communicating while de-emphasizing the learning of concepts or facts.
4. If, in planning an activity, sufficient manipulative materials are unavailable or if these materials are too sophisticated to be placed in the hands of children, then *don't* use this activity or unit. A lesson consisting of little more than teacher-pupil verbalization can contribute little or nothing to the objectives of sciencing.

With these "four commandments" in mind, let us turn to the three phases or types of sciencing activities; formal, informal, and incidental sciencing and consider each in greater detail.

I. Formal Sciencing

"Formal sciencing" is the most carefully planned phase of sciencing. The teacher plays a central role "behind the scenes," but only a minimal role when "on stage." That is, she plans lessons, obtains the necessary materials, presents the materials to the children, then steps back as much as possible and lets the children do the work, make the discoveries and, hopefully, have the fun.

The children use simple materials initially to develop basic investigative skills (process skills) such as observing and classifying. They then use the process skills to investigate and learn about a very small number of science-related concepts (product understandings). In other words,

319

formal sciencing consists of two segments: the building of process skills and the development of product understandings. Each segment contributes some unique quality to the total effectiveness of the sciencing experience for children. Therefore each segment must be consciously planned for and included in the day-to-day implementation of sciencing activities. The following section provides a relatively detailed description of the process and product segments of sciencing.

A. Development of Process Skills

The most important dimension of "formal sciencing" involves the active participation of young children in the processing of data that comes to them through the use of their senses. This phase builds process skills. There are over a dozen processes that are used by adults in the solution of both simple and complex problems. Often we hear these called the processes of science—though a more accurate statement would label them as the processes of decision making. Four processes seem particularly appropriate for young children who are attempting to come to grips with the natural and man-made world. The first of these and the most basic process of all is *observing*. Observing is the fundamental building block for all of the other processes and thus must be stressed in every way possible throughout *all* of the various activities carried out in sciencing. The other three processes within the framework of understanding of a preschool or primary level child are *inferring*, *classifying*, and *communicating*. A description of each of these four processes follows:

1. *Observing.* By observing, a child learns to examine objects using all or as many of his five senses as possible: seeing, hearing, smelling, tasting and feeling. For example, a child may observe a melting ice cube and make 20 or more observations based on what he sees, feels, tastes, hears or touches. He may observe a burning candle and report what he sees and smells. Some activities that might be used to help children understand and use the process of observing are included in Table 1.
2. *Inferring.* When observations of an object or a system are limited, a child should learn to use the limited observations plus appropriate previous experiences to discover additional information or explanations about the objects or the systems. Information that is generated in this way is called inference and the process used by the child in making an inference is termed inferring. It is useful for a child to understand this concept, the ways in which inferences are made, the limitations of inferential information, and how it differs from observation. Furthermore, he comes to understand that inferences are sometimes less accurate than observations. He must be willing to risk being "wrong" when he makes an inference.

    Some activities that help children understand the meaning of inference and help them differentiate observing from inferring are included in Table 2.
3. *Classifying.* A set of objects may be classified by a child into a series of groupings and subgroupings. The child usually calls this sorting,

TABLE 1.

Process	Materials Suggested	Activities
Observing: Visual	Colors (paints, crayons, food coloring), living plants, seeds, leaves, rocks, minerals, pieces of wood (sawdust from the wood), small animals, fish.	Multiple opportunities to examine objects visually; look for general and specific properties, changes in appearance.
Observing: Smell	Perfumes, fresh-cut flowers, plants, common household products with distinctive odors, fresh fruits, fresh vegetables.	Describe smells; use the sense of smell to identify and describe objects.
Observing: Touch	Cloth material of varying textures, wood of varying grains; various grades of sandpaper, objects of various temperatures.	Use the sense of touch to increase the quality of one's observations.
Observing: Taste	Variety of foodstuffs, harmless drinkable liquids.	Taste a variety of edible products to increase the accuracy of one's observations. Identify characteristics of objects on the basis of taste.
Observing: Hearing	Musical instruments, variety of noise makers, phonograph records (music and sound effects), tape recorder.	Identify voices and commonly heard sounds. Identify degree of loudness, pitch, quality. Increase child's awareness of sounds around him and how they enable him to make better observations.

and even preschool children are able to sort a group of objects on the basis of one property or dimension such as color, hardness or size. Some children are able to sort on the basis of more than one property or dimension—but this ability is rather unusual in preschoolers. It is important that a child be allowed to decide on his own classification scheme and not have a scheme imposed on him.

In Table 3 are some suggested activities that should help children understand that classification schemes are man-made and that there is more than one way to sort a set of objects.

4. *Communicating.* A child should be encouraged to tell how and what he has observed, inferred or classified in order to clarify his thinking and build his skill of interacting with others. The child should be encouraged to communicate with his peers as well as with teachers and adults in the classroom. (See Table 4.)

TABLE 2.

Process	Materials Suggested	Activities
Inferring	"Gift box," sealed bags of materials.	Infer what is in the gift box or sealed bag without looking inside.
	Variety of clear liquids.	Infer which liquid is water without smelling or tasting the various liquids.
	Closed container with small living insect inside.	Is the object inside the container alive?
	Sound effects (records or tapes).	Infer whether noise is being made in the city or in the country; describe object making noise from its sound.
	Hot and cold objects.	Infer how objects became hot or cold. Is entire object hot or only part of it?

TABLE 3.

Process	Materials Suggested	Activities
Classifying	Bags of buttons, bags containing a variety of materials; sandpaper squares consisting of a variety of grades and painted a variety of colors; tagboard pieces in a variety of shapes, sizes, and colors; bags of rocks; shells.	Have children sort materials according to properties of their own choosing. Encourage children to think about and tell why they sorted objects in the way that they did. Also encourage them to try to find another way to sort their objects.

B. Development of Product Understandings

The product understandings are essentially the "what" of science—the facts and the concepts that make up the scientific body of knowledge. For a variety of reasons, product understandings ought not to be emphasized in the preschool program. In keeping with the basic goal of making sciencing activities realistic for young children, many topics were evaluated in order to find appropriate content material for this phase of the formal sciencing program. Four science-related topics were found that seem sufficiently broad, yet basic enough, to be within the intellectual grasp of preschool and early-primary children. Furthermore, these four topics seem to lend themselves well to involving children with materials that are relatively simple to use and easy to obtain.

I will list the four topics and suggest some materials that could be used in implementing the topics. I will not delineate specific activities for

TABLE 4.

Process	Materials Suggested	Activities
Communicating	Any and all of the materials used in developing the skills of observing, inferring, and classifying can be used to develop this process skill. In addition, small sets of objects composed of specific properties can be used to help children develop a useful vocabulary for communicating. The sets may include: shiny and dull objects; hard and soft; rough and smooth; heavy and light; hot and cold; fat and thin; noisy and quiet.	Describe materials and/or recognizable objects; name materials and objects; tell about perceived relationships among materials and objects. Learn descriptive terms.

several reasons. First, teachers can, with an understanding of the objectives of sciencing, come up with creative activities that will present these topics and materials to children. Second, children differ, materials available differ, teachers differ from place to place, year to year and sometimes day to day. In developing activities, keep in mind that all children should be actively and physically involved in these activities to the maximum extent possible. (See Table 5.)

In summary, two segments must be considered in planning and carrying out "formal sciencing." These are: 1) the process skills to be employed by the children; and 2) the content material that children can find meaningful and that can serve to increase their awareness of the world around them. We will now turn to another phase of sciencing: "informal sciencing."

II. Informal Sciencing

"Informal sciencing" is a second phase of the total preschool sciencing program. The most prominent features of "informal sciencing" are the emphasis on total individualization and the complete openness in its implementation. This phase of sciencing may come fairly close to what many teachers of preschool programs usually call science.

A corner or section of a room should be established as the "sciencing center." In addition, an outdoor area should be developed as an important extension of the indoor center. In these areas, carefully selected materials can be placed in containers and made available to children who desire to work with them. There should be no predetermined objectives and no directions for a child to follow. The only desired outcomes are that children will feel free to take a set of materials, spend some time with

TABLE 5.

Topic	Materials Suggested
1. Objects are alike, objects are different. How are some objects in a set alike? How are they different?	Rocks, twigs, leaves, coins, glasses of water (add various food colors), common toys, small insects, fruits, animal pictures, flowers, assorted yard goods, buttons, seeds, two-dimensional shapes, assortment of tiles, building blocks, small musical instruments or noise makers.
2. Objects have definite properties. What are some common properties of objects? a. color b. shape c. size d. bounciness e. shine f. texture g. smell h. sound (pitch, tone, loudness) i. hardness	Felt pieces (variety of shapes and colors), wooden dowels, two- and three-dimensional shapes, pieces of cloth (variety of colors, shapes, textures,) common fruit, cords, metallic pieces, plastic or ceramic tiles, paint color cards, rug samples, phonograph and records, bells, super ball, rubber ball, clay, sand paper, food coloring, perfume, other materials with a distinctive odor.
3. Some objects are living, some are not. How can you tell if an object is living? How can you tell if it is not living?	Common insects, mealworms, small rodents, algae, rocks, aquatic plants, seeds, seedlings, sand, soil, aquarium, goldfish, fossils, crystals, (e.g., sugar, etc.) mechanical toys, living plants, plastic flowers, sponges, common fruits and vegetables.
4. Some objects are solid, some are liquid, some are gas. How are solids alike? How are liquids alike? How are gases alike? How are solids, liquids and gases different from one another?	Talcum powder, sand, salt, sugar, wood, metal, plastic, ice, oil, glycerin, water, rubbing alcohol, balloons filled with oxygen, air, carbon dioxide, freon or steam.

these materials manipulating them in a variety of ways; and in some way find this activity to be an intellectually challenging and rewarding experience.

The teachers' role in this kind of sciencing is basically to provide the necessary materials and some free time during each day so that children who desire to involve themselves in this activity may do so. In other words, the role of the teacher in the actual day-to-day implementation of informal sciencing is fairly minimal. However, she is responsible for setting up and maintaining materials in the sciencing center and for making children aware that the center is a place where they are encouraged to work on their own with science-like equipment. In addition, the teacher should watch the sciencing center out of the corner of her eye and intervene if she sees that a child is obviously becoming frustrated or doing something that might endanger himself or others.

In order to facilitate maximum freedom for a child to work with the science equipment, all materials should be carefully selected and made readily accessible to the child. It is therefore suggested that materials be placed in color-coded containers and that the containers be stored on a convenient shelf where children can reach them without difficulty. I suggest color-coding the containers for several reasons. First, the child can more readily get what he needs without hunting through a dozen containers. Color-coding can help organize equipment into logical units or topics. Second, color-coding will assist the teacher in maintaining and checking out the quantities and conditions of specific materials. Third, color-coding can be very attractive and the eye-appeal may serve to draw some children to the sciencing center who might otherwise be indifferent to this kind of activity. Fourth, the coding may help children in naming and identifying colors.

The key to the success of informal sciencing is, of course, the quantity and quality of materials available in the "center." If there are insufficient quantities of materials or if the equipment is so sophisticated that it far exceeds the child's intellectual and motor capabilities, this phase of the program will be predestined to failure. The following groups of materials represent the kinds of simple, yet challenging things that are appropriate to the objectives of informal sciencing and useable by preschool children.

1. *Simple electrical equipment:* small battery holders, dry cell batteries, quantities of wire (with alligator clips at each end) small D.C. motors and simple switches.
2. *Magnets:* variety of magnets, magnetic and nonmagnetic materials, iron filings, small compasses.
3. *Electro-magnets:* battery holders, batteries, variety of nails, bell wire, magnetic and nonmagnetic materials, compasses.
4. *Living organisms and related materials:* one-gallon plastic aquarium, aquatic plants, guppies, snails, magnifying glasses, seeds and containers for planting; small animals such as rabbits, gerbils or guinea pigs; terraria to be set up in plastic containers; small reptiles and amphibians.
5. *Floating and sinking materials:* aquaria, variety of objects some of which float and some that sink, oil-base clay (to be made into a variety of shapes), overflow can, small plastic graduated cylinders, variety of metal cylinders of different densities, string.
6. *Sound making materials:* variety of noise makers, rubber bands and cigar boxes, heavy glass bottles (into which water can be placed), tin cans and string; simple musical instruments.
7. *Outdoor studies:* simple weather equipment such as a wind vane, rain gauge, anemometer, thermometer; gardening; collecting insects, leaves, flowers; fossil hunting; bird watching.

Not every child will be interested in participating in this phase of sciencing. That is to be expected. Some children may spend an hour working with some simple equipment. Others may show waning interest after minutes or seconds. This too is to be expected. Some children will be full of questions about what they are doing or what they have seen. As a teacher of younger children it is advisable to answer as few of these questions as possible. Suggest that they might continue their work or try some new approach to finding answers. Remember, in sciencing you are less interested in "what" and more concerned with "how" the children find out. "Informal sciencing" is a very useful technique for making children aware of the importance of "how."

II. Incidental Sciencing

The third phase of the preschool sciencing program is based on opportunism. Occasionally, while out on a walk, on the way to or from school, or in some unpredictable manner, a child will come across an object or observe some natural phenomenon that greatly arouses his interest. He may bring an object to the classroom (I wonder how many preschool and kindergarten teachers have had a child come to class with a dead sparrow in his hand?). He may excitedly describe the gigantic bolts of lightning and claps of thunder observed during yesterday's thunderstorm. A friend or relative may have brought him an unusually attractive rock in which a fossil crinoid stem has been imbedded. His mother may have given birth to a new baby brother or sister. In the case of the dead sparrow, does one say to a child, "get that dead bird out of my classroom!" or perhaps, "Isn't that nice, Johnny. Now flush it down the toilet." Or does a teacher use that moment to light a spark of interest in as many of the children as possible by saying, something like, "I wonder what happened to the bird? Could any of you suggest what might have happened?" In this instance children are given a chance to infer a cause and effect relationship. We aren't concerned about the actual cause of death. We are concerned with why the child believes the bird was run over by a car or hit by a b-b pellet.

"Incidental sciencing" is unpredictable and open. It is not an every day happening. It is not planned by the teacher. It is the result of some occurrence that has captured the imagination of one or more children and is capitalized upon by an alert teacher.

BENEFITS FROM SCIENCING

There are a number of ways in which sciencing is likely to influence children in a positive way. These include:

1. *Promoting intellectual growth.* Thanks to the work of Piaget and others, new and better insights into the growth of intelligence in children are being made. For example, Piaget has described the order of stages through which all children pass as they learn to function at more sophisticated levels. He has provided guide lines for identifying the stage at which a particular child is operating at a particular time. More importantly, the basic building blocks necessary for promoting higher levels of thinking in children have been identified (Piaget, 1965).

It is in this area that sciencing can be of great benefit to preschool children. In order to reach the stage of thinking at which logic rather than physical appearance dominates a child's thinking, the child must be able to recognize and understand certain observable phenomena. These include the following: 1) Relatively large and recognizable objects such as a glass of water or a cube of sugar are composed of smaller particles—droplets of water or crystals of sugar. In addition, the droplets or the crystals can be rearranged to form a different shaped glass of water or different shaped lump of sugar. Moreover, the child should sense that in changing the shape of a glass or the dimensions of a lump, the composition of the basic units are in no way affected—that is, the water droplets are still water droplets and crystals of sugar are still crystals of sugar. Furthermore, the child should experience and understand that while two objects look very different on the surface, that is, have a very different outward appearance, the smaller units that make up the two objects may be identical. For instance, rock candy and a cube of sugar do not look at all alike as we normally observe them. If, however, the rock candy and the sugar cube are ground up and compared under a magnifying glass, the rock candy sugar crystals cannot be distinguished from the sugar cube sugar crystals. At the atomistic level (smallest distinguishable particles) they are identical— made up of the same "stuff." 2) Objects that are short and fat can contain just as much material as objects that are tall and skinny. 3) Objects can be sorted (classified) into groupings on the basis of more than one property. 4) Objects can be physically changed in some way, then returned to their original form or shape. 5) Objects can be arranged in an order from most to least and least to most based on one or more properties possessed by the objects.

It has been demonstrated that some children who have had experiences involving these five phenomena (atomism, multiple relationality, multiple classification, reversibility and serial ordering) have achieved higher levels of logical thinking, in some cases more quickly and in others with greater facility. (Sigel & Roeper in Sigel & Hooper, 1968). A large number of the activities suggested in the preceding sections were designed specifically to provide the child with experiences involving these factors. As a result, it is likely that these experiences are useful in promoting the attainment of higher levels of logical thinking.

2. *Potential for success in school.* A child who has had experience in sciencing may show improvement in his readiness to read. Evidence indicates that sciencing sharpens a child's ability to make visual discriminations, particularly in picking out similarities and differences among highly similar objects (Neuman, 1970). Sciencing helps build such basic concepts as big, small, round and square—all of which are useful in word and letter recognition. Vocabulary development through use of science-related words is another facet of reading readiness affected by sciencing. Serial ordering and physical sequencing of objects provide the child with a left to right orientation, useful in promoting success in reading. In addition, a child who is given an opportunity to manipulate a variety of materials is likely to develop motor

skills necessary for later success in a variety of school situations. Hand-eye coordination and small muscle development can be enhanced by experiences in which a child fits small objects together or connects a wire to a battery terminal in order to make a light go on. Science materials are sufficiently interesting and challenging to encourage a child to try working with them even though total muscle control is not yet well developed. The result is that the child may improve his motor skills as a concomitant of working with the science equipment.

3. *Development of a more positive self-image.* If sciencing is carried out as it is intended, it should contribute substantially to sustaining children's interest and curiosity about the world around them. In essence, a child who is sciencing is acting the part of a scientist—on a somewhat small scale. Because activities involving the direct manipulation of a variety of objects is stressed, the scientific procedures of observing, inferring, classifying and communicating become a natural part of a child's repertoire of skills. In addition, because the child does a good deal of individual exploring with his own materials, he soon begins to realize that there is often more than one correct approach to a problem and often more than just one solution. He learns to look for answers that are supported by observable evidence. And most of all, he begins to learn that he can be successful in sciencing. After all, he's not looking for right or wrong answers. He is merely reporting his observations or his inferences that are based on those observations. He is classifying objects on the basis of self-selected criteria. He is sharing with others what *he* feels is worth communicating.

It is an accepted fact that "nothing succeeds like success." Sciencing, as it is described in this paper, should provide every child with a chance to succeed at some level or in some manner. In fact, all activities should be designed in such a way that the success of every child is the prime objective. Teachers should consciously plan experiences that are failure-proof. As a result, children will know that they have been successful in school related activities; and sciencing will become a useful vehicle for developing a healthy and positive self-concept as well as a more positive feeling about school.

Admittedly, there are many "important things" to do in preschool and primary program. However, sciencing does provide a variety of unique and challenging experiences for children; experiences that no other activity can do or do as well. The value of sciencing should be recognized by all teachers and administrators, so that it can become an integral part of school programs designed for young children.

REFERENCES

Neuman, Donald. "The Effect of Kindergarten Science Experiences on Reading Readiness." Unpublished research report to U.S. Office of Education, 1970.
Piaget, Jean. *The Child's Concept of Number.* New York: Norton, 1965.

Sigel, Irving, Roeper, Anna Marie & Hooper, Frank. A training procedure for acquisition of Piaget's conservation of quantity: A pilot study and its replication. In Irving Sigel & Frank Hooper (Eds.) *Logical Thinking in Children*. New York: Holt, Rinehart, & Winston. 1968.

CONSTANCE KAMII
RHETA DEVRIES

30. Piaget, Children, and Number

I. THE NATURE OF NUMBER

In Piaget's theory, number is an example of logico-mathematical knowledge, which is an aspect of knowledge that is different from both physical and social (arbitrary) knowledge. The logico-mathematical nature of number will be discussed first in contrast with physical knowledge and then with social (arbitrary) knowledge.

Piaget makes a fundamental distinction between two types, or poles, of knowledge—physical and logico-mathematical. Physical knowledge is knowledge about objects in external reality. The color and weight of a pencil are examples of physical properties *in* objects which can be known by observation. The knowledge that a pencil will roll when pushed is also an example of observable, physical knowledge about objects in external reality.

When, on the other hand, we are presented with 2 pencils and note that there are 2 pencils, the "twoness" is an example of logico-mathematical knowledge. The pencils are indeed observable, but the "twoness" is a *relationship* created mentally by the individual who puts the 2 objects into a relationship. If the individual did not put the objects into a relationship, each pencil would remain separate and distinct for him or her. The "twoness" is neither *in* one pencil nor *in* the other. It is a relationship, and this relationship is not observable, as it does not have any existence in external reality. Other examples of relationships created by the individual are "longer than," "heavy as," and "different in color."

Piaget's view about this logico-mathematical nature of number is in sharp contrast with that of the proponents of "modern math." One typical modern math text (Duncan, Capps, Dolciani, Quast, and Zweng 1972) states, for example, that number is "a property of sets in the same

From Constance Kamii and Rheta DeVries, *Piaget, Children, and Number* (Washington, D.C.: NAEYC, 1976), pp. 5–24, plus notes and references. © Constance Kamii and Rheta DeVries 1976 by permission of the authors.

way that ideas like color, size, and shape refer to properties of objects" (p. T30). Accordingly, children are presented with sets of 4 pencils, 4 flowers, 4 balloons, and 5 pencils, for example, and are asked to find the sets that have the same "number property." This exercise reflects an assumption that children learn number concepts by abstracting "number properties" from various sets in the same way they abstract color or other physical properties of objects.

In Piaget's theory, the abstraction of color from objects is considered very different in nature from the abstraction of number. The two are so different, in fact, that they are distinguished by different terms. For the abstraction of physical properties from objects, Piaget uses the term *simple* (or *empirical*) abstraction. For the abstraction of number, he uses the term *reflective* abstraction. In simple abstraction, all the child does is focus on a certain physical property of the object and ignore the others. For example, when he abstracts the color of an object, the child simply ignores the other properties such as shape, size, and weight. Reflective abstraction, in contrast, involves the creation of mental relationships between/among objects. Relationships, as we said earlier, do not have an existence in external reality. Numbers for Piaget are thus created by reflective abstraction. The term *constructive* abstraction might thus be easier to understand than *reflective* abstraction—to indicate that this abstraction is a veritable construction by the mind rather than a focus on properties that already exist in objects.

The distinction between the two kinds of abstraction may seem trivial and academic while the child is learning small numbers, say, up to 10. When he goes on to large numbers such as 999 and 1000, however, it becomes clear that it is impossible to learn every number all the way to infinity by abstraction from sets of objects or pictures! Numbers are learned not by abstraction from sets that are already made but by abstraction as the child constructs relationships. Because these relationships are created by the mind, it is possible to think of numbers such as 1,000,002 even if we have never seen 1,000,002 objects in a set.

Number for Piaget is a synthesis of two kinds of relationships the child creates among objects. One of these relationships is ordering, and the other is class inclusion. All teachers of young children have seen the common tendency among children to count objects by skipping some and counting some more than once. When given 8 objects, for example, a child who can recite, "One, two, three, four . . ." correctly up to ten may end up claiming that there are 10 things by "counting" as shown in Figure 1(a). This tendency shows that the child does not feel any logical necessity to put the objects in an order to make sure he does not skip any or count the same one more than once. The only way we can be sure of not overlooking any or counting the same object more than once is by putting them in an order. However, one does not have to put the objects literally in a physical order to put them into an ordered relationship. What is important is that they be ordered mentally as shown in Figure 1(b).

If ordering were the only mental action on objects, the objects would not be quantified, since the child could consider one at a time rather

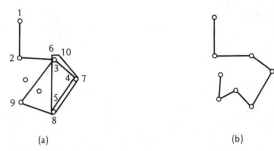

FIGURE 1. (a) The way many four-year-olds "count." (b) The mental ordering of the objects shown in Figure 1(a).

than a group of many at the same time. To quantify the objects as a group, he or she has to put them into a relationship of class inclusion as well. This relationship, shown in Figure 2, means that the child mentally includes "one" in "two," "two" in "three", "three" in "four," etc. The child thus may be presented with 8 objects, but he or she will "see" a set of 8 only if he or she puts all 8 of them into a single relationship.

Piaget's theory of the logico-mathematical nature of number is also in contrast with the common assumption that number concepts can be taught by social transmission like arbitrary social knowledge, especially by teaching children how to count. Social knowledge is knowledge which is built neither by observation of physical phenomena (physical knowledge) nor by the creation and coordination of relationships (logico-mathematical knowledge) but by social consensus. Examples are the knowledge that Christmas comes on December 25, and that a chair is called a "chair." The characteristic of social knowledge is that it is mostly arbitrary. The fact that Christmas comes on December 25 rather than on December 20 is an example of the arbitrariness of social knowlege. The fact that there is any Christmas at all is another example of the arbitrary nature of social knowledge. There is no physical or logical reason for December 25 to be considered any different from any other day of the year. The fact that a chair is called "chair" is likewise completely arbitrary. In another language, the same object is called by another name. It follows, therefore, that social knowledge can be taught only by social transmission.

People who believe that "number facts" should be taught by social transmission fail to make the fundamental distinction between logico-mathematical and social knowledge. In logico-mathematical knowledge,

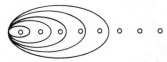

FIGURE 2. The structure (relationship) of class inclusion in the child's conception of number.

nothing is arbitrary. For example, 2 + 2 gives the same result in all cultures. In fact, every culture that builds any mathematics at all ends up building exactly the same mathematics, as mathematics is built on the internal consistency of a deductive system in which absolutely nothing is arbitrary. To cite another example of the nonarbitrary nature of logico-mathematical knowledge, in all cultures, there are more animals than cows.

In conclusion, Piaget's view is in contrast with the belief that there is a "world of number" into which each child must be socialized. To be sure, even two-year-olds can see the difference between a pile of 3 blocks and one of 10 blocks. This, however, does not imply that number is "out there" in the physical world, to be abstracted by simple (empirical) abstraction. By the same token, even though there is consensus about the sum of 2 + 2, number is not "out there" in the social world, to be learned by social transmission. We must be aware that the arithmetic we can teach directly is limited to certain arbitrary social conventions, such as how to say, "one, two, three, four," and the details of specific computation, such as 5 + 5, which can be taught only after the child himself has constructed the logic underlying the addition of two numbers.

If the child cannot create relationships such as "five" in his mind, no amount of verbal counting or drill will enable him or her to construct the notion of "five." While we thus believe with Piaget that number concepts are not directly teachable, we do not draw the pedagogical implication that the only thing the teacher can do is set back and wait. There are certain things he or she can do to encourage children to construct number concepts. These are discussed in Section II as principles of teaching that we derive from Piaget's theory of number.

II. PRINCIPLES OF TEACHING

1. Teach Number Concepts When They Are Useful and Meaningful to the Child

We have emphasized elsewhere (Kamii and DeVries, 1977) the most basic principle of teaching we derive from Piaget's constructivism: Promote the child's autonomy. If children develop by constructing their own knowledge and morality, they must be encouraged to act out of their own choice and conviction. Thus, we would not advocate that young children between the ages of four and six have a time set aside just for math. Rather than doing math because the teacher says to do it, children should be encouraged to think about number when they feel a need and interest. All children between four and six years old seem to be intensely interested in number when its use is at the right level for them. They spontaneously count the presents they receive and the marbles they own, and argue about who has more blocks than they have. They also adore songs and board games involving counting. In Kamii and DeVries (1976), we discuss the kinds of situations in which the teacher can capitalize on this spontaneous interest.

2. Use Language That Elicits Logical Quantification and the Comparison of Groups

Logical quantification is contrasted here with numerical quantification. An example of using the language of logical quantification is "Bring *just enough* cups for everybody at your table," instead of saying "Bring six cups." Although we feel it is good for children to learn how to count, we feel that when the teacher is trying to get children to construct beginning number concepts, it is best to avoid telling them to count. The reason for this belief is that, for preoperational children, the ability to count is one thing, and quantification is quite something else. In the conservation of elementary number task, for example, many Level II children count the two equivalent rows correctly, but still say that there are more in one row! Some children at this point occasionally look embarrassed and confess to having made a mistake. Most Level II children, however, see no contradiction between saying that each row has eight, and saying that the bottom row has more.

Counting thus helps the Level II child only once in a great while to conserve. If it helps him or her, this is because the child's level of cognitive development in logico-mathematical knowledge is already quite high, and he or she is very close to conserving anyway. If, on the other hand, the child's cognitive development is low, no amount of counting can help him or her to conserve. Counting for this child is like saying, "Mark, John, Suzy, Mary, Bobby, . . . Judy," in the right order, and answering the question "How many?" by repeating the last name in the series. Thus counting causes the child to focus on each object and its name in the series, rather than the entire set. This is why we say that counting is one thing, and quantification is quite another thing.

When asked in the conservation task, "Are there as many here as here?" the child compares the two sets in the best way he or she can. If the child does not have the logico-mathematical structure of number (which is built by ordering objects and putting them into a relationship of class inclusion), the best way he or she can quantify the sets is by comparing the spatial frontiers of the two sets. Similarly, when the teacher asks a child to "bring just enough straws . . ." the child will quantify in the best way he or she can. If the child can use counting, he or she will. If the child has not yet constructed his or her notion of number, and therefore cannot see the use of counting, the child will still reason about the numerical issue in some way. He or she may use one-to-one correspondence, or grab a fistful and end with too many or not enough. Still, the child has thought in some way about a quantitative problem.

Thus, we recommend that the teacher avoid asking a child to count because this gives a "trick" or half of the solution, rather than encouraging him or her to figure out what to do. Other examples of language that elicit logical quantification and comparison of sets are:

1. Do we have *enough* for everybody to have one?
2. Do we have *too many* cups?

3. Do you have *as many* chips (or the *same amount*, or the *same number*) as I have?
4. Who has *more?*
5. Bobby has *less* than you do.

3. Encourage Children to Make Sets with Movable Objects

When we encourage children to focus on only one set of objects at a time, we limit their possibilities for thinking about quantity. The only type of question we can ask about a single set is of the kind "How many are there?" or "Can you give me eight?" We thus can only end up encouraging children to count the objects. As explained in Principle 2, encouraging children to count is not a good way to help them begin quantifying groups of objects. A better approach is to ask them to compare two sets.

There are two ways of asking children to compare sets: by asking them to *make a judgment* about the equality (or nonequality) of sets that are already made, and by asking them to *make a set* that has the same number as another set. The second approach is far better for two reasons. First, when a child is asked to make a judgment about two ready-made sets, his reason for comparing the sets is that the adult wants an answer to the exercise he or she chose for the child. Comparing ready-made sets is a passive activity in which the child is limited to only three possible responses: The two sets are the same; one has more; or one has less. When the child has to *make* a set, in contrast, as when he or she is asked to bring just enough straws for everyone at the table, the child starts with zero, takes one, one more, one more, etc., *until he or she decides when to stop.* This kind of decision necessary to the physical making of a set has more educational value because there is a greater degree of freedom in starting with zero and knowing exactly when to stop the action of "adding one more." In making sets, children have a chance to order the objects actively and group them.

The value of encouraging children to make sets implies that some commonly used materials are inappropriate for teaching elementary number. Workbook pictures such as Figure 3 and Cuisenaire rods (Kunz 1965) are examples of such unfortunate materials.

Exercises such as the one shown in Figure 3 are undesirable because they preclude any possibility for the child to move the objects and make a set. Moreover, such an exercise easily elicits the kind of reasoning that yields the right answer for the wrong reason. For example, when asked how they knew the right answer to Figure 3, many children explain, "You draw lines like this, and put an X on the set that has one left over." Such children may or may not have the slightest idea about which set has *more.* If they do, this is usually because they already have the ability to quantify objects. If they don't, the exercise is useless because children do not learn to make quantitative judgments by drawing lines on paper.

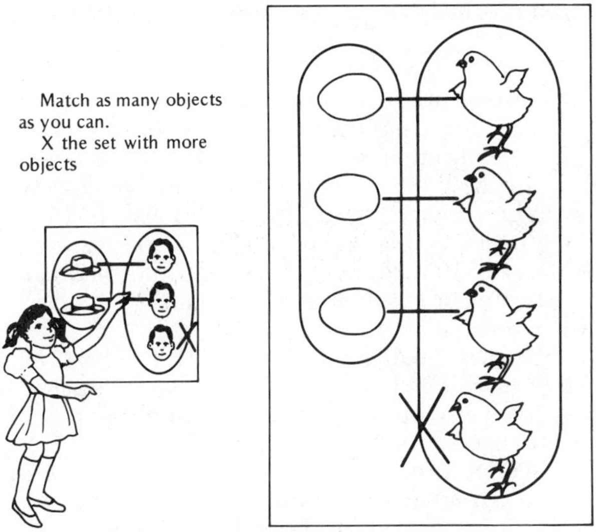

FIGURE 3. An example of a typical workbook page.

Cuisenaire's approach to teaching number with rods reflects the common confusion between discrete and continuous quantities. For Cuisenaire, the 1-cm rod stands for "one," the 5-cm rod stands for "five," and the 10-cm rod stands for "ten." For Piaget and most young children, however, each of these rods can only be "one," since it is a single, discrete object. Number involves the quantification of discrete objects, and therefore cannot be taught through length, which is a continous quantity.[1] Giving such a ready-made "two," "three," "four," etc., to children is worse then giving them ready-made sets such as Figure 3. At least these are sets of discrete objects.

Montessori (1912), Stern (Stern and Stern 1971), and many others, too, made seriated rods proportioned according to the same principle as the Cuisenaire rods. This principle is to make the second rod twice as long as the first one, the third one three times as long as the first, etc. Advocates of teaching number with such rods believe that by ordering the rods, children learn about the number series, including the idea that "one" is included in "two,' "two" is included in "three," etc. Piaget's research shows that, in reality, when the child arranges the rods from the longest to the shortest, or vice versa, all he or she learns is the crutch of how to use the stairstep shape to judge whether or not his arrangement is correct. This shape is an observable spatial configuration, which the child can use as a source of external feedback. In logico-mathematical knowledge, feedback can come only from the internal consistency of a logical system constructed by the child. This system, as can be illustrated by the system of class inclusions, is not observable. Ability to arrange objects by trial-and-error based on feedback from the configuration is thus not the same thing as the development of logic.

4. Get Children to Verify an Answer Among Themselves

As stated above, arithmetic does not have to be transmitted from one generation to the next like social (arbitrary) knowledge, since all children in all cultures construct the same arithmetic if they construct any at all. Therefore, if children are encouraged to think about numerical quantity, they are bound to construct notions which will eventually lead them to right answers. When a child brings "just enough straws . . .," therefore, the best thing for the teacher to do is to refrain from giving direct feedback and encourage the same child or other children to check the answer. When children are confronted with an idea that conflicts with their own, they are motivated to think about the problem again, and either revise their idea or argue for it. Therefore, an important principle of teaching is to bring disagreements to children's attention by asking for many opinions or by mentioning casually to a child that someone else has a different idea.

When we teach number by being the only source of feedback, we unintentionally teach many other things, such as how to read the teacher's face for signs of approval. Such teaching amounts to education by conformity to the person in authority. This is not the way children can develop confidence about their own ability to figure things out. Piaget (1948) vigorously opposes this kind of teaching and insists that the emotional block many students develop about math is completely avoidable.

5. Figure Out How Children Are Thinking

If children make an error, it is usually because they are using their intelligence by reasoning in their own way. Since every error is a reflection of the child's thinking, the teacher's task is not to correct the answer, but to figure out why the child made the error. Based on this insight, the teacher can sometimes correct the process of reasoning, which is not the same thing as correcting the answer. For example, if the child brings one less than "just enough straws . . .," the reason may be that he or she did not count himself or herself. Preoperational children often have difficulty considering themselves as both the counter and the counted. When they count the others, therefore, they frequently do not count themselves. When they distribute straws and find they are one short, a casual question such as, "Did you count yourself when you counted the children?" may be helpful.

Just as there are many ways to get the wrong answer, there are many ways to get the right answer, and not all of them are based on logical reasoning. One illustration of this is a study by Piaget (1941, Chapter 8) of how children divide 18 counters between 2 people. He found three different (levels) of getting the right answer, only the last one of which is based on logical reasoning. Below are the three levels:

Level I: A global (intuitive) method. The child divides the counters in a rough, global way and may by accident give 9 to each per-

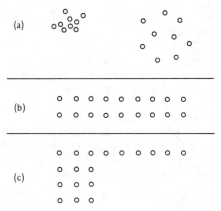

FIGURE 4. The division and arrangement of 18 counters.

son. This is an example of getting the right answer for the wrong reason. After thus dividing the counters, however, the child may end up saying that there are more in one bunch, especially if the spatial configuration is changed as shown in Figure 4(a).

Level II: A perceptual (spatial) method. The child spatially puts the counters in one-to-one correspondence as shown in Figure 4(b). After thus dividing the counters, however, he or she usually ends up saying that there are more in one set if one of the arrangements is changed as shown in Figure 4(c).

Level III: A logical method. The child gives one (or more) to each person alternately until all 18 of the counters are exhausted. The spatial correspondence is unnecessary and irrelevant when the child's logic has thus developed.

By observing the child's behavior, the alert teacher can infer whether the child is approaching a problem in a global, perceptual, or logical way. On the basis of this kind of continual study, the teacher can give problems to each child at a level that is truly appropriate for him or her.

6. Encourage Children in a General Way to Put All Kinds of Objects, Events, and Actions into Relationships

Number concepts are not isolated ideas that develop independently of all the other relationships the child creates and coordinates. The child's construction of the class-inclusion structure may serve to illustrate this point. Class inclusion is a cognitive structure characterized by mobility of thought which enables us to think about "five," for example, in relation to "one," "two," "three," "four," "six," "seven," etc. (Figure 2). The ability to coordinate the elements in a hierarchical system requires thought which is both mobile and well-structured.[2]

Mobility of thought develops as the child put things and events into relationships and structures them in his or her daily life. For example, bedtime may be the same very night except Fridays and Saturdays. There may be items of clothing (such as underwear) which are for every day of the year, and others which are only for parties or Sunday school. In playing a game like bowling, too, the child may notice that the target is missed by rolling the ball too far to the right sometimes, and too far to the left at other times. These are examples of the countless situations in daily life where the child can put elements of his or her reality into hierarchical relationships. The hierarchical relationships develop by the coordination of more limited local relationships, such as "I missed the target again." The child who has created and coordinated many relationships in his daily life is probably the one who is highly "ready" to construct number concepts—even by the worst teaching method.[3]

Notes

1. A continuous quantity such as a length can be quantified only by introducing an arbitrary unit which is not given in the object. The logical structure of serial inclusion is the same in number and length. In number, however, the unit is given by the discrete object. Continuous quantities may, therefore, be of use to later work in mathematics, but they are completely inappropriate for the teaching of beginning elementary number.

2. The reader is referred to Inhelder and Piaget (1959, Chapters 1, 2, and 4) for a fuller understanding of the significance of this statement.

3. This emphasis on the child's creating and coordinating relationships implies that number should be taught in the context of a total curriculum which is not limited to the teaching of number. The reader interested in a broader curriculum is referred to Kamii and DeVries (1977).

References

Duncan, E. R.; Capps, L. R.; Dolciani, M. P.; Quast, W. G.; and Zweng, M. J. *Modern School Mathematics: Structure and Use.* Teacher's annotated ed., rev. ed. Boston: Houghton Mifflin, 1972.

Inhelder, B., and Piaget, J. *The Early Growth of Logic in the Child.* New York: Harper & Row, 1964. (First published as *La Genèse des Structures Logiques Élémentaires, Classification et Sériations.* Neuchâtel: Delachaux et Niestlé, 1959.)

Kamii, C. "Evaluation of Learning in Preschool Education: Socio-Emotional, Perceptual-Motor, Cognitive Development" In *Handbook on Formative and Summative Evaluation of Student Learning,* edited by B. Bloom, J. Hastings, G. Madaus. New York: McGraw-Hill, 1971.

Kamii, C., and DeVries, R. *Piaget, Children, and Number.* Washington, D.C.: NAEYC, 1976.

Kamii, C., and DeVries, R. "Piaget for Early Education." In *The Preschool in Action,* edited by M. C. Day and R. K. Parker. 2nd ed. Boston: Allyn and Bacon, 1977.

Kunz, J. *Modern Mathematics Made Meaningful with Cuisenaire Rods.* New Rochelle, N.Y.: Cuisenaire Co. of America, 1965.

Lavatelli, C. *Early Childhood Curriculum: A Piaget Program.* 2nd ed., Teacher's Guide. Boston: American Science and Engineering, 1973.

Montessori, M. *The Montessori Method.* New York: Schocken, 1964. (First published in English, New York: F. A. Stokes, 1912.)

Piaget, J. *The Child's Conception of Number.* New York: W. W. Norton, 1965. (First published with A. Szeminska as *La Genèse du Nombre chez l'Enfant.* Neuchâtel: Delachaux et Niestlé, 1941.)

Piaget, J. *The Moral Judgment of the Child.* New York: The Free Press, 1965. (First published as *Le Jugement Moral chez l'Enfant.* Paris: Alcan, 1932.)

Piaget, J. *To Understand Is to Invent* New York: Gross Publications, 1974.

Stern, C., and Stern, M. B. *Children Discover Arithmetic.* New York: Harper & Row, 1971.

Introduction to Early Childhood Administration

Part III

OVERVIEW

Because the past decade has seen a proliferation of early childhood programs, considerable attention is given in Part III to the successful administration of these programs. The quality of administration that is provided in any early childhood program is basic to the effective and efficient functioning of the program and, as a result, the creation of early childhood centers that can better serve the nation's children. Integration of theory and research, along with practical material, is included in Part III in order to aid the modern early childhood administration toward unifying theory and practice in daily administrative activities.

In addition, this section is an attempt at providing the early childhood administrator with information about some of the tools and techniques by which an administrator can best achieve the stated goals of his center. Attention has been directed at including readings from business administration as well as educational administration in an attempt at offering the reader a global view of the administrative process. Readers may want to consider the arrangement of the articles in Part III as an aid in developing a systematic process of administration.

RENÉE YABLANS-MAGID
31. The Process of Administering Early Childhood Programs

Much has been written in the past decade regarding the importance of the child's early years. New research and a new body of knowledge have prompted the growth of early childhood programs at an exponential rate. These programs have been launched in churches and synagogues, in storefronts, in the basements of city housing projects, in private homes, in elaborately built structures, in hospitals and factories, in public schools, and in state and federal facilities. In many instances, it appears as though the individuals involved with early childhood programs felt that the mere desire for establishing an early childhood center was all that was necessary for the success of the center and its program. Little attention has been paid to the importance of the process of administering an early childhood center and to the positive results of effective administration. The purpose of this article is to provide the new early childhood administrator with an overview of the administrative process and of the importance of this process to the success of the program.

At the heart of the administrative process are people, and the success of an administrator is founded on getting things accomplished through people. The tools of the administrator are those of planning, operating, and evaluating the program in order to provide the best quality care and education of young children. The process of effective administration requires a dynamic administrator and reflects the leadership dimension of that individual. Administrators may adopt a variety of leadership behavior, from democratic to autocratic behavior. The important consideration for an administrator is to recognize that no single leadership pattern is a panacea. The wise administrator recognizes the need to select a leadership pattern, namely, a way of behaving within the group that feels comfortable and is appropriate to the situation and the people involved.

The tools of administration—planning, operating, and evaluating— must be an ongoing process. An administrator cannot assume that when a particular administrative function is completed, it can then be forgotten. In the real world, events occur not in simplistic terms nor merely on paper, but with the speed of lightning and with anything but simplicity. Unless the effective administrator recognizes the need to monitor consciously and carefully the ongoing process of planning, operating, and evaluating the program, confusion may be the result, and the success of the center will be diminished.

"Failing to plan means planning to fail." Planning is the primary ingredient in the administrative process, because it determines the nature of all other functions that will follow. The planning function involves the development of five major components, the first of which is a long hard look at the purpose or need for an early childhood program in the community of your choice. In other words, why institute a center? Why bother? Ask yourself these all-important questions before you as an administrator go one step farther:

1. Does the community need an early childhood program?
2. Does the community need a different type of early childhood program?
3. Do present societal conditions demand an early childhood program in the particular community?

In searching for answers to the above questions, utilize every available source of information at your disposal: public schools, news media, religious organizations, people residing within the community, community leaders, census reports, local business leaders, local and state early childhood organizations. At the conclusion of this process, the answers will be different for each individual but certainly founded on the knowledge that the optimum growth and development of all children is important.

Once an individual has established the need and/or the purpose for an early childhood center, the second step is the development and commitment to a personal philosophy of early childhood education. This is nothing more than stating what you believe about how young children develop, how and in what type of environment they best learn. Once the above questions have been explored and answered to your personal satisfaction, you can then formulate your plans for the future.

The third step in the planning process demands a well-defined plan of action that will help you achieve your purpose. This is not to be confused with methodology. A plan of action is a statement of meaningful goals and objectives that are further extensions of one's philosophy and are more closely defined. Having a well-defined philosophy is useless if you do not have goals and objectives that reflect this philosophy. Perhaps you find you cannot meet all of your stated goals and objectives. Perhaps the situation is altered by imposed limitations, such as a lack of money, time, or facilities. Do these conditions indicate that the initial plan of action was ineffective? Not necessarily. One must remember that an effective administrator recognizes the need for an ongoing planning process, and it is this ongoing process that allows for necessary adjustments when and where appropriate. In this era of rapid change, the ability to adapt to a changed situation and to resist the pain of change allows an administrator to maintain a realistic but positive perspective of where his/her program is heading.

The fourth step in the planning function is the development of written policies and procedures. Remember, you have spent much time in developing goals and objectives, but without clear-cut policy and procedure statements as a guide to defining the future direction and intent of your program, you, as an administrator, may constantly find that you are spending precious time in "fighting fires" instead of administering a healthy program. Establishing policies and procedures is not intended as a lesson in extraneous paperwork but should provide a deliberate attempt at moving toward your objectives.

Policies and procedures are especially important when applied to those areas that continually occur in the administration of a center, such as admissions policies, health and safety policies, and personnel policies. Well-written policies can provide for an optimum socio-emotional climate, one where all staff members are aware of the expectations of the administration and one where people have a greater understanding of the rules and regulations governing the center. Policies and procedures can allow an administrator to be more systematic in budgeting and using precious time.

The fifth step in the planning function, often overlooked as significant in the planning process, is managing the budget. "Budget has been defined as telling money where to go rather than where it went" (Fulmer, 1974, p. 171). It is naive to believe that even the smallest early childhood center does not require a budget. In a time of inflation, rising costs, and increased shortage of materials, it may in fact be more difficult to manage a budget. However, it becomes more crucial that the dynamic administrator pay particular attention to budgeting on a systematic basis. A budget can be managed if an administrator is continually aware of the needs of staff and children and keeps accurate records of where funds are going.

For an administrator, the greatest challenge in the planning process is being able to utilize effectively all the resources that are available. All early childhood centers, regardless of size, reflect the effort of more than one individual; therefore, planning must include the cooperative effort of all persons involved with the program. The successful administrator, when involved in the planning process, needs to be secure enough to accept the variety of ideas and experiences of staff, parents, children, and other community persons.

Probably the most exciting part of an administrator's responsibility is operating a carefully planned early childhood program. The administrator can integrate the theories of administration with the practical aspects of administration. He or she can implement the plan and organize the program. At this point, the dynamics of working with people toward a common purpose is at its best. As Peter Drucker (1946, p. 26) has said, "An institution is like a tune; it is not constituted by individual sounds, but by the relations between them."

How often have you walked into an early childhood center filled with children and immediately known that good things for children were happening? This experience resulted from careful organization, selective staff recruitment and development, and the adoption of a curriculum designed to benefit children. The administrator who believes that good education doesn't just happen but is made to happen can create a program where people do feel instant pleasure and where children can feel worthwhile and successful.

In order to utilize efficiently the human resources within your program, it is vital to organize your program. In all institutions, organization charts are useful, for they are an attempt to represent reality on paper.

However, the administrator who allows a simple line drawing to guide him/her through daily activities may not always attain the desired results. An organization chart, when clearly defined and understood, tells a good deal about an early childhood center to the people involved in the program. Organization charts should depict

1. A way of dividing up tasks to be accomplished.
2. Responsibility for tasks.
3. One means of communication.
4. Authority for decision making.
5. Relationships within the program.
6. The uniqueness of the program.

Organization charts are not intended to

1. Box people in and limit freedom.
2. Create a static program status.
3. Be different from the planned program objectives.

The organization chart is a helpful tool in achieving program objectives, in allocating time, and in spelling out responsibilities. It must never be a replacement for effective, ongoing communication and the development of all-important interpersonal relationships with all individuals involved in the program. The organization chart is an important tool for everyone in the organization: administrators, teachers' aids, volunteers, cooks, and janitors, but it is not the blueprint that makes the program hang together.

What in fact does allow a program to hang together? It is that factor noted earlier in this article: people! The "people factor" is that special ingredient that makes each program a unique one. The "people factor" begins with the planning function, is carried through the operating function, and is involved in the evaluation process. How does the "people factor" affect the administrative process?

The "people factor" begins from the moment an administrator selects the staff. The kind of program the administrator views as all-important for children will determine the people who are recruited, selected, and retained. The person with a long list of degrees and impressive credentials may in fact not be the best person for the job. It is important to select staff members who understand and agree with the philosophy that is compatible with that of the early childhood center and who appear as though they can easily work together with the parents of the children enrolled in the program, with you, the administrator, and with other staff members. An administrator has a responsibility to select staff members who can succeed within the program and, in turn, make the program successful. This is accomplished through an ongoing process of staff development, cooperation, guidance and, acceptance of the unique qualities of all people.

Staff development can be viewed as a nonthreatening procedure if it begins on the day a person is selected for a position. Honest job interview techniques are essential. When people know what is expected of them, the emotional and educational climate is set for a supporting, honest, ongoing relationship. Staff development should not be an isolated function reserved only for a few occasions designated on your personal calendar. In fact, staff development occurs each day that an administrator and staff member work together. Staff development can be appreciated when an administrator is genuine and authentic in relationships with other people. Supportive and accepting feelings should be the nature of all adult relationships. It is expected that this attitude will then be extended to the adult-child relationships within the program.

The administrator as the educational leader must respond to many and varied situations that arise on a daily basis in any early childhood center. It is naive to expect that problems will rarely occur and that an administrator will always respond with the correct solution. However, it is this writer's opinion that the number of people problems can be decreased when open and honest relationships are a vital part of the staff development function.

Up to now, the discussion of relationships has primarily dealt with administrator-staff relationships. Little has been said about parents, parent involvement, and parent-school relationships. The administrator and the staff must never minimize the importance of the role parents play within the total early childhood program. Parents are a natural resource of any program and should be valued. Parents, administrators, and staff all share a common bond, that of attempting to provide the very best education for young children. Some parents may want to be directly involved in the daily activities of the center, some may not, and others may indicate a lack of time or ability. Provisions must be made within the program's objectives to include all parents in some way. Ira Gordon (1969, p. 178) indicates a number of ways parents can be involved in early childhood programs:

1. Parents as an audience in conferences, newsletters, workshops, seminars, and so on.
2. Parents as a reference. All parents can provide important information regarding their child.
3. Parents as teachers in the home.
4. Parents as volunteers in the classroom.
5. Parents as trained, paid aids.
6. Parents as part of the decision-making body.

As we noted in the discussion of the administrator's function, staff relationships, initial impressions, and contacts are important. Parents, too, should always be respected, valued, and treated with the same open, honest approach. An effective administrator must maintain a balance and continuity in all relationships, a task not easily accomplished but well worth the effort.

In discussing the administrative process, much emphasis has been placed on the tools and techniques that the administrator must possess to get the job done. In fact, at times the administrative process appears to be mechanical. However, the reader needs to be reminded that the tools of the administrator—planning, operating, and evaluating—are irrelevant if they do not help to build "a children's place" where children are thought of first and where the development of children is enhanced in a meaningful way.

Therefore, the development of a curriculum in the administrative process is crucial but not difficult if the administrator remembers the following points:

1. What is the philosophy of the program?
2. What are the goals and objectives unique to the program being administered?
3. How will the program best meet the needs of the children in a particular community?

With the above goals firmly in mind, the decisions regarding curriculum become a natural conclusion in the planning and operating process. The daily activities, the variety of experiences, the layout of the classroom, the involvement of teachers, aids, and volunteers, the availability of children's materials, the scheduling of activities, and the role of the children in the total program—all are part of the process of attempting to achieve desired program goals and objectives and contribute to the optimum learning experience for children.

Evaluation is an inherent part of the administrative process and a logical conclusion in the discussion of administration. It is essential that readers view evaluation as a growth process, one of creating opportunities for novel, innovative, and better ways to administer an early childhood center. Evaluation is not only an integral part of the ongoing administrative process but a means of providing everyone in the early childhood program with an opportunity to analyze the philosophy, goals, and objectives of the program in light of current conditions. Once again, all people in the program have an opportunity to gather new information and new evidence to help establish priorities, permit new value judgments, communicate the future of the program, and honestly assess the growth and development of the children and staff. This approach to evaluation encourages active participation on the part of teachers, parents, volunteers, aids, and children. It is this active participation that helps to confirm feelings of trust, openness, honesty, and a commitment to quality early childhood education.

Evaluation is also a means of coping with change, an inevitable component of our culture and the one constant in present-day society. Evaluation is not a means of avoiding new techniques, allowing a stagnant program to create a negative climate, or making comparisons for no logical reason. Evaluation should go beyond just measurement and statistics, those familiar components that in the past have often confused the evaluation process and in many circumstances turned evaluation into a negative process. As the reader can observe, evaluation is best seen as a beginning rather than an end. Evaluation is the component that can allow for renewal of the administrative process.

REFERENCES

Butler, Annie L. *Early Childhood Education: Planning and Administering Programs.* New York: D. Van Nostrand, 1975.

Castetter, William B. *Administering the School Personnel Program.* New York: Macmillan, 1968.

Decker, Celia A., and Decker, John R. *Planning and Administering Early Childhood Programs.* Ohio: Charles E. Merrill, 1976.

Drucker, Peter F. *Concept of the Corporation.* New York: John Day, 1946.

Drucker, Peter F. *The Practice of Management.* New York: Harper & Row, 1976.

Fulmer, Robert M. *The New Management.* New York: Macmillan, 1974.

Goode, John M. (Ed.) *Readings in Education Management.* New York:American Management Association, 1973.

Gordon, Ira. Developing parent power in E. Grotberg (Ed.) *Critical Issues in Research Related to Disadvantaged Children.* Princeton, N.J.: Educational Testing Service, 1969.

Koontz, Harold, O'Donnell, Cyril O. *Principles of Management,* 5th Ed. New York: McGraw-Hill, 1972.

Parker, Ronald K. *The Preschool in Action.* Boston: Allyn & Bacon, 1972.

THE PLANNING PROCESS

Planning is the critical factor in administration and the primary task of the early childhood administrator. Planning is that administrative function that helps to determine in advance what needs to be accomplished. It consists of determining one's philosophy, setting short- and long-range objectives, developing policies and procedures to achieve the goals, and utilizing the vast quantity of human resources at the administrator's disposal. Logically, planning is the initial stage in the administrative process, but revisions should be made as often as alternative courses of action demand.

The administrator is the key individual in the planning function. He is responsible for making things happen. An effective administrator makes things happen by exercising competent leadership. In the reading by Tannenbaum and Schmidt, the authors stress the importance of a leader who not only knows himself but who is also flexible and can adapt his leadership skill and style to meet the needs of a particular situation and group. McAfee's article acknowledges the importance of the leader's role but also stresses the importance of involving many individuals in the planning process—parents, volunteers, teachers, and children.

Planning demands a wide variety of considerations: Determining one's philosophy, scheduling, establishing regulations, budgeting, and making policy. With these important areas in mind, the reader will be wise to look carefully at the articles by Weber, the Deckers, Butler, and Bogue and Saunders.

The reader will not find a cookbook for planning success in this chapter; instead the reader will discover some necessary ingredients for developing a basic framework for planning that will allow the new administrator to develop an individual plan, because, unlike any other center, each early childhood center is a unique combination of program, children, administration, and all personnel.

ROBERT TANNENBAUM and WARREN H. SCHMIDT

32. How to Choose a Leadership Pattern

- "I put most problems into my group's hands and leave it to them to carry the ball from there. I serve merely as a catalyst, mirroring back the people's thoughts and feelings so that they can better understand them."
- "It's foolish to make decisions oneself on matters that affect people. I always talk things over with my subordinates, but I make it clear to them that I'm the one who has to have the final say."
- "Once I have decided on a course of action, I do my best to sell my ideas to my employees."
- "I'm being paid to lead. If I let a lot of other people make the decisions I should be making, then I'm not worth my salt."
- "I believe in getting things done. I can't waste time calling meetings. Someone has to call the shots around here, and I think it should be me."

Each of these statements represents a point of view about "good leadership." Considerable experience, factual data, and theorectical principles could be cited to support each statement, even though they seem to be inconsistent when placed together. Such contradictions point up the dilemma in which the modern manager frequently finds himself.

NEW PROBLEM

The problem of how the modern manager can be "democratic" in his relations with subordinates and at the same time maintain the necessary authority and control in the organization for which he is responsible has come into focus increasingly in recent years.

Earlier in the century this problem was not so acutely felt. The successful executive was generally pictured as possessing intelligence, imagination, initiative, the capacity to make rapid (and generally wise) decisions, and the ability to inspire subordinates. People tended to think of the world as being divided into "leaders" and "followers."

NEW FOCUS

Gradually, however, from the social sciences emerged the concept of "group dynamics" with its focus on *members* of the group rather than solely on the leader. Research efforts of social scientists underscored the

Robert Tannenbaum and Warren H. Schmidt, "How to Choose a Leadership Pattern," *Harvard Business Review*, March–April 1958, Copyright © 1958 by the President and Fellows of Harvard College; all rights reserved.

350

importance of employee involvement and participation in decision making. Evidence began to challenge the efficiency of highly directive leadership, and increasing attention was paid to problems of motivation and human relations.

Through training laboratories in group development that sprang up across the country, many of the newer notions of leadership began to exert an impact. These training laboratories were carefully designed to give people a firsthand experience in full participation and decision making. The designated "leaders" deliberately attempted to reduce their own power and to make group members as responsible as possible for setting their own goals and methods within the laboratory experiences.

It was perhaps inevitable that some of the people who attended the training laboratories regarded this kind of leadership as being truly "democratic" and went home with the determination to build fully participative decision making into their own organizations. When ever their bosses made a decision without convening a staff meeting, they tended to perceive this as authoritarian behavior. The true symbol of democratic leadership to some was the meeting—and the less directed from the top, the more democratic it was.

Some of the more enthusiastic alumni of these training laboratories began to get the habit of categorizing leader behavior as "democratic" or "authoritarian." The boss who made too many decisions himself was thought of as an authoritarian, and his directive behavior was often attributed solely to his personality.

NEW NEED

The net result of the research findings and of the human relations training based upon them has been to call into question the stereotype of an effective leader. Consequently, the modern manager often finds himself in an uncomfortable state of mind.

Often he is not quite sure of how to behave; there are times when he is torn between exerting "strong" leadership and "permissive" leadership. Sometimes new knowledge pushes him in one direction ("I should really get the group to help make this decision"), but at the same time his experience pushes him in another direction ("I really understand the problem better than the group and therefore I should make the decision"). He is not sure when a group decision is really appropriate or when holding a staff meeting serves merely as a device for avoiding his own decision-making responsibility.

The purpose of our article is to suggest a framework which managers may find useful in grappling with this dilemma. First we shall look at the different patterns of leadership behavior that the manager can choose from in relating himself to his subordinates. Then we shall turn to some of the questions suggested by this range of patterns. For instance, how important is it for a manager's subordinates to know what type of leadership he is using in a situation? What factors should he consider in deciding on a leadership pattern? What difference do his long-run objectives make as compared to his immediate objectives?

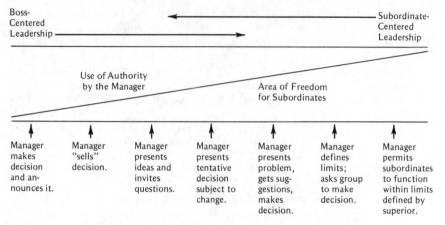

| Boss-Centered Leadership | | | | | | Subordinate-Centered Leadership |

Exhibit 1. Continuum of leadership behavior.

RANGE OF BEHAVIOR

Exhibit 1 presents the continuum or range of possible leadership behavior available to a manager. Each type of action is related to the degree of authority used by the boss and to the amount of freedom available to his subordinates in reaching decisions. The actions seen on the extreme left characterize the manager who maintains a high degree of control while those seen on the extreme right characterize the manager who releases a high degree of control. Neither extreme is absolute; authority and freedom are never without their limitations.

Now let us look more closely at each of the behavior points occurring along this continuum:

- *The manager makes the decision and announces it.* In this case the boss identifies a problem, considers alternative solutions, chooses one of them, and then reports this decision to his subordinates for implementation. He may or may not give consideration to what he believes his subordinates will think or feel about his decision; in any case, he provides no opportunity for them to participate directly in the decision-making process. Coercion may or may not be used or implied.
- *The manager "sells" his decision.* Here the manager, as before, takes responsibility for identifying the problem and arriving at a decision. However, rather than simply announcing it, he takes the additional step of persuading his subordinates to accept it. In doing so, he recognizes the possibility of some resistance among those who will be faced with the decision, and seeks to reduce this resistance by indicating, for example, what the employees have to gain from his decision.
- *The manager presents his ideas, invites questions.* Here the boss who has arrived at a decision and who seeks acceptance of his ideas provides an opportunity for his subordinates to get a fuller explanation of his thinking and his intentions. After presenting the ideas, he invites

questions so that his associates can better understand what he is trying to accomplish. This "give and take" also enables the manager and the subordinates to explore more fully the implications of the decision.

- *The manager presents a tentative decision subject to change.* This kind of behavior permits the subordinates to exert some influence on the decision. The initiative for identifying and diagnosing the problem remains with the boss. Before meeting with his staff, he has thought the problem through and arrived at a decision—but only a tentative one. Before finalizing it, he presents his proposed solution for the reaction of those who will be affected by it. He says in effect, "I'd like to hear what you have to say about this plan that I have developed. I'll appreciate your frank reactions, but will reserve for myself the final decision."

- *The manager presents the problem, gets suggestions, and then makes his decision.* Up to this point the boss has come before the group with a solution of his own. Not so in this case. The subordinates now get the first chance to suggest solutions. The manager's initial role involves identifying the problem. He might, for example, say something of this sort: "We are faced with a number of complaints from newspapers and the general public on our service policy. What is wrong here? What ideas do you have for coming to grips with this problem?"

The function of the group becomes one of increasing the manager's repertory of possible solutions to the problem. The purpose is to capitalize on the knowledge and experience of those who are on the "firing line." From the expanded list of alternatives developed by the manager and his subordinates, the manager then selects the solution that he regards as most promising.[1]

- *The manager defines the limits and requests the group to make a decision.* At this point the manager passes to the group (possibly including himself as a member) the right to make decisions. Before doing so, however, he defines the problem to be solved and the boundaries within which the decision must be made.

  An example might be the handling of a parking problem at a plant. The boss decides that this is something that should be worked on by the people involved, so he calls them together and points up the existence of the problem. Then he tells them:

There is the open field just north of the main plant which has been designated for additional employee parking. We can build underground or surface multi-level facilities as long as the cost does not exceed $100,000. Within these limits we are free to work out whatever solution makes sense to us. After we decide on a specific plan, the company will spend the available money in whatever way we indicate.

---

[1]For a fuller explanation of this approach, see Leo Moore, "Too Much Management, Too Little Change," HBR January–February 1956, p. 41.

- *The manager permits the group to make decisions within prescribed limits.* This represents an extreme degree of group freedom only occasionally encountered in formal organizations, as, for instance, in many research groups. Here the team of managers or engineers undertakes the identification and diagnosis of the problem, develops alternative procedures for solving it, and decides on one or more of these alternative solutions. The only limits directly imposed on the group by the organization are those specified by the superior of the team's boss. If the boss participates in the decision-making process, he attempts to do so with no more authority than any other member of the group. He commits himself in advance to assist in implementing whatever decision the group makes.

KEY QUESTIONS

As the continuum in Exhibit I demonstrates, there are a number of alternative ways in which a manager can relate himself to the group or individuals he is supervising. At the extreme left of the range, the emphasis is on the manager—on what *he* is interested in, how *he* sees things, how *he* feels about them. As we move toward the subordinate-centered end of the continuum, however, the focus is increasingly on the subordinates—on what *they* are interested in, how *they* look at things, how *they* feel about them.

When business leadership is regarded in this way, a number of questions arise. Let us take four of especial importance:

- *Can a boss ever relinquish his responsibility by delegating it to someone else?* Our view is that the manager must expect to be held responsible by his superior for the quality of the decisions made, even though operationally these decisions may have been made on a group basis. He should, therefore, be ready to accept whatever risk is involved whenever he delegates decision-making power to his subordinates. Delegation is not a way of "passing the buck." Also, it should be emphasized that the amount of freedom the boss gives to his subordinates cannot be greater than the freedom which he himself has been given by his own superior.
- *Should the manager participate with his subordinates once he has delegated responsibility to them?* The manager should carefully think over this question and decide on his role prior to involving the subordinate group. He should ask if his presence will inhibit or facilitate the problem-solving process. There may be some instances when he should leave the group to let it solve the problem for itself. Typically, however, the boss has useful ideas to contribute, and should function as an additional member of the group. In the latter instance, it is important that he indicate clearly to the group that he sees himself in a *member* role rather than in an authority role.
- *How important is it for the group to recognize what kind of leadership behavior the boss is using?* It makes a great deal of difference.

Many relationship problems between boss and subordinate occur because the boss fails to make clear how he plans to use his authority. If, for example, he actually intends to make a certain decision himself, but the subordinate group gets the impression that he has delegated this authority, considerable confusion and resentment are likely to follow. Problems may also occur when the boss uses a "democratic" facade to conceal the fact that he has already made a decision which he hopes the group will accept as its own. The attempt to "make them think it was their idea in the first place" is a risky one. We believe that it is highly important for the manager to be honest and clear in describing what authority he is keeping and what role he is asking his subordinates to assume in solving a particular problem.

- *Can you tell how "democratic" a manager is by the number of decisions his subordinates make?* The sheer *number* of decisions is not an accurate index of the amount of freedom that a subordinate group enjoys. More important is the *significance* of the decisions which the boss entrusts to his subordinates. Obviously a decision on how to arrange desks is of an entirely different order from a decision involving the introduction of new electronic data-processing equipment. Even though the widest possible limits are given in dealing with the first issue, the group will sense no particular degree of responsibility. For a boss to permit the group to decide equipment policy, even within rather narrow limits, would reflect a greater degree of confidence in them on his part.

DECIDING HOW TO LEAD

Now let us turn from the types of leadership that are possible in a company situation to the question of what types are *practical* and *desirable*. What factors or forces should a manager consider in deciding how to manage? Three are of particular importance:

- Forces in the manager.
- Forces in the subordinates.
- Forces in the situation.

We should like briefly to describe these elements and indicate how they might influence a manager's action in a decision-making situation.[2] The strength of each of them will, of course, vary from instance to instance, but the manager who is sensitive to them can better assess the problems which face him and determine which mode of leadership behavior is most appropriate for him.

Forces in the Manager

The manager's behavior in any given instance will be influenced greatly by the many forces operating within his own personality. He will, of

[2]See also Robert Tannenbaum and Fred Massarik, "Participation by Subordinates in the Managerial Decision-Making Process," *Canadian Journal of Economics and Political Science*, August 1950, pp. 413–418.

course, perceive his leadership problems in a unique way on the basis of his background, knowledge, and experience. Among the important internal forces affecting him will be the following:

1. *His value system.* How strongly does he feel that individuals should have a share in making the decisions which affect them? Or, how convinced is he that the official who is paid to assume responsibility should personally carry the burden of decision making? The strength of his convictions on questions like these will tend to move the manager to one end or the other of the continuum shown in Exhibit I. His behavior will also be influenced by the relative importance that he attaches to organizational efficiency, personal growth of subordinates, and company profits.[3]
2. *His confidence in his subordinates.* Managers differ greatly in the amount of trust they have in other people generally, and this carries over to the particular employees they supervise at a given time. In viewing his particular group of subordinates, the manager is likely to consider their knowledge and competence with respect to the problem. A central question he might ask himself is: "Who is best qualified to deal with this problem?" Often he may, justifiably or not, have more confidence in his own capabilities than in those of his subordinates.
3. *His own leadership inclinations.* There are some managers who seem to function more comfortably and naturally as highly directive leaders. Resolving problems and issuing orders come easily to them. Other managers seem to operate more comfortably in a team role, where they are continually sharing many of their functions with their subordinates.
4. *His feelings of security in an uncertain situation.* The manager who releases control over the decision-making process thereby reduces the predictability of the outcome. Some managers have a greater need than others for predictability and stability in their environment. This "tolerance for ambiguity" is being viewed increasingly by psychologists as a key variable in a person's manner of dealing with problems.

The manager brings these and other highly personal variables to each situation he faces. If he can see them as forces which, consciously or unconsciously, influence his behavior, he can better understand what makes him prefer to act in a given way. And understanding this, he can often make himself more effective.

Forces in the Subordinate

Before deciding how to lead a certain group, the manager will also want to consider a number of forces affecting his subordinates' behavior. He will want to remember that each employee, like himself, is influenced by many personality variables. In addition, each subordinate has a set of

[3]See Chris Argyris, "Top Management Dilemma: Company Needs vs. Individual Development," *Pesonnel*, September 1955, pp 123–134.

expectations about how the boss should act in relation to him (the phrase "expected behavior" is one we hear more and more often these days at discussions of leadership and teaching). The better the manager understands these factors, the more accurately he can determine what kind of behavior on his part will enable his subordinates to act more effectively.

Generally speaking, the manager can permit his subordinates greater freedom if the following essential conditions exist:

● If the subordinates have relatively high needs for independence. (As we all know, people differ greatly in the amount of direction that they desire.)
● If the subordinates have a readiness to assume responsibility for decision making. (Some see additional responsibility as a tribute to their ability; others see it as "passing the buck.")
● If they have a relatively high tolerance for ambiguity. (Some employees prefer to have clear-cut directives given to them; others prefer a wider area of freedom.)
● If they are interested in the problem and feel that it is important.
● If they understand and identify with the goals of the organization.
● If they have the necessary knowledge and experience to deal with the problem.
● If they have learned to expect to share in decision making. (Persons who have come to expect strong leadership and are then suddenly confronted with the request to share more fully in decision making are often upset by this new experience. On the other hand, persons who have enjoyed a considerable amount of freedom resent the boss who begins to make all the decisions himself.)

The manager will probably tend to make fuller use of his own authority if the above conditions do *not* exist; at times there may be no realistic alternative to running a "one-man show."

The restrictive effect of many of the forces will, of course, be greatly modified by the general feeling of confidence which subordinates have in the boss. Where they have learned to respect and trust him, he is free to vary his behavior. He will feel certain that he will not be perceived as an authoritarian boss on those occasions when he makes decisions by himself. Similarly, he will not be seen as using staff meetings to avoid his decision-making responsibility. In a climate of mutual confidence and respect, people tend to feel less threatened by deviations from normal practice, which in turn makes possible a higher degree of flexibility in the whole relationship.

Forces in the Situation

In addition to the forces which exist in the manager himself and in his subordinates, certain characteristics of the general situation will also affect the manager's behavior. Among the more critical environmental pressures that surround him are those which stem from the organization, the work group, the nature of the problem, and the pressures of time. Let us look briefly at each of these:

Type of Organization

Like individuals, organizations have values and traditions which inevitably influence the behavior of the people who work in them. The manager who is a newcomer to a company quickly discovers that certain kinds of behavior are approved while others are not. He also discovers that to deviate radically from what is generally accepted is likely to create problems for him.

These values and traditions are communicated in many ways—through job descriptions, policy pronouncements, and public statements by top executives. Some organizations, for example, hold to the notion that the desirable executive is one who is dynamic, imaginative, decisive, and persuasive. Other organizations put more emphasis upon the importance of the executive's ability to work effectively with people—his human relations skills. The fact that his superiors have a defined concept of what the good executive should be will very likely push the manager toward one end or the other of the behavioral range.

In addition to the above, the amount of employee participation is influenced by such variables as the size of the working units, their geographical distribution, and the degree of inter- and intra-organizational security required to attain company goals. For example, the wide geographical dispersion of an organization may preclude a practical system of participative decision making, even though this would otherwise be desirable. Similarly, the size of the working units or the need for keeping plans confidential may make it necessary for the boss to exercise more control than would otherwise be the case. Factors like these may limit considerably the manager's ability to function flexibly on the continuum.

Group Effectiveness

Before turning decision-making responsibility over to a subordinate group, the boss should consider how effectively its members work together as a unit.

One of the relevant factors here is the experience the group has had in working together. It can generally be expected that a group which has functioned for some time will have developed habits of cooperation and thus be able to tackle a problem more effectively than a new group. It can also be expected that a group of people with similar backgrounds and interests will work more quickly and easily than people with dissimilar backgrounds, because the communication problems are likely to be less complex.

The degree of confidence that the members have in their ability to solve problems as a group is also a key consideration. Finally, such group variables as cohesiveness, permissiveness, mutual acceptance, and commonality of purpose will exert subtle but powerful influence on the group's functioning.

The Problem Itself

The nature of the problem may determine what degree of authority should be delegated by the manager to his subordinates. Obviously he will ask himself whether they have the kind of knowledge which is needed. It is possible to do them a real disservice by assigning a problem that their experience does not equip them to handle.

Since the problems faced in large or growing industries increasingly require knowledge of specialists from many different fields, it might be inferred that the more complex a problem, the more anxious a manager will be to get some assistance in solving it. However, this is not always the case. There will be times when the very complexity of the problem calls fòr one person to work it out. For example, if the manager has most of the background and factual data relevant to a given issue, it may be easier for him to think it through himself than to take the time to fill in his staff on all the pertinent background information.

The key question to ask, of course, is: "Have I heard the ideas of everyone who has the necessary knowledge to make a significant contribution to the solution of this problem?"

The Pressure of Time

This is perhaps the most clearly felt pressure on the manager (in spite of the fact that it may sometimes be imagined). The more that he feels the need for an immediate decision, the more difficult it is to involve other people. In organizations which are in a constant state of "crisis" and "crash programming" one is likely to find managers personally using a high degree of authority with relatively little delegation to subordinates. When the time pressure is less intense, however, it becomes much more possible to bring subordinates in on the decision-making process.

These, then, are the principal forces that impinge on the manager in any given instance and that tend to determine his tactical behavior in relation to his subordinates. In each case his behavior ideally will be that which makes possible the most effective attainment of his immediate goal within the limits facing him.

LONG-RUN STRATEGY

As the manager works with his organization on the problems that come up day by day, his choice of a leadership pattern is usually limited. He must take account of the forces just described and, within the restrictions they impose on him, do the best that he can. But as he looks ahead months even years, he can shift his thinking from tactics to large-scale strategy. No longer need he be fettered by all of the forces mentioned, for he can view many of them as variables over which he has some control. He can, for example, gain new insights or skills for himself, supply training for individual subordinates, and provide participative experiences for his employee group.

In trying to bring about a change in these variables, however, he is faced with a challenging question: At which point along the continuum *should* he act?

Attaining Objectives

The answer depends largely on what he wants to accomplish. Let us suppose that he is interested in the same objectives that most modern managers seek to attain when they can shift their attention from the pressure of immediate assignments:

1. To raise the level of employee motivation.
2. To increase the readiness of subordinates to accept change.
3. To improve the quality of all managerial decisions.
4. To develop teamwork and morale.
5. To further the individual development of employees.

In recent years the manager has been deluged with a flow of advice on how best to achieve these longer-run objectives. It is little wonder that he is often both bewildered and annoyed. However, there are some guidelines which he can usefully follow in making a decision.

Most research and much of the experience of recent years give a strong factual basis to the theory that a fairly high degree of subordinate-centered behavior is associated with the accomplishment of the five purposes mentioned.[4] This does not mean that a manager should always leave all decisions to his assistants. To provide the individual or the group with greater freedom than they are ready for at any given time may very well tend to generate anxieties and therefore inhibit rather than facilitate the attainment of desired objectives. But this should not keep the manager from making a continuing effort to confront his subordinates with the challenge of freedom.

CONCLUSION

In summary, there are two implications in the basic thesis that we have been developing. The first is that the successful leader is one who is keenly aware of those forces which are most relevant to his behavior at any given time. He accurately understands himself, the individuals and group he is dealing with, and the company and broader social environment in which he operates. And certainly he is able to assess the present readiness for growth of his subordinates.

But this sensitivity or understanding is not enough, which brings us to the second implication. The successful leader is one who is able to be-

---

[4]For example, see Warren H. Schmidt and Paul C. Buchanan, *Techniques that Produce Teamwork* (New London, Arthur C. Croft Publications, 1954); and Morris S. Viteles, *Motivation and Morale in Industry* (New York, W. W. Norton & Company, Inc., 1953).

have appropriately in the light of these perceptions. If direction is in order, he is able to direct; if considerable participative freedom is called for, he is able to provide such freedom.

Thus, the successful manager of men can be primarily characterized neither as a strong leader nor as a permissive one. Rather, he is one who maintains a high batting average in accurately assessing the forces that determine what his most appropriate behavior at any given time should be and in actually being able to behave accordingly. Being both insightful and flexible, he is less likely to see the problems of leadership as a dilemma.

ORALIE McAFEE

33. Planning the Preschool Program

A suitable curriculum for early childhood education cannot be contained in a workbook, textbook, kit or program guide. It must be planned by the teacher or teachers with the needs of a particular group, and the particular children in the group, in mind.

To some, written plans have the taint of rigidity and regimentation, antithetical to the notion of a curriculum based on children's interests and needs. And of course they can be if slavishly followed or used as a "course of study" which is identical from year to year.

However, the thesis of this article is that written plans, properly prepared and flexibly used, are a useful tool to make the early childhood classroom function more smoothly and purposefully. For the role of the teacher has changed and is still changing. As parents, volunteers, students, paraprofessional assistants, cooks, nurses, researchers and special consultants become a part of the classroom team, it is the teacher who has the final responsibility for utilizing these human resources in a way that will be of maximum benefit to children. Written plans can help achieve this goal. No matter how well formulated are the plans in the teacher's mind, they are difficult for others to follow. And in all honesty,

Reprinted by permission, from *Curriculum Is What Happens: Planning Is the Key*, edited by L. L. Dittmann. rev. ed. Copyright © 1977, National Association for the Education of Young Children, 1834 Connecticut Avenue, N.W., Washington, DC 20009.

we as teachers must admit that the discipline of *advance* planning is likely to result in *better* planning.

In the following discussion, the teacher is referred to as the planner, since it is usually the teacher who pulls suggestions, needs and insights into an operational form. However, all regular members of the classroom team should be involved as much as feasible.

FORM OF ORGANIZATION

Use any form of organization that works. Teachers and assistants may want to experiment with several types and will probably decide to use a combination. Plans may be organized:

Around the primary responsibility of the adults.

- Miss James will be responsible for snacks and art.
- Mr. Valdez will be responsible for the block area and science center (magnifying and reducing lenses today).

Around areas of interest centers in the room.

- In the block area, the transportation equipment will be out—add new airplanes.
- In the art area, give children choice of red or blue paper for pasting, have scissors and scraps out for collage.
- In the reading-listening area, *The Carrot Seed* book and record. Have carrot seeds and carrots there to look at. Recall having carrots for lunch yesterday.

Around blocks of time.

- From 9:00 until 10:30, there will be available:
Chalk and chalkboards for drawing.
Blocks.
Dramatic play (add new hats, put hand mirror close by).
Hammer boards.
New picture books from library (put table close).
Nesting cups—spread on floor ordered according to size.
    If children stack, help them count, talk about
    largest and smallest, top and bottom.
Colored cubes—partially sort according to color, see if children "catch on."

Around the stated objectives of the school.

- Self-awareness (two metal hand mirrors out near "dress-ups"; use with "I See You" song at snack time).

362

- Expressing feelings and ideas through art media (brush painting, red, yellow and blue paint available).
- Developing language skills (with interested children, place "Gumby" in various locations; have the children say where he is: "Under the bookshelf," "Behind Willie").

Each of these has some advantages and disadvantages. Organizing around objectives, for example, keeps one focused on goals, but gives little guidance on "who will do what, when shall we do it, and how shall we manage the day." A workable combination is to start with blocks of time. Within those, plan what activities will be emphasized in each area and which adult will probably be responsible for supervision and interaction. Usually those activities that are listed are in addition to, or a variation on, the activities and equipment that are "standard." Periodic review of objectives during planning will keep long range goals in mind; a brief listing on the plans of short range goals will show how these are being implemented.

Regardless of the type of organization used, several important elements must be considered as planning begins.

CONSIDERATIONS IN PLANNING

Consider the needs of children, both individually and as a group. A group composed of children from impoverished rural backgrounds may have needs very different from an urban group of the same economic level. In turn, a group composed mainly of children from homes with plenty of money and "things" may have still different needs. A highly diverse group, either in age, cultural and economic background or intellectual development, will necessitate very careful planning if the needs and interests of each child are met.

Research and observation both afford overwhelming evidence of the differentiating effects of the various subcultures in which children are reared. No longer can teachers say "children are children," and provide identical experiences for each one. Planning should recognize these differences.

Groups containing many children with limited experiences and an even more limited vocabulary will need experiences to enlarge their world *plus* plans to help the children comprehend and express in words what they are experiencing.

Children who have not yet learned to listen to a story as a group should be given preliminary experiences to help them learn, but the three or four children who are ready for stories can be read to as they express an interest. If a teacher or paraprofessional cannot be freed to read to them, advance planning will have assured that their favorite stories are recorded on a cartridge or standard tape recorder, ready for listening.

The needs of individual children are also more likely to be met when planning is done. For instance, a volunteer who has received instructions and materials ahead of time can work on a one-to-one basis with four-year-old Bobby, whose language development is so retarded that his own mother can't understand him. The child who needs some special attention from an adult to help him "get started" should be considered as the teacher plans where adults will be assigned at the beginning of the day. The child who is having a difficult time adjusting to school but who feels secure playing with pegboards and pegs, should be considered when the teacher plans what equipment should be out on a given day.

Consider the disposition of time each day and throughout the year. To provide for variation in children's interests, in attention span, in style and speed of activity, long stretches of time are needed.

Planning within long stretches of time each day makes discipline easier. The less the teacher has to interrupt the children's work to line up, move to another activity, or come together as a group, the fewer discipline problems will develop. The free choice of activities that the children are allowed when they first come might extend for an hour and a half or even longer. This doesn't mean that the same toys and art materials that were out at 9:00 are still there at 10:30, although they could be. They are changed, sometimes by the child, sometimes by the teacher, as the children lose interest or another interest is introduced.

A long stretch of time is needed for the achievement of long range objectives. If a child is to be allowed to work at his own pace, rather than at a pace dictated by the teacher or a time schedule, enough time must be allowed for him to do so. One cannot decide to be "through" developing a healthy self-image by Christmas, or "through" sorting and classifying by Easter. A program based upon the idea that children are interested in learning, and learn most when they are interested, must allow enough time for a balance of interests and activities over a longer period of time than a day or a week. This is analogous in some ways to Davis' classic study showing that children who had not built up prejudices about foods picked well-balanced diets when offered a variety of natural foods, but the balance was apparent only over a long period of time (Davis, 1939).

A child may spend "too much" time in the block area the first month, and only gradually move away to other areas. Over a period of a year, however, he might well have a fairly good balance of activities. Of course, this places extra responsibility on the teacher for making sure that every activity available is a worthy component of the curriculum, which is determined by the program objectives.

Consider the available resources and the way these resources can be used to best advantage—the community, natural resources, books, songs, fingerplays, and both traditional and innovative equipment.

Resources are the learning materials for the child. The way they are used, how often they are used, or even whether they are used at all, has an impact upon the learning environment in a particular classroom. The teacher, then, must have in mind what learning she hopes is going to take place, and structure the environment in such a way that this is likely to happen.

Such planning makes possible the correlation of field trips, books, songs and activities to make it easy for the child to make connections, see relationships, to discover the picture in a book, "just like we saw at the airport."

It allows for continuity and sequencing. A child does not discover and start to use certain materials one day, only to find that it doesn't show up again for a month. Nor is he expected to maintain interest in activities that stay at the same level of difficulty week after week. Resources can be used in a variety of ways to maintain children's interest and provide challenge. If the same equipment, songs, games or stories keep showing up on the plan book again and again, the teacher can be sure that she needs to bring out some new equipment, suggest new uses for old, or change the books and songs. As the children master the simplest activity with outdoor equipment, for example, it should be changed around, combined or simplified to provide more challenge and a different kind of experience.

Consider the areas of the indoor and outdoor learning environment and the activities that are likely to be occurring there. This involves placement of various activities so they are properly supervised, placement of adults so they can give proper supervision and arrangement of equipment and activities so that one activity does not interfere with another.

With two teachers in the room, three or four activities requiring close supervision or teacher-child interaction would not be planned for the same time. A new piece of equipment which required careful supervision until the children learned how to use it safely, such as the woodworking bench, would not be put out at the same time as fingerpainting and a ball-rolling activity to help children say their own and each other's names. The ball-rolling, however, might be done later in the morning, when the wood working and fingerpainting have been put away, some of the children are having juice, and some need a new activity as an orderly transition to group time. Such commonsense planning makes it easier for the child to know and do what is expected of him, and easier for the teacher to handle the activities in a calm, relaxed manner. If, for example, there are new books on the shelves, and the children are likely to ask to be read to, then a record player set up close by would almost certainly interfere with the reading. The teacher could, however, read to interested children and by facing into the room, supervise another nearby activity such as pegs and pegboards, puzzles or other relatively quiet manipulative toys.

Plans must be made for teachers, assistants and volunteers to function at the position and in a way that will enable them to be most useful. For example, if a game requiring teacher-child interaction is planned, then plans must also be made for an adult who knows the procedure to be there.

Possible rough spots in the daily schedule can be anticipated and minimized with careful planning. Suppose the whole group is seated at the table for a birthday party and the next activity is a "story time" in a different part of the room. How are you going to get the children there with a minimum of confusion, and without their losing interest in what comes next? This type of planning involves the flow of children and activities from one area to another, and the transition from one activity to another. The experienced teacher plans this automatically, knowing that new "dress-ups" will stimulate play and the table that was in that area yesterday had better be moved to provide more room; or that transition from juice to group time requires carefully chosen activities to prevent disorganization. Until a teacher has reached that point, planning helps.

Consider the objectives of the program, both long and short range. The achievement of objectives is directly related to how explicitly they have been defined and how carefully the learning experiences have been developed to achieve those objectives. Incidental or accidental learning is not enough. Whether the objective is a rather nebulous one such as "improving the child's self-image," or a very specific one such as learning the meaning of "the same as" and "different from," the objective is far more likely to be achieved if it is planned for, the necessary equipment and supplies are available, and the teacher and assistants know how to guide and respond to children.

The objectives of educational programs for young children are often couched in deliberately nonspecific terms. But global objectives are more likely to be attained if at least some components can be operationally defined. Then planning toward these goals can proceed.

Consider the method or methods to be used. The teacher's philosophy about what young children should learn and how they learn is reflected in the way the problem is planned. The way the needs of the children are met, the way the resources are used, the way available time is allocated, the way the components of the program go together and function in action constitute a method, or more likely, a combination of methods. Do children acquire and clarify their concepts by being told and shown, or by encountering "specific instances" of those concepts in their play, with acquisition and clarification coming through use and appropriate verbal interaction with adults and other children?

The teacher who believes that children want to learn and like to learn should have plans to reflect that conviction. The teacher who believes that children learn best with extrinsic rewards and punishments will let this guide her planning. The teacher who talks of individual differences yet who has all the children making identical pictures within the same span of time will probably manifest this inconsistency elsewhere also.

Planning can help implement one's philosophy of early childhood education. If that philosophy is unformed or a bit shaky, careful, thoughtful planning can help form and stabilize (but not solidify!) the philosophical foundations which uphold any educational structure.

At no other level of education does a teacher have so much freedom and so few constraints concerning content, method and expected outcomes. Inherent in this freedom is both challenge and responsibility for careful, imaginative, resourceful planning for the education of young children.

REFERENCES

Bernard, Harold W. *Human Development in Western Culture.* Boston: Allyn & Bacon, Inc., 1966.

Davis, Clara. Results of the self-selection of diets by young children. In W. E. Martin & C. B. Stendler (Eds.). *Readings in Child Development.* New York: Harcourt, Brace & Co., 1954, 69–74. Reprinted from *Canadian Medical Association Journal,* 1939, 16, 257–261.

Hellmuth, J. (Ed.). *The Disadvantaged Child.* Seattle: Special Child Publications, 1966, 1968, Vols. 1 & 2.

Krauss, Ruth. *The Carrot Seed.* New York: Harper & Row, 1945. Record from Children's Record Guild (1003), 45 rpm.

Nimnicht, Glen, McAfee, Oralie & Meier, John. *The New Nursery School.* New York: General Learning Corp., 1969.

Read, Katherine. *The Nursery School: A Human Relationship Laboratory.* Philadelphia: Suander, 1966.

Todd, V. E. & Heffernan, H. *The Years Before School.* New York: Macmillan Co., 1964.

EVELYN WEBER

34. The Function of Early Childhood Education

No curriculum decisions are more at issue in early childhood education, as indeed in education at many levels, than the objectives of the program. Should the purpose of education be to enhance the whole person? This question has been answered affirmatively by innovators of the various levels of early childhood education as they came into being—first kindergarten, then nursery school, now programs for infants and toddlers.

As Friedrich Froebel conceived the kindergarten, the aim of education was individual self-realization. He wrote: "The child, the boy, man, indeed, should know no endeavor but to act at every stage of development wholly what this stage calls for" (Froebel, 1889). Froebel's frequently reiterated invitation, "Come, let us live with our children," implied a deeper living with them, encompassing an appreciation of the child's nature, an ability to enter into his activities and interests. Psychological as well as physical nurture was early stated as an objective of nursery schools, viewed not just as a substitute for home care, but as an extension of home life enriching to the total development of all children (Owen, 1923). The new phenomena of our time, programs for infants and toddlers, are supported by the belief that optimum human development requires supportive and enriching physical and psychological environments as early in life as possible. Clearly, education for the early years of

Reprinted by permission from *Young Children,* Vol. 28, No. 5 (June 1973), pp. 265–274. Copyright © 1973, National Association for the Education of Young Children, 1834 Connecticut Avenue, N.W., Washington, D.C. 20009.

a child's life came into being as a means of supporting and enriching his optimum growth.

THEORY AND THE DOWNWARD EXTENSION OF EDUCATION

Gradually, attention has moved closer to the initial stages of human development, to the kind of nurture, beginning in infancy, which is expansive and supportive of the fully functioning person. As this movement has spanned more than a century, each new extension of education into a younger age level has naturally reflected the preponderance of theoretical study and social concern of the particular historical period in which its growth took place. Kindergartens, for example, increased rapidly in the decades around the turn of this century under the aegis of a broad social concern. A humanitarian impulse in the 1880s and 1890s spurred the desire to alleviate the distress of many people drawn to the cities by increased industrialization. Kindergartens, as well as settlement houses, seemed one answer to the poverty and squalor experienced in urban slums. They were part of a vision of fostering the perfectibility of man and society through education. Small wonder that this vision led to the development of a curriculum to bring about change in social behavior (Weber, 1969, pp. 127–133). A reshaping of the curriculum carried out by leaders in kindergarten education brought it in line with their conceptions of behavior compatible with democratic principles—responsibility, cooperation and respect.

The development of nursery schools spreading rapidly in the 1920s, coincided with an augmented consideration of the emotions. Deeply responsive to psychoanalytic theory, nursery school teachers began to relate certain postulates to the handling of behavior problems, to the release of feelings through artistic expressions, to a search for the causes of behavior which were deemed to be largely emotional (Weber, 1969, pp. 167–169). This early involvement with one theory of the emotions has been expanded and modified to embrace new theoretical understandings; nevertheless, the clear recognition was there that learning cannot be divorced from the affective components of growth.

Early in the decade of the 1960s, psychological research and study veered sharply to focus overwhelmingly on cognitive growth. Benjamin Bloom's synthesis of existing research revealed the early years as significant for intellectual growth. Bloom concluded that "at least for extremes of environment there are clear-cut differences in the levels of intelligence reached by children." (Bloom, 1964). The effects of environment appear to be greatest in the early and more rapid periods of intellectual development: these include all of the first five years of growth. Influential also in centering attention upon cognition are the writings of J. McVicker Hunt. As a direct result of his analysis of the work of Jean Piaget, Hunt emphasizes the importance of all the early years including those from birth to 24 months. Inspired by this new influence, research and programs for the very young have proliferated (Weber, 1970).

This alliance between a continuously expanding knowledge of child growth and concern for his welfare, then, has been responsible for each downward extension of educational programs. It is easy to see historically why so many lay people believe social adjustment to be the main purpose of the kindergarten. Or, one can understand why the nursery school concentrated so heavily on the child's emotional well-being, or why programs for infants and toddlers are now searching for appropriate intellectual stimuli.

THE PRIMARY YEARS AS PART OF EARLY CHILDHOOD

It becomes clear that early childhood education must give consideration to all the years, as well as the environments encountered, from birth through kindergarten age. But it does not end there. Physically and psychologically, it includes the next few years, until around the ages of seven or eight. Early childhood leaders have long considered that the period of a child's life between the ages of four to eight was psychologically one. While we know that growth is all of a piece without evidence of discrete stages and that individual development is highly idiosyncratic, there are reasons to believe that the primary years are more akin to early childhood than to the later elementary school period. Piaget's conception of intellectual growth gives support to this. After a period of sensorimotor learning (from birth to 18-24 months), a second period lasting until the seventh or eighth year begins, during which are developed the foundations of logical thought—or, in Piaget's terminology, the child moves in a preoperational way toward the formation of mental operations proper. During this period, when logical deduction is not yet possible, the child needs numerous experiences for acting on objects in a first hand manner. Both physical and logic mathematical experiences are essential to lead to the processes of abstraction necessary to reach the stage of formal operations. Not through language, but through actions on objects does the child eventually become able to make logical deductions (Piaget, 1969, p. 37). This holds for the six-, seven- and eight-year-old as well as the four-and five-year old. Hans Furth argues that the primary years should focus upon action-oriented and action-dependent functioning which supplies the foundations for logical knowing schemes (Furth, 1970).

This period is marked by the formation of what Piaget calls "the symbolic function" (Piaget, 1969, p. 31), which enables the child to represent objects or events not present by evoking them through substitute objects or signs. The symbolic function enables the learner to extend the means of thought and is one big step in decentering from the immediacy of sensorimotor action. Other decentering occurs during this period which opens up expanded social possiblities for the child. A gradually increased mobility of thought enables the child to take the view of another person and replaces egocentrism with cooperative social enterprises (Hunt, 1961, pp. 216-217). Thus, some important social transformations accompany the intellectual changes at about the age of seven or eight.

When the child has reached distinctions between his own behavior and that of others, he gains a clearer concept of rules. At about the second or third grade, he becomes engrossed in group play, particularly active games requiring skill, which become highly satisfying experiences (Gordon, 1969). It is clear that the eight-year-old is acquiring more achievement-oriented and independent behavior and that peers reinforce this social growth toward independence (McCandless, 1967). Such growth is not possible until "increased mobility of thought permits the child to shift rapidly between the views of others and himself. (Hunt, 1961, p. 217). Research on social development and study of the cognitive growth of the child both indicate significant transformation occurring sometime around the ages of seven to nine, the precise age influenced by cultural as well as individual differences. These are representative of significant factors which make it realistic to include the primary grades in the span of early childhood education.

THE PURPOSES OF PRIMARY EDUCATION

The purposes of traditional primary education have not coincided with the personal, holistic approach of those working with younger children. With a different history and with goals, established essentially in an earlier era, the emphasis has been education dedicated largely to gaining knowledge. At the primary school level, this meant the acquisition of skills which enabled the learner to study: the young child learned to read so that at a later time he could read to learn. Community pressures for early attainment of reading skills has led many a first grade to center their efforts so entirely in this direction that they are operated with a singleness of purpose.

Reaching down into the kindergarten, programs of reading readiness were urged by those who placed great merit on early literacy. Work book exercises became part of some kindergarten curricula. While the deferred values of a readiness program did not square with the developmental point of view of those concerned with the totality of growth, others began to consider readiness for first grade as the primary function of the kindergarten.

Not until the decade of the 1960s has direct skill teaching been recommended for children under six. Augmented by a conception of compensatory education stemming from new social urgencies, some newcomers to the field of early childhood education are attempting to design compensatory programs for economically deprived children which pay off rapidly in skill achievement. They tend to define deprivation in terms of the acquisition (or lack of it) of specific measurable skills. The goals of the projects become the skills required at a later grade level and these become the direct focus for specific training in the preschool years. Again, a singleness of purpose tends to crowd out recognition of the complexity of human growth.

Two major curricular reform movements have worked, however, to bring primary classrooms (as well as those for older children) into a conception of function more allied to the holistic approach of most preschool classrooms: progressive education and what is commonly called "open" education today. Progressive educators thought of the child's life as an integral one having unity and completeness within the child's own psychological world (Dewey, 1902). They viewed each learner as reacting as a whole to any experience and taking away from it multiple learnings: attitudes and values, social understandings, physical skills as well as intellectual meanings. They reacted against a curriculum divided into topics, lessons and specific facts and formulae which seemed to fragment the world of the learner. The learner was placed at the central core of the learning process with the goal of education the release of the human spirit in educational experiences which respected the individual potential of each child. Growth was considered an individual matter both in respect to the free play of individual thinking and in creative ways to express that thinking. Objectives were necessarily long-range and multiple.

While for many reasons progressive education did not succeed in influencing the curriculum of great numbers of primary classrooms with lasting impact, it provided a legacy full of dynamism. Part of this dynamism reaches into the "open classroom," though there is little direct recognition of the relationship. Perhaps this is just as well, for we are beyond the progressive era with new insights and much more research documentation to build upon. However, it is in the trend toward "open" education, growing most rapidly at the primary level, that one finds a new affirmation of the function of the school to educate the total person and to help him attain his full potential.

The integrated day permits a "wholeness" to learning experiences, for learnings are not compartmentalized along subject matter lines. The British report of *Children and Their Primary Schools* contains this statement: "The idea of flexibility has found expression in a number of practices, all of them designed to make good use of the interest and curiosity of children, to minimize the notion of subject matter being rigidly compartmental and to allow the teacher to adapt a consultative, guiding, stimulating role rather than a purely didactic one."[1] The person is at the heart of the curriculum. Indeed, a concept of nurturance seems to predominate which includes an active part for the learner in his own learning. In the same document the aims of primary education are stated: "A school is not merely a teaching shop, it must transmit values and attitudes. It is a community in which children learn to live first and foremost as children and not as future adults."[2] The curriculum of the British primary or open school is planned in light of the potentialities of children in their environment; it is a living situation with a wide range of educative alternatives.

RESOLUTION OF THE ISSUE—PSYCHOLOGICAL EVIDENCE

Should the school stand solely as a training ground for the mind or should the school serve as a multipurpose, developmental agency promoting individual self-actualization? Perhaps it would be well to raise the question here of whether these two points of view need to be considered so mutually exclusive. Proponents of specific curricula tend to imply that the school can only do one or the other. Actually this need not, in-

[1]Central Advisory Council for Education (England) *Children and Their Primary Schools.* London; Her Majesty's Stationery Office, 1967. P. 198.
[2]*Ibid.*, P. 187.

deed, *must* not be so. Increasing amounts of psychological research reveal the affective and cognitive components of growth to be so inextricably bound together that we can no longer think of working with the child as a disengaged intellect. Nevitt Sanford sums up contributions from personality theory: "First the personality functions as a whole. This is not just a slogan. We must not permit educators categorically to separate the intellectual or the cognitive from the rest of personality. Conceptually, they may do this. Cognition, feeling, emotion, action and motivation are easily separated by abstraction, but no single one of these can function independently of the others" (Sanford, 1967). Anyone who has worked closely with young children will recognize the utter necessity of dealing with feelings, drives, curiosity, imaginative play and a whole range of affect-laden behavior. In older children, facades tend to hide such behavior, but their impact upon learning is just under the surface.

Those who argue for an exclusively cognitive mission for the school frequently make the assumption that this aspect of growth is neglected in more child-centered classrooms. Often this is based upon a fear that if children do not meet traditional age-grade standards in basic skills, they are not being fitted to grapple with the world as it will eventually confront them. Arbitrary grade standards, designed decades ago, dominate the thinking of many people as they judge the effectiveness of teachers and the growth of children. Such standards, set to embrace all children, have the effect of homogenizing them, of ignoring the vast differences in individuals at any age level.

No single empirical set of facts provided by research on human development is more firmly established than the idiosyncratic nature of growth. That individuals differ enormously is evident by research on assessment of abilities, traits, attitudes and classroom performances. One style of learning may be more suitable for one child than another. Rates of learning differ from child to child. The direct implication of the extensive empirical inquiry which can be marshaled to support these statements argues for the abandonment of traditional age-grade achievement standards.

That academic skills are ignored in "open" classrooms during the integrated day is a misconception, which fails to recognize the learning process in operation. It is a process of learning which recognizes that each child has a unique personal history, comes to learning with distinct interests and drives, builds cultural skills of effective functioning in different manners and varying rates. With these differences recognized appropriately within the classroom, there is promise that the quality of learning, the depth of skills, the commitment to ideas and the personal usefulness of knowledge will be increased. An unreal timetable of skill acquisition can well be discarded in order to achieve more functional learning.

NEW PSYCHOLOGICAL UNDERSTANDINGS

Though ultimately living in our society requires effective language skills, new psychological understandings question whether early skill acquisition constitutes the best training ground for the mind. The work of Jean Piaget reveals the early childhood period as one in which the child is constructing a logical way of thinking. His research leaves no question about the avenue to knowledge and logical thinking: it is through direct active transactions with the objects and people in his world. The environment replete with materials for the discovering of ideas and relationships together with a multi-age grouping within the classroom, offering a wider age span for interactions, extend direct possibilities for intellectual expansion. In one sense, the child in this environment is actually constructing his own learning abilities, moving through preoperational toward more logical operations in handling ideas, for it is through his own efforts that the child comes to logical understanding of his world. Language and active interaction need close association, but instruction through language alone and divorced from active interactions is not likely to have much lasting value. Furthermore, to focus entirely on abstract symbols offering little opportunity for direct interaction with environmental stimuli may even interfere with the growth toward logical thinking.

This leads to the exciting recognition that the same classroom environment which nourishes the mind through providing the underpinnings of logical thought is also the one that provides sound ego support and expanding social awareness. The same active learning patterns which enable the child to gain knowledge and test its reality through exploration, manipulation and investigation contribute also to positive ego strength. This style of learning which releases the child's curiosity and encourages him to try out his capacities contains its own instrinsic reward and generates further motivation to active learning. The pleasure from such learning supports a positive self-concept and feelings of competence. Barbara Biber underscores the significance of this: "The core of ego-strength is competence, and, subjectively, the sense of competence, and this is the fruit of action: what is learned by action and the effect of action on the physical and human universe." (Biber, 1967).

Social collaboration, the ability to engage in truly cooperative enterprises, is dependent upon the child's being able "to dissociate his point of view from that of others and to coordinate these different points of view" (Piaget, 1968). For the child to arrive at this ability at around the age of seven or eight, he needs to gradually grow out of his earlier state of social and intellectual egocentricity. Slowly he decenters his thinking about objects by moving from concentration on a single striking feature to taking into account other important aspects, and thus is able to reason about them more logically. Socially, the child slowly acquires an other-role orientation and begins to see the necessity to justify his own reasoning and convey it to others. True discussions become possible and contribute to cooperative enterprises. These transformations come only at the end of the early childhood period but surely the conditions which make them possible should be a part of education in the early years. They take place in an activity-oriented classroom where children are at liberty to work alone or in groups and to talk while working. "It is social interaction which gives the ultimate *coup de grace* to childish egocentrism," is the way John Flavell puts it (Flavell, 1963). In repeated interpersonal interactions in which the child must again and again recognize the role of another (especially those involving arguments), the child becomes not only intellectually but more socially competent.

The preponderance of evidence from psychological inquiry argues for the broader conception of function in early childhood education, for basically the same classroom conditions provide for all avenues of growth. In a learning environment where the child is continually transacting in a variety of ways, the opportunities are there for promoting progressive thinking in an ever more logical manner, for moving from egocentric to increasingly cooperative behavior, for seeing oneself less as the center of the universe but building a growing esteem for one's own competence, for extending the learner's motivation to keep on learning, for becoming an expansively unique and creative person. From the psychological evidence accumulating, it seems time for us to stop arguing about the function of early childhood education and to get on with solving the problems essential to providing the most appropriate action-oriented, transactional learning environment.

All areas of growth then become the concern of all levels of early childhood from birth through about the age of eight or nine. Kindergarten goals can no longer be regarded as essentially social in nature, though, if this is the child's first experience in group living, great care will be given to interpersonal relationships. The absolutely essential attention given to the psychosocial adjustment of nursery school children can merge with expanded goals. Both levels must address themselves to providing the environment appropriately supporting cognitive functioning. Already expanding programs for infants and toddlers are searching for this environment while building upon what is know about other areas of growth. Primary classrooms allied to the "open" school movement already are concerned with the broader conception of function.

As educators come more generally to understand the psychological underpinnings which support a curriculum for the totality of individual growth, education will move toward increasing numbers of action-oriented, child-centered classrooms. To bring about this evolutionary change it will be necessary to increase the knowledge and allay the fears of parents whose faith has become unduly tied to fallacious age-grade standards.

Not only does the psychological evidence point to a resolution of the issue of purpose, but as new insights are utilized in a classroom intent upon all-round nurturance, the curriculum will be more in line with the natural tendencies of children. And, at last, children will experience a continuity in education from birth through the ages of eight or nine.

PHILOSOPHICAL BASES

While psychological evidence seems to converge toward a single direction, the same convergence may not be true of philosophical bases. Throughout history, as today, philosophic statements delineate the divergent points of view: education that transmits the cultural heritage and trains individuals to take on the roles of lawyers, teachers, engineers, dentists—or education that fosters the development of complete human beings with a sense of integrity and a coherent set of values and personal goals. With the latter view we find Commenius, Froebel, Dewey and Whitehead, all denoting the seamless coat of learning and an ideal image of a functioning, curious, creative, problem solving, personally and socially sensitive individual. Schooling for the child under six has tended to be associated with this view. On the other side is the Thomist view which has exerted extensive influence on American education including the primary grades. It is this tradition which holds those who support direct skill learning in the primary grades more, however, because it is tradition than because they have consciously analyzed the meaning of this tradition.

Contemporary statements continue the cleavage. In a recent statement, an Educational Policies Committee contends that "the development of every student's rational powers must be recognized as centrally important."[3] In a direct answer to the Educational Policies Commission, Theodore Brameld disagrees, not with the statement as a goal but with its limitations. Brameld believes the major goal of education to be the development of world citizenship which provides education "a thrilling opportunity to share in the creation of a new epoch by and for mankind" (Brameld, 1961, p. 14). A personal note is given by Brameld when he sees the path ahead "in the emergence of newly cooperative processes of teaching and learning that encourage students to reach group decisions and thus to choose deliberately and consciously from among the crucial normative options confronting our time" (Brameld, 1961, p. 13). Alice Miel effectively relates this to young children when she urges a curriculum which develops children who care for themselves and others around the world and who move into the future with a concern for the higher values in our society (Miel, 1962).

There is only one of these philosophic positions which is congruent with the evidence of psychological theory as touched upon briefly in the preceding section: it is that position which pins its faith upon the worth, dignity, integrity and uniqueness of each person. It is an ethical stance. Twenty years ago John Childs wrote: "Those educators who have combined the psychological principles of democracy and have developed the conception that the supreme aim of education should be the nurture of an individual who can take responsibility for his own continued growth have made an ethical contribution of lasting worth." (Childs, 1950). Linking this to the current scene, James Macdonald states firmly: "Moral concerns are grounded in a form of personalism . . . the open school has no rationale for existence unless one sees another as a whole person (or a whole child)." (Macdonald, 1970).

A heightened concern for the ethical values inherent in educating the whole child is well documented in the expanding educational literature analyzing the dehumanizing influences of our schools. Scholarly research, as well as popularly written observations, reveal the psychological inadequacy of the traditional curriculum by demonstrating the devastat-

---

[3]Educational Policies Commission of the National Education Association. The central purposes of American education. *NEA J.*, L, Sept. 1961, 16.

ing effects upon the mental health of many children.[4] Previously unpublicized features of school life are now being discussed, such as the ritualistic and cyclical quality of the classroom day, the overwhelming focus upon mistakes and deficiencies, the immediate demands to meet adult requirements, the pervasive spirit of evaluation—all failing to recognize and to utilize the child's own strengths, his personal way of attaining maturity according to his capacities and limitations. Such an analysis caused one writer to reverse his conception of the function of the school:

> It was not until I was well into the writing . . . that I began to realize what a metamorphasis had taken place in me and in my thinking about education . . . . I thought I knew what the purpose of education should be: namely, intellectual development. . . .
>
> I was wrong. What tomorrow needs is not masses of intellectuals, but masses of educated men—men educated to feel and to act as well as to think (Silberman, 1970).

A renewed humanism is pressing urgently for education embracing the totality of human potentialities. In all its infinite complexity, education for the release of the human spirit is an imperative. More than ever before, we know this must begin in early childhood.

REFERENCES

Biber, Barbara. A learning teaching paradigm integrating intellectual and affective processes. In Eli M. Bower & William G. Hollister (Eds.), *Behavioral Science Frontiers in Education*. New York: John Wiley, 1967. P. 132.

Bloom, Benjamin S. *Stability and Change in Human Characteristics*. New York: John Wiley, 1964. P. 79.

Brameld, Theodore. What is the central purpose of American education? *Phi Delta Kappan*, XLIII, Oct. 1961, 13-14.

Childs, John. *Education and Morals*. New York: Appleton Century Crofts. 1950. P. 15.

Dewey, John. *The Child and the Curriculum*. Chicago: University of Chicago Press, 1902. Pp. 5-6.

Flavell, John. *The Developmental Psychology of Jean Piaget*. Princeton, N.J.: Van Nostrand, 1963. P. 157.

Froebel, Friedrich. *The Education of Man*. (Trans. William N. Hallmann) New York: D. Appleton & Co., 1889. P. 30.

Furth, Hans G. *Piaget for Teachers*. Englewood Cliffs, N.J.: Prentice-Hall, Inc., 1970. P. 25.

Gordon, Ira J. *Human Development*. New York: Harper & Row, 1969. Pp. 165-166.

Hunt, J. McVicker. *Intelligence and Experience*. New York: Ronald Press, 1961. Pp. 216-217.

[4]Cf. Holt, John. *How Children Fail*. New York: Pitman, 1964. Jackson, Philip W. *Life in Classrooms*. New York: Holt, Rinehart & Winston, 1968. Kozol, Jonathan. *Death at an Early Age*. Boston: Houghton Mifflin. 1967. Minnehin, Patricia; Biber, Barbara; Shapiro, Edna & Zimiles, Herbert. *The Psychological Impact of School Experiences*. New York: Basic Books, 1969.

Macdonald, James. The open school: Curriculum concepts. In Georgianna Engstrom (Ed.). *Open Education: The Legacy of the Progressive Movement.* Washington: National Association for the Education of Young Children, 1970. P. 24.

McCandless, Boyd R. *Children: Behavior and Development.* New York: Holt, Rinehart & Winston, 1967, 2d ed. Pp. 435-436.

Miel, Alice. Let us develop children who care about themselves and others. *Audiovisual Instruction,* VII, June 1962, 355-357.

Owen, Grace. The aims and functions of the nursery school. In Grace-Owen (Ed.), *Nursery School Education.* New York: E. P. Dutton, 1923. P. 19.

Piaget, Jean. *Science of Education and the Psychology of the Child.* New York: Viking Press, 1969. Pp. 31-37.

—.*Six Psychological Studies.* New York: Vintage Books, 1968, P. 39.

Sanford, Nevitt. The development of cognitive-affective processes through education. In Eli M. Bower & William G. Hollister (Eds.), *Behavioral Science Frontiers in Education.* New York: John Wiley, 1967. P. 79.

Silberman, Charles E. *Crisis in the Classroom.* New York: Random House, 1970. Pp. 6-7.

Weber, Evelyn. *Early Childhood Education: Perspectives on Change.* Worthington, Ohio: Charles A. Jones Publishing Co., 1970. Pp. 55-70.

—.*The Kindergarten: Its Encounter with Educational Thought in America.* New York: Teachers College Press, 1969. Pp. 127-133.

EPILOGUE AND PROLOGUE

To take a firm philosophic stance for the wholeness of learning and for personal nurturance as the heart of the curriculum provides the support for building a curriculum with a consistent humanism. It clarifies the bases for curriculum decisions.

The unresolved problems of carrying out such a curriculum on a day to day basis, however, are vast. It most certainly does not mean giving unlimited freedom to young children but rather giving them help in the use of "responsible freedom." A laissez-faire curriculum is not the answer. This we have learned; but we need a great deal more knowledge about how to assist children in making more effective transactions with their learning environment. How can we help the young child experience a deep and creative involvement with his world, which will lay the foundations for an attitude of commitment to mankind's highest hopes? In what ways can we help the learner, within the limitations of his ego-centricity, develop more effective modes of communication? Is he ready to become involved in decision-making skills? To answer these, and similar questions, and to relate the answers to programs for young children we need knowledge and understandings.

The Center for Young Children at the University of Maryland is attempting to develop such knowledge that may aid curriculum workers in fostering aspects of learning not well understood. If, for example, education is to concern itself with the uniqueness of persons, we need to be able to communicate much more effectively. The Center for Young Children has focused recently on the nonverbal behavior of the three- to five-year-old and its meaning for teachers. Such new information can help educators provide more appropriate action-oriented, child-centered learning environments essential to the humanistic philosophic position. Louise Berman, in her article "Not Reacting but Transacting: One Approach to Early Childhood Education," describes the work of the center in its efforts to provide new knowledge.

This effort to derive new understandings applicable to curricula for young children needs to be duplicated throughout the country. Let us multiply attempts to obtain new understandings at centers directly involved in work with learners wherever extensive philosophic and psychological support is available. E.W.

CELIA A. DECKER and JOHN R. DECKER

35. Considering Regulations

The continuing growth of facilities and schools for young children has necessitated increased emphasis on regulations for insuring that not only are minimum standards met but that existing standards for quality care and instruction are raised. Regulations are the rules, directives, statutes, and standards that prescribe, direct, limit, and govern early childhood programs.

The characteristics that follow are generally representative of such regulations.

1. Regulations cover all aspects of a program—administrative organization, facilities, personnel, funding, and services offered.
2. The various regulations apply to different types of early childhood programs. Some regulations govern private programs (e.g., licensing and incorporation); others may affect federal and state funded programs (e.g., direct administration and Interagency Day Care requirements); and some regulations must be met by virtually all programs (e.g., fire safety and sanitation requirements, zoning, transportation, the Civil Rights Act, local board regulations, and regulations concerning staff qualifications).
3. Regulations vary in their comprehensiveness; for example, licensing regulations cover the total program but certification requirements affect only the educational preparation of the staff.

From Celia A. Decker and John R. Decker, "Considering Regulations," in *Planning and Administering Early Childhood Programs*, Charles E. Merrill Publishing Company, 1976, pp. 24-42. Reprinted with permission of Charles E. Merrill Publishing Company.

4. Most regulations are mandatory; one exception is accreditation which is self-regulation, and thus not mandatory.
5. Regulations come from various sources. Federal agencies regulate some early childhood programs because they provide funds through various grants and titles. State agencies regulate some early childhood programs because they provide funds. State laws regulate public programs because public school education is a state responsibility. Local governments regulate some programs through community ordinances and health and safety codes. The judiciary system regulates some early childhood programs through its decisions affecting civil rights and the responsibilities of agencies and schools.

REGULATIONS GOVERNING PRIVATE EARLY CHILDHOOD PROGRAMS

Licensing and incorporating are regulatory procedures that are unique to private early childhood programs. They are means for insuring that minimum standards are met by those proposing to establish child care and/or instructional programs not funded, and hence not regulated, by federal or state agencies or through public school systems. Each state develops its own licensing and incorporation procedures and defines what is meant by a private child care facility. This term usually includes a facility that accommodates a few children in the owner's home to one that may have several hundred children. Both licensing and incorporation regulations tend to be comprehensive in nature; that is, these regulations usually include all aspects of planning and administering privately operated early childhood facilities.

Licensing

Licensing is the procedure by which an individual, an association, or a corporation obtains from their state child care licensing agency a license, or authorization, to operate, or to continue operating, a child care facility. A licensed facility is recognized by the state agency as having met minimum standards for child care.

Protection of children is the basis for licensing. Private child care agencies are classified as either "voluntary or philanthropic" or "proprietary or commercial."[1] Licensing is not concerned with child care facilities under public auspices. Public agencies are expected to implement their own standards and exercise supervision over their own facilities. An outline for licensing private child care service would include these elements:

people, operations, structure, and materials—the accountable administering agency, the place in which the service takes place, and the program which is conducted there.[2]

Historical Note

Licensing originated in New England when a board of charities was created in 1863 to inspect and report on various child care facilities. The first licensing law was passed in Pennsylvania in 1885; however, general interest in licensing did not begin until the early 1900s when public scandals over the abuse of children in some child care facilities caused concern. This concern led to regulations for minimum standards of care and supervision of the publicly subsidized agencies. By 1920 most states had some regulation of child care. As a result of the federal grant-in-aid funds of 1935, state child welfare departments were able to procure better qualified personnel; day care facilities were brought under child care licensing statutes; social workers took an active interest in protective services; and licensing was identified as a state child welfare function.[3,4,]

In the bulletin, *A Survey of State Day Care Licensing Requirements*, these data were reported:

1. There are three major categories of day care facilities licensed in the United States: *family day care homes*, a category in forty-eight state regulations; *group day care homes*, a category in nine state regulations; and *day care centers*, a category in fifty state regulations. The categories are not similarly defined in the various states, however.
2. State licensing of family day care homes is not mandatory in eleven states. Licensing of day care centers is voluntary in one state and the licensing regulation has been overturned in another state.
3. In some states, licensing requirements are not imposed for all cities and counties.[5]

The Licensing Agency

According to Class,[6] the licensing agency is a regulatory agency with both quasi-legislative and quasi-judicial authority. The quasi-legislative powers include the responsibility for the establishment of standards and the quasi-judicial powers include the responsibility for making decisions to issue or deny a license application and for conducting hearings in grievance cases. The major tasks of the licensing agency are

(a) interpreting the fact that child care is an activity affecting public interests and is therefore recognized by the State as an area of regulation; (b) formulating and reformulating licensing standards which will reduce the risk of improper care; (c) evaluating each applicant's situation to decide whether or not to issue the license; and (d) supervisory activity to maintain conformity to standards and, usually, consultation to upgrade care.[7]

Licensing of child care facilities is the responsibility of a particular state department such as the Department of Public Welfare, of Social Services, of Health, of Social Services and Health, and of Health and Welfare. Other departments, however, may be responsible for licensing; for example, each of these departments issue licenses in at least one state: Board of Pensions, Environmental and Community Services, Departments of Children and Family Services, of Employment and Social Services, of Institutions and Agencies, of Institutions, and of Human Resources.

Child Care Service License

The different types of child care facilities may be covered by a general or differential licensing law. Differential licensing laws have varying standards for these types of programs; day care (family day care homes, group day care homes, and day care centers); educational facilities (private kindergartens and programs that carry the term *school* in their title); foster care (foster homes and group foster homes); child placing institutions; residential facilities; children's camps; and handicapped children's centers.

In most states the term *day care center* includes any early childhood program having these characteristics:

1. Operated as either nonprofit or profit making by any person(s), association, corporation, institution, or agency.
2. Opened for any part of or all of the daylight hours, but less than twenty-four hours.
3. Enrolling a specified minimum number (e.g., four, five, or seven) of children not related to the operator and/or conducted away from the children's homes. (The minimum number of children and the place of operation are used to make a distinction between day care services and babysitting services.)

The term *day care center,* in most states, does not include the following:

1. Kindergartens and/or nursery schools operated under public school auspices.
2. Kindergartens and/or nursery schools registered with the state department of public instruction. (Usually these are operated in conjunction with private and/or parochial elementary schools.)
3. Nurseries or other programs in places of worship during religious services.
4. Day camps as defined by the various state codes.

Thus, in most states, privately operated nursery schools and kindergartens that are individually owned and/or church-supported programs are considered day care centers and are under the licensing regulations of their state. If the state code includes the local nonpublic school nursery and/or kindergarten as an educational institution and provides for the registration of the program with the state department of public instruction, then the privately owned nursery school and/or kindergarten is exempt from licensing regulations as a day care center.

Features of Day Care Center Licensing Laws

The regulations for day care centers will be the focal point for this discussion concerning licensing laws. The features of these regulations are similar to those of family and group day care homes, differing only in regard to the number of children regularly enrolled. The regulatory laws governing day care centers differ widely from state to state and in order to learn the specific regulations of a state you should contact the state's licensing agency and request a copy of the regulations. Although state regulations do vary, there are two common features. First, the licensing regulations in most states are very specific in the areas pertaining to the physical health and safety of the child and are more lax in the area of program content. For example, health and safety regulations may state the required room temperature or the specific items to be included in the first aid kit, and a program regulation may be that the program content "contribute to total development." Second, the licensing regulations in most states cover the following areas: the licensing law and procedure, organization and administration, staffing, plant and equipment, health and safety and program.

The Licensing Law and Procedure

Each state manual contains information concerning the law which gives the licensing agency its quasi-legislative and quasi-judicial authority. The section in the manual on procedure contains all or some of the following items:

1. Terms such as *day care center* and *care-giver* are defined.
2. Institutions which must be licensed (e.g., day care centers) and those which are exempted (e.g., Sunday schools and public school kindergartens) are delineated; the penalty, usually a misdemeanor, for operating without a license is also stated.
3. Procedures are described for obtaining and submitting an application for a license.
4. Statements of fees, if any, charged for license application are given. Renewal fees are charged in some states.
5. Bases for application approval are explained. In most states these bases include the ability of the applicant: (a) to show need for the program; (b) to demonstrate that the minimum standards for child care or instruction have been met; (c) to give evidence of adequate financial stability; and (d) to indicate probability of permanence in the proposed organization. In some states a center that has not met all requirements and is engaged in active processes of meeting the requirements may obtain a provisional license.
6. The duration of a license and explanation of the procedure required for renewal are explained. In most states a license must be renewed each year; a few states require a renewal every two years. In some states a provisional license must be renewed every three to six months; and in other states it cannot be renewed.
7. Bases for revoking a license are explained, and statements concerning grievance policies or appeals are given. There is a penalty for operating after a license has been revoked.
8. A statement that a license must be posted in the center is made.
9. Conditions that require notification of the licensing agency are out-

lined: (a) change in location of the facility, in administration, in services offered, or in enrollment after the license was granted; (b) serious accident; (c) fire; (d) civil action taken against an institution or an employee; and (e) closing of the center.

Organization and Administration

State licensing laws require than an applicant indicate the purposes and sponsorship of the organization and if it is profit or nonprofit making.

All state licensing laws require that administrative authority be clearly placed. In profit-making organizations, the requirements may be that the authority reside in one person or that an advisory board must be formed and be comprised of individuals who can be of professional assistance. Usually a nonprofit organization must operate under a governing board which is composed, at least in part, of the people it serves.

Policies concerning children must be included in a description of the organization of a center. Although these policies vary from state to state, they usually embody these details:

1. The center's admission and termination of service policies must be stated and conform with state regulations. Once an admission policy is adopted by the center and approved by the licensing agency, a change in this policy by the center requires application for another license. In some states day care centers cannot serve children under a minimum age which ranges from four weeks to three years, and over a maximum age which ranges from school age to sixteen years. Not all state licensing regulations use age as a criterion for receiving services of a center but may use phrases such as "ready for group activity," "children who are likely to benefit from the services available," or "consideration must be given to children who need care."

2. A procedure for admission must be written: for example, in some states an interview with a parent may be required before admission.

3. In most states a nondiscrimination provision with respect to race, sex, creed, color, or religion must be adopted before a license can be issued.

4. A fee policy must be written and made available to parents. Fees charged depend on services offered and on whether the organization has been established for profit or nonprofit purposes. Often in nonprofit organizations, fees are charged in keeping with a parent's ability to pay on a sliding scale basis and in keeping with the actual cost of operation.

5. A center must state its child-staff ratio and the maximum number of children to be cared for or instructed in one group. Those numbers must conform to the state licensing regulation.

6. Finally, state licensing laws require a center to show financial solvency for immediate and continuous operation. Continuous operation is often defined as three months.

Staffing

Regulations concerning staffing usually include the following: the categories of personnel needed; child-staff ratio required; age, educational, health, character, and temperament requirements of staff; and personnel records which must be kept. The trends in staffing requirements are as follows:

1. Personnel needed include a director who must be in charge and who must assume total responsibility for the center. One state requires that centers with forty or more children hire a nonteaching director. A majority of states stipulate that two or more care-givers or instructors be on duty at all operating times. In all states, auxiliary staff must be hired when their services are required (e.g., for meals) or offered (e.g., for transportation). Some states mandate and others suggest the use of parent volunteers.

2. The child-staff ratio is based on care-giving or instructional staff only. The maximum size of the group is often specified. Usually when a combination of ages is provided with services under one care-giver or instructor, the ratio is calculated on the basis of the youngest child in the group. Two representative examples of child-staff ratios and the maximum group sizes are as follows:

Age of Children Children	Child-Staff Ratio	Maximum Group Size
Birth - 18 months	3:1	6
19 - 35 months	4:1	8
36 - 53 months	7:1	14
54 - 71 months	10:1	20
2½ - 4 years	10:1	10
4 - 5 years	20:1	20
5 - 6 years	20:1	20
School-age children	25:1	25

3. Each member of the staff must have certain personal qualifications:
   a. *age.* In most states the minimum age required for directors and main care-givers or instructors is eighteen or twenty-one years and the maximum age permitted is sixty-five or seventy years. Assistant care-givers or instructors, who are never alone with children, must be a minimum of sixteen or eighteen years of age.
   b. *education and experience.* Minimum educational and experience requirements are given in most state licensing manuals. In most states directors and main care-givers or instructors must have a high school certificate; a few states require two years beyond high school with courses in child development and nutrition; one state requires a bachelor's degree and two years teaching experience; and another state requires that centers called schools have at least one teacher whose qualifications include a high school certificate and college hours in child psychology, family relations, nursery school curriculum and procedures, and student teaching. In many states, assistant care-givers or instructors must be able to read and write. In all states auxiliary professional staff (e.g., nurses and dietitians) must have the educational competencies required in their respective fields. Finally, most states require that a plan for staff training and development be submitted to the licensing agency.

c. *health.* All states require a physical examination including evidence that a staff member is free of tuberculosis. The results of the examination must be signed by a physician and placed on file in the center.

d. *character and temperament.* Various terms are used to describe the character and temperament of employees. Some of the terms used are "mature," "warm," "friendly" and "have a liking for children." A majority of states do not permit the hiring of any staff member convicted of a crime.

4. Personnel record keeping is a requirement in all states. Personnel records, containing information on each regulation concerning the staff, are kept in the day care center and must be made available to the licensing agency upon request.

Plant and Equipment

Many licensing regulations concerning the physical plant begin with descriptive statements such as the plant should be "safe, sanitary, and comfortable," "roomy, conducive to the development of children," or "not where any conditions exists which would be injurious to the moral or physical welfare of a child or children."

Before application can be made for a license, a potential applicant must meet local zoning, health, and fire department as well as state health department requirements. Although the licensing agency has no authority over these local and state requirements, it can make further location requirements. Some of the statements found in various licensing laws are that the "front must be twenty feet or more wide with a door," "not located with aged, infirmed, or incapacitated," and "programs for children under two and one-half years must be on the ground floor."

A majority of the states have regulations concerning both room size and number needed for care-giving or instruction and concerning other rooms needed in the center. States vary on the amount of indoor space required; generally a minimum of twenty-five to thirty-five square feet per child is stated. A separate care-giving or instructional room is required for each maximum number of children who can be under one care-giver or instructor. In cases where the law mandates children of certain ages be separated, a room must be provided for each age group. Most states prescribe separate bathrooms for children and staff, isolation quarters for an ill or disturbed child, a kitchen, and office space.

Environmental control regulations are included in licensing. These controls include heating and cooling regulations, such as "central heating and air conditioning" and "no fireplaces," amount of window space, room temperature requirements, and light intensity.

Regulations for drinking water and sanitary facilities are included in all licensing laws. Drinking fountains or separate or disposable glasses are required in all states. In most states minimum regulations for bathroom facilities vary between ten to fourteen children per toilet and basin. Facilities for bathing children are suggested in the licensing standards of some states.

The outdoor space regulations often stipulate the amount of space required, with most states prescribing a minimum of forty to one hundred square feet per child. Some of the other regulations (or recommendations in some states) for the outdoor space include that the grounds be adjacent to the indoor area; be clean, drained, and fenced in; have various types of surfacing (e.g., sand and grass); and have open and shaded areas.

Other physical plant regulations that most, if not all, licensing manuals incorporate are that kitchen facilities must conform to health and sanitation requirements; telephones must be installed; and medicines and/or cleaning equipment must be stored in places where children cannot reach them.

Equipment regulations, on the whole, are not as specific as physical plant requirements. Many states require one chair per child and prescribe one cot (or sometimes a mat) per child who remains in the center during a resting time. Other equipment regulations are that the center be "equipped adequately" or "suitable for the age range," have "suitable furniture and arrangement," have "low shelves," and use "easily cleaned equipment." Some licensing manuals provide a list of suggested equipment to be used with children of certain ages or developmental stages.

Health and Safety

All early childhood programs, both public and private, are charged with the protection of children under their care. Licensing agencies are concerned with this protection mandate and have required many health and safety standards be met before they license a private institution. The trends in health and safety requirements are as follows:

1. All states have regulations concerning the health of staff and enrolled children and require that appropriate written records covering these regulations be on file. In most states employees are required to have a general physical examination before being hired and an annual tuberculosis examination. Some states require certain immunizations for their staff and all states require food handlers to obtain a permit. In short, all staff members must obtain a physician's statement that they are in good physical and mental health. In all states a child must be given a general physical examination, have specified immunizations, and be given a tuberculosis examination before being initially admitted to a center. A daily check of each child is required, for a center cannot care for a child with an acute illness or communicable disease. When a child becomes ill at the center, he must be isolated from other children until parents are able to remove him. All states have strict requirements concerning staff members administering medicine to a child. Accurate and current medical records must be kept on file in all states. When handicapped children are admitted to a center, adequate staff must be provided to care for their specific needs.
2. Local and state health and sanitation requirements must be met before application can be made for a license. (It should be noted that other sanitary regulations were discussed under the topic, "plant and equipment.")
3. Transportation regulations must be followed. All states require that

each driver and vehicle be properly licensed. Other transportation regulations are not uniform from state to state. Most states require off-street loading and unloading; set a maximum number of children who can be transported in the various types of vehicles; set a minimum number of supervisors who must ride in the transporting vehicle; state that a child cannot be left unattended in a vehicle; and require the center to have proper insurance coverage. Some states specify the maximum amount of time, ranging from thirty minutes to one hour, that a child can ride to and from the center. Many other safety precautions are found in the licensing manuals, such as safety locks on doors of the vehicle and seat belts for each occupant.

4. Emergency medical care must be planned. Although regulations do vary, most states require emergency-assistance phone numbers be posted by the telephone at all times. Some states require that centers not employing full-time medical staff have at least one staff member who has a current American Red Cross Standard First Aid Certificate or its equivalent; and some states specify supplies to be included in a first aid kit. One state has the regulation that a center can have no more nonambulatory children or infants than can be carried by adults.

5. Nutritional requirements must be met. All states prescribe the fraction or percent, usually one-third to one-half, of the daily food needs a child must receive at the center; the types of food which must be served; the length of time between meals and snacks, which is usually one main meal every four or five hours and a snack two to two and one-half hours after a meal; and that menus be posted and kept on file. States permitting the enrollment of infants in centers specify the time periods for feeding infants and require that infants be held while taking a bottle. Finally, all state health and sanitation requirements must be met in the preparation and serving of food.

Program

As has been previously mentioned, program regulations tend to be more lax than most other areas of licensing regulations. General areas of program regulations include program content, scheduling and planning, and guidance of children.

Infants are to receive verbal stimulation, cuddling, encouragement, and play. Program content for young children is described in most licensing manuals in terms of suggested activity areas such as art, language development, music, block building, dramatic play, science, and manipulative play. Some states specify "no formal learning experiences" and no television viewing.

Common program planning and scheduling regulations include adequate play periods, outdoor playtimes, free-choice and teacher-determined activities, and rest periods. Posting of the schedule and regularity of program is required in several states.

Many states stipulate "no harsh discipline" and give suggestions for guidance of children. Some examples of these suggestions are: discipline cannot be associated with food, rest, or toileting; children should be given choices; staff members should use positive remarks; and corporal punishment should not be used.

Incorporation

Incorporation, necessary for private nonprofit and/or profit-making organizations, is regulatory in nature in that through the process of incorporation, states investigate the character and goals of, and require reports from, those seeking to incorporate. The corporation is subject to licensure and public regulation.

REGULATIONS GOVERNING PUBLIC EARLY CHILDHOOD PROGRAMS

Early childhood programs that are publicly funded are not subject to licensure. Instead, all publicly funded programs such as public school and federally supported early childhood programs receive regulations from a state or federal agency, respectively. A specified state or federal agency is required by law to prepare regulations. Because publicly funded programs are self-monitoring (i.e., answerable to elected officials only), program quality depends upon citizen involvement to cause the elected officials to be truly accountable to the public taxpayer.

Public School Regulations

Public school education in the United States is a state function. State control is exercised through legislation and through guidelines or directives from the state department of education. As was discussed in chapter 3, the states delegate portions, and these portions vary significantly among the fifty states, of the school's operation to local school districts. Specifically, the major areas of state control are as follows:

1. The state creates local school districts and vests them with specific legislative powers.
2. There is legislative control over curricular content via legislation concerning what may or may not be taught, legislative approval of course offerings, and regulations regarding textbook adoption.
3. Certification of administrators and teachers is delegated to the state education agency by legislative authority.
4. Except for Mississippi and South Carolina, state legislatures have established compulsory attendance laws.
5. State aid comes to local schools with regulations regarding the expenditure of these funds; local noncompliance could mean the withholding of state aid.
6. Building construction programs are regulated by various state agencies.
7. There are state regulations concerning the transportation of children.
8. The state legislature delegates authority to the state board of education, the chief state school officer, and/or to the state department of

education to approve or accredit local school systems (i.e., local school systems are accredited on the basis of meeting state standards although some state education agencies may work with regional accrediting agencies).

The Federal Interagency Day Care Requirements

The federal government became involved in early childhood programs in 1933 under the Federal Emergency Relief Administration. Today, the federal government is even more involved in early childhood programs with its extensive funding of Head Start and with grants to research programs involving young children. Because government involvement is of a funding nature, one type of government regulation is funding standards. These standards, which are levels of quality for which the government is willing to pay, are ultimately a form of direct regulation. The 1968 funding standard, the Federal Interagency Day Care Requirements, is a major regulation involving federally supported early childhood programs. It is an effort to insure the same quality of day care services to children regardless of which federal agency provides the monies. This federal regulation is rather comprehensive in nature for it includes standards concerning teacher-child ratios; the number of children treated as a group; services offered to the children; qualifications and in-service training of staff; and parent participation.

Although the intent of developing guidelines is to provide quality services, the guidelines may inhibit some quality services from being offered by not considering the needs for diverse programs, by being incompatible with guidelines used in other programs, and by requiring uniform fund expenditures for programs in various communities. Furthermore, in some states, licensing regulations have been brought in line with the Federal Interagency Day Care Requirements and private proprietors have had to meet the more stringent requirements without subsidy.

REGULATIONS GOVERNING ALL EARLY CHILDHOOD PROGRAMS

Although private and public early childhood programs each have their unique regulations, there are various types or categories of minimum regulations that are common to all programs. Generally speaking, these regulations concern: (1) physical safety; (2) prevention of discrimination; (3) program standards; and (4) staff qualifications.

There is some overlap in the regulations imposed by the various agencies of the federal, state, and local governments. When there are regulations of a similar nature under more than one jurisdiction, an early childhood program must be in compliance with each regulation. For example, a private early childhood program is subject to the fire safety standards of the local city code and the state licensing law. Furthermore, to help insure that both standards are met, most state licensing agencies require that an application for licensure of an early childhood program include proof of compliance with all applicable city ordinances.

389

Fire Safety and Sanitation Requirements

The statutory base for fire safety and sanitation requirements rests in public safety and public health laws, which may be municipal ordinances or state regulation with local enforcement. All public and private early childhood facilities must meet fire safety and sanitation requirements. Certificates of public safety and public health inspections are usually required by licensing authorities as precondition for the license.

Zoning Regulations

Zoning, a local regulation, regulates the location of an early childhood facility. Early childhood programs are often zoned out of residential neighborhoods because of noise factors and out of commercial areas because they are not considered as good places for children. Generally speaking, as density of population increases, zoning regulations become more stringent.

Transportation

In each state the agency which regulates matters pertaining to motor vehicles has the legal mandate to protect people who are transported in buses and private vehicles. In some states special regulations are devised for day care transportation. These regulations are in addition to those required for licensure.

The Civil Rights Act of 1964, Title VI

Any program which uses federal funds must sign an "Assurance of Compliance to the Civil Rights Act." This assurance means that there will be no discrimination on the basis of color, race, national origin, or sex in the employment of staff or the admission of children to a federally funded program. Since much of state licensing is indirectly paid for with federal funds, if the Civil Rights Office finds that any child is excluded from a licensed facility on the basis of discrimination, the exclusion is a denial of his rights, for he has not benefited from federal funds used to license the facility. If an early childhood program refuses to comply with this act it could lose its federal funds.

Local Board Regulations

Each faculty and staff member employed by an early childhood program is governed by the regulations of its governing board, which must be in keeping with the restrictions and authorizations of federal, state, and local laws, directives, and guidelines. The governing board's regulations may include such things as: (1) educational requirements in addition to state certification requirements; (2) salary and related benefits; (3) absences and leaves granted; (4) promotions; (5) evaluations of staff; (6) grievance policies; (7) housing of program; (8) equipment used in program; (9) curricular assistance given to teachers (e.g., detailed course outline, in-service training, resource personnel, or no curricular assistance); (10) plan of staffing for instruction (e.g., self-contained classroom, team teaching, or departmentalized staffing); (11) teaching and nonteaching duties; (12) nature of communication with public (e.g., publicity, citizens' visits or participation in schools); (13) administrative, instructional, and discipline requirements to be employed in working with children (e.g., attendance regulations, methods of determining and reporting children's progress, and discipline, including punishment guidelines); and (14) each administrative and supervisory employee's responsibility in giving direction to faculty and staff.

Regulations Concerning Administrator Qualifications

Administrators of public school early childhood programs must hold their state administrator's certificate which grants legitimate authorization to administer a school program. Administrators of private early childhood programs need not hold an administrator's certificate unless the program is educational in nature. The state education agency issues various types of administrator certificates, such as an elementary principal's certificate, secondary principal's certificate, general principal's certificate and superintendent's certificate. Several states are working toward certification requirements for an early childhood education administrator's certificate. Generally, certification requirements for administrators are:

1. All states require teaching experience (usually three years).
2. States require from fifteen semester hours of graduate work to a master's degree in school administration. Graduate credit is required in courses such as curriculum, supervision, general administration, and specialized fields of administration (e.g., school law and school finance).
3. Many states require two or three years of school administrative experience as a prerequisite for a superintendent's certificate.

Any other qualifications established by the local board or accrediting agency to which the program belongs must be met by administrators of early childhood programs.

Directors, the administrators of private early childhood programs, must meet the educational and experience requirements of their state's licensing law. In some states the minimum educational requirement for a director is a high school diploma, but in other states two years or more of college work must be completed. Minimum experience requirements for directors range from no experience to two years of successful experience in an early childhood program.

Regulations Concerning Teacher and Paraprofessional Qualifications

A teacher of young children performs many roles every day, including functioning as a language model, an arouser of artistic sensitivity and creativity, a relater of knowledge, a questioner, a stimulator of curosity, a learning diagnostician, a guidance counselor and mediator of conflicts, a diplomat with parents, an administrator of a classroom, and more. The teacher also has total responsibility for all that happens to children in the school setting. Because the quality of education is also the teacher's responsibility, there are regulations that help insure that qualified teachers and paraprofessionals are placed with young children.

Certification of Teachers in Public School Early Childhood Education Programs

Certification is the function of granting authorization to teach. Certificates may be standard or provisional and are limited to special fields (e.g., music) and/or levels of instruction (e.g., elementary grades). In most states the state legislature delegates certification responsibilities to the state department of education; these responsibilities usually include: (1) the power to issue, renew, or revoke a certificate; and (2) the task of writing minimum requirements for each type of certificate or to develop guidelines for institutions of higher education to follow in planning a program for prospective teachers. Although the bases for certification are left to each state, most certification standards specify United States citizenship; age and health requirements, earned college degree with special course requirements, and possibly a recommendation from the institution of higher education.

Historical Note

When American kindergartens were first established, prospective kindergarten teachers received their training in Germany and other European countries. The growing kindergarten movement, however, necessitated the establishment of kindergarten training schools in the United States with the first training institution founded in Boston in 1868. These schools offered instruction in Froebelian theory and methods and on-the-job training in kindergarten classrooms. "The training given emphasized the kindergarten as a unique form of education apart from and having nothing in common with the school."[8] In the decade from 1890 to 1900, many public schools adopted kindergartens. The kindergarten training schools were continued as private, self-supporting institutions, because the normal schools were not able to supply the increasing demand for trained teachers.

Many educators realized the desirability of employing state certified kindergarten teachers rather than having the kindergarten work "carried on by people who play a piano and love dear little children."[9] Consequently, many colleges and universities reorganized to meet the needs of students preparing to teach kindergartens. By 1925, in the forty states which had kindergarten legislation, all states had teacher certification laws for kindergarten except for Alabama, Kentucky, Louisiana, Oklahoma, and Tennessee. Most of the certificates were based upon a high school diploma and a two-year professional program, and were special subject certificates valid only for teaching in the kindergarten. In California, Illinois, Michigan, Ohio, and Wisconsin, however, a kindergarten-primary certificate based on a two-year professional program was issued.[10] Recently, the following profile was developed concerning certification for early childhood personnel:

20 states have certification requirements for prekindergarten teachers.
 2 states have certification for prekindergarten paraprofessionals.
47 states have certification for kindergarten teachers.
 6 states have certification for kindergarten paraprofessionals.
11 states require state certification for day care personnel.
31 states accept elementary certification for kindergarten and/or prekindergarten usually with an additional endorsement.[11]

Special Features of Certification Requirements

There are several types of early childhood education teaching certificates. A few states offer a nursery or nursery-kindergarten certificate; others offer a kindergarten or a kindergarten-primary (e.g., K-2, and K-3) certificate. However, as has been noted, thirty-one states accept an elementary (e.g., K-6, K-8, and K-9) certificate or an elementary certificate with an additional endorsement. The requirements for an endorsed elementary certificate usually include two or more early childhood education courses and student teaching in an early childhood program in addition to the requirements for an elementary certificate. This type certificate is becoming more popular, because educators are beginning to realize that early childhood education personnel need specialized training within the elementary education framework. Most states offer only one type (elementary or endorsed elementary) of early childhood education certificate; however, in some states there is more than one type (K-6, N-2, and K-3) of certificate granted.

Generally, early childhood education certification requirements are as follows:

1. Approximately sixty semester hours in the areas of physical and biological sciences, language and literature, mathematics, the social and/or behavioral sciences, and humanities.
2. Most certificates require between twenty-four and thirty semester hours of professional education courses including courses in: (a) introduction to education and/or early childhood education including history and philosophy; (b) human growth and development including guidance; and (c) curriculum content, methods of teaching, and materials and equipment used in teaching.
3. The majority of states require at least three (some states five to eight) semester hours of student teaching in an early childhood education program and additional student teaching in a primary or intermediate level or grade.

4. Many states recommend that course electives be taken in these areas: the psychology of the exceptional child, abnormal psychology, psychology of learning, mental hygiene, parent/community relationships, linguistics, nutrition, speech correction, and school administration and/or supervision.

Prospects for Upgrading Requirements

An *ad hoc* committee on the preparation of nursery school and kindergarten teachers, composed of the National Education Association's Department of Elementary-Kindergarten-Nursery Education, the NEA's National Commission on Teacher Education and Professional Standards, the American Association of Colleges for Teacher Education, the American Home Economics Association, the Association for the Education of Young Children, the National Association of State Directors of Teacher Education and Certification, the National Kindergarten Association, and Project Head Start, was convened to explore problems of providing competent personnel for nursery schools and kindergartens. The committee recommended the following ideas for further study:

1. Certification dependent upon demonstrated competence.
2. Recognition of differentiated staff roles (e.g., teacher aide).
3. Elimination of permanent certificates.
4. Greater opportunities for in-service education for all personnel.
5. Emergency-type certificates should be granted to permit able people to pursue the requirements while working within the profession.[12]

Hansen's analysis of forty-four kindergarten teacher-training institutions indicated that these institutions planned changes toward more appropriate student-teaching programs, additional early childhood courses, better screening of candidates, increased observation and participation in kindergarten programs, efforts to strengthen related subject-matter courses, and provisions for more materials for teaching methods courses.[13]

Staff Qualification Required by Licensing Regulations

The educational qualifications of personnel employed in child care facilities under private control are determined by each state's licensing regulations. In most states directors and care-givers or instructors must have a high school certificate; a few states require college education, usually two years, with course work in child development, curriculum, organization and administration, and methods and materials used with young children.

Licensing regulations often require that assistant care-givers or instructors be able to read and write or have a high school diploma. Professional personnel on the auxiliary staff (e.g., nurse and psychologist) must meet the requirements of their respective specializations.

American Montessori School Certificate

Because the American Montessori Society, Inc., is a national private agency, the instructional staff of a Montessori school would have to meet the licensing code requirements of the state or, in some states, the requirements of the state board of education. In addition to the state's regulations, the American Montessori Society has its own certification requirements:

1. A degree from an accredited four-year college or equivalent foreign credential is required, but no specific field of study is stipulated.
2. About 300 clock hours of academic work including workshops or seminars in: (a) the historical and philosophical foundations of American education and the relationship of Montessori education to current knowledge of child development; (b) knowledge of Montessori theory, philosophy, and materials for instruction as presented in seminars and as seen in observation of laboratory classes; and (c) training in language arts, mathematics, science, art, music, social studies, and motor perception.
3. An internship of nine months in a site approved by the "course director" under an approved "American Montessori Society supervisor" during which the intern is observed by a "training program representative."[14]

Child Development Associate

In an effort to maximize competence of paraprofessionals working in programs for young children, the Child Development Associate (CDA) program was created by the Office of Child Development. The CDA program was planned to upgrade the skills of individuals already working with young children in Head Start, Follow Through, and day care centers, but who lack formal education in child development and early childhood education. The creators of the program hope that eventually these individuals will hold a nationally awarded credential (rather than a state certificate) certifying professional competence for working with children, ages three to five years, in a group setting. Rather than act as an aide, the CDA will be able to care independently for children.

The prospective CDA may receive training through college-planned programs, field work-study and supervised field-work programs; however, regardless of the training received he will have to demonstrate competence in terms of performance with young children. Six general categories of competencies were developed on the assumption that these broad competencies would not violate divergent educational views or cultural backgrounds of various child care programs:

a. Setting up and maintaining a safe and healthy learning environment
b. Advancing physical and intellectual competence
c. Building positive self-concept and individual strength

d. Organizing and sustaining the positive functioning of children and adults, in a group, in a learning environment
e. Bringing about optimal coordination of home and center child-rearing practices and expectations
f. Carrying out supplementary responsibilities related to children's programs[15]

The Child Development Associate Consortium, Inc., a private corporation of organizations involved in child care and early childhood education, is charged with the responsibilities of developing competency assessment and formulating a credential model for the Child Development Associate who is assessed as competent.

ACCREDITATION

Accreditation is a voluntary process of self-regulation. It means that the educational or child care facility has met minimum standards set by the accrediting agency. There are no legal penalties for inability to meet accreditation standards; rather it means failure to gain professional status. Early childhood programs which are accredited by a particular association or agency are not necessarily superior to other programs, although they may be because accredited programs have voluntarily pursued a degree of excellence.

In order to receive accreditation, the personnel of an early childhood program must: (1) apply to the accrediting association; (2) evaluate its facility, staff, and program to be assured it meets or exceeds the association's standards; (3) request a visit and be reviewed by a committee selected by the accrediting association; and (4) accept accreditation when approved by the accrediting association. Accreditation is a continuous process because programs are accredited only for a short period of time. Before the expiration date, a program that desires to remain accredited must repeat the process.

Public schools are necessarily accredited by the state education agency. Because early childhood programs in public schools are considered part of the elementary school, these programs are accredited with the elementary schools in a local school district. In addition to the various state education agencies, early childhood programs that are part of elementary schools may be accredited by the Southern Association of Colleges and Schools. (Among the six regional accrediting associations, only the Southern Association of Colleges and Schools has an arrangement for accrediting elementary schools.)

The Child Welfare League of America, Inc., has an accreditation program. League accredited membership is open to public (e.g., state) and private (e.g., church and charitable organizations) child welfare agencies. Local private early childhood programs licensed by these accredited agencies warrant public confidence in their administration and professional competence.

NOTES

1. Norris E. Class, *Licensing of Child Care Facilities by State Welfare Departments* (Washington, D.C.: U.S. Department of Health, Education, and Welfare, Office of Child Development, Children's Bureau, 1968), p. 7.

2. *A Survey of State Day Care Licensing Requirements* (Washington, D.C.: The Day Care and Child Development Council of America, 1971), p. 6.

3. Class, *Licensing of Child Care Facilities*, pp. 56-60.

4. *A Survey of State Day Care Licensing Requirements*, pp. 5-6.

5. Ibid., pp. 11-13.

6. Class, *Licensing of Child Care Facilities*, p. 6.

7. Ibid., p. 9.

8. Margaret Cook Holmes, "The Kindergarten in America: Pioneer Period," *Childhood Education* 13 (1937): 270.

9. "Marked Kindergarten Progress in the Northwest," *Childhood Education* 1 (1925): 303.

10. Nina C. Vandewalker, "Facts of Interest About Kindergarten Laws," *Childhood Education* 1 (1925): 325.

11. "Where Are We Now?," *Young Children* 28 (1973): 288-M.

12. Helen H. Hartle, "Early Childhood Programs in the States," *Compact* 3 (1969): 19.

13. Harlan S. Hansen, "Analysis of Forty-Four Kindergarten Teacher-Training Programs in Five Upper-Midwest States—Iowa, Minnesota, North Dakota, South Dakota, Wisconsin," *Childhood Education* 47 (1971): 281-82, 284, 286.

14. *Approved Teacher Training Programs* (New York: American Montessori Society, 1973).

15. "The Development of the Child Development Associate (CDA) Program," *Young Children* 28 (1973): 140.

FOR FURTHER READING

Class, Norris E. *Licensing of Child Care Facilities by State Welfare Departments*. Washington, D.C.: U.S. Department of Health, Education, and Welfare, Office of Child Development, Children's Bureau, 1968.

Committee on Infant and Preschool Child of the American Academy of Pediatrics. *Standards for Day Care Center for Infants and Children Under 3 years of Age*. Evanston, Ill.: The American Academy of Pediatrics, 1971.

Morgan, Gwen G. *Regulation of Early Childhood Programs*. Washington, D.C.: The Day Care and Child Development Council of America, 1973.

National Association for the Education of Young Children. "Preparation Standards for Teachers in Early Childhood Education." *Young Children* 23 (1967): 79-80.

A Survey of State Day Care Licensing Requirements. Washington, D.C.: The Day Care and Child Development Council of America, 1971.

ANNIE L. BUTLER

36. Managing School Finances

Good early childhood education is expensive, bringing up children is expensive—and the cost to the community and the family is even greater in later years if the early years of childhood are neglected. These facts must continuously be repeated if children are to be the beneficiaries of good early childhood programs. Opening and operating an early childhood program is a business arrangement, and anyone considering such a venture should enter into it informed about skills that are necessary to succeed. Any private individual who decides to open a nursery school or kindergarten must follow all established legal procedures for opening a business. The Internal Revenue Service will expect him to be accountable for all money spent and received, just as in any other business.

HOW PROGRAMS ARE FINANCED

Public funds are not available for financing preschool programs on a widespread basis. Financing, therefore, is usually a problem that must be faced before any program becomes operational. The common sources used to finance a program are parents' fees, funds from local community chests or from other local fund-raising campaigns, government appropriations for special purposes or for specified populations, endowments, fund-raising by the particular program, and occasional special gifts.

Parents' Fees

The majority of nursery school programs and many day care centers are financed by parents' fees. Many kindergarten programs are also financed by the parents in states which do not allow state aid to kindergarten programs. Cooperative schools, private schools, and church-sponsored schools are largely financed by parents' fees. The fees which are assessed must be in accordance with the expected expenditures. Fees must provide the income which will be expended to run the program, usually allowing a small cushion for emergencies. Private schools as a rule are the most expensive, sometimes charging $800 to $1,000 for the year's tuition. Costs to the family are often cut by having groups of children that attend two days a week and groups that attend three days a week. Most private schools must obtain funds to provide the program as well as some profit for the

From *Early Childhood Education: Planning and Administering Programs* by Annie L. Butler © 1974 by Litton Educational Publishing Inc. Reprinted by permission of D. Van Nostrand Company.

owner. Often the quality of the program varies depending on the extent to which the owner is committed to good education for children compared to how interested he is in making a profit. Making a profit on an early childhood program is not easy because there are limits to the fees young families can afford to pay, and because good programs are expensive to operate. During the initial years of a program particularly, planning to make an appreciable profit is unrealistic.

The cooperative school is able to charge lower fees than the private school because of the contribution the parents make in services as assistant teachers and as officers, committee chairmen, and committee members. The church-sponsored school if it is also a cooperative school is likely to be the least expensive, as it frequently has both the contribution of services by parents and the contribution of space and sometimes equipment by the church. No profit is usually involved in either of these types of program, with the exception of the money the leadership thinks necessary to take care of emergencies, pay bills during the summer, and get the program going the following year. Such programs often maintain a small savings account for these purposes. The account helps each incoming group of parents feel secure in making a few purchases and financial commitments before the tuition for the year is paid.

Assessing fees for day care programs is a much more complex process. All parents with children in day care may not pay the same fee, because of differences in income; therefore, information about the family must be obtained before fees for an individual child can be determined. Several factors determine the fees paid to a day care center, including the auspices of the center, the financing available, and community attitudes toward working mothers and the care of young children outside the home. Fees are much related to the fact that public funds are not permanently available on a widespread basis. In many day care centers, fees must equal costs plus profit, if one is to be made. Even though some community support may be available, the community agency which supplies the support may expect the day care center to supply a part of its budget through its own efforts. There is also a prevailing point of view that parents should pay whatever they can afford.

Before setting fees, information has to be collected about operating costs, about the community, and about the families the program expects to serve. If a program already is in operation, its costs should be converted to a unit cost for care or a cost per child per day.[1] An accountant or auditor familiar with the program will be able to suggest an appropriate method for arriving at this figure by calculating the indirect costs such as utilities, payroll service, insurance, administrative salaries, office supplies and many others.

Community factors which affect the setting of fees are prevailing wage and salary rates, the cost of living, and the distribution of work opportunities by categories such as professional, technical, clerical, and unskilled. The fee schedule in a community having low wages and salaries, a low cost of living, and a large number of semi-skilled workers would

---

[1]Macolm S. Host and Pearl B. Heller, *Day Care Administration*, No. 7, Child Development Series (Washington, D.C.: Office of Child Development, 1971), pp. 133.

be lower than a fee schedule in a community where wages, salaries and the cost of living are higher, and a large number of persons are employed in professional and technical positions.

Situations vary enough so that each school's policy-making body will have to decide its own fee schedule to conform to particular requirements and conditions. Some decisions must be made in relation to: setting of fees for a family from which more than one child is enrolled; how fees should be computed, whether by the week, semi-monthly, or monthly; how absences should be treated; how delinquent accounts should be handled; how fees will be collected, where and by whom; how the money will be protected until it arrives at the bank or other respository.[2]

The policies regarding the collection and handling of fees must be consistent. The procedure should be business-like and receipts should be given to parents as fees are paid. Delinquent fee accounts should be reported promptly and not permitted to continue. Policies should call for prompt exploration of the causes of delinquency and may permit adjustments, especially in case of a partially subsidized day care program. Parents should be encouraged to correct delinquent accounts promptly so that the account does not grow to a size they feel they can never pay off.

Public Funds

Public funds for early childhood education are available largely for the support of kindergartens in public schools in states which have permissive laws. Very little public money has been made available to programs for four-year-olds. Some money is appropriated, through government agencies, for use with specific groups of preschool children who qualify, such as children of working mothers, children from low socio-economic backgrounds, and children of migrant workers. Since this money has limitations imposed on its use, only certain segments of the population are reached by it. This money may be available to public agencies such as the public schools, or it may be made available to private institutions which meet the criteria and the standards of the program. Growing recognition of the need for public programs available for all children is leading to widespread effort to pass legislation which would make funds available for this purpose.

Government agencies sometimes make specific contributions to early childhood programs through providing surplus food, free school lunches, and medical care. Also, space for day care centers is sometimes made available in public housing projects; other public space is made available to programs as an "in-kind" contribution.

Fund-Raising

Often early childhood programs benefit from an annual campaign for public support, such as the Community Chest Drive. Such funds usually

[2]*Ibid.*, p. 134.

do not fully support a program. They are more often designed to make up the difference between an agency's anticipated income from all other sources and its estimated annual expenses. This is a fluctuating amount which must be negotiated each year and is at all times based on the total funds obtained during the drive. Such funds often enable day care programs to subsidize the fees paid by low-income families so that it is possible to set fees in accordance with the families' ability to pay.

Individual programs may also conduct fund-raising campaigns of their own. They may sponsor theater benefits, rummage sales, book fairs, bake sales, or card parties. Often such efforts are more satisfactory if the fund-raising event is planned to raise money for some specific purpose, such as a large, expensive piece of equipment or scholarships for children of low-income families. Some of these projects are well established in the community and have excellent support. Communities sometimes support these fund-raising ventures in recognition of the program's contribution to community life and its importance to children.

Endowments and Other Special Gifts

Some long-established day care programs and nursery school programs are fortunate enough to have continuing income from endowments or property belonging to the corporation. Usually such property has been acquired at the bequest of some individual or foundation that had a special interest in perpetuating the program. To have this source of income is very important to a program. It considerably reduces fees that must be charged to families it serves, particularly if many of these families cannot afford to pay the usual fees.

One-time gifts of small amounts of money for a specific purpose, such as money to supplement the equipment budget or to purchase a certain piece of equipment, are occasionally received by nursery schools and day care centers that are nonprofit. An individual may give money in memory of someone previously associated with the program, or may provide a scholarship for a child whose parents cannot afford to enroll him in the program. Such gifts are helpful if appropriately designated, but cannot be relied on to make a major contribution to actual operating expenses.

Occasionally programs are funded with research and development funds from private foundations, if the purpose of the project is to develop a certain type of program. Research funds may be obtained to support a specific project operating in conjunction with the program. Such funds would not actually support the program but could make it more stable through the research and recognition received.

THE COST OF OPERATING A SCHOOL

The plan for the school budget should be based on an estimate of actual expenditures. During the first year of operation, the estimates will not always be accurate for such costs as supplies and food. With records of actual expenditures, however, a more accurate budget can be prepared for the next year. Keeping accurate financial records is an important part of any business venture. If the person who is to keep the records has not had bookkeeping training or experience, he should obtain help in setting up the bookkeeping system and keeping it accurately. It should be possible to tell at any time how much money the school has, in each of its budget categories.

Some of the categories that should be included in a school budget are as follows:

1. Salaries, wages, and employee benefits.
2. Rent or mortgage payment.
3. Insurance.
4. Utilities—heat, light, water, and gas.
5. Food.
6. Educational equipment.
7. Educational supplies.
8. Household equipment.
9. Household supplies.
10. Office supplies.
11. Publicity.
12. Postage, telephone, and transportation.
13. Professional development.
14. Other services and goods.

Salaries

Salaries make up the largest single item in the school budget. Salaries may vary considerably from one community to another, but the proportion of the budget allocated to salary expenses is usually eighty percent or more.[3] Schools that want to be competitive in the selection of staff will find that their salaries must not lag far behind those of other schools. As the staff is the key to the quality of the program, there should be little economizing on staff, either in the number employed or in the quality of their professional competence.

In making estimates of salaries for budgets, payments for social security and any other retirement plans should be included. Unemployment insurance and medical and hospital insurance should also be included if applicable. An allowance should be provided for normal salary increments according to the policy adopted by the school's board or director. Salary estimates must also include funds to pay substitutes in case of absence or during vacations.

[3]Dorothy B. Boguslawski, *Guide for Establishing and Operating Day Care Centers for Young Children* (New York: Child Welfare League of America, 1968), p. 19.

Rent or Mortgage Payment

The second largest expense in the operation of a school is housing, unless some of the funds for housing can be obtained as an in-kind contribution. If a building is to be purchased for the school, a sum of money will be needed for a down payment, and possibly for repairs or alterations to the building. If the building is rented, some expense may still be necessary for minor alterations, such as partially removing walls to create larger rooms or increasing the number of toilets in the bathroom. Estimates of cost should be obtained from local contractors. Before getting estimates of costs, health and safety inspections should be made so it is known exactly what additional costs will be necessary. Some additions that may be necessary are fencing around the play yard, floor covering for the classrooms, additional exits, doors that open outward, and protection for windows and stairwells.

Insurance

An insurance agent should be consulted to determine the best insurance coverage for the school. The person consulted should be an independent agent, who would be able to make available the policies of several companies. Responsible administrators of a school acknowledge insurance to be an essential cost. Some of the kinds of insurance which should be considered are property insurance or tenants' insurance, which covers fire and theft, accident insurance for children, liability for staff, and public liability for any vehicles operated by the school. Often a fidelity bond is obtained for those persons who are responsible for the handling of funds.

Utilities

Heat, light, water, and gas are utilities which will be a part of the expense of every school, except where one or more of these is included in rental for a building. In some cases, an installation fee will be necessary, but these fees should be fairly stable over a period of years, except if rates change or the size of the school changes.

Food

Expenditures for food are minimal in schools which are open for only two or three hour sessions. In an all-day program, a basic amount for food should be allotted and careful records kept to establish a cost per child per meal. The possibility of reimbursement for school lunches and milk under the School Lunch Program should also be investigated. If storage space is available, buying food in quantity in conjunction with another school or agency can result in substantial savings. It is well to check health department regulations regarding the storage of food before purchasing in quantity, particularly if perishable or frozen food is involved.

Educational Equipment

Equipment means all items which are permanent in the educational program. This includes furniture for the classroom, blocks and other relatively permanent pieces of equipment, toys, books, records, and tricycles. In an initial budget this category represents a considerable expense, as it includes equipment for both indoor and outdoor activities. Although costs will vary considerably, depending on quantity, shipping charges and local resources, budget estimates should include approximately one hundred and ten to one hundred and twenty-five dollars per child for a half-day program.[4] If the program is all day, additional costs will be thirty-five to fifty dollars above the costs of a half-day program to take care of cots, linen, and food service equipment such as dishes and silver, depending on whether these are considered household equipment or educational equipment.

Often costs for equipment can be reduced by having such items as book shelves and toy storage shelves, housekeeping equipment, outdoor climbing apparatus, and possibly tables, constructed locally. Ample money should be allowed in the budget to insure that these items are well constructed and made of the best materials for the purpose, so that they will not need to be replaced for many years. Items used by children need regular cleaning and the finish should be able to withstand hard wear. Often repairs cannot be easily made and constant use ruins inferior products.

The equipment purchased with the initial equipment allotment should include as many of the items of basic equipment as possible, as well as large and expensive items which should not soon have to be replaced. If this is done, the yearly budget for replacement of equipment items can be kept to a minimum. It will always be necessary to replenish the supply of such things as dolls, puzzles, books, records, and small toys at regular intervals. For this kind of replacement approximately three to five hundred dollars per group annually should be allowed.

Educational Supplies

The need is constant for the replacement of expendable instructional supplies. Paint, paper, science materials, and clay fall into this category. If the program gives children many opportunities to work with materials, the materials must be there in abundance and in variety. These items should be conserved without causing the children to feel that they

[4]National Council of State Consultants in Elementary Education, *Education for Children Under Six* (Cheyenne, Wyoming: National Council of State Consultants in Elementary Education, 1968), p. 47.

cannot have what they need for their projects. The cost of expendable supplies is estimated at two hundred and fifty to three hundred dollars per group annually.[5]

If at all possible, small amounts of petty cash should be available to teachers for the purchase of small items which they could not plan for ahead of time and which they will probably have to buy again. Usually the money spent in this way should be limited, and teachers should know the limits. Accounting for petty cash is difficult, and money spent in this way in a large school could, if permitted, become a sizeable budget item. It is equally undesirable if a teacher must spend her own money for every item she needs for the classroom. For example, if the class is planning to make jello, the teacher should not have to buy the jello, and if the school has a half-day session, it would not be on hand unless ordered in advance by the director with other food supplies.

Household Equipment and Furnishings

All-day programs must have a kitchen fully equipped for the preparation of meals and with adequate sanitary conditions. A small half-day program can manage nicely with a small kitchen unit where juice can be refrigerated and where cooking projects can be carried out. A refrigerator is a necessity for all programs to keep food which will be served to the children as snacks.

If the facility has conference rooms, offices, isolation rooms or clinics, furniture must be provided for these. The budget should provide for the purchase of sturdy equipment. Rooms in schools not occupied by a class should be put to multiple uses. Furniture should reflect anticipated uses.

Household Supplies

The chief expenditure for household supplies is for various kinds of paper goods such as toilet tissue, facial tissue, paper napkins, and paper cups. Good record keeping for the first year will provide a sound estimate of the funds needed for these items. For the first year an estimate will be based on the number of children and the amount used during the first few weeks.

Other items include the soaps, cleansers, and other supplies needed for cleaning and sanitation. These must be stored in places to which children do not have access; consequently, the supply which can be purchased at one time may be limited.

Office Supplies

Office supplies needed for a small school are minimal. It may be more economical to have materials duplicated for parents than to employ sec-

---

[5]*Ibid.*, p. 48.

retarial help to do them at the school. Most schools do not need much more than the usual desk supplies and school forms.

Publicity

Every school that is just getting started must find some way of informing people of its existence. Newspaper ads and printed posters are two ways that the school can advertise its services. An ad may be placed in the newspaper in the spring, when applications for fall enrollment are being taken. If allowed to run for one or two days, it may be enough to obtain the required number of applicants. Often attractive posters or flyers giving information about the school can be put in places such as grocery stores and laundromats, which are frequented by young parents. If a school is located in a church or community building, publicity can easily be circulated to the membership or to the people using the building for other purposes. In deciding about appropriate publicity, questions must be asked about the program and the people for whom it is intended, as well as the usual avenues that are used for reaching these people.

From time to time, it becomes necessary to advertise positions that are available at the school. The dossiers of prospective teachers may be obtained from the educational placement offices of colleges or universities or by informing other early childhood educators of the vacancy. Prospective aides, cooks, custodians, and maids can be obtained through the U.S. Employment Office or it may be advantageous to run an ad in the help-wanted column of the local paper.

Publicity will have to be given to fund-raising projects. This is usually done through newspaper ads, posters, and radio publicity, if there is a local station with current-events coverage for the community.

The best publicity that a program can have is the recommendation of young parents satisfied with the program. Young parents often take the recommendation of their friends and do not search further for a school for their children.

Postage, Telephone, and Transportation

Time and energy can be saved if the early communication with parents is done by mail. Forms can be mailed out which parents complete and return to the school. The medical form can be mailed early so that the parent has the form when she is ready to take the child to the doctor.

Even more communication will be by telephone. If the school is to maintain close contact with the family, telephone calls must be made back and forth. Budgeting should provide for a business telephone and should include occasional long distance calls. While it is unlikely that the school will make a large number of long distance calls, they may be necessary in connection with the employment of a teacher or with materials ordered from out-of-town companies.

If the school provides transportation for the children to and from school, this must be a budgeted item. Parents might be charged extra for this service, or it might be included in the tuition. Not all schools wish to assume responsibility for transportation. Schools often help parents become acquainted with other parents in the same locality, so that they may organize car pools, or they may refer parents to a company or individual who contracts directly to provide transportation. Charges are then made directly to the parent without the involvement of the school in the arrangements.

Almost all schools have allocated funds for transportation for school trips. For the protection of the children it is usually necessary to use public transportation or to employ a bus or taxi driver who has licensing and insurance. Although most of the trips taken by young children should be in the school's immediate vicinity, a few longer trips will be taken and must be considered in planning the budget.

Professional Development

One way to encourage teachers to attend professional meetings and workshops is to pay for transportation and registration. Money may also be budgeted for tuition in professional courses taken at a university or vocational school. Often professional materials are purchased, such as professional books, magazines, or tapes of speeches that have been delivered at conferences. Money budgeted for this purpose contributes to the long-term development of the staff and school.

Other Services and Goods

An additional budget item is maintenance of equipment. Even the best equipment wears out, and sometimes minor repairs at the proper time can keep it in use for much longer. The amount which should be budgeted for equipment repair is estimated at ten percent of the original cost of the equipment.[6]

A second type of miscellaneous expense is licensing or registration of the program. This expense occurs infrequently and will not be very large, unless the services of an attorney are required, as in the case of the school's being incorporated.

PURCHASING MATERIALS

Skillful purchasing and distributing of materials is one way that the administration can contribute creatively to the school's effectiveness and efficiency. The careful selection and purchase of supplies can support the kind of program that is considered best for the children. It is possible to support the creative efforts of staff and to encourage variety and innovation in the program in this way.

[6]*Ibid.,* p. 48.

Purchasing Practices

Even very small schools require purchasing from a variety of sources. Because of this, it may be very difficult for them to obtain really good buys, unless someone is available to take advantage of bargains when they appear. Even the small school should keep enough cash in its account to permit it to receive discounts on bills. Sometimes vendors will offer a two percent discount if bills are paid within ten days after they are rendered. The amount of cash on hand should also be large enough to allow for purchases of special supplies from auctions or from surplus property stores. Charge accounts should be established only after the vendor has shown that he will provide a range of items required by the school at competitive prices.

Materials and supplies that do not function properly are false economy. Items such as paper towels that do not absorb moisture readily, and paper that cannot be erased without smudges, only frustrate and hinder the staff. They may save money in the original purchase, but in terms of staff time and satisfaction a great deal is lost. If the quality is the same, the school does not usually need to pay for fancy or separate packaging. The storeroom can protect items against damage and keep them clean, if they are stored in boxes or wrapped in plastic.

All major purchases should require the approval of the director of the program. Usually it is better to have one person make major purchases, although if the purchases are for a particular classroom, approval of the staff member who will use them is wise. Purchasing by too many members of the staff is very expensive in terms of staff time and may cause overexpenditure in some budget categories. Usually it is the director who has full knowledge of the budget allocations and decides whether or not an item can be accommodated within the budget.

Some programs are eligible for tax-exempt status. If this is possible, the school should file a tax-exempt certificate with each vendor with which it has a charge account. Staff members who make cash purchases should also be supplied with a copy of the certificate. Considerable money can be saved over a period of time if the school is tax-exempt.

Purchasing from neighborhood stores is desirable so long as these merchants can meet the school's requirements adequately. It may be that a slight increase in costs is offset by savings in time and transportation. Schools should not feel under obligation, however, to purchase locally when they can benefit from wholesale or quantity prices elsewhere.

Distribution of Supplies and Equipment

A centralized storage space where supplies and equipment are accessible can do much to contribute to the financial management of a school. Centralized storage permits all portable equipment to be cared for and kept in the best possible condition with minimum cost and time. Fewer pieces of portable equipment, such as film projectors and audio-visual machines, are needed if stored in a central location.

Central storage also enables the school to keep inventories more easily and to note when items have to be reordered before the supply is completely exhausted. Necessary measures may be taken to prevent the depletion of certain materials that are badly needed. Items that remain unused on the shelves for exceptionally long periods can be identified. It may be that these materials had been ordered specifically for an upcoming event. It may be that teachers did not know that such materials were available. It could be discovered which items were unsuitable or of inferior quality, or to what possible use they could be put, or how they might be disposed of or resold.

If centralized storage is used, it is very important for the users of the supplies to know that those who make the purchases are sensitive to the needs of the different components of the program so that the practice of hoarding is not established. Large quantities of any kind of supply in one classroom can defeat the purpose of centralized storage, as well as create problems for others who need the materials.

Supplies and equipment should be distributed in a way that is both flexible and business-like. This is simple enough for a school with one or two classrooms, where the personnel work closely together in planning the program. But in large schools and day-care centers, a lot of time could be wasted trying to find out who has what and how long they plan on using it. Equipment that is shared by several classrooms should be checked out for the time it will actually be used. Information on when it will be returned should be part of the reservation procedure so any staff member can tell what equipment is available. Some equipment and supplies will be duplicated, but buying exactly the same equipment for each room is not a good practice when the purchase of similar but different material could enlarge the variety available to any one classroom.

Teachers and other personnel must have access to the storeroom when the program is in session. Some regular procedure for keeping the storeroom open should be worked out. Sometimes it it difficult for storeroom personnel and purchasing personnel to understand that the purpose of equipment and supplies is for the use of the children. It is also sometimes difficult to get teachers to fill out requisitions or make written requests for materials that are needed. Someone should be responsible for reconciling invoices for incoming stock with requisitions for outgoing stock, and the inventory. If this is not done at regular intervals, some materials can disappear and perhaps not be missed until it is too late to do anything about it.

The inventory of equipment should be made each year prior to the school's budget development sessions. This will help to identify what is available for the next year and what amounts need to be budgeted. Budgets cannot be made entirely on the basis of the inventory, as it is necessary to make provision for unforeseen contingencies. It is estimated that a desirable inventory level is one that will carry an organization through two months of operation.[7]

[7]Malcolm S. Host and Pearl B. Heller, p. 156.

PAYROLL

Every school has a responsibility to honor scrupulously its obligations to its employees. One of the most important obligations is to pay its employees on time. This is important not only because it is evidence that the management is conscientious about its fiscal affairs but also because it is closely linked to the morale of the staff. How the payroll is managed is a vital administrative tool for making the partnership work between the administration and the staff.

Before selecting the time and length of the pay period, it is wise to investigate local practices. The number of employees who are paid wages, community practices related to rent payment and credit collection, and the cost of living may be factors that affect the length of the pay period. In many areas it is customary to pay those who earn wages rather than salaries every two weeks. In some areas, salaried employees are also paid twice monthly.

Whether employees are paid wages or salaries, they should know the basis used to compute their daily pay rate. Wages are usually based on an hourly rate. In the case of salaries, the daily rate is obtained by dividing the monthly salary by the number of working days in a month. If this information is clear to the employee, misunderstanding and resentment can be prevented when deductions for absences must be made.

Another practice which helps to prevent misunderstanding is to provide the employee with a payroll check which has a stub showing the kinds and amounts of deductions which have been made. Although employees have been told in advance what deductions will be made, it often comes as a surprise when they see how much is deducted from their checks.

Policies regarding vacations and sick leave should be made very clear. An annual statement should be presented to the employee showing how much sick leave and vacation time has accumulated. Policies may vary widely from one school to another. A school that is in session for only nine or ten months does not have to be concerned about vacations other than those which occur during the school year, such as Thanksgiving and Christmas. A school such as a day care center, which operates the year round, must plan to provide vacation time for its employees, which may mean hiring substitutes. There are also policies about the maximum amount of vacation time that may be accumulated, since an organization must eventually pay for vacation time. Employees who resign are entitled to their accumulated vacation time.

Sick leave is viewed somewhat differently from vacation leave. Most schools allow a minimum, ranging from five days per year to one day per month, for sick leave without loss of pay. If employees have used their sick leave judiciously and undergo a lengthy illness, they will often be given special consideration. If sick leave has been used when there was doubt of actual illness, an employee may not be given such consideration. There should be policies that indicate how much sick leave may be accumulated from one year to the next.

Records of hourly employees should be carefully kept. These records need not be any more complex than a regularly kept time sheet showing the time one reports for work, leaves for lunch and leaves work. There should also be records of overtime, if that is permitted. Policies should be clear on whether employees are to be paid for overtime or given time off instead.

Certain records regarding the payroll are required by law. Annual statements of taxes withheld from each employee's earnings are to be sent to him no later than January 31 of the year following the year in which wages or salaries were paid. W-2 forms, on which this information is to be supplied, are obtained from the Internal Revenue Service. Social Security taxes also require records and quarterly reports which must be filed accurately and on time. The school must deposit the money withheld from salaries in a separate bank account to avoid any suspicion of co-mingling of federal funds with other funds of the school. Co-mingling of federal funds is prohibited by law and violation of this statute carries severe penalties.

Careful records are necessary to administer the payroll responsibly. The school is accountable for all the money that it takes in, and since the payroll makes up a larger portion of this money than any other expense, the greatest care is required in this category.

E. G. BOGUE and ROBERT L. SAUNDERS

37. The Educational Manager: Artist and Practitioner

For years, observers of organizational life have dealt caustic verbal blows to policy makers and policy manuals. It has been said that the last act of a dying organization is to issue a greatly enlarged policy manual. Why, then, in the face of all this advice, do organizations continue to insist on the development and use of written policy guides and manuals? Formal policy must offer some advantage in organizational function.

Actually, policy is very much like any other management tool. It can be used or abused. And the abuse is more frequently related to the user than to the tool itself. Thus, the question is not necessarily whether one should have codified policy or not, but rather what policies are needed and how they can be put to work for more effective organizational function.

From E. G. Bogue and Robert L. Saunders, *The Educational Manager: Artist and Practitioner,* "Policy As a Management Tool," Charles Jones Publishing Company, pp. 127–140. Reprinted with permission by E. G. Bogue and Robert L. Saunders.

POLICY DEFINITION AND ADVANTAGES

Justin G. Longenecker defines policy as a guide for management action.[1] Daniel Katz and Robert Kahn say that policy should include goals and objectives along with the procedures for achieving these goals.[2] William H. Newman defines policy as a "general plan of action that guides members of the enterprise in the conduct of its action."[3] James H. Donnelly, Jr., and others suggest that policy making is a phase of the planning function of management; that policy is the principal instrument for reflecting the basic objectives of an organization; and that it is an important management tool for ensuring goal-oriented behavior.[4] In summary, policy describes the general goals of organizations—their reason for existence—and provides a guide to decision making for achievement of goals.

A frequent difficulty in policy writing is that of recognizing levels of policy. For example, Herbert Simon suggests that there should be three levels of policy in organizations.[5]

1. Legislative Policy—the ethical premises of management.
2. Management Policy—broad nonethical rules laid down by top management.
3. Working Policy—other rules of action and behavior.

As an illustration of the changing levels of abstraction, consider this. A university or a school system may state its intent to provide equal employment opportunity as a matter of legislative policy. As a matter of management policy, it may suggest that 50% of all new teachers hired during a year be members of minority groups. As a matter of working policy, it may prescribe the recruiting procedures that will lead to the realization of both management and legislative policy.

We should note that the level of abstraction is reduced as one begins to interpret policy in an organization—and therein lies some of our greatest difficulties and causes of abuse. It is one thing, for example, for a college governing board to promote the personnel policy that "all faculty shall have a weekly teaching load of at least 12 course hours or its equivalent" but quite another to interpret in an operational sense what "equivalent" means. A noble aim is expressed in the policy that teachers should be accessible to students, but quite a different motive may be given to the interpretation which says that all teachers must be in their offices until 4:30 p.m.

Similarly, it is possible for two educational organizations to have the same general policy for direction and quite different operating policies. For example, two colleges may give allegiance to the traditional goals of instruction, research, and service. But in the interpretation and implementation of that policy, one may decide to have an open admissions policy and another a selective admissions policy. Two urban school systems may subscribe to the same learning goals, with one being tightly centralized in its structure and operation and the other being totally decentralized. This is not unique to educational organizations. Business and industrial organizations can subscribe to the same directional policy but operate on widely divergent marketing and production policies.

Formal and Informal Policies

The policy expressed in a manual is just one manifestation of organizational beliefs and practices. In most organizations, and most certainly in educational organizations, there is an informal, implicit set of policies at work. They may not be in the book, but they are just as real and just as effective. For example, in one school system there was a formally published procedure for teachers to request transfers to another school. The policy described the criteria to be employed in such decisions and the forms and procedures as well. In actual practice, however, teachers were aware of "board feeling" that to request a transfer was equivalent to requesting assignment to lower regions of Hades.

In a university there was an institutional and formally published policy concerning change-of-address procedures, including the last dates to add and drop courses. However, there was considerable variance in the informal policy held by two different colleges of the university. In one college, student applications for change of course were treated impartially and with dispatch. In the other, the attitudes of the dean and faculty were such that a student hesitated to request any change of course, no matter what his reason. These two informal policies yielded interesting differences in student performance and failure rates—even though neither of them was formally described in university policy statements.

Advantages of Published Policies

Policy is basically designed to define organizational direction, to outline management intent, and to provide a guide for decision making. Some of the reasons for publishing policy in formal guides or manuals are:

1. *Delegation of Authority.* Policy amounts to an extension of managerial authority and thus permits decisions to be made without constant reference to higher authority.
2. *Efficiency in Decision Making.* If the routine and recurring decisions in an organization can be made on the basis of policy, the manager's time is not wasted in dealing with decisions which are repetitive.
3. *Economy of Management Effort.* Published policy should enable decisions, especially recurring ones, to be made deeper in the organization. Thus, the top-level educational manager should be freed to spend more of his time and energy in managing exceptions and in planning.
4. *Consistency and Equity in Decision Making.* Differing judgments can result in unequal treatment of employees, particularly in the

413

critical areas of workload and rewards. Written policies should encourage equity and consistency of interpretation and application.

5. *Continuity and Training.* Procedures located only in the head of one who has left the organization are singularly hard to retrieve. An urban school system learned this lesson the hard way when its director of computers and administrative processing resigned. There was no documentation of either policy or procedure—which suggests that a new director was probably needed anyway. The absence of documentation created major disruptions in the system operation. These disruptions were at least tolerable until checks for teachers and administrators were one week late.

6. *Better Human Relations.* The human relations advantage may not be immediately apparent or even believable, for it is in this area that policy most frequently seems abusive. However, policy should have a rationale and philosophical base that leads to a better understanding of reasons for actions and consequently better human relations.

The Manager and Policy Formation

Speaking of the role of the educational manager in policy development, Robert Hutchins said that the "administrator must accept a special responsibility for the discovery, clarification, definition, and proclamation of the [institution's] end. But he does not own the institution."[6] Roald F. Campbell and others pointed out that the "community, [governing board] and the chief administrator are directly involved with policy formation."[7] The nature of this interaction is described by Calvin Grieder, Truman Pierce and K. Forbis Jordan.

. . . in policy making and legislation [by the governing board] there is a reciprocal relationship between the board and school personnel . . . If policies and legislation are to guide administration, those who make policies and legislate must know what administration requires. Hence policy making and legislation must be guided by what administration knows about the schools. The executive must point the way for those who have responsibility for education. Legislation can energize administration; administration alone can inform legislation.[8]

Certainly, the educational manager has responsibility for policy initiative at the level of "management" and "working" levels previously mentioned. We believe also that he has responsibility to work with governing agencies in the development of legislative policy. A leadership role in policy formation has a solid foundation in practice and is safely short of usurping a governing board's prerogative in establishing policy.

POLICY ABUSES AND DYSFUNCTIONS

All of us are familiar with ways in which the policy tool is abused. A quick review of illustrative cases may suggest guidelines for improving the quality of policy.

Inadequate Concept of Policy Definition

Some policy manuals and guides are not policy at all but sets of procedures. Newman points out that the distinction between what is policy and what is procedure may well depend upon the perspective from which the content is viewed.[9] Occasionally, policy manuals may contain not only policy but job descriptions. The policy manual of one university devoted large portions to descriptions of major academic and administrative positions. There was no policy that dealt with the responsibilities of key academic personnel and major program areas. For example, there was no visible policy in such areas as promotion, tenure, evaluation, and curricular review. Yet one could easily find such vague and useless statements as "The Vice President for Academic Affairs coordinates with the other vice presidents on matters of concern to the University." What constituted "matters of concern" was a mystery insofar as the formal policy manual was concerned.

Development of Policy for Exceptions

Educational managers are prone to develop policy for handling exceptions rather than for general decision situations. Because managers deal so frequently with the exception, it is easy to develop policy on this basis. For example, the research director of a large university discovered that scientists in one of the research institutes were using the university computer for personal consulting work. Ignoring the fact that there were no abuses in the other six research bureaus and centers, the director published a policy which contained an elaborate set of control processes for any research use of the computer.

In reviewing financial records, the deputy superintendent in a large city school system found that a high school principal had equipped his school with an expensive laboratory in astronomy. That his high school had at best a mediocre program in basic physics did not stay this principal from investment in rather esoteric equipment. Infuriated at this exhibition of poor judgment, the deputy superintendent "promulgated" a systemwide policy requiring all purchase requisitions to be approved at the superintendent's level. This, of course, penalized the other principals who had exercised balanced judgment, convinced them that the superintendent's staff only existed to make life hard for them, and probably did little to correct the judgment of the single offender.

Policy as an Artificial Protector of Status

Educational organizations abound with policies that serve no productive function other than artificially protecting academic status. Colleges frequently limit maximum student load to 16 or 18 credit hours. The theory is that no student can do a respectable job with a greater load, especially in view of the rigor of college work. This premise ignores the fact that many bright and energetic students can well handle more course work, but they have to fight their way through policy and process just to earn the right to try. In reality, rigorous educational programs would make it improbable that a student would take more than eighteen hours. But we ensure the "status" of our program through a policy which prohibits students from trying to test the rigor of our programs. We thus produce a self-fulfilling prophecy; namely, that if we do not permit students to try we can be comfortable that indeed we do have rigorous, high quality programs.

This kind of policy nonsense is rampant in graduate programs as well. Ordinarily, advanced degree work should keep the fulltime student adequately occupied. But we ensure an artificial rigor by policies which do not permit full-time students to hold jobs which require more than 15 to 20 hours a week of work. Of course, many intelligent and energetic students will carry full loads and moonlight jobs without our knowledge. They simply circumvent the policy.

No better example of this dysfunction exists than the matter of course prerequisite systems. Instead of defining prerequisites in terms of skills and knowledges required for successful performance, we define them in terms of other courses. In some disciplines, it is possible for a student to perform quite well without having had a parade of undergraduate courses in that discipline. But this is troublesome to our academic prestige, so we establish a pseudo prestige by insisting that a student show a long list of undergraduate hours before we will permit him to take graduate work.

Policy as a Punitive Tool

Senior colleges in one state decided that they should adopt some policy which would discourage the newly emerging community colleges from infringing on senior college prerogatives. That is, they did not want community colleges to offer more than two years of work or to entertain aspirations of becoming senior institutions. These senior institutions, therefore, promoted a policy which said that students could transfer no more than 60 course hours from a community college. On the surface, this would seem to serve exactly the purpose the senior institutions had in mind.

But this policy had a senseless effect on students. Here is a true illustration. One student, needing only a freshman level course in general biology to graduate, was told he could not take the course in his hometown, regionally accredited community college. The student had already transferred 60 hours from a community college. Hence, he must travel 100 miles to attend a senior college for one class.

Use of Policy as a Substitute for Managerial Courage

In some institutions, policy is invoked as a substitute for managerial courage. Managers can develop a policy to get at a single offender without

416

having to deal with him on a face-to-face basis. The principal in a large elementary school noticed that two teachers were habitually late. Rather than engage the issue head-on, she published a policy which required that *all* teachers sign in when they arrive and sign out when they leave, thereby adding another control on the teacher who is on time and providing a challenge for the two late teachers, who within a week found a way to cheat the process.

Policy as a Substitute for Good Judgment

Policy can become a substitute for exercising good judgment in some situations. For example, in one university the official policy was that married women were not permitted to change their name of record unless they could present a notarized statement of the change. To accommodate students, one of the clerks in the registrar's office was a notary public. Students were treated to the curious process of being turned down by the first clerk, sent two steps left to get a notarized statement, and then moved back two steps with the notarized statement for the official change. Whatever the original philosophy behind this policy, it had clearly been bent all out of shape. Perhaps the reason for this kind of behavior is that no provision had been made for exceptions.

Newman suggests that policy flexibility can be ensured only when exceptions to policy can be made quickly enough to secure the benefit of concession.[10] If we cannot respond quickly, then we promote the kind of rigidity exemplified in these illustrations.

Inadequate Communication of Policy Rationale

A student enters the registrar's office of First Rate College and requests that a copy of his transfer work from Excel College (from which he had recently transferred) be sent to a prospective employer. The records clerk informs the student that college policy will not permit her to send a transcript from Excel, that she can only send a transcript from First Rate College. The student asks why. "Because it's against our policy," replies the records clerk, as she brandishes the college policy manual in her right hand. Exit one angered student.

Now just a moment taken to explain the rationale behind this policy would have helped everyone. The student might have been calmed if he could have understood that past abuses by students had caused registrars to agree not to release transcripts from other institutions because registrars have no way of knowing whether a student has outstanding obligations, especially financial ones, for which the record is being held. Unfortunately, however, no one ever bothered to explain this rationale to the records clerk; hence, she could hardly pass it on to the student.

That the communication of policy is important is emphasized by Longenecker:

Policies often affect many who are not directly involved in their formulation. Managers at lower levels, for example, are expected to apply policies adopted at "headquarters." Employees including managerial personnel, are also expected to conform to policies regulating personal behavior. This creates a need for communication of policies to all personnel who are concerned with them.[11]

In the matter of educational policy, Robert L. Saunders and others have dealt with both the philosophical and research bases for communication and involvement in policy matters. They point out that more adequate decisions are likely to emerge when those affected by the policy are involved in its development.[12]

Overprescriptive Policy

There are organizational tasks of a technical and sensitive character which demand close adherence to prescribed rules. This may be especially the case in the flow of information and materials which must eventually be automated for computer analysis. However, we occasionally will write policy which is overprescriptive for the situation.

An electrician in a county school system was nearly electrocuted when he fell across a high voltage line and was saved only when a carpenter working nearby pulled the main power switch. With noble purpose, the director of plant published a policy which in effect said that maintenance personnel must work in pairs. It is at least questionable whether the policy increased safety, but there is no question that it had a negative effect on the efficiency of maintenance operations. Even the locksmith who is called over to unscramble the tumblers in the lock of the superintendent's door must take along his helper. Such a policy is clearly overprescriptive and, to emphasize a point previously made, a substitute for good judgment.

Maintenance of Obsolete Policy

In some of our educational organizations, expensive resources are wastefully spent because obsolete policies are still in effect.

The president of a small college was infuriated that two faculty members gave exams early in the summer term and left the campus two days before the term was over. Substituting policy for courage, he published a policy which in effect said that both instructors and students must be present on the day in which final exams were officially scheduled. Ten years later, two deans are following this policy to the letter with an interesting ritual. They have departments which give exams prior to regularly scheduled finals, and these exams serve as a final for the course. In each case, however, the instructors and students in these departments are required to show up at the time published in the schedule of classes. They sign a piece of paper which indicates that they were there and then leave.

Unfortunately, inattention to policy evaluation and revision is all too prevalent. Martin K. Starr has pointed out that lawyers and judges are employed full-time to provide interpretation of social policy and spend little time in evaluation of policy, which is a legislative and executive function. In organizations, however, these two obligations are entrusted

418

to the manager. Thus, educational managers should not only attend to the interpretation of policy but remain vigilant to the need for policy evaluation and revision.[13]

IMPLICATIONS FOR POLICY ACTION

What ideas can be extracted from these illustrations of policy abuses that will help educators improve the quality of policy performance? Let us structure these ideas into four phases of policy activity: policy development, policy communication, policy execution, and policy evaluation.

Policy Development

The first phase of policy activity is that of policy development. We need to keep several ideas before us. The first of these is to ensure that what we publish is indeed policy and not procedures or job descriptions. Policy should outline points of organizational direction, management intent, decision processes, and personnel involvement. Properly developed policy will in fact provide operational definitions of positions by describing the ways and means by which various positions are involved in decision processes.

A second concept to guide our action is recognizing that educational organizations are organic in nature. That is, parts of the organization are interdependent. Consequently, there are few matters of policy that do not have complex action roots. This idea suggests broadly based involvement in policy development.

Another notion is that some freedom is necessary for efficiency. We should not freeze the initiative and good judgment of effective personnel by publishing policy designed to control the actions of a small number of ineffective persons. Policy should not be used, therefore, as a punitive tool but as a tool to facilitate organizational operation.

Policy Communication

Policy communication is a cyclical process. It begins in the formulation phase, continues in the execution phase, and starts around again in the evaluation phase. There are a number of ideas to guide us. First, the effectiveness of a policy can hinge on a single word or phrase. The wording, style, and tone of written policies should receive rigorous review so that the policy will elicit positive feelings rather than hostile responses.

The responsibility for execution of policy often falls to those who have had little involvement in the policy development stage. We do well to remember that involvement builds allegiance. But it does more—it protects the quality of policy decisions. Successful policy action is more probable if those who are affected by policy actions are involved, or at least represented, in the development deliberations.

Finally, we will want to keep in mind that many managerial attempts to produce efficiency can have quite an opposite effect in action—especially if the philosophical base on which the policy is built is shaky or if the communication of policy rationale is poor. Thus, we can expect to see few instances in which it is sufficient to put a policy in action by the simple expedient of a memo or transmittal letter. The more thorough and personal policy communication can be made, the more likely we are to obtain the desired performance.

Policy Execution

Good policy will usually represent some compromise between philosophical elegance and administrative simplicity. There are some educational managers who have a hard time understanding this. But the simple truth is that the philosophical elegance of a policy has little value unless the intent of that policy can be translated into actions which are capable of being managed. This, of course, usually means that policy leaves some room for judgment. And well it should, because policy is not a substitute for good judgment on the firing line and it is not a substitute for managerial courage needed to deal with poor judgment. It is true that policy should encourage equity in the decision-making process; but if we attempt to write policy that will in action remove all initiative, risk taking, and judgment, we create organization automatons.

Policy Evaluation

No managerial tool reaches obsolescence so quickly as policy. Our system of policy activity should provide a means of ensuring continual review, evaluation, revision. The best judges of policy function are those who must use it. Our system should provide for feedback from the operating level and responsive action when a policy becomes obsolete. Managerial sensors should identify those times and places where existing policy has become dysfunctional and isolate those personnel who use policy as a recipe rather than a guide.

SUMMARY

Policy is a management tool. It can be used to indicate organizational goals, value positions, and ways of achieving these goals. Policy can be both formal and implicit. Properly and artistically applied, policy can promote delegation of authority, efficiency and consistency in decision making, and better human relations. It can facilitate training and continuity of organizational functions.

But policy can be abused and frequently is. It can become a recipe rather than a guide, an excuse for inaction and poor judgment, a substitute for managerial courage, a punitive tool rather than a facilitating one. Policy can be narrowly conceived and poorly communicated.

The effective educational manager will develop an artistic touch in the use of policy as a management tool. He will work to formulate policy which is the product of broadly based thinking and involvement, combining philosophical soundness with administrative simplicity, balanced in prescription and freedom.

Notes

1. Justin G. Longenecker, *Principles of Management and Organizational Behavior* (Columbus, O.: Charles E. Merrill, 1969), p. 101.

2. Daniel Katz and Robert L. Kahn, *The Social Psychology of Organizations* (New York: John Wiley and Sons, 1966), p. 260.

3. William H. Newman, *Administrative Action: The Techniques of Organization and Management* (Englewood Cliffs, N.J.: Prentice-Hall, 1963), p. 40.

4. James H. Donnelly, Jr., James L. Gibson, and John M. Ivancevich, *Fundamentals of Management: Functions, Behaviors, Models* (Dallas: Business Publications, 1971), p. 72.

5. Herbert Simon, *Administrative Behavior* (New York: The Free Press, 1965), p. 59.

6. Robert M. Hutchins, "The Administrator," *The Works of the Mind*, Robert B. Heywood (ed.), (Chicago: University of Chicago Press, 1974), p. 151.

7. Roald F. Campbell, Edwin M. Bridges, John E. Corbally, Jr., Raphael O. Nystrand and John A. Ramseyer, *Introduction to Educational Administration*, 4th edition (Boston: Allyn and Bacon, 1971).

8. Calvin Grieder, Truman M. Pierce, and K. Forbis Jordan, *Public School Administration*, 3rd edition (New York: The Ronald Press, 1961), p. 127.

9. Newman, *Administrative Action*, p. 42.

10. Ibid., p. 44.

11. Longenecker, *Principles of Management*, p. 107.

12. Robert L. Saunders, Ray C. Phillips, and Harold P. Johnson, *A Theory of Educational Leadership* (Columbus, O.: Charles E. Merrill, 1966), pp. 84–85.

13. Martin K. Starr, *Management: A Modern Approach* (New York: Harcourt, Brace, Jovanovich, 1971), p. 429.

THE OPERATING PROCESS

There is a saying among administrators: "Plan the work and work the plan." In operating an early childhood center, the administrator is doing just that; he is "working the plan"; he is putting into action the established goals, objectives, policies, and procedures of the center. Operating a center entails literally hundreds of activities on a day-to-day basis. To aid the new early childhood administrator with these activities, readings in this chapter were selected that deal primarily with those areas of center operation that an individual initially will have to consider to accomplish established goals and objectives.

Making the most constructive use of the total human resources available is at the heart of operating an early childhood center. As Gross and Katz suggest in their articles, an administrator must not forget the all-important dynamics of the early childhood teacher. The early childhood teacher must possess those qualities that provide warm and stimulating opportunities for young children.

As the "swinging door" concept of recruitment and staffing become obsolete, staff training is an increasingly important facet of running a center. Kaplan-Sanoff provides models for the all-important training and development of early childhood personnel.

Pickering's article is not only practical but innovative in its approach to curriculum development in early childhood education. Its step-by-step procedure for curriculum design will be welcomed by all individuals involved with early childhood education.

Teacher-parent relationships are a subject that has long been an area of importance in working with young children. However, the increasing number of young children in early childhood facilities makes teacher-parent relationships a growing area for concern. Handler acknowledges the need for cooperative and productive relationships among teachers and parents to assure the best educational opportunities for children.

One need not be a nutritionist to consider the relationship between human growth and proper nutrition, according to Sinclair. As a result, it is necessary for administrators to look carefully at the food services within their centers.

DOROTHY WEISMAN GROSS

38. Teachers of Young Children Need Basic Inner Qualities

There has been much, not to say overriding, concern these days with the education of very young children. How children learn and what we should teach them are subjects of much research and discussion. But comparatively little has been said about who is to do the teaching. State departments and boards of education proliferate long lists of course requirements for licenses and certificates, implying that a "qualified" teacher is one who has two credits in Arts and Crafts and three in Educational Psychology. Universities evolve complex courses of study for training teachers, often neglecting matters of personality and attitude. The heart of the matter—the inner qualities needed for working effectively with young children—has been strangely overlooked. Let us explore here some of those basic inner qualities.

First, there is enjoyment in learning. This is one way of saying what Fritz Redl put more vividly as "children want some adult in a clear-cut role of somebody who feels it is fun to watch them learn." After all, one central issue in education, even in preschool education, is love of knowledge for its own sake, the conviction that knowing, by itself, can bring delight. Clearly, if we wish our children to love learning we must provide them with teachers who love learning. A teacher who likes to learn will take steps on her own to increase her knowledge through courses, reading, professional conferences, participation in art and music.

A teacher who enjoys seeing children—and parents—learn will study environments, physical and human, which best encourage learning and attempt to establish them. A teacher who is fascinated with the processes involved in solving problems can be relied on to invent the structure necessary to facilitate that problem-solving. Parent seminars and staff meetings, organization of routines and carefully planned placement of materials are, after all, forms invented to help people find out things.

The oft-cited requirement that teachers should love children is questionable without further definition. Love for children, in an educational sense, is most appropriately the effort the teacher makes to help children understand themselves and the world. In other words, a teacher should base her relationship to a child on the curriculum she creates out of a knowledge of his personal and developmental needs.

The question of how a teacher can distinguish a child's needs and decide on a proper curriculum for him leads to the second quality needed,

Reprinted by permission from *Young Children*, Vol. 23, No. 2 (Nov. 1967), pp. 107–110. Copyright © 1967, National Association for the Education of Young Children, 1834 Connecticut Avenue, N.W., Washington, D.C. 20009.

the ability to distinguish between personal and others' needs. The way in which a teacher uses her needs, predilections and idiosyncrasies to help children learn depends, in the first place, on her becoming aware of herself as a person. The implications are manifold: The teacher who can keep a clear picture of herself as distinct from the children she teaches will be less likely to use the children to satisfy her own needs for affection and more able to plan curriculum suitable for them. She will be more able to help parents find their own directions in living with and guiding their children. She will be less likely to interpret children's and parent's behavior as either personal tribute or personal threat and sees its significance, instead, in its relation to their own learning drives. It must be obvious that little change can occur in curriculum unless there are changes in the thinking and behavior of teachers.

But if, as research on children's learning has suggested, maturing in children is stimulated by mastery of skills and knowledge, i.e., immersion in the real events of every day and learning how to handle them, so, too, may it be with teachers. Not only must a teacher train herself in self-awareness but she must have knowledge about how young children learn, the third point. A recognition of the importance of self-discovery, of room for error, of concrete experience, of supportive structure in children's learning must be part of the professional equipment of every teacher of young children. Based on these, she must know appropriate material and how to create curriculum. While keeping clear about the aims of the school, she must be able constantly to adapt and invent curriculum so that it flows with the tide of the children's learning.

This leads to the fourth point, that the teacher of young children must have a personality which is comfortable with open-endedness. This is a rare trait to find in combination with the others but a necessary one. In a school appropriate for young children, there would be much moving about, touching, testing, questioning, guessing, noise. Answers would become new questions and few timetables would be set for achievements. Order would exist but of an organic kind, not openly obvious. For a teacher to function effectively in such a setting requires an ability to draw strength from inner order, a disposition which is challenged rather than threatened by openness, and a talent for creating meaning out of seemingly unconnected experiences. A good teacher of young children may be slow-moving or quick, voluble or silent, gregarious or shy, impulsive or measured, intense or gentle. There is room for much variation in personality. But the basic inclination towards the unanswered question—the journey rather than the arrival—is a necessary quality in one who would work with young children.

Finally, if a teacher is to work effectively with young children, she must take pleasure in working with parents. Nor is this so simple, implying as it does that her own attitudes towards authority have reached at least a minimum level of maturity. Fear of parents, open or veiled hostility towards them, condescension, disrespect of their opinions are still all too common among teachers. Working with children who are still so subject to the influence of their parents is a difficult task for a teacher. She must be nondefensive and flexible enough to accept parents' ideas

424

and contributions while developing the self-confidence and professional maturity to give them the help they need and want. Exaggeration of either—surrender of standards in attempts to be "friendly" or arrogation of all knowledge and authority—will mitigate against the health of the learning situation for the children.

Only one of these qualities is dealt with in any degree in most teacher-training programs—understanding of how children learn. Some attempt is usually made, through course work and/or field work in schools, to expose prospective teachers to the developmental and learning ways of young children. Rarely are any of the others even considered. But without some degree of self-knowledge and flexibilty, deep interest in learning for its own sake, and honest acceptance of children's homes and parents, concern with how children learn becomes meaningless and even mechanical.

We have moved, since the early days of teacher training, from emphasis on curriculum—the *what* of education—through stress on methods of teaching—the *how*—to concern with the child. Now, influenced by the Cold War and our own Civil Rights struggle, we are involving ourselves again with what to teach. Is it not time to add to these traditional concerns a deep examination of what is needed in the teacher of young children?

LILIAN G. KATZ

39. Teaching in Preschools: Roles and Goals

In general, evaluative research on early childhood education is typified by tests of aspects of children's behavior before and after attendance in a program without reference to the possible effects on children of teachers and their behavior.

However, there is no shortage of literature *about* teaching in preschools. At least a dozen recent books and scores of articles have carried discussions about teachers, especially about the "good" or "effective" teacher. In these discussions many terms appear to describe the behavior of teachers: *teaching style,*[4,5,6] *teaching methods,*[7] *teacher approach,*[8] *teacher pattern,*[9] *teacher role,*[3] *teacher tempo and manner,*[10] and

From Lilian G. Katz, "Teaching in Preschools: Roles and Goals," *Children* (now *Children Today*) Vol. 17 (March–April 1970), pp. 42–48. Reprinted with permission of Lilian G. Katz and *Children Today*.

teacher personality.[11] Often the same author uses several of these terms interchangeably.

Because this confusion of terms makes the task of synthesis and analysis complex and difficult, I have found it useful to make a basic distinction between two aspects of teaching: teaching *role* and teaching *style*.

The term *role* refers to that aspect of the teacher's behavior that concerns *the duties, responsibilities, and functions expected of the teacher by her clients and herself*. The term *style*, on the other hand, refers to that aspect of the teacher's behavior that might be called the *individual rendering with which the teacher's role is performed*. For example, the role of the teacher—her functions, duties, and responsibilities—might be to instruct, but her style of instructing might be humorous, warm, authoritarian, or cold.

The role concept has been extensively discussed in educational literature.[12] It provides a fairly simple way of examining and thinking about many different kinds of social positions and the expectations of behavior that surround these positions. One of the important elements in this concept is that the social roles, or the kinds of behavior expected of people in specific social positions, are largely independent of the particular persons occupying the positions at any given time. Thus, whether the teacher is Mrs. Smith or Miss Jones, she is expected to carry out certain tasks and to behave in certain expected ways. The behavior expected of the person performing the role of teacher remains the same.

While the teacher's role is concerned with her functions, duties, and responsibilities towards her clients—children, parents, and employers— the teacher's style is concerned with *how* the role is performed and, therefore, involves individual differences. Such qualities as humor, warmth, creativity, passivity, and spontaneity, for example, can be thought of as aspects of teaching style.

ROLE MODELS

Over the years, teachers of young children have followed three basic role models:

1. *The maternal model* puts major emphasis on keeping children safe, comfortable, busy, and happy. A major responsibility of the teacher is to help the children become what is popularly called "well behaved." This model represents the teacher as a kind of mother substitute who is expected to fulfill the mother's responsibilities, duties, and functions while the child is away from home.
2. *The therapeutic model* puts major emphasis on helping children express inner feelings, work out tensions, and resolve whatever inner conflicts may be impeding their early development.[13] This model has had a strong and productive place in the development of preschool education. The teacher focuses her attention on the children's mental health[14] to "correct any defective socialization processes and to

strengthen the child's ego functioning."[15] Moustakas describes the teacher's role in this way:

> . . . to help children grow both as unique individuals and as important members of the group, to help them feel comfortable in expressing themselves, and to help them develop a positive attitude toward school . . . to help children resolve their tensions and conflicts.[16]

3. *The instructional model* puts major emphasis on the deliberate transmission of information and knowledge and the conscious training of children to develop skills—that is, on direct instruction or structured programs.

Each of these three role models—maternal, therapeutic, and instructional—has its own variants. Each also has its own particular strengths and weaknesses. Although the maternal model still exists in practice, it is not generally being advocated today.[10] On the contrary, recent research has stimulated efforts to help mothers become better teachers or to adopt a teacher role model.[17,18] The maternal role is sometimes referred to disparagingly as "custodial care" or "glorified babysitting."

The therapeutic model still enjoys an important place in early childhood education.[19] However, some shifts in emphasis seem to be occurring. We are moving away from building a protective and psychologically safe environment around the vulnerable young child and toward helping him develop the strategies and strength for coping with his natural environment.

THE "IN" MODEL

No doubt elements of all three models are followed by all teachers. Certainly, people do not come in "pure" types of anything! However, current trends seem to indicate that the instructional model is "in." But I sense a great resistance to it among teachers whose nursery school training and experience are rooted in the pre-Sputnik, pre-Head Start era.

The instructional role presents three major problems: problems stemming from confusion between academic and intellectual goals; problems of teaching style; and problems relating to teacher-client relations.

Since the function of the instructional role model is to transmit knowledge and skills to the children in a premeditated fashion, the curriculum is not left to emerge when the children's interests are spontaneously expressed or awakened, as it is in the therapeutic model. The teacher plans what knowledge and skills are to be taught and learned before she meets the individual children in her class.[20,21]

I find it useful to distinguish between academic and intellectual goals associated with the instructional model. With academic goals, the effort is to help children adjust to school, develop testable skills, and learn to conform to the daily routine and expectations of the typical public school classroom—that is, to acquire the role of pupil. Gracey, writing of kindergarten as an "academic boot camp," says:

> The unique job of the kindergarten in the educational division of labor seems rather to be teaching children the student role . . . the repertoire of behavior and attitudes regarded by educators as appropriate to children in school . . . the learning of classroom routines . . . all the command signals and the expected responses to them.[22]

This function of teaching the pupil role, now being urged upon nursery schools, works toward academic rather than intellectual goals.

With intellectual goals, the effort is, through guiding and encouraging curiosity about the environment, to help children develop skills in problem seeking and problem solving—that is, to acquire the role of learner. The emphasis is on the children's motivation to learn, rather than their motivation to achieve.

Planners with intellectual goals may also have *a priori* commitments to specific knowledge and skills to be learned by the children, but they are more likely than planners with academic goals to be sensitive to stages of learning, individual differences among children in learning styles, and children's readiness for specific kinds of learning. Certainly the academically oriented planners are interested in the children's intellectual growth. But the intellectual goals are often "lost in translation," and such losses very likely stem from the fact that intellectual stimulation depends on the teacher's style rather than on her role.

EFFECTS OF STYLE

As I have already mentioned, the term *teaching style* is a way of talking about the differences between teachers within any given role model. For example, the Montessori method is a specific variant of the instructional role model. The Montessori literature defines the duties, functions, and responsibilities of the teacher; but if you see more than two or three Montessori teachers at work, you will certainly see differences in style. Similarly, among teachers who use the Bereiter-Englemann method, you can see great variations in style. Some teachers are alert and enthusiastic and work with humor, zest, and warmth; some are dull, sullen, or grimly serious; and some are detached or authoritarian.

Similarly teachers who follow the therapeutic role model show great variations in style. Some are more active or intrusive than others, some are more stable and so forth. Such individual differences in style exist even though the teachers perceive their functions and responsibilities in very much the same way.

Research thus far has not produced direct evidence regarding the effects on children of different teaching roles and styles. The results of some studies suggest that a teacher's style may be a stronger determinant of the effects of her work than the role model she follows. Moreover, we do not know whether certain role models tend to attract people with particular style inclinations—warmer people, for example, to the therapeutic model, or serious people to the instructional model—or whether there is no inextricable linkage between role and style. These questions have not yet been studied.

Conners and Eisenberg studied the behavior of 38 Head Start teachers in a 6-week summer Head Start program in Baltimore in 1965.[23] All the teachers in their sample were experienced public school teachers. Trained observers recorded the "discrete episodes" in their behavior:

> Each statement of the teacher to a child or the group was recorded vertabim. An episode was defined as a change in the triangular relationship between teachers, children, and the environment.[23]

The episodes recorded in this way were scored on the basis of their "values"—the implicit goals that these activities were judged to serve, such as the development of the concept of self, consideration for others, intellectual growth, or neatness. On the basis of these scores, the teachers were classified as placing a high, medium, or low value on each of these goals. In addition, the teachers were given an overall rating combining ratings on warmth versus coldness, permissiveness versus restrictiveness, activity versus passivity, and variety versus lack of variety.

The children's growth was assessed by administering the Peabody Picture Vocabulary Test (PPVT) at the beginning and at the end of the Head Start program. The results indicated that the children whose teachers were rated "high" on valuing intellectual growth and were *also* rated as "warm" showed the greatest growth in intelligence as measured by the PPVT. Those whose teachers placed a high value on intellectual growth but were not rated as warm did not achieve appreciable growth; nor did those whose teachers received a high rating on warmth but a low rating on valuing intellectual growth.[23]

These findings seem to support the proposition that the instructional *role* has a positive effect on children if the *style* of the teacher is warm.

Beller's study of Head Start teachers supports this proposition. Beller looked at teachers regarded by their supervisors as "good" or "poor" in an effort to determine their effects on children's skills in solving problems. He reports that the children whose teachers—

> . . . made less distinction between work and play, who were more flexible in their classroom arrangements and more flexible in programming their instruction performed better on our problem-solving task. . . .[6]

Since these teachers were largely the ones regarded as "good teachers," it would seem to be their teaching styles that distinguished them from the "poor" teachers.

Prescott and Jones studied 104 teachers in Los Angeles centers, as well as the children in their care.[10] The children's behavior was rated on a 5-point scale according to level of interest and involvement in their activities. The results indicate that children's level of interest and involvement is high "when teachers behave in certain specific ways." The researchers report:

Positive responses from children are highly related to encouragement. They are also related to teacher emphasis on verbal skills, and to lessons in consideration and creativity and pleasure, awe and wonder. They are negatively related to restriction, guidance, and lessons in control and restraint and rules of social living.

Thus some evidence is emerging to support the proposition that the instructional model, both in its academic and intellectual variants, can be performed with warmth and can carry a therapeutic effect for children needing it. However, more empirical studies of teacher behavior and its effects on children are urgently needed before any teacher role model can justifiably be denounced. Reports emanating from the modern British infant schools suggest that the instructional model, with a strong intellectual emphasis, can be performed in such a way that teachers maintain great respect for and enjoyment of children. Respect and enjoyment seem to be elements of teaching style.

Perhaps one of the most serious problems with the now popular instructional role model is that the role is easily "packaged" and "sold," but that the all-important style elements—such as flexibility, warmth, enjoyment, and encouragement—are neglected. They are aspects of teaching not easily "packaged." There is some evidence that such neglect of style can have deleterious effects on children.[10,24]

Of course, the roles and styles of teaching are not the only determinants of the outcomes of preschool education. Size of center as measured by the number of children served, type of sponsorship, and the quality and quantity of physical space and equipment are important factors in determining what the teachers and children do.[10] Climate too is a factor. The same teachers vary significantly in their behavior in winter and spring.[25]

Another aspect of preschool centers that has not been studied in relation to its effect on children is the distribution of decision-making authority. An example of this came up during a recent visit I made to a Head Start day care center in the midwest. I sat down to have lunch with the children at the center. The children were very friendly, and the food was very good.

"What is this red stuff we're eating?" I asked the little boy next to me.

"Jello," he answered.

"Where did it come from?" I asked.

"Out there," he said, pointing in the direction of the kitchen.

"Where do the people out there get it?"

"From the tree."

"What kind of a tree?"

"A jello tree."

"Have you ever seen a jello tree?"

"Uh huh."

"Where did you see a jello tree?"

"Downtown," he answered.

"On T.V.," said another boy at the table.

"On a apple tree," said another.

Later I suggested to the young teacher that the children might be included in preparing their food: some could stir, some could watch, or taste, or measure, and so forth. The teacher replied, "You talk to the cook."

As it turned out, the cook was an awesome woman. She had a territory, her own area of command, and *nobody* was allowed in that territory, certainly not dirty little boys with dirty little hands! (She was unaware that the State health regulations were on her side.) The teachers were afraid to cross her. Until it was suggested to them, they did not realize that jello could be prepared in the classroom. I am sure they have been making jello with the children ever since!

My friends with elementary school backgrounds tell me that janitors have a similar sense of autonomy which sometimes conflicts with the elementary classroom teachers' authority.

TEACHERS AND PARENTS

This brings me to the third problem associated with the instructional role model: the relationships between teachers and their clients.

Whenever I ask a group of preschool teachers "Who is your client?," the response is invariably "the child." This seems reasonable, since the child is the direct recipient of the teachers' services. But like people in other professional roles, teachers have many different clients. They include the parents, the children, the school board, and the community. It seems to me the primary client is really the parent.

Nursery school teachers have long emphasized the building of close relationships with parents, and on the whole, they have worked with parents who were receptive to their views on preschool education. But today the differences between the expectations of parents and preschool teachers constitute one of the most serious issues facing the profession of preschool education.

Many nursery school teachers, especially those who were in the field of nursery education before Head Start, have a sophisticated and complex view of the nature of learning and development. Some actively try to help parents see the soundness of their views, methods, techniques, styles, and goals in working with young children. They talk of children's learning through play, through self-selected activities, creative activities, exploration, and experimentation. They make complex assumptions about the psychodynamics of growth and development, and the meaning of children's behavior.

Many parents find it hard to understand the concepts behind the teachers' methods and so they complain when they see children "just playing" in the classroom. Preschool teachers are under great pressure—sometimes open, sometimes indirect—to prepare children for school. They are responsible to parents who seek some tangible evidence that they are in fact preparing children for the role of pupil. Caldwell has pointed out that "mothers are looking for professional leadership to design and provide child-care facilities that help prepare their children for today's achievement oriented culture."[18] Many parents are expecting teachers to perform a kind of teacher role and adopt a kind of teaching style that the teachers do not like.

In my review of research I found no systematic study of the conflicting expectations of parents and teachers in Head Start. However, I did run across some informal reports of such problems. In an extensive survey of summer Head Start programs in Massachusetts in 1965, Curwood reported on the basis of interviews with parents that "most of the (Head Start) programs, even with a minimal child development emphasis, failed to meet the parents' expectations for more formal education."[26]

In another study, Wolff asked teachers and parents to suggest improvements in the Head Start curriculum.[27] The teachers listed such items as "more materials, more time on emotional and social development" while the parents suggested "more teaching, more work including ABC's and numbers." Similar problems are brought out in Polly Greenberg's sensitive and moving account of Head Start in Mississippi:[28]

> We had to interpret parents' insistence on having children learn ABC's to mean they were insisting that the children learn *reading*. . . . If CDGM [Child Development Group of Mississippi] planners were going to claim to be deeply concerned with community values and parents' ideas, we could not stoically resist parental convictions that reading is critically important.

Sieber and Wilder[29] studied the teacher role preferences of the teachers and parents of first, fifth, and 10th grade children in regard to four basic role models: content oriented; control oriented; discovery oriented; and sympathy oriented. In brief, they found that the younger the child, the more the mother is likely to prefer a "control oriented" teacher, and that this is especially true of the mothers from "working class" families. Only 36 percent of the mothers interviewed preferred the "discovery oriented" teacher role, but 56 percent of the teachers interviewed identified themselves with this model. Moreover, 69 percent of the mothers differed with their children's teachers in their preference of teacher role models. The researchers suggest that as the participation of parents increases in the schools, the level of dissatisfaction will also increase.

Unfortunately, no study of this kind has been carried out with Head Start teachers and parents. However, I would hazard a guess that the disagreement between the teachers' and the mothers' preferred teacher role in Head Start would reach about 80 percent.

IMPLICATIONS FOR THE FUTURE

The first impression gained from our current, but limited, knowledge is that the role models to which teachers are committed may not be as important to their effectiveness with children as their individual styles of teaching. However, from the evidence now available, the instructional role model cannot be ruled out entirely. Perhaps a fresh conceptualization is needed: something like that implied in Caldwell's term "nurcher" from the verb "to nurture"[18]—the adoption of an instructional role performed with style characteristics that facilitate growth—to help children become both learners *and* pupils.

The second implication that might be drawn from current knowledge is that if nursery school teachers continue to emphasize goals other than teaching the child the pupil role—even though they adopt a healthy mixture of a therapeutic role plus an intellectual emphasis—they will lose the very parents who most need their help, their skill, and their understanding. Whatever may be wrong with the public schools, preschool educators have no right to deny the child's need to acquire the social role of pupil.

Finally, a most important implication of current research findings is that when the child is taught his ABC's, colors, shapes, and school-type tasks, something may be set off between the child and his parent that could make a profound difference in his development. It may be that having her child come home with a specific skill increases his mother's confidence in his future and that a mother's confidence in her child's future has continuing positive effects on his development.

The most important question for a preschool teacher to ask herself concerning her role, style, and goals may be: *What am I doing to increase the mothers' confidence in the future of their children?* Perhaps the resistance to current pressures is a reflection of the preschool educator's sensitivity to children; but unless there is just as sensitive a response to their parents, what is done for the children may be lost.

Notes

[1]Nehrt, R. C.; Hurd, G. E.: Preprimary enrollment of children under six, U.S. Department of Health, Education, and Welfare, Office of Education, Washington, D.C. 1969.

[2]Sears, P. S.; Dowley, E. M.: Research on teaching in the nursery school. *In* Handbook of research on training (N. L. Gage, ed.). Rand McNally, Chicago, Ill. 1963.

[3]Katz, L. G.: A study of the changes in behavior of children enrolled in two types of Head Start classes. Unpublished doctoral dissertation. Stanford University, Stanford, Calif. 1968.

[4]Rashid, M.: The teacher, teacher style and classroom management. Paper presented at the Head Start Research Seminar, Washington, D.C. July 1968.

[5]Garfunkel, F.: Teaching style: the development of teaching tasks. Head Start Evaluation and Research Center. Boston University, Boston, Mass. 1968.

[6]Beller, E. K.: Teaching styles and their effects on problem solving behavior in Head Start programs. Study V. Head Start Evaluation and Research Center. Temple University, Philadelphia, Pa. n.d.

[7]Gage, N. L.: Teaching method. *In* Encyclopedia of educational research, 4th Edition. (R. Ebel, ed.) The Macmillan Co., New York, N.Y. 1969.

[8]Reichenberg-Hackett, W.: Practices, attitudes and values in nursery group education. *Psychological Reports*, October 1962.

[9]Prescott, E.; Jones, E.: Patterns of teacher behavior in preschool programs. Unpublished paper presented at the biennial meeting of the Society for Research in Child Development. Santa Monica, Calif. 1969.

[10]_____: Group day care as a child rearing environment: an observational study of day care programs. Pacific Oaks College, Pasadena, Calif. 1967.

[11]Rosen, J. L.: Personality and first year teachers' relationships with children. *School Review*, September 1968.

[12]Wallen, N. E.; Travers, R. M. W.: Analysis and investigation of teaching

methods. *In* Handbook of research on teaching. (N. L. Gage, ed.) Rand McNally, Chicago, Ill. 1963.

[13]Read, K. H.: The nursery school. W. B. Saunders Co., Philadelphia, Pa. 1960.

[14]Gans, R.: Young children at the turn of this era. *In* Early Childhood Education. (N. B. Henry, ed.). Forty-sixth Yearbook, Part I. National Society for the Study of Education. Chicago, Ill. 1947.

[15]Mattick, I.: Adaptation of nursery school techniques to deprived children: some notes on the experiences of teaching children of multiproblem families in a therapeutically oriented nursery school. *Journal of the American Academy of Child Psychiatry*. October 1968.

[16]Moustakas, C.: The authentic teacher. Howard A. Doyle Printing Co., Cambridge, Mass. 1966.

[17]Hess, R. D.; Shipman, V.: Early blocks to children's learning. *Children*, September–October 1965.

[18]Caldwell, B. M.: What is the optimal learning environment for the young child? *American Journal of Orthopsychiatry*, January 1967.

[19]Biber, B.; Franklin, M.: The relevance of developmental and psychodynamic concepts to the education of the preschool child. *Journal of the American Academy of Child Psychiatry*, January 1967.

[20]Gray, W. W.; Klaus, R. A.; Miller, O. J.; Forrester, B. J.: Before first grade. Teachers College Press, New York, N.Y. 1966.

[21]Bereiter, C.; Englemann, S.: Teaching disadvantaged children in the preschool. Prentice Hall, New York, N.Y. 1966.

[22]Gracey, H. L.: Learning the student role: kindergarten as academic boot camp. *In* Readings in introductory sociology. (D. H. Wrong and H. L. Gracey, eds.) The Macmillan Co., New York, N.Y. 1967.

[23]Conners, K.; Eisenberg, L.: The effect of teacher behavior on verbal intelligence in Operation Head Start children. Johns Hopkins University School of Medicine, Baltimore, Md. 1966.

[24]Katz, L. G.: Teachers and children in two types of Head Start classes. *Young Children*, September 1969.

[25]Wilensky, M.: Observational techniques in preschool classrooms. Institute for Developmental Studies, School of Education, New York University, New York, N.Y. 1966.

[26]Curwood, S. T.: A survey and evaluation of Project Head Start as established and operated in communities of the Commonwealth of Massachusetts during the summer of 1965. Final report.

[27]Wolff, M.: Is the bridge completed? *Childhood Education*, September 1967.

[28]Greenberg, Polly: The devil has slippery shoes: a biased biography of the Child Development Group of Mississippi. Macmillan Company of Canada Limited, Toronto, Ontario. 1969.

[29]Sieber, S.; Wilder, D.: Teaching styles: parental preference and professional role definitions. *Sociology of Education*. Fall 1967.

MARGOT KAPLAN-SANOFF

40. Theory and Practice: A Model for Staff Training and Development in Early Childhood Education

As money for staff training and development is drastically reduced in most early childhood programs nationwide, the problem of developing economical and effective staff training becomes of paramount importance. What skills do new teachers and those teachers just beginning to work in early childhood need to develop to become quality teachers of young children?

Many of these teachers had no intention of working with young children. College graduates seeking jobs in early childhood settings are often trained in elementary education, and professionals and paraprofessionals enter the field for economic and social reasons wholly unrelated to their knowledge of and interest in young children. Suddenly, these teachers find themselves in the unenviable position of having to develop a workable teaching method that satisfies both supervisors and parents. It is no wonder that they often end up teaching for survival, adapting strategies from other teachers that seem to work rather than developing a defensible teaching philosophy. Teachers often settle for ad hoc, trial-and-error methods that seem to provide some measure of success. In the long run, however, these ad hoc solutions do not provide the most effective tool for classroom management or for child learning. A teacher without an overall framework tends to give children mixed messages about her expectations for them and about their own level of worth. Moreover, a teacher who lacks a coherent theory of learning makes her job far more difficult, for she has no fixed or rational basis for making the many daily decisions that confront her in teaching.

Although it is questionable whether any staff development and training program can make novice teachers feel totally at ease with their new responsibilities, certainly these programs can encourage teachers to confront their own beliefs about learning and help them to apply those beliefs consistently in the daily workings of the classroom. At present, staff development tends to be parceled out into sessions that compartmentalize theory and practice, making it difficult for teachers to integrate the two areas. But to be most successful, training should introduce teachers to a wide range of theoretical perspectives on the teaching/learning process and suggest the kinds of classroom strategies that derive from them. This is not to say that training should dictate specific teaching strategies or styles to teachers; rather, it must make teachers cognizant of the theoretical assumptions that underlie their classroom practices so that those practices will be congruent with the individual teacher's beliefs. What follows in this essay is a brief model of how this integration can be accomplished in early childhood education. I will first discuss the major theoretical perspectives on child learning and then consider the strategies and teacher behaviors that are consistent with these perspectives.

THEORETICAL PERSPECTIVES ON LEARNING

Romantic Model

The prevailing view of development in the 1960s held that intelligence is fixed at birth and that the rate of development is predetermined. There is little need for early stimulation since genetic endowment sets clear limits both on the child's intellectual development and his rate of growth. The child is seen as a flower, blossoming naturally if given sufficient nurturance. Psychologists and educators perceived the child as actively controlling his predetermined destiny, while the environment remains essentially passive, merely supporting his physical growth. Unique self-identity is the goal of education—to develop inner feelings of security, self-worth, and trust. Kohlberg (1972) termed this orientation towards teaching the "romantic" or "bag of virtues" strategy and identified it with the early social action and Head Start programs that stressed "the emotional and social development of the child by encouraging self-confidence, spontaneity, curiosity, and self-discipline" (Grotberg, 1969). But perhaps the best educational example of this philosophical view was A. S. Neill's *Summerhill*. To Neill, the teacher's role is to create an unconflicted environment in which the child can learn about himself through uninterrupted play and exploration.

ACTIVE	PASSIVE
Child	Environment

Behavioral Model

In the 1960s, the research findings of Benjamin Bloom (1964) and Samuel Kirk (1958) shed new light on the notion of genetic endowment determining potential. Although these researchers granted that the outer limits of potential are certainly determined by heredity, they reported that the rate of intellectual development can be altered by changing the environment. Working with young retarded children, Kirk was able to accelerate significantly the rate of their intellectual development by providing a stimulating preschool experience. This new knowledge of the variability of human potential led many educators to reverse totally their earlier view of the environment as being passive and unimportant. Instead, they conceptualized the child as a static switchboard, a passive organism through which the environment actively transmits facts, rules, and values. The task of the teacher becomes the transmission of knowledge through direct instruction and imitation; the teacher literally pours facts into the empty vessel of the child's mind. As Bereiter (1972) strongly argued, children "must learn to be taught." Learning becomes the acquisition of a successive chain of behaviors, each behavior specifically taught to the child

436

through a stimulus-response paradigm. The teacher provides the stimulus (a question, a problem) to which the child responds with the correct answer; the teacher then reinforces the response.

TEACHER: This is a fork. What is this?
CHILD: This is a fork.
TEACHER: Good talking.

The output or rote memorization of the child becomes the focus of instruction. One can only observe and evaluate the specific terminal aspects of behavior; inferred social growth or intervening cognitive processes can not be seen and are therefore ignored. The metaphor of the switchboard allows for only teacher input and child output, not the mysterious workings of the inner "black box" (Levitt, 1968). Incidental learning also becomes invalid since the goal is not predetermined by the teacher, nor can the results be measured or evaluated.

ACTIVE	PASSIVE
Environment	Child

Because the child only responds to the input of others, his desire to learn is naturally perceived as being externally motivated by tangible rewards or the avoidance of unpleasant consequences. Thus the goal of education in this behavioral approach is the acceleration of learning in areas crucial to academic achievement; it is a highly task-oriented approach to the teaching of specific knowledge. The child's behavior is evaluated by his conformity to societal norms, that is, all four-year-olds must learn to recite the alphabet. Necessarily future-oriented, the behavioral model analyzes the skills that a child needs to be successful and then systematically teaches those skills by a lock-step approach. The curriculum is fixed and the child molded to it. The scope and sequence of many reading and math readiness programs are predicated on this idea; all children need to learn the names of the letters and numerals before they can learn to read and add. There is basically one approach to the acquisition of knowledge, and it can accommodate only a limited range of individual differences in children.

Whereas Neill (1960) argued the ultimate importance of social growth —"if the emotions are free, then the intellect will take care of itself"— behaviorists like Bereiter (1972) saw success in the cognitive domain as a prerequisite for the development of self-concept. In other words, self-image is enhanced by learning how to recite the alphabet. There is also little room for spontaneous play in this no-nonsense approach to education. Whatever play does exist is usually adult-initiated and adult-prescribed, for example, Bereiter and Englemann's (1966) suggestion that the teacher deliberately "trick" the children with wrong answers to obvious questions.

Developmental Model

However, Bloom's findings that the environment can affect human development led to a third model of child learning. According to Piaget

(1952) and Hunt (1966), learning is conceptualized as an interaction between an active environment and an equally active child. The child is pictured as a computer, an information processor with a capacity for storing information and for retaining a vast repertoire of strategies that can be used to process data from the environment. The child is actively involved in his own learning. Out of his large repertoire of possible mental operations, the child selects those operations most appropriate to a given situation. In other words, the child both manipulates and is manipulated by the environment through a continuous interaction between his thought processes and the responses he receives from the environment.

ACTIVE   ACTIVE

Child initiates interaction ⟵——————— Stimulates environment to respond

Environment responds to child's initiation

Feedback Loop

In this model, thought is dependent on experiences with/and feedback from the environment. With the child's maturity, this sensorimotor approach to learning becomes more internalized, the child using pictorial and linguistic symbols for manipulation rather than actual concrete objects. As such, inner behavior and incidental learning are taken quite seriously; though processes and actions on objects are regarded as the true index of learning, rather than mere rote performance or self-identity.

Education is defined as the progression of the child through invariant, ordered, sequential stages of growth with the goal of attaining a higher level or stage of functioning. The sequence of stages is assumed to be the same for all children, although individual children may fluctuate greatly in the rate at which they proceed through each stage. These sequential stages are also hierarchical; attainment of a preceding stage is a prerequisite for success in the next stage of growth. Thus knowledge of the sequence of skill development provides a broad framework in which to define the present operating level of the child and to project which experiences the child needs to progress to the next highest stage of development. The teacher's role is to provide a "proper match" between the child's present level of operation and those challenges in the environment that further his development by causing him to question his thinking and reorganize his inner mental structures (Hunt, 1966).

Yet not every change in behavior is considered growth; changes in structures have to lead to greater differentiation, integration, and adaptation (Kohlberg, 1972). Piaget (1952) postulated that young children are intrinsically motivated to achieve that higher level of development. From his perspective, internal mental structures need to be used; metaphorically, these structures need aliment or nourishment to grow, and the environment provides that nourishment. Children are pulled towards the novel and complex stimuli in the environment, and, in their efforts to extract meaning from these events and to resolve the conflict between what is known and what new data are presented, children achieve greater integration of thought processes (Berlyne, 1960).

In this developmental model, spontaneous, self-initiated play is vital to child learning. Play allows active manipulation of the environment and clarifies thinking through social interaction. Since peers are better able to provide the proper match for the child than an older adult, play becomes the primary way for children to test out their thoughts on others in the environment.

STRATEGIES FOR TEACHING

From this discussion of theoretical perspectives, it becomes possible to define specific teacher behaviors and strategies that derive from a particular model of child learning. Because the child controls much of his own learning in the romantic model, the teacher's role is that of passive observer. She prepares the classroom so that children can learn on their own in an unconflicted environment, and she rarely intrudes upon the child even when she sees him demonstrating intellectual confusion in play. Intervention to protect the rights of the child still remains unobtrusive, consisting of the teacher visually looking on, placing herself physically near the child, or using nondirective statements (Wolfgang, 1976). Evaluation of learning is also within the child's domain, because the teacher may be unaware of the goals the child has set for the learning experience. For example, the teacher observes two children building in the block area. As they stack blocks to make their tower, they count, 1-2-6-7." However, the teacher merely continues to observe, noting that sequential counting has not yet been achieved. She does not intervene. From her perspective, the socialization and linguistic skills being exercised by the two children are far more important than a rote performance of facts. Because her role is primarily that of an observer, she feels no responsibility for providing exercises in play to correct the child's misconceptions (Almy, 1967).

On the other hand, the behavioral teacher makes most of the decisions on what and how skills will be learned. The teacher sets the stimulus, often demonstrating to the children a model of what she expects, and the children respond to that stimulus automatically. She then rewards those children whose products have met her expectations. There is usually one correct response to the stimulus, with the evaluation of learning based upon teacher perceptions and cultural correctness. Emphasis is on a structured approach to achieving a terminal behavior. Thus the teacher chooses the activity—"Today we're going to make Halloween pumpkins"—and displays her finished pumpkin as an example. She then provides the specific materials needed to imitate her pumpkin—"You will each get one orange circle, black paper, scissors, and paste."—and reinforces those children who immediately begin to copy her model. The children's end results are evaluated for their conformity to a single standard of correctness, the teacher's. Workbooks and programmed texts function in much the same way, demonstrating the first correct answer and then providing those materials that the child will need to complete the task. From a behavioral perspective, teachers function as controllers, transmitters of information, and evaluators of child performance.

Consistent with the view that children gain knowledge about how the world works through concrete and mental operations on objects, developmental teachers emphasize the value of the child's active manipulation of materials and ideas. And although the teacher functions as an observer, noting the individual activities of children, she also functions as a facilitator, subtly guiding the children's growth by providing an environment that ensures the proper match between each child's present level of operation and the next highest stage of development. Learning, then, is a process of mutual decision making between teacher and child; the teacher creates a supportive environment in which the child pursues his own interests in learning. Whereas the motivation to learn is essentially intrinsic, the developmental teacher acknowledges her role as a guide, presenting the child with new experiences and challenges to help him achieve his preset and incidental goals. Thus, teaching strategies remain extremely open-ended, relying on the child's initial interest and interactions with the environment. As a facilitator, the teacher helps the child in his learning through open-ended questioning strategies— "What would happen if . . ."—and the presentation of new information and material—"See if this tape will help your collage to stick." Rather than assuming there is only one correct answer to a question, the teacher supports numerous responses and solutions to problems. And because she assumes that internal cognitive processes are more important than verifiable correct answers, she stresses divergent thinking and problem-solving rather than conformity or self-identity.

Although advocates of each of these theoretical models tend to treat their positions as separate and distinct from the others, these models represent merely three fixed points along a single continuum of teaching beliefs. The continuum illustrates the range of teacher beliefs concerning the degree of teacher-child control and the role of motivation in child learning.

BEHAVIORAL	DEVELOPMENTAL	ROMANTIC
High Teacher Control of How and What Is Taught	Mutual Decision Making on Goals	High Child Control with Free Exploration
• child as passive responder	• child active within given limits of equally active environment	• teacher as passive observer
• extrinsic motivation necessary for children to learn	• intrinsic motivation to gain control over the environment	• intrinsic motivation to create, explore, and grow

FIGURE 1.

After examining their assumptions about how children learn, it then becomes possible for teachers to locate their unique positions along the continuum. Teachers need not identify completely with any one of the three established theoretical positions; rather they can choose an intermediate position somewhere between the extremes. Thus, a teacher who believes in mutually decided contracts between children and teacher, but who also rewards with stars on the finished contracts, might be placed somewhere between the behavioral and developmental models.

The idea of the continuum also serves a secondary function, helping teachers identify both their current teaching behaviors and their ideal teaching beliefs. By identifying the differences between actual classroom behavior and theoretical teaching beliefs, teachers and their supervisors can begin to analyze how to make practices and beliefs more congruent, in other words, how to move from point A to point B along the continuum.

When confronted with this idea of choosing a theoretical position and teaching strategies consistent with that position, teachers often complain that the learning materials chosen by the school force them into a specific teaching style over which they have no control. This complaint, however, is rarely valid, for teachers who blame school administrators and parents for their own unwillingness or inability to use materials in divergent ways are merely begging the issue. Whatever tasks and materials are assigned by the school or funding agency can be approached from differing perspectives; teachers who can identify their own theoretical teaching style can also use the prescribed materials and texts in ways that are consistent with their style. Thus, if the school demands completion of a readiness workbook, then the developmental teacher could individualize her approach so that instead of reviewing a concept with the entire class before completing a page in the workbook, she could let the children work at their own pace, completing pages as they progress.

Teachers must also understand the implications of each theoretical position so that their goals and expectations for child learning are congruent with their teaching strategies. If the teacher wants the children to complete all work in a certain way within a specific time period, then she must also accept a certain lack of creativity within her classroom, and she must understand that creative thinking will probably not increase as the year goes on. However, if she values creativity, she must accept that assigned work might not be finished at the same time or with the same dispatch that she might want. It becomes crucial for each teacher to establish priorities based upon her theoretical position so that she does not set conflicting goals for herself or for the children.

Teachers who can identify their theoretical assumptions and classroom strategies related to child learning have several distinct advantages over those teachers who must continually flounder among diverse, and often conflicting, educational approaches. Most importantly, those teachers who can identify their positions are able to make daily educational decisions based upon a rational, consistent framework of beliefs. Answers to such a variety of questions as how to serve meals during the school day, how to keep records, and how to arrange the classroom can be derived from those essential beliefs. Thus, if one assumes that children are intrinsically motivated to learn and that in striving to gain control over the environment, they need adult guidance, then meals might be serviced family style with each child serving himself, records might include lists of activities initiated by the child, and the classroom might be organized so that children could choose freely from a broad array of materials the ones that provide the proper match for their developmental needs. Conversely, a behavioral teacher might serve meals herself, perhaps from the head of the table. She might maintain exact records of observable performance—"correctly identified 3 out of 5 colors from the color board"—and her room might be clearly divided into teaching areas where materials used for learning are available only upon teacher direction.

Second, teachers with a firm understanding of theoretical perspectives are able to justify their positions of teaching to their supervisors, principals, and parents. Whether she wants a sand table to help children develop social, motor, and cognitive skills or a box of toy reinforcers for a token economy, the teacher who can explain her goals for teaching and how her strategies will achieve those goals will have a higher probability of getting administrative and parental support.

Finally, teachers who are able to acknowledge a firm theoretical orientation are also in a position to evaluate their own teaching performance. Thus, the behavioral teacher who stresses facts and correct answers can evaluate her teaching in terms of the children's conformity to her standards: "Are they able to respond to my questions with the correct answers?" Similarly, the developmental teacher with her emphasis upon cognitive operations and divergent thinking can judge her teaching based upon the children's ability to problem-solve creatively and to learn independently within the classroom.

Clearly though, before teachers can begin to evaluate their own assumptions about child learning and the teaching strategies that are consistent with those beliefs, training programs must first provide a comprehensive curriculum that will encourage teachers to integrate theoretical positions with daily teaching practices. Although it is outside the scope of this article to present a detailed proposal for such a curriculum, several general guidelines can be suggested. First, training programs must stop compartmentalizing theory and practical application. Rather than exploring the linguistic capacities of young children in one theoretical session and the specific techniques for teaching language arts and reading in another session, training should provide a comprehensive approach that helps teachers integrate theoretical positions about cognition with techniques that convey language concepts to young children. Training must also provide extensive exposure to varying teaching models through visits, films, and speakers so that teachers can observe different teaching strategies firsthand and make informed decisions about their own teaching style. Finally, supervisors and trainers must firmly support the independent decision-making skills of teachers. If the goal of staff development is to train teachers who can articulate and defend their own beliefs about the teaching/learning process, then trainers and supervisors must allow these teachers the freedom to explore various, and even opposing, teaching styles and the openness to question age-old assumptions about teaching and learning.

References

*Almy, M. "Spontaneous Play as an Avenue for Intellectual Development." *Young Children* 22 (1967): 265–276.

Bereiter, C. "Moral Alternatives to Education." *Interchange* 3 (1972): 25–41.

Bereiter, C., and Englemann, S. *Teaching Disadvantaged Children in the Preschool.* Englewood Cliffs, N.J.: Prentice-Hall, Inc., 1966.

Berlyne, D. *Arousal, Conflict and Curiosity.* New York: McGraw-Hill Book Company, 1960.

Bloom, B. *Stability and Change in Human Characteristics.* New York: John Wiley & Sons, Inc., 1964.

Grotberg, E. *Review of Research, 1965 to 1969.* Office of Economic Opportunity Pamphlet 6108-13. Washington, D.C.: Research and Evaluation Office, Project Head Start, Office of Economic Opportunity, 1969.

*Hunt, J. M. "The Epigenesis of Intrinsic Motivation and Early Cognitive Learning." In *Current Research in Motivation*, edited by Ralph N. Haber, pp. 335-370. New York: Holt, Rinehart and Winston, 1966.

Kirk, S. *Early Education of the Mentally Retarded.* Champaign, Ill.: University of Illinois Press, 1958.

Kohlberg, L., and Mayer, R. "Development as the Aim of Education." *Harvard Educational Review* 42 (1972): 449-496.

*Levitt, E. "Process and Product: Two Views on Cognition in Children." *Young Children* 23 (1968): 225-231.

Neill, A. A. *Summerhill.* New York: Hart Publishing, 1960.

Piaget, J. *The Origins of Intelligence in Children.* Translated by M. Cook. New York: International Universities Press, Inc., 1952.

*Wolfgang, C. "Teaching Preschool Children to Play." In *Quest: Learning How to Play*, edited by D. Seidentop. Monograph 26. Washington, D.C.: NAPECW-NCPEAM, 1976.

DENNIS A. PICKERING

41. Curriculum Leadership in Early Childhood Education

The ultimate goal for a curriculum leader in early childhood education must be the individual development of all those human beings who are either directly or indirectly involved in the curriculum process. These individuals include not only the children who are the recipients of the program under consideration but also the staff and parents who are either directly or indirectly involved in implementing the curricular plans. Being a successful curriculum leader therefore requires one to possess certain skills and attributes that will enhance this individual development process. Such leadership skills seem to center upon

1. One's ability to guide others systematically in the fulfillment of the fundamental steps in the curriculum development process.

2. One's understanding and use of both mass and individual communication skills throughout this development process.
3. One's understanding of and ability to apply the principles of planned change while working with staff and others.
4. One's ability to utilize the dynamics of informal as well as formal power while completing each of the curricular steps.
5. One's ability to utilize proper group process skills throughout the development procedure.

Let us now look at the interplay of these five factors as a curriculum leader attempts to enhance the human development process that is so essential if significant advances are to take place in the programs being offered to our youth.

STEPS TOWARD CURRICULUM DEVELOPMENT: INDIVIDUAL DEVELOPMENT

The fundamental steps in the curriculum development process must be clearly understood by those individuals who are to be directly and indirectly involved in formulating an early childhood education program. These individuals include both the professional staff who are actively involved in designing and implementing the program and the parents and others who are providing input and support to such a program development effort. In communicating the fundamental steps in curriculum to others, this author has found that it is often helpful if the leader formulates a workable curriculum model such as the one illustrated in Figure 1. Such a model will not only provide participants with a basic understanding of the steps and their order but will also give them some idea of the inner relationships among each of the steps as well. Before any consideration is given to the fulfillment of the various steps, basic consensus on a workable model is needed so that all those involved can envision where the process is leading them.

The process of acquiring consensus may require the leader and others not only to explain the model to the entire group in a mass communication setting but also to discuss it with individuals on a one-to-one basis. This is especially true of those individuals who constitute the informal power of the group. These individuals often have a great deal of influence on the decisions made by the group. Without a careful assessment by the curriculum leader of the attitudes and perceptions of these informal leaders, one is likely to make decisions that will ultimately jeopardize the impact of the development process on each individual.

It must also be kept in mind that all individuals are not likely to adopt or adapt the process model at the same time. Careful consideration to providing adequate time and encouragement for the acceptance of the procedure is time well spent. It should be pointed out that the model illustrated in Figure 1 is only suggestive of the model that might be formulated by your group. The key issue here is to take adequate time to determine what the process is to be, so that you do not have to utilize group time later in debating what constitutes the next step in the curriculum process.

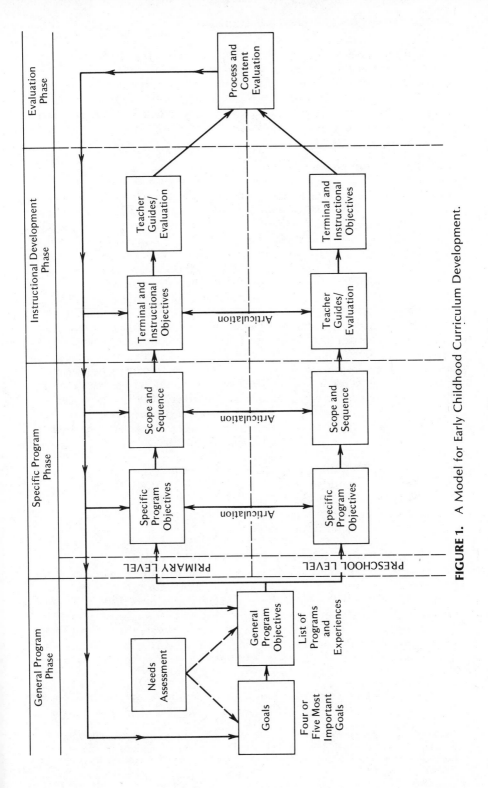

FIGURE 1. A Model for Early Childhood Curriculum Development.

445

For illustrative purposes, let us now look more closely at the design of such a curriculum process model. In the model illustrated in Figure 1 ("A Model For Early Childhood Curriculum Development"), participants can see that they will be guided through four stages: the General Program Phase, the Specific Program Phase, the Instructional Development Phase, and the Evaluation Phase.

General Program Phase

In the General Program Phase, participants in the process are involved in coming to an agreement upon four or five of the most important goals for the education of children in the early years, from about ages two through eight. One way to complete this task is to allow each individual involved in the planning process to list what he or she sees as the four or five most important goals for an early childhood education program.[1] After each individual has completed his or her own list, a composite of the various statements is then formulated. The individuals will then cluster into small groups and proceed to give priority to the goals identified in the composite list in order to come up with the four or five most important goals for the program. This individual-to-group consensus process has proven to be quite successful because it gives participants an initial personal commitment before allowing the dynamics of the small groups to have its impact upon their final decision. It has also been found that by focusing the group's attention upon the four or five most important goals, it is much easier to guide it toward a consideration of the key programs and experiences to be offered. Examples of some goals that have been selected in the past for inclusion on such a list are:

1. To enhance a child's curiosity about the world around him.
2. To promote a positive self-concept.
3. To provide opportunities for social development.
4. To encourage the development of readiness skills in the basics.
5. To encourage good health habits.

Once the group has determined the goals that it feels are the four or five most important ones, it is then ready to identify the general program objectives. This is a list of the various programs and experiences that it anticipates will fulfill each of the goals stated. When working with parents and staff on this step of the process, the curriculum leader is likely to find that various individuals will strive to incorporate their own beliefs on what is most important in a comprehensive early childhood education program.[2] Some are likely to emphasize a more structured program

---

[1]This group may vary but should include the entire instructional and support staff plus possibly several lay representatives, including parents of children in the age groups under consideration.

[2]What the curriculum leader will be hearing are elements of the true philosophy of the participants. You will note that the model being illustrated does not ask participants to produce a formal statement of philosophy. Originally, a statement of philosophy was requested

and others may emphasize a less structured play program format. Through careful assessment of the various sentiments of the group, proper use of group dynamics, and the support of the informal leadership of the group, the curriculum leader will be able to guide participants toward a list of acceptable programs and experiences. In listing such general program objectives, it is often helpful to use a format similar to the one illustrated in Figure 2. Such a format will assist participants in identifying those programs and experiences that will help to fulfill the goals established originally.

For additional assistance in completing the General Program Phase of identifying goals and general program objectives, a needs assessment can be conducted in order to identify the perceived and real needs of the children affected by the program. The results from such an assessment can be very beneficial in identifying the key goals and basic programs to be developed.

Goal I: To enhance a child's curiosity about the word around him.

    A.   To provide readiness programs* in the areas of:

These would be
your General
Program
Objectives

        1.
        2.
        3.

    B.   To provide specialized experiences** in the areas of:

        1.
        2.
        3.

Goal II: To promote a positive self-concept.

    A.   To provide readiness programs in the areas of:

        1.
        2.
        3.

    B.   To provide specialized experiences in the areas of:

        1.
        2.
        3.

*Programs here are identified as a developmental sequence of experiences over a set period of time. The time may be a semester, a year, several years, or the entire educational program.

**Specialized experiences are occasional opportunities to acquire specialized skills that are not necessarily dealt with in a developmental sequence.

FIGURE 2.   Format for general program objectives.

early in the process model. It was found that the typical outcome from such an exercise was of very little value to the group. The informal approach being advocated in what they believe about the various issues being addressed. If a formal statement of philosophy is desired, it has been found that after the participants have spent a considerable amount of time working together as a team, they are quite capable of expressing what really are their agreed-upon beliefs.

Specific Program Phase

Once the general program objectives are listed, the curriculum leader is ready to take an identified program area and develop it. For illustrative purposes, let us take the area of readiness in science. One begins by identifying the specific program objectives. In science, such specific program objectives might include

1. Promoting an awareness and appreciation of living things.
2. Enhancing one's understanding of the earth and the universe.
3. Developing an actual awareness about the concepts of matter and energy.

Once these areas are clarified, one can then direct his/her attention to the actual scope and sequence of that particular program area.

The first step in the scope and sequence construction process is to identify the specific areas of the program under consideration. This identification is actually an abbreviated statement of your specific program area objectives (See Figure 3—Part A). Next, you will need to identify the developmental, grade, or age levels being considered (See Figure 3—Part B). In developing an early childhood education program, definite attention needs to be given not only to the age or developmental levels being taught but also to the educational levels following this program. Therefore, when you are working on such a curriculum program, it is strongly recommended that you project several age or developmental levels on the chart. When parents communicate with you, they will have a much better understanding of why you are planning what you are for their children. The third step in the construction of a scope and sequence chart is to identify the facts, skills, concepts, and generalizations that constitute the final outcomes for each of the designated areas (Figure 3—Part C). The fourth step is the identification of the developmental sequence of the skills (Figure 3—Part D). This identification indicates when the skills are first introduced and when final instruction or mastery takes place. The actual flow of the skill should be determined in accordance with basic principles of learning and child growth and development.

In carrying out the entire scope and sequence development phase, it is strongly recommended that the curriculum leader organize participants into small groups by the grade, age, or developmental level that they teach. (Lay participants can be distributed among each of these groups.) Once each of these groups has made its initial commitment, have single representatives from each group get together and formulate a rough draft of the entire chart. Dialogue in small groups made up of participants from the various levels will follow. Through such a process, the author has found much more participation by each individual within the study. Individual development therefore has usually been enhanced due to this increased dialogue and initial commitment.

Part B. Identify the developmental, grade or age levels**

(Part D. Developmental Sequence)

(Part A.
Specific Areas)

I. Living Things*

A. Explain why plants
and animals are living
things.

B.

C.

(Part C.
Example of a
fact, skill,
concept or
generalization
named as a
final outcome)

II. Earth and the Universe*

(Part A.
Specific
Areas)

III. Matter and Energy

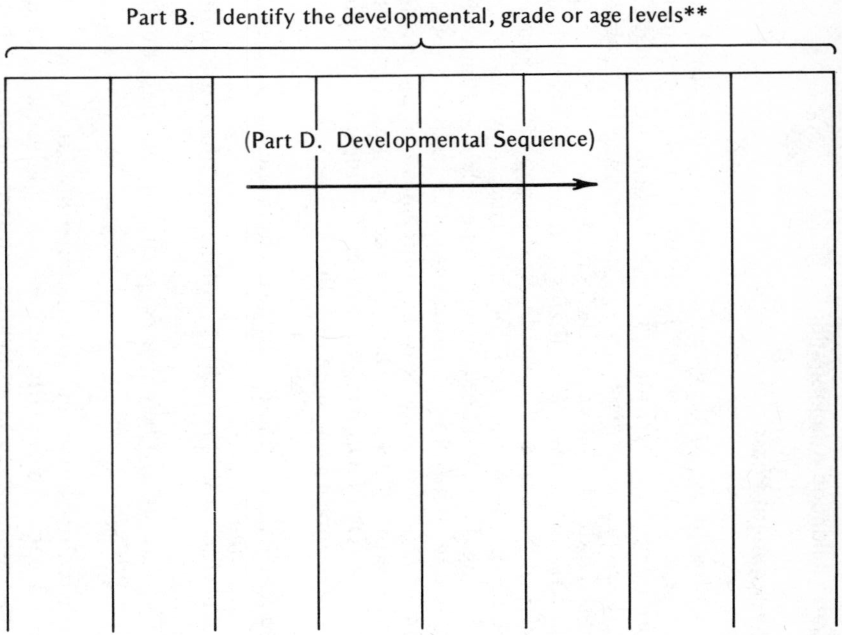

(Part A.
Specific
Areas)

*Taken from the specific program area objectives for science which were listed earlier in this article.
**Most staffs are oriented to think in terms of grade or age levels. If one of these two designations is selected, attention to the developmental
levels of a child should still be kept in mind.

FIGURE 3.   Format for a scope and sequence chart.

449

Instructional Development Phase

Once the scope and sequence of the program have been identified, the curriculum leader is ready to move on to the Instructional Development Phase. This phase involves the writing of terminal and instructional objectives and the development of lesson plans that include learning activities that meet the individual needs of each child.

Terminal objectives are written by utilizing statements directly from the scope and sequence chart. For example, in the scope and sequence illustrated in Figure 3, one would have the following objective for the first item under Living Things: The student will be able to explain why plants and animals are living things. Instructional objectives are then written as statements of intermediate learning outcomes that the teacher feels children will need in order to accomplish the terminal objectives.[3] For the terminal objective (T.O.) concerning living things, the instructional objectives (I.O.) might be written as follows:

> T.O. The student will be able to explain why plants and animals are living things.
>
> I.O. The student will be able to explain why plants are living things.
>
> I.O. The student will be able to explain why animals are living things.

As one works with both terminal and instructional objectives, one will find the need to go back occasionally and identify additional instructional objectives for certain terminal outcomes children continue to have difficulty with in the program. On the other hand, one may find the need to consolidate or even eliminate certain instructional objectives when children display the capabilities of handling larger segments of the learning task.

After completing both terminal and instructional objectives, the curriculum leader is ready to move on to the writing of daily lesson plans. A format that this writer has designed and implemented with a great deal of success in working with teachers at all levels of instruction is the Teacher Guide Page (See Figure 4). In utilizing the Teacher Guide format, one has a clearly stated terminal and instructional objective at the top of the lesson plan page as illustrated. Possible activities include free exploratory play are then briefly stated to remind the teacher of the alternatives available. Emphasis is placed upon creating activities that will meet the learning-style attributes of all the children who are to be involved in the program. Various evaluative procedures are then provided for assessing the outcomes of the students. The Guide pages can be designed in such a way that they are cumulative guides. As the teacher develops alternative ways of teaching a certain aspect of the program, he or she lists

---

[3]Richard W. Burns, in his book *New Approaches to Behavioral Objectives*, provides a complete explanation of how to write terminal and instructional objectives. Second ed. (Dubuque, Iowa: Wm. C. Brown Company, Publishers, 1977).

```
┌─────────────────────────────────────────────────────────────┐
│                        TEACHER GUIDE                         │
│                                                              │
│  T.O.   The student will be able to explain why plants and   │
│         animals are living things.                           │
│                                                              │
│  T.O.   The students will be able to explain why plants are  │
│         living things.                                       │
│                                                              │
│  Possible Activities                                         │
│                                                              │
│  1.   Grow beans in paper cups.                              │
│  2.   Bulletin board on plants.                              │
│  3.   Draw pictures of plants.                               │
│  4.   Filmstrip entitled "Plants."                           │
│  5.                                                          │
│  6.                                                          │
│  7.                                                          │
│                                                              │
│  Evaluation                                                  │
│                                                              │
│  1.   Ask children to explain why plants are living things.  │
│  2.                                                          │
│  3.                                                          │
│  4.                                                          │
└─────────────────────────────────────────────────────────────┘
```

FIGURE 4.

the various means under the activities section. In other words, the Teacher Guides develop as a teacher grows in his or her ability to adapt that segment of the program to the individual needs of the learner. This same process holds true for the evaluation section as well. As a teacher becomes more aware of alternative procedures in evaluating student outcomes, they are listed.

It has been found that the Guide pages can be sequenced according to the needs of the students being taught. If one student or a small group of students requires certain skills before proceeding to other skill areas, activities from the appropriate Guide pages can be assigned. Guide pages, in other words, provide one with a greater opportunity for individualizing one's instruction through alternative teaching strategies.

Evaluating Phase

The final phase of the model is the evaluation of the curriculum process and content. Process evaluation has to do with the systematic assessment of both the attitudes and value changes that have taken place in those involved in designing and implementing the program. These changes can oftentimes be observed in the behavioral changes of faculty, such as the willingness to try something new and to develop nonverbal abilities. Changes in parents can be observed in their verbal and behavioral support for the program that is going on.

Content evaluation has to do with the success one has in fulfilling the terminal outcomes identified in the scope of the program. Content evaluation is affected by the various methodologies utilized, the organizational sequencing of the learning experiences, and the actual materials provided in the instructional setting.

SUMMARY

The role of the curriculum leader in early childhood education is that of coordinating a curriculum procedure that ultimately leads to the individual development of all those who are directly and indirectly involved. This human development process can have a tremendous impact upon the staff who have control over the "real"curriculum that takes place when the classroom doors close; upon the parents who can provide within the home environment continual support for what is being taught; and upon the children who are growing proportionately to the quality of the program that has been formulated. Through the careful and well-planned use of the five factors identified at the beginning of this article, it has been proposed that the curriculum leader is more likely to fulfill this ultimate curriculum leadership goal.

ELLEN HANDLER

42. Teacher-Parent Relations in Preschool

The structural determinants of teacher-parent interactions have not been extensively investigated even though the subject has assumed a special importance in the context of school decentralization. Across the country, plans are being implemented to alter the administrative structure of school systems to encourage maximum feasible participation by client groups in the decision-making process. Yet there is little information on the relationship of the structure of formally organized socialization settings to client participation and on the effects of client participation on the socialization process that occurs in these settings. The purpose of

From Ellen Handler, "Teacher-Parent Relations in Preschool." *Urban Education*, Vol. VI, No. 2/3 (October 1971), pp. 215-231. Reprinted with permission of Ellen Handler and *Urban Education*.

this paper is to present a typology of teacher-parent interactions derived from a study of a variety of differently organized preschool institutions. It is hoped that some of the salient features that can be extracted from a study of preschools as a natural experimental setting may increase our understanding of such factors in the elementary and secondary public school contexts as well.

BACKGROUND

Most of the past work on teacher-parent interactions has focused on individual differences between parents who did and who did not participate in organizations that fostered such interactions. Hausknecht (1962), for instance, investigated the social characteristics of members of PTAs and other civic organizations. Hollingshead (1949) noted that the content of teacher-parent interactions varied depending on the socioeconomic status of the parent. Such factors have an important bearing on the subject. However, in order to explain variability in teacher-parent interactions more fully, it is necessary to evaluate structural factors as well.

Authors such as Waller (1932), Becker (1957) or Parsons (1959), who have concerned themselves with structural determinants of teacher-parent relations, have recognized a natural conflict between teachers and parents arising out of their respective role requirements. According to this formulation, the teacher's expectations of and behaviors toward the child arising out of her universalistic, specific, affectively neutral relationship are not appreciated by the parent, who relates to the child in a particularistic, diffuse, affectively charged manner. These authors clearly regard the parent as a nuisance rather than as a threat to the teacher. They point out that the underlying conflict is handled through a variety of techniques whereby the parent is kept at a distance and his involvement with the educational system is limited so that the teacher can educate the child in accordance with professional principles (Sykes, 1953).

The above analysis, which will be called the "traditional" model throughout the remainder of this paper, is predicated on a definition of the function of the public school which is no longer universally accepted and it depends on certain structural features that are not applicable to all educational institutions.

The traditional function of the elementary school has been to acculturate the young by teaching them middle-class behaviors, values, and norms, to enable the children to gain a competitive advantage in the struggle for upward mobility (Williams, 1960; Sexton, 1967; Grambs, 1965). Teachers were considered the authoritative source of these middle-class ideals. If parents disagreed with teachers, they could either be educated themselves, through settlement house programs, for example, or they were ignored. The latter option could be legitimated by recourse to notions of professional autonomy (Becker, 1962). Although elementary schools have traditionally been subject to local control through lay boards, these latter structures have reinforced the middle-class orientation of the schools through selected requirement of personnel (Charters, 1953).

Furthermore, although many children have always dropped out of the educational process, this was regarded as less important than the fact that others succeeded.

As a result of the Civil Rights Movement of the 1950s and 1960s, the function of the school was redefined to conform with new concerns. School dropouts became more important than school successes. Investigation showed that school failures were disproportionately concentrated in disadvantaged sectors of the population (Deutsch et al., 1967; Passow et al., 1967). These children differed from the middle-class majority not only in school-related skills but, as Reissman (1962) pointed out, in culture as well. The middle-class character of the schools was redefined from an asset to a liability (Sexton, 1961) because it was regarded as a major obstacle to academic achievement of low-socioeconomic-status children.

Closely related to the above was a reassessment of the values of professionalism. The autonomy of the professional was challenged not only in the schools but in medical practice (Friedson, 1960) and in social agencies as well (Haug and Sussman, 1969).

The resulting decentralization program was designed to make schools more "successful" as educational agencies by increasing their responsiveness to culturally determined values of their client groups through citizen, and especially parent, participation in educational decision-making. Thus, the redefinition of the function of the schools pointed to a new source of conflict between parents and teachers—i.e., cultural differences associated with socioeconomic status—and sought solutions to newly "discovered" educational shortcomings by creating channels for more effective parent participation in the educational process.

The changing role of the public school is reflected in Litwak and Meyer's (1965) "balance theory" of school-community coordination. The authors describe a variety of mechanisms whereby schools attempt to optimize relations with parents by maintaining (or increasing) social distance with middle-class, highly involved parents. This theory indicates that schools recognize the importance of gaining the cooperation of uninvolved parents in order to enhance the achievement motivation of their students. However, it does not necessarily imply a basic shift in the balance of power between teachers and parents, a point to which we will return later.

The "traditional" model of teacher-parent relations is most closely associated with the earlier definition of the function of the public school and also with certain structural features which are common to public primary schools but not to preschool institutions. For instance, elementary school attendance is required by law and assignment to a given school and class does not depend on client preference. Most elementary schools are publicly supported and free to the client. Decision-making is generally not visible to client groups. Most clients find it difficult to localize or to influence the decision-making process, and many crucial decisions are made by persons such as school board members and superintendents of schools with whom the client has virtually no contact.

Preschools differ from elementary schools in all these respects. Attendance is voluntary, and the parent has considerable choice in selecting a school within the limits of his ability to pay. Preschools vary in price for service, but most schools are not free. Until Headstart was established, free or almost free services were very limited in supply and restricted to the poor. Most preschools are relatively small autonomous institutions with few hierarchical levels. Decision-making is highly visible and is usually carried out by the director, who, in many cases, serves as the parents' main source of contact with the school.

Whereas public elementary schools are relatively uniform with respect to these structural features, preschools are highly varied. For this reason, preschools offer a natural setting for investigating the effect of structural factors on parent participation in educational decision-making. We will attempt to show through our analysis of teacher-parent relations in different types of preschools that the "traditional" model is a special case rather than a generic description of the subject.

In the process, we may be able to suggest cases for the two unused, logical possibilities in Carlson's (1964) typology of schools by (1) client control over own participation and (2) organizational control over client admission. In the elementary and secondary school situation, the two common types are the public school, where the client lacks control over his participation and the school lacks control over his admission, and the private school, where client participation is voluntary and so is organization acceptance of the client. In the preschool situation, however, there are examples where client participation is voluntary but acceptance by the organization is mandatory (Headstart). Also, because of market factors, there are situations where client participation is almost involuntary, because of lack of alternatives, and where the organization has considerable control over client admission (subsidized day care centers).

However, the present study cannot serve as a direct extension of Carlson's paradigm, because his primary concern is with the student's willingness to involve himself in the educational process. In the preschool situation, student involvement is less problematical because of the age of the child. The focus in this study is on the parent. He is also a client, but one who presents different types of problems and cannot be "tracked" or "dumped" into a vocational program if he does not cooperate.

METHODOLOGY

This study is based on an analysis of preschool institutions by a combination of research methods. Seven schools in one midwestern community were studied in detail, mainly through repeated, lengthy (two or three hour) periods of observation in all classrooms, and through wide ranging interviews (one to two hours) with all 21 teachers. Observations were carried out at functionally different times of the school day, including periods of maximum teacher-parent interactions—i.e., when the children were brought and fetched. Parent meetings also were observed and recorded in field notes. All teachers were asked to respond freely and with maximum detail to the following questions:

1. How often do you talk to parents?
2. Where and how do you talk to parents—i.e., in formal conferences at the school, home visits, group parent meetings, telephone calls after school hours, and the like?
3. Who initiates the contacts?
4. What kinds of things do you discuss?
5. Do you ever disagree with a parent on a subject related to your school or your work?
6. What happens if you disagree?

After the typology of teacher-parent interactions began to emerge, a group of five additional institutions was studied, but more selectively, with respect to specific hypotheses. The purpose was to determine whether the emerging theoretical schema had wider applicability than for the seven institutions on which it had been based. Also, at this time additional corroborating data were sought through interviews with parents and board members and through analysis of documents pertaining to the institutions such as charters and contacts with teachers.

Through these various means, material was sought specifically bearing on decision-making within the institutions. For the purposes of this study, only a few crude parameters of this complex process were considered. The typology distinguishes between decisions that are *central* to the educational process, such as those concerning basic educational goals and personnel policy, from decisions that are *peripheral* to the educational process, such as decisions concerning entertainment for special occasions or format of parents' meetings. The contrary to participation in decision-making was defined as compliance with demands originating with the other party. Using these three points of reference, it seemed possible to construct an imaginary continuum of involvement in decision-making. At the low end, involvement is confined to compliance with demands. An intermediary position entails involvement limited to decisions that are peripheral to the educational process and the high end involves formulation of central educational policy decisions.

The typology also distinguishes the party that initiates the bulk of teacher-parent interactions. This factor does not have intrinsic significance, but it serves as an indicator of the relative power of the different parties. According to Homans (1950), the party with the greater power tends to initiate more contacts with the party of lesser power than vice versa. Since the typology will be used to suggest differences in the relative power of teachers and parents, this factor should provide useful corroborating evidence.

It is apparent that this typology touches only a few of the main features of teacher-parent interactions in preschool settings. Also, the four cases to be described below should be considered roughly analogous to Weber's "ideal types" (Gerth and Mills, 1958) since few situations fit the model in all respects.

THE TYPOLOGY

Type I is a preschool setting where teachers are clearly in charge and parents follow rules. Contact between teachers and parents is minimal and generally initiated by teachers. As one teacher explained, "To them [the parents] we stand right next to God." Parents do not question policy and procedures even when they could be clearly justified in doing so, for instance, in a case where a child was severely bitten by another. Virtually all decisions are made by the staff. Content of teacher-parent interactions revolves largely around compliance with staff-formulated rules. For instance, parents are asked to arrange for transportation for their children, to pay fees on a given schedule, to pay fines for lateness, and to provide extra sets of clothes.

This type is exemplified by the subsidized day care center. Client fees are generally low and depend on the family's ability to pay. Typically, this type of institution is set up to serve children of low-socioeconomic-status working mothers. The organization does not depend on client fees for its continued existence. Eligibility for such programs is determined by the organization and is based on financial need and activity of the mother. Usually children are not accepted unless the mother is working or incapacitated. Such facilities are in great demand, and waiting lists are a common feature. Although client participation is voluntary, the limited supply of such services and lack of viable alternatives virtually eliminates client discretion to participate.

Type II might best be described as a standoff. Despite the rhetoric to the contrary, central decision-making remains with the staff, but, in contrast to the previous case, parents are not expected to comply with demands. Very few, if any, demands are made on parents because experience has shown that parents do not comply. For instance, regarding transportation for children, whereas in type I institutions parents are usually expected to make their own arrangements, in type II programs, transportation is usually provided or the children do not come.

Decision-making is a sensitive issue. In theory, parents are supposed to be involved in all its facets. In practice, parent participation is usually limited by a variety of factors. For instance, teachers are required to make home visits to facilitate parent participation, since few parents venture into the school or attend meetings, even when money payment "to cover babysitting expenses" is offered as an inducement. In effect, however, home visits are usually brief social affairs, unrelated to school events and policies, but sufficient to satisfy formal requirements. The various parent advisory groups which are a prominent feature of the organizational blueprints are sparsely attended. Their agenda consists largely of peripheral issues such as whether parents prefer a panel or a single speaker for future meetings.

A second technique that affects parent involvement is that of cooptation. The official guidelines give priority to hiring indigenous personnel, including parents, to staff the programs. As a result, parents who are sufficiently interested to attempt to influence the programs are recruited as staff and become spokesmen for the educational "establishment." The process of informal cooptation, as described by Selznick (1966), has been characteristic of many of the poverty programs, although they were designed specifically to be responsive to the clientele they served rather than to the professionals who directed them (Van Til and Van Til, 1970).

Parent education can also serve to deflect parent involvement in decision-making. For instance, a teacher related that in the course of a home visit a mother had unexpectedly complained that her child was not receiving sufficient academic training at the nursery school. The teacher responded by showing the mother how she (the mother) could teach her child, using materials that were readily at hand. By interpreting the mother's complaint into a request for parent education, the teacher had deflected the mother's attempted participation and had furthered the legitimate organizational goal of parent education. In this type of school, most of the teacher-parent interactions are initiated by the teachers, as was true of type I schools.

One example of type II schools is compensatory education programs like Headstart. These are usually part-day programs completely supported by public funds. All preschoolers of eligible families—i.e., those whose income falls below a stipulated maximum—may attend if they choose to do so. Such organizations need to induce client participation in order to legitimate their requests for public funding. In Carlson's (1964) terms they are less "domesticated" than public schools where client participation is assured by law. Accordingly, we should expect to find a variety of "linking mechanisms" (Litwak and Meyer, 1965) to induce parent cooperation. Teacher visits are a prime example of the "detached worker" mechanism. The present case serves as an excellent example of one possible result of the "balance" strategy. Parent participation is encouraged in a variety of ways.

Type III come closest to a relationship between equals or a partnership. Interaction between teachers and parents tends to be informal and lively, initiated about equally by either party, and concerned with any and all aspects of the school. Both parties reserve the right to accept or reject the suggestions made by the other. Both parties make demands on each other, some of which are met, whereas others are rejected. Usually, the two parties work out a satisfactory division of labor regarding their responsibility for child-rearing tasks. If such an understanding does not emerge and disagreements become frequent and serious, the parties tend to terminate the relationship by removing the child from the school.

One example of this type is the small, proprietary day care center, especially under circumstances where the demand for such facilities more or less equals the supply. These centers are supported by client fees and offer an all day service to children of middle-class working parents.

Type IV is the polar opposite of type I. Here parents play a more dominant role in decision-making than do teachers. The amount of teacher-parent contact varies, but it is frequently extensive and primarily parent-initiated. Parents play a dominant role at formal meetings where central policy questions are discussed, including limits to the teachers' sphere of activity; e.g., parents often prohibit activities that have even faintly religious overtones. When teachers in this type of preschool are highly trained, they are frequently concerned about parental infringement on their professional autonomy. This is especially serious where parents also formulate and carry out personnel policies, so that teachers are dependent on their clients not only for educational guidelines but also for their employment, promotions, and salaries.

In type IV schools, a variety of mechanisms may be used to protect teachers against parental interference, such as designating a third party to act as buffer between teachers and parents, or using esoteric language for teachers' communication with parents. These mechanisms are described by Litwak and Meyer (1965) as compatible with the "locked door" position in school-community relations. Their purpose in both the elementary school and the type IV preschool is essentially the same, to keep the middle-class, highly involved parent at a distance. However, the situation is more difficult in the preschool because the parent has greater potential power. Since the preschool needs the parent to provide continuing financial support to maintain the school, the staff must avoid antagonizing the parent so that he will not withdraw his child. Some schools respond to the problem by frankly sacrificing professional expertise for responsiveness to client desires by hiring teachers on the basis of their potential ability "to get along with parents."

The most extreme example of this type is the cooperative nursery school, although many part day private nursery schools share some of the above characteristics. These schools depend on client fees and offer an educational or other supplementary service to middle-class children whose mothers are typically full-time homemakers.

DISCUSSION

When the four types are combined in a 2 × 2 matrix, as in Figure 1, two major differentiating dimensions emerge. These can be translated into social power concepts as follows: According to Blau (1964), power depends on the ability of one party to control resources on which the other is dependent. In the preschool context, teachers always control the services of the institution (care or education of children) and are always dependent on outside sources for financial support. The power situation of parents, however, varies depending on structural factors. In types III and IV (right-hand column), parents provide financial support for the organization, in contrast to types I and II (lefthand column), where they do not. In types I and III (top row), parents are more dependent on the service provided by the teachers because it enables them to fulfill role obligations associated with their employment. In types II and IV (bottom row), the preschool program provides only a nonessential, supplementary enrichment experience. Accordingly, it is not surprising that parent power seems greatest in type IV, where parents provide financial support without being dependent on the service. Conversely, parent power seems lowest in type I, where parents do not provide financial support and yet are highly dependent on the service.

Returning now to the "traditional" model of teacher-parent relations,

Source of Support

	By Outside Funds	By Client Fees
Long	Type I Subsidized day care center	Type III Private day care center
Short	Type II Compensatory education (Headstart)	Type IV Private hursery schools (Coops)

Length of Day

FIGURE 1. Typology of teacher-parent relations.

it becomes apparent that this description fits most nearly the type I situation. The factors producing the configuration are different from the elementary school situation because client participation is more voluntary and organizational control over client admission is greater in subsidized day care centers than in the elementary school. Nevertheless, of the four types, this is clearly the situation where parents have least power to exert influence over the education process.

Changes in teacher-parent relations that can be anticipated as a result of decentralization schemes will probably depend on the amount of alteration in basic structural factors. If decentralization results chiefly in setting up new channels for parent participation, e.g., advisory committees and the like, the outcome may be a proliferation of techniques whereby parent participation is formally encouraged and informally discouraged, as was noted in type II. Linking mechanisms such as those described by Litwak and Meyer (1965) can be used either to produce a more cooperative clientele, for instance through parent education, or an educational system that is substantially more responsive to the values and goals of its clientele. The latter is more likely to happen if decentralization includes parental options in choice of school (a true freedom-of-choice system), and especially if such choice is accompanied by expansion of educational services so that supply exceeds demand. In the extreme case where public funds would no longer be allotted directly to the institution but given to the client to be spent at the institution of his choice, as Friedman (1962) has advocated, a more basic shift might occur, whereby teacher-parent relations would become more similar to types III and IV.

However, if the basic purpose of decentralization is to produce a more flexible, innovative educational process through increasing parent participation, then this study does not provide grounds for optimism. In type IV schools, where parent power was greatest, the introduction of innovations depended on congruence of values among parents and between parents and teachers. Parents could not compel teachers to adopt innovations against their better judgment, and teachers were dependent on parental support to carry out educational schemes they considered professionally desirable. Therefore, unless a variety of type I schools is available within a community, which would permit some sorting of teachers and parents by educational goals and values, the scope of innovation may be limited to negative types of changes. In the type IV schools studied, it seemed relatively easier to persuade teachers to eliminate a given activity or to permit children greater freedom to follow their own inclinations than to introduce new, structured programs (such as academic training) because of the virtual veto power of a parent minority. Despite the wealth of equipment and rhetoric to the contrary, many type IV schools offered little beyond the minimum program needed to fulfill licensing requirements.

On the other hand, in type I organization studied, a radical shift in educational policy occurred when a more highly trained director was hired. The new director reported that the main source of constraints was the old staff, who were reluctant to change established practices.

At this point, it may be instructive to consider differences in innovativeness between type I and type IV preschools in terms of Carlson's (1964) paradigm. According to his theory, the rate of innovation is lower in public than in private schools because public school clients are involuntary participants, whereas private school clients are not. A question raised by the present study is whether client control over his own participation is the main determinant of the rate of innovation. The study of preschools suggests that under certain circumstances innovation may be high where client participation is involuntary (type I) and may be low where it is not (type IV). Perhaps one of the main deterrents to innovation in public schools is the cumbersome bureaucratic machinery that processes all decisions. Accordingly, we might suggest that the rate of innovation may be related rather to the degree of professional autonomy, at least to the extent that new ideas are related to professional expertise. This formulation points to the possibility that there are different types of innovation. Those that relate to professional expertise, such as techniques of teaching, might result from a different set of factors than those that relate to responsiveness toward low-status or minority group clients, such as new hiring policies favoring minority groups. The concern here is with the former rather than the latter type of innovation.

According to this formulation, a decentralization program that involved a shift in power between parents and teachers could result in less rather than more innovation if it followed the type IV pattern. This would be especially likely if teacher-parent disagreements were exacerbated by cultural differences in addition to normal, role-related conflict. In preschool institutions, cultural sources of conflict are minimized because, in general, parent power is greatest in types III and IV, where teachers and parents share values and norms associated with their common middle-class status. In type I and II schools, where teachers and parents are most likely to differ in class-related values because parents tend to be lower-class while teachers tend to be middle-class, parents are relatively less powerful.

In contrast, public school decentralization programs are often designed specifically to increase the power of parents in those situations where socioeconomic status differences between teachers and parents are widest, and conflicts in expectations of teacher role performance are most likely to arise (Sieber and Wilder, 1967). Thus, the potential for conflict may be greater in elementary schools as a result of decentralization than in any of the four types of preschool situations described in this paper. Under these circumstances, potential gains from greater parent input in decision-making could be negated and could even result in an educational program of greater inferior quality than before.

CONCLUSION

This paper has attempted to analyze the structural determinants of teacher-parent relations by means of descriptive data from preschool institutions. Four types were delineated to illustrate differences in the power of parents vis-à-vis teachers. The "traditional" model of unquestioned teacher dominance was found to fit mainly into one of four types, thus suggesting its limited applicability. The discussion pointed to structural factors that underlie the typology and attempted to show how these might be applicable for the elementary school situation. Some of the implications of these factors for the socialization process were discussed in order to demonstrate the importance of this largely unexplored subject for understanding and planning of educational institutions.

REFERENCES

Becker, H. S. (1962) "The nature of a profession," in Education for the Professions. Sixty-First Yearbook of the National Society for the Study of Education, Part II. Chicago: University of Chicago Press.

——— (1957) "The teacher in the authority system of the public school," in B. E. Mercer and E. R. Carr (eds.) Education and the Social Order. New York: Rinehart.

Blau, P. M. (1964) Exchange and Power in Social Life. New York: John Wiley.

Carlson, R. O. (1964) "Environmental constraints and organizational consequences: the public school and its clients." Behavioral Science and Educational Administration. N.S.S.E. 63, part 2.

Charters, W. W. (1953) "Social class analaysis and control of public education." Harvard Educational Rev. 23.

Deutsch, M. et al. (1967) The Disadvantaged Child: Studies of the Social Environment and the Learning Process. New York: Basic Books.

Freidson, E. F. (1960) "Client control and medical practice." Amer. J. of Sociology 65.

Friedman, M. (1962) Capitalism and Freedom. Chicago: University of Chicago Press.

Gerth, H. H. and C. W. Mills (1958) From Max Weber: Essays in Sociology. New York: Oxford Univ. Press.

Grambs, J. D. (1965) Schools, Scholars and Society. Englewood Cliffs, N.J.: Prentice-Hall.

Haug, M. R. and M. B. Sussman (1969) "Professional autonomy and the revolt of the client." Social Problems 17, 2.

Hausknecht, M. (1962) The Joiners: A Sociological Description of Voluntary Association Membership in the U.S. New York: Bedminster.

Hollingshead, A. B. (1949) Elmtown's Youth. John Wiley.

Homans, G. C. (1950) The Human Group. New York: Harcourt, Brace.

Litwak, E. and H. J. Meyers (1965) "Administrative styles and community linkages of public schools: some theoretical considerations," in A. J. Reiss, Jr., Schools in a Changing Society. New York: Free Press.

Parsons, T. (1959). "The school class as a social system: some of its functions in American society." Harvard Educational Rev. 29 (Fall).

Passow, A. H., M. Goldberg and A. J. Tannenbaum (1967) Education of the Disadvantaged: A Book of Readings. New York: Holt, Rinehart & Winston.

Reissman, F. (1962) The Culturally Deprived Child. New York: Harper & Row.

Selznick, P. (1966) TVA and the Grass Roots: A Study of the Sociology of Formal Organizations. New York: Harper & Row.

Sexton, P. C. (1967) The American School: A Sociological Analysis. Englewood Cliffs, N.J.: Prentice-Hall.

——— (1961) Education and Income. New York: Viking.

Sieber, S. D. and D. E. Wilder (1967) "Teaching style, parental preferences and professional role definitions." Sociology of Education 40, 4.

Sykes, G. (1953) "The PTA and parent-teacher conflict." Harvard Educational Rev. 23, 2.

Van Til, J. and S. B. Van Til (1970) "Citizen participation in social policy: the end of the cycle?" Social Problems 17, 3.

Waller, W. (1932) The Sociology of Teaching. New York: John Wiley.

Williams, R. M. (1960) American Society: A Sociological Interpretation. New York: Aldred A. Knopf.

LINDA REGELE-SINCLAIR

43. Providing Food Services

So closely and intricately interwoven into a strand within the individual are both physical nature, which requires food and that nature which we call intellectual development, that it will not do to keep them separate. (1)

The children of any society are its wealth, for in them is embodied the hope of a culture for a better fiture. If children are denied access to good,

From Linda Regele-Sinclair, "Providing Food Services," in Child Care: A Comprehensive Guide; Model Programs and Their Components, Vol. II, ed. S. Auerbach (Human Sciences Press, 72 Fifth Avenue, New York, N.Y. 10011; 1976), pp. 230–241. Reprinted with permission of Human Sciences Press and the author.

nutritious food they also will be denied an opportunity to become fully involved in their environment. Therefore, the first concern of any day-care program should be to ensure that each child receives the proper amount of food needed to sustain both physical and intellectual growth.

Because children in day care receive a substantial part of their daily food needs in the center, much attention should be given to the planning and operating of a meal program.

It is equally important for day-care centers to encourage children to become interested in food and actively involved in its preparation. It may be said then that food not only sustains life but it also can educate a child about life.

The relationship between human growth and proper nutrition has long been understood. A study done by John Boyd-Orr in 1936 demonstrated that the height of a controlled group of children varied according to the social class of the child. He suggested that the difference in height could be attributable in part to heredity but that "environmental differences particularly related to nutrition were probably highly influential in producing the observed gradient in height."[2]

Other investigations, such as those showing the relationship between inadequate nutrition in early life and its effect upon the growth of tissues and organs have added to an ever-growing body of knowledge surrounding proper nutrition and its relationship to growth development.

The foods that children eat will affect not only their physical growth but also their own sense of well-being, their joy in being alive, and their ability to learn. A child can discover much about himself through food. Foods are symbolic and can carry a strong emotional message for children. Probably most importantly, foods represent love and security.

These are important concepts for homes or centers which care for children during the day to keep in mind when planning a meal program. For as Evans, Shub, and Weinstein state in their book *Day Care,* "Any day care facility has the responsibility to provide a program which facilitates children's optimal growth and development."[3]

But just how does a day-care home or center ensure an interesting and adequate food program?

WHERE TO BEGIN: OR HOW TO GET FOOD TO YOUR CENTER

For most centers the prospect of running an adequate meals program means finding more money. More money may mean increasing fees charged to parents or investigating what is available to centers in federal food assistance.

The Special Food Service Program for Children, sponsored by the Department of Agriculture (USDA), is designed to help nonprofit private and public day-care and Head Start centers operate meal programs. It provides cash, commodities, and equipment money to any eligible, nonprofit center for the operation of a food program.

The Special Food Service Program (Section 13 of the National School Lunch and Child Nutrition Act) was introduced in Congress by Representative Charles Vanik (Ohio) in early 1968. Later that year the bill became law. It authorized a pilot food service program for day care to be operated for three years.

With the passage of the Special Food Service Program for Children legislation, Congress and USDA took their first step towards seeing that children cared for outside of their homes would be guaranteed the right to nutritious food and good health.

The Special Food Service Program is administered by the USDA. The USDA has the responsibility to formulate the rules and regulations which define how the program is to operate. It also administers the program on the state level. The state department of education is responsible for collecting claims, reimbursing centers, and providing technical assistance wherever it is needed. Sixteen state departments of education are prohibited by law from administering the programs outside of the public school system. In each of those states, the regional office of the USDA assumes the state agency's responsibility.

Originally Congress intended that the program should focus on centers serving primarily children from low-income families. Today the program has been broadened and the Special Food Service Program is available to:

any private, nonprofit institutions or public institutions such as child day care centers, settlement houses or recreation centers which provide day care, or other child care where the children are not maintained in residence for children from areas in which poor economic conditions exist and from areas where there is a high concentration of working mothers.[4]

The program includes private, nonprofit institutions providing day-care services for handicapped children. Unfortunately, family day-care homes are not presently eligible for the Special Food Service Program.

The Special Food Service Program for Children provides a cash reimbursement for each meal served plus varying amounts of donated commodities. If a state so chooses, it may set aside up to 25 per cent of its apportioned funds for food preparation and storage equipment to be used by participating centers or potential program sponsors. This nonfood assistance is made available in the form of one-time grants for the purchase of kitchen equipment or, in the case of leased equipment, as a regular subsidy for a given period of time. Many states have chosen not to allocate money for equipment and have thereby restricted program expansion.

Some day-care and Head Start centers may also qualify as "especially needy" centers. Centers showing severe need must demonstrate that the per meal reimbursement rate received is insufficient to carry on an effective feeding program. Centers designated especially needy can receive "financial assistance not to exceed 80 per cent of the operating costs of such a program, including the cost of obtaining, preparing and serving the food."

To apply for participation in the Special Food Service Program, a center must fill out a series of applications and forms. Upon approval the center must sign a statement agreeing to abide by the rules and regulations for basic operation of a meals program. Under the regulations children must be guaranteed the right to receive a free or reduced price meal, if they are eligible. Centers may not discriminate against children receiving free and reduced price meals and must also agree to prepare meals which meet the specified meal requirements set by the USDA. These are referred to as Type A meal standards.

Type A meals provide for minimal necessary nutritional intake. The department suggests that centers use the following as meal guidelines:

1. Age: 1-3, breakfast—½ cp. milk, ¼ cp. fruit or juice, ½ slice bread or equivalent or ¼ cp. cereal.

2. Lunch/supper—½ cp. milk, 1 ounce meat or equivalent quantity of an alternative, ¼ cp. vegetable, fruit or both, ½ slice bread or equivalent.

3. Snacks—½ cp. milk or juice, ½ slice bread or equivalent.

4. Age: 3-6, breakfast—¾ cp. milk, ½ cp. juice or fruit, ½ slice bread, ½ cp. cereal or equivalent.

5. Lunch/Supper—¾ cp. milk, 1½ ounces meat or equivalent, ½ cp. vegetable, fruit or both, ½ slice bread or equivalent.

6. Snacks—½ cp. milk or juice, ½ slice bread or equivalent (nuts, fruits, etc.).

After a center has been approved for assistance it will receive a reimbursement of 36¢ for lunch or supper; 18¢ for breakfast; and 12¢ for snacks. If commodities are available, centers will receive what the state delivers.

The federal government also sponsors the Special Milk Program, which is open to any nonprofit private or public center. Applications for the Special Milk Program are available from each state department of education. The program currently provides centers with 5¢ for every pint of milk served. Centers may also be reimbursed for the full cost of the milk if it is served to a child who is eligible for free meals.

The responsibility of a center for providing a meal program does not end with getting the financing for food and seeing that it is prepared. A center should build a meals program which embodies all the benefits of food.

FOOD, MEALS, AND CHILDREN'S NEEDS

Bruno Bettleheim once said, "Food is the greatest socializer." Food can serve as an excellent vehicle for learning. Involving a child in preparing and eating a meal offers the opportunity of enhancing and enlarging his world.

Children learn about the world by doing, feeling, seeing, and tasting. Food can serve as a good example of texture, shapes, and color. It can help to teach word skills and new concepts. Buying and preparing food helps the child learn math skills. Scientific concepts of life and growth can be taught by planting a vegetable or herb garden. A sense of love, sharing, care, and communication can be expressed and experienced in the actual eating of the meal.

Food consumption is strongly influenced by custom habit. Each cultural group tends to have its own strong preference for certain foods and cooking. People eat the food they like, when they can get them; that is, they eat the food which they find attractive in taste and flavor. . . . Each cultural group tends to regard its own habits as the normal and natural ones . . . food habits are, in fact, very deeply rooted in each culture.[5]

Children's tastes may be broadened by introducing them to a wide range of foods. The preparation of ethnic foods is a particularly good way not only to broaden children's tastes but to help them learn about other people and cultures. A day-care center in Minneapolis that has Native American, Afro-American, and white children has published a small recipe book with the favorite recipes of each child who participates in the center. Each parent was asked for his or her child's favorite recipe (one which was simple enough for the children to help prepare). Each day a different meal was prepared, stressing whose favorite food it was, what culture it came from, and so on. This experience served both as a means of communication and an introduction to different foods for all the children in the center.

In any meals program a center should see that the children enjoy eating their food and are getting nutritionally adequate meals. The best way to do this is to consider the children's food needs.

The Maryland state licensing agency suggests that "a variety of foods and snacks which appeal to children and which meet children's daily nutritional needs shall be served at intervals of not more than three weeks apart."[6]

The meal should be an enrichment of the child's total personality. If the mechanics of eating are difficult, a child may become frustrated and lose any interest or desire to eat. Therefore, tables, chairs, and utensils should be manageable, as should the size of the food portion. If a child requires a particular diet, all measures should be taken to ensure that the child gets the necessary meal and at the same times does not feel left out.

The involvement of teachers, aides, and staff in preparing and eating the meal is critical. A meal shared by all can be a highly rewarding experience. It can offer everyone—children and adults alike—a chance to interact and communicate with one another around a common, shared experience.

It is also important for the staff to closely examine how the meal experience is used. Are meals a time of socializing and educating or are meals used as bribes, punishments, and rewards? Do staff members eat with the children—and do they eat the same foods as the children?

Snacks can also be a time during which staff and children interact. A snack might be a simple food that the children help to prepare. The preparation experience can encourage new knowledge about foods, their preparation, texture, and odor. Children also learn skills in measuring, in mixing, and in following directions.

Food and its importance in a day-care program should not be confined to just meals and snacks. Other activities such as field trips related to food; stories, games, and songs about food; discussions and participation in food preparation; parties, holidays, and ethnic foods; food-related art work; and growing vegetables can help to further extend children's interest in and knowledge of foods.

HOW CAN A CENTER CONTINUE TO MAKE FOOD AN INTERESTING AND SPECIAL PART OF THE DAY?

To focus on food as one of the more important educational tools, the staff of a center may feel that continual information is needed—and it is. Not everyone is born a nutritionist or an economist or a sociologist or knows what kind of food assistance is available to centers and how to apply for it.

This is an area where, potentially, the state licensing office can play an important, progressive role in providing centers with sources of information which will ensure quality care. Most states and counties have nutritionists on their public health staff available on a consulting basis. Many county agent offices have home economists on staff also available upon request. Use them.

A small number of the day-care center staff, with the assistance of the resource people, could put together a series of workshops, which could be offered both to day-care center staff and parents. The workshops could include nutrition information as it relates to the food supply, production, and distribution; the politics of food; food assistance programs; control of the food economy and its affect on food costs; and eating habits.

There are many resources, both public and private, which can be tapped to assist in putting together and running food workshops. If a center or centers are interested in pursuing nutrition/food education on a more long-term basis, there are various funding sources which could be tapped to support these efforts.

Locally, centers could contact the United Way, local foundations, the Jaycees, Kiwanis Club, the American Legion, and local businesses to request nutrition education money. Prior to contacting any potential funding source, the center(s) should prepare a brief statement of their problem, a plan of how the funding source can help correct the problem, and a cost figure.

Very often funding sources make money available on a one-time basis. Some thought should be given to sources of continual funding if food and nutrition training is held to be a useful endeavor.

A WORD ABOUT FAMILY DAY-CARE HOMES

Although this article has focused primarily on day-care centers, children and nutrition should be no less important a concern in family day-care homes. Family day-care mothers and fathers should take the same time and care in planning meals and food activities as do day-care center staff. In some ways the day-care mother or father is at a distinct advantage in having the opportunity to more fully involve the children in preparing and eating the meal.

Yet family day-care homes are not eligible to participate in the Special

Food Service Program. Therefore, family day-care mothers and fathers are required to rely upon the fees received from parents and money from their own pockets to pay for food. Now there is a great deal of interest in seeing that family day-care homes are included under new SFSPC legislation.

Regarding nutrition and food-training activities planning, the situation varies from county to county, city to city, state to state. Some areas send extension agents into the homes of family day-care mothers and do on-the-spot training. In other areas there are no organized services available to family day-care mothers. And in still other areas, family day care is well organized and mothers attend classes, receive certificates in early childhood education, and continually participate in workshop updates.

Although training varies from place to place, attempts should be made both by the family day-care mother and responsible agencies to see that children in family day-care homes are accorded the same food and nutrition benefits as children in day-care centers.

Food is the basis of life. It is one of the better socializers for children. Without good food and adequate nutrition starting at an early age, children are handicapped in their ability to learn and experience the world around them.

Yet offering adequate food to children is not enough. Children are constantly tempted by fast foods. Formulated foods are rapidly replacing good, wholesome, natural food. Advertising preys on children's minds, enticing them to demand sugar-coated cereals and oversweet cakes or soft drinks. And always, our society says, *fast*—eat fast, eat on the run.

Children must be, as we all must be, educated to make good food choices. A day-care center or family day-care home which realizes this need and does something about it can offer much more to the growth of a child than two pieces of enriched white bread with bologna could ever do.

NOTES

1. Bettleheim, Bruno. *Food to Nurture the Mind*. Washington: The Children's Foundation, 1970. p. 23.

2. Birch, Herbert G., "Malnutrition and Early Development." Edith Grotberg, editor, *Day Care: Resources for Decisions*. Washington, D.C.: Day Care and Child Development Council of America.

3. Evans, E. Belle, Shub, Beth, and Weinstein, Marlene. *Day Care: How to Plan, Develop, and Operate a Day Care Center*. Boston: Beacon Press, 1971. p. 113.

4. 1973 Regulation for Special Food Service Program for Children, p. 4, 225.7(b).

5. Aykroyd, W. R. *Food for Man*, London: Pergamon Press, 1964. p. 75.

6. Maryland State Licensing Regulations, "Food Service."

BIBLIOGRAPHY

Amidon, Edna A. *Good Food and Nutrition*. New York: John Wiley, 1946.
Aykroyd, W. R. *Food for Man*. London: Pergamon, 1964.
Barry, Erick. *Eating and Cooking Around the World*. New York: John Day, 1963.

Bettleheim, Bruno. *Food to Nurture the Mind.* Washington: The Children's Foundation, 1970.

Birch, Herbert G. "Malnutrition and Early Development." *Day Care: Resources for Decisions,* ed. Edith Grotenberg. Washington: Day Care and Child Development Council of America.

Borgheses, Anita. *The Down to Earth Cookbook.* New York: Scribner's, 1973.

Child Welfare League of America. *Standards for Day Care Service.* New York: Child Welfare League of America, 1968.

Croft, Karen B. *The Good for Me Cookbook.* San Francisco: R. & E. Associates.

Evans, E. Belle, Shub, Beth and Weinstein, Marlene. *Day Care: How to Plan, Develop, and Operate a Day Care Center.* Boston: Beacon Press, 1971.

Fenton, Carol and Kitchen, Nermine. *Plants that Feed Us.* New York: John Day, 1971.

Goodwin, Mary and Pollen, Gerry. *Creative Food Experiences for Children.* Washington: Center for Science in the Public Interest, 1974.

Hille, Helen H. *Food Groups for Young Children Cared for During the Day.* Washington: Children's Bureau Publication #386, Supt. of Documents, USGPO, 1960.

Levine, Lois. *The Kids in the Kitchen.* New York: Macmillan, 1968.

Maryland State Licensing Regulations, "Food Service," Baltimore.

Maternal and Child Health/Maryland State Department of Health *Newsletter.* Baltimore: March, 1965.

Tannahill, Reay. *Food in History.* New York: Stein & Day, 1973.

THE EVALUATION PROCESS

Evaluation should be a realistic means of providing information for determining the progress and effectiveness of any early childhood center. Evaluation is a continuous part of the administrative process, because it endeavors to improve a program and also to stress areas of competence and success. There is a responsibility on the part of the administrator, and all other center personnel, to identify continually areas of strength and weakness within the center and to be optimistic in analyzing situations and finding appropriate solutions. It is certainly not a surprise that no one person or program is perfect. It is the evaluation process that encourages activity to aid in developing a more efficient program, one that continually meets the needs of children.

Evaluation should not only be a means of contrasting and comparing individuals. As Yonemura and Katz suggest in their articles, supervision as an evaluative tool should serve to provide the framework for continued professional growth and development of all personnel. Boehm's article provides a focus for the importance of evaluating a center's program in light of realistic and attainable goals. Harms deals with the specifics of evaluating the physical environment of early childhood centers and the ways it affects the opportunities for children to maximize their learning experience. Because personnel in early childhood centers have a responsibility to parents to be open and honest in their assessment of children, the reader will find it helpful to read Butler's article on reporting children's progress.

MARGARET V. S. YONEMURA

44. Supervision in Early Childhood Education

Early childhood programs are expanding throughout the country. States previously without kindergartens are introducing them into their school systems. Day Care, Headstart and Parent Child Centers, as well as Operation Follow Through in the first grades of inner city public schools, are offering new educational opportunities for children. With this expansion, there is a need for increased staff, both on the teaching and the supervisory levels. To cope with the shortage of supervisory personnel, teachers who show competence in teaching are generally assumed to be good candidates as supervisors, even though they may not have the specific training, experience or skills required.

There is little doubt that quality supervision of early childhood programs is crucial to instituting and maintaining high standards of education for young children. With so many new teachers, paraprofessionals and parents entering education, the role of the supervisor is highly significant. This paper questions the prescriptive role usually adopted, often reluctantly, by many supervisors and proposes an alternative model and pursues some of the implications if it were adopted.

Supervision of the type known as "prescriptive" appears to be burgeoning in many early childhood settings. Such supervision is viewed by many teachers, as contributing minimally to their job performance and professional development. It does little to build their self-esteem which Argyris (1964) feels ". . . is developed by dealing with the world competently in such a way that a person can assign the solution of the problems to himself, to his abilities, to his efforts, to his work."

Teachers who were asked to recount their experiences in supervision have given us the following quotes which illustrate what typically "is" in all too many settings.

Teacher 1: Never had a supervisor, but the Asst. Principal came in twice for purposes of evaluation. Didn't like this. Objected to his coming in unannounced. I have a reputation for not pushing children. He came in and would say things like "Is this how far you've gone? The *other* teachers are way ahead of you."

This is an example of hit-or-miss supervisory observations with on-the-spot judgments, often of negative value to the teacher. Judgments are apparently made without regard to the teacher's competence or professional judgment. They assume the teacher is a functionary who performs tasks clearly delineated administratively which she is expected to carry out.

Reprinted by permission from *Young Children*, Vol. 24, No. 2 (Dec. 1968), pp. 104–109. Copyright © 1968, National Association for the Education of Young Children, 1834 Connecticut Avenue, N.W., Washington, DC 20009.

Apparently, the supervisory objectives are to oversee the teacher at work and to inject as motivation a drive to compete with other teachers. The teacher is given a harsh reminder that she is falling short of job expectations, but she is given no help.

Teacher 2: Never had a supervisor. First principal came in one day, sat in the back of the room and wrote and wrote and never came in again but once. He was amazed at the control I had. This principal was critical because there were too few charts and bulletins and the windows were not open enough. When he opened the windows, all the papers flew all over the place, the children complained of the draft, and this principal never came into the room again to criticize.

This again illustrates supervisory contact in which dismal, indirectional communication (supervisor to teacher) was occupied with noneducational trivia. This supervisory behavior violated the principle that the teacher is a professional practitioner and cannot have her job done for her. The supervisor, as insensitive critic, is rejected by the teacher.

Teacher 3: I was very fortunate. Had excellent experiences with three marvelous people in three different settings respectively. Supervisors were principals. Had daily contact such as lunch, visits in room and office. They provided materials, professional magazines, introduced new things at staff meetings. I was never afraid to ask and was very comfortable. Experience with supervisors was so good because they were this kind of person.

It is a relief to turn to a positively oriented supervisory relationship. But it must be noted that these contacts were informal, not regularly scheduled, and indicate the generally low priority given to regular supervisory activity. Perhaps this is related to the view, not wholly realistic or workable, that the teacher is an autonomous professional without need of supervision. The final remark about her experience with supervisors being so good because "they were this kind of person" contains shades of the good-teachers-being-born-not-made. It is likely to lead to the same problems. So very few of us are born good at anything. If this is accepted as given, systematic training and study can be seen as imperatives for educating both supervisors and teachers.

Teacher 4: Worked as assistant teacher. Teacher was better supervisor than the real supervisor. She discussed the situation immediately. The supervisor always fell asleep when she came in to observe. Teacher gave the kind of help everyone should get. Felt lucky to get that kind of support.

This response raises some question about the lines of supervision. There is ample documentation that teachers receive most help from other teachers. Each setting might clarify its supervisory structure so that the actual supervisor becomes recognized as such and one teacher is not saddled with two supervisors, an untenable plight.

Teacher 5: In settlement house, much supervision. Supervisor always there, always available—not coming in and observing negatively. Very compatible, offered suggestions. Lack of supervision was regarded as deprivation.

473

One can detect the recurrent theme of supervision as being experienced negatively by the teacher only by inference in this record from the comment that the supervisor was always there, "not coming in and observing negatively."

PAST EXPERIENCES

Prescriptive supervision is so prevalent that, even when teachers reject its underlying ethic, it appears in many cases to be the only model upon which they can draw when they are called upon to act as supervisors.

Lacking alternatives, newly appointed supervisors often use their own experiences as a model for their supervisory practices. Thus, the teacher who will describe her own supervision as prescriptive and time wasting, when asked to role play a supervisory conference will, within three to five minutes, usually step into the very role she claims to reject as a supervisory model. It is a "telling," prescriptive, although a well-intentioned, role. Likewise, the use of a prescriptive model was evident in a group of students in a supervision course who were given a case study of a new teacher in an early childhood setting. They were asked to role play the supervisor and to write an ideal script of a supervisory conference with this beginning teacher, giving, in addition, their agenda for the conference. The agenda were well conceptualized with verbal acknowledgement of the underlying dynamics of learning, change and growth in individuals. In most cases, however, the scripts were no sooner off the ground than the supervisor's role became very much one of "telling how" and prescribing. It seems that despite the best of intentions, the tendency to do as one has been done to is the dominant mode.

Many supervisors who prescribe to teachers have thoroughly rejected the *tabula rasa* concept of the child. Yet, they seem to proceed with a teacher, as if she were a clean slate upon which they could write. With the paraprofessional, sometimes the slate is not only clean, but it is much smaller so that the supervisor or supervisory teacher can only anticipate giving a diminished message.

Some early childhood programs for young children legitimize this prescriptive supervisory role. Teachers are told and trained what to do, when and how—and then with disarming naivete told to feel free to use their imaginations. These are programs in which small children are told what to do, when and how, and—if they are disadvantaged—it is assumed they have no ideas that are of school-learning importance. In such programs, supervision becomes a checking up process in order to assess the effectiveness of the limited educational goals conceived and sought.

There are other concepts of education and of supervision, and these rest on different conceptual bases about supervisory behavior, the individual, the group and the teacher. The model of supervision proposed here is derived from a view of the individual and the group as having, admittedly varying, degrees of useful potential. Tapping this potential is a major function of supervision.

Eric Hoffer (on a television program in September 1967) described how a group of derelicts loafing on a street in Los Angeles during the Depression were "scooped up" into a truck and sent out to build the San Bernadino road. They were dumped out in the mountains—unselected, uninterviewed and unsupervised individuals. They organized nonetheless. They divided up jobs and *dished out* responsibilities and proceeded to accomplish the job. The *innate capacities of an individual and a group have to be believed in order to become and be.* When supervisors accept this idea, supervision does not become the skill of making men do a job they would otherwise not get done or a chore that keeps wandering noses to the grindstone.

John Dewey saw the teacher's role as one that was ". . . to induce a vital and personal experiencing" in children. Bruner (1960) repeats this theme by seeing an outcome of teaching as giving students "a sense of excitement about discovery." There is no one way that such teachers can be developed, but they are unlikely to be nurtured unless the school system, as symbolized in its supervisory personnel, perceives this kind of behavior as valuable. If it does, it will avoid major doses of prescriptive supervision which are likely to rebound in dominative teacher classroom behavior. Since, within an organization, the supervisor in the hierarchy is a powerful role model, the prescriptive supervisor is likely to unleash prescriptive tendencies in many of the teachers with whom she works. Anderson (1946) showed in his studies of dominative teacher behavior in a nursery school that it seemed to lessen the children's ability to show initiative, the initiative that is an essential component of "personal experiencing" and a "sense of discovery." The model of supervision presented here, then, supports behaving toward teachers as if they have initiative as well as the drive to be competent.

IMPLICATIONS OF NEW MODEL

The implications of this guiding principle for supervisory behavior are many. It means first and foremost learning where the teacher is in her thinking.

As early childhood educators begin learning to match young children's "cognitive structures" or "action patterns" with the content of the curriculum, how ironic it all becomes if the supervisory move cannot be matched to the teacher's stage of development. Determining this can be a needle-in-a-haystack enterprise if supervisory encounters are unfocused: Hit and miss chats on the run, or other versions of "instant" supervision, are not effective as the basis for this model of supervision. It has to be planned, conscious, and supervisor-teacher directed. Planning becomes indispensable and it is reflected in the schedule priority of the supervisor's day. "The highly specialized nature of supervision, and the skills and knowledge required, are little understood, or are disregarded, by the schools. Supervision, with helpful intent, requires an enormous amount of time" (Shaplin, 1963). Supervisors are too frequently burdened with administrative chores of such depressing proportions that the time for supervision is miserly.

An example may help to make explicit the ramifications of this model of supervision as it applies to one everyday supervisory task: classroom observation of a teacher by the supervisor. This would first of all be planned in advance—the time and the focus of the observation—by both teacher and supervisor. It might focus on the behavior of one child, a running record documenting as objectively as possible what the child is doing. The supervisor becomes a camera, almost, noting what the child is doing without psychologyzing, sociologizing or moralizing about it. Marginal notes of what the teacher is doing and where she is give some relevant ecological data.

ALLOW TEACHERS TO SELF-CORRECT

Even one such observation develops many tentative but significant hunches for the supervisor about a teacher's level of functioning. The record will be suggestive of many places to begin feeding-in information, raising questions and clarifying values. The prescriptive supervisor would know where to begin. But it is the teacher's move, not the supervisor's, now. The teacher needs time to read and think over the carbon copy of the running record before she meets with the supervisor—again at a planned time—to discuss the record. Since it is her behavior that may need to be modified, her hunches, her views, and her questions need to be given priority.

In working with various groups of supervisors-in-training and supervisors, I have found one of their unanimous satisfactions is the discovery that they can utilize the ability of most teachers to self-correct and self evaluate. For example, during supervisory conferences when teachers have read the raw data provided by a running record of a child in the class, they will make such comments as "I don't ask any open-ended questions, do I?" or, conversely, "That was a good question, wasn't it?". "Why didn't I see that Lewis was approaching me for information on four occasions?" Teachers can generally see for themselves many places where they can raise questions about what they are doing, or feel encouraged about what may have daunted them in their thinking.

Having themselves witnessed the behaviors that need changing, they are *ready* for supervisory help of a different order from the elementary prescriptive. This is the time when the supervisor, based on a careful diagnosis, can assess what is likely to have most impact as the next small sequential step in the supervisory relationship. It may be just the question, "Can you see some alternative ways of teaching in this situation so that x condition will be prevented?" Maybe alternatives, new information, materials will be needed. The supervisor who is abreast of the research on teaching and who is soundly educated in the early childhood field can be invaluable in this way to the teacher's professional growth.

ACCEPTING TEACHER'S VIEWPOINT

Accepting this nonprescriptive but integrative model of supervision is an intellectual challenge. The hardest step is to begin to listen and hear and understand the teacher's point of view and ideas. Early childhood teachers are sensitive to latent meanings in children's behavior but this sensitivity must become part of their supervisory behavior for working with adults. The next step is to relate the teacher's goal to those of the school. It is not a matter of letting the teacher go her own way. Rather, it is helping her make explicit the rationale for what she does, removing the unexamined nature of her biases by raising questions, feeding in information, talking about, describing, showing, providing liberal amounts of *feedback* (Raths & Leeper, 1966). This feedback can be plain (running and anecdotal records) or fancy (tapes and videotapes). But give her every chance to self-correct. The teacher's ideas, then, have to be weighed and balanced against the school's or agency's goals to see if they are compatible. New teachers, particularly, are well served by the kind of supervision which enables them early in their careers to maintain their own style and integrity. Didactic supervision may drive them into building moat-ringed castles in which they have to muster their defenses against the attacks of the do-as-I-do enemy of professional integrity and the destruction of what little autonomy the teacher possesses.

New staffing arrangements are part of the present and future for early childhood settings. The challenge is to display the same respect and belief in the individual teacher and paraprofessional as the profession has built in the individual child.

References

Anderson, H. H. & Brewer, J. J. *Studies of Teachers' Classroom Personalities, II: Effects of Teachers' Dominative and Integrative Contacts on Children's Classroom Behavior.* Applied Psych. Monographs, 8, 1946.

Argyris, C. *Integrating the Individual and the Organization.* New York: John Wiley & Sons, 1964, p. 26.

Bruner, J. *The Process of Education.* Cambridge: Harvard Univ. Press. 1960, p. 73.

Raths, J. & Leeper, R. (eds.). *The Supervisor: Agent for Change in Teaching.* Washington, D.C.: Assn. for Supervision & Cur. Develpm., N.E.A., 1966.

Shaplin, J. T. Practice in Teaching. *Harvard Educ. Rev.*, 33, 1, 1963, pp. 43–44.

LILLIAN G. KATZ
45. Developmental Stages of Preschool Teachers

Preschool teachers can generally be counted on to talk about developmental needs and stages when they discuss children.[1] It may also be meaningful to think of teachers themselves as having developmental sequences in their professional growth.[2]

There may be at least four developmental stages for teachers. Individual teachers may vary greatly in the length of time spent in each of the four stages outlined here and schematized in Figure 1.

STAGE 1: SURVIVAL

During Stage 1, which may last throughout the first full year of teaching, the teacher's main concern is whether she can survive. This preoccupation with survival may be expressed in questions the teacher asks: "Can I get through the day in one piece? Without losing a child? Can I make it until the end of the week? Until the next vacation? Can I really do this kind of work day after day? Will I be accepted by my colleagues?" Such questions are well expressed in Ryan's enlightening collection of accounts of first-year teaching experiences.[3]

The first full impact of responsibility for a group of immature but vigorous young children (to say nothing of encounters with their parents) inevitably provokes teachers' anxieties. The discrepancy between anticipated successes and classroom realities intensifies feelings of inadequacy and unpreparedness.

During this period the teacher needs support, understanding, encouragement, reassurance, comfort, and guidance. She needs instruction in specific skills and insight into the complex causes of behavior—all of which must be provided on the classroom site. On-site instructors may be senior staff members, advisors, consultants, or program assistants who know the beginning teacher and her teaching situation well. Training must be constantly and readily available. The trainer should have enough time and flexibility to be on call as needed. Schedules of periodic visits that have been arranged in advance cannot be counted on to coincide with crises. Cook and Mack[4] describe the British pattern of on-site training given to teachers by their headmasters (principals). Armington also tells how advisors can meet the needs of these teachers.[5]

Reprinted from Lilian G. Katz, "Developmental Stages of Preschool Teachers," *Elementary School Journal*, Vol. 73 (1972), pp. 50–54. By permission of The University of Chicago Press. Copyright 1979 by The University of Chicago.

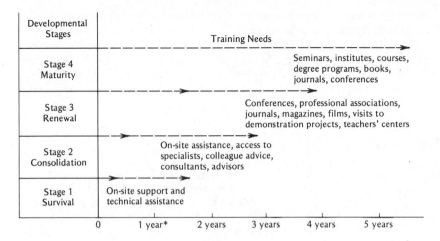

Developmental Stages	Training Needs					
Stage 4 Maturity			Seminars, institutes, courses, degree programs, books, journals, conferences			
Stage 3 Renewal			Conferences, professional associations, journals, magazines, films, visits to demonstration projects, teachers' centers			
Stage 2 Consolidation		On-site assistance, access to specialists, colleague advice, consultants, advisors				
Stage 1 Survival	On-site support and technical assistance					
	0	1 year*	2 years	3 years	4 years	5 years

*Some periods approximate

FIGURE 1. Stages of development and training needs of preschool teachers.

STAGE 2: CONSOLIDATION

By the end of the first year the teacher has usually decided that she can survive. She is now ready to consolidate the gains made during the first stage and to differentiate tasks and skills to be mastered next. During Stage 2, teachers usually begin to focus on individual children who pose problems and on troublesome situations. The teacher may look for answers to such questions as: "How can I help a shy child? How can I help a child who does not seem to be learning?"

During Stage 1, the beginning teacher acquires a base line of information about what young children are like and what to expect of them. By Stage 2, the teacher is beginning to identify individual children whose behavior departs from the pattern of most of the children she knows.

During this stage, on-site help continues to be valuable. A trainer can help the teacher by exploring a problem with her. Take the case of a young teacher from a day-care center who was eager to get help and asked: "How should I deal with a clinging child?" An on-site trainer can observe the teacher and the child at the center and arrive at suggestions and tentative solutions fairly quickly. However, without firsthand knowledge of the child and the context, an extended give-and-take conversation between the teacher and trainer may be the best way for the trainer to help the teacher interpret her experience and move toward a solution of the problem. The trainer might ask the teacher, "What have you done so far? Give examples of some experiences with this child during this week. When you did such and such, how did the child respond?" Other suggestions for helping children are offered by Katz.[6]

At this stage, the teacher may find that she needs information about specific children or about children who pose problems. It will be helpful if she has a wide range of resources. Psychologists, social workers, health workers, and other specialists can strengthen the teacher's skills and knowledge at this time. Exchanges of information and ideas with more experienced colleagues may help teachers master the developmental tasks of this period. Opportunities to share feelings with other teachers at the same stage of development may reduce some of the inadequacy and the frustration the beginning teacher feels.

STAGE 3: RENEWAL

Often, during the third or fourth year of teaching, the teacher begins to tire of doing the same things. She asks questions about new developments in the field: "Who is doing what? Where? What are some of the new materials, techniques, approaches, and ideas?" Perhaps what the teacher has been doing for each annual crop of children has been adequate for them, but she herself finds the seasonal Valentine cards, Easter bunnies, and pumpkin cutouts no longer interesting. If it is true that a teacher's own interest in the projects and the activities she provides for children contributes to their educational value, then her need for renewal and refreshment should be taken seriously.

During this stage, teachers find it rewarding to meet colleagues from various programs on both formal and informal occasions. Teachers at this developmental stage are particularly receptive to experiences in regional and national conferences and workshops. Teachers at Stage 3 profit from membership in professional associations and participation in their meetings. Teachers are now widening the scope of their reading, scanning magazines and journals, and viewing films. During this period they may be ready to take a close look at their own classroom teaching through videotape recording. This is also a time when teachers welcome opportunities to visit other classes, programs, and demonstration projects.

Perhaps it is at this stage that the teachers' center has the greatest potential value.[7, 8] Teachers' centers are places where teachers can meet to help one another learn or relearn skills, techniques, and methods. At these centers, teachers can exchange ideas and organize special workshops. From time to time specialists in curriculum, or child growth, or any other area of concern are invited to the center to meet with teachers.

STAGE 4: MATURITY

Some teachers may reach maturity, Stage 4, within three years; others need five years or more. The teacher at this stage has come to terms with herself as a teacher. She now has enough perspective to ask deeper and more abstract questions, such as: "What are my historical and philosophical roots? What is the nature of growth and learning? How are educational decisions made? Can schools change societies? Is teaching a profession?" Perhaps she has asked these questions before. But with the experience she now has, the questions represent a more meaningful search for insight, perspective, and realism.

Throughout maturity, teachers need an opportunity to participate in conferences and seminars, and perhaps to work toward a degree. Mature teachers welcome the chance to read widely and to interact with educators working on many problem areas on many levels. Training sessions and conference events that teachers at Stage 2 enjoy may be tiresome to the teacher at Stage 4. Similarly, introspective and searching seminars that teachers at Stage 4 enjoy may lead to restlessness and irritability among the beginners at Stage 1.

It is useful to think of the growth of preschool teachers (and perhaps other teachers, also) as occurring in stages, linked generally to experience gained over time.

The training needs of teachers change as they gain experience, as they move from one stage to another. The issues dealt with in the traditional social foundations courses do not seem to address themselves to the early survival problems that are critical to the inexperienced teacher. However, for the maturing teacher, those same issues may help deepen her understanding of the total complex environment in which she is trying to be effective.

The location of training should change as the teacher develops. At the beginning of the new teacher's career, training resources must be taken to her so that training can be responsive to the particular (and possibly unique) developmental tasks and working situation she faces in her classroom. As the teacher moves on past the survival stage, training can move to the college campus.

The timing of training should be shifted so that more training is available to the teacher on the job than before it. Teachers say that their preservice education has only a minor influence on what they do day to day in their classrooms. The complaint suggests that strategies acquired before employment may seldom be used under the pressures of the job.

It is often said that experience is the best teacher. To make sure that the beginning teacher has informed and interpreted experience should be one of the major roles of the teacher trainer.

NOTES

1. Lilian G. Katz and Mary K. Weir. *Help for Preschool Teachers: A Proposal.* Urbana, Illinois: ERIC Clearinghouse on Early Childhood Education, 1969.

2. This paper was produced pursuant to a contract with the Office of Education, United States Department of Health, Education and Welfare. Contractors undertaking such projects under Government sponsorship are encouraged to express freely their professional judgment. Points of view or opinions stated do not, therefore, necessarily represent official government position or policy.

3. Kevin Ryan (editor). *Don't Smile until Christmas: Accounts of the First Year of Teaching.* Chicago, Illinois: University of Chicago Press, 1970.

4. Ann Cook and Herbert Mack. *The Headteacher's Role.* New York: Citation Press, 1971.

5. David Armington. "A Plan for Continuing Growth." Newton, Massachusetts: Educational Development Center (mimeographed, no date).

6. Lilian G. Katz. "Condition with Caution," *Young Children.* In Press.

7. Arlene Silberman. "A Santa's Workshop for Teachers," American Education, 7 (December, 1971), 3-8.

8. Stephen K. Bailey. "Teachers' Centers: A British First," *Phi Delta Kappan, 53* (November, 1971), 146-49.

ANN E. BOEHM

46. One Model for Developing a Prekindergarten Assessment Program

With the recent growth of prekindergarten programs for the disadvantaged has come increasing concern regarding their effectiveness. It has been questioned whether such programs "work"—whether in fact they improve children's overall readiness for school. Another question centers around the type of program that is most effective.

The majority of current research studies assessing the effectiveness of prekindergarten intervention programs have based their evaluation on changes in scores on standardized tests of intelligence, reading readiness, or language abilities (Deutsch, 1965; Gray & Klaus, 1965; Kohlberg, 1965; Weikart, 1967). Generally, positive gains have been reported as a result of such programs. However, followup studies dealing with the long range effect of prekindergarten programs after kindergarten or first grade have demonstrated conflicting and often disappointing results (DiLorenzo, Salter, & Bradley, 1968; Green, 1969).

Serious doubts have been raised as to the value of changes in IQ scores as measures of program success. Glick (1968) discussed the variability in IQ scores on the part of deprived children, and suggested that the change in scores may be the result of motivation or understanding how to take the tests. Furthermore, such testing measures assess only part of a program's overall goals. Passow noted at the National Conference on the Education of the Disadvantaged (1966) that although new program ideas are being attempted, old and inappropriate evaluation techniques are still employed.

The nature and appropriateness of experiences are other factors in determining a program's effectiveness. Evaluation of prekindergarten programs and assessment procedures rarely have been utilized by prekindergarten programs which *match* teaching and curricular materials to the individual needs of the pupils. Such a goal has been fundamental to the development of the assessment program to be described.

HISTORY AND GOALS

The question of program effectiveness has been an important issue facing a prekindergarten program located in an urban setting near New York City. This program encountered many of the same problems as those found in the larger urban setting. Of the approximately 900 children who reach the age of 4 during any one year and live in this city, 150 children from low income families are served by the prekindergarten program. This program is one of 48 New York State funded experimental prekindergarten programs. There are 10 classes of 15 children, each meeting for a half-day session 4 days per week. On the fifth day, in-service courses are held for the teachers and other staff members. A teacher certified in early childhood education and a teacher aide work with each class. Classrooms are located in four elementary school buildings and the program is considered an integral part of that school.

In order to evaluate the effectiveness of this prekindergarten program, it was necessary to raise the question, "Effective in relationship to what?" Better performance on standardized intelligence tests or readiness tests? The attainment of curricular goals? While these two questions are not mutually exclusive, the problem of assessment has been approached from the second point of reference.

The first source of information used was the teachers' written curricular reports. In these reports, the teachers' educational goals for children were indicated and grouped into the following categories: (a) improved social interactions, (b) emotional development, (c) cognitive development, (d) increased ability to cope with the problems of classroom life, (e) increased expression of ideas and thoughts through language, and (f) physical-motor development.

Another source of information was an investigation of the conditions and/or skills necessary for success in kindergarten and first grade. Based on teacher interviews and a survey of curricular materials, such conditions and skills included: (a) following directions consisting of multiple components, e.g., color all of the little triangles green, (b) comprehending what is read and heard, (c) understanding basic concepts such as "big" and "small," (d) differentiating beginning and ending sounds of words, (e) meeting success with beginning reading, (f) learning basic mathematical concepts, (g) expressing thoughts in spoken words and through the written symbol, and (h) developing emotional and social maturity.

Through discussions with teachers, aides, and other staff personnel, the goals of the prekindergarten assessment program were set to:

1. Select or devise measurement instruments relevant to 3 and 4 year old children from many backgrounds.
2. Measure those aspects of children's functioning which appear related to later school success.
3. Utilize measures in a diagnostic manner so that the levels of children's functioning can be determined with regard to strengths and weaknesses.
4. Provide information to teachers which will help the teacher modify and/or develop curricula to meet specific needs of children.
5. Devise a series of teacher administered tasks which are adequately delineated to measure some of the above goals.

Other major purposes of the assessment program have been to compare the growth of a child *with himself* during the course of the school year, compare the functioning of the individual child with that of his prekindergarten class as a whole, and evaluate the success of the program in attaining selected curricular goals.

INVENTORY OF SKILLS AND FUNCTIONING

Integrating the information gained from teachers' curriculum reports, the survey of curricular materials used in prekindergarten, kindergarten, and first grade, and discussions with teachers, an Inventory of Cognitive Skills and Visual-Motor Functioning* was developed.

The following areas were covered in the Inventory.

1. Knowledge of body parts.
2. Identification of color and shapes.
3. Number concepts such as the recognition of the number of concrete or pictured objects presented.
4. Information from pictures and comprehension of simple stories.
5. Relational concepts such as "same" and "different."
6. Following directions containing multiple components such as "Find the ball that is big and red."
7. Copying geometric forms.
8. Gross motor functioning.

The final section of the inventory deals with the child's overall behavior during testing. A rating scale dealing with behavioral factors—such as "attention span" and "ease of relationship"—which might affect the child's performance, is therefore an integral part of each inventory.

The design of the inventory was such that each of the major areas tested was broken down into levels of difficulty. Therefore, if a child encountered difficulty at one level, the task was broken down into simpler levels so that the point of difficulty could be determined, particularly in terms of

*Additional information about the *Inventory of Cognitive Skills and Visual-Motor Functioning* may be obtained from The Experimental Pre-kindergarten Program, City School District, New Rochelle, New York.

materials or instructions. For example, a child was asked to identify a number of basic colors with the question at level 3 being, "What color is this dress?" At level 3, it was necessary for the child to make an identification among colors and provide the color label. If the child met difficulty at level 3, the label was provided and the evaluator moved to level 2 with the question, "Show me the dress that is red." The child at level 2 was expected to make only the correct identification of the color. If difficulty continued to be met at level 2, the evaluator then moved to level 1 and placed a colored square before the child and asked him to, "Find me another one like this" or "Where does this go?" At level 1, the child needed only to match the color correctly. He did not have to identify a specific color or provide a label.

Aspects of a child's cognitive development, approach to learning, physical-motor development, and verbal expression are assessed in part by the inventory (corresponding to points *c* through *f* of the teacher's educational goals for children). Observational reports and teacher conferences are used to supply further information regarding the social and emotional growth of the child.

THE DEVELOPMENT PROCESS

The first form of the inventory was administered individually by the writer to a sample of 50 children during October and November (pretest) and May and June (posttest) of the 1966-67 school year. Upon completion of the fall testing, the results were reported to teachers, aides, and other prekindergarten personnel. They, in turn, questioned the meaning, necessity, and representativeness of the questions.

During a number of inservice sessions, the nature and meaning of "assessment" was discussed. Assessment was defined as evaluating the level of a child's functioning, both his strengths and his weaknesses, in areas related to the curriculum.

Assessment procedures employed a task analysis approach which broke down the same task into levels of difficulty so that if a child did not meet success at one level, he might enjoy success at another. Thus tasks involved in the assessment were viewed not as an "all or none" entity but as containing several degrees of attainment. The inventory was not just "another test" which would yield another intelligence quotient; it was a source of data useful for program planning. After completion of the end of year testing, teachers were able to compare the child's functioning against himself from the beginning to the end of the school year. Teachers indicated that although daily interactions with children provided insight into many of the areas assessed, the inventory provided a systematic check for all children in the class.

TEACHER ADMINISTRATION

Next in the process of development (1967-68) was the refinement of the inventory, instructions, and scoring criteria so that teacher administration would be feasible. Administration of the inventory by teachers was desirable because teachers and aides would have immediate feedback regarding the functioning of each child, his style and approach to the tasks presented, and his reactions to success and difficulty. The psychologist and supervisor could then discuss the results in terms of the child's strengths and areas needing development, teacher impressions of the child, and program planning for that child. Thus the goal of *matching* a curricular program to the needs of the child could be fostered by this procedure.

Before administering the inventory, teachers and classroom aides attended a one day training session. Directions and scoring criteria were clarified where possible. For example, teachers pointed out that a child would never see a "group" of ice cream cones, and he would be more familiar with the word "pile." The direction was changed to read: "Show me the piles of boxes that are the same." Teachers were also requested to note suggestions or areas of difficulty which occurred during testing.

It was anticipated that the total testing time per child would range between 12-15 minutes. The teachers and aides administered the inventory during the first 2 weeks of school, testing 3 or 4 children during any one day in their classroom setting. Complaints arose about the length of the test, inadequacy of the pictured material, and the disruptive aspects of testing during class time. Suggestions were also made to clarify directions, eliminate items which yielded inadequate information, and provide ideas for better pictorial representations. At this point, the prekindergarten staff began to view the assessment inventory as *their* inventory, one that reflected their recommendations and criticisms.

A major criticism of the form of the inventory described above (1967-68) was the difficulty which occurred as a result of administration during class sessions at the beginning of the school year. Children were in the process of adjusting to the routines of classroom life at this time and teachers stated that it was difficult to devote the necessary time to assessment. As a result of the criticisms and suggestions made, in the 1968-69 school year the inventory was administered during the registration period the week before classes began.

PARENT INTERACTION

An important modification suggested by the teaching staff was to have parents present during the testing session. This modification was made an integral part of the assessment procedures during the 1969-70 school year. This gave the teacher the opportunity to interpret to the parent that:

1. No child is expected to answer all questions correctly, since the tasks assessed are among the skills to be developed during the prekindergarten year. Furthermore, the same battery will be administered at the end of the child's prekindergarten experience. In such a manner the child's progress in relation to himself can be determined.
2. The prekindergarten experience involves more than play, for it has specific cognitive goals.

3. Each child has strengths and areas needing development in planning his curriculum.

Some parents were pleased to observe their children's levels of learning. Others were concerned that their children should know everything, viewing the inventory as a test to be "passed."

Parent and teacher communication was facilitated by this interaction with the inventory providing a stimulus for the discussion of curricular goals. Many parents indicated that they did not know the areas measured were important for success in school. Parent interaction with younger children in these families should benefit from this exposure.

END-OF-YEAR TESTING

The end of year testing takes place during the last 2 weeks of school. Two days are set aside for the testing with half of the children in any one class present each day. The teacher and aide are able to manage the smaller class group successfully as well as to test each of the seven or eight children present.

Comparing the child's progress from the beginning to the end of the school year on each of the subareas assessed has enabled the prekindergarten teacher to specify factually gains made as well as areas in need of further development. Such information has been passed on to kindergarten teachers so that more meaningful follow-through programs can be developed.

RESULTS

Teacher, aide, and parent interaction in the development of a prekindergarten assessment program has facilitated the development of a workable inventory which provides meaningful information to teachers. The prekindergarten staff has moved from viewing testing as a task to provide data which slots children into groups to viewing testing as an assessment procedure and a basis for educational communication with parents. Discussions regarding the fairness of items have now moved to discussions in which questions are raised such as, "How representative is the inventory of what is taught in your classroom?" and "What doesn't the test measure that would be useful?" Another benefit of this interaction has been additional concentration on the learning process. The task analysis approach of breaking down tasks into their multiple components is now used by the teaching staff in developing curricular approaches and materials.

The assessment consultant has gained insight into the curricular goals and concerns of the prekindergarten staff. An ongoing dialog with the staff has resulted. This same approach, although requiring considerable time, can serve as a model for developing other assessment procedures.

REFERENCES

Deutsch, M. *Institute for developmental studies: Annual report.* New York: New York Medical College, 1965.

DiLorenzo, L., Salter, R., & Bradley, J. *Pre-kindergarten programs for the disadvantaged. A third-year report on an evaluative study.* New York: State Education Department, December 1968.

Glick, J. Some problems in the evaluation of preschool intervention programs. In R. D. Hess and R. M. Bear (Eds.), *Early education.* Chicago: Aldine, 1968. Pp. 215-222.

Gray, S. W., & Klaus, R. A. An experimental preschool program for culturally deprived children. *Child Development,* 1965, 36, 887-898.

Green, M. Follow-through study of children who attended the Great Neck Pre-kindergarten center for disadvantaged pre-schoolers during 1967-68 school year and are attending kindergarten in the Great Neck schools during 1968-69. Great Neck, N.Y.: Great Neck Public Schools, 1969 (duplicated).

Kohlberg, L. Montessori with the culturally disadvantaged: A cognitive-developmental interpretation and some research findings. In. R. D. Hess and R. M. Bear (Eds.), *Early education.* Chicago: Aldine, 1968, Pp. 105-118.

US Department of Health, Education, and Welfare. *National conference on education of the disadvantaged.* Report of a national conference held in Washington, D.C., July 18-20, 1966. Washington, D.C.: US Government Printing Office, 1966.

Weikart, D. P. Preschool programs: Preliminary findings. *Journal of Special Education,* 1967, 1, 163-181.

THELMA HARMS

47. Evaluating Settings for Learning

It is very helpful during an evaluation to look at the environment from a child's point of view. To a child, everything that is present in a setting is a stimulus. He responds to what is really there, not only to what we as adults

Reprinted by permission of *Young Children,* Vol. 25, No. 5 (May 1970), pp. 304-306, 308. Copyright © 1970, National Association for the Education of Young Children, 1834 Connecticut Avenue, H.W., Washington, D.C. 20009.

are aware is there. The way people treat him is as real a part of his environment as the materials on the shelves or the space provided for block building. The teacher's tone of voice, the way she walks and her facial expression contribute to the overall atmosphere. Similarly, the child's interaction with other children is an important component of the school setting. Everything present in the environment, even the spacial arrangement, communicates to the child how to live in that setting. Materials that are in good condition and placed far apart on open shelves tell a child that the materials are valued, that they are meant to be considered, and that a child may take them off the shelf by himself. When they are taken off the shelf, they leave a big, empty space so it is easy to put them back where they belong. What kind of a message does a child get from open shelves crowded with an odd assortment of materials, few with all the pieces put together? What kind of a message does he get from a closed cupboard?

Physical environment is a powerful means of communication. To sensitize yourself to physical environment, set yourself the task, every time you walk into a new setting, of reading the messages contained in the room arrangement. The room with a speaker's stand in front of rows of chairs tells us something about the predicted relationship of teacher to student, and student to student in the class. Chairs in a circle imply another kind of learning interaction.

Children respond to the messages given to them by the physical environment, the activities and the time schedule, so we must become increasingly aware of the total environment we are creating for them. Often problems occur because contradictory messages are being simultaneously sent out by the different components making up the environment. The teacher may be trying to prevent running and sliding while the large, slick expanse of floor in the center of the room is inviting the children to run and slide. Improvement in the children's use of materials in that situation might require a reorganization of the physical environment rather than improvement in interpersonal skills or changes in activities or time schedule. In another school, however, the physical environment may be well defined, the interpersonal atmosphere warm and accepting, but the children may need the challenge of more complex activities, or they may need longer periods of unbroken time to become involved in the activities offered. Each setting for learning needs to be looked at individually because it is a unique combination of children.

SUGGESTIONS FOR USING THE CHECKLIST

The following list of questions is organized into four categories. Each category contributes in a major way to the environment as experienced by the child. The questions are meant to help you identify both strengths and problems in your own setting. Many schools have found it helpful to give each staff member a checklist to think about for several days before the evaluation meeting. Then, when the entire staff meets, each person is prepared to share his observations and suggestions.

EVALUATION CHECKLIST

The Physical Environment

1. Can quiet and noisy activities go on without disturbing one another? Is there an appropriate place for each?
2. Is a variety of materials available on open shelves for the children to use when they are interested? Are materials on shelves well spaced for clarity.
3. Are materials stored in individual units so that children can use them alone without being forced to share with a group?
4. Are activity centers defined so that children know where to use the materials?
5. Are tables or rug areas provided for convenient use of materials in each acitivity center?
6. Is self-help encouraged by having materials in good condition and always stored in the same place?
7. Are cushioning materials used to cut down extraneous noise—rug under blocks, pads under knock-out bench?
8. Are setup and cleanup simple? Are these expected parts of the child's activity?
9. Have learning opportunities been carefully planned in the outdoor area? Painting, crafts, block building, carpentry, gardening, pets, sand and water all lend themselves to learning experiences outdoors.
10. Is the children's work displayed attractively at the child's eye level?
11. Do the children feel in control of and responsible for the physical environment?

The Interpersonal Environment

1. Is there a feeling of mutual respect between adults and children, children and children?
2. Is the physical environment enough under control so that the major part of the adults' time is spent in observing or participating with children?
3. Can children engage in activities without being disturbed or distracted by others?
4. Do adults observe children's activity and intervene only when it is beneficial to the child?
5. Do adults have "growth goals" for each child based on the needs they have observed in each child? Is individualized curriculum used to reach these goals?
6. Do children feel safe with one another?
7. Is competition avoided by arranging materials in individual units, limiting the number of children participating in an activity at one time, insuring the fairness of turns by starting a waiting list on which the child can see his name keeping his place in line?

8. Do the adults show children how to help themselves? Are children encouraged to learn from one another?
9. Are there opportunities for children to play alone, participate in a small group, and participate in a large group?
10. When limits are placed, do adults use reasoning and consistently follow through? Are limits enforced?
11. Are the adults models of constructive behavior and healthy attitudes?
12. Is there an overall warm interpersonal environment?

Activities to Stimulate Development

1. Are there many opportunities for dramatic play: large housekeeping corner, small dollhouse, dress-up clothes for boys as well as girls?
2. Is there a variety of basic visual art media: painting, drawing, clay, salt-flour dough, wood-glue sculpture, fingerpaint, collage?
3. Is music a vital part of the program: records, group singing, instruments, dancing?
4. Is language stimulation varied: reading books, games with feel boxes, flannel boards, stories, questions and answers, conversation, lotto games, classification games? Are limits enforced through verbal control and reasoning?
5. Are there small manipulative toys to build eye-hand coordination and finger dexterity?
6. Are there some opportunities to follow patterns or achieve a predetermined goal: puzzles, design blocks, dominos, matching games?
7. Do children do things like cooking, planting seeds, caring for animals?
8. Are field trips planned to give experience with the world around us? Is there adequate preparation and follow-up after trips?
9. Are there repeated opportunities for children to use similar materials? Are materials available in a graded sequence so that children develop skills gradually?
10. Are children involved in suggesting and planning activities? How is free choice built into the program?
11. Are new activities developed by teachers as they are suggested by the interests of individual children?
12. Is the range of activities varied enough to present a truly divergent curriculum? Are there opportunities for learning through exploration, guided discovery, problem solving, repetition, intuition, imitation, etc.? Is there provision for children to learn through their senses as well as verbally?

Schedule

1. Is the time sequence of the school day clear to both teachers and children?
2. Has the schedule been designed to suit the physical plant and particular group of children in the school?

491

3. Are long periods of time scheduled to permit free choice of activities and companions?
4. Are other groupings provided for in the schedule, e.g., small group activities, one to one adult-child contacts, larger group meetings, etc.?
5. Is the schedule periodically reevaluated and modified? Are changes in schedule and the reasons for these changes made clear to both staff and children?

EXTENDING YOUR EXPERIENCE

Visiting other schools and using the checklist as an observation guide is a good way to extend your experience. There are also some helpful films and books you might want to use as resource materials. A selected list of films, books and pamphlets to extend your experience with environment follows:

Films

"My Art is Me." Univ. of California Film Media Center, Berkeley, Calif.
"Organizing for Free Play." Project Head Start, Office of Economic Opportunity, Washington, D.C.

Books

Almy, Millie C. *Ways of Studying Children.* New York: Teachers College Press, Columbia University, 1959.
Ashton-Warner, Sylvia. *Teacher.* New York: Simon & Schuster, 1963.
Pitcher, E. G., Lasher, N. G., et al. *Helping Young Children Learn.* Columbus, Ohio: Charles E. Merrill Books, 1966.
Read, Katherine. *The Nursery School: A Human Relations Laboratory.* Philadelphia: W. B. Saunders Co., 1960.

Pamphlets

"Space, Arrangement, Beauty in School." #101, Association for Childhood Education International, 3615 Wisconsin Ave., N.W., Washington, D.C. 20066.
"Let's Play Outdoors." #101, National Association for the Education of Young Children, 1834 Connecticut Ave., N.W., Washington, D.C. 20009.
"Nursery School Settings—Invitation to What?" #102, NAEYC.
"Space for Play: The Youngest Children." #111, NAEYC.

48. How to Evaluate and Report Individual Progress

Perhaps there is no more significant educational issue today than that which concerns providing the highest quality education for three- and four-year-olds. Quality education and evaluation go hand in hand, because evaluation is an essential ingredient of all good teaching. Nursery school teachers, in particular, need to be good evaluators of children's behavior and needs, since they usually exercise a high degree of autonomy in planning educational programs for their children.

WHAT IS EVALUATION?

Evaluation, a conscious and systematic approach to the appraisal of a child's behavior, should lead to definite action designed to facilitate the child's progress. Many nursery school teachers need to improve their evaluative abilities. Some speak glibly in general terms about how a child is growing or progressing but are very vague about the evidence of a child's improvements or problems in growing and learning. Other teachers study their children in detail, spending hours recording behavior, but they never take the next step of analysing the records for evidence of growth or clues for planning. (3:325).

Evaluation is based on objectives. The teacher must have a clear understanding of the objectives she is trying to achieve. Such objectives, if they are well selected and well stated, can encourage the teacher to be quite creative in planning and can facilitate the development of a well-rounded program for the children. Objectives provide a guide but do not imply the procedure for meeting objectives. Many nursery school teachers have the idea that objectives make for a rigidly structured program. This is nonsense—a statement of objectives can be made sufficiently comprehensive to include all important areas of development.

The way a teacher plans gives the program its flexibility or rigidity. For example, if the objective is for the school to provide understandings of simple quantity, the teacher might sit the children down in a circle and have them take turns counting each other or objects she would provide, an approach quite highly structured for many three- and four-year-olds. A more suitable approach would be to take advantage of those opportunities to count that arise when children stack blocks, set out juice supplies,

From Annie L. Butler, "How to Evaluate and Report Individual Progress," in *Nursery School Portfolio,* 1969. Reprinted by permission of Annie L. Butler and the Association for Childhood Education International, 3615 Wisconsin Avenue, N.W., Washington, D.C. Copyright © 1969 by the Association.

discuss the number of guppies in the aquarium or count the number of persons who may work at the workbench at a given time. Records can be kept of how far a child can count. All the children need not count the same thing or at the same time. A reason some teachers have had difficulty interpreting nursery school programs to parents and community is that the teachers themselves are not clear about objectives and sometimes cannot distinguish the difference between *methods* and *objectives.*

Objectives need to be interpreted in terms of each individual child's behavior. For example, an objective might be to help the child sustain interest in a self-selected activity. Jim may have an attention span of exactly one minute for most activities while Sam may stay with any of several activities for as much as 20 minutes. The teacher would not expect the same behavior of both. She would deliberately plan activities she thought would hold Jim's interest for a longer time, but she would most likely concentrate in her planning and guidance on some other aspect of Sam's behavior, such as his tendency to withdraw from other children. Specific experiences planned for Jim would depend on her interpretation of what would have definite appeal to him. The evaluation should be made in terms of each child and of his progress in his own right. Evaluation is not a matter of comparing one child to another or the results of what is done in one classroom with what is done in another classroom.

Objectives need to be defined in behavioral terms. If a teacher is to be specific about evaluation, she must know what behavior is consistent with the typical pattern of development. While the three-year-old's frequent need for reminders to respect the rights of other children may consume much of the teacher's time, she continues to make positive suggestions regarding sharing, secure in the knowledge that this behavior is common for three-year-olds, and that as they have additional experience with children under proper guidance they acquire the desired social skills. In order to give the needed guidance the teacher must be able to describe clearly the behavior and the circumstances under which it occurs. She must be able to place it on the developmental continuum.

Evaluation and teaching are closely interrelated. Guiding the teaching-learning process of nursery school children is a matter of setting goals, planning and providing experiences, evaluating behavior and then setting new goals. Within recent years, much has been done to improve the resources available for curriculum planning. The teacher can easily find suggestions for activities to provide for a class. The missing link is frequently the lack of instruments to help in determining the developmental status of the children. Teachers need quite specific information about the children to determine the curriculum experiences that are in the best interests of the children and those that may bore them or result in unreasonable pressures.

QUESTIONS TO BE ASKED IN EVALUATING

The nursery school teacher is concerned about the child's behavior in all areas of his development. Categories usually approximate the areas of physical, emotional, social and intellectual development. One reason for evaluation is to make sure that one area is not being neglected in favor of others.

The following questions may be helpful to the teacher in evaluating behavior of nursery school children:

A. *Evaluation of Self-concept*
 1. In what ways does the child recognize his own feelings?
 2. What kind of controls, appropriate or inappropriate, does the child exercise over his behavior?
 3. How does the child show dependence and independence?
 4. To what extent does the child become involved in activity?
 5. How does the child respond to new experiences?
 6. How does the child respond to success and failure?

B. *Relationships with Other People*
 1. What skills does the child have in joining a group of children?
 2. To what extent does the child show sensitivity to the feelings of others?
 3. In what situations does the child show respect, or lack of respect, for the rights of others?
 4. How does the child relate to small groups of children?
 5. How does the child respond to total groups of children?
 6. How does the child respond to total group activity?
 7. How dependable is the child in complying with the specific demands of a situation such as walking with a group on a trip?
 8. How does the child react to school personnel?

C. *Ability to Cope with the Physical Environment*
 1. How well does the child use large-muscle apparatus?
 2. How well does the child coordinate bodily movements?
 3. What skills does the child have in doing real things such as dressing and undressing?
 4. How does the child respond to art media and other materials available in the classroom?
 5. How much responsibility can the child take for taking care of materials?

D. *Evaluation of Intellectual Ability*
 1. How does the child express curiosity?
 2. How does the child communicate ideas?
 3. How does the child organize information?
 4. What does the child find humorous?
 5. What does the child understand about size, shape, simple quantity and time relationships?
 6. How does the child respond to books and stories?
 7. How does the child respond to fanciful ideas?
 8. How does the child use new ideas and suggestions?
 9. What creative activity does the child engage in?

Each teacher can make up her own set of questions after she has compiled a complete statement of objectives. After she has a clear picture of the child's behavior in relation to the objectives, she has the basis for planning experiences specifically for each child.

WHOSE VALUES ARE IMPORTANT?

A teacher evaluates children's growth and she also evaluates her own way of working. More important, she helps the child to evaluate and feel satisfaction from his own activity. Her comments invite the child to discuss his activity or his product and encourage him to set his own standards. She values his products because he made them not because they are pleasing to her. She is careful with praise that might cause the child to rely on her evaluation rather than his own.

REPORTING TO PARENTS

A further function of evaluation is to report progress to parents and to plan with them regarding the child's future development. Contact between parents and teachers needs to be a two-way process from home to school and from school to home. The teacher needs to be especially aware of barriers that have to be overcome if communication is to be effective. Often the parents feel the school should contact them; many times the teacher wishes the parents would invite her to their home. Sometimes, even teachers who feel strongly that the teacher-parent relationship is important do not feel confident to initiate the contact. Parents likewise do not take the initiative because they have the idea that the teacher is too impersonal, distant or hurried. Experience with Head Start has shown that if accepted by the teacher, parents are very responsive.

Many of the ways in which parents and teachers communicate with each other are informal. Home visits and conferences before the child enters school help teacher and parent in becoming acquainted and give the teacher insight into the background of the child. It is also important for the parent and the child to visit school, before the child enters, to become acquainted with the facilities. Some teachers see the parents each morning when the child is brought to school. Such casual visits enable the teacher to acquire many cues as to the child's behavior and the parent's attitudes. In schools where parents participate as teaching assistants there are still more contacts to provide greater insight for both the teacher and the parent. "The value of the casual contacts should not be underestimated; they make a significant contribution to the parent-teacher relationships by establishing rapport, paving the way and providing a means for scheduling the planned conference at a later date" (2:379). The informal contacts help the teacher, the parent and the child to share common interests and talk freely together.

These casual contacts should not replace the scheduled conference. The regularly scheduled conference, because it affords opportunity for two-way communication, is the best means for reporting a child's progress. Prior to

496

the conference, the teacher studies the child's records and prepares for the conference. She provides a place where problems, progress, plans and follow-up activities can be discussed without interruption. Both parents and teachers feel freer to reveal their true feelings, if they feel they cannot be overheard and that the discussion is confidential. It is good to remember that both teacher and parent have a kind of "expertise" about the child. The nursery school teacher is probably the first objective observer of the child. But it is important for her to know that the parents are more important in the life of the child than the teacher. Only as these important persons in the child's life are able to share their impressions can the child receive maximum benefit. It is never a matter of the teacher telling the parents what to do or how to raise their children. Teachers and parents are co-workers.

WRITTEN REPORTS

Written reports can never communicate as effectively as conferences, although it may be desirable that there be a written report in addition to the conference. In many schools there is a belief in the necessity of a written report which remains a part of the child's permanent record. The report if submitted to parents should be in the form of a letter describing the child's progress and his strengths and weaknesses. The parent will feel more receptive to what will follow if the letter starts with something complimentary or positive about the child.

THE NEXT STEP

Attendance in the nursery school is the first step in helping the child establish relationships outside the home. Kindergarten is the next big step. The nursery school teacher can take a number of steps to help. Many nursery schools provide opportunity for the children to visit the school they will attend, to talk to the teacher, to become familiar with the facilities and see the materials they will use.

A conference between the teacher, the parent and the kindergarten teacher will help to provide for satisfactory adjustment. The nursery school teacher can make an important contribution through the sharing of her records of activities and her assessment of the child's progress that will assist the new teacher to guide his growth so that it will not be interrupted. The wise teacher knows that to be successful she must build on all that has gone on before; therefore, it is important for the nursery school to provide some basic information to the school the child will enter. Someone must take the initiative. This person may well be the nursery school teacher.

REFERENCES

1. Butler, Annie L., *An Evaluation Scale for Four and Five-Year-Old Children*, Bulletin of the School of Education, Indiana University, Vol. 41, No. 2. March, 1965.

2. Leeper, Sara Hammond, et al., *Good Schools for Young Children,* Macmillan, New York, 1968, 465 pp.

3. Wills, Clarice, and Lindberg, Lucile, *Kindergarten for Today's Children,* Follett Publishing Company, Chicago, 1967, 401 pp.

Appendix

AGENCIES AND ASSOCIATIONS

American Academy of Pediatrics
P.O. Box 1037
Evanston, Ill. 60204

American Parents Committee
52 Vanderbilt Ave.
New York, N.Y. 10017

American Psychological Association (APA)
1947 Rosemary Hills Drive
Silver Springs, Md. 20910

Association for Childhood Education International (ACEI)
3615 Wisconsin Ave., NW
Washington, D.C. 20016

Association for Supervision and Curriculum Development (ASCD)
Suite 1100
1701 K St. NW
Washington, D.C. 20036

Black Child Development Institute
Suite 514
1028 Connecticut Ave. NW
Washington, D.C. 20036

Center for Parent Education
55 Chapel St.
Newton, Mass. 02160

Child Development Associate Consortium (CDAC)
Southern Bldg., Suite 500
805 Fifteenth St. NW
Washington, D.C. 20005

Children's Book Council
67 Irving Place
New York, N.Y. 10003

Children's Bureau
U.S. Dept. of Labor
Washington, D.C. 20210

Children's Defense Fund
1520 New Hampshire Ave.
Washington, D.C. 20036

Child Welfare League of America
Dorothy L. Bernhard Library
67 Irving Place
New York, N.Y. 10003

Council for Exceptional Children (CEC)
1920 Association Dr.
Reston, Va. 20091

Day Care and Child Development Council (DCCDC)
1012 Fourteenth St. NW
Washington, D.C. 20005

Day Care Facts
U.S. Dept. of HEW
Office of Child Development
400 Sixth St. SW
Washington, D.C. 20201

Education Commission of the States
Research Center
300 Lincoln Tower
1860 Lincoln St.
Denver, Colorado 80203

Education Development Center (EDC)
55 Chapel St.
Newton, Mass. 02160

ERIC Clearinghouse of Elementary and Early Childhood Education
University of Illinois
805 W. Pennsylvania Ave.
Urbana, Illinois 61801

Information Center on Children's Cultures
U.S. Commission for UNICEF
331 E. 38th St.
New York, N.Y. 10016

National Association for Child Development and Education
Suite 810
500 Twelfth St. SW
Washington, D.C. 20024

National Association for the Education of Young Children (NAEYC)
1834 Connecticut Ave. NW
Washington, D.C. 20009

National Education Association (NEA)
1201 Sixteenth St. NW
Washington, D.C. 20036

National Piaget Society
University of Delaware
Newark, Delaware 19711

Office of Child Development (OCD)
U.S. Dept. of HEW
Donahue Building
400 Sixth St. NW
Washington, D.C. 20201

Office of Education
400 Maryland Ave. SW
Washington, D.C. 20202

Parent Cooperative Preschool International
P.O. Box 40123
Indianapolis, Indiana 46240

Parenting Institute
1609 Poplar St.
Philadelphia, Pa. 19130

Society for Research in Child Development (SRCD)
University of Chicago
5801 Ellis Ave.
Chicago, Illinois 60637

Superintendent of Documents
U.S. Government Printing Office
Washington, D.C. 20202

RESEARCH CENTERS

Arsenal Family and Children's Center
40th & Penn Ave.
University of Pittsburgh
Pittsburgh, Pa. 15224

Bank Street College of Education
Research Division
610 W. 112th St.
New York, N.Y. 10025

Center for Early Development and Education
University of Arkansas
College of Education
815 Sherman St.
Little Rock, Arkansas 72202

Child Behavior Research Lab
Brown University
Providence, R.I. 02912

Child Development Center
Howard University
2217 Fourth St. N.W.
Washington, D.C. 20001

Child Development and Mental Retardation Center
University of Washington
Seattle, Washington 98195

Appendix

Child Study Center
Brown University
Box 1857
Providence, R.I. 02912

Child Study Center
Yale University
333 Cedar St.
New Haven, Conn. 06510

Children's Center
Syracuse University
100 Walnut Place
Syracuse, N.Y. 13210

Demonstration and Research Center for Early Education
George Peabody College for Teachers
Box 151
Nashville, Tenn. 37203

Frank Porter Graham Child Development Center
University of North Carolina
Chapel Hill, N.C. 27514

Fels Research Institute for the Study of Human Development
Yellow Springs, Ohio 45387

Gesell Institute of Child Development, Inc.
Yale University
310 Prospect St.
New Haven, Conn. 06510

Institute of Child Development
University of Minnesota
Minneapolis, Minnesota 55455

Institute for Child Development and Experimental Education
University of New York
33 W. 42nd St.
New York, N.Y. 10036

Institute of Child Study
Indiana University
Bloomington, Indiana 47401

Institute of Child Study
University of Maryland
College Park, Maryland 20742

Institute of Human Development
1203 Tolman Hall
University of California
Berkeley, California 94720

Harold E. Jones Child Study Center
2425 Atherton St.
Berkeley, California 94704

Kansas Center for Research in Early Childhood Education
University of Kansas
Lawrence, Kansas 66045

John F. Kennedy Child Development Center
4200 E. Ninth Ave.
University of Colorado
Denver, Colorado 80220

Merrill-Palmer Institute
71 E. Ferry Ave.
Detroit, Mich. 48202

National Institute of Child Health and Human Development
U.S. Dept. of HEW
9000 Rockville Park
Bethesda, Maryland 20014

Pacific Oaks College
714 W. California Blvd.
Pasadena, California 91105

Index

Authors

Almy, Millie C., 221, 308, 439

Baumrind, D., 162, 277
Beller, E. K., 429
Bereiter, C., 303-304, 428, 436, 437
Berlyne, D. E., 307
Berman, Louise, 378
Bettleheim, Bruno, 466
Biber, Barbara, 373
Bloom, Benjamin, 8, 18, 20, 368, 436, 437
Boehm, Ann E., 482-487
Bogue, E. G., 349, 411-421
Boyd-Orr, John, 464
Brameld, Theodore, 375
Bruner, Jerome, 42, 223, 305-306, 307, 475
Butler, Annie, 349, 398-411, 493-498

Caldwell, Bettye, 431
Campbell, Roald F., 414
Childs, John, 375
Connors, K., 429

Decker, Celia, 378-397
Decker, John, 378-397
Dewey, John, 370, 375, 475
Donnelly, James H., 412
Drucker, Peter, 344

Eisenberg, L., 429
Englemann, S., 219, 428, 437
Erikson, E., 110, 225, 226, 238, 242, 243, 289

Fantz, R. L., 106
Flavell, John, 373

Freud, S., 23, 109
Froebel, F., 367, 375
Furth, Hans, 369

Gesell, A., 90
Gordon, Ira, 346, 369
Grieder, Calvin, 414
Gross, Dorothy, 422, 423-425

Handler, Ellen, 422, 452-463
Harms, Thelma, 488-492
Hebb, Donald, 24, 33
Hess, R. D., 253, 278
Hoffer, Eric, 474
Holt, John, 375
Hunt, J. McVicker, 23, 223, 230, 305-306, 368, 369, 438
Hutchins, Robert, 414

Jordan, K. F., 414

Kagan, J., 261, 262, 264, 306
Kahn, Robert, 412
Kaplan-Sanoff, Margot, 105, 422, 435-443
Katz, Daniel, 412
Katz, Lilian, 3, 277, 422, 425-434, 478-482
Kirk, Samuel, 436
Kohlberg, L., 180, 188, 281, 436, 438

Longenecker, Justin G., 412

Macdonald, James, 375
Magid, Renee Yablans, 342-348
McAfee, Oralie, 349, 361-367
McCandless, Boyd R., 370

505

Subjects